THIS CATALOGUE IS RESPECTFULLY DEDICATED TO MRS. KAY KIMBELL

Kimbell Art Museum

Catalogue of the Collection 1972

Kimbell Art Foundation Fort Worth Texas

Kimbell Publication One
First Edition

International Standard Book Number
0-912804-00-9

Library of Congress Catalog Card Number
73-177945

Designed by Laurence Channing, Boston
Published in 1972 by Kimbell Art Museum
Will Rogers Road West, Fort Worth, Texas 76107
Printed and bound by Brüder Hartmann, Berlin

Color Photography by Robert Wharton, Fort Worth.
Black-and-White Photography by Robert Wharton, Fort Worth; Osvaldo Böhm, Venice; John Rewald, New York, and Dieter Widmer, Basel.

Photography Credits:
Bibliothèque Nationale, Paris
Boymans Museum, Rotterdam
British Museum, London
Gemäldegalerie, Dahlem, Berlin
The Pierpont Morgan Library, New York

Table of Contents

Preface and Acknowledgments

This initial catalogue of the Kimbell Art Museum collection is the result of a splendid team effort on the part of the museum's entire staff. Although particular entries for specific objects were actually written by every individual staff member who is a professional art historian, including the director, individual identification of the authors has been eschewed in favor of a corporate recognition as a better expression of the spirit and working method that produced the book. The cooperative nature of the research process, the cross-pollination of ideas and interpretations, innumerable successive proof readings of every entry by various persons involved, and a marvelous willingness to maintain a mutual style were all extremely rewarding aspects of the project.

Inevitably, however, in order to achieve the level of organization needed to complete such a production, certain tasks, to a greater or lesser degree, had to be assumed by different members of the team. For overall planning and supervision of research, as well as maintenance of consistent form and quality of illustrations, our gratitude goes to David M. Robb, Jr., Curator. To him also goes the credit of having written the largest number of individual entries. His assistants, Ellen Oppenheim and Nell Johnson, carried out impeccable research at a truly scholarly depth and tirelessly wrote articles that are both solidly documented and admirably elucidating. Also, the well-researched and beautifully expressed entries written by Ruth Wilkins are firm evidence that we will be able to build our public education program on a sound scholarly foundation. We are thankful to our curator's wife, Frances Robb, who produced, with seemingly no ill effects on their domestic life, entries that reveal her own competence as a professional art historian and excellent critical writer. To our Director of Museum Program, Max Sullivan, fell the complicated tasks of production, scheduling and coordination of the diverse contributions from writers, designer, photographer, business office and printer. With his profound knowledge of all the factors essential to an ambitious publication, he ordered the work superbly. None of the foregoing efforts could finally be effective if our language were not right: spelling, grammar, punctuation, word selection, consistency of usage, proper form, style. All these ultimate elements came under the beneficent but sternly alert eye, mind and red pencil of our experienced Editor, Shirley Spieckerman. She received invaluable assistance, especially in the areas of foreign references and the index, from our very knowledgeable Librarian, Ilse Rothrock. All of this material had to be typed, proofed and corrected, over and over again; and our heartfelt thanks for the lion's share of this labor goes to Pamala Freeze and Carolyn Naumer. The importance of photography in a catalogue of the visual arts is self-evident, and prime recognition for both the quantity and high quality of this work goes to Robert Wharton.

No museum staff, and especially one as relatively small as ours, can hope to encompass the range of specialized knowledge required to arrive at authoritative conclusions concerning all the art objects of such variety as those discussed in this catalogue. Fortunately, our many friends and colleagues in other institutions who do possess these various special competences have been unbelievably generous in sharing their knowledge with us.

Especially because of necessary research on the large number of British paintings from the original Kimbell private collection, we would like to acknowledge the substantial assistance and guidance provided us by Robert R. Wark of the Huntington Gallery in California and Ellis K. Waterhouse of the Paul Mellon Center for Studies in British Art, London. For critical help in general, but also for sharing his profound experience in the Dutch and Flemish field, we owe our gratitude to Seymour Slive of Harvard University.

Numerous other persons generously gave their advice, supplied otherwise inaccessible information, clarified difficult iconographic identifications, or translated inscriptions in such languages as Chinese that are beyond the Kimbell staff's linguistic abilities.

In the field of Ancient European art, Herbert A. Cahn of Basel and Cornelius C. Vermeule of the Museum of Fine Arts, Boston, offered extremely helpful advice.

Regarding our few, but important, Medieval objects, the opinions of Harry Bober, Institute of Fine Arts, New York; Richard Randall, Walters Art Gallery, Baltimore; Harvey Stahl, Metropolitan Museum of Art, New York, and Derek H. Turner, British Museum, provided welcome guidance.

The many catalogue entries in the large sections covering western European art from the Renaissance through the Baroque and Rococo reflect invaluable opinions and information from the following: Craig Felton, New York; the late Harry D. M. Grier, The

Frick Collection; Carolyn Hurt, Library, the Art Institute of Chicago; Michael Jaffe, Cambridge University; William Jordan, Southern Methodist University; Michael Mahoney, Trinity College, Connecticut; Edgar Munhall, The Frick Collection; Marcel Roethlisberger, University of Geneva; Richard Wallace, Wellesley College; and Federico Zeri, Rome.

Further assistance in researching the British pictures was freely given by Kenneth Garlick, John Hayes and Richard Ormand, all of London, and by Jules D. Prown of the Paul Mellon Center of British Art and British Studies, Yale University.

In the area of nineteenth-century painting, although the opinions of a host of connoisseurs have been helpful, we want especially to thank Jeannine Baticle of the Louvre and Lorenz Eitner of Stanford University.

Indispensable services were provided which enabled us to complete entries on objects of Asian art, by: Molly Garrett Bang, Harvard; Emma C. Bunker, Colorado State University; Pramod Chandra, University of Chicago; Neil Chassman, Southern Methodist University; Richard Ettinghausen, New York University; Donald Jenkins, Art Institute of Chicago; Jean Gordon Lee, Philadelphia Museum; Max Loehr and his colleagues, Mrs. Fumiko Cranston and Harvey Molé, Harvard; John A. Pope and Harold P. Stern, Freer Gallery, Washington, D.C.; Henry Trubner, Seattle Art Museum; Father Harrie Vanderstappen, University of Chicago; and Hugh Wass, Mills College, California.

Conservators who have treated works in the collection, and whom we would like to thank for services that go beyond the essential physical preservation of objects, are William Suhr, New York, Jack K. Flanagan, Houston, and, most recently, Perry C. Huston who joined our staff in 1971.

While acknowledging with deep gratitude all the invaluable assistance we have received, full responsibility for all content of the catalogue rests with the Kimbell Art Museum staff.

R. F. B.

Introduction

As Velma Kimbell has frequently said, "Kay always wanted to share what he had with others." This is what he had in mind when he created the Kimbell Art Foundation in 1936, some time after he had commenced to collect art privately. The circumstances of his beginnings as a collector, in contrast to what has happened during the intervening four decades or so, is beautifully illustrative of cultural growth in the city of Fort Worth and the private generosity that has made it possible.

During the 1930s, the only institution exhibiting qualitatively selected works of art to the public on some regularly scheduled basis was the Fort Worth Art Association, the spirited volunteer organization that later established the Fort Worth Art Center Museum, which is currently expanding its fine, small 1954 building with a splendid new wing. The Art Association's exhibitions during that earlier period were held in a second-floor lobby area of the downtown Fort Worth Public Library, and it was at one of the opening receptions of a show in this facility that Kay Kimbell fell under the gracious spell of English eighteenth-century painting. He was so enamored of one picture that he wished he could take it home. Mr. Bertram Newhouse of the noted New York gallery bearing his name, and a major lender to that show, was introduced to Mr. Kimbell, and when the exhibition closed the desired picture went to the Kimbell residence instead of back to New York. Thus began a long, friendly association between Mr. and Mrs. Kimbell, the elder Mr. Newhouse and his two sons, Clyde and Ross. With their help the Kimbells gathered together many fine examples of later European Renaissance, French nineteenth-century, and American nineteenth-century art. But first love remained the most constant, British painting in the grand tradition; and trips to the Huntington Gallery in California or The Frick Collection in New York only served to bolster this enthusiasm over the years.

As more and more pictures were added, they not only graced the walls of the Kimbells' home, but, through the Foundation, as well as the corporation, a great many were continuously on loan to leading regional institutions. For thousands of youths at nearby colleges and universities, exposure to Kimbell Gainsboroughs, Corots, Van Dycks or Innesses constituted the students' first and, in many cases, only contact with original works of art. Dozens of other works, carefully selected for pertinence to the institution's function, were always on view at churches of different denominations, the public library, and rooms used for meetings and general congregation.

As is perfectly natural to developing collectors whose roots go deep into the soil of the western United States, many paintings in the original early collection turned out to be excellent depictions of the colorful cowboy-and-Indian frontier by Remington and Russell, plus many majestic views of the West's awe-inspiring natural wonders by such masters as Thomas B. Moran. Occasionally a superb genre scene recording America's bucolic past, such as William Ranney's "On The Wing," was added because of its sheer quality and nostalgic appeal. But with their inherent taste for European Baroque and the English aristocratic style, the Kimbells garnered more than 200 objects in this tradition while viewing with favor the burgeoning collection of western American art being developed by their friend Mr. Amon G. Carter, Sr., who, by the time of his death in 1955, had created one of the most notable collections in existence in this special field. Expansion, and an extension of the purview of this collection, has been vigorously carried forward by the Carter Foundation since the opening of the Amon G. Carter Museum of Western Art in 1961. Meanwhile, in response to an inevitable and widespread demand, the Art Center Museum has become one of the most vital and progressive forums in the country for the presentation and interpretation of international contemporary art in all of its bewildering variety and novelty.

With one museum successfully devoted to American art and another imaginatively dealing with the always-difficult modern scene, to say nothing of the archaeologically and ethnographically interpreted art objects in the Fort Worth Museum of Science and History, the desired areas of emphasis for the new Kimbell Art Museum were obvious. The direction already taken by Mr. and Mrs. Kimbell had pointed the way: European art in all ramifications of its grand classical sweep from ancient times down through the early years of the twentieth century would best complement what was already being done well by the other three local institutions. Through this division of labor, in educational programs as well as collecting, the public's opportunity for cultural enrichment could be immeasurably extended with the greatest economy and efficiency.

The opportunity for Kimbell Art Museum to seize every possibility in effecting its part in this broad program for public benefit stems very largely from the wisdom displayed by Mr. Kimbell in the directives contained in his will. Upon his death in 1964, his executors, now trustees of the museum, were charged, as simply and directly as possible, to create an art museum of the first class within the city of Fort Worth. With that same breadth and objectivity of administrative point of view that helped him to amass a fortune in grain, food processing and merchandising, oil, insurance, and a host of other pursuits, he delegated the authority and the means to achieve his long-felt aim; and he did so with a minimum of restrictions and the maximum flexibility. With tremendous generosity, coupled with faith in both the importance and attainability of the goal, Mrs. Kimbell gave her entire share of the community property to the Kimbell Art Foundation, the sole purpose of which is support of the museum. Moreover, since 1966 when the Foundation began implementing the project with a professional staff, construction of a suitable museum building, and a rounding out of the collection, she has devoted her attention, time and energies diligently to the proper resolution of the problems posed by these many activities.

The exhilarating freedom and the very magnitude with which the founders conceived their dream have stimulated much added impetus and quality from other sources. When the city officials of Fort Worth realized the potential of the project, they gave 9½ acres of land to the Foundation as a site for the building and its gardens. The architect of that structure, Louis I. Kahn of Philadelphia, was inspired to design one of the most thrilling and functional edifices yet produced during a career that has placed him among the most renowned architects of the world; the building itself is as much a creative work of art in its own right as the masterpieces it shelters and displays. The trustees of the Foundation fully supported the museum's professional staff and provided them with the indispensable freedom and flexibility to seek aggressively, find, study and acquire art of quality for the collection, to work imaginatively with the architect, and to create an educational program pertinent to the times, the community and sister institutions.

Of paramount importance, however, is the collection—the art, for which all other aspects of the project exist. The open-minded and resilient philosophy that permeates the entire undertaking has permitted the nature of the collection itself to change, and to fulfill demands that otherwise might have gone unsatisfied. For example, heretofore it has been practically impossible for citizens of the vast region of the Southwest to see and increase their understanding of the cultures of India, China, Southeast Asia, or Japan as evinced in major examples of their visual arts. The Kimbell Museum has made a strong start at filling this lack, and many oriental objects of revealing significance can now be seen and studied in this part of the nation. To a degree, comparable observations could be made about such special areas as Romanesque or Gothic art.

Historical comprehensiveness, however, to say nothing of mere size of the collection, is not the objective. It is only the quality of the individual work of art in all its uniqueness that can help define a culture, a period, a master, or a medium, and, through that definitiveness, give us a better appreciation and understanding of our historical heritage, the nature of the physical world we inhabit, or our fellow men who produced these objects out of circumstances so different from our own. Today's world urgently needs to avail itself of this communicative function in art. But even more important is the sense of fulfillment and reward that can come from the purely aesthetic reaction to a work of art of high quality, no matter what its form, technique or derivation. Into the life where this experience can occur frequently, there comes a large measure of satisfaction and a faith in lasting values. Believing in the significance of this experience for the betterment of our society, we of the Kimbell Art Museum will continue to collect, preserve, exhibit, study and teach at the highest level of which we are capable.

Richard F. Brown
June, 1972

Notes to the Catalogue

This catalogue of the Kimbell collection is intended to provide information for both the interested general reader and the art historian. In each entry the salient visual qualities of the work are discussed and, when pertinent, related to those of other works of comparable age or by the same artist. Other aspects of the object may be mentioned, such as its historical importance, its relative date in the artist's career, other known versions or replicas, information on the artist as it relates to the work or on the identity of a known sitter. Much of this may hold particular interest for the art historian who seeks documentation on crucial or controversial aspects of various objects.

Entries are initially classified by world area, then arranged in approximate chronological sequence. The "British Eighteenth Century" section is an exception; it reflects the focus of Mr. Kay Kimbell's collecting interests and begins with one anomalous seventeenth-century work. Works of known artists are ordered primarily by years of birth, except those in the twentieth-century section which are arranged according to the date of each work. Artists' names are given in the familiar form with longer forms shown in the text. Variant titles and those in foreign languages are included in notes and references.

Mediums and supports are briefly indicated in conventional forms. Dimensions are given to at least the nearest eighth inch, followed by the equivalent centimeters. Height precedes width (or diameter) followed by depth. Measurements shown are the present extent of the original work; sculpture dimensions do not include bases of later date unless noted.

In the final sections of each entry, the following standards have been observed:

Inscription includes all markings on the work which are thought to be in the artist's own hand and any later inscriptions which elucidate the history of the object.

Description identifies major visual elements in the work, especially those not clearly discernible in illustrations. Right and left are those of the viewer unless otherwise indicated.

Condition begins with a term indicating the object's general physical condition relative to other works by the same artist or of similar materials or age. Those few considered in *excellent* condition are completely intact, without initial imperfections or subsequent blemishes affecting their appearance, except for normal effects of aging. Those designated in *very good* condition are substantially intact; any blemishes, repairs or imperfections are superficial and located in areas of secondary visual interest. Works in *good* condition may have had minor imperfections initially or suffered minor unredeemable losses or damage that has been repaired. Those in *fair* condition are relatively intact, with the original appearance of a portion of the work transformed in some respect.

Exhibitions include significant public exhibitions of the work and confirmation of any illustration of it in an exhibition catalogue. Earlier long-term loans of paintings in the Kimbell Bequest to institutions in the Fort Worth area are not usually recorded.

Collections identify persons and organizations that have previously owned the work. Brackets enclose names of commercial vendors. The histories of some works are not complete, pending further verification. The final line indicates the means of acquisition by Kimbell Art Foundation: "Foundation Acquisition" identifies works acquired since October, 1965, and "Kimbell Bequest" designates works collected by Mr. and Mrs. Kimbell. The alphabetical prefixes signify:

AP – acquired since the appointment of the museum's professional staff.
APX – acquired through exchange of other works owned by the Foundation.
ACF – selected by Mr. and Mrs. Kimbell and acquired by the Foundation.
ACK – acquired by Mr. and Mrs. Kimbell and given to the Foundation.
ACC – acquired by the Kimbell Corporation and lent to the museum.
AG – given to the Foundation since October, 1965.

Each registration number concludes with numerals indicating the year and order of acquisition, as well as alphabetical suffixes for some works with two or more parts.

Notes and References to books and periodicals are in conventional form. References to exhibition catalogues include the name of the organizer and/or writer of the catalogue (when known) and the exhibition's title, organizing or publishing institution, city and dates.

David M. Robb, Jr.
June, 1972

EUROPE

Female Figure
From the Cyclades Islands
About 2500–2000 B.C.

White marble, 16 in. high (40.6 cm.)

This slender, elegant *Female Figure* from the Cycladic Islands in the Aegean Sea dates from the beginning of the monumental sculpture tradition in the third millennium B.C. Although similar figures vary in height from two to more than forty inches,[1] relatively few are as large as the Kimbell work. These nude figures were created for about 500 years during the Early Bronze Age and perhaps well into the Middle Bronze Age; despite this period of duration, the conventions of their position and treatment remained relatively constant.[2] Consequently, it is difficult to date them precisely but current scholarship places the Kimbell figure in the first period of Early Cycladic art, about 2500–2000 B.C.[3]

Because this figure has both flat and rounded surfaces on which details are incised as well as rendered in relief,[4] it exemplifies the Spedos variety or the "folded-arm figurine" type, the most important and numerous form in Cycladic sculpture. It originated in the period of the Keros-Syros culture of the Cyclades Islands that was contemporary with Early Helladic culture on the Greek mainland and Early Minoan culture of Crete. Shaped with an abrasive rock from a thin rectangular slab of fine or coarse-grained marble, this highly stylized figure is more naturalistic and graceful than the earlier, more rigid "fiddle idols" with rounded shoulders and bases.[5]

The distinctive elegance of the Kimbell figure is established by the rhythm of gentle curves and carefully balanced symmetry of the parts. The curvature of the thighs echoes the lyre-shaped head surmounting the massive, tapered neck. The face is dominated by a long beak-like nose, its simplicity enhanced by the absence of eyes, mouth, or ears. Below the summarily indicated breasts, the horizontal accent of long parallel forearms is repeated in the light incisions about the waist and groin. A vitality is imparted to the profile by the slant of the head and the slightly flexed legs. Despite the absence of the lower legs and angled feet, which may have been deliberately broken off in a funerary rite,[6] a total image is easily visualized.

These Cycladic figures are generally considered to be images of deities, although their exact religious or symbolic significance is not known. They are most often found in excavated cist burial sites where they were placed on their backs as offerings, along with utilitarian objects, to accompany the dead. They may also have served as idols for the living before interment.[7]

The abstract qualities of the figurines combined with the intrinsic beauty of the raw material make them readily appealing to the modern eye. The sculpture of twentieth-century artists, such as Constantin Brancusi, Hans Arp, and Archipenko reflects the flat surfaces, simplified rendering of forms and balanced design of these ancient idols.

Wreathed Male Head

From Cyprus
First quarter of Fifth Century B.C.

Limestone, 6 1/4 in. high (16 cm.)

Description: Sculpted nude female figurine. She has slightly rounded shoulders and modeled arms folded at the waist, left above right. Breasts are indicated lightly, and the pubic triangle is lightly incised. The head is a flat oval squared off at the top and rounded at the chin; it tilts upward and backward on a tapered neck. The nose, the singular facial feature, projects from the convex surface of the face. The slightly flexed legs are missing below the knees; there is a grooved cleft between the slightly bulging thighs. No backbone is indicated, although the arms and neckline are incised on the back.

Condition: Very good. The clean breaks at the neckline and across the brow have been repaired. The legs are missing below the thighs.

Exhibitions: Thou Shalt Have No Other Gods Before Me, the Jewish Museum, New York, May 3–Sept. 6, 1964, cat. no. 220, illus. *Beyond Europe,* Saidenberg Gallery, New York, March 27–May 22, 1971, cat. no. 3, illus.

Collections: Ben Heller, New York, by 1955.
Gift of Ben Heller, AG 70.2.

Notes:

1 Colin Renfrew, "The Development and Chronology of the Early Cycladic Figurines," *American Journal of Archaeology,* vol. 73, January, 1969, p. 1.

2 Renfrew, pp. 24–26.

3 Unpublished opinion of Edith Porada, Professor of Art and Archaeology, Columbia University, New York.

4 Christos Doumas, *The N. P. Goulandris Collection of Early Cycladic Art,* Athens, 1969, p. 83.

5 Renfrew, pp. 9–11, 15–21, 24.

6 Cornelius C. Vermeule, III, "Recent Museum Acquisitions, Greek and Roman Sculptures in Boston," *Burlington Magazine,* vol. 113, January, 1971, p. 37–38.

7 Doumas, p. 92; Renfrew, pp. 24–26.

The Kimbell *Wreathed Male Head* is from Cyprus, dating from the Cypro-Archaic Period which saw the introduction of monumental sculpture to the island. Although smaller than life-size, this head has an imposing presence and sense of imperturbability which suggest a mixed Greek-oriental heritage.

By the Cypro-Archaic Period, Cyprus had already become established as a crossroads in the trade between East and West, having been exposed since earliest antiquity to successive waves of foreign conquest, migration and colonization. Early influences included those of the Anatolians, Hyksos and Egyptians, followed by the Mycenaeans at the end of the fifteenth century B.C. and the Achaeans after the fall of Troy, about 1200 B.C.[1] Henceforth, Cyprus was carried irreversibly into the sphere of the Greek world, which by the eighth century extended to the shores of Asia. The Archaic Period in Cyprus was marked by a notable flowering of the arts, strongly Eastern in inspiration. This is particularly apparent in Cypro-Archaic pottery where a new freedom of decoration expressed itself in highly original motifs. This same vigor and freshness of vision carried over into Cypro-Archaic sculpture.

The Cypriot *Wreathed Male Head* can, therefore, be considered to relate to the art of the contemporary Greek world, whose culture it shared. Indeed, it bears a marked resemblance to the heads of certain kouroi, statues of standing male youths, which were a prevalent subject in Archaic Greek art.[2] On the basis of its features alone, the Kimbell head corresponds to the late kouros type, which has been classified by G. M. A. Richter as the Ptoon 20 Group, dated about 520–485 B.C.[3]

Like the Greek kouros, the Kimbell head represents an ideal of masculine beauty. The circling laurel wreath, a symbol of triumph, rests on his head like a diadem. His hair below the wreath falls in rows of tight curls which suggest Mesopotamian influence. His eyes are perhaps the most strikingly oriental feature, widely spaced and elongated. His "archaic smile" (which in Greek examples often appears simpering) is not an expression of weakness, but rather one of heroic acceptance. His chin juts forward strongly, conveying a sense of determination. His cheekbones are prominent; his features have a roughhewn quality suggesting virility and a rudimentary strength. This latter derives, in part, from the soft limestone material, which does not lend itself to over-refinement.

The vitality of the Kimbell head becomes apparent when compared with the *Wreathed Male Head* in the Cyprus Museum, Nicosia,[4] which is a later work, more mechanical in execution. Another *Head of a Young Man with Laurel Wreath,*[5] also in the Cyprus Museum and dated fifth century B.C., is more classical in conception, while revealing a strong Eastern flavor in the stylization of its curls and headdress.

The Kimbell *Wreathed Male Head* represents Cypriot sculpture at its moment of highest artistic achievement. Its Greek origin is unquestionable, while it retains a serene, unfathomable presence which bespeaks its close ties with the Orient.

4 *Description:* A wreathed head of a young man, about one-half life-size, in limestone. His face is framed by rows of curls which fall over his low forehead. His eyes are large and almond-shaped; his lips form an enigmatic smile. In profile, his chin meets the line of his lips.

Condition: Good. The head has been irregularly broken off from its body. The nose is almost completely lost, and there are additional minor losses to the surface of the piece.

Exhibitions: Weltkunst aus Privatbesitz, Kölner Museen, Cologne, May 18–Aug. 4, 1968, cat. no. A 55.

Collections: [Elie Borowski, Basel.]
Foundation Acquisition, AP 72.5.

Notes:

[1] Tony Spiteris, *The Art of Cyprus,* trans. by Thomas Burton, New York, 1970, p. 88.

[2] Gisela M. A. Richter, in collaboration with Irma A. Richter, *Kouroi: Archaic Greek Youths,* 2nd ed., London, 1960. p. 1.

[3] This group is characterized as follows: the skull is spherical; the ear is in the correct position and well shaped; the eye is set horizontally, with recess at the corner indicated; both lips are well shaped, the upper lip protruding markedly over the lower; the hair is short or rolled up at the back. See: Richter, p. 133.

[4] Spiteris, p. 182.

[5] Spiteris, p. 178.

Funerary Statue of a Young Female Attendant
About 340–330 B.C.

Marble, 45 1/4 in. high (115 cm.)

Funerary sculpture flourished in Attica from the second half of the fifth century B.C.,[1] introducing into Greek art themes which were intensely human, expressing for the first time a sense of mortal suffering and the sadness of death. The dead were memorialized in intimate scenes which evoke a mood of pensive sorrow and melancholy. Most commonly, the deceased was presented taking leave of a companion, the two figures facing one another in a final act of farewell. The companion could be a member of the family or even a devoted servant. The deceased was always idealized and ennobled, portrayed with a sense of detachment and withdrawal from this world. Mourning was expressed in highly restrained terms, almost never as a deep emotion or unrestrained grief.

The Kimbell statue of a young draped female figure is believed to have been a member of such a funerary pair. She displays a stately grace and air of solemnity as she stands poised with her weight on her right leg. The jewelry box, which she holds in her left hand, suggests that she served as a companion to a lady of high standing or a priestess. Her body sways rhythmically as she appears to offer the box to this unseen person.

This theme is familiar in Attic funerary art and is fully acted out in the *Sepulchral Monument of Hegeso*, National Museum, Athens, from the end of the fifth century B.C.[2] Hegeso, the deceased, is seated to the right of the stele facing her maidservant, who approaches bearing an open jewelry case. Hegeso examines a necklace, as the two are quietly engaged in an activity which was commonplace during the lifetime of the deceased.

In an early fourth-century B.C. Attic *Tombstone of an Unknown Woman*,[3] National Museum, Athens, this same exchange is repeated. The deceased is again seated on the right; her attendant stands before her on the left and with bowed head presents the jewelry box. Although the same compositional elements are present in this later version, the figures appear to move more freely in space, existing almost independently of the background and of each other.

If the Kimbell figure is to be viewed as part of a further development of this same theme, she must be considered as the young female attendant standing to the viewer's left. She carries the open jewelry box high in her left hand, just under her bosom, suggesting that she is in the act of presenting it to a standing figure, rather than a seated one. The mistress presumably appeared to the right, considerably taller than the young attendant. Both figures were sculpted completely in the round and free of the background, probably set in a deep niche which would have provided the atmosphere of a small shrine.

Even when viewed alone and out of context from her original role, the Kimbell statue stands on her own merits as a monumental figure, exemplifying the classical ideals of serenity, harmony and balance as conveyed through the human form. Her dignified bearing is reminiscent of the maidens from the solemn Panathenaic procession of a century earlier.[4]

Similarly, almost 2,000 years later in a climate engendered by the Italian Renaissance, these same majestic forms reappear multiplied many times over on the walls of another monument. At Arezzo, in recreating *The Legend of the True Cross*, the Umbrian artist Piero della Francesca peopled a world of heroic figures, truly classical in conception. The Kimbell statue and Piero's St. Helena,[5] to isolate but one example, bear a common heritage. Both stand as symbols of human dignity, timeless figures which have meaning for all ages.

If the form and stylistic elements of the Kimbell funerary statue presage Piero's St. Helena, then surely they derive from the maidens in the Parthenon frieze. Like them, the stance of this figure is one of calm repose. Her simple gown falls into natural folds, caught up beneath her bosom, giving her a youthfully slim, long-legged appearance. Dated about 340–330 B.C.,[6] she is perhaps a more elegant figure than her fifth-century counterpart, higher-waisted, more slenderly proportioned. Her pose is more relaxed; this becomes particularly apparent when viewed from the back. She is much closer in conception to the *Torso of Artemis*, a copy of an almost contemporary work by Praxiteles, dated 346–345 B.C., now in the Landgrafen-Museum, Kassel.[7] Both have the same rhythmical swing to the body, and the drapery falls in similar patterns, the folds grouped mostly on the side of the supporting leg. Both display the pervading softness and languid grace characteristic of the Attic spirit of the fourth century B.C.

Description: Life-size standing figure of a young woman, headless, in white marble. She stands on her right leg, her left knee bent. Her weight shifts accordingly, her right hip protruding markedly. Her gown follows the contours of her body and falls into soft folds. It is high-girdled, secured by a cord which crosses her back and shoulders. She holds an open, paneled box in her left hand.

Condition: Good. The head is broken off at the neck. The right forearm and elbow are missing. There are additional losses in the back shoulder area, the fingers on the left hand, at the base around the feet, and in the jewelry box. Various abrasions occur on the back surface of the gown.

Exhibitions: None known.

Collections: [Elie Borowski, Basel, Switzerland.] Foundation Acquisition, AP 72.3.

Notes:

1 Funerary art continued until an anti-luxury decree, enacted by Demetrius of Phaleron between 317 and 307 B.C., forbade the erection of sculptured gravestones in Attica. See: Gisela M. A. Richter, *A Handbook of Greek Art*, London, 1969, pp. 129, 162.

2 Reinhard Lullies and Max Hirmer, *Greek Sculpture*, New York, 1960, p. 84, no. 187, pl. 187. This tombstone is dated early fourth century by Margarete Bieber, *The Sculpture of the Hellenistic Age*, rev. ed., New York, 1961, p. 9.

3 Lullies and Hirmer, p. 86, no. 202, pl. 202.

4 Maidens from the frieze of the Parthenon, about 442–438 B.C. See: Richter, p. 117, illus. 144.

5 Kenneth Clark, *Piero della Francesca*, 2nd ed. rev., London, 1969, pls. 89, 91.

6 This statue has been dated 340–330 B.C. by Ernst Berger, Director of the Antiken Museum, Basel, while Vagn Paulsen, former head of the Ny Carlberg Glyptothek, Copenhagen, prefers a mid-fourth century B.C. date.

7 Bieber, fig. 42.

Head of a Female Child
About 300 B.C.

Marble, 6 11/16 in. high (17 cm.)

Each age has its own conception of childhood which is recorded visually through its art, and this early Hellenistic head with its softly defined features and wispy hair realistically captures the essence of young girlhood. This child is not portrayed as a miniature adult, nor is she over-sentimentalized; she is presented naturalistically, with a sense of freshness and grace which is appropriate to the subject.

Hellenistic art was multifaceted; it examined nature in all its aspects, presenting man from infancy to old age, sometimes with lightness and gaiety,[1] often with pitiless realism. Although children had occasionally been represented in preceding periods, they now became favorite subjects. Boys and girls of all ages were portrayed in a striking variety of poses—playing with their toys and pets,[2] dancing gracefully or even gently sleeping.[3] Children of the Hellenistic period were seldom stereotyped; they ranged from smiling innocents with cherubic faces to weary slave boys drowsing beside their lanterns.[4] All were treated with insight and understanding.

The Kimbell head is not an idealized image; the girl's features are distinctly individualized, evoking a quality of sweetness and uncorrupted purity. Her high forehead is serene and untroubled; her full cheeks complete the rounded contour of the face. Her eyes are deeply set, giving her an air of dreamy repose which can be compared to the *Head of a Sleepy Child*, Glyptothek, Munich.[5] Her hair is caught back by a diadem which suggests that she might have been a child of the gods,[6] or one dedicated to a particular god.

7

The Kimbell *Head of a Female Child* was originally part of a full-length statue, which could have served some ceremonial purpose. In attempting to visualize how the body of the figure might have appeared, the viewer can turn to such contemporary examples as *Girl with Pet in Pouch of her Dress*, in the Metropolitan Museum of Art, and the *Figures of Girls Dedicated to Eilithyia at Agrae*, in the National Museum, Athens.[7] All of these draped figures realistically retain the chubby proportions which mark very young children.

Description: Head of a female child, about two-thirds life-size, in white marble. She wears a headband and her short hair curls gently around her ears and the nape of her neck. She has a high forehead, a small but well-structured nose, and soft lips. The contours of her face are those of a very young child.

Condition: Good. The head has been broken off from its body at the neck. There are losses in the tip of the nose, the chin area and top of the diadem; various abrasions and incrustations are visible on the surface of the piece.

Exhibitions: None known.

Collections: [Elie Borowski, Basel.]
Foundation Acquisition, AP 72.4.

Notes:

1 For a discussion of rococo trends in Hellenistic art see: Margarete Bieber, *The Sculpture of the Hellenistic Age*, rev. ed., New York, 1961, pp. 136–56.

2 Bieber, fig. 543.

3 Gisela M. A. Richter, *The Metropolitan Museum of Art Handbook of the Greek Collection*, Cambridge, Mass., 1953, pl. 102.

4 Bieber, figs. 546, 548–49.

5 Bieber, fig. 547.

6 A child wearing a diadem is so described by Wolfgang Helbig, *Führer durch die öffentlichen Sammlungen klassischer Altertümer in Rom*, 4th ed., ed. by Hermine Speier, Tübingen, 1966, cat. no. 1985, p. 738.

7 Bieber, figs. 541–42.

Crouching Aphrodite

About 50 B.C.

Marble, 25×13 7/8×19 3/8 in. (63.5×35.3×49.2 cm.)

The Kimbell statue of the *Crouching Aphrodite* is a highly evocative work, immediately calling forth those qualities which characterize the Greek goddess of beauty and love. The pale flesh tone of the marble contributes to the sensual character of the torso. The contours of the nude female body are full and lifelike, the surface of the stone suggesting the texture and soft feeling of flesh. The intimacy of the pose and smaller-than-life scale of the figure combine to present the goddess in very human terms.

While the complete nudity of Aphrodite seems a commonplace to our twentieth-century eyes, one must not forget that the goddess of love first appeared in Greek art as a fully draped figure, at once exalted and remote. It was not until Praxiteles created his most celebrated work, the Aphrodite of Cnidus, about 364 B.C., that the goddess was presented for the first time entirely nude, laying aside her robes in preparation for the ritual bath. The fame of this statue, in antiquity, was such that many sailed to the island of Cnidus expressly to see it.[1]

Beyond Praxiteles, the humanization of the goddess was carried to its ultimate expression during the Hellenistic period, when the image of Aphrodite as a crouching figure was introduced by the artist Doidalsas, who was active in the mid-third century B.C. as court sculptor to King Nikomedes of Bithynia. Doidalsas portrayed the goddess in an intimate pose crouching in her bath, looking over her right shoulder, awaiting a shower of water to be poured on her back. King Nikomedes had tried in vain to purchase the original Cnidian statue, and the creation of this second renowned Aphrodite is probably related to his failure to secure the first.[2] Neither of these two innovative sculptures, well documented through literary references, has survived to the present. However, their character is known by copies, often broadly interpreted and executed in a variety of materials–marble, bronze and terra cotta.

The Kimbell *Crouching Aphrodite* retains the closed pyramidal form of its third-century B.C. prototype. The lower part of the body and legs face in one direction, the body twists, and the neck turns sharply in the opposite direction, to her right. While the head and both arms are missing, one can speculate that the figure's right arm was probably drawn across her breast, while the left might have rested in her lap. The most faithful copy of the original Doidalsas composition is thought to be that found in Vienne, France, now in the Louvre.[3] The Kimbell Aphrodite is very close to this version in the delicate modeling of the back and breasts and delineation of the soft folds of flesh across the abdomen. Two additional copies exist in the Louvre,[4] and a particularly appealing version, with part of the head intact, can be found in the Museo delle Terme, Rome.[5] Another copy, less well preserved, is in the Metropolitan Museum of Art, New York.[6] In spite of variations in the opposing movement of arms and legs, all of these compositions retain the rather chaste, gathered-in pose of the original which, in effect, shields the figure's nudity from the viewer.

Genre subjects such as the *Crouching Aphrodite* were in great demand for the decoration of Roman gardens and baths, and the Kimbell statue, thought to date from about 50 B.C., might well have served such a purpose.[7]

Description: Smaller than life-size figure of a crouching nude woman, in white marble. The head is broken off at a 45-degree angle to her right. The portion of softly curling locks which cling to the remaining left nape of the neck suggest that the face of Aphrodite must have been youthfully idealized. The body appears to be in an almost kneeling position, its weight supported on the left leg, with the right leg folded underneath almost horizontally.

Condition: Good. The neck was broken off from the torso but has been rejoined. Her right arm is broken at the line of her breast; her left arm is irregularly broken through the shoulder. There is an older break and small loss in the outer top left calf and another loss in the left hip. The surface of the piece is generally in good condition with some abrasion and minor pitting, principally on the shoulder. Some fissures run through the marble. The surface texture varies greatly; the under surfaces of the breast, knees, legs and underarms are extremely smooth, the outer surfaces having weathered. In spite of losses of head and limbs, the essential quality of the crouching figure remains unimpaired.

Exhibitions: None known.

Collections: [Charles Lipson, Boston.]
Foundation Acquisition, AP 67.9.

Notes:

1 Gisela M. A. Richter, *The Sculpture and Sculptors of the Greeks*, 4th ed. rev., New Haven, 1970, p. 200.

2 Margarete Bieber, *The Sculpture of the Hellenistic Age*, rev. ed., New York, 1961, p. 82.

3 Bieber, figs. 290–91. The Doidalsas sculpture was reproduced on contemporary coins (see: Richter, fig. 823), which indicate the presence of the figure Eros in the original composition, presumably holding a mirror for the goddess. The presence of Eros is suggested in the Vienne version by the small hand resting on the goddess' back (see: Bieber, p. 83). No such presence is indicated in the Kimbell sculpture.

4 Bieber, figs. 292–93.

5 Richter, *Sculpture*, fig. 822.

6 Richter, *The Metropolitan Museum of Art Handbook of the Greek Collection*, Cambridge, Mass., 1953, fig. 122c.

7 The popularity of this theme continued well into the imperial period, as evidenced by the crouching Aphrodite discovered at Hadrian's villa, referred to above as the version now in the Museo delle Terme, Rome.

After Skopas (Greek), about 370–330 B.C.
Head of Meleager
50 B.C. to A.D. 50

Marble, 11 3/4 × 8 × 9 1/2 in. (29.8 × 20.3 × 24.1 cm.)

Meleager, the mythological hero struggling against his fate, was as appropriate a subject of fourth-century Greek art as today's anti-hero is expressive of the late twentieth century. As intrepid leader of the Calydonian boar hunt, Meleager was nonetheless doomed to death by his mother, Althaea, as punishment for taking the lives of her brothers.[1] Artists of the fourth century preferred such themes, which humanized the gods and depicted mythological heroes caught up in the sufferings and imperfections of man.

The Kimbell head of Meleager is a Graeco-Roman copy of a full-length statue by the Greek sculptor Skopas who worked in the mid-fourth century B.C. The original work included the entire torso, a hunting dog and the head of a Calydonian boar.[2] In the Kimbell head, Skopadic stylistic details are evident in the low forehead, which protrudes noticeably over the bridge of the nose, and the heavy roll of flesh curving outward from the brows.[3] Skopas, along with Praxiteles and Lysippos, was one of the three great artists of his age and was notable for introducing the element of intense human emotion into the static forms of earlier Greek classicism. His work is known to us today primarily through copies, literary sources of the period, and sculptural fragments from the temple of Athena Alea at Tegea and the east face of the Mausoleum of Halicarnassus.[4]

This head of Meleager is more than a mere physical likeness of an impassively idealized youth. From the tilt of the head and the parted lips, the viewer is aware that the work expresses a yearning quality, a kind of suppressed inner agitation. The eyes are deeply sunken underneath swelling brows. The pupils are not indicated, but the gaze seems directed upwards, and one feels that, were the nose complete, the nostrils would probably be dilated. Such indications of human feeling were first suggested in Skopas' work and were to be carried to their ultimate expression in the unrestrained emotionalism of the late Hellenistic period.

Greek statuary became very popular in Rome after the second century B.C., when conquering Roman armies brought back quantities of plundered Greek art. Copies of these works through the first century B.C. are thought to have been executed by Greek artists "who had come from their impoverished homelands to prosperous Italy where work was plentiful."[5] The Kimbell Meleager, thought to date from 50 B.C. to A.D. 50,[6] was presumably made for a Roman patron, possibly by a Greek hand.

Additional copies of the Meleager statue are to be found in Berlin, in the Vatican, and in the Fogg Art Museum, Harvard University. A head of Meleager also exists in the Villa Medici in Rome.[7]

Portrait Head of Marcus Aurelius

About A.D. 170

Marble, 14 3/8 × 9 7/8 × 10 1/4 in. (36.5 × 25.1 × 26 cm.)

Description: A life-size head of a young man in white marble. The head is turned sharply toward the left shoulder, emphasizing the powerful neck. The face is sensual, with full, parted lips. The hair curls in a rather unruly manner, which gives a further sense of motion and turbulence to the piece. The use of the drill is limited, and the hair is less carefully delineated in the back.

Condition: Good. The neck is broken off unevenly, indicating that the head was once part of a full-length statue. There are various losses in the surface of the piece, including a substantial portion of the nose. The lips and chin are abraded, but these losses do not degrade either the essential form or expressive quality of the whole.

Exhibitions: None known.

Collections: Auction, Münzen und Medaillen, Basel, May 6, 1967, lot no. 201. [Charles Lipson, Boston.] Foundation Acquisition, AP 67.10.

Notes:

[1] Robert Graves, *The Greek Myths*, New York, 1955, pp. 263–68.

[2] George M. A. Hanfmann, *Classical Sculpture*, in the series, *A History of Western Sculpture*, consultant ed., John Pope-Hennessy, New York, 1967, pp. 320–21, illus. nos. 158, 166.

[3] Margarete Bieber, *The Sculpture of the Hellenistic Age*, rev. ed., New York, 1961, p. 24.

[4] Bieber, pp. 23–28. See: Reinhard Lullies and Max Hirmer, *Greek Sculpture*, New York, 1960, pp. 90–92, for a more complete discussion of the relief panels from the Mausoleum at Halicarnassus, illus. no. 214–17.

[5] Gisela M. A. Richter, *The Sculpture and Sculptors of the Greeks*, 4th ed. rev., New Haven, Conn., 1970, p. 247.

[6] Dated by Cornelius C. Vermeule in letter to Ruth S. Wilkins, March 3, 1972.

[7] Bieber, p. 24–25.

Marcus Aurelius Antoninus, Roman Emperor from A.D. 161 to 180, was both soldier and philosopher, and it is this dual nature embracing both the active and the contemplative which portraitists strove to capture. These qualities are evident in the Kimbell portrait head which dates from about A.D. 170, when Marcus was approaching his fiftieth year and had been emperor for almost a decade.[1]

The style of the hair is particularly significant, as this is among the earliest portraits of Marcus in which the hair is swept up from the hairline and temples, no longer falling over the forehead as in youthful representations. The thick moustache curling up at the ends also links this portrait to those of his mature years. Marcus' face, however, remains broad and full, as yet showing no sign of the elongation and gauntness which age and prolonged warfare brought to his appearance.[2]

Like many heads of the Antonine period, the smooth polished surface of the face is in marked contrast to the massive modeling of the hair and beard. The three-dimensional treatment of the thickly curling hair is heightened by the use of the drill, creating deep holes, particularly at the top and sides. However, both hair and beard are closely integrated to the head. Neither approach the attenuated, flamelike forms which are to be found in some later or even posthumous portraits. The eyes remain the most expressive feature, gazing outward into the distance, suggesting the inner life of the Stoic philosopher. The details of the face, hair and beard relate the Kimbell head to the portrait of Marcus Aurelius in the panel relief, *Clementia*, Museo dei Conservatori, Rome. It is presumably earlier than the long-faced portrait bust, *Imperatori 38*, from the Museo Capitolino, Rome.[3]

Numerous portraits of Marcus Aurelius are known to us, and for the most part they present a consistent image. From his youth onwards, he is portrayed in a somber, reflective manner, seemingly mindful of the gravity of his future responsibilities.[4] Perhaps the earliest portrait of Marcus is to be found in the *Relief of the Imperial Succession*, from the Great Antonine Altar at Ephesus. In what is believed to be the adoption of the Antonines by Hadrian, Marcus is portrayed as a youth of seventeen, standing to the right of Antoninus Pius as his adopted son and successor.[5] Marcus, therefore, became the subject of Imperial Roman portraiture at an early age.

The purpose of imperial art was the glorification of the emperor, who stood as the symbol of Rome's power and majesty. According to the Stoic philosophy of the day, the ruler was the chosen servant of the state, and in Marcus Aurelius, with his strong sense of duty and austere self-discipline, the imperial ideal of the second century found its appropriate expression.

Marcus Aurelius has been referred to as the saint of pagan history, representing Roman strength tempered by Greek humanity.[6] The Kimbell portrait reflects this concept in achieving a powerful, larger-than-life physical presence, in no way lessened by the deeply human, introspective quality of the man beneath.

Description: Over life-size head of a middle-aged man in white marble. The hair curls upward from the forehead, parted in the center. The beard, also divided in the center, falls into four spiral curls on each side. The face is smooth and unlined with the inner corners of the eyes defined by drill marks, the pupils and irises indicated. The neck is excessively thick and powerful.

Condition: Fair. The neck is cut back at an angle (2 3/4 in.) from the bottom edge of the beard. It then breaks unevenly up to the back edge of the hairline. There are various losses in the surface of the face, including virtually the entire nose, parts of the brow, the upper and lower lids of his left eye. His right eye is almost completely obliterated. On the top of the head, slightly to the back and to the viewer's right, a hole (3/4 in. diam.) is drilled toward the center of the head to a depth of approximately 3 1/2 in.

Exhibitions: None known.

Collections: Auction, Münzen und Medaillen, Basel, May 6, 1967, lot no. 201. [Charles Lipson, Boston.] Foundation Acquisition, AP 67.11.

Notes:

1 While the dates of the northern wars are open to controversy, it is known that Marcus Aurelius was in Rome in A.D. 169, the year in which his co-emperor Lucius Verus died. This portrait probably dates from this period, before his return to the frontier in A.D. 170.

2 Inez Scott Ryberg, *Panel Reliefs of Marcus Aurelius*, vol. XIV of *Monographs on Archaeology and Fine Arts*, New York, 1967, p. 23.

3 Wolfgang Helbig, *Führer durch die öffentlichen Sammlungen klassischer Altertümer in Rom*, 4th ed., ed. by Hermine Speier, Tübingen, 1966, p. 142.

4 For a youthful portrait, see: *Portrait of Marcus Aurelius as a Youth*, Antiquarium del Foro, Rome, in which Marcus is portrayed with a somewhat dreamy expression, curly locks, and the slightest indication of a beard.

Portrait Head of Faustina the Younger

After A.D. 161, probably before A.D. 180

Marble, 13 1/4 × 10 5/8 × 9 5/8 in. (33.6 × 27 × 24.5 cm.)

Roman portraiture, one of the great artistic achievements of the ancient world, serves as both a mirror and a measure of its times. As a tool of Imperial Roman propaganda, it played a vital role in exalting not only the reigning emperor but members of the imperial family as well. Faustina the Younger, daughter of the Emperor Antoninus Pius, was given in marriage to Marcus Aurelius in A.D. 145. The Kimbell portrait head of Faustina skillfully achieves the ennoblement of the empress by presenting her not as an ordinary woman but as a priestess of the imperial cult.

Faustina's appearance is familiar to us from contemporary coins, where she is first presented as the daughter of Pius, later as empress in her own right and, after her death, as the divine Faustina. The inscriptions on the reverse of these coins ascribe to the empress such traditional Roman virtues as Concordia, Pietas and Pudicitia (harmony, goodness and modesty). These various issues of coins are significant because they record the official portrait types from which they were derived and thereby serve to document the changing iconography of Faustina.[1]

The Kimbell head is thought to portray Faustina as a young empress in her early thirties, shortly after the succession of Marcus Aurelius in A.D. 161.[2] Her face has the spareness and refinement associated with her earliest portraits, but her features display a new sharpness and definition. While this remains a youthful portrait, it no longer has the same soft, girlish qualities which characterize heads such as that of Faustina in the Museo Capitolino, Rome, which is thought to be the portrait type created on the occasion of her marriage when she was about fifteen years of age.[3] Interestingly, however, the Kimbell portrait lacks the full-cheeked, matronly appearance which usually characterizes Faustina at this time of her life.[4] Consequently, the Kimbell portrait head might well be a posthumous image presenting a youthfully idealized Faustina as a divine being, rather than as the young empress in the role of priestess.

The distinctive feature of the Kimbell portrait is the headband, from which emerge the bases of three portrait busts, the heads of which are now missing. This type of priestly headdress is associated with the rites of the imperial cult in the Roman provinces of Asia Minor, where the emperor and his family were worshipped as part of the state religion. It has been suggested that the three figures on the headband may have represented prominent members of the Antonine family, with Hadrian in the center, Antoninus Pius to the viewer's left, and Marcus to the right.[5]

The Kimbell portrait head is thought to come from Asia Minor, which might relate to the fact that Faustina died in A.D. 175 at Halala in Cappadocia while accompanying her husband on his tour of the eastern provinces. Halala was forthwith renamed Faustinopolis, and divine honors were accorded to Faustina by the Roman Senate.[6]

Description: Life-size head of a young woman, white marble with sand-colored incrustations. Her hair is divided in the middle, falling in soft waves parallel to the part. She wears a mantle drawn up over her head, on top of which rests a diadem, directly above a string of beads. The back of the head is finished with great delicacy and careful attention to

[5] J. M. C. Toynbee, *The Art of the Romans*, vol. 43 of *Ancient People and Places*, ed. by Glyn Daniel, New York, 1965, p. 65. See: Cornelius C. Vermeule, *Roman Imperial Art in Greece and Asia Minor*, Cambridge, Mass., 1968, pp. 95–123, for a complete discussion of the Great Antonine Altar at Ephesus.

[6] A. S. L. Farquharson, *Marcus Aurelius: His Life and His World*, New York, 1951, p. 10.

Additional References:
For a complete discussion of the iconography of Marcus Aurelius, see: Max Wegner, *Die Herrscherbildnisse in antoninischer Zeit*, Berlin, 1939, pp. 166–210, pls. 14–33. Jale Inan and Elisabeth Rosenbaum, *Roman and Early Byzantine Portrait Sculpture in Asia Minor*, London, 1970, pp. 76–77, pls. XXVII–XXIX.

Undated Roman denarius. Based on Faustina's hair style, this coin probably dates from about A.D. 147–48. Kimbell Art Museum

decorative detail, with the mantle falling into regular folds, over which lie the crossed ties of the headdress.

Condition: Good. Various losses include those in the headpiece; the mantle, in front, notably to the viewer's left, less so to the right; and the upper back head area to the viewer's right. The lower half of the nose is missing, as is the chin. The mouth, which was originally strongly structured, has been abraded, and losses to both the upper and lower right lips turn what was probably originally a bland expression into a strange smile.

Exhibitions: None known.

Collections: [Mathias Komor, New York.]
Foundation Acquisition, AP 69.18.

Notes:

1 See: Harold Mattingly, *Antoninus Pius to Commodus*, vol. IV of *A Catalogue of Coins of the Roman Empire in the British Museum*, London, 1968.

2 Cornelius Vermeule, "Three Imperial Portraits in America: Nero, Britannicus, and Faustina II from Asia Minor," *Boston Museum Bulletin*, vol. LXVII, 1969, p. 121.

3 Wolfgang Helbig, *Führer durch die öffentlichen Sammlungen klassischer Altertümer in Rom*, 4th ed., ed. by Hermine Speier, Tübingen, 1966, p. 143, cat. no. 1303.

4 Helbig, p. 89, cat. no. 1234.

5 For a detailed discussion of the possible identity of the three figures on Faustina's headband, see: Vermeule, "Three Imperial Portraits," pp. 121–24.

6 Vermeule, *Roman Imperial Art in Greece and Asia Minor*, Cambridge, Mass., 1968, p. 282.

Additional References:
For a discussion of the iconography of Faustina the Younger, see: Max Wegner, *Die Herrscherbildnisse in antoninischer Zeit*, Berlin, 1939, pp. 210–25, pls. 34–38.
Jale Inan and Elisabeth Rosenbaum, *Roman and Early Byzantine Portrait Sculpture in Asia Minor*, London, 1970, pp. 77–79, pls. XXVIII–XXXI.

Funeral Portrait Head
Probably from Egypt
About A.D. 200–250

Stucco, 11 9/16 × 7 5/8 × 5 1/2 in. (29.4 × 19.4 × 14 cm.)

The Kimbell funeral portrait stands symbolically between two worlds–the crumbling Roman Empire and the newly emerging Christian church.

This head, with its highly individualized features, follows the Roman tradition of realistic portraiture. Its proportions and modeling of the nose and mouth derive from classical antecedents as exemplified in the second-century Roman *Portrait Head of Marcus Aurelius*, Kimbell collection, whose heroic assurance is tempered by a pensive, questioning mood. The Kimbell funeral head, from the first half of the third century, carries this element of brooding introspection to its furthest limit. This new expressionistic quality is conveyed primarily through the treatment of the eyes, which are strikingly inlaid with a glass-like material and make no pretense at being naturalistic. The eyes do not actually focus; the eye to the viewer's right looks out obliquely while the left eye stares straight ahead. Along with the taut modeling of the face, they create the appearance of a man in anguish, seemingly haunted by his view of this world, who looks past it to a personal spiritual vision beyond.

The Kimbell *Funeral Portrait Head* is thought to be Eastern Mediterranean in origin and was probably made in the Nile Valley during the Roman period (30 B.C.–A.D. 395).[1] The thin, sensitive face bespeaks a sense of asceticism, an advanced degree of awareness. Its introspective quality reflects the new religious ferment and the political turbulence of the age. This derives from the emergence of Christianity and other mystery religions from the Near East, which introduced such new concepts as personal salvation and an individual's direct relationship with deity. A strong element of mysticism, a daily expectation of miracles, contributed to this heightened religious climate which pervaded the entire Roman world during the first centuries of our era.[2]

The Kimbell portrait head was made to cover the skull of a mummy and as such is hollow inside. The earliest plaster funeral heads date from the beginning of the Roman period and are thought to have come mostly from Middle Egypt. The Kimbell head appears to have rested level with the body. More commonly, however, in later examples the head was raised at an angle, giving the appearance of a man lying on a pillow.[3]

Another funeral portrait head, which is comparable to the Kimbell example in its expressive quality, is the painted plaster mask from Hu (Diospolis Parva), early first century.[4] Now in the British Museum, it displays the same facial characteristics–aquiline nose, full lips, staring eyes–and perhaps an even deeper sense of cataclysmic terror. A charming funeral bust of a woman in the Louvre is of interest primarily because it includes the entire upper body and hands. It is later than the Kimbell head, but completely lacking in spiritual content. It reflects the pagan quality which persisted in such Hellenized Egyptian towns as Antinoe, where the piece was excavated.[5]

One might be led to speculate that the subject of the Kimbell head was a Copt, a native Egyptian in a land conquered by the Romans in 30 B.C. By the time Christianity had become established in Egypt in the late second century, the oppressed Copts had embraced the new faith with a religious fervor amounting to fanaticism.[6]

Whether or not the subject was a Christian, however, is immaterial. What does matter is that he lived at a time in history which saw the breakup of the Roman Empire and the first stirrings of a new order which placed emphasis on individual spiritual values. The expression on this man's face suggests that he was a witness to these events.

Description: A life-size funeral portrait head of a man, in white stucco, with traces of paint and gilding. The face is remarkable in that the two halves are completely unlike and, when viewed in profile from either side, presents a completely different expression. The mouth is drawn downward to the viewer's left; the top right lip curls upward almost into a sneer. The pink color of the lips is retained. The aquiline nose is sharply defined; the right nostril curves upward. The left ear is higher than the right and not as well delineated; its lobe is bulbous and unfinished.

The face is framed by a row of somewhat flattened curls, decoratively arranged in individual strands. A second row of curls, more sketchily rendered, is attached to the left side and acts as a transition between the head and its base. There are traces of brown pigment affixed to the hair, which probably served as a base coat for the gilding. Traces of gilding also cling to certain areas of the beard. In contrast to the hair, both the moustache and beard are modeled in low relief. The forehead is low and indented just below the hairline. Sharp ridges form the eyebrows; they are completely conventionalized, with no attempt to indicate hair. The almond-shaped eyes are large and compelling, with prominent lids. They are inlaid with a creamy pinkish substance which might be a fired clay or glass paste, or a finer sifting of the stucco. The irises are a translucent green inlay; the pupils are black, possibly obsidian. The eyelashes are outlined in black and appear to have been a separate inlay, very thin and inserted with great precision.

Condition: Excellent. Except for the relatively minor loss of gilding to the hair and beard, the face is in pristine condition. There appears to be a separation of the second row of curls in the back left section of the head and possibly some losses to the hair in this area.

Exhibitions: None known.

Collections: [Ben Heller, Inc., New York.]
Foundation Acquisition, AP 70.5.

Notes:

1 This head could also have come from Syria, which had close ties with the Nile Valley during the third century. Like the entire Eastern Empire, Egypt and Syria shared a Graeco-Roman heritage, and the Kimbell head relates to certain funeral reliefs from northern Syria in such details as the treatment of the hair and beard, the delineation of the brows, the high-bridged nose, heavy lids, and the hypnotic quality of the intensely staring eyes.

2 Ranuccio Bianchi Bandinelli, *Rome: The Center of Power*, trans. by Peter Green, London, 1970, pp. 310, 322–24, 338–39.

3 *A General Introductory Guide to the Egyptian Collections in the British Museum*, London, 1964, p. 229.

4 *Guide*, p. 230, fig. 82.

5 *Koptische Kunst: Christentum am Nil*, Villa Hügel, Essen, 1963, pp. 218–19, cat. no. 40, illus. See also: Kazimierz Michalowski, *The Art of Ancient Egypt*, London, 1969, p. 337, color illus. 139, and *L'Art Copte*, Petit Palais, Paris, 1964, p. 63, cat. no. 18, illus.

6 Klaus Wessel, *Coptic Art in Early Christian Egypt*, New York, 1965, pp. 65–72.

Wall Paintings from the Chapel of St. André de Bagalance, near Avignon
Middle of the Twelfth Century
Dry fresco on plaster, transferred to canvas and mounted on wood, 12 ft. 4 3/4 in. × 10 ft. 2 in. × (depth) 11 ft. 3 in. (376.2 × 310.2 × 343.2 cm.)

Romanesque art embodied the first style to achieve universal diffusion throughout Western Europe since the decline of the Roman Empire, and it was, in large measure, a conscious effort to revive the ancient classical principles. During all the centuries of the so-called Dark Ages the ideal of glorious Rome never died, but constant turmoil prevented any revival from coalescing, no matter how brilliant certain renascences were. However, as the first millennium of the Christian Era drew to a close, the confluence of many factors provided a period of sustained stability and broad communication which permitted a new cosmopolitan art to emerge. The Christianization of Vikings and Visigoths had been effected and the Magyars had been evicted from Central Europe. The Moors and Byzantines were held at bay by the Norman kingdom of Sicily, as Spain began her reconquest over the Mohammedans. The great pilgrimage roads of southern France and Spain were thronged, and the Holy Land was won on the First Crusade by the year 1100. The large monastic orders were finally achieving unified leadership in a movement of profound spiritual intensification. In support of all these activities there arose such colorful enterprises as the wide-ranging Orders of the Knights Templars and the Knights of St. John of Jerusalem.

The Chapel of St. André de Bagalance may bear the imprint of the activity of one of these military orders. In the apex of the ceiling is represented the *Lamb of God* carrying, not the usual Latin Cross, but the cross of equal arms (in the sixteenth century to become known as the Maltese Cross). Shortly after 1120, the *Lamb of God* thus depicted was adopted as their distinctive emblem by the Knights of St. John of Jerusalem, an order that is known to have founded numerous priories and hospitals along the pilgrimage roads of southern France. A justification for such a startlingly intimate fusion of military orders and the purely spiritual was set forth by no less a leader than St. Bernard of Clairvaux in his *De laude novae militiae* (about 1135).

Whatever the instigation for founding the chapel, it is referred to as having already existed for some time in a document of the early thirteenth century. In 1212 (Archives Vaucluse, H., St. Catherine, 89) and in a parchment dated 1229 preserved at St. Michel de Frigolet, the church is called St. André de Tybel (or Tibel). That this reference is to one and the same place is signaled in another document from the end of the eleventh century (Archives Vaucluse, G., 698, p. 89.7) where it is evident that Bagalance is a toponym. There are local records from the thirteenth century of a Bagalance family. One other thirteenth-century record (Archives Vaucluse, G., 219, 12) is dated 1274.

Located about five miles south of Avignon, in the district of Barbentane, much of the stone structure of the little chapel still stands. That an even earlier church stood on the same spot is indicated by the presence of some of its foundation stones (eleventh century?), which were removed, recut to size, and used in the present church. Recently, in a commercial gravel pit dug into the side of the hill that supports the chapel, the remains of a prehistoric stone hut were uncovered. In another hill that stands above the church, recent official archaeological excavations have discovered remains of what must have been a fortified town *(oppidum)* dated by Henri Rolland to about 700 B.C. Since both the present railroad line and the main north-south highway use this particular cut through the rocky terrain, it seems safe to assume that it has been a thoroughfare for as long as men have been in the region, including the era of Romanesque pilgrimages.

There exists a complete chronological list of ecclesiastics who were in charge of the chapel from the end of the fifteenth century down to 1789 when the French Revolution discontinued its religious use. On the night of February 21, 1720 (Archives Communales de Barbentane, g. g. 5, f. 2 V), "Brother Stephen Colon, hermit of the hermitage of Barbentane, in the quarter of Bagalance, was found stabbed to death at the age of thirty-five, and was buried at Barbentane..." Thereafter, people came to know the church only as "Chapel of the Hermitage," ignoring its real name, "St. André de Bagalance."

Since there was an abbey dedicated to St. Andrew nearby at Villeneuve-les-Avignon, the small chapel was probably a priory church dependent upon it. Nevertheless, consistent with the universality of the Romanesque movement, the themes for the apse decoration of this minor church display an amazing canonical constancy to frescoes in other religious houses of whatever size or importance throughout Western Europe. Stylistic elements also strive for constancy, including a color range severely restricted to earth pigments, a strict schematization of scenes, and abstract treatment of details. There is also general submission to the law of frontality, a conventional repetition of images and very little attempt at three-dimensional space. Not in spite of,

JOA
NES
MARC
VS
LVCAS

but *because* of this restraint, the fresco cycle deftly achieves its primary doctrinal goal, and does so within a total effect of monumental unity conducive to the serenely contemplative ideal of the age.

Description: There are five scenes, each contained within its own field by broad decorative borders in varying geometric patterns. The lowest field, running completely around the apse, contains the *Twelve Apostles*, all standing and all looking upwards in contemplation of the image of Christ in heaven. Every apostle carries a Gospel Book, the only one with an additional distinctive attribute being Peter who holds a large key. Above at the right is shown the *Annunciation to the Virgin.* Above at left is a putative subject, probably the *Ordination of the Chapel.* In the place of glory, above the window at the back, is *Christ in Majesty* surrounded by the symbols of the four evangelists, the name of each inscribed alongside his symbol. At the apex of the vault, on the ceiling, is the *Lamb of God* carrying the cross of equal arms. In the lower tier to the right is a painted wall niche to contain the holy altar vessels, in the lunette above which is an owl with outstretched wings.

Condition: Good. When religious use of the chapel was discontinued at the end of the eighteenth century, the walls were subsequently covered with successive layers of whitewash which served to protect the frescoes and also prevented them from being known. The building was used to house farm animals, fodder and agricultural equipment. This is probably why the whole level next to the ground is worn away. Otherwise, the losses are surprisingly small: the heads of two apostles, seven irregular patches toward the extremity of the *Christ in Majesty* motif, a round section between the legs of the *Lamb of God,* and ten irregular losses in the lower tier, including one at the right that largely obliterates the painted wall niche.

The paintings, and the thin layer of underlying plaster which the paint only partially penetrated, have been transferred to canvas, and these have been mounted on nine panels of laminated wood which, when assembled, present the frescoes in their original shape and dimensions.

Collections: Foundation Acquisition, AP 71.1.

The Barnabas Altarpiece
Painted about 1250–60
Tempera and oil on panel; central panel, 35 3/4 × 22 5/8 in. (91 × 57.5 cm.); left panel, 35 3/4 × 14 3/4 in. (91 × 37.5 cm.); right panel, 35 3/4 × 14 9/16 in (91 × 37 cm.).

For an understanding of the combination of styles and influences that shaped *The Barnabas Altarpiece* it is helpful to see it in at least a general historical context. In England from the close of the Romanesque period through the decades that saw the creation of a Gothic style (roughly 1200–85), there was a pervading cosmopolitanism. Englishmen were participating strongly in the Crusades. Constantinople fell in 1204, driving renewed Byzantine influence across Western Europe. King John (brother of Richard the Lion-Hearted) lost control of Normandy to the French early in the century, and many of the populace moved northward across the Channel. John's son, King Henry III, married Eleanor of Provence, and together they supported a great period of cultural activity; scores of foreign artists and craftsmen were imported in an effort to make Westminster Abbey a cathedral second to none (1245–70). At the Treaty of Paris (1259) all of southwestern France was ceded to the English. King Henry's son, Edward I, married Eleanor of Castile, and they consummated an important treaty of commerce with Flanders in 1274. King Haakon IV of Norway (1224–62), seeking to bolster his autocratic regime, tirelessly pursued a policy of triangular political and cultural exchange between France, England and Scandinavia.[1]

These elusive threads in England's past are interwoven in the pattern of art history. For example, the most influential English manuscript illuminator of the century, Matthew Paris, was so surnamed because he learned his art at the French capital before practicing it at the Abbey of St. Albans near London until his death in 1259. He inserted into one of his own school's manuscripts a most noble drawing of the apocalyptic Christ, done by a certain Brother William, an Englishman who was one of the earliest followers of St. Francis, near whom he is buried at Assisi. In an entire group of English psalters the format of the pages is derived from French stained glass window techniques. A fresco series from a small church at the foot of the Pyrenees in Aragon may very well have been designed by the so-called Morgan Master of the Winchester school. The great Vatican inventory of 1295 lists far more rich pieces of English embroidered vestments made in the thirteenth century than from any other country.

Because of this welter of cultural intercourse it is not surprising that it has taken some time to determine England as the country of origin for *The Barnabas Altarpiece*. In addition to the attritions of time from such an early epoch, in Britain there was the iconoclasm of the Reformation. Practically nothing except manuscripts is left with which to compare. This rarity, of course, makes the Barnabas triptych all the more important historically, and it has occasioned a sustained analysis on stylistic and technical grounds by many medieval scholars.

During the nineteenth century, when the panels were little known in the Hochon collection in France, they were simply accepted as French,[2] as they still were when exhibited in the important exhibition, *La Vierge dans l'Art Français*, at the Petit Palais in 1950.[3] Those in charge of the exhibition followed the analysis of French Inspector of Monuments Historiques, Louis-Philippe May, who had argued in an article of 1948 that the triptych was Burgundian and related to manuscripts from Cluny datable about 1200.[4] As such, they were exhibited once again in 1952–53.[5] In another whole group of general history books and encyclopedias the panels were used as illustrations.[6]

As a result of these exhibitions and publications, *The Barnabas Altarpiece* began to receive the attention of the most authoritative scholars in the Gothic field. Prof. Ellen Beer of the University at Bern at first proposed a Norwegian attribution, but, upon careful study and examination of the panels after cleaning, she strongly supported England as the place of origin and asserted that, because the altarpiece is English, "it is one of the earliest pieces extant..." and "the unique and ancient character of the piece makes it of primary importance."[7] Another strong voice in negating the Scandinavian source was that of Aron Andersson of the Central Office and Museum of National Antiquities, Stockholm, who stated that if it were Scandinavian "a picture by the same hand... would be expected to exist in Norway, which is not the case." He supports the English origin and dates it between 1250–70.[8]

The possibilities of Spain were brought up by both Richard Randall of the Walters Art Gallery and Prof. Harry Bober of New York University, Randall perceptively relating the retable to a group of paintings in a mixed style best illustrated by "a French manuscript for a Spanish queen [Blanche of Castile]," (Morgan Library, Ms. M. 240).[9] In this regard, it is interesting to note that Chandler R. Post, when shown the altarpiece, assigned it to France and excluded it from consideration in his monumental *History of Spanish Painting*.

D. H. Turner of the British Museum, who has studied the Barnabas panels after cleaning and given a more comprehensive and precise consideration to them than anyone else, asserts that they are "undoubtedly English work of the third quarter of the thirteenth century."[10] He did further research in collaboration with Dr. Beer, the two scholars concluding that "we are inclined to a date in the 50s rather than the 60s."[11] Supporting this opinion all along has been Prof. T. S. R. Boase of Magdalen College, Oxford, who strongly asserts: "It is clearly a most important addition to the corpus of thirteenth century English work . . . and it must be one of the earliest of our surviving panel paintings."[12]

A number of other authorities in Gothic studies have declared themselves rather precisely in this same vein,[13] thus substantiating *The Barnabas Altarpiece* as perhaps the earliest surviving English painting on panel, the famous Westminster Retable being datable about 1470 or later. And the latter, although once obviously superb, is in extremely poor condition.

Inscription: On bottom margin of St. Peter panel: BARNABAS; on bottom of central, or Virgin, panel: BARNABAS: EPS:
The identity of a bishop by this name has not yet been established,[14] but he undoubtedly was the donor of the altarpiece.

BARNABAS

BARNA BAS : EPS

Description: The altarpiece consists of three panels, now separate from each other. The central panel contains the Virgin offering her left breast to the Christ Child, an unusual motif for this early a time; but other examples of it are to be found in the Amesbury Psalter of about 1250 (Bodleian Library, Oxford, Ms. 6), and the Psalter for Guisborough Priory, Yorkshire (Bodleian, Ms. Laud. Lat. 5., fol. 11). The architectural throne in the latter manuscript is quite similar to the one on which the Barnabas Virgin and Child sit, with gold-embroidered bolster cushion at the back and a "Romanesque" tiered masonry structure, narrowly fenestrated, flaring outward at the top. The Virgin's exaggerated open gold crown, curving at a rakish angle, is paralleled in a number of English manuscripts of the period, including the above-mentioned Guisborough Psalter.

The Virgin is clothed in a white robe and headdress, with a red mantle bordered in gold. The two saints wear similar vestments, whereas the Child is covered by a thin, pale lavender-pink tunic. All three male personages carry a bound, strapped Bible in their left hands, while each of the saints carries in his right hand a large version of his respective symbol: double keys for Peter, a pointed sword with gold hilt for Paul. This combination of subject matter was sometimes used in key places, such as the dedicatory page of a Bible, or central medallion of a chasuble (Prologue page of Bible of William of Devon, for example, about 1250; Clare Chasuble, Victoria and Albert Museum, about 1272–94). The artist was not quite up to the sophistication of showing Peter's hand holding his book through the cloth of his garment, and the resulting awkwardness reminds one of the thirteenth-century northeast Italian New Testament at Oxford where Peter does the same thing (Bodleian, Canon. Bibl. Lat. 14). It was an occasional medieval gimmick, seldom very successful, applied to other personages as well (cf. Bodleian, Lyell Ms. 71, by Hugues de Fouilly, ca. 1300). The shallow, so-called "drop" Gothic arches of the painted architecture, in addition to the throne, and the piled-up buildings behind the arches, still have some of the Romanesque about them, while the column bases, capitals and foils of the central arch have a whiff of Byzantine.

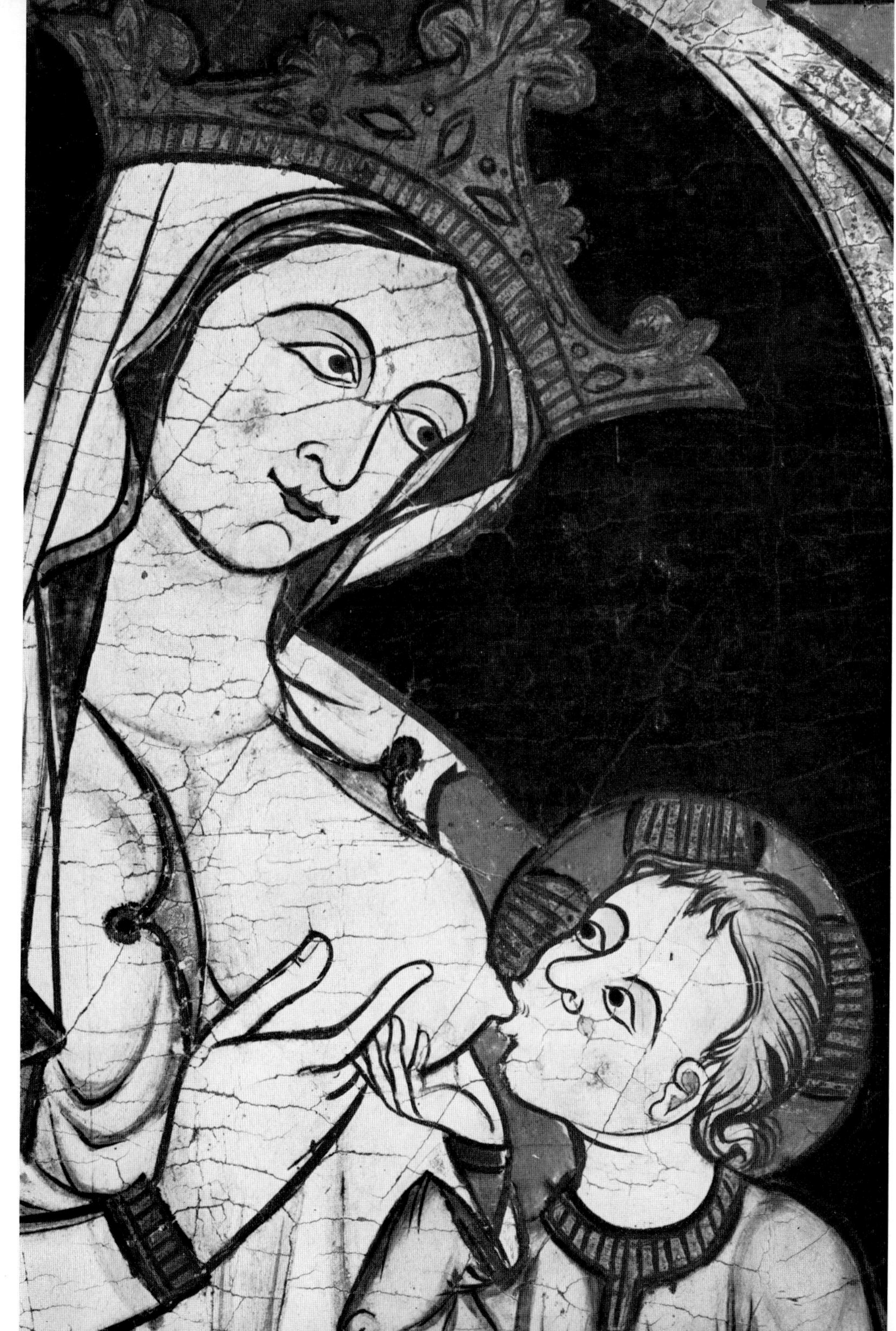

What is being described seems to fit quite well what D. H. Turner calls the "Anglo-French" style that stands apart from the main line of development and takes its strongest influence from northwestern France.[15] It is a transitional, or middle, phase of early Gothic evolution that occurred just past the middle of the century. In its spatial and psychological relationships also it represents a midpoint of development. The figures are no longer completely separated from each other and bound by their own spatial enclaves, but neither do they visually engage each other, or the viewer. However, the vivacity of facial expression, gesture, and action is a yearning toward the fuller humanism of the mature Gothic. Whereas the technique is less painterly than the Westminster Retable, the vigor of color and line has the freshness and charm of all things at the threshold.

Condition: Fair. During 1967–68 the panels were cleaned and stabilized at the Swiss Institute for Art Research, Zurich; analyses of pigment colors were carried out at the Doerner Institute, Munich, and Prof. S. Rees-Jones of the Courtauld Institute, London, conducted a technical examination.[16] The wood of the primary supports was determined to be willow, another argument in favor of an English origin. A secondary support of parqueted pine had been affixed during the 19th century; this was removed. Each panel had been nearly pulverized by the action of wood worms, but each was successfully impregnated with wax resin, strengthened with balsa strips, and sealed. Areas of splintering had occurred at a number of the edges, and these were filled with wax resin with an admixture of sawdust, then regessoed, and inpainted without imitating the original crackle pattern, so that the repainted edges can easily be seen. All old accretions, yellowed varnish and nineteenth-century repaint were removed. About a third of the distance up from the bottom of each panel, running horizontally across all three, there are rough, round bumps in the paint structure caused by the heads of large nails that had been driven through the panels to join them by a horizontal toggle at the back. The nails oxydized, expanded and caused the protuberances. The remnants of a ledge at the bottom, plus the fact that the tops of each panel have been sawn off, surely indicate that they were the middle range of a three-tiered altarpiece originally.[17] Indeed, there is the very end of a big toe just left of center at the top of the Paul panel, and the tip of a finger (?) near the lower left corner of the Virgin panel. This may be all we will ever see of Barnabas Episcopus; based upon custom of the time in manuscripts in England (cf. Matthew Paris' *Enthroned Virgin and Child* showing the artist himself kneeling at their feet, British Museum, Royal Ms. 14 CVII, fol. 6, and the aforementioned "Bible of William of Devon" where a cleric kneels at the bottom) and usage in extant altarpieces elsewhere in Europe, Barnabas might be expected to be found there at the feet of the Virgin and under his own name.

Exhibitions: Petit Palais, *La Vierge dans l'Art Français*, Paris, 1950, cat. no. 1, illus. no. 10. Galerie Charpentier, *Cent Peintures Religieuses*, Paris, 1952, cat. no. 2, illus.

Collections: M. Hochon, Paris, to 1903. [Galerie Georges Petit], Paris 1903. Philippe Gangnat, Paris. Maurice Clement de Coppet, Geneva, by 1962.
Foundation Acquisition, AP 69.6 a, b, c.

Notes:

1 Harry Fett, "L'Influence Française dans l'Art Norvégien," *Gazette des Beaux Arts*, vol. VI, 1922, p. 218. See also: A. A. F. Lindblom, *Peintures Gothiques en Svede et en Norvège*, Paris–London, 1916.

2 Galerie Georges Petit, sale catalogue, *Collection de M. Hochon*, Paris, June 12, 1903, no. 14, illus.

3 Jacques Dupont and Jean Verrier, *La Vierge dans l'Art Français*, Petit Palais, Paris, 1950, cat. no. 1, illus. no. 10.

4 Louis-Philippe May, "Le Triptyque Barnabas, un tableau Romano-Gothique," *France Illustration*, Paris, December, 1948, numerous illus.

5 Galerie Charpentier, *Cent Peintures Religieuses*, Paris, 1952, cat. no. 2, illus.

6 Camille Enlart, *Manuel d'Archéologie*, sec. 2, "Religious Architecture"; chapter 10, "Altars and Altar Screens," Paris, 1920, p. 837. Stanislas Fumet, *Art et Style*, vol. 26, 1953, chapter 3, illus. Librairie Larousse, *Histoire de France*, Paris, 1954, vol. 1, plate facing p. 224. L.-P. May, *Analysis of Harmonious Structure Based on Pythagoras*, Paris, 1960, p. 10, illus. nos. 1–2. *Nouveau Petit Larousse Illustré*, Librairie Larousse, Paris, 1971, p. 891, "Retable," illus.

7 Ellen Beer, "Gotische Buchmalerei," *Zeitschrift für Kunstgeschichte*, Munich and Berlin, 1968, "England," p. 325; also cf. letter of Sept. 30, 1965.

8 Aron Andersson, letter, Aug. 22, 1968.

9 Harry Bober, letter, Oct. 22, 1968; Richard Randall, letter, Jan. 16, 1969.

10 D. H. Turner, letter, Dec. 13, 1966.

11 Turner, letter, Sept. 29, 1967.

12 T. S. R. Boase, letters, June 9, 1964; Dec. 3, 1965.

13 See letters of: Donald King, Victoria and Albert Museum, Oct. 12, 1965, who relates style to English embroideries of the period. Prof. Kurt Gerstenberg, Würzburg, Pfingsten, 1966. Prof. Otto Pächt, University of Vienna, Feb. 21 and March 9, 1967. Peter Strieder, Germanisches National-museum, Nuremberg, Jan. 9–Feb. 6, 1969. Harvey Stahl, Metropolitan Museum of Art, New York, Jan. 20, 1969. F. Ph. Verdier, University of Montreal, Feb. 20, 1969.

14 Letter of Donald King, Victoria and Albert Museum, Oct. 1, 1965.

15 Turner, *Early Gothic Illuminated Manuscripts*, British Museum, London, 1965, p. 14.

16 Dr. Thomas Brachert, *Untersuchungsbericht*, Schweizerisches Institut für Kunstwissenschaft, Zurich, 1968.

17 Mojmir Frinta, "The Closing Tabernacle–A Fanciful Innovation of Medieval Design," *Art Quarterly*, vol. XXX, no. 2, 1967, p. 103, note 16; p. 117.

Giovanni di Paolo, about 1400/3–1483
Madonna and Child, with St. Margaret and St. Catherine of Alexandria
Painted about 1445–60

Egg tempera on gesso panel, 15 1/4 × 8 in.
(39 × 20 1/2 cm.)

Giovanni di Paolo di Grazia was born during those very years that are traditionally designated as the dawn of the Italian Renaissance, and his long, active career spanned the period which produced modern humanism, individualism, naturalistic investigation of the world and man, and the disciplines of an unprecedented intellectual rationality. The Florentines were leaders in this movement, but Giovanni was born and spent his whole life in Siena, the indolent city-state of ultraconservatism with a decided distaste for progressive innovation, logical analysis, or the worldly. The mystical spirit of St. Catherine of Siena (1347–1380) still held sway, and while Giovanni was in mid-career (1461) she was canonized. The artist more than likely stood in the Campo before the Palazzo Pubblico to witness the preachings of San Bernardino of Siena (1380–1444). The Sienese deliberately clung to the other-worldliness of the Gothic age, and most of their artists throughout the fifteenth century continued the endeavor to symbolize the spirituality of that age while elsewhere there was enthusiasm for mathematical perspective, scientific anatomy, and the revival of ancient Greece and Rome.

An unavoidable awareness of developing Renaissance styles, plus this conscious tendency to archaism, inevitably led Giovanni to considerable eclecticism. He is thought to have been trained first in the shop of Taddeo di Bartolo, and also perhaps in the *bottega* of Paolo di Giovanni Fei. Certainly he was strongly influenced as a young artist by Gentile da Fabriano, who was working in Siena in 1424–25. He took some of his conceptions and much of his iconography from the great Sienese masters of a hundred years earlier, especially the Lorenzetti and Simone Martini. In

addition, as we know from surviving manuscripts, Giovanni was an accomplished miniaturist, and he not only developed a minute technical precision through this branch of his art, but received a diversity of new ideas by examining examples of this transportable art form. The confluence of all these factors in the mind of one who must have had a singularly mystical temperament produced a style utterly unfettered by logic and immune from a constant stylistic allegiance. Giovanni was left with an extremely loose, flexible medium that he used impulsively, according to his own fantasy, with the result that he became one of the most individual artists of his century.

The Kimbell picture undoubtedly is the central panel of a little portable altarpiece, the two folding wings of which are missing. It is characteristic of Sienese taste in its finely wrought small scale and insistent use of the timeless, spaceless gold background which adds to the conventionalized but richly decorative design. The artist ignored linear perspective and made no attempt to create a real volume of space in which the figures could stand, the bodies and draperies being molded by an abstract light that leaves them as though they were in very shallow relief upon a flat ground. This essential two-dimensionality, however, is enriched by a wealth of lovingly and precisely rendered detail, such as the wreaths of roses, brocaded textiles, or ermine minivers on St. Catherine's robe. Consonant with the essential flatness, but weaving all the represented details together, is a complex composition of sinuous calligraphic lines that display Giovanni's refined, meticulous draftsmanship. The profile contours of the figures provide much of this distinctive linear design, but closer contemplation reveals a delightfully rich concentration of this lyrical Gothic motif in the less obvious areas within the figures. Where areas of gold leaf meet areas of paint, these lines are accentuated by the medieval technique of "marking out" *(ritagliare)*, in which the lines of demarcation are actually incisions into the gesso of the panel.

The diminutive personages, gracefully posed and elegantly garbed, innocently breathe the languid air of a courtly place and time that is being superseded. Their fragile, elongated figures and strangely introspective faces seem to be a more realistic version of the traditional Sienese-Byzantine form and augment the little panel's quality as a symbol of a supernatural world.

Description: Seated on a throne covered with a cloth of red and gold, the Madonna holds in her lap the nude Child who turns to look at Saint Margaret standing at the right with the conquered dragon beneath her feet. Saint Catherine of Alexandria is at the left holding a fragment of the toothed wheel upon which she was martyred. Both saints are crowned with double wreaths of roses. Saint Catherine wears a red robe lined with ermine. Saint Margaret's robe is light blue, lined with green; her gown, red and gold. The background is gold with some of the red bole ground showing through.

Condition: Good. The panel underwent technical treatment in late 1969–70, during which cleavage areas were laid down, and the whole was infused from the back with wax resin. A new surface coating was formed. Numerous old small losses, scattered, were found to have been retouched with tempera long ago; these were left. The small triangular section at the top is a replacement.

Exhibitions: Masterpieces of Art, New York World's Fair, May–October, 1939; catalogue by George H. McCall, "European Paintings and Sculpture from 1300–1800," p. 72, no. 146. *Art*, "Golden Gate International Exposition," Palace of Fine Arts, San Francisco, 1940, no. 109, illus. p. 21.

Collections: Chigi-Saraceni, Siena. Leon Somzée, Paris, until at least 1904. Dan Fellows Platt, Englewood, N. J., before 1911.
Foundation Acquisition, AP 66.7.

References: Catalogue des Monuments d'Art Antique ... Tableaux Anciens ... composant les Collections de Somzée, Deuxieme Partie: Tableaux Anciens des Ecoles Italienne, Flamande, Française, Brussels, May 24, 1904, no. 286; pl. XXIV, facing p. 6.
F. Mason Perkins, "Dipinti italiani nella Raccolta Platt Parte I," *Rassegna d'arte*, vol. XI, no. 1, January, 1911, p. 3.
Joseph Breck, "Some Paintings by Giovanni di Paolo: II," *Art in America*, vol. II, no. IV, June, 1914, pp. 283–84, illus. p. 285, fig. 3.
F. M. Perkins, "Dipinti senesi sconosciuti o inediti," *Rassegna d'arte*, vol. XIV, no. 7, July, 1914, p. 165, note 1.
Osvald Siren, "Giovanni di Paolo di Grazia," in *Allgemeines Lexikon der bildenden Künstler*, eds., Thieme and Becker, Leipzig, 1921, vol. XIV, p. 136.
Raimond van Marle, *The Development of the Italian Schools of Painting*, The Hague, 1927, vol. IX, p. 451, note 2.
Bernard Berenson, *Italian Pictures of the Renaissance*, Oxford, 1932, p. 245.
B. Berenson, *Pitture italiani del Rinascimento*, Milan, 1936, p. 157.
John Pope-Hennessy, *Giovanni di Paolo*, New York, 1938, pl. XXIV b, pp. 94, 112, also note 93.
Cesare Brandi, *Giovanni di Paolo*, Florence, 1947, p. 87, note 73.

Giovanni Bellini, about 1430–1516
Madonna and Child
Painted about 1470–75

Tempera and oil on panel, 32 3/8 × 22 3/4 in. (82.5 × 58 cm.)

Giovanni Bellini, most likely an illegitimate son of painter Jacopo Bellini (about 1400–1472), became the grand patriarch of Venetian art before the end of his long career. He was the most powerful influence upon both Giorgione and Titian, and many of the principal developments in the subsequent history of art are unimaginable without taking Giovanni Bellini's contribution into account. He commenced working about the middle of the fifteenth century in a belated International Gothic style that his father had learned as an assistant in the shop of Gentile da Fabriano, a style to which Giovanni's brother Gentile clung, at least partly, until the end of his life. The whole Bellini family studio was then affected by the stoic and sculpturesque forms of Mantegna who, at Padua in 1453, married Jacopo's daughter Nicolosia. Also during the fifties and sixties of the quattrocento, the Bellinis absorbed much of the intellectual and classical legacy of Florentine art, partly through Mantegna and partly through Tuscan artists working in the Veneto. But Giovanni went on enlarging and enriching his vision and technique with influences from Piero della Francesca, Antonello da Messina and northern European masters who were far advanced in the experience of working in oil, with the result that he transformed the art of Venetian painting into a majestic instrument of poetic expressiveness in sonorous color, light, and shadows. Marco Boschini, writing in 1660, summed it up with an hyperbole difficult to deny: "...with his colors, he was the first to make living paintings. Giambellino may be called the spring of all the world in the art of painting, for all freshness is derived from him, and without him art would be winter."[1]

From a period relatively early in the master's career, the Kimbell *Madonna and Child* is suffused with that spirit of springlike freshness and innocence that one associates with the quattrocento generally, as opposed to the more complex visual sophistication of the High Renaissance to which Bellini himself was one of the greatest contributors. The Virgin here is among the very youngest and most prophetically wistful of the many examples from Bellini's hand. The tenderness of subject is directly achieved, as the Child actually *sings* the psalm his Mother is teaching him from the book lying before them.

The overall composition is simple and classical, the space shallow and planar, with a dramatic separation of the different planes accomplished by such devices as the large shadow cast by the Madonna on the cloth of honor behind her. Although marvelously delicate and fine, the Child's curly blond hair still has something of that archaic severity derived from Mantegna and the Tuscan sculptors, as do the edges and folds of the draperies. There is still a whisper of the "primitive" in the partly gold ground and flat, embroidered cloth of honor, as well as in the perfectly round halos made of thin gold lines. The upper layer of the paint structure, in oil, achieves a pristine translucence and pearly lightness, even though it was applied with a sharp-pointed brush in multiple straight strokes that recall the traditional tempera technique. These elements combine to form a paradigm of that moment in the history of art when Early Renaissance conventions were being transformed into a fuller, living humaneness.

Sometime prior to 1866 the picture was acquired from a private collection in Bergamo by Otto Mündler (1811–70) who, although little known today, was one of the most influential connoisseurs of the nineteenth century. A German-born resident of Paris, he not only put together an impressive collection of his own[2] but, as official agent on the Continent for the National Gallery, under the director Sir Charles Eastlake, he helped acquire some of the greatest Renaissance treasures in the London institution. He wrote many brilliant articles in the earliest German journals devoted to art history, was among the first to understand and appreciate El Greco, gave Jacob Burckhardt some of his ideas relating art to general history, drove the young von Bode mad with competitive jealousy, and advised and sold important pictures to a number of mighty private collectors.[3] Thus, shortly after he had acquired the Bellini, it went into the collection of Prince Napoleon III in Paris. The Franco-Prussian War, the Commune, and the collapse of the Second Empire forced dispersal of the Royal Collection, however, in 1872.[4] The Kimbell painting was sold to an undisclosed buyer, and it disappeared completely for nearly a hundred years.

Just before it passed from Mündler to Prince Napoleon, however, it was published in a very laudatory article in the *Gazette des Beaux-Arts*.[5] It was illustrated in the article, in those days before the invention of half-tone reproductions from photographs, with an engraving by Ferdinand Gaillard, who, in addition to being a painter and distinguished print-maker, was a broadly traveled authority on the painting techniques of the old masters. Interestingly, he was among the earliest experimenters in the photogravure process. In any case, the Kimbell *Madonna and Child* was considered a lost picture by all art historians, and the only visual knowledge of it available to students of Bellini was Gaillard's engraving. Although some writers remained unaware of the "lost" painting, the more painstaking and astute always referred to it, and some illustrated it with a reproduction of the engraving.[6] After its recent rediscovery in a private collection in Europe, it is published here for the first time since 1866.

All the literature on Bellini that referred to the Kimbell picture, of course, related it to the version of the same subject in the Church of Santa Maria dell' Orto, Venice. Now, once again, the two have been examined comparatively. There are a number of details that differ. The dell' Orto version has three inscriptions of Greek letters, as in certain other "Greek Madonnas" by Bellini. The parapet is plainer in its marbled veining, and it does not rise as high into the picture. The book is missing, and the cord that ties the Madonna's gown at the waist is thinner, straighter, and does not have the looped knot with dangling free ends. The Virgin's transparent white veil has different folds and catches highlights in a different pattern; it runs across the dell' Orto forehead in a flatter manner and follows the curving line of the eyebrows much more closely. The Child's tunic is a deep mauve tone, whereas in the Kimbell version it is blacker than the Mother's mantle; the manner of picking out the highlights on the mantle with multiple straight strokes by a pointed brush is more pronounced in the dell' Orto picture. The large shadow that the Kimbell Madonna casts upon the cloth of honor is not in the other painting. The overall tonality of the dell' Orto version is in a lower register, and the modeling is darker.

BELLINI, GIOVANNI
Madonna and Child, Santa Maria dell'Orto, Venice

GAILLARD, FERDINAND
Madonna and Child
Engraving after the Kimbell painting, 1866, Bibliothèque Nationale, Paris

Emmanuele Cicogna determined that the *Madonna and Child* in Santa Maria dell' Orto was once placed above an altar dedicated to Luca Navagero, Governor of Udine, who died in 1488.[7] Crowe and Cavalcaselle, recognizing the discrepancy between the late date of such a dedication in relation to the earlier style of the picture, suggested that the Navagero family could have acquired a picture for the altar done some years before.[8]

Inscription: Signed, bottom center: IOANNES BELLINUS

Description: Standing behind a balustrade or parapet of richly veined Verona marble, the Virgin supports the Christ Child with her left hand beneath his right thigh and right hand around his chest. He leans back to sing, with his left hand across his breast and right hand dangling down to touch the index finger of his Mother. He is partially covered by a black tunic bordered in gold embroidery and clasped at his right shoulder with a round gold button inset with a red stone. The Madonna wears a gold-bordered, nearly black, greenish mantle, a red dress, and tissue-thin white veil that covers her head, as does the mantle. Two vertical edges of a flat gold ground appear at each side of a black, central cloth of honor richly embellished in repeating and intertwined oval floral motifs in gold. A book (Psalter?) lies on the right side of the parapet, and it is held open to the desired page by a metal device affixed to the book's stiff cover. Bellini's signature appears at bottom center upon a represented rectangle of slightly creased paper; the second "L" in the last name is slightly more elevated than the first, a detail, according to Morelli, which indicates the picture is an autograph work.[9]

Condition: Excellent. Cleaned and revarnished in 1969–70, the picture was found to have no major losses. A single area of fairly modern overpaint consisted of a cuff of embroidered gold that covered the originally plainer left forearm of the Madonna; this was removed. In her left eye was the only abraded area that required some superficial treatment. A number of old, small spot damages are scattered irregularly, most detectable on the Virgin's right cheek, the Child's right temple, and in the area of his legs; these were left untreated. Two vertical splits in the panel have been stabilized and required minimal inpainting. The original supporting panel, which developed a convex warp, is remarkably solid and remains uncradled.

Exhibitions: None known.

Collections: Private collection, Bergamo. Otto Mündler, Paris, before 1866. Prince Napoleon III, to 1872. Missing, to 1969.
Foundation Acquisition, AP 71.6.

Notes:

1 Marco Boschini, *La Carta del Navegar Pitoresco*, critical edition, ed. by A. Pallucchini, Venice, 1966, p. 665.

2 After Mündler's death there were three sales of his collection: Hotel Drouot, Nov. 27, 29, 30, 1871, a few very rare copies of the catalogue being still extant.

3 Editorial, "Eastlake's Travelling Agent," *Burlington Magazine*, vol. LXXXIII, September, 1943, p. 211.

4 Christie's, *Works of Art from the Collection of His Royal Highness, the Prince Napoleon*, London, May 9, 1872.

5 *Gazette des Beaux-Arts*, Paris, vol. XX, 1866, p. 288.

6 George Gronau, *Giovanni Bellini*, vol. 36 of *Klassiker der Kunst*, Stuttgart, 1909, p. 206. Gronau, "Bellini" in *Allgemeines Lexikon der bildenden Künstler*, eds., Thieme and Becker, Leipzig, 1909, vol. III, p. 260. J. A. Crowe and G. B. Cavalcaselle, *A History of Painting in North Italy*, ed. by Tancred Borenius, 1912, vol. I, p. 151, no. 2. "Eastlake's Travelling Agent," p. 211, no. 2, pl. I. Rodolfo Pallucchini, *Giovanni Bellini*, Palazzo Ducale, Venice, 1949, cat. no. 79, p. 122. Luitpold Dussler, *Giovanni Bellini*, Vienna, 1949, p. 33. Fritz Heinemann, *Giovanni Bellini e i Belliniani*, Venice, 1959, vol. I, no. 26, p. 6; illus. vol. II, no. 54b, p. 76. Stefano Bottari, *Tutta la Pittura di Giovanni Bellini*, Milan, 1963, vol. I, p. 139.

7 Emmanuele A. Cicogna, *Delle Iscrizione Veneziane*, Orlandelli ed., Venice, 1827, vol. II, pp. 260–61.

8 Crowe and Cavalcaselle, p. 151.

9 Giovanni Morelli [I. Lermolieff], *Critical Studies of Italian Painters*, trans. by C. J. Ffoulkes, London, 1892–93.

Giovanni Bellini, about 1430–1516
Christ Blessing
Painted about 1490–95

Tempera and oil on panel, 23 1/4 × 18 1/2 in.
(59 × 47 cm.)

30 Until fairly recently in its known history the essential qualities of Bellini's art were hidden from view on this panel of *Christ Blessing*. Sometime before it first became known, in the Cunningham collection in England, where it had arrived at an undetermined date prior to 1849, the picture had been heavily overpainted. The largest area of repaint covered much of the torso with a white robe in order to minimize the nudity of the holy figure, and there were many other retouchings scattered generally throughout the composition. Until 1958 this disfigurement remained on the panel, plus multiple layers of dark yellow varnish which had become heavily pockmarked. During the subsequent cleaning process, it was also found that the surface of the paint structure itself was considerably obscured with dirt. With the picture in this poor condition, the heirs of Richard Fisher, Esq., put it up for auction as a work by Basaiti, an artist traditionally used as a catchall for works difficult of attribution.[1–2]

The panel went to the collection of Josef H. Dasser in Switzerland, where it was cleaned. Once rid of the accretions of time and the ravages of man, the painting was found to be in surprisingly excellent condition, and the exquisite subtleties of representation and technique, as well as Bellini's expressive power, were once again fully appreciable. Antonio Morassi studied the painting at length, and as the result of his research published an extensive article about it in *Arte Veneta*.[3] He not only recognized the picture as a "profoundly expressive" image of Christ by Bellini, but, based upon a comprehensive analysis of the picture in relation to other works by this master, and its date of execution (1490–95) in relation to chronological events in the painter's life, he identified this panel with the "*effigie del Salvatore in atto di benedire*" that Bellini gave to the Church of Santo Stefano in Venice, as mentioned by Carlo Ridolfi in his *Le Maraviglie dell'arte* published in 1648.[4] Rodolfo Pallucchini, in his superb monograph on Bellini published in 1962, agreed wholeheartedly with Morassi that this picture "has been rightly restored to Bellini" and that "valid reasons" identify it with the Santo Stefano image of Christ.[5] Fritz Heinemann, in his monumental two-volume catalogue of Bellini and all of his followers, agreed also,[6] as did the International Committee for the Venetian Art Exhibition at the National Museum in Stockholm,[7] as well as the Austrian scholar of Bellini, Luitpold Dussler, who, after the Stockholm exhibition, published and illustrated the picture in *Pantheon*.[8] Although Giles Robertson is unconvinced by the arguments identifying this picture with the one for Santo Stefano and thinks it a "high quality" work from Giovanni's studio,[9] there is general authoritative acceptance of it as published here.

Description: The following is excerpted from Morassi's description, upon which it would be difficult to improve: "Christ, risen from the sepulchre, is shown only to the waist, in frontal position, the right hand raised in the act of benediction, the left hand bearing the staff of the banner. A pale lilac drapery falls from the shoulder over the arm in large folds; a white lining enfolds the waist. His glance is sweetly fixed upon the spectator; the parted hair, falling with hardly a wave upon the shoulders with hieratic simplicity of line, almost suggests an archaic 'Pantocrator.' The solemn and pure, gentle tranquillity of this Christ is profoundly expressive, emanating a mysterious fascination, divine and human at one and the same time.

"By now almost free from the world, and with soul already among the things of Heaven, He seems materialized with a diaphanous purity, in which flesh becomes light... His youthful torso, of an ineffable chastity, delineated with a purity of line and modeled with supreme subtlety of shading, blooms from the enfolding drapery like a luminous lily of amber transparency... evoking the idea of... an eternal and profound symbol.

"... the landscape background may be counted among the more profoundly felt and laden with poetic mystery that issued from Giovanni's brush. The sun has set behind the circle of hills, and the horizon is no longer red; it is being transmuted... into the first moments of night. The shadows, in fact, have already invaded the earth. Three small figures wrapped in mantles, certainly the 'holy women,' hasten toward home; the shepherd presses his flock toward the fold, but two little rabbits, symbols of love, still delay to play among themselves. A bell tower stands out against the sky in order to sound afar the vesper chimes. Upon a large tree with withered limbs is perched a solitary bird (a magpie, a blackbird?), still that symbol of life everlasting in the darkness."[10]

Condition: Good. The results of the most recent cleaning process (1958–59) are detailed in the catalogue text above. With those later additions removed, the paint layer in its present condition reveals a vertical checking pattern consistent with wood grain throughout the painting. There are still some older, small repairs and strengthening in the head, edge of the drapery, and torso, which were not removed with the above-mentioned overpaint. There is one larger loss (repaired) in the upper right corner. The picture is on an uncradled wood panel that was held with nails and brown paper, some of which still adheres to the back.

Exhibitions: Konstens Venedig, Nationalmuseum, Stockholm, October, 1962–February, 1963, p. 62, cat. no. 56.

Collections: Church of Santo Stefano, Venice (cf. A. Morassi in *Arte Veneta,* below). Cunningham, English consul in Venice, who brought the panel to England prior to 1849. Richard Fisher, Esq., England. Mrs. Gunhilda Fisher, England. [Sotheby's], London, 1958. Josef H. Dasser, Zurich. Foundation Acquisition, AP 67.7.

Related Versions: Although this *Christ Blessing* is certainly comparable, in part, to the image of Christ in such paintings as the *Resurrection* for the Church of San Michele at Murano (now Berlin) and a few bust-length depictions (Madrid, for example), and perhaps even more to the Christ figure in *The Baptism* in Santa Corona, Vicenza, this theme of Christ blessing, seen as Saviour of the world, triumphant and isolated, is unique in Bellini's career. As Felton Gibbons, as well as Morassi, has pointed out, this singularity indicates a picture more surely by the master's hand only, for the shop pieces usually exist in many versions.[11] The well-known half length of Christ in the Louvre (ex-Orloff collection), on the grounds of early date and theme represented, caused Morassi to reject the traditional identification of it as the picture given to Santo Stefano. Most authorities date it to the time when Bellini would barely have arrived in Venice (first mention, 1459) and, as a youthful artist just beginning his career in a new city, he could hardly have developed the kind of relationship with a religious house (Augustinians) that would result in such a donation. On the contrary, it would have been most likely for the aging master of the 1490s, and as documents indicate, already beset with infirmity and with the hereafter on his mind, to have made such a gesture with just such a subject as that of the Kimbell picture. Further, the theme of the Louvre picture is really a "Cristo

Dolente," a "Cristo Piagato," in the spirit of the Pietà, not an "effigie," as Ridolfi called the one at Santo Stefano in 1648.

Notes:

1 Sotheby's, sale catalogue, London, 1958.

2 For discussions of the fictionalizations of art history resulting from this practice, see George Gronau, *Giovanni Bellini*, vol. 36 of Klassiker der Kunst, Berlin and Stuttgart, 1930; and Rodolfo Pallucchini, *Giovanni Bellini*, Milan, 1962.

3 Antonio Morassi, "Scoperta d'un Cristo Benedicente del Giambellino," *Arte Veneta*, no. XII, Venice, 1958, p. 45 ff.

4 Carlo Ridolfi, *Le Maraviglie dell'arte, ovvero le Vite degl'illustri Pittori Veneti e dello Stato*, Venice, 1648, von Hadeln ed., 1914–24, i., p. 71.

5 Pallucchini, ... *Bellini*, pp. 92, 153, fig. 162.

6 Fritz Heinemann, *Giovanni Bellini e i Belliniani*, Pozzo, Venice, 1962, p. 57, cat. no. 191 bis., fig. 86.

7 Nationalmuseum, Stockholm, *Konstens Venedig*, October, 1962–February, 1963, p. 62, cat. no. 56.

8 Luitpold Dussler, "Berichte-Schweden," *Pantheon*, Heft 2, 1963, p. 153, fig. 113.

9 Giles Robertson, *Giovanni Bellini*, Oxford and London, 1968, p. 113. See also: Verlag F. Bruckmann, Munich, Kunstkalender 1965, illus. for month of April.

10 Morassi, p. 48.

11 Felton Gibbons, letter to Richard F. Brown, June 1, 1967.

Andrea Mantegna, 1431–1506
The Risen Christ between St. Andrew and St. Longinus
Engraved about 1495–1500

Engraving on paper, 15 × 13 1/8 in. (38.1 × 33.3 cm.)

In the history of early engraving Andrea Mantegna is a pioneer and this particular engraving is a landmark. As William Ivins said, "In this Risen Christ between Saints Andrew and Longinus the three-dimensional flat picture makes its triumphal appearance in engraving. It is one of the epoch-making prints, as it showed that in the hands of a major artist engraving was capable of producing pictures with as great and as serene emotional power and life as any other artistic medium... Its technique is that of Mantegna's pen drawings, severe, restrained, taking no count of textures or color."[1] These qualities are enhanced by the inherent nature of engraved lines whose incisive clarity is obtained by cutting metal from the engraving plate with a sharp burin. Furthermore, like Mantegna's paintings, this print is imbued with an atmosphere of austere grandeur that derives from its spare rendering, clear outlines and the imposing presence of figures seen from below.

The scene shows Christ standing before a simply carved sarcophagus with his hand raised in blessing. He looks downward with a doleful expression, as do Saint Andrew and Saint Longinus standing at his sides. The upward view of this scene imparts a majesty to the image which is enhanced by the solid modeling of the figures. The severity of the composition is emphasized by the strong axes developed by the arms of the cross, Longinus' left arm and the curved pennant, all of which direct attention to the figure of Christ. This stately dignity is energized by the rhythmic arrangement of feet; the upraised heels of Longinus and Christ are complemented by Andrew's right foot which projects forward and down, over the edge of the ground plane. The placement of Andrew's foot, a subtle exception to pictorial convention, also heightens the illusion of space that is suggested by the concise modeling of the figures and by the darker shading in the background.

Mantegna moved to Mantua in 1459 where he remained the rest of his life and received several of his most important painting commissions. The print reflects his Mantuan roots because the two subordinate figures have particular associations with this town in North Italy. Its principal church, Sant'Andrea (designed by Leon Battista Alberti in the 1470s), is dedicated to Saint Andrew, who is identified in this print by the large cross on which he was martyred. The patron saint of Mantua is Longinus, by tradition the soldier whose lance pierced the side of Christ at the crucifixion. Subsequently forgiven, and converted to Christianity, he is honored for bringing to Mantua the relic of the Blood of Christ now enshrined in the high altar of the church of Sant' Andrea. In this print he is identified by his military dress and long lance.

These Mantuan associations and the distinctive composition have inspired several differing hypotheses about the original purpose of the design seen in this print. One suggests that it was the basis for statuary intended perhaps for the high altar of Sant' Andrea.[2] According to a recent proposal, the original design would be more appropriate "for a fresco situated high above a door."[3] Differences of scholarly opinion about the precise date of this print and the actual engraver of its plate should also be noted. Nonetheless, whether dated in "the early 1490s"[4] or "probably about 1500,"[5] and whether

the plate was cut by Mantegna himself or by technicians especially trained by him[6] is beside the main point: there is unanimous consent that the powerful design of this engraving, and that of only six others, could have been originated only by Mantegna.

Watermark: Shield with initials: P.S.[7]

Description: Upward-looking view of three standing, full-length figures: St. Andrew steadying a bulky wooden cross, Christ with his right arm raised in blessing and holding a tall staff with a small banner, and St. Longinus, with his hands and bent head in a prayerful attitude, holding a long lance upright against his right side. Behind the legs of Christ is seen the end panel of the sarcophagus, the cover of which is leaning against the side. Longinus' helmet lies at his feet just in front of the tomb cover. About the figures the background is shaded by fine lines, diagonally disposed and parallel to each other.

Condition: Excellent. The heavy, clear inking indicates that it is a relatively early impression. The very clean paper, which is free of repairs, has larger extant margins than most other recorded impressions of this print,[8] many of which have been considerably trimmed. The exceptionally wide lateral margins include the line of the plate edge at the upper left; nearly all the open space above and below the composition has been retained.

Exhibitions: None known.

Collections: George Cumberland, London, until about 1827 when he gave it to the Royal Academy of Arts, London,[9] where it remained until sold in 1965. [William H. Schab, New York.]
Foundation Acquisition, AP 71.8.

Notes:

1 William M. Ivins, Jr., *Notes on Prints*, New York, 1930, p. 51.

2 Paul Kristeller, *Andrea Mantegna*, London, 1901, p. 402. Giuseppe Fiocco, *Mantegna*, Milan, 1937, p. 101.

3 E. Tietze-Conrat, *Mantegna, Paintings – Drawings – Engravings*, London, 1955, p. 242.

4 Tietze-Conrat, p. 242.

5 A. M. Hind, *Early Italian Engraving . . .*, London, 1948, part II, vol. V, pp. 6, 16, cat. no. 7.

6 The latter view is persuasively argued by Tietze-Conrat, p. 241–42.

7 Hind, watermark no. 77.

8 The large margins of this impression are exceeded by those of only one other recorded impression, the only known impression with an intact plate mark; it is in the Rijksprentenkabinet, Amsterdam, and measures $17\frac{1}{4} \times 13\frac{3}{8}$ in. (43.8 × 34 cm.). See: *L'Incisione europea dal* XV *al* XX *Secolo*, Turin, Galleria Civica d'Arte Moderna, April–June, 1968, cat. no. 55.

9 George Cumberland, *An essay on the utility of collecting the best works of the ancient engravers of the Italian School, accompanied by a critical catalogue . . . now deposited in the British Museum and Royal Academy in London . . .*, London, 1827, no. LX.

Additional Reference:
Adam Bartsch, . . . *Maîtres Italiens*, vol. 13 of *Le Peintre-Graveur*, Vienna, 1803–21, vol. 13, p. 231, cat. no. 6.

After Hans Memling, about 1434–1494
St. John the Baptist
St. John the Evangelist
Painted in the late Fifteenth or early Sixteenth Century

Oil on panel, each $24\frac{3}{4} \times 7\frac{7}{8}$ in. (63 × 20 cm.)

At the time of his death Hans Memling was eulogized as "reputed to have been, at the time, the most accomplished and excellent painter of the whole Christian world,"[1] yet a century later the Dutch biographer Carel van Mander mentioned him only in passing. This abrupt decline was occasioned in part by the exaggerated success his gentle, conventional works enjoyed during the artistic détente in Bruges during the 1470s and 1480s,[2] and in part to the limitations of Memling's own talents. "Following generations," as Friedländer observed, "thought his creations weak and pale."[3] He was not an especially innovative painter, and he never rose above an eclectic dependence on the genius of his teacher Roger van der Weyden, but he did create a body of work that is well executed, temperate and agreeably harmonious. His religious subjects are marked by a "general air of youthful innocence and amiable civility"[4] in which contrast and individuality are softened into an image of unobtrusive serenity. These mild qualities appealed to romantic taste in the nineteenth century when Memling's work came to be esteemed as the epitome of medieval art in northern Europe.

The two Kimbell panels are nearly contemporary copies[5] of the inner wings of Memling's triptych of about 1485, the *Madonna Enthroned* in the Gemäldegalerie in Vienna.[6] The panels are quite close to their Vienna prototype; slender, ascetic figures stand in identical attitudes in the same narrow, slightly skewed Gothic archways before parklike landscapes typical of Memling. Details such as the oak leaf molding above the archways, the knobbed capitals, and the tiled floor are similar to the Vienna *Madonna Enthroned*. One unexplained difference does stand out, however; the Kimbell panels include a tiled area in the foreground, found in other works by Memling, which does not appear in the Vienna triptych.[7] Other variations are evident in the overall tonality of the paintings, changed from a soft yellow to a cool grey, and in the facial types, from which an emphasis on bony structure is absent. The subjects of the paintings, the two saints John, are "frequently associated in the iconography of the Middle Ages and of the Renaissance, not only because they bear the same name but because it was believed that the date of the Evangelist's death coincided with the anniversary of the Baptist's birth."[8]

Although the artist of the Kimbell panels was quite conscientious as a copyist and basically successful in penetrating Memling's formal idiom, in some details he betrays both a misunderstanding of Memling's intent and somewhat differing stylistic concerns. One detail, the chalice held by John the Evangelist,[9] is conspicuously different. In the Vienna painting its bowl is smooth and unadorned, its foot broad and low, in keeping with the pervasive harmony of the whole. In the Kimbell panel not only is its place in space rather ambiguous, but its bowl is ornately worked, its stem embellished with jewels and its foot tall and narrow. This type of chalice appears in another early copy of the Memling *Madonna Enthroned*, the Morrison Triptych, now in Toledo, Ohio.[10] Painted about 1520, it is a freer version containing numerous stylistic changes that reveal interests in movement, variety and complexity typical of the sixteenth century. These concerns appear only timidly in the Kimbell panels in the form of the chalice and in the slightly more complex drapery, floor tiling and postures. The quiet verticality of Memling's Evangelist, whose space-displacing form fills the archway, is replaced in the Kimbell Evangelist by a more angular posture that is emphasized by the greater thinness of the figure. The religious content of the paintings also reflects the changing climate of belief. The Kimbell saints seem posed and self-conscious where Memling's saints are lost in that ". . . vision of pure and naive beauty, of religious fervor and profound mystic peace"[11] which filled the Middle Ages. Such differences, however subtle, reveal a final inability to recapture the serene spirit of Memling's art.

Description: In both panels a youthful saint stands in a narrow Gothic archway, with a view through the room behind of sky, meadows and trees. The grey archways, bordered above with an oak leaf and acorn motif, are skewed so that more shows of the outer sides; there is a puzzling discrepancy in their heights. The random tiling of the floors–grey, yellow, green and brown–is brought forward below the threshold to the foreground. Across the small, empty rooms behind the figures, single colonettes support carved beams that frame the blue sky and green grass beyond.

In *St. John the Baptist* the prophet is turned slightly to his left and points with his right hand to the white lamb on his left arm. He wears a grey cloak over a short brown hairshirt; his brown hair and beard are short and curly. His lips are barely parted and he looks down at the lamb. The yellow tiling in the floor of this panel is somewhat paler than in the other.

In *St. John the Evangelist* the apostle, turned slightly to his right, looks at his right hand raised in a gesture of blessing and holds in his left a gold chalice. His cloak is green over a long red-orange robe, and his hair is a light brown. A tile in the lower left corner bears an ambiguous pattern which might have been related to the design of the now-missing center panel.

Condition: Very good. The paint layer in both panels is well preserved with small scattered areas of filling and inpainting; the entire surface has a characteristic very fine age craquelure. Although planed down and mounted on a cradle, the panels are apparently in their original dimensions: about the edges of the painted area there is an upturned lip of paint, suggesting that the panel was painted in its original frame.

Exhibitions: None known.

Collections: Said to have been in the collection of Emperor Charles v at the Monastery of Yuste near Plasencia, Spain, 1500–1558, and to have been bought in Spain by Baron Taylor for King Louis Philippe of France in 1850.[12] [Spanish Art Gallery], London, 1920. [T. Harris], London, 1932. [Erich Newhouse], New York, 1935. Private American collection, 1936–about 1965. [Newhouse Galleries, Inc., New York.]
Kimbell Bequest, ACF 65.1 and ACF 65.2.

Notes:

1 Rombouts de Doppere, notary at St. Donatian's in Bruges, 1494, trans. in Erwin Panofsky, *Early Netherlandish Painting*, Cambridge, Mass., 1966, p. 347.

2 Panofsky, p. 347.

3 M. J. Friedländer, *Die altniederländische Malerei*, Berlin and Leiden, 1924–37, vol. VI, p. 56, trans. in Panofsky, p. 347.

4 Friedländer, *Early Netherlandish Painting*, vol. VI, part I: *Hans Memlinc and Gerard David*, trans. by Heinz Norden, New York, 1971, p. 33.

5 Friedländer, . . . *Memlinc and* . . . *David*, part I, p. 46, pl. 36, no. 9 c.

6 Friedländer, . . . *Memlinc and* . . . *David*, part I, cat. no. 9, pls. 32–34. The Vienna triptych is one of the three late versions of a composition first executed in 1468; the inner wings of this earlier altarpiece also depict John the Baptist and John the Evangelist.

7 For example, on the shutters of the altarpiece of the Crucifixion in Lübeck; see Friedländer, . . . *Memlinc and* . . . *David*, part I, cat. no. 3, pls. 9, 12–13.

8 Louis Réau, *Iconographie de l'art chrètien*, Paris, 1958, vol. III, part II, p. 713 (translated from the French).

9 The chalice is part of his legend, referring to an abortive attempt to poison him.

10 Friedländer, *Early Netherlandish Painting*, vol. VII: *Quentin Massys*, trans. by Heinz Norden, New York, 1971, cat. no. 81, pl. 69.

11 J. Huizinga, *The Waning of the Middle Ages*, Garden City, N. J., 1954, (originally published 1924), p. 242.

12 Unconfirmed vendor information.

Barthel Bruyn, the Elder, 1493–1555
Hermann Sudermann, Burgomaster of Cologne, with his Sons and St. Thomas
Elisabeth Hupp Sudermann with her Daughters and St. Ursula
Painted in 1525–30
Oil on panel, each 25×14 in. (63.5×35.5 cm.)

Barthel Bruyn worked in Cologne from 1515, introducing there an important school of portrait painting that remained active long after his death. The style of painting he brought to Cologne was Netherlandish in character, reflecting Bruyn's early study with the Haarlem painter Jan Joest and the strong influence of his contemporary Joos van Cleve. Unlike most portrait painters of the period, such as Lucas Cranach and Hans Holbein, Bruyn had no connections with any court; his subjects and patrons were the burghers of Cologne, whom he portrayed with sympathy and understanding. He also executed numerous altarpieces, the donor portraits of which constitute an important category in his portrait œuvre.

The Kimbell panels once formed part of such an altarpiece, the central panel of which is now missing; they depict members of the prominent Sudermann family of Cologne.[1] The dark, simple attire of the men is appropriately earnest and sober, in contrast to the more lively atmosphere of the feminine panel, evoked by the jewelry, the bright colors of the ornamented dress and the curving lines of the sweeping drapery. St. Ursula, whose angel-supported mantle shelters the women, figures prominently in paintings of the Cologne area because it was there that she was martyred with her attendant virgins. St. Thomas has no comparable ties to Cologne; when depicted as in this panel, holding a carpenter's square, he is the patron of builders and architects, a reference perhaps to Hermann Sudermann's occupation or accomplishments.

The Gothic concept of donor portraits in which tiny figures kneel with eyes devoutly upraised beneath a towering saint has here yielded to the Renaissance consciousness of personality. The saints, human in scale with unidealized, even prosaic features, would hardly seem to occupy a different level of reality. St. Thomas appears as a gentle and rather grandfatherly protector with a striking resemblance to Hermann Sudermann. (Dürer has given us the supreme example of this humanistic conception of the divine in his painting *The Four Apostles*, done in 1526.) The strength of Bruyn's portrait art can be seen in the way he has captured convincing and unpretentious likenesses of specific individuals; Hermann and Elisabeth Sudermann are especially impressive in their pious air of bourgeois dignity, self-awareness and reserve, qualities which frequently come through in Bruyn's work as he attempted to please his conservative patrons. Typical of his earlier work, the portraits of the male members of the family are more lifelike and varied than those of the females.[2] Even among the very similar faces of the little girls, however, Bruyn has attempted to distinguish each by slight differences of expression. Naturalism takes precedence, at the expense of religious content: the assembled donors convey a sense of individual isolation and self-conscious piety very different from the unquestioned commitment of figures in donor paintings of the Medieval period.

These panels were painted in the middle years of Bruyn's artistic activity, probably closer to 1530 than 1525;[3] the short haircut of the men was a fashion introduced about 1528.[4] The abundance of local color is both typical of his middle period and indicative of the baroque tendencies of the Late Gothic that appear more explicitly in his large altarpieces. In this period he abandoned the oval,

gothic faces of his earlier work for broader, fleshier ones. The stylization of the little girls' faces with their high, domed foreheads, soft, full lips and fine pallor is typical of this period, as is the lank hair and leathery skin quality of St. Thomas and Hermann Sudermann.[5] Bruyn, like most artists of the sixteenth century, concentrates the individuality of his sitters in their faces; bodies are insignificant and hands are merely sketched in or rendered schematically, for example, when raised in prayer.[6] Clothes are executed in detail, however, as an important indication of rank and well-being. Italian influences, more evident in his later works, are apparent here in the monumental drapery of St. Thomas.

Description: Hermann Sudermann and his five sons kneel in the foreground, with St. Thomas the Apostle standing behind them, under an open blue sky with wispy clouds. A blue-green hilly landscape appears in the distance on the right and a rocky promontory on the left. The elderly St. Thomas, dressed in a red cloak over a blue tunic, holds a book in his left hand and a carpenter's square in his right. Hermann Sudermann, a dark-haired man about 40, kneels at a prayer bench[7] on which appears the Sudermann escutcheon, yellow above with white chevrons on a red field below.[8] He and his sons wear black mantles with collars closed high at the neck over delicate white shirts. He also wears a black, fur-lined cape with slits for sleeves and a large, open fur collar.

Elisabeth Sudermann with her seven daughters behind her kneels at a similar prayer bench whose escutcheon, featuring a bird, is identified as that of the Hupp family. St. Ursula, holding a book in her right hand and two arrows in her left, stands behind them with two angels holding out her crimson, ermine-lined mantle. The left angel wears yellow, the right one pinkish-red. St. Ursula wears a gold brocade lorica-shaped garment over a blue skirt and the diadem and jeweled ear ornaments which appear in other Bruyn paintings of this saint.[9] Trees fill the background on the right under the blue sky with wispy clouds. Elisabeth Sudermann is dressed in black; her eldest daughter wears the habit of a nun. The younger girls wear identical dresses of scarlet banded with black, with pleated white shirts, gold embroidered hoods and gold necklaces. Elisabeth's hood is black and gold with transparent white lappets pinned up beneath.

Condition: Very good. Both panels are cradled.[10] The paint surface has developed a very fine crackle system throughout; the varnish layer has tinted yellow. Some abrasions along the edges of the left panel and small scattered losses in the right panel have been filled and inpainted. Numerous *pentimenti* are visible in both panels, especially in the area around the prayer benches.

Exhibitions: Gemälde alter Meister aus Rheinisch-Westfälischem Privatbesitz, Galerie Stern, Düsseldorf, Germany, Feb. 24–March 31, 1934, cat. nos. 15, 16, pl. 5.

Collections: Rhenish-Westphalian private collection, until at least 1934. [Roland, Browse & Delbanco], London, 1938–39. [Kleinberger & Co., Inc.], New York. Walter P. Chrysler, Jr., collection, New York, by 1955. [Newhouse Galleries, Inc., New York.]
Kimbell Bequest, ACF 65.3 and ACF 65.4.

Notes:

1 W. Baumeister, "Die Rolinxwerd und ihr Verwandtenkreis," *Mitteilungen der westdeutschen Gesellschaft für Familienkunde,* vol. VIII, part I, cols. 23, 24, informs us Hermann Sudermann was Burgomaster of Cologne ten times between 1541 and 1568. At the time this work was painted he held a seat on the city council which he had occupied since 1521; his later title of Burgomaster has been anachronistically applied to this painting.

2 Hildegard Westhoff-Krummacher, *Barthel Bruyn der Ältere als Bildnismaler,* [Munich and Berlin], 1965, p. 26. Much of the information about Bruyn and his period has been derived from this source.

3 Horst-Johs Tümmers, *Die Altarbilder des älteren Bartholomäus Bruyn,* Cologne, 1964, p. 74, cat. nos. A 59, A 60, places these panels in the period 1525–30.

4 Westhoff-Krummacher, p. 47.

5 Westhoff-Krummacher, pp. 24–25.

6 Westhoff-Krummacher, pp. 76–78.

7 This same type of prayer bench appears in another altar shutter of this period with a donoress and St. Catherine; see Tümmers, cat. no. A 69, p. 77, who notes that details of it are borrowed from the right wing of an altarpiece by Joos van Cleve in the Kunsthistorisches Museum in Vienna.

8 Baumeister, col. 24, states that the traditional Sudermann chevron is silver.

9 For example, the painting of St. Ursula in the Wallraf-Richartz Museum in Cologne (Tümmers, cat. no. A 61).

10 Tümmers, p. 74, reports that an Annunciation scene in grisaille was said to be painted on the reverse of these two panels. However, no trace of this Annunciation is now evident.

Additional References:

K. G. Pfeill, "Gemälde alter Meister," *Die Christliche Kunst,* vol. 30, 1933–34, p. 301.
Pantheon, vol. 13, 1934, p. 125, notice of Galerie Stern exhibition.
Wallraf-Richartz Museum, *Barthel Bruyn 1493–1555,* Cologne, 1955, p. 29, cat. nos. 68, 69 (listed but not exhibited).

Corneille de Lyon, about 1510–1574/75
James V of Scotland
Painted about 1537

Oil on panel, 6 3/4 × 5 3/4 in. (17.2 × 14.6 cm.)

By about 1534 when Corneille de Lyon had established himself in the town of Lyon, he apparently was an accomplished portraitist, for he became painter to the Dauphin, later Henry II, about 1540 and also served Charles IX. Little is known about Corneille except that he came to France from The Hague and was quite possibly influenced by the Flemish artist, Joos van Cleve, who visited the French Court about 1530 to paint Francis I and his second wife, Eleanor of Portugal.

With his contemporary François Clouet, the son of Jean Clouet, Corneille helped to introduce the tradition of miniature portraits in France at the beginning of the Renaissance.[1] In this age, which placed new emphasis on the individual and humanism, there was a great demand, especially in the courts, for portraits which were small in scale and could either be easily transported or hung in small rooms designed expressly to hold them; sometimes, they were even set into the woodwork. Painted on wood or porcelain, these portraits continued the pictorial conventions of two small-scale art forms: illuminated manuscripts, in which bright colors are combined with intricate detailing and patterning, and the circular or oval medals and cameos that were revived in the Early Renaissance from antique models, in which careful attention is paid to the subject's physiognomy.[2]

Among Corneille's portraits, relatively few of the sitters have been identified with any certainty. The subject's identity in the Kimbell portrait as *James V of Scotland* is, however, fairly well established by its strong resemblance to two portraits in England, one in the National Trust at Polesden Lacey, Surrey,[3]

and another at Hardwick Hall, Derbyshire.[4] The Kimbell portrait was probably painted in 1537 at the time of James' marriage in Paris to the eldest daughter of Francis I, Madeleine, who died within six months. His remarriage in 1538 to Mary of Guise united Scotland and France as allies against England. Shortly thereafter, James waged war on his uncle, Henry VIII of England, only to be defeated at Solway Moss; he died within a month at Falkland on December 14, 1542.[5]

Despite the intimate scale of the Kimbell portrait, dignity and grandeur are imparted to this royal sitter. Depicted bust-length and turned slightly to his right, the king is placed before a luminous green background where shadows are simulated at the top and left sides. Although his costume is treated in a summary manner, his face was probably painted from life because few, if any, chalk preparatory studies by Corneille survive. Its convincing plasticity is created by delicate detailing and naturalistic modeling, and the variety in light and texture is created by a proficient use of transparent glazes which recall Corneille's Flemish heritage.[6] These elements are typical of Corneille's work throughout his career but evoke an especially gemlike quality in the Kimbell portrait.

Description: Bust-length portait of a young man about 25 years old. Placed before a green background with dark green shadows, he is turned slightly to his right in a three-quarter view. He wears a black jacket with random light orange decorations at the shoulders and on the sleeves. Two silver drawstrings with tassels hang from the high collar, which has a white ruffle framing his face. He has pale flesh, rosy cheeks and lips, and blue-green eyes. His hair, moustache and beard are light auburn. A fluffy white feather with brown and grey shading extends over the right side of his flat, black hat.

Condition: Very good. The permanent cradle members have slightly distorted the surface plane; the paint surface has developed a normal crackle system with some very slight cupping.

Exhibitions: None known.

Collections: Private collection, France. [Schaeffer Galleries, Inc., New York.]
Foundation Acquisition, AP 66.1.

Notes:

1 Anthony Blunt, *Art and Architecture in France, 1500 to 1700*, 2nd ed., Baltimore, 1970, p. 64.

2 Graham Reynolds, *English Portrait Miniatures*, London, 1952, pp. 1–2.

3 Photo 521–19, Frick Art Reference Library, New York; *Catalogue, Polesden Lacey*, Surrey, 1950, pp. 3, 18, illus. no. 15.

4 Anonymous British artist, *James V and his Second Wife Mary of Guise*, about 1540, 43 × 56 1/2 in., Sir John Gore, "Pictures in National Trust Houses," *Burlington Magazine*, vol. 111, April, 1969, supplement, p. 244; illus. in *Encyclopædia Britannica*, vol. 12, 1962, p. 860.

5 Since his second marriage was performed only by proxy in France and in a second ceremony in June, 1538, soon after Mary's arrival in Scotland, it is unlikely that the portrait was painted at the later date. Their only surviving child became Mary, Queen of Scots, immediately after her father's death.

6 Blunt, pp. 65–66.

Jacopo Tintoretto, 1519–1594
The Raising of Lazarus
Painted in 1573

Oil on canvas, 26 1/2 × 30 1/2 in. (67.5 × 77.5 cm.)

Jacopo Robusti was the son of a Venetian silk-dyer, and he therefore became known as Il Tintoretto. He was apprenticed to the great master of color, Titian, who prematurely ended their association out of jealousy over the younger artist's precociousness and burgeoning popularity. According to the writer Pietro Aretino, a friend of both painters, trouble between the two was intensified because of the youth's overly aggressive and arrogant nature. Once on his own, however, Tintoretto became an artist much in demand, a happy circumstance that steadily increased until the end of his days. He literally covered the walls of the great palaces, churches and *scuole* of Venice with acres of painted canvas, being helped in this incredible production by five of his eight children who became painters also. In spite of his seemingly limitless energy, Tintoretto spent his whole life in his native city without experiencing any outstanding events. We know for sure of only one journey, that which he made to visit the court of the Gonzagas at nearby Mantua in 1580 when he was more than sixty.

For years it has been assumed that Tintoretto must have gone to Florence and Rome about 1547, but there is no documentary proof of this unless one accepts as such the many drawings, indubitably by Tintoretto, of monuments in those cities, especially the famous sculptures of Michelangelo.[1] However, there are critical arguments that indicate these could have been done from casts, from drawings by Daniele da Volterra who was working in the Veneto, or from the full set of drawings depicting these monuments done by Vasari and sent to Pietro Aretino in 1535.[2] In any case, augmenting the grand tradition of Venetian colorism, the second component of

Tintoretto's style became central Italian Mannerism, the progenitor of which was Michelangelo. According to Ridolfi (1642), Tintoretto had a sign posted in his studio that said, *Il disegno di Michelangelo, ed il colorito di Tiziano.*

By the time the Kimbell *Raising of Lazarus* was painted Tintoretto had achieved his characteristically dramatic synthesis of these divergent stylistic elements. We know the date of the picture because it was commissioned by a wealthy Venetian named Antonio da Mula to go in his library along with four portraits that were to be overdoors, and the contract for this commission exists, with a date of February 6, 1573.[3] Mary Pittaluga identified this particular canvas as the one named in the contract by relating subject, size, shape and the number of figures (twenty) specified.[4] Because of paint decomposition resulting from age, there have been some who could count only nineteen figures, one figure in the background, right of center, being extremely faint (see *Condition*). No other picture by Tintoretto of this subject bears comparison with the contract, and most authorities since M. Pittaluga accept the identity of the picture with the contract.[5]

In 1901 Henry Thode, troubled by the presence of the strongly foreshortened nude figure semi-reclining at the left end of the sarcophagus, thought that the subject might be "Christ at the Pool of Bethesda."[6] Accordingly, in the catalogue of the Holford Collection it was listed as "Christ the Physician."[7] At the Burlington House Winter Exhibition of 1960 it was again called "Christ at the Pool of Bethesda," in spite of the fact that all other intervening literature employed the Lazarus title.[8] Although there may be an iconographic reason for the presence of the figure, it has not been determined. The use of such a figure for compositional purposes is ubiquitous in the master's works, especially when an event or miracle is being depicted that calls for a dense concentration of people in a great variety of poses. There are, moreover, a large number of subjects from all periods in the painter's lifetime into which such a figure was introduced in a surprising manner and with absolutely no iconographic necessity; for example, the two nude men at either side of the Dresden Museum's *Christ and the Adulteress*, or the semi-nude child and man at the foot of the steps in *The Last Supper* in Santo Stefano, Venice, or the foreground reclining semi-nude in the Munich Pinakothek's *Crucifixion*.

The wide variations of interpretation the Lazarus theme has received throughout the history of art, as pointed out by Louis Réau,[9] result from the fact that minimal information is given about the event, by only one Evangelist (John 11:44). Tintoretto's earliest version of the subject, a large picture in the Leipzig Museum done about 1560, has a figure very similar to the one in the Kimbell work; but the composition is entirely different, with the man reclining semi-nude in front of the sarcophagus and seen from the back.

The huge *Raising of Lazarus* now in the Lübeck Museum also has this figure, again seen from the back, kneeling at the feet of Christ. Although the Lübeck picture is in tall, vertical format, there are many other pictorial elements that precisely parallel the Kimbell painting, including the violently epileptic tossing of the awakening figure of Lazarus. The Lübeck version is signed and dated 1576, three years after the commission contract with Antonio da Mula for the Kimbell version. All authorities now agree that the Lübeck canvas, done for a Netherlandish family who installed it in Lübeck's Church of St. Catherine in a specially made frame with the family escutcheons and date of 1578 carved upon it, is substantially by the hand of assistants in Tintoretto's shop.[10] The chronological relationship of the Kimbell and Lübeck examples, their difference in size, the similarities of pictorial motifs, plus the difference, especially of geographical location, between the two clients, all indicate a connection between the two in which the smaller version (or drawings for it?) was used as a kind of *modello* for the larger shop work. Although such a consideration must remain hypothetical, the identity of the subject as Lazarus becomes certain if one compares all of Tintoretto's versions of this theme[11] with the only two pictures he did of *Christ at the Pool of Bethesda*, one (dated 1559) in the Church of San Rocco, the other (datable 1578–81) in the Scuola of San Rocco, which hangs near the master's final version of *The Raising of Lazarus* that was among the last things done for the Scuola (1578–81).

That final version from Tintoretto's old age is a masterpiece in a pantheon of masterpieces, and, consistent with the stylistic development of most great artists, it is the most romantic, dramatic, and freely painted of all. The proportions and general arrangement of the composition differ considerably from the Kimbell version, but the figure of the kneeling Mary Magdalen is a mirror image. Although done, at most, seven or eight years earlier, the Kimbell Lazarus united those same disparate elements of form and color in a dramatic synthesis dominated by powerful light, and it thus achieves a spiritually intense expressiveness with natural means that was the goal of Tintoretto's entire career and made him the greatest harbinger of the Catholic Reformation and the Baroque age.

Description: With a beckoning gesture, Christ strides inward from the extreme left of the scene towards an ancient stone sarcophagus, out of which rolls a sallow Lazarus who flails legs and arms wildly, as though awakening from a nightmare. His eyes stare glassily, not yet capable of focus, while the cloth in which he was wrapped for burial drops away, leaving him mostly nude. The two men who were assisting and holding Lazarus are obeying Christ's command to release him. Directly in the center foreground, richly dressed and reclining on the ground, is Martha, one of the sisters of Lazarus. Mary, the other sister, leans inward from the lower right corner of the scene, her arms stretched wide in a gesture of ecstatic transport at the miracle she beholds. A nude male figure, seen in bold foreshortening, sits on the ground at the left end of the sarcophagus with a staff in his right hand. In the background stand fourteen of the throng of Pharisees who witnessed the event with great anxiety because of its political import. These, plus the six foreground figures, constitute the total of twenty named in the contract. The whole scene, vaguely following John the Evangelist's suggested setting, is under a hill or grotto overhung with vegetation.

Condition: Fair. Although there are no major damages or large localized losses in the paint structure, the vicissitudes of time have been unkind to the aesthetic surface generally. Evidently, considerable abrasion was suffered sometime early in the picture's history. In addition, a loss of covering power and some decomposition of hue increased as the paint aged, and at some time (perhaps nineteenth century?) many areas were strengthened and some overpainted. Old traction cracks were filled and painted. At a second, or even third, time of treatment, there must have been considerable cleavage, so the canvas was lined, and some additional reinforcing of certain detailed areas of the paint layer was added at the time. An old, lower level of varnish (to this date not removed) seems partially decayed and probably slightly tinted. A half-inch of canvas was added at top and bottom, probably at the time of lining, which, judging by the nature of the organic adhesive and tacking to the stretcher, was probably done early in the twentieth century.

To some authorities the results of this technical condition have been disconcerting, but surely Pittaluga went too far, after identifying the picture in the 1573 contract and stating that it was "obviously" by Tintoretto, in asserting that it was "ruined."[12] With full knowledge of what the erosion of 400 years has done, one still can appreciate the expressive relationships between delicate glazes and rough scumbles, the heightening of the drama of this miraculous moment through violent contrasts of light and dark, the tormented *chiaroscuro* within the darks which suggests the anguished import of the event, the impassioned brushwork continuing over a succession of alternating kinds of surfaces that augments the feeling of troubled movement in the figures, and the coherent discipline of a carefully structured and phrased abstract composition that subsumes the whole.

Exhibitions: Venetian Art, New Gallery, London, 1894–95. Loan, National Museum, Budapest, 1939–46. *Exhibition of Venetian Pictures,* King's Lynn, Norfolk, 1959. *Italian Art and Britain,* Royal Academy, London, 1960, no. 65.

Collections: Antonio da Mula, Venice, 1573. Sir G. L. Holford, Westonbirt, Gloucestershire, until at least 1924. First Viscount Rothermere, London, until about 1960. Dr. James Hasson, London, 1963.
Foundation Acquisition, AP 66.2.

Notes:

1 Nikolaus Pevsner, *Barockmalerei,* Potsdam, 1928, p. 67.

2 D. F. von Hadeln, *Zeichnungen des Giacomo Tintoretto,* Berlin, 1922, p. 26.

3 F. Galanti, *Atti della Reale Accademia di Belle Arti in Venezia,* 1876, p. 87. Also see: Galanti, *L'Arte,* Venice, 1899, p. 500.

4 Mary Pittaluga, *Il Tintoretto,* Bologna, 1925, pp. 203, 272.

5 Erich von der Bercken, *Die Gemälde des Jacopo Tintoretto,* Munich, 1942, p. 113.

6 Henry Thode, *Tintoretto,* Leipzig, 1901, pp. 110, 139.

7 *Holford Collection Catalogue,* London, 1924, no. 58, p. 68, pl. 56.

8 *Italian Art and Britain,* Royal Academy Exhibition, London, 1960, no. 65.

9 L. Réau, *Iconographie de l'Art chrétien,* Paris, 1957, tome II, p. 386 ff.

10 Pittaluga, p. 273. Also, von der Bercken, p. 114.

11 There are two more versions, in addition to those discussed here: (1) Somewhat earlier in date than the Kimbell picture, compositionally quite different, once in the Farrar collection, London, and now unlocatable; (2) A large (approx. 8 ft.) horizontal treatment of the subject with strongly elongated, manneristic figures, out of a French private collection, and now in the art market.

12 Pittaluga, p. 272.

Additional References:

J. B. S. Holborn, *Jacopo Robusti Called Tintoretto,* London, 1903, p. 103.
Mrs. A. Bell, *Tintoretto,* London, 1910, p. 44.
Evelyn M. Phillipps, *Tintoretto,* London, 1911, p. 159.
F. P. B. Osmaston, *The Art and Genius of Tintoret,* London, 1915, p. 188.
Erich von der Bercken, *Jacopo Tintoret,* Munich, 1923, vol. I, pp. 202–4, 274; vol. II, pl. 12.
Jacques Lassaigne, *Tintoretto,* New York, n. d., pl. 24.
Hans Tietze, *Tintoretto,* London and Innsbruck, 1948, p. 376 (where it is incorrectly stated that Osmaston doubted the attribution).
Bernard Berenson, *Venetian School,* vol. I of *Italian Pictures of the Renaissance,* London, 1957, p. 178.

El Greco, 1541–1614
St. John the Evangelist
Painted about 1612–14

Oil on canvas, 28 3/8 × 21 3/4 in. (71.7 × 55.2 cm.)

The Kimbell *St. John the Evangelist*, dated about 1612–14,[1] characterizes the late style of El Greco (Domenico Theotocopuli) which is a synthesis of Byzantine, Venetian, and Mannerist influences. Representing the apostle who became one of the most persuasive and aggressive advocates of Christianity, El Greco has depicted him as an alert, beardless young man, haggard from the rigors of his calling. He looks down to his left while his hand, much like the attenuated figures of Byzantine icons, or votive images, gestures in the opposite direction. The angular composition derives not only from abstractly patterned Byzantine art but also from convoluted Mannerist works. The accentuated modeling, ranging from strong darks to extreme lights, reflects the sumptuous modeling of sixteenth-century Venetian painting, as does the brilliant richness of the dissonant colors: the saint's acid green tunic, symbolizing spiritual initiation, and his luminous rose mantle, symbolizing his love of action. The flickering, tortuous brushstrokes, peculiar to El Greco's style, help to create a visionary intensity for this image of one of the earliest martyr saints.

The Kimbell work was painted as part of an *apostolado*, a group of thirteen paintings of uniform size depicting Christ and the twelve apostles, which had once occupied the small parish church in Almadrones, Spain, near Guadalajara.[2] Shown half-length and without attributes or symbols, these saints resemble those in other *apostolados* by El Greco.[3] The identity of the Kimbell St. John is clearly established by the color, costume, and pose which correspond to three more depictions of the saint by El Greco from this period. These are in the Prado Museum,[4] the Toledo Cathedral,[5] and the Museo del Greco.[6] In these three versions, the figure of the youthful saint is shown three-quarter length holding a chalice with a serpent coiled near the opening of the vessel. The consistent color and compositional schemes of the various *apostolado* series, all done around the first decade of the seventeenth century, suggest that El Greco intended the image of Christ to be located centrally in the apse of the church, flanked by six apostles on each of the adjoining walls.[7]

Although seventeenth-century history of the Almadrones series has not been established, its subsequent history is reasonably well documented. In the eighteenth century, it was acquired by a charitable foundation set up by Don Miguel del Olmo, Bishop of Cuenca, who gave the series to the provincial church in Almadrones. There it remained in obscurity until the Spanish Civil War when, between 1936 and 1938, nine extant paintings of the series were discovered by soldiers who took them to the fort at Guadalajara by order of the Marquis of Lozoya. Here they were identified as works by El Greco. Because they were in a somewhat deteriorated condition, they were sent to the Prado to be cleaned and relined.[8] Four were retained for the Prado collection;[9] the remaining five, including the Kimbell painting, were sold and are now located in public collections.[10]

Like other paintings in the Almadrones series and other large projects attributed to El Greco, the Kimbell painting was probably produced out of a workshop situation organized to satisfy a demand for a great variety and number of religious pictures from all sorts of clients at that time. Since few pictures by El Greco are historically documented as being solely by his own hand, it would seem reasonable to conclude that the series was done by the master with the help of members of his shop. Among scholars of El Greco, the Kimbell work has been highly regarded by José Camón Aznar,[11] but not by Harold E. Wethey who is not known to have examined it personally.[12]

Inscription: Upper right: cursive initials (delta theta) of El Greco's name in Greek.

Description: Half-length frontal portrait of St. John the Evangelist. The saint has a meditative expression; his elongated head is inclined to the left. He has a sallow complexion, dark sunken eyes, and brown hair. Contrasting with his chartreuse robe is a light vermilion mantle which falls in broad folds diagonally from his left shoulder to his attenuated, outstretched fingers. He stands in a shallow space before a dark brown background.

Condition: Good. The painting has been relined and cleaned. It has been skillfully filled and inpainted where scattered losses have occurred, particularly at the edges which had been rubbed by the frame.

Exhibitions: Twenty-One Paintings from the Kimbell Art Foundation, Fort Worth Art Association, March 3–26, 1953, cat. no. 5.

Collections: Parish Church, Almadrones, Spain, to 1936 or 1938. Spanish Government, 1937–38 to 1949. [Newhouse Galleries, Inc., New York.]
Kimbell Bequest, ACF 52.4.

Notes:

[1] Harold E. Wethey, *El Greco and His School*, Princeton, 1962, vol. II, pp. 106–8.

[2] Wethey, vol. II, p. 107.

[3] The San Feliz series, ca. 1610–15, 27 3/4 x 21 in. (70 x 53 cm.), Oviedo, Spain, and the Henke series, ca. 1610–15, 24 1/2 x 19 3/4 in. (62 x 50 cm.), various locations. See: Wethey, pp. 211–13.

[4] Ca. 1595–1600, 40 x 30 1/2 in. (102 x 77 cm.), Madrid. See: Wethey, vol. II, p. 135; vol. I, pl. 245.

[5] 1605–10, 39 3/8 x 30 in. (100 x 76 cm.), Toledo. See: Wethey, vol. II, p. 103; vol. I, pl. 211.

[6] Unfinished at the time of the artist's death in 1614, 38 1/4 x 30 1/2 in. (97 x 77 cm.), Toledo. See: Wethey, vol. II, pp. 104–5; vol. 1, pl. 222.

[7] Wethey, vol. II, pp. 101–2.

[8] Wethey, vol. II, p. 107.

[9] The Saviour and Saints James Major, Paul, and Thomas.

[10] Saints Matthew, Simon, and Luke are in the collection of Clowes Foundation, Indianapolis; Saint Andrew is at the Los Angeles County Museum of Art.

[11] José Camón Aznar, *Dominico Greco*, Madrid, 1950, vol. II, pp. 986, 997.

[12] Wethey, vol. II, p. 107.

Additional Reference:

Enrique Lafuente Ferrari, "El Greco: Some Recent Discoveries," *Burlington Magazine*, vol. 87, December, 1945, pp. 292–301.

Joos de Momper, 1564–1635
Travelers in a Mountainous Landscape
Painted about 1590–1620

Oil on panel, 18 × 29 1/2 in. (45.7 × 74.9 cm.)

A jewel-like warmth and an elegant spaciousness are the salient and endearing qualities of the distinctive mountain pass landscapes painted by Joos de Momper.[1] Among several different types of landscapes that he painted, these rugged mountainous scenes are perhaps his most attractive and certainly his best-known works. It seems likely that they were inspired by his recollections of Alpine scenery that de Momper had seen while traveling to northern Italy. He is thought to have made this trip in the 1580s before returning to his native Antwerp by 1590 when he was married. Subsequently, he seems to have remained in Antwerp and Flanders for most of his life, achieving a comfortable success and a favorable reputation that is evident in his election as dean of Antwerp's Guild of St. Luke in 1610. Probably taught by his father, de Momper developed a painting style that remained impressively consistent throughout his life. Among the very few of his paintings that can be accurately dated, little change in style is evident between early and later works; consequently, only approximate dates are usually indicated for most of his works.[2]

De Momper's impressive command of expressive Mannerist conventions is clearly evident in this fantasy landscape. An unreal but very atmospheric sense of space is positively evoked by the distinct zoning of foreground, middle distance and background into the typical brown-green-blue triad of tones. The darker mountains and foliage stand forward from the light greenish-yellow tones of the valley and the very pale blue tones of the hazy distant mountains and the cloud-filled sky. The scene is dramatized by the strong contrast of the foliage-edged cliffs against the sky and by the converging diagonals of cliff face, meandering path and distant ridge which draw the eye through the rich coloring of the exaggerated distances. Nonetheless, a benign intimacy pervades this spacious vista. It is evoked by meticulously painted details such as the foliage, the small birds flying about the sky, the transparent veils of splashing water and by the small scale of the travelers ascending the pass. It should be noted, however, that these figures are probably the work of a different artist. As the writer of the major study of landscape painting of this period[3] has observed: "There is not the least doubt that Momper is the author of this painting, which is a particularly good work. The landscape . . . is doubtless of his hand; the human figures are certainly by another hand, as is the case almost always with Momper's paintings, probably by Jan Brueghal or another artist close to him."[4]

Description: View through a forested, rocky mountain pass of a wide valley and a distant mountain ridge. Ascending from the valley on a well-worn path is a long file of eleven travelers, including mounted horsemen, animal tenders and back-packers, as well as three heavily burdened donkeys and a small dog. Waterfalls cascade in narrow veils down steep, rugged cliffs at the left and right. At the side of the path, leaning over a small stream fed by the falls at the left, is a rustic wooden cross with a small bird perched on the crossarm. Five small birds fly about the lightly clouded, pale blue sky. The scene is painted in warm tones of green and brown except for the greenish-yellow tones of the valley floor and the pale, greyish-blue tones of the distant ridge. Varying shades of red in the rustic dress of the travelers accent the foreground.

Condition: Very good. There is a very narrow, carefully inpainted, horizontal crack across the middle of the panel and some scattered, superficial strengthening in the sky. The figures and the landscape are in pristine condition, and the varnish is thin and clear. The panel is mounted on a cradle.

Exhibitions: None known.

Collections: Count Philippe de Limbourg-Stirum, Brussels.
[Otto Wertheimer, Paris.]
Foundation Acquisition, AP 70.23.

Notes:

1 His first name is shown variously in contemporary records with Joos being more common than Josse, Joost or Judocus. See Gregory Martin, "Joos de Momper, II," *National Gallery Catalogues: The Flemish School*, London, 1970, pp. 96–97. This thoroughly documented summary of de Momper's life is the basis for the biographical details in this entry.

2 A similar mountain pass landscape, dated about 1610–20, is recorded in *Catalogue of European and American Paintings and Sculpture in the Allen Memorial Art Museum*, Oberlin, Ohio, 1967, pp. 111–12, fig. 50. It also gives references for other mountainous landscapes by de Momper located in Chicago, Dresden and Cologne.

3 Joseph Alexander Graf Raczyński, *Die flämische Landschaft vor Rubens*, Frankfurt am Main, 1937.

4 Raczyński, letter to Otto Wertheimer, May 26, 1970.

Francisco de Herrera, about 1590–1656/57
Saint Andrew
Painted about 1639–40

Oil on canvas, 45 3/4×36 in. (116.2×91.4 cm.)

Francisco de Herrera the Elder is considered one of the major exponents of Early Baroque Realism in Spain. Active in Seville from at least 1610 to about 1648, he was influenced by Juan de Roelas (ca. 1560–1625) to abandon the prevailing timid and conventional style of the Andalusian region for a bolder, freer manner which soon became a major quality of the Sevillian school.[1] Herrera's sharply individualized style of realism significantly influenced other artists, particularly his use of somber yet rich colors applied with vigorous, lively strokes calculated to give an immediate effect at a distance.[2]

Considered one of Herrera's best works,[3] the Kimbell *Saint Andrew* exemplifies the master's style of Baroque Realism. It depicts one of the first disciples of Christ who converted so many people to Christianity that in A.D. 70 the Roman governor of Patrae in Greece, fearing a popular uprising, had Andrew arrested and crucified on an x-shaped cross.[4] The transverse timbers of the cross are partially visible at the left behind his head and alluded to by the quill and rolled parchment crossed in front of his book. Reading from Hebraic scriptures, *Saint Andrew* is a type frequently found in Herrera's oeuvre: the massive, masculine figure is forcefully characterized as an old man with deep-set eyes, greying hair and beard, and a tanned, weatherbeaten complexion. He is silhouetted against a landscape setting in the background, where parallel spatial planes are defined by sharp contrasts of light and shade, preventing them from flowing smoothly and atmospherically into one another. Herrera organized the composition compactly, building up the forms with opaque strokes of somber-colored pigments applied in a free but deliberate manner. The forms, no longer meticulously rendered with muddy colors as in his earlier works, are washed by a golden brown light which is diffused over the canvas.

These stylistic characteristics suggest a date of about 1639–40, placing the Kimbell painting at the end of Herrera's second Sevillian period (1629–39) when he did his best and strongest works.[5]

Inscription: Across the bottom of the painting:

S. ĀDREAS
ET IN IESVM CHRISTV̄ FILIV̄ EIVS VNICV̄, DOMINVM NOSTRV
II.

(St. Andrew, and in Jesus Christ his only son, our Lord)
The long marks over several letters denote abbreviations, a common practice in the sixteenth and seventeenth centuries.

Description: Old man seated in a landscape setting reading Hebraic scriptures. Wearing an orange-brown jacket with a cream-colored drape over his shoulders, he has greying hair and beard and a ruddy complexion. His head rests on his right hand while his left hand holds the pages of the large open book before him. To his right are two sheets of cream-colored parchment with writing on them. The book and sheets are placed on the flat surface of a rock as are the black inkhorn in the center foreground and the rolled sheaf of parchment with a white quill resting on it to the left, partially obscured by a plant. A wooden cartouche with an inscription carved into it spans the immediate foreground. In the upper left corner is a roughhewn, x-shaped, wooden cross of dark brown. Immediately behind the saint the ground is strewn with rocks, and in the distance is a precipice revealing a landscape vista at the upper right.

Condition: Very good. The original canvas has been trimmed to the paint area and relined. There is general crazing with some cupping and possible cleavage in the face, also filling and inpainting on all edges and in scattered areas such as dexter wrist, hair, book, scroll, background, plaque. The varnish has slightly darkened, yellowed, and decayed. Beneath the present painting, recent x-ray examination has revealed the presence of underlying painting, an inverted head toward the bottom right of the canvas and a sketchy head at the upper left. The crackle system throughout the canvas is consistent, suggesting that these heads are roughly contemporary with the present image.

Exhibitions: Extended loan to Texas Christian University, Fort Worth, Spring, 1958–October, 1968.

Collections: Acquired in Spain in 1850. Private collection, Paris. [Newhouse Galleries, Inc., New York.]
Kimbell Bequest, ACF 58.2.

Notes:

1 John S.Thatcher, "The Paintings of Francisco de Herrera, the Elder," *Art Bulletin*, vol. 19, 1937, p. 328.

2 Thatcher, p. 353.

3 Unpublished opinion of José Gudiol, Director, Instituto Amattler de Arte Hispánico, Barcelona, Spain.

4 George Ferguson, *Signs & Symbols in Christian Art*, New York, 1961, p. 103.

5 For a detailed discussion of this period in the artist's oeuvre, see: Thatcher, pp. 338–49.

Peter Paul Rubens, 1577–1640
The Triumph of David
Painted about 1638

Oil on panel, 23×31 ½ in. (58.5×80 cm.)

Sir Peter Paul Rubens, in his person and life-style, as well as in his "beloved profession" of painting, probably defines the Baroque era better than any other artist. His father was a doctor of jurisprudence and minor diplomat whose widow saw to it that their sons received solid educations in the classical tradition, enriched tremendously in the case of the future painter during his decade of travel and study abroad, mostly in Italy. Handsome, gracious and courtly of manner, a complete master of six languages, and endowed with prodigious energy, Rubens easily became a trusted favorite at the courts of Mantua, Genoa, Madrid, Antwerp, Paris and London. Often during his career he clandestinely negotiated ticklish diplomatic missions while overtly visiting a foreign capital to paint portraits or a large decorative series. With this background he very consciously understood his own exuberant age that established the concept and political fact of large nation-states, that laid the foundations of modern scientific discovery, and that began the unprecedented expansion into the New World. He was also a devout Catholic who fully participated, intellectually and aesthetically, in the Counter-Reformation. In order to embrace this astounding richness and variety, he became one of the most immensely creative eclectics in history; and to satisfy the enormous demand for pictures that expressed his age so well, Rubens became the greatest art impresario.

He had the administrative ability to organize the production of a large studio in Antwerp that included painters, engravers, decorators, book illustrators and other craftsmen, many of whom bore some of the most famous names in art history,

RUBENS, PETER PAUL
Pen Drawing for Return of David, Boymans Museum, Rotterdam

including Van Dyck, Jordaens, Snyders, Jan Brueghel and Wildens. Rubens was the "inventor" of themes and designs that were then carried out by specialists in the studio, with the master supervising to a greater or lesser degree. There were many large pictures and whole related series of them, of course, that Rubens did entirely with his own hand, depending upon the importance of the client and/or the master's own interest and availability. There were some for which Rubens gave the studio the merest sketch, and the finished product would leave the shop without a touch by the master. Usually, once a project was decided upon, Rubens in his private studio would produce an oil sketch, or "modello," painted swiftly and directly upon a gessoed wood panel. He developed astonishing powers to achieve complete expression of an idea by sketching directly in paint. This smaller initial version would then be taken to the studio to be used as a model for production of the full-scale final version, with the master adding corrections as work progressed, and then the final touches. Connoisseurs prize the "modelli" because in them one can see the master's exhilarating process of invention at work, with all of its freedom and assurance. They are small only in physical size.

The "modello" of *The Triumph of David* was done about 1638 when Rubens turned to a celebration of two Old Testament heroes, Moses and David. As Michael Jaffé admits, we know nothing of the original commission for this unique combination of rare subjects.[1] The "modello" for *Moses Rejoicing After the Crossing of the Red Sea* is in the Staatliche Kunsthalle, Karlsruhe, and it is the same size as the David panel. The two subjects, twin episodes in the deliverance of the Chosen People, similarly treated and on panels of the same dimensions, were evidently projected as a pair.[2] A large version of the Moses is unknown; however, a large version of the David, reasonably attributed to Theodor van Thulden (1606–69), is in the Gallery of Schwerin, Mecklenburg (inv. no. 714). Curiously, the companion piece to it, also at Schwerin and attributed to Van Thulden, is a different Moses subject, the *Finding in the Bulrushes*. Both these large paintings may have been done after Rubens' death, without his supervision and without following his originally intended program.[3]

"A David coming into Jerusalem with the head of Golias, by Lucas van Leyden" was item 176 in the inventory of Rubens' possessions after his death in 1640.[4] Although Van Leyden's composition is different from the Kimbell panel, it is possible that the presence of the sixteenth-century picture in his collection stimulated Rubens to treat the subject.

As Justus Müller Hofstede has shown, Rubens adapted his group of the women of Jerusalem in the David panel from a picture by Orazio Gentileschi (1562–1647) who was working in London for Charles I during Rubens' last visit there.[5] Gentileschi's canvas, now lost, was *Apollo Listens to the Playing of the Muses*, and Rubens' pen drawing from it is now in the Boymans Museum, Rotterdam (cat. no. V. 57).[6] An unlocated chalk drawing (22 × 23 cm.) of the same title may be related to this David panel; it is recorded in the Villeneuve sale, Paris, 1842.

Description: David, carrying the severed head of the slain Goliath, with the huge sword of the vanquished slung over his shoulders, approaches the city gate, out of which have come the women of Jerusalem to rejoice and honor their hero with music, dancing and the strewing of flowers in his path. The architecture of the gate, as in numerous late pictures, is similar to the portal of Rubens' own home, the Castle of Steen. Two male figures, suggesting the throng that suddenly was freed from mortal dread of the Philistines, rush from the city, pointing to the victorious host of Israel seen marching homeward in the middle distance. The trunks, branches and foliage of a cluster of trees at the center repeat in pictorial metaphor the rhythmic attitudes, movements and gestures of the central group of figures. The breathless, triumphant spirit of the moment is heightened by the swirling openness and freedom of the brushwork and the flickering "changeant" colors of the multi-hued drapery. And the cadence of joyful music is measured by Rubens' brilliant placement of bodies and treading feet.

Condition: Excellent. Cradled on the back to contain three horizontal cracks, one two inches below top edge, two others across center. Slight bowing due to warpage, side to side. Two losses, filled and inpainted, lower right corner.

Exhibitions: None known.

Collections: Possibly an 18th-century British collection (cf. *Related Versions*), because of the number of copies in Britain. Possibly the painting sold: "Vente X," Paris, Nov. 19, 1772; *Le Triomphe de David après la défaite de Goliath,* panel, 32 x 22 p. [59.5 x 86.6 cm.]. M. Coulouma, Rouen, 1840 (when presented to him as a wedding gift). M. Coulouma, the son.
Foundation Acquisition, AP 66.3.

Related Versions: (1) Theodor van Thulden used this modello for his large picture of the same subject which is in the Gallery in Schwerin, inv. no. 714. (2) A late 18th-century copy by Alexander Runciman is in the collection of Sir John Clerk, Penicuik House, Midlothian. See Ellis Waterhouse, *Painting in Britain, 1530–1790,* no. 166 a, illus. (3) A third copy, attributed to "Franken" (on copper 18 x 15 in.), was sold at Christie's, London, Dec. 18, 1964. (4) Another copy, attributed to Thomas Stothard, sold at Christie's, Nov. 18, 1966, cat. no. 26. (5) M. A. Immenraet also made a copy that is now in the Von Nivkl Collection, Budapest.

Notes:

1 Michael Jaffé, "Rediscovered Oil Sketches by Rubens-II," *Burlington Magazine,* vol. CXI, September, 1969, p. 529, fig. 10.

2 Jaffé, p. 537.

3 Jaffé, p. 537.

4 Franz Wolter, *Oud Holland,* vol. V, 1926, pp. 226–28, Abb. 1. Through an engraving by Jan van Saenredam and a painting in a private collection, the appearance of the Lucas van Leyden *David* is known.

5 Justus Müller Hofstede, *Pantheon,* vol. III, May–June, 1965, p. 165, no. 14. The Gentileschi painting (Abb. 2) is illustrated.

6 This drawing bears, in addition to color notes penned by Rubens himself, a later inscription, "van tulden," which is certainly not the attribution. Van Thulden may have owned the drawing.

After Frans Hals, 1581/85–1666
The Rommel Pot Player
Painted after about 1615–18

Oil on canvas, 41 3/4 x 31 5/8 in. (106 x 80.3 cm.)

This well-known painting is considered to be one of the best of numerous surviving versions of a lost work that Frans Hals painted about 1615–18.[1] Probably painted with Hals' consent, it is certainly based on his original composition. The earthy subject and carefree mood are characteristic of a group of genre works that Hals painted early in his career. Hals' treatment of figures constitutes an innovation in this traditional mode of Dutch painting; their large scale and proximity to the viewer, their sympathetic observation and unrestrained joy were intended to involve the viewer more than earlier, more restrained, genre studies had done. In this painting, in spite of some ambiguities that warrant the qualified attribution, these Halsian qualities are quite evident, particularly in the main figure.

The major figure is an ebullient musician whose rugged face, gnarled hands and somber clothing are painted in broad, sure strokes that imbue his coherently modeled figure with energy and vitality. He laughs in a nearly toothless grin as he amuses the enthralled children with the groaning sounds of his crude homemade instrument, a rommel pot,[2] which he cradles against his stomach. This dark earthenware pot is partially filled with water and its mouth is covered by a taut skin which vibrates, producing a resonant gurgling whine that is best compared to the squeal of a stuck pig.[3] Despite an ambiguous dark stroke which projects formlessly from the back of the musician's head (between his hat and collar),[4] the assured rendering of this merry beggar seems, indeed, quite close to that of Hals' own facile hand.[5]

The five children surrounding the musician are uniquely disposed in this painting compared to its other versions. All but one look toward the musician. The two boys in front of him each offer a coin in a fist while the winking boy at the right extends an open hand of outrageous size. Although the broadly painted modeling of the four boys is generally convincing, facial details are less definitive than those of the central figure. Several thinly painted areas reveal *pentimenti* (such as in the head of the small boy in the foreground). In contrast, the face of the young girl who looks to the viewer with a winning smile is painted in assured strokes comparable to those of the figure of the musician. This vigorous rhythm of juxtaposed figures, the accents of bright color and vivid facial expressions evoke a mood of unadulterated joy.

The unrestrained carnival mood is appropriate to the subject of the painting which may represent an incident in the pre-Lenten celebration of Shrovetide, the three days before Ash Wednesday. Indeed, it could be an illustration of the Dutch proverb inscribed on a later engraving of a more surly rommel pot player:[6]

"Many fools run around at Shrovetide
To make a half-penny grunt on a rommel pot"

The musician in the Kimbell painting is easily identified as a fool; the long white-tipped foxtail trailing from his battered hat is a "fool's foxtail," a motif that Hals used with similar meaning in another contemporary painting.[7] The coins offered by the boys to the musician may well be halfpennies that will soon "grunt" for a moment on the head of the rommel pot before being pocketed by the player.

This Shrovetide theme and the exceptional emphasis on the spontaneous joy of children, along with the dense composition and the generally somber colors, are characteristic of Hals' work of about 1615–20. A Hals painting with a related carnival theme, *Shrovetide Revellers*, dates about 1615; the original version of the Kimbell work was probably painted several years later. Hals' paintings of children are among his most distinctive works; in *The Rommel Pot Player* "they take leading roles for the first time."[8]

Description: Five laughing children crowd about a merry, bearded street musician. In his left hand he holds a rommel pot, an earthenware jar covered by tautly stretched skin, that is pierced by a thin stick which he grasps in his right hand. He wears a floppy, wide-brimmed dark grey hat with a long foxtail and a baggy, dark grey coat with a rust-colored lining that shows at the cuffs and neck where a white collar is revealed. The children are dressed in clothes of similar somber tones. At the right, a boy wearing a rumpled, rust-colored cap winks one eye, sticks out his tongue and extends the open palm of his left hand. At the left, the two boys nearest the musician, one bareheaded and the other with a wide-brimmed brown hat, face him; each offers a coin in an extended hand. Behind them the fourth boy regards the musician; the tips of the fingers of his right hand can be seen on the shoulder of a small girl in a white cap who faces the viewer with a cheerful smile. In the background two summarily sketched haggard faces, barely discernible, peer through a doorway at the left of a brown wall from which a reddish-brown ceramic jug hangs at an oblique angle just to the left of center.

Condition: Fair. Inpainting of a network of small losses is evident in the sleeves and the front of the musician's jacket, the brim of his hat and about the edges of the canvas. The canvas has been trimmed to its present dimensions; the thumb of the boy at the right and the hand and ear of the boy at the left have been cropped. The surface varnish is generally clear except for a small clouded area above the head of the boy at the left and some slight discoloration in other dark areas.

Exhibitions: Works by Early and Modern Painters of the Dutch School, Guildhall Corporation, London, 1903, cat. no. 173 *(The Man with the Rumble)*, illus. *Twenty-One Paintings from the Kimbell Art Foundation*, Fort Worth Art Association, March 3–26, 1953, cat. no. 8, illus.

Collections: Sir Frederick Cook, Doughty House, Richmond, Surrey, by 1903; descended to: Sir Francis Cook until after 1946. [Newhouse Galleries, Inc., New York.] Kimbell Bequest, ACF 51.1.

Related Versions: The complex relation of approximately twenty known versions and copies of this painting precludes a meaningful discussion here because their history and attribution are not clear. However, some distinctive aspects of the best-known variants are worth noting. None of them seems as close to Hals' early style as the Kimbell painting. The image of the musician is similar in most of the versions but the number, dress and pose of the children and the background vary considerably. A small panel in the Art Institute of Chicago, attributed to Judith Leyster, has five children in similar poses but their dress is different and the faces are more summarily painted. Among the deviations: the winking boy wears a fur cap and has pulled in his tongue; the small boy has curly hair and there are three (rather than two) old crones in the doorway.[9] In a slightly larger version at Wilton House, six children are differently arranged in a dense composition; the little girl is closer to the musician, looks toward him and holds a coin, while the lusty chap at the right pummels his closed right fist into his left hand.[10] A very broadly painted close-up view of the musician alone was in the Van Gelder Collection, Uccle, Belgium.[11]

Notes:

1 C. Hofstede de Groot, ... *Verzeichnis der Werke der hervorragendsten holländischen Maler des* XVII. *Jahrhunderts*, Esslingen and Paris, 1910, vol. III, p. 138, cat. no. 137–5. Wilhelm von Bode and M. J. Binder, *Frans Hals: His Life and Work*, trans. by M.W. Brockwell, London, 1914, vol. I, p. 26, cat. no. 10; vol. II, pl. 6. Seymour Slive, *Frans Hals*, London, 1970, vol. I, pp. 36–39, fig. 20.

2 Rommel derives from the Dutch verb *rommelen* meaning "to rumble."

3 Slive, vol. I, p. 37.

4 Several other aimless strokes can be noted: a dark vertical stroke on the frame of the door and some diagonal strokes on the upper arm of the boy in the foreground.

5 It would be tempting to suggest that Hals painted this figure and assistants painted the subordinate areas. However, Slive, p. 8, explicitly remarks that Hals does not appear to have followed this practice; nothing is known about his studio practice or his direction of copyists.

6 The engraving by Jan van de Velde (ca. 1593–1641) is illustrated by Slive, vol. I, p. 37, fig. 19.

7 The figure of "Peeckelhaering" in Hals' *Shrovetide Revellers* (Metropolitan Museum of Art, New York) holds a foxtail in his right hand. See: Slive, vol. I, p. 36; vol. II, pl. 8.

8 Slive, vol. I, p. 38.

9 15 × 12½ in., Hofstede de Groot, cat. no. 137–4. Slive, vol. I, p. 37, fig. 21.

10 43 × 34 in., Hofstede de Groot, cat. no. 137–6. Sidney, 16th Earl of Pembroke, ... *Paintings and Drawings ... at Wilton House*, London, 1968, p. 42, cat. no. 107, pl. 68.

11 Joséphin Peladan, *Frans Hals*, Paris, 1912, illus. facing p. 100. The Kimbell painting is briefly mentioned on p. 101. See also Von Bode and Binder, cat. no. 14, pl. 8b.

Additional References:

Wilhelm R. Valentiner, *Frans Hals*, vol. 28 of *Klassiker der Kunst*, 2nd ed., Stuttgart, 1923, p. 300, illus., p. 24. He considers the Kimbell version the closest to the lost original and also suggests that the children may represent Hals' children.

Maurice W. Brockwell, *Catalogue of the Cook Collection*, [London?], 1932, vol. II, p. 44, cat. no. 265.

Numa S. Trivas, *The Paintings of Frans Hals*, London, 1941, appendix, no. 3, pl. 154. He considers this painting to be a variant of a lost original work.

Frans Hals, 1581/85–1666
Portrait of a Man
Painted about 1643–45

Oil on canvas, 34 5/8 × 25 5/8 in. (87.9 × 65.1 cm.)

By the mid 1640s, when this portrait is thought to have been painted,[1] Frans Hals' painting style had evolved from an exuberant mode to one of sobriety and dignity. Even so, the very personal and distinctive qualities of his style were recognized and admired by his contemporaries. In 1648 it was said of Hals: "... by his extraordinary manner of painting which is uniquely his, he virtually surpasses everyone. His paintings are imbued with such force and vitality that he seems to defy nature herself with his brush. This is seen in all his portraits ... they are painted in such a way that they seem to breathe and live."[2] Today, Hals' deft, straightforward style and trenchant characterizations make his portraits among the most appealing in the history of European painting.

In this portrait of a stalwart Dutch burgher, Hals has used very effective pictorial means to construct a powerful image of a mature, worldly man; his resolute character is readily perceived even though his identity is unknown. The stolid respectability of his monochromatic dress is reinforced by the somber background and low-keyed skin tones. The heavy eyelids and the puffed flesh about them, fluently modeled with long assured strokes, draw the viewer's attention to the clear, steady gaze of the pupils. Vitality and energy are communicated by the terse strokes that form the bushy eyebrows, the elegantly trimmed moustache and beard, and the soft curling locks. The plastic modeling of the face is equally revealing of a forceful personality, particularly the brilliant contrast of dark shadows and bright highlights with the flat, pristine whiteness of the crisply starched collar. Strength

and tension are emphasized by the very summary strokes of the gnarled hand.

The flat, triangular composition is direct and economical yet equally subtle. Established by the sloping shoulders and edges of the collar, it creates a solid form within which the subdued rhythm of folds in the dark clothing clearly defines his chest and arms. The bright accent of the left hand solidly anchors the composition, counterbalancing the highlights in his face and collar. Thrust forward toward the viewer, this hand establishes the front base of a solidly three-dimensional pyramidal composition with an apex at the sitter's face.

The same hand firmly holds a distinctive attribute of the man's interests or profession. However, the rapid abstract rendering of this feathery golden object inhibits its definitive identification and allows a variety of interpretations. Possibly a glove, a swatch of cloth, or a bouquet of tail-feathers from a grouse,[3] its hue and ragged texture are also close to the burst heads of ripe grain, suggesting that the man may have been a grain merchant or brewer who wished to indicate his means of success in his portrait. However, in other Hals' portraits no precedents appear that corroborate any of these possibilities. No grain merchant has been identified, and among the half a dozen brewers painted by Hals, only one or two are "in a traditional pose with gloves or a glove in hand."[4]

The brief known history of this painting includes one of those rare instances in which an unknown painting is recognized as a definitive work by a major artist. It is only since 1963 that Hals scholars have established that this previously unrecorded painting is an authentic work and worthy of exhibition at the Frans Halsmuseum, where it was shown for several months in 1965.

Description: Half-length portrait of a man about 40 to 50 years old. His dress, including a tall wide-brimmed hat, is coal-black, except for the large white wings of a broad collar. Buttoned down the front with glistening black buttons, his cloak drapes loosely over his arms which are crossed in front. A glimpse of his right hand is visible beneath the rumpled folds over his left arm. In his left hand he grasps some loosely painted golden yellow matter, possibly grain. His eyes are dark and his bushy eyebrows, waxed moustache and closely trimmed beard are light brown, streaked with grey and yellow highlights. Behind his right ear, long curving locks of grey-streaked hair extend from beneath his hat with a strand of black hair just in front of the ear. The dark, nearly black, background is tinged with green.

Condition: Good. Relatively little abrasion was evident when the painting was cleaned and relined. There is some filling and inpainting: a one-inch diameter loss at his left temple and hat, several losses in the upper left quarter, an L-shaped tear in the right center, a two-inch scratch to the left of his hand and a few scattered small losses.[5]

Exhibition: Frans Halsmuseum, Haarlem, the Netherlands, April–May, 1965.

Collections: "A country house in Gelderland," the Netherlands, during "the second half of the nineteenth century." Mr. L. Hofman of Zutphen, who sold it about 1930 to Mr. Van Mourik; with Mrs. M. C. van Mourik-Spoor, Huize Midwijk, Vorden, until auction, October, 1962, sold to: Mr. Th. J. van Beukering, Arnhem.[6] Auction, [J. C. Derkson], Arnhem, July 19, 1963, sold to: Mr. and Mrs. Leonid Hotinov, Muiderberg (Amsterdam), who sold it to Mrs. Gisela Kemperdick, Kaster (Cologne), Austria; sold by her at auction, [Christie's], London, Nov. 26, 1965, lot 70. Foundation Acquisition, AP 65.2.

Notes:

1 Seymour Slive, *Frans Hals*, London, 1970, vol. II, pl. 241; vol. III (to be published), cat. no. 158. See also notes by C. C. Vieten in *Die Weltkunst*, vol. XXIV, no. 23, Nov. 15, 1964, p. 990, and vol. XXXV, no. 10, May 15, 1965, p. 403, illus.

2 Theodorus Schrevelius, *Harlemias*, 1648, (trans. by Slive, vol. I, p. 8).

3 The feathers were suggested by H. P. Baard, "Wedergeboorte en lotgevallen van de 'Hotinov-Hals'," *Oud-Holland*, vol. LXXX, 1965, pp. 213–14, 216.

4 Slive, letter to David Robb, Feb. 9, 1972.

5 Baard, pp. 211–16, discusses the painting's condition and publishes two illustrations, figs. 2, 4, of the painting before conservation.

6 The history before 1963 is based on the provenance shown in the Christie's auction catalogue, Nov. 26, 1965, lot 70, and the historical summary given by Baard, pp. 211–12, 216.

Massimo Stanzione, about 1585–1656
Madonna and Child
Painted in the 1630s

Oil on canvas, 50 1/8×38 1/8 in. (127.4×96.8 cm.)

In the second quarter of the seventeenth century, Naples was second only to Rome as the center for artistic developments of the Italian Baroque style. In this southern Italian city, a distinctive style developed which depended on two powerful influences: Caravaggism from Rome and Bolognese Classicism. The native Neapolitan artists were inspired to break away from a prevailing academic Mannerist mode by the examples of Caravaggio's paintings which he had done for churches and private patrons during his visits to Naples in 1607 and 1610.[1] From the 1630s on, however, the primary influence was Bolognese Classicism which was brought to Naples by followers of the Carracci brothers, such as Domenichino, Giovanni Lanfranco and Guido Reni.[2]

Current studies of the Neapolitan Baroque are equivocal. Massimo Stanzione, one of the major figures of the second-generation Neapolitan painters, is frequently misclassified as a member of the *Caravaggisti*, or followers of Caravaggio. His work does have some similarities, which he derived from his teacher Giovanni Battista Caracciolo, called Battistello (who founded Neapolitan Baroque painting of the seicento on the basis of Caravaggio's influence[3]), and from several trips he made to Rome.[4] Stanzione developed independently, however, and his work appears to owe allegiance more to the classically oriented principles developed by the Carracci in Bologna.[5] The decorative, mannered elegance of his work is what influenced younger artists of this period, particularly his student Bernardo Cavallino.

Stanzione's brand of Neapolitan Classicism is manifest in the Kimbell *Madonna and Child* by the mood of lyrical serenity. The figures are arranged pyramidally in a shallow space and look directly at the viewer. The Madonna, seated gracefully in a classicizing pose, is intimately related to the Child by the tilt of her head. Stanzione's interest in elegant costumes is evident in the Madonna's variously textured ensemble whose flowing but rather bulky draperies tend to emphasize the tangibility of her figure. The subtle variations of the rich colors are complemented by tightly controlled impasto effects.[6]

Stanzione's isolation of the two figures before a dark, unmodulated background and use of a strong light from an unseen source at the left reveal his Caravaggesque roots. However, the light is modulated evenly across the figures, creating subtle changes of tone instead of spotlighting a dramatic scene with abrupt changes in *chiaroscuro*. The more natural lighting is indicative of a prevailing taste in Baroque art rather than a definite reaction to Caravaggesque emotionalism.

Inscription: Lower left on pedestal: EQ MAX [Eques Maximus][7]

Description: Three-quarter-length view of the Madonna and the Christ Child. The Madonna is a pretty young woman with brown hair and brown eyes who is seated before a plain background which shades from dark raw umber at the left to grey-green at the right. Her dress is dark red and her blue mantle with dark blue shadows drapes over her legs and her right arm. A beige diaphanous scarf is at the neckline of her dress. A misty green shawl with shadows of red, simulating velvet, drapes over her left shoulder across to the Child's torso and down to the pedestal. Her turban-like headdress is beige silk with blue stripes. The nude Child with light brown hair and brown eyes stands on a fluted pedestal while his right foot rests on his mother's thigh. They both look out at the viewer, their heads tilted slightly to the right of the canvas.

Condition: Fair. The painting has been relined but the relining canvas, which is very dry, brittle, and decayed, is impressed into the original surface. There is some scattered cleavage and several insignificant losses, a condition which will be ameliorated during conservation treatment that is scheduled for the near future. At that time it is anticipated that the ambiguous rendering of the Infant's hair will be resolved.

Exhibitions: None known.

Collections: Fuerstlich Liechtensteinsche Gemaelde Gallerie, Vienna, Austria, and Vaduz, Liechtenstein, by 1873. [Newhouse Galleries, Inc., New York.] Kimbell Bequest, ACF 56.1.

Notes:

1 Alfred Moir, *The Italian Followers of Caravaggio*, Cambridge, Mass., 1967, vol. I, pp. 157–59.

2 Rudolf Wittkower, *Art and Architecture in Italy, 1600 to 1750*, 2nd rev. ed., Baltimore, 1965, pp. 230–31. See also: Richard E. Spear, *Caravaggio and His Followers*, Cleveland, 1971, pp. 17–25.

3 Moir, pp. 159–65.

4 The first trip, 1617–18; the second trip, 1623–25. See: Moir, p. 166.

5 Spear, pp. 17–25.

6 Moir, p. 167.

7 This is the signature Stanzione used after he was knighted in 1625. See: Moir, p. 166, note 42.

Additional References:

G. F. Waagen, *Die vornehmsten Kunstdenkmäler von Wien*, Vienna, 1866, p. 264.
Catalogue of the Fuerstlich Liechtensteinsche Gemaelde Gallerie, Vienna, 1873, no. 59.
Bryan's Dictionary of Painters and Engravers, London, 1910, vol. V, p. 116.
John Denison Champlin, Jr., *Cyclopedia of Painters and Paintings*, New York, 1892, vol. IV, p. 217.
Helen Comstock, "Liechtenstein Collection Madonna," *Connoisseur*, vol. 137, no. 544, June, 1956, p. 289, illus.

Jusepe de Ribera, 1591–1652
Saint Matthew
Painted in 1632

Oil on canvas, 50 1/2 × 38 1/2 in. (128.2 × 97.8 cm.)

Single figures of saints are subjects frequently found in seventeenth-century Spanish painting. Jusepe de Ribera's painting of *Saint Matthew* is an excellent example of the interest of Baroque painters in realism for both religious and aesthetic purposes. Painted in Italy in 1632, close to the end of Ribera's early, more Caravaggesque phase of artistic activity,[1] it epitomizes his highly influential early Baroque style.

Born in Játiva, Spain, a village near Valencia, Ribera left for Italy early in his career and, after a circuitous route, settled in the Spanish viceroyalty of Naples by December, 1616.[2] He remained there the rest of his life, except for possible sojourns in Rome.[3] In spite of his great ability to absorb Italian influences, Ribera retained a distinctly Spanish flavor in his work which is less sensuous than that of his Italian contemporaries. As one of the foremost painters of his time, he was commissioned to paint many works, especially for the Carthusian monastery of San Martino in Naples, for succeeding viceroys and presumably for Philip IV of Spain whose collection included many religious paintings by the Spanish artist. It is through these latter works that he exerted a tremendous influence on seventeenth-century Spanish painters, especially Diego Velásquez and Francisco de Zurbarán.[4] His painterly style which combines virtuoso brushwork with plastic volumes set a new precedent for Baroque realism. The physical veracity of his intensely spiritual images was very much in keeping with Counter-Reformation dogma.

The powerful sense of drama in the Kimbell *Saint Matthew* is evoked by Ribera's emphasis on the

dignity of the individual and by a stark composition combined with strong lighting and sculpturesque modeling. Although the saint is more aristocratic in appearance than Ribera's usual choice of homely, peasant types, his intense, meditative expression reflects the compassion and personal dignity with which Ribera endowed his subjects, thus fulfilling one of the principal aims of the Counter-Reformation. The simplicity of composition is achieved by Ribera's selectivity in a minimum of details identifying the subject (a cross and the apostolic attribute, Saint Matthew's Gospel Book) and an uncomplicated composition with the static figure placed before a dark, neutral background. He does not rely in this early period on the typically Baroque compositional device of the diagonal for drama, nor does he include secondary figures to create a narrative situation as he was to do in his succeeding years.[5] The sharp light from one side which spotlights the figure flows across the forms, modeling them, and creates murky shadows. This lighting device, called tenebrism, is an element which Ribera inherited from Caravaggio, the most influential Neapolitan painter when Ribera arrived in southern Italy. Other Caravaggesque elements which Ribera adopted are the earth-toned coloration, warm tonality and emphasis on volume.

Ribera's use of the *alla prima* method of painting allowed him the freedom and fluidity which became his hallmark. Working the whole composition simultaneously, he rapidly applied layer upon layer of dense, liquid pigment to achieve a textured surface with glistening highlights.[6] Painting directly from his model,[7] he used quick brushstrokes and vigorously built-up impasto to achieve the sensitive articulation of the saint's ruddy face and hands, and of the book which he holds. These areas are complemented by the numerous, small, curving strokes used to describe the saint's softly curling locks and his grizzled beard. In contrast, controlled strokes of great breadth powerfully convey the ample substance of the thick folds in his black cloak, which, in turn, is played against the thinly painted planes of the lighter-toned russet mantle over his right side, providing variation in texture and color that focuses attention on the head.

Inscription: Lower right: *Jusepe de Ribera, espagñol F 1632*

Description: Three-quarter-length portrait of the apostle, Saint Matthew. He stands just right of center in the composition before a dark brown, unarticulated background. Looking to his left, the saint has dark brown eyes, a ruddy complexion weathered by time, brown hair which is greying, and a grey beard. Wearing a black cloak, he is partially draped by a russet mantle over his right shoulder. He holds a heavy, brown, leather-covered book with his left hand, the fingers of his right hand resting on its ochre pages. In the lower right corner a brown, wood cross lies flat on a greyish-tan rock. The strong raking light, which comes from an unseen source high at the left, models the forms and picks up highlights on the saint's forehead, nose, hair and beard, white undercloak, hands, and the book.

Condition: Very good. It is painted on very coarse canvas which has been relined; there is a normal craquelure pattern throughout the paint layer and the varnish is yellowed by age. Abrasions have been filled and inpainted, particularly evident in the flesh areas.

Exhibitions: *Exposition d'Art Ancien Espagnol*, Galerie Jean Charpentier, Paris, 1925, cat. no. 83, illus. p. 137.

Collections: [M. Sano, Paris.] Lord Wimborne, Cranford Manor, Wimborne, Dorset, England, November, 1867, to [Christie's] sale, London, March 9, 1923, cat. no. 50. [Sedelmeyer], Paris, 1925. Jean Deschamps, Paris. [Newhouse Galleries, Inc., New York.]
Foundation Acquisition, AP 66.10.

Related Version: A possible study for the head is illustrated by Carlos Sarthou Carreres, *J. José de Ribera y su arte: El Españoleto y su Patria*, Valencia, 1947.

Notes:

1 Elizabeth du Gué Trapier, *Ribera*, New York, 1952, p. 2.

2 He was married at this time. See: Lorenzo Salazar, "La patria e la famiglia dello Spagnoletto: Nuovi documenti," *Napoli Nobilissima*, vol. III, 1894, p. 98.

3 George Kubler and Martin Soria, *Art and Architecture in Spain and Portugal, and their American Dominions, 1500 to 1800*, Baltimore, 1959, p. 238.

4 Kubler and Soria, p. 238.

5 Trapier, p. 2.

6 See Kubler and Soria, pp. 238–40, for a description of the master's painting method.

7 Trapier, p. 1.

Additional Reference:

A Catalogue of the Pictures at Cranford Manor in the Possession of Lord Wimborne, London, 1888, p. 68, no. 163.
August L. Mayer, *Jusepe de Ribera, Lo Spagnoletto*, Leipzig, 1923, p. 197 (as "lost").
Craig McFadyen Felton, *Jusepe de Ribera, a Catalogue Raisonné*, unpublished doctoral dissertation, University of Pittsburgh, 1971, pp. 206–7, cat. no. A-34.

Jan van Goyen, 1596–1656
View of Arnhem
Painted about 1645–48

Oil on panel, 14 1/8 × 24 3/8 in. (35.9 × 61.9 cm.)

Jan van Goyen was the most innovative contributor to the rise of pictorial realism in Dutch landscape painting of the seventeenth century. Dispensing with allusions to classical themes and traditional formulas in composition and color, he evolved a more empirical conception of landscape painting that found a ready market with bourgeois patrons. This new style is characterized by views with low horizons under large expanses of moist sky, the vast plains of Holland seeming to stretch to infinity, punctuated by small towns that barely rise above the level fields. With Salomon van Ruysdael and Pieter Molijn, Van Goyen developed a monochromatic palette, representative of the Tonal Phase of Dutch landscape painting, which allowed emphasis on atmospheric effects.[1]

Painted at the height of the Tonal Phase in the early 1640s, the Kimbell landscape shows the town of Arnhem[2] viewed from the northwest. The larger church is the Groote Kerk, built in 1452, while the one to the left with twin towers is the St. Walbergkerk. Across the Rhine River to the right is the town of Huissen, and in the distance beyond in Germany is the Eltener Berg with its ancient abbey.[3] More topographically accurate than most of Van Goyen's landscapes, this view was probably based on rapid chalk drawings of the scene that he made while traveling through the Netherlands and along the Rhine River. In his studio he embellished these views by judicious placement of genre groups derived from quick studies.

Beyond the groups of travelers who accentuate the lighter area of the left foreground, this painting is dominated by the broad expanse of the distant horizon, all of which is conveyed with the utmost economy of means. The central motif of buildings in the town of Arnhem provides a scale that is a defining foil for the summarily painted buildings at the horizon in the center and at the right edge. The crisp outlines of the compactly massed spires and town are silhouetted against the light horizon and the luminous sky with rolling white clouds which create a sense of great breadth and height. The small groups of peasants, which provide scale and color contrast, are placed casually and picturesquely in the composition and integrated into the landscape. Sketched in with a light touch, they and the land are painted in Van Goyen's bold, vivacious and very fluid technique. The sky is rendered with quick, whirling strokes that evoke a moist atmosphere which seems to veil everything while the land is described by a delicately balanced, almost monochromatic scale of values consisting of luminous grey-green tonalities with brown shadows. The subtle distribution of broad areas of light and shade provides a sense of spaciousness and quietude.

Inscription: None apparent.[4]

Description: View of the town of Arnhem looking southeast toward the Rhine River. Large windblown, white clouds dominate the pale blue sky which occupies nearly three-quarters of the painting. In the center of the earthen-hued terrain of the foreground, five brown cows graze in isolation under the observation of a shepherd resting on a small hill at the right. Groups of travelers along a rough road leading toward Arnhem dominate the left foreground. In the middle distance, the town of Arnhem stretches from the center to the far right. Painted in medium grey-greens with dark grey accents, a large church with a tower, another church with twin towers and a smaller building with a steeple rise above houses and other small buildings with pitched roofs. These architectural elements skirt a pale blue body of water at the far right on which there are two tiny boats. The far distance is painted in muted grey-greens which become paler as the horizon meets the sky. Trees are suggested along the low-lying plains and a town with a church is discernible at the far right.

Condition: Excellent. The well-preserved paint layer had some very minor abrasions in the sky which were inpainted when the panel was cleaned and mounted on balsa wood backing in late 1970.

Exhibitions: Seventeen Masterpieces of the Seventeenth Century, Schaeffer Galleries, New York, 1939.[5] M. Knoedler & Co., Inc., New York, 1950. *Life in Seventeenth Century Holland*, Wadsworth Atheneum, Hartford, Conn., Nov. 21, 1950–Jan. 14, 1951, cat. no. 21, pl. III.

Collections: Fr. Gluck, Budapest, by 1887.[6] [Alfred Brod, Ltd.], London. [M. Knoedler & Co., Inc.], New York, by 1950. Private collection, England. Private collection, Paris. [Galerie les Tourettes, Paris.]
Foundation Acquisition, AP 66.4.

Notes:

1 See: Jakob Rosenberg, Seymour Slive, and E. H. Ter Kuile, *Dutch Art and Architecture: 1600 to 1800*, Baltimore, 1966, pp. 148–50.

2 Arnhem, as well as the towns of Rhenen and Nijmegen, is frequently seen in paintings by Van Goyen and those of other artists. See: Wolfgang Stechow, *Dutch Landscape Painting of the Seventeenth Century*, London, 1966, pp. 8, 41.

3 *Life in Seventeenth Century Holland*, Wadsworth Atheneum, Hartford, Conn., Nov. 21, 1950–Jan. 14, 1951, cat. no. 21.

4 Although the Wadsworth Atheneum catalogue indicates that this painting is initialed and dated 1645, no inscription could be located in a recent examination of the painting. See also: Stechow, p. 3.

5 A. M. Frankfurter, *Art News*, vol. 37, Feb. 4, 1939, p. 21, illus. (In this review of the Schaeffer Gallery exhibition, the Kimbell painting is illustrated but its caption confuses it with another view of Arnhem by Van Goyen, now in the Ten Cate Collection, Almelo, Holland, which is much larger and a rather different view with much more emphasis on diagonal movement.)

6 Cornelis Hofstede de Groot, *Verzeichnis der Werke der hervorragendsten holländischen Maler des* XVII. *Jahrhunderts*, Esslingen and Paris, 1923, vol. 8, cat. no. 12, p. 9.

Additional References:

Walther Bernt, *Die niederländischen Maler des 17. Jahrhunderts*, Munich, 1948, vol. I, cat. no. 322, illus. (*The Netherlandish Painters of the Seventeenth Century*, London, 1969, vol. I, cat. no. 444, illus.)
Anna Dobrzycka, *Jan van Goyen 1596–1656*, Poznan, 1966, pp. 52, 130, cat. no. 277, illus. p. 210, fig. 75.
Hans-Ulrich Beck, *Jan van Goyen, Gemälde und Zeichnungen*, monograph in preparation to be published in Amsterdam in 1972.

Anthony van Dyck, 1599–1641
Self-Portrait, about age 15
Painted about 1614

Oil on panel, 14 3/8×10 1/8 in. (36.5×25.8 cm.)

Anthony van Dyck was precocious: he entered the Antwerp Guild of St. Luke at the age of ten; eight years later he was enrolled as a master. During these years he is known to have worked in the Antwerp studio of Peter Paul Rubens, but the nature of their association is not definitely established. It seems likely that after receiving guidance from Rubens, possibly as a pupil, Van Dyck rapidly advanced to an independent status by the time he was nineteen years of age. Whether as student, disciple or collaborator, he learned much from Rubens.[1] This interacting association makes definitive identification of Van Dyck's early works a rather challenging task; some of them, including this panel, have been attributed to Rubens.[2] The Kimbell painting, which has only recently been attributed to Van Dyck,[3] is one of two self-portraits that Van Dyck did before 1620 (when he went to England); the other one, now in the Akademie der Künste in Vienna, is quite well known and regarded as Van Dyck's earliest self-portrait.[4]

The Kimbell portrait was painted about 1614, a year or so later than the Vienna painting. In both, the youth is recognizably the same: the high cheeks, long straight nose and firm chin vary only as might be expected in about two years of adolescent growth.[5] Moreover, the attitude is the same, an inquiring look over the shoulder. In the Vienna painting this pose communicates a strong personality, full of confidence and an ingenuous innocence. In the Kimbell painting the large expanse of muffling folds of the cloak and the white collar, together with the partly shaded face, impute a guarded reserve to this image. He looks out with a "watchful, self-protective air," giving the impression of the slightly disdainful self-confidence of a maturing adolescent. While less endearing a youthful image than the earlier Vienna painting, the Kimbell painting is strong, vibrant and quite engaging. Its compelling assurance, particularly the smoothly glazed modeling of the face, as well as its iconographic affinity with the Vienna painting, certainly mitigates the meager record of its history.

However, the physical condition of the painting and a related drawing present a rather complex art-historical puzzle. The barely discernible wide-brimmed hat is recent overpaint, but the shadow it casts across the brow is quite old and integral with the original surface. In the initial stage of this portrait, there was apparently no hat—only the face, a full head of hair, and the white collar. Apparently dissatisfied with this design, the artist decided to embellish it, and a drawing in the Albertina Collection, Vienna, has been identified by Michael Jaffé as Van Dyck's solution.[6] It shows three modifications that focus further attention on the face: the hat that covers the hair on the crown and part of the forehead, the subdued shadow cast by the wide brim over the remaining forehead and the figure's right eye, and the painting of the cloak over the lower end of the white collar (the *pentimento* of which can be seen beneath). Of these three additions, only the last two remain today.

The original hat was removed many years later after the overpaint had discolored the underlying flesh tones of the forehead. Perhaps the underlying hair was striking through the hat and misled a restorer to regard it as a later "tasteful" addition. Although extensive scraping of the background was necessary to remove the hat, the hair and forehead remained relatively intact. When the restorer realized the implications of the shadowed brow and the discolored forehead, he applied a protective varnish layer and painted on the second hat. In 1971 when the overpaint of the second hat was removed, revealing the original head of hair, the same conditions were encountered: the paint in the shadow across the brow was old, quite hard and integral to the adjacent areas. It was finally concluded that without the hat the shadow made no visual sense at all; therefore, the present hat, the third one, was applied to the panel as unobtrusively as possible.

Description: Bust-length head of a young man looking over his left shoulder. His dark grey eyes look directly at the viewer while his partly shaded face, seen in three-quarter view, is framed by long wavy locks of brown hair with yellow highlights. Covering his neck is a stiff white lace collar which rises from the enveloping folds of a dark grey cloak. The background is an opaque, very dark brown.

Condition: Fair. The face, neck and cloak are in very good condition with only a few scattered minor losses and some slight abrasions on his right cheek. When a layer of discolored varnish was removed in 1971, it revealed relatively recent overpaint that constituted the entire rendering of the hat and large areas of the background. Removal of the overpaint revealed the repair of a vertical crack one inch from the right edge, a large area around the head that had been scraped to the white ground, beneath the hat, a previously obscured high forehead and a considerable amount of hair. Although slightly discolored, the substantially intact rendering of the forehead and hair definitely appeared to be contemporary with areas that had not been overpainted. However, because the paint layer of the shadow laid across the forehead and right eye was very hard and of comparable age with the underlying flesh tones, it was decided to reapply the hat. The original oak panel had been planed to a very thin layer and remounted on a second supporting panel and a cradle.

Exhibitions: None known.

Collections: Said to have been in a private collection, Madrid.[7] Frederick W. Mont, New York, by 1954.[8] [Newhouse Galleries, Inc., New York.]
Kimbell Bequest, ACF 55.1.

Notes:

[1] See the detailed discussion by Gregory Martin, "Anthony van Dyck," *National Gallery Catalogues: The Flemish School,* London, pp. 26–27; also Michael Jaffé, *Van Dyck's Antwerp Sketchbook,* London, 1966, vol. I, pp. 16, 47.

[2] It was attributed to Rubens when it was acquired; however, it does not seem to have been published with a Rubens attribution.

[3] Jaffé, p. 47–48; p. 105, note 89; p. 115; p. [12], fig. 1. Martin, p. 33, note 22, concurs with Jaffé's attribution and dates the Kimbell panel about 1614.

[4] 25.8 × 19.5 cm. See: Gustav Glück, *Van Dyck,* vol. 13 of *Klassiker der Kunst,* Stuttgart, 1931, p. 517, p. 3, illus; and [Margarethe Poch-Kalous], *Akademie der Bildenden Künste in Wien: Katalog der Gemälde Galerie,* Vienna, 1961, cat. no. 142, pl. 14. Both date the painting about 1613. Jaffé, p. 47, suggests that the Vienna painting shows Van Dyck at about 13, or 1612–13.

[5] Jaffé, p. 48, suggests that the Kimbell painting dates a year or so later than the Vienna painting or about 1613–14.

[6] Pen and wash and chalks, 13.9 × 12.1 cm., Graphische Sammlung Albertina, Vienna, no. 8655. Jaffé, p. 48, p. 106, note 90, frontispiece. Jaffé mentions that Otto Benesch agreed with him in attributing this drawing to Van Dyck.

[7] Vendor's information.

[8] Jaffé, p. 105, note 89.

Additional Reference:

Götz Eckhardt, *Selbstbildnisse niederländischer Maler des 17. Jahrhunderts,* Berlin, 1971, pp. 70, 180, pl. 62 (*Jugendliches Selbstbildnis mit Hut*).

Anthony van Dyck, 1599–1641
Portrait of a Cavalier, age 57
Painted in 1634

Oil on panel, 28 3/4 × 21 7/8 in. (73.1 × 55.6 cm.)

By the 1630s Anthony van Dyck had achieved considerable, and well deserved, success. His brilliant technique and colorful, elegant style had brought him numerous commissions in Flanders, Italy and England. The lively poses, worldly expressions, and dexterously painted dress of his sitters established a sophisticated portrait mode that reverberated through succeeding generations of European painters. In England he achieved exceptional success, though he lived there a relatively small portion of his career. He was patronized by James I and especially by Charles I for whom he painted a magnificent array of portraits that are still in the royal collection and by whom he was knighted in 1632.

In March of 1634 Van Dyck is thought to have left England and worked mostly in Brussels before returning to England by June, 1635.[1] Whether this half-length portrait of an unknown man was painted in London or in Brussels remains to be established. It is attributed to Van Dyck[2] on the basis of the trenchant characterization of the sitter, the lively composition and the fluid brushwork whose quality compares favorably with that of Van Dyck's portraits of *Philippe Le Roy* (1630)[3] and the *Cardinal Infante Ferdinand* (1634).[4] The confident mien of the man in this portrait is manifest in the alert tilt of the head, the firmly modeled face and the assured attitude of his hand. An elegant design is established by the overlapping curls of his long, disarrayed locks, the balanced outline of his collar, and the curved guard of his highly polished sword. The painting's warmth derives from the ruddy flesh tones, the rust-brown of the freely brushed background and the leather-gloved hand. In short, Van Dyck has communicated his awareness of the man's successful mastery of his milieu. All that is known of the sitter is that he was 57 years old and that he was probably a soldier. The former is indicated by the inscription and the latter by the relaxed assurance of his hand which could come only from long familiarity with a sword.

Inscription: Upper left: ÆT^s. 57.
1634
.

Description: Half-length portrait of a man with long black hair, streaked with grey, and a scraggly moustache and goatee. The nearly frontal view of his face is enlivened by a slight turn to his right, toward which his brown eyes also are directed. The flaring wings of a large white collar rise about his throat, embrace his neck and project out above his shoulder. A black cape envelops his shoulders and torso, in front of which his left hand, in a tan glove, rests lightly on the hilt of a sword. The white ground can be seen through the vigorous brushwork of the thinly painted rust-brown background in which the partial impression of a handprint is visible at the top edge.

Condition: Good. Although the rather thin paint layer has suffered from surface abrasion in the highlights of the cape, in the wisps of hair and about the edges, the painting is in generally sound condition. A thin vertical scratch, now inpainted, runs through his left forehead into his hair. At the time of a 1970 laboratory treatment to inhibit some incipient cleavage in the upper right corner, the original oak panel, 1/4-inch thick, was removed from a cradle and secured with wax resin to a balsa maple wood support. Overpainted alterations which had previously obscured the date in the inscription and filled in the space between the collar and the man's right shoulder were also removed at that time.

Exhibitions: None known.

Collections: Baron Nathaniel Meyer de Rothschild, Vienna, until 1905; descended to his nephew, Baron Alphonse Mayer de Rothschild of Vienna and Paris.[5] Confiscated during the German occupation; recovered in May, 1945, from a salt mine in the Loser Plateau in Austria[6] and returned to the Rothschild heirs. [Newhouse Galleries, Inc., New York.] Kimbell Bequest, ACF 59.6.

Notes:

[1] Gregory Martin, "Anthony van Dyck," *National Gallery Catalogues: The Flemish School*, London, 1970, p. 27.

[2] Michael Jaffé kindly shared his favorable opinion of the attribution in a letter of Dec. 14, 1971.

[3] Wallace Collection, London. See: Gustav Glück, *Van Dyck*, vol. 13 of *Klassiker der Kunst*, Stuttgart, 1931, p. 329, illus., and *Wallace Collection Catalogues: Pictures and Drawings*, 16th ed., London, 1968, pp. 103–4, cat. no. P-94. illus.

[4] Museo del Prado, Madrid. See: Glück, p. 423, illus., and Martin, p. 27.

[5] A label, formerly located on the cradle until it was removed in 1970 and preserved, bears the Rothschild coat of arms and the printed text: SCHILLERSDORFER SCHLOSS-INVENTAR No. 242 (ink figures), indicating that it once hung in the Austrian castle belonging to the Rothschild family.

[6] "A plan for loot. . . How Hitler intended to dispose of the 'purchased' Rothschild collections," *Illustrated London News*, vol. 207, no. 5542, July 7, 1945, pp. 24–25, two illus.

Salomon van Ruysdael, 1600/02–1670
Landscape with Ruins of Egmond Abbey
Painted in 1644

Oil on panel, 26 1/2 × 38 1/2 in. (67.3 × 97.8 cm.)

Landscape with Ruins of Egmond Abbey, a work of Salomon van Ruysdael's mature phase, was probably painted in his studio at Haarlem where he lived most of his life. Like the great majority of the best Dutch landscapes about the middle of the seventeenth century, it is distinguished by a subtle particularization of atmosphere and light that is achieved by a superlative balance of tonal contrasts and enhanced by a sensitive disposition of compositional accents.

The Kimbell painting is typical of Ruysdael's specialization in the category of landscape painting of rural scenes. Beneath a majestically sweeping sky which occupies the canonical two-thirds of the composition, a low horizon spans the breadth of the picture. Rising above the horizon in the center, the ruins of Egmond Abbey[1] form a prominent foil to the landscape and sky.

Ruysdael used several compositional devices to establish perspective. The movement of figures across the foreground, such as the dark-coated dog running along the patch of sunlit earth, leads the eye through the painting into the distance. Providing notes of local color that contrast with the muted tonal harmonies of the landscape and sky, the small-scale, rather schematically rendered people and animals repeat a motif frequently found in Ruysdael's œuvre.[2] Another device to establish spatial definition is the vertical accent formed by the large group of trees dominating the left side. Counterbalancing the distant view, this innovative device, identified as the "one-winged" solution or the "heroic tree motif," was introduced by Ruysdael as an enlivening variation of the expansive panoramic view. It modifies the diagonal pattern of the road receding from the left foreground into the middle distance at the right while the silhouette of the thin, lace-like foliage provides a dark contrast against the lighter, colorful sky.[3] Thus, a greater sense of distance and a wider perspective is achieved by these space-clarifying devices.

Like his contemporary from The Hague, Jan van Goyen, Ruysdael employed subdued tonalities and monochromatic harmonies of browns, greens, and greys in a style that reflects the influence of Esaias van de Velde on both artists. However, by the 1640s, Ruysdael's landscapes were distinguished by a greater emphasis on local color in massed areas and more deliberately structured compositions.[4] This gives them a monumentality and sobriety that is enhanced by his meticulous technique, which contrasts with Van Goyen's dashing brushwork.

Description: Landscape with figures, animals and the ruins of an abbey church. In the center foreground, a black and brown covered carriage drawn by three brown horses is led by a man wearing a red coat and a brown, broad-brimmed hat with light blue feather. He rides a dark brown horse at whose feet is a small, dark brown dog. Walking behind the carriage is a man dressed in dark brown and three dogs. They traverse a light brown path with a pale blue puddle at the left, bounded at the lower right by dark brown, low bushes and at the left by a small ridge with brown brush, surmounted by trees with thin foliage. Two large trees dominating the left side lean diagonally toward the center of the composition; they have gnarled brown and grey bark and muted green and brown leaves. At the far right before light green trees, a man in an ochre jacket riding a white horse, a standing figure with a staff, and a small white dog trod down a beige dirt path following several brown cows. In the middle distance, a light green field with bound sheaves of pale yellow wheat stretches before rows of green and brown trees at the horizon through which clusters of light red houses can be seen at various intervals. Rising above these, and silhouetted against the pale blue sky, dappled with white, light grey, and pale violet clouds, are the light tan masonry ruins of Egmond Abbey, its twin towers still intact.

Condition: Very good. The paint is applied with low impasto. The panel has been rejoined along two clean horizontal splits and cradled. A minor loss near the figures at the right and two losses in the area of the woods at the horizon have been filled and inpainted. There is some abrasion along the lower edges.

Exhibitions: None known.

Collections: Max Flersheim, Paris.[5] Ivar Kreuger, Stockholm, to sale, Sept. 14, 1932, lot 77, illus. Private collection, United States.[6] [Schaeffer Galleries, Inc., New York.] Foundation Acquisition, AP 66.5.

Notes:

1 Egmond Abbey was a twelfth-century Romanesque church that was almost totally destroyed before the seventeenth century.

2 An almost identical representation of this motif appears in Ruysdael's *View of Amersfoort,* 1634, whose location is unknown. See: Wolfgang Stechow, *Dutch Landscape Painting of the Seventeenth Century,* London, 1966, pl. 59.

3 Stechow, pp. 39, 55.

4 Jakob Rosenberg, Seymour Slive, and E. K. Ter Kuile, *Dutch Art and Architecture, 1600 to 1800,* Baltimore, 1966, p. 151.

5 Wolfgang Stechow, *Salomon van Ruysdael, eine Einführung in seine Kunst, mit kritischem Katalog der Gemälde,* Berlin, 1938, p. 95, cat. no. 239.

6 Information supplied by vendor.

Claude Lorrain, 1600–1682
A Pastoral Landscape
Painted in 1677

Oil on canvas, 22 1/2 × 32 3/8 in. (57.2 × 82.2 cm.)

Claude Gellée (called Claude Lorrain after his birthplace in the province of Lorrain, France) lived most of his life in Rome. At the age of 77, he painted *A Pastoral Landscape* for Prince don Lorenzo Colonna (1637–89), a leading connoisseur and art collector in seventeenth-century Rome and Claude's most important patron.[1] This commission is recorded by Claude in his *Liber Veritatis*, a book containing annotated drawings of all his paintings after 1636.[2] The volume, now in the British Museum, is an extraordinary document in the history of art, as it provides exceptionally detailed information about a major artist's conceptual process and his patrons. From it, we learn that Claude painted at least nine pictures for Colonna between 1663 and 1682. *A Pastoral Landscape*, the eighth, is unusual because it is the smallest and the only one with an unidentified subject.[3]

As in many of Claude's late paintings, the subject probably alludes to classical history or mythology. Perhaps the old shepherd is recounting a legend about the *genii loci* of the peaceful valley—the gods, goddesses, nymphs and fauns—who lived there harmoniously before the crumbling ruins were built. Although the setting is not a specific location, the ruins might allude to the Roman Campagna, where the Colonna family originated. The painting's poetic mood, with its serene blue sky, pastoral motifs and "antique" landscape, suggests that the subject has a legendary and peaceful theme.

The composition heightens this harmonious mood. Claude apparently achieved these balanced proportions and spatial relationships by overlapping squares the height of the canvas across the width of the painting to locate the two major vertical accents—the left edge of the tall trees and the soaring face of the temple on the right. Between them is a central axis of open space given depth by diagonal axes. One is formed by the sheep at lower right, the narrating shepherd, and the upper edges of the two trees; the other, by the river course, the middle of the trees, and the foliage above the temple on the right.

There is a related system of balanced proportions which, as Marcel Roethlisberger notes,[4] is often quite complex in Claude's later works. The placement and scale of major motifs was apparently determined by dividing the width of the painting in fifths. The round temple is one-fifth from the left edge and the horizon, two-fifths from the bottom; the figures cover one-fifth of the width.

This rational ordering is textured by a system of balanced colors and tones. Small areas of intense color are contained within larger areas of more modulated tones. The subtle rhythm of alternate light and dark areas complements the integrated system of axes and proportions.

This coherent integration was evolved by Claude in a series of preparatory drawings recently identified by Roethlisberger. The earliest, a sketch of 1673, shows the figures before a hill surmounted by a temple, but the foliage is heavier, the vista shallower, the town and the bridge omitted.[5] Probably it was an independent work to which Claude returned at the time of the second, more agitated drawing of about 1675, in which the composition is reversed,[6] deep space is suggested and a tree in the middle distance corresponds to the two in the painting.

The third drawing introduces the sheep, the bridge and a round tower at the right, but there is only one figure and a rather abrupt sequence of space.[7] The fourth drawing, probably the study for the painting, includes the tall trees on the right, the round temple and water on the left, although the details are larger and the space as a whole is narrower. There are no animals and classical temple, and the figures are different: a shepherd kneels, extending an offering to a standing couple.[8] Traces of squaring with diagonals in chalk suggest that the painting's system of proportions was first investigated in this drawing. A fifth drawing is the record drawing for the *Liber Veritatis*.

Inscription: Lower right center, somewhat abraded:

CLAVDIO IV[F]
ROMA 1677

Description: Landscape of cool green and brown tones with a group of five small figures on the right. A seated, elderly shepherd holding a staff, with a dog lying at his side, is speaking (or chanting), accompanied by a piping girl seated beside him. A young herdsman, dressed in brown and leaning on a staff, and two young girls, one holding a tambourine, stand listening. Color accents in the clothing are in blue and red. A flock of sheep is scattered on both sides of the foreground, and beyond a river to the left is a herd of cattle. Two tall, slender trees dominate the picture's middle ground. On the horizon to the left, a round temple stands in the midst of a town in ruins and, to the right, beyond a thicket of trees, are the columns of a second temple in ruins. Spanning the horizon between is a fortified bridge beyond three tiny figures seated on the river bank. The background is a blue sky with puffy white clouds.

Condition: Good. A heavy layer of yellowed varnish and some discolored repaint was removed when the painting was relined and cleaned in 1969. Some very old, slightly darkened repaint (visible in the trees, the distant landscape and around the figures) was not removed as it adheres firmly to the original paint surface. An old tear about four inches long along the left side and several very minor losses in the sky were inpainted.

Exhibitions: None known.

Collections: Commissioned by Prince don Lorenzo Onofrio Colonna, Rome; remained in the Colonna family until after 1787;[9] probably sold in 1798.[10] Sir Andrew Corbet, Adderly Hall, Shropshire, until 1835; descended to his son, Richard Corbet,[11] and to Sir Roland James Corbet, until about 1915. [Leger], London, in 1946. [Frederick Mont], New York. [Newhouse Galleries, Inc., New York.]
Foundation Acquisition, APX 67.4.

Related Version: A "poor small copy" made before 1800 is in a private collection, Rome.[12]

Notes:

1 Marcel Roethlisberger, *Claude Lorrain – The Paintings: Critical Catalogue,* New Haven, 1961, vol. I, pp. 34, 374–75.

2 Claude's drawing of *A Pastoral Landscape* is on blue paper and is *Liber Veritatis* drawing no. 190. On the back is inscribed: *quadro facto per Ill.mo et eccll. / sig.re Contestable Collonna / Claudio Gellee / 1677.* See: Roethlisberger, *Paintings,* p. 37, cat. no. LV 190, p. 445, and Roethlisberger, *Claude Lorrain: The Drawings,* Berkeley, 1968, vol. I, p. 406, no. 1105; vol. II, pl. 1105.

3 Roethlisberger, *Paintings,* p. 446.

4 Roethlisberger, *Paintings,* p. 31.

5 Musée Lorrain, Nancy, 1.50 x 2.30 cm., Roethlisberger, *Drawings,* no. 1060.

6 Norton Simon, Inc., Museum of Art, Los Angeles, 1.86 x 2.61 cm., Roethlisberger, *Drawings,* no. 1102. Roethlisberger, *The Wildenstein Album,* Paris, 1962, cat. no. 26. Roethlisberger, *The Claude Lorrain Album...,* Los Angeles County Museum of Art, 1972, cat. no. 59.

7 British Museum, London, no. 00. 6–123, H. 302, 1.97 x 2.51 cm., Roethlisberger, *Drawings,* no. 1103.

8 The Louvre, Paris, no. RF 4, 594, 1.85 x 2.61 cm., Roethlisberger, *Drawings,* no. 1104.

9 It was still in the Colonna gallery in 1783 *(Catalogo dei quadri... Casa Colonna,* 1783, no. 467, *paese con figurine)* and 1787 (W. von Ramdohr, *Ueber Mahlerei... in Rom,* Leipzig, 1787, vol. II, p. 78, wrongly as *Judgment of Paris,* figures by Maratti). See Roethlisberger, *Paintings,* pp. 375, 446.

10 Roethlisberger, *Painting,* pp. 375, 446, gives the subsequent history of the painting.

11 Label on the back of the painting.

12 On panel, 11 3/4 x 17 3/4 in. (30 x 45 cm.), I. Faldi, *La Quadreria della Cassa Depositi e Prestiti,* Rome, 1956, no. 80, as "after Claude." See Roethlisberger, *Paintings,* p. 447.

Additional Reference:

Roethlisberger, "Lorrain (Claude Gellée) dit Claude," *Encyclopedia Universalis, Paris,* 1971, vol. V., illus.

Rembrandt van Rijn, 1606–1669
St. Jerome Reading in an Italian Landscape
Etched about 1653–54

Etching and drypoint on white paper, second state, 10 7/16 × 8 5/16 in. (26.6 × 22.9 cm.)

This idyllic view of *St. Jerome Reading in an Italian Landscape* is the latest in date and perhaps the most compassionate rendering among Rembrandt van Rijn's seven etchings of this venerable scholar. In his earlier interpretations Rembrandt showed St. Jerome on his knees in earnest prayer or reading at a table and, somewhere nearby, the lion that he befriended by extracting a thorn from its paw. However, none of these views emphasize the subtle rapport between beast, man and nature that provides the sense of cohesive intimacy in *St. Jerome Reading in an Italian Landscape.* Although St. Jerome is thoroughly absorbed with the text that he reads and is seemingly oblivious of his surroundings, the lion looks toward St. Jerome, while gingerly raising his wounded paw. Even though the beast is apparently reluctant to disturb the saint, this backward glance of the lion establishes a positive association between the two figures.

Rembrandt's exceptional command of the expressive range of the etching medium can be clearly seen by contrasting this print to its preliminary drawing, now in Hamburg.[1] As Christopher White has observed, Rembrandt used a loaded reed pen to make thick strokes on the drawing "in exactly the same way as the drypoint burr was employed on the identical places in the print." However, he transformed the drawing's outline rendering by modulating the range of tonal values in the etching with a more developed pattern of shadows that gives it a rich sense of depth and volume.[2]

The lion's fur is rendered with a dense pattern of heavily inked crosshatching; in contrast, St. Jerome is indicated with spare black lines, without modulations, except about his shadowed head. To unify this wide range of tones, Rembrandt used drypoint to emphasize and clarify significant features. The buildings in the distance, the edge of the tree, the lion's mane and his raised paw all bear the heavier inking of drypoint outlines to make them stand out from their surrounding areas. After his initial proofs, Rembrandt added additional drypoint lines to the strut of the bridge to strengthen the dark tones at the right side of the print; these lines identify this impression as the second and final state of this print.[3] Furthermore, Rembrandt often varied his inking and type of paper; in this impression the relatively small amount of ink left on unmarked areas enhance the contrasts of black ink lines on white paper.

Rembrandt's choice and treatment of the setting contribute enormously to the serene mood of this scene. Instead of showing St. Jerome near a cave, in a wilderness, or seated at a desk indoors, Rembrandt placed him in the foreground of a rural landscape that is dominated by a large tree at the left and by a cluster of crisply detailed farm buildings on the brow of the hill in the background. The architecture of these buildings, and Rembrandt's rendering of them, is very similar to those of idealized landscapes in the backgrounds of sixteenth-century Venetian painting and may have been directly inspired by Rembrandt's known reworking of a drawing by Domenico Campagnola that is now in Budapest.[4] These buildings are positively integrated into the distant hill by the subtle interplay of darks and lights, just as the dark textures of the lion are associated with the shadowed middle ground and the outlined figure with the highlighted foreground. By

these subtle means the quiescent mood of the landscape becomes a revealing mirror of the temperate thoughts of the scholar and timorous attitude of the patient lion. That this print would be so imbued with this heightened sense of poetic mood is quite understandable because the print dates from the early 1650s,[5] the period of some of Rembrandt's most expressive graphic inventions.

Description: An intimate view of a forested landscape with a figure at the left, a lion in the middle, a stream at the right and buildings in the distance. At the lower left, an elderly bearded man, dressed in a long loose robe and wearing a wide-brimmed hat, rests his left arm on a large, flat rock as he reads a book. On the rock to the right stands a lion, seen in rear view, with a raised left front paw. A massive tree trunk with heavy foliage behind rises above the figure at the left, while the upper right side is dominated by a cluster of buildings perched on a bluff above the stream. Below the buildings, and to the right of the lion, are two small outlined figures, seen against the rail of a sloping wooden bridge that crosses over the stream on a pair of stilt-like wooden piers. The creamy white paper is of French origin; its watermark is a foolscap with figure 4 and three balls, without initials.[6]

Condition: Excellent. The lines in this brilliant impression are solidly inked and very clear. The paper is trimmed almost to the edge of the intact plate mark.

Exhibitions: None known.

Collections: Two unidentified collectors' marks are on the reverse. [William H. Schab, New York.] Foundation Acquisition, AP 70.17.

Notes:

1 Christopher White, *Rembrandt as an Etcher*, London, 1969, vol. I, pp. 220–22; vol. II, fig. 340. See also: O. Benesch, *The Drawings of Rembrandt*, London, 1957, vol. V, cat. no. 886, fig. 1095.

2 White, vol. I, p. 221.

3 Illustrations of the first and second states are given by K. G. Boon, *Rembrandt: The Complete Etchings*, New York, [1963], pls. 247–48.

4 White, p. 220, note 32; vol. II, fig. 339.

5 White dates this etching in 1654; previous scholars have dated it about 1653.

6 This watermark is quite similar to French watermarks of 1632 and 1656, illustrated by W. A. Churchill, *Watermarks in Paper . . .*, Amsterdam, 1935, nos. 339, 355.

Additional References:

A. Bartsch, *Catalogue Raisonné de toutes les Estampes qui forment l'Œuvre de Rembrandt*, Vienna, 1797, cat. no. 140.
Arthur M. Hind, *A Catalogue of Rembrandt's Etchings*, London, 1923, cat. no. 267.
George Biörklund, *Rembrandt's Etchings: True and False*, 2nd ed., Stockholm, London and New York, 1968, cat. no. BB 53–31.
Kenneth Clark, *Rembrandt and the Italian Renaissance*, London, 1966, pp. 117–21.

Juan de Arellano, 1614–1676
A Basket of Flowers
Painted about 1670–76

Oil on canvas; 32 3/16 × 40 9/16 in. (81.7 × 102 cm.)

A Basket of Flowers epitomizes the work of Juan de Arellano, the Late Spanish Baroque master from Madrid whose reputation rests on his flower paintings *(floreros)*. In this work, he employs a horizontal format in which he arranges objects symmetrically before a dark, neutral background and illuminates the whole with a strong light from an unseen source at the left. The objects are those found repeatedly in his paintings: a reed basket abundantly filled with brightly colored flowers and placed on a stone ledge on which insects crawl. Drama is achieved by the sharp light which produces a pronounced *chiaroscuro* effect, giving the objects a plastic character and emphasizing their elegant silhouette against the plain background.

The subject matter, the charming coloristic effects and the painterly technique appealed to both intellectual and fashionable clients who made Arellano's specialty most lucrative. Deliberately conceived as a decorative work with no symbolic connotations, the Kimbell work is typical of paintings which Arellano produced in quantity in his Madrid workshop with the aid of assistants.[1] It is very tentatively dated about 1670–76 because of its apparent stylistic affinities to one of Arellano's few dated works, a similar painting of the same title, dated 1672, in the collection of Sir William Wiseman, New York.[2]

The luxuriant abundance of Arellano's *florero* paintings is in contrast to the extreme stylization and theatricality of another strain of Spanish still life painting, the *bodegón*, which is characterized by hermetic, austere depictions of food accompanied either by figures or household objects. Originally

Juan, de Arellano

a disparaging term (connoting a low eating place), *bodegón* has become the accepted term for this type of still life which was brought to its apogee by Juan de Zurbarán and Juan Sánchez Cotán. The *bodegón* and *florero* emerged as independent art forms in Spain about 1600, shortly before Dutch seventeenth-century artists established still life painting as a genre equal in importance to landscape and portrait painting.

Inscription: Lower left: *Juan de Arellano*

Description: Still life of flowers on a brown stone ledge before a grey-green unarticulated background. The golden reed basket holds a bouquet of flowers arranged informally but with a regularity to the design which gives the composition its cohesiveness. A profusion of blossoms is also revealed in the basket's interior through its openwork reeding. The flowers, painted in the primary color scheme of red, yellow and blue, include carnations, tulips, cornflowers, roses, violets, and daffodils. Insects on the flowers are a butterfly at the upper left, a dragonfly at the upper right and a moth at the lower left. On the ledge near the base of the basket are a caterpillar and butterfly, and two tulips overlap its edge at the left.

Condition: Good. Evidence of minor craquelure acquired with normal aging and some repainting around canvas perimeter where stretcher has made marks in the canvas.

Exhibition: The Museum and the Private Collector, Fort Worth Art Center, April 4–May 1, 1966.

Collections: "Purchased in Spain at the end of the eighteenth century by a member of the Waldhausen family of Austria" in whose hands it remained until the twentieth century.[3]
[Newhouse Galleries, Inc., New York.]
Lent by Kimbell, Inc., ACC 65.1.

Notes:

1 See *The Golden Age of Spanish Still-life Painting, late 16th through early 19th centuries*, the Newark Museum, Dec. 10, 1964–Jan. 26, 1965, illus. nos. 1–5, and Ramón Torres Martín, *La Naturaleza Muerta en la Pintura Española*, Barcelona, 1971, fig. no. 4, repr. no. 10, pls. 53–56.

2 George Kubler and Martin Soria, *Art and Architecture in Spain and Portugal and their American Dominions, 1500 to 1800*, Baltimore, 1959, pl. 163a.

3 Information supplied by the vendor.

Salvator Rosa, 1615–1673
Pythagoras Emerging from the Underworld
Painted in 1662

Oil on canvas, 51 5/8 × 74 3/8 in. (131.2 × 189 cm.)

On July 29, 1662, Salvator Rosa wrote from Rome to his friend Ricciardi that he had just completed a pair of canvases eight palmi long to send to the exhibition at San Giovanni Decollato.[1] He identified the paintings as showing two events from the life of Pythagoras and remarked that these paired subjects "succeed miraculously." In September, 1663, the eminent banker Don Antonio Ruffo attempted to purchase the pair at 300 scudi for his collection in Messina, but he did not acquire them until March, 1664, when he doubled his original offer.[2] At that time he entered in his notebook the sizes of the paintings and scale of the figures which help to established that the Ruffo purchases were the Kimbell *Pythagoras Emerging from the Underworld*, and its pendant, *Pythagoras and the Fishermen*, now in Berlin.[3] The Kimbell painting, long missing, has recently been identified,[4] restoring to us a work in which Rosa took obvious and justifiable pride.

Rosa greatly preferred his paintings of histories and allegories to the landscapes and battle scenes for which he was better known. Didactic subjects were not only considered more noble but they allowed him scope for his strongly held philosophical ideas. Conceding little to popular taste, he sought lofty and moralizing subjects which were often rather esoteric.[5] The stern moral teachings of the Greek philosopher Pythagoras (sixth century B.C.) were similar to those of the Stoics whom Rosa admired; furthermore, Pythagoras fulfilled the seventeenth-century philosophical "concept of the scholar-magician who by intuition, genius and divination plumbs the secrets of nature."[6] Indeed, Rosa, who demonstrated in his paintings "his belief in the

intuitive, irrational, inspired and mysterious qualities of his own genius,"[7] may well have equated himself with Pythagoras.

In his letter to Ricciardi, Rosa described the Kimbell painting as showing "Pythagoras leaving his underground habitation, awaited by his sect of men and women, saying to them that he had returned from Hades." His most likely literary source for the scene is the narrative given by Diogenes Laertius (VIII, 41): "Pythagoras, on coming to Italy, made a subterranean dwelling and enjoined on his mother to mark and record all that passed, and at what hour, and to send her notes down to him until he should ascend. She did so. Pythagoras some time afterwards came up withered and looking like a skeleton, then went into the assembly and declared he had been down to Hades, and even read out his experiences to them. They were so affected that they wept and wailed and looked upon him as divine, going so far as to send their wives to him in hopes that they would learn some of his doctrines; and so they were called Pythagorean women."[8] Doubtless, Rosa also had in mind Diogenes Laertius' vivid description of the tortured souls of Homer and Hesiod which Pythagoras saw in Hades, because a perturbed and ominous mood pervades the Kimbell painting.[9] The subject of the Berlin painting is taken from a different source, Plutarch's *Moralia*, where Pythagoras' purchase and subsequent release of a catch of fish is described and two interpretations are given, one being that he "paid a ransom for them as for friends and relatives who had been captured,"[10] and the other that he tried thereby "to accustom men to refrain from cruelty and rapacity in connexion with dumb animals."[11]

The two paintings are apparently linked by a common reference to the afterlife and perhaps may have been intended to illustrate two different concepts of the fate of the soul. The Berlin painting seems to illustrate Pythagoras' concept of the soul's immortality. In contrast, the Homeric concept of the unhappy fate of the dead is implied in the Kimbell painting not only by its possible allusion to the horrific scenes that Pythagoras had just seen in Hades but also in the three indistinct figures of men huddled in the shadow of the tomb at the left. Lower than the other figures and unnoticed by them, they observe the scene with sad faces as if they were shades of the underworld condemned forever to stand apart from the living. In both paintings Pythagoras represents the man of superior knowledge and moral virtue who sees the vicissitudes of fortune and death, a typical Rosa theme.

The Kimbell painting is a good example of Rosa's late, mature style. "Beginning late in the 1650s, he produced a series of ... compositions in which his usually expansive landscape settings were reduced to constricted backdrops for life-sized figures that in pose and characterization came more and more to imitate Poussin's classicizing style, a convention that was thought most fitting for the presentation of grave and elevated subjects."[12] In this painting the setting infuses the scene with exceptional drama; the murky colors of the trees and rocks and extremes of lighting establish an unsettled mood, intensified by the consternation expressed on several faces and the theatrical gestures of the figures. They are disposed in a "frieze-like grouping in a shallow space,"[13] found in many of Rosa's late works, but in this instance Rosa has arranged them according to a concept of Pythagorean number theory. Starting with the isolated single figure of Pythagoras and progressing to the men kneeling at the slab, the three leaning figures behind, then four standing figures and finally five figures at the left, they form a sequence of 1 + 2 + 3 + 4 + 5. When such a sequence is expressed graphically, forming a symmetrical triangle, it reveals at a glance the sum of the successive numbers. Representing numbers in areas was a basic step in the direction which ultimately led to the Pythagorean discoveries in geometry and music. Thus, not only in his choice of subject but also in its presentation, Rosa had opportunity to display the intellectual sophistication in which he delighted.

Inscription: On the back: *S. Rosa* (now covered by the lining canvas).

ROSA, SALVATOR
Pythagoras and the Fishermen, Gemäldegalerie, Dahlem, Berlin

Description: Precipitous landscape beneath lowering skies with an agitated group of men and women among fragmentary ruins. They attend the appearance of a man in a ravine at the lower right who emerges between two trees with a horrified expression. The fourteen figures in the group at left are about two-fifths of the height of the painting and arranged laterally in an undulating rhythm. The three prominent figures are picked out by a strong raking light that enters from the left: a man wearing a cream-colored toga, striped with blue, who turns back to look at his companion at the extreme left; a woman in profile with both arms upraised, dressed in a grey-blue classical gown with an ochre shawl around her head and shoulders, and a man wearing an umber toga who, with back to the viewer, kneels over a stone slab at the edge of the ravine. The other figures appear by twos and threes somewhat to the rear. The coloring of the figures is echoed in nearby objects; for example, the umber of the kneeling man's toga warms the faces of the people around him and highlights an adjacent branch; and the colors of the dress of the woman in profile appear in highlights in the cliffs behind her and the stones and trees in the foreground. The funerary character of the forbidding landscape is suggested by the sepulchral urn at left, which is decorated with an indistinct motif and surmounts the tall pedestal of the tomb. The sombre tonality of the foreground is accented by the dramatically lighted sky which is filled with clouds of dark ultramarine and cream.

Condition: Excellent. The original canvas consists of two pieces joined horizontally approximately $5\frac{3}{4}$ inches from the top. A 10-inch vertical line of overpaint, located 10 inches from the right edge and beginning eight inches from the bottom, is possibly a tear in the canvas. There is minor strengthening in several of the figures and other small scattered areas of overpaint. The painting was relined by William Hisgrove and cleaned in 1969 by Gabrielle Kopelman, under the supervision of Mario Modestini.

Exhibitions: San Giovanni Decollato, Rome, 1662. Possibly British Institution, 1821, cat. no. 38, *Pythagoras in the Cave.*[14]

Collections: Don Antonio Ruffo, Messina, from 1664. Possibly C. H. Tracy, England, by 1821.[15] George Roche family, Louisville, Ky., since the nineteenth century. [Newhouse Galleries, Inc., New York.] Foundation Acquisition, AP 70.22.

Notes:

1 A. De Rinaldis, *Lettere inedite di Salvator Rosa a G. B. Ricciardi*, Rome, 1939, letter 107, quoted in Luigi Salerno, *Salvator Rosa*, Milan, 1963, p. 97, who states that Rosa also mentions these paintings in another letter to Ricciardi of Sept. 16 as being among the five he will send to San Giovanni Decollato.

2 Vicenzo Ruffo, "La galleria Ruffo nel secolo XVII in Messina," *Bolletino D'Arte*, vol. 10, 1916, p. 177, note 2. The dimensions of the paintings given in Ruffo's notebook (folio 15) were $5 \times 7\frac{1}{2}$ palmi and in an inventory of his collection 5×7 palmi, discrepancies with Rosa's dimensions that are accountable in part by the differences between Roman and Neapolitan palmi. See also: Francis Haskell, *Patrons and Painters*, New York, 1963, p. 209, who states that in Ruffo's palazzo "his pictures were arranged according to a symmetrical pattern, and he was often anxious to make up pairs."

3 Stiftung Preussischer Kulturbesitz, Staatliche Museen, *Gemäldegalerie: Verzeichnis der ausgestellten Gemälde des 13. bis 18. Jahrhunderts in Museum Dahlem*, Berlin, 1966, p. 100, no. 1/59 (127×187 cm.); illus. in Salerno, pl. 68. Another *Pythagoras and the Fishermen* with smaller figures, belonging to the Chatsworth collection, sold at Christie's, June 27, 1958, lot 16.

4 Michael Mahoney of Trinity College, Hartford, Conn., and Richard Wallace of Wellesley College both identified this work as the painting mentioned in Rosa's letter and provided much valuable assistance in locating references to the painting.

[5] The life of Pythagoras would not have been so abstruse in the seventeenth century as might appear today; at least six translations and editions of Diogenes Laertius came out in the sixteenth century. See A. Delatte, "La Vie de Pythagore de Diogène Laërce," *Mémoires de l'académie royale de Belgique, second series*, 17, 1922, p. 97.

[6] Salerno, p. 40.

[7] Richard Wallace, "The Genius of Salvator Rosa," *Art Bulletin*, vol. 47, no. 4, December, 1965, p. 480.

[8] Diogenes Laertius, *Lives of the Eminent Philosophers*, VIII, 41, trans. by R. D. Hicks, Cambridge, Mass., and London, 1958, vol. II, p. 356.

[9] Lady [Sidney] Morgan, *The Life and Times of Salvator Rosa*, London, 1824, vol. II, p. 151, without quoting a source, lists the subject of the Kimbell painting as Pythagoras "relating to them his visit to the infernal regions, and his interview with Hesiod."

[10] Plutarch, *Moralia* 729 D, trans. by Edwin L. Minar, Jr., F. H. Sandbach and W. C. Helmbold, Cambridge, Mass., and London, 1959, vol. IX, p. 179.

[11] *Moralia* 91 C, trans. by Frank Cole Babbitt, Cambridge, Mass., and London, 1928, voll. II, p. 33.

[12] Michael Mahoney, "Salvator Rosa's *Saint Humphrey*," *The Minneapolis Institute of Arts Bulletin*, vol. 53, no. 3, 1964, p. 62.

[13] Wallace, "Salvator Rosa's 'Death of Atilius Regulius,'" *Burlington Magazine*, no. 109, part 2, July, 1967, p. 395.

[14] Algernon Graves, *A Century of Loan Exhibitions*, London, 1913–15, (1970 reprint), vol. II, p. 1136.

[15] Graves, vol. II, p. 1136.

Gérard ter Borch, 1617–1681

Portrait of a Gentleman

Painted about 1667–68

Oil on canvas, 18 1/2 × 14 1/2 in. (47 × 36.8 cm.)

Having traveled about Europe as a young man, Gérard ter Borch settled in Deventer after being married in 1654. There he appears to have remained the rest of his life, painting charming genre scenes and developing, in the 1660s, an innovative mode of small-scale portraits distinguished by a subtle psychology and dignified restraint. Carefully posed within discreetly defined interior spaces, his figures wear fashionably elaborate dress of subdued tones, often greyish blacks, with judicious accents of brighter colors and pristine white shirting and accessories. Their faces and dress are painted with a meticulous concern for discrimination of contrasting textures, delineation of detail and three-dimensional definition of shapes. The reserved attitudes of Ter Borch's sitters and the rich orchestration of the low-keyed tones of their elegant dress endow these portraits with an enormous dignity and a considerable presence that belies the relatively small size of his paintings. These qualities are clearly revealed in this portrait of a man[1] and the companion portrait of his wife[2] that were painted by Ter Borch about 1667–68.

The male portrait is particularly impressive. The strong delicate modeling of flesh in the face and hands, the clear outline of his firmly set jaw and, above all, the direct open look of his dark eyes clearly convey the gentleness and vigor of a confident man in the fullness of life. His forthright glance is enhanced by the simplicity of his elegantly cut dress, which is precisely painted in a composition of whites, muted greys and blacks that focuses attention on the face. The fresh whiteness of his shirt and delicately embroidered collar is played against the narrow range of blacks that describe the remarkably palpable fringe that hangs softly about his waist and his sleeve. Because of the effectiveness of these subtle details in conveying an image of a vital personality it is surprising to note that S. J. Gudlaugsson, the writer of the admirably comprehensive monograph on Ter Borch's paintings, regarded the accessories in this painting as the work of an assistant, quite possibly Ter Borch's half-sister, Gesina. This apparent inconsistency between the beguiling appearance of the painting and Gudlaugsson's qualified appraisal of it may be the result of his apparently incomplete knowledge of the painting and its companion.[3]

Among Ter Borch portraits of the 1660s these two portraits are unusual in one respect. Although the calculated pose, compositional accessories and dress of the figures are typical and quite consistent with the pictorial conventions that Ter Borch evolved, the three-quarter-length view is uncommon. Most of his portraits were full-length views of figures carefully set in the midst of a sparsely furnished domestic interior. The close-up view of figures in the Kimbell pair (accompanied by a slight reduction in painting size) and the simplified setting (reduced to one object on a partially viewed table and a neutral background) give the figures in this pair an intimacy of contact with the viewer that heightens their psychological immediacy.

The distinctive format and the remarkably consistent quality of painting in these two portraits, particularly of the man, suggest that there might be some basis for reconsidering Gudlaugsson's designation of them as nearly identical partial repetitions of full-length versions, the man now in the museum at St. Omer[4] and the lady in Paris.[5] The Kimbell portraits and the full-length versions are in accord in pose and dress but they vary in some details of setting, with the Kimbell paintings being substantially simpler. The dull violet color of the table covering is, however, identical in all four paintings, contrary to the incomplete description given by Gudlaugsson. Moreover, not only was Gudlaugsson's assessment of both Kimbell paintings apparently based on second-hand knowledge but examination of the full-length versions when they were recently exhibited together in Paris[6] suggests that in the Kimbell version of the man, the modeling of the face and hand and the definition of the black fringe about the waist is more solidly rendered than in the full-length version at St. Omer.[7]

Inscription: Lower left, a barely visible monogram: large *G* with small *T* and *B* superimposed.

Description: Three-quarter-length view of a man with soft, dark brown hair falling below his shoulders and his right hand held at his waist. His body is turned to his left and he looks directly at the viewer. He has a ruddy complexion; his eyes are hazel and he is clean-shaven except for a closely trimmed, inverted-V moustache. About his neck is a broad sheer white collar with delicate floral designs embroidered across the bottom. Over a loosely fitted, full-sleeved white shirt with embroidered cuffs he wears a black sleeveless vest, whose small black buttons are fastened only beneath the collar. His left arm is hidden beneath the long folds of a black cape over his left shoulder; over his right forearm the edge of the cape is fringed with heavy broad strips. A similar but longer fringe encircles his waist and embellishes the lower end of a black sash hanging over his pleated black skirt. At the lower right, a black hat rests on a table draped with a dull violet fabric that falls in a crisp heavy fold to the bottom edge of the painting. A dark olive green tone, slightly paler about the head, covers the background.

Condition: Excellent. There is a very small amount of strengthening at the edges of the hair. Some tiny losses scattered in the face and skirt have been filled and inpainted.

Exhibition: The Louvre: Musée de l'Orangerie, Paris, 1911, cat. no. 153.[8]

Collections: Max Kann, Paris, to sale: March 3, 1879, lot no. 64.[9] Baron d'Erlanger, Paris, by 1912.[10] [Th. Fischer], Lucerne, 1927.[11] Pöhlmann collection, Berlin, 1931. Private collection. [H. Terry-Engell Gallery, London.] Foundation Acquisition, AP 70.24.

Notes:

1 S. J. Gudlaugsson, *Geraert ter Borch: Katalog der Gemälde*, The Hague, 1959–60, vol. II, pp. 198–99, cat. no. 216–II; vol. I, p. XIX, illus. 2.

2 Gudlaugsson, vol. II, cat. no. 217–II; vol. I, pl. XIX, illus. 3.

Gérard ter Borch, 1617–1681
Portrait of a Lady
Painted about 1667–68

Oil on canvas, 18 5/8 × 14 1/2 in. (47.3 × 36.9 cm.)

[3] Inquiries at the time of acquisition indicated that Gudlaugsson had not had the opportunity to examine this pair of paintings prior to publication of his book in 1959–60. Information in his entry supports this conclusion: his most recent record of the paintings was a 1931 collection and he acknowledges that his color notes are based on previously published (and inconsistent) records. Unfortunately, Mr. Gudlaugsson died shortly after the paintings were acquired but before arrangements could be made for him to examine them.

[4] Gudlaugsson, vol. II, cat. no. 216–I; vol. I, p. 351, illus.

[5] Gudlaugsson, vol. II, cat. no. 217–I; vol. I, p. 351, illus.

[6] J. F. [Jacques Foucart], "Borch, Gérard Ter," *Le Siècle de Rembrandt* . . . , Musée de Petit Palais, Paris, Nov. 17, 1970–Feb. 15, 1971, cat. nos. 21 and 22, illus.

[7] However, as Gudlaugsson observes, vol. II, p. 198, identification of the St. Omer man as the original companion of the Paris lady may not be accurate since this hypothesis involves interpretation of possibly contradictory nineteenth-century sale records and, in addition, these two portraits are of slightly different dimensions. This suggests that there may be a *third* version of the man, now missing.

[8] Armand Dayot, *Grands et petits maîtres hollandais*, 1912, [pl. ?] no. 16; Gudlaugsson, cat. no. 216–II; Foucart, cat. no. 21.

[9] Gudlaugsson, vol. II, cat. no. 216–II.

[10] Cornelis Hofstede de Groot, . . . *Verzeichnis der Werke der hervorragendsten holländischen Maler des* XVII. *Jahrhunderts*, Esslingen, 1912, vol. 5, cat. no. 321.

[11] This and the subsequent collection is given by Gudlaugsson, vol. II, cat. no. 216–II.

Ter Borch's portrait of this lady, like the companion portrait of her husband, employs a number of expertly controlled pictorial devices to create an image of decorum and respectability. Her forthright pose and the direct glance of her eyes effectively convey an assurance and self-confidence that is aptly complemented by a coolness of temperament evoked by her somber expression and half-lowered eyelids. Her carefully arranged dress of subdued greys and black is brilliantly contrasted with the immaculate whiteness of the delicately embroidered scarf and sleeves. All the fabrics and her accessories, particularly her lustrous black jewelry, are painted with a meticulous precision that gives them substance and sensuous appeal. Complementing this image of gentleness and propriety is an isolated still life rendering of a jewel box on the table. Its flat planes and brassy tones and the sweeping curve of the string of glistening pearls form an attractive foil to the supple fabrics of the lady's dress.

While the male companion to this portrait has slightly more presence overall than its full-length counterpart, this portrait of the wife[1] and its full-length version, now at the Sorbonne, Paris,[2] have different strengths. The more carefully detailed still life in the Kimbell version is certainly more tangible and assertive than in the Sorbonne painting (where a fan is added) and the subtle modulation of background tones about the figure in the Kimbell portrait creates a more intimate space than does the complex ambience of the Paris version (whose background includes a carved doorway and a chair). The facial modeling, dark fabrics and embroidery are of comparable quality in both portraits, but the full-length format of the Paris version gives greater prominence to the rich gold brocade and the glistening satin folds of the lady's long underskirt. Comparisons of this type suggest that a thorough investigation of possible connections between the Kimbell and the full-length versions might establish that the two sets were perhaps created concurrently for related families.

Identification of the sitters in this and its companion portrait would certainly further such an investigation. Unfortunately, the known historical record of the Kimbell panels dates only from the nineteenth century. However, it is possible that portraits of Joan de Wilde and his wife recorded in the 1672 inventory of the estate of Frerick Fredericks Bannier were the full-length versions of the Kimbell paintings. If so, a possible explanation is suggested for the origin of the knee-length versions now in the Kimbell collection. This format, uncommon in Ter Borch's oeuvre, might be related to the fact that Joan de Wilde's wife was Ter Borch's stepdaughter, Aaltje Dams, born in 1625 of his wife's first marriage.[3]

Inscription: Lower right, a barely visible monogram: a large *G* with small *T* and *B* superimposed.

Description: Three-quarter-length portrait of a mature woman, turned to her right and looking at the viewer. Her oval-shaped head is accented by a long nose, high forehead and the curving edges of a small black cap. Covering most of her brown hair (which is pulled tightly and braided on the back of her head), the cap is pinned by a small circular brooch formed of lustrous black jewels like those in her long earrings and the ring of her left little finger. Her arms are bent slightly at the elbows; both hands pull back the opening of the pleated overskirt of her black gown to reveal a cream-colored satin underskirt banded with gold brocade. A sheer white scarf, richly embroidered with floral designs and secured by four fine string ties, covers her shoulders. The very full sleeves stop at the elbow revealing puffed white undersleeves with embroidered edging that is secured with black string ties. To her right is a partial view of a table draped with a dull violet fabric, on which lies a low-legged, rectangular, brass-colored box, from which streams one curving strand of pearls. A dark olive green tone, paler about the sitter's head, covers the background.

Condition: Excellent. There is a very small amount of inpainting in the folds of the tablecloth and in the face.

Exhibitions: The Louvre: Musée de l'Orangerie, Paris, 1911, cat. no. 154.

Collections: Max Kann, Paris, to sale: March 3, 1879, lot no. 63. The subsequent history is the same as that of the pendant.
Foundation Acquisition, AP 70.25.

Notes:

1 S. J. Gudlaugsson, *Geraert ter Borch: Katalog der Gemälde,* The Hague, 1959–60, vol. II, p. 199, cat. no. 217–II; vol. I, p. 148, pl. XIX, illus. 3.

2 Gudlaugsson, vol. II, p. 199, cat. no. 217–I, vol. I, p. 351, illus.; see *L'Œil,* no. 192, December, 1970, p. 9, for color illus.

3 Gudlaugsson, vol. II, pp. 50, 199. However, because the portraits may not represent de Wilde and his wife it has been observed that the arms shown above the door in the full-length Paris version are not those of the de Wilde family. See J. F. [Jacques Foucart], "Borch, Gérard ter," *Le Siècle de Rembrandt,* Musée de Petit Palais, Paris, Nov. 17, 1970–Feb. 15, 1971, cat. no. 22.

Bartolomé Estéban Murillo, 1617–1682
The Immaculate Conception
Painted about 1670–80

Oil on canvas, 66 5/16 × 42 7/8 in. (168.5 × 190 cm.)

Bartolomé Estéban Murillo, a Sevillian painter of religious subjects as well as of genre scenes and portraits, was considered one of the greatest Spanish artists during his lifetime and well into the nineteenth century. His work fell into disfavor, however, around the time of Impressionism because his subject matter was considered overly sentimental.[1] While his themes may not appeal to twentieth-century taste, one can appreciate his exceptional mastery of felicitous design and rich color schemes.

The subject of this painting, *The Immaculate Conception,* was one of the most frequent themes commissioned by the Catholic Church during the Counter-Reformation when religious art was intended not only to embody religious concepts but also to inspire exaltation in the faithful. Consequently, this theme played an important role in Baroque art, especially after rules on its iconography and representation were formulated early in the seventeenth century. These rules, instituted in 1615 by Pope Paul V and published in 1649 by Francisco Pacheco, painter and advisor to the Inquisition, portray Mary as conceived by divine intervention; thus, she was herself free from original sin and worthy to be the mother of the Saviour. As the personification of grace and purity, she had to be represented in the most attractive, decorous, and intelligible form that visually expressed this abstract theological belief.[2] Murillo and his Italian contemporary, Guido Reni, are generally credited with establishing the most popular pictorial form for this subject.

Closely following the tenets set by the Catholic Church, the majestic and radiant Virgin in the Kimbell *Immaculate Conception* is portrayed as a beautiful young maiden in a central ascendant position. Her traditional white tunic has shimmering silvery shadows, and her deep blue mantle, which drapes her almost completely, swirls behind her in a typically Baroque undulating movement. These forms are modeled with fluid brushstrokes and moderate impasto; the rich, cool colors are modified by halftones and shadows. These painterly qualities are also found in the gold scarf which encircles her shoulders and in the major attribute of the Immaculate Conception, the silvery crescent moon with upturned horns at the Virgin's feet, supported by a grey cloud. With her eyes raised in adoration toward the heavens, the Virgin's face, which expresses her innocence, and her hands, folded to her bosom in a gesture of piety, are modeled softly and clearly, giving a human immediacy to this spiritual subject.

Subordinate areas are rendered with thinner paint, drier brushwork, and warmer, more delicate hues. The sun, expressed as rays of light around her head, illuminates the atmospheric background, creating a mandorla around her. The loosely brushed outlines of the five cherubim grouped beneath her in various attitudes meld into the airy, mistlike space. They bear symbols of purity and of the Passion of Christ–lilies, the flower of the Virgin, roses, and palm leaves–while the choir of seraphim at the top poke their heads out of the clouds, the natural veil of the blue sky used as a symbol of the unseen God.[3]

Probably commissioned for a church in Seville, where Murillo spent most of his life, the Kimbell painting exemplifies Murillo's late *Vaporoso* style.[4] The light fluid brushwork and the facile draftsmanship which complement the gracefully flowing composition distinguish this work from the more studied style of his earlier paintings, such as the Cleveland *Immaculate Conception*.[5] One of numerous versions of this devotional subject by Murillo, the Kimbell painting probably dates from the early or middle 1670s, although precise chronological classification is difficult because he rarely signed or dated his paintings.

This impressively scaled painting is thought to be contemporaneous with at least three other versions of this subject painted in Murillo's late style: the *Immaculate Conception of the Capuchins* (Seville Museum),[6] the "Walpole" *Immaculate Conception* (Hermitage Museum, Leningrad),[7] and the "Half-Length" *Conception* (Prado Museum, Madrid).[8] Not only is the Kimbell painting stylistically similar to these three versions but it would appear that the idealized model, thought to be Murillo's daughter, is the same in all four versions.[9]

Description: Placed centrally in a vertical format, a young woman stands with a white crescent moon and a grey cloud at her feet. Viewed frontally, she turns slightly to her left, hands folded across her bosom. Her head is tilted upward to her right. She has long brown hair, parted in the center, and brown eyes. A dark blue drapery covers most of her long white robe, and she wears an ochre scarf around her shoulders. The cool tonalities of her white robe shaded with greys and her deep ultramarine blue mantle contrast dramatically with the warm tonalities of the golden ochres and umbers of the vaporous, shallow space behind her.

The warm-cool tonality contrasts are repeated in the five cherubim that float beneath her. One looks downward from behind her robe at the left, with only his head and left shoulder visible. Of the two cherubs in the lower left corner, one leans backward, facing the viewer; he is draped in a yellow cloth and holds three white lilies. Leaning forward over his left side, below the left horn of the moon, the other cherub holds three white roses. Of the two cherubs at the right looking upward to the central figure, the one to the right of the crescent is shown full-length, obscuring all but the face of the cherub behind him. He leans back, his feet pushed toward the viewer and his right hand extending upward to the figure. He holds cream-colored palm leaves in his left hand, and there is a pink drapery over his left side. Eight seraphic heads hover above the central figure, four in each corner.

Condition: Excellent. The margins of the original canvas have been trimmed to the edge of the painted area, probably when it was relined. Normal fine age craquelure is evident throughout the painting. Scattered losses have been filled and inpainted and old varnish remains, especially in the darker areas.

Exhibitions: British Institution, London, 1839, cat. no. 108. *Seventeenth and Eighteenth Century Paintings,* Hazlitt Gallery, London, June 3–27, 1969, cat. no. 13, illus.

Collections: John Blackwood, England, by 1760; descended to his widow, then to her niece, then to William C. Cartwright, Aynhoe Park, Northamptonshire, England, by 1886.[10] Lady Cartwright, to 1969.
Foundation Acquisition, AP 69.14.

Related Prints: James McArdell did a full-length mezzotint "from the original belonging to John Blackwood, Esq." A half-length mezzotint of 1839 by Coombs, with all the heads omitted, and a lithograph by Lafosse, with one cherub and all the seraphic heads omitted, have also been recorded. See: G. Goodwin, *James McArdell,* London, 1903, cat. no. 216; and *Seventeenth and Eighteenth Century Paintings,* Hazlitt Gallery, London, June, 1969, cat. no. 13.

Notes:

1 George Kubler and Martin Soria, *Art and Architecture in Spain and Portugal and their American Dominions, 1500 to 1800,* Baltimore, 1959, p. 273.

2 Anna Jameson, *Legends of the Madonna,* London, 1852, pp. 49–50.

3 According to the rules, the horns of the moon point downwards, but Murillo frequently reversed their direction, perhaps for compositional reasons. In addition, he sometimes depicted the Virgin with her hands clasped together in prayer. In the Kimbell painting, as in most of his representations of this subject, he omitted several traditional attributes–the customary diadem of 12 stars around her head, the cord of St. Francis, and the vanquished dragon. These few deviations do not make the image less orthodox.

4 Kubler and Soria, pp. 277–78.

5 Nancy Coe Wixom, "The Immaculate Conception," *Cleveland Museum of Art Bulletin,* vol. 47, no. 7, September, 1960, pp. 163–65, color illus. on cover.

6 August Liebermann Mayer, *Murillo,* vol. 22 of *Klassiker der Kunst,* 2nd ed., Stuttgart, 1923, p. 135.

7 Mayer, p. 77.

8 Mayer, p. 76.

9 Theodore Crombie, *Seventeenth and Eighteenth Century Paintings,* Hazlitt Gallery, London, June, 1969, cat. no. 13.

10 Luis Alfonso, *Murillo,* Barcelona, 1886, p. 203.

Additional References:

Edward Davies, *The Life of Bartolomé E. Murillo,* London, 1819, p. xcii.
Charles B. Curtis, *Velázquez and Murillo,* 1883, p. 131, no. 33.
Paul Lefort, *Murillo et ses Elèves,* Paris, 1892, p. 71, cat. no. 33.
S. J. Ignacio Elizalde, *En Torno a las Immaculadas de Murillo,* Madrid, 1955, p. 146.
"Current and Forthcoming Exhibitions," *The Burlington Magazine,* vol. 111, June, 1969, p. 398.
Theodore Crombie, "Baroque and Bristol Cream," *Apollo,* vol. 89, June, 1969, pp. 468–69, illus. p. 469.

Aelbert Cuyp, 1620–1691
Landscape with Windmill
Drawn about 1650–60

Red chalk on white paper, 7 1/16 × 11 7/16 in. (18 × 29.1 cm.)

The red chalk medium of this drawing is unusual among Dutch seventeenth-century drawings. There are very few extant sanguine landscapes, and this drawing is the only one known that is attributed to Aelbert Cuyp.[1] His experimentation with red chalk is not surprising, for he was one the first artists in Holland to use crayons instead of such traditional techniques as pen and ink.[2] His typical drawing medium was black crayon with occasional ink washes.

Since sanguine drawing was common in Italy at this time, Cuyp's use of the medium in this distinctive drawing may indicate his increased interest in Italian pictorial conventions in the late 1640s and 1650s. Born in Dordrecht where he lived most of his life, Cuyp is not known to have visited Italy. His paintings of this period, however, are distinguished by serene moods and a moist, golden atmosphere that may have been inspired by the Italianate scenes of Claude Lorrain and Jan Both.[3]

The tranquil mood of this landscape is evoked by several stylistic means that are characteristic of both Cuyp's paintings and drawings from the late 1640s to about 1665, after which his artistic activity abated. The panoramic vista is created by the orderly sequence of rows of stratified foliage that recede deep into the distance and stretch laterally across the view. The extension of these rows to the farthest edges of the drawing, unimpeded at the left and behind the tree at the right, contributes equally to a positive evocation of palpable space. Drawn in progressively softer strokes and lighter tones, the foliage in the middle distance and the upward slope of the valley in the far distance recede

dramatically behind the treetops in the foreground, the windmill and the large tree, all of which are rendered in more intense color and with crisp, definite outlines.

These emphatically contoured edges are perhaps related to the distinctive "light lines" at the edges of forms in Cuyp's painting, where their contrasting color contributes enormously to the serene moist atmosphere of his paintings.

Description: Panoramic view across an extensive valley with a windmill in the near left center and a tall tree at the far right. Just past the bare downward slope of the foreground is a bank of foliage formed by the tops of a row of trees and shrubs. Rising above the treetops is the four-vaned windmill; beside it to the left is the low, chimneyed roof of a cottage nestled among the trees. Like the windmill and the treetops, the tree at the right (whose foliage extends beyond the edge of the drawing), is heavily worked with strong outlines and emphatic contours. In the valley beyond are lightly drawn fields bordered by rows of shrubs and trees and occasional low buildings. In the distance, the upward slope of the valley rises to form a lightly indicated low ridge with a higher hill at the right beyond the large tree. Very light shading articulates the sky. The paper bears no watermark.

Condition: Very good. The color is fresh and strong. Some foxing in the sky has been bleached, and several small tears on the right edge have been repaired. The paper is trimmed to the border.

Exhibition: A Collection of Fifty Master Drawings ..., William H. Schab Gallery, New York, 1969, cat. no. 16, illus. on back cover.

Collections: [William H. Schab, New York.] Foundation Acquisition, AP 70.16.

Notes:

1 Prof. J. H. Van Gelder will include this drawing in his forthcoming monograph on Cuyp.

2 [Carlos van Hasselt], *Dessins de Paysagistes Hollandais du* XVIIe *Siècle, ... l'Institut Néerlandais de Paris,* Brussels, Rotterdam, Paris and Bern, October, 1968, to May, 1969, p. 33.

3 Cuyp was "deeply indebted to Jan Both" (who had studied with Claude in Italy), but his understanding of Claude's classical restraint was more profound than Both's. See Wolfgang Stechow, *Dutch Landscape Painting of the Seventeenth Century,* London, 1966, pp. 62–63.

Jan van Huysum, 1682–1749
Flower Still Life
Painted first half of the Eighteenth Century

Oil on canvas, 29 3/8 × 21 1/2 in (74.7 × 54.6 cm.)

Flower Still Life by Jan van Huysum[1] is a superb example of this Dutch specialist's luxuriant flower pieces, the highly finished, enamel-smooth paintings which gained him an international reputation. Its primary function is to delight the eye with delicacy of realistic detail and sensitive rendering of texture. Van Huysum also intended it to instruct the viewer; therefore, he grouped flowers which bloom in different seasons. Although the variety of flowers seems overwhelming, the visual selectivity is typically Dutch in comparison to the sumptuous abundance in Flemish still life painting. As one of the rare Dutch still life artists who was active as a draftsman, van Huysum worked out the details from nature in drawings which exhibit a spontaneous, broad touch not found in the paintings.[2] The asymmetrically structured composition, which achieves a loose, natural-appearing flower arrangement, and the lively *chiaroscuro* effects continue preceding traditions of this genre. However, the light background and overall light tonality are unique to van Huysum; his use of cool colors, dominated by saturate blues and vivid greens, is his greatest innovation and creates the light, airy effects which conform to eighteenth-century rococo tastes.[3]

Van Huysum's works continue the tradition of still life painting which began with the fifteenth-century Flemish artists who delighted in careful rendering of objects which played a subordinate, but highly symbolic, role in their religious paintings. By the mid-sixteenth century, the biblical subject had become no more than a pretext for the depiction of beautiful objects, and in the seventeenth century, the still life emerged as a separate genre.[4] The Dutch mania for flowers stimulated its development and created a popular market for such works of art among the Dutch middle class.[5] Although interest in the still life was gradually waning in its appeal toward the end of the century, it was revived by the freshness of van Huysum's decorative paintings. Active in Amsterdam in the first half of the eighteenth century, the artist was called by his contemporaries "the phoenix of all flower painters." He had numerous close followers and inspired generations of decorators of porcelain and crockery.[6]

Inscription: Lower right: *Jan van Huysum*

Description: Flowers in a vase which stands on the sill of a balustrade. The background is a verdant landscape with a rivulet of water cascading behind a vase on a grey, stepped pedestal at the right and a taupe-colored, draped female caryatid figure at the upper left. The vase is a short, round, brown earthenware vessel with a palmette design in low relief around the lower portion. In front of the vase on the left lie white flowers–a rose, hydrangea and hibiscuses–and, on the right, a large red peony. The flowers in the vase are roses, peonies, hydrangeas, morning glories, primroses, forget-me-nots, buttercups, poppies, sweet peas, tulips, irises, delphiniums, cornflowers, asters, field daisies, marigolds, lantana and fritillaria.

Condition: The canvas was for a long time attached to a thin wood panel which was removed in 1968–69 when the canvas was lined with a secondary canvas support. The wood panel is retained in the study collection.

Exhibitions: None known.

Collections: Count von Shoenborn, Pommersfelden, Germany. M. Haro Collection, Paris, to 1892.[7] Foundation Acquisition, AP 70.21.

Notes:

[1] Alternate spelling: Jan van Huijsum.

[2] Jakob Rosenberg, Seymour Slive, and E. H. ter Kuile, *Dutch Art and Architecture: 1600–1800*, Baltimore, 1966, p. 217.

[3] Walther Bernt, *The Netherlandish Painters of the Seventeenth Century*, London, 1970, p. 61.

[4] Max J. Friedländer, *Landscape, Portrait, Still-Life*, New York, 1963, pp. 279–80.

[5] Friedländer, p. 278.

[6] Rosenberg, Slive, and Ter Kuile, p. 217.

[7] Sold at Haro auction, Paris, May 30, 1892, lot. no. 25. See C. Hofstede de Groot, ... *Verzeichnis der Werke der hervorragendsten holländischen Maler des* XVII. *Jahrhunderts*, Stuttgart and Paris, 1928, vol. X, p. 364, cat. no. 120 (*Blumen in einem Pokal auf dem Gesims einer Balustrade*). A mark from the Haro Collection was located on the former backing which was removed when cleaned in 1968–69.

Additional Reference:

M. H. Grant, *Jan van Huysum, a Catalogue Raisonné*, Leigh-on-Sea, England, 1954, p. 23, cat. no. 81 *(A Goblet with Flowers)*.

Philippe Mercier, 1689–1760
The Concert
Painted about 1740

Oil on canvas, 48 1/2 × 60 3/8 in. (123.2 × 153.3 cm.)

The son of French Huguenots who emigrated to Berlin, Philippe Mercier was trained on the Continent and sometime between about 1720 and 1725 went to England, where he was court painter to Frederick, Prince of Wales, from 1727 to 1736. Through his introduction to England of the French rococo taste of Watteau and Chardin, and his innovation of the small conversation piece (about 1725) and the domestic "fancy" picture (about 1737), he exerted an influence more profound than that of many greater artists.

Mercier painted during his career several works based on the theme of a concert in which the harmony of the instruments becomes a metaphor for the harmony of feeling uniting the players. The Kimbell painting belongs to a group of these concert scenes executed around 1737–40, which his biographer George Vertue described as "conceited plaisant Fancies & habits . . . mixt modes really well done—and much approvd off."[1] These later pictures, which are among his best works, reveal a stylistic move away from the delicacy of Watteau toward the broader handling of Chardin, evident in the Kimbell painting in the facial types and in details such as the carefully rendered lute held by the boy in the lower right. This painting most closely corresponds to *A Music Party* in the Tate Gallery[2] and *A Musical Party*, formerly in the collection of Monsignor Patrick Browne, Dublin.[3] The three share a like setting of monumental columns with glimpses of indistinct vistas beyond and large figures crowded into the foreground with *repoussoir* elements such as the table, recorder and guitar in *The Concert*. The most pronounced similarities are to be found between the Kimbell painting and Monsignor Browne's: the lady with her chin raised and her head turned with eyes averted; the man with a violin who gazes at her, and the boy in the background whose face is tightly framed on three sides. Mercier in his later work frequently painted figures cut off by the borders of the painting, as well as figures who look directly out at the viewer. His figures characteristically have large eyes, beestung lips and noses which seem slightly skewed on their faces, evident here in the central figure of the lady standing. In the Kimbell work the luscious blues, browns and yellows that reflect the influence of Chardin tie together an otherwise rather awkward composition and give the painting a bright, cheerful effect consonant with the musical diversion of the handsome, youthful figures.

Description: Nine half-length figures grouped around a table singing and playing instruments in a garden setting. Three women holding music are flanked on the left by a man playing a recorder and on the right by a violinist looking intently at the woman to his right. Four boys on the right turn away from the musicians; one lays his recorder down on the table and another still holds his lute. In the background on the right are the bases of two monumental columns, on the left the voluted base of a large vase with sketchily rendered trees between. The table in the foreground, covered by a green cloth, has two books resting on it at the left near the beribboned neck of a guitar projecting up in the immediate foreground. The figures are dressed in Van Dyck costumes in rich, soft colors: the woman leaning on the table in blue, the two flanking men in shades of brown, the boy with a recorder in blue with a dull yellow cape, and the boy with a lute in red.

Condition: Fair. There is extensive overpaint and strengthening in numerous areas including two vertical inpainted areas at bottom center and bottom right.

Exhibitions: None known.[4]

Collections: E. M. Hodgkins, Paris, until about 1914–17.
[Arnold Seligmann, Rey & Co.], Paris and New York.
[Newhouse Galleries, Inc., New York.]
Kimbell Bequest, ACF 41.6.

Notes:

[1] George Vertue, *Notebooks*, vol. III, p. 82, quoted in *Philip Mercier*, City Art Gallery, York, England, June 21–July 20, 1969, and Iveagh Bequest, Kenwood, Hampstead, England, July 29–Sept. 28, 1969, p. 36.

[2] Iveagh Bequest, Kenwood, cat. no. 73, (addenda), illus.

[3] Christie's, sale catalogue, *Important Pictures by Old Masters*, London, June 21, 1968, lot 95, illus.

[4] According to unconfirmed vendor information, it was at some time exhibited at the Minneapolis Institute of Art.

Canaletto, 1697–1768
Venice: The Grand Canal at Santa Maria della Carita
Painted about 1726–30

Oil on canvas, 18×24 7/8 in. (45.8×62.8 cm.)

The enduring charm of the widely varying scenes of Venice appealed enormously to travelers of the eighteenth century. Viewed at leisure from a gently gliding gondola, the bright sun, the sparkling water and the ornate architecture created a distinctive ambience unlike that of any other European city on the "Grand Tour." Paintings of these picturesque scenes found a ready market among the foreign visitors, and the wealthier ones acquired groups of these views, particularly of the Grand Canal, the major water route that winds through the island of Venice.

As a young man, Giovanni Antonio Canale, known as Canaletto, was well trained to paint these views. From his earliest known Venetian scenes, painted in the mid-1720s, it is readily apparent that his prior experience as a designer of operatic and theatrical settings (of which very little is known) had made him thoroughly familiar with the drama that can be evoked by discreet modulations of perspective, color and light. By the late 1720s his superb control of these techniques and his exceptional facility as a draftsman had established him as recognized master of "dramatized topography" and brought him numerous commissions, including four well-known series that date from the late 1720s and early 1730s.[1] This painting is from one of these series, a now dispersed group of at least eight Venetian views that were in the collection of the Princes of Liechtenstein by 1780,[2] and may have been acquired about 1740 directly from Canaletto by Prince Joseph Wenzel (1696–1772).[3]

The view is looking east toward the entrance to the Grand Canal from the Bacino. At the right is the pinnacled facade of the mid-fifteenth-century church, Santa Maria della Carita (now part of the Accademia di Belle Arte) and to its left beyond the shadowed plaza stands its tall bell tower (now demolished) and the dome of Santa Maria della Salute in the distance. Canaletto's subtle balance of shadows, lively figures, and architectural detail imbues this painting with a positive sense of light and space, which is still quite perceptible despite losses of paint in the sky that have weakened the original overall effect of a once splendidly palpable atmosphere. This clear articulation of space is still evident in the luminous shadows cast by the church at the compositional focus of the painting formed by the converging diagonals of the quay and the parapet of the bridge in the foreground. Painted in bright colors and informally posed, the scattered figures give the architecture a human scale by accenting the sunlit space with their shadows and enlivening the scene with movement. They are foils to the regularity of the crisply painted architectural details that are clear even in the buildings in the far distance. The precise structural patterns, the rhythm of diagonals and the vitality of the figures are stabilized by the areas of cool shade cast on the buildings at the sides and bottom of the scene.

Canaletto painted at least three slightly different views of this scene and his apparently faithful record of changes in architectural detail establishes that the Kimbell view was painted after June, 1726, and before 1735. In the well documented 1726 view, now in Montreal,[4] the edge of the quay in the foreground is intact and there is a low stone wall enclosing the nearby square column. By the time of the Kimbell painting[5] repairs had begun on the quay stonework, which lies askew along the edge of the quay, and the enclosure about the square column is being dismantled. Clearly postdating the Montreal and Kimbell paintings is the third, more expansive, view of the scene that is now in the royal collection at Windsor Castle, London. It has been variously dated as before 1730[6] and in the mid-1730s;[7] it was definitely painted by 1735 when an engraving of it was published. In this latest view, the quay has been rebuilt and the paving about the column relaid without an enclosing wall. Moreover, one architectural detail is deliberately omitted in the London painting; the sculptural figure that surmounts the rightmost pinnacle of the church facade in the Kimbell and Montreal paintings is not in place, having either fallen or been removed after they were painted.[8]

Description: A scene on the Grand Canal, Venice, looking east, dominated by the facade of Santa Maria della Carita at the right. In the lower right foreground a footbridge leads to a large open square before the church. Beyond the church are its bell tower and a glimpse of the dome of Santa Maria della Salute. On the left, among the buildings across the open water of the canal, is the Palazzo Cavalli. Several gondolas ply the canal. Isolated groups of figures are scattered about the square, two men are fishing at the edge of the quay (which is under repair) and a dog, dwarf and two servants are on the bridge. The sky is pale blue with creamy white clouds.

Condition: Fair. There are numerous areas of inpainting in the sky and scattered losses in the buildings, now inpainted, particularly along the canvas edges.

Exhibition: Kunstmuseum (?), Lucerne, Switzerland, 1948.[9]

Collections: Possibly acquired from Canaletto about 1740 by Prince Josef Wenzel (1696–1772) of Liechtenstein. Recorded from 1780 to 1948 in the collection of the Princes of

Liechtenstein, Vienna.[10] [Frederic W. Mont], New York. [Newhouse Galleries, Inc., New York.]
Kimbell Bequest, ACK 52.3.

Notes:

[1] Two of the series, those at Woburn (22 paintings) and at Windsor Castle (14 paintings), are still intact; the other two have been dispersed. See W. G. Constable, *Canaletto . . .*, Oxford, 1962, vol. I, pp. 104, 109–12.

[2] Listed by Constable, vol. I, p. 112. The dimensions of this painting accord with those shown in the 1780 catalogue, *Galerie de Son Altesse François Joseph Chef et Prince Regnant de la Maison de Liechtenstein*, cat. nos. 195–206: "Douze vues de Venise . . . hauts 18 pouces sur 24 de largeur."

[3] It is not certain when the series entered the Liechtenstein collection. See Constable, vol. II, p. 185. Another painting in the series (now in the Toledo Museum of Art) bears a Liechtenstein inscription dated 1740. See: Barry Flannegan, *Painting in Italy in the Eighteenth Century*, Art Institute of Chicago and others, 1970, p. 56, cat. no. 17.

[4] Constable, vol. I, pl. 42; vol. II, cat. no. 194.

[5] The painting has been dated between 1726 and 1730 by Constable, vol. I, pl. 42; vol. II, p. 266, cat. no. 195, while Lionello Puppi, *The Complete Paintings of Canaletto*, London, 1970, cat. no. 41 A, illus., dates it "1726–28?". However, the date and number of other paintings in the Liechtenstein collection have not been definitively established; the Toledo painting from this series has been dated in the late 1730s by Flannegan, cat. no. 17.

[6] Constable, vol. I, pl. 42; vol. II, cat. no. 196.

[7] Michael Levey, *The Later Italian Pictures in the Collection of Her Majesty the Queen*, London, 1964, pp. 58, 61, cat. no. 380, pl. 142.

[8] Noted by Levey, p. 58.

[9] Constable, vol. II, cat. no. 195.

[10] See A. Kronfeld, *Führer durch die Fürstlich Liechtensteinische Gemäldegalerie in Wien*, Vienna, 1927, cat. no. 216, and other catalogues of the collection dating from 1870 to 1948.

Canaletto, 1697–1768
The Molo, Venice
Painted about 1735

Oil on canvas, 24 1/2 × 39 7/8 in. (62.3 × 101.3 cm.)

The reputation of Giovanni Antonio Canale, called Canaletto, and his mature style of painting were firmly established by the mid-1730s, when he painted this Venetian scene. In fewer than ten years he had developed a distinctive painting style that transformed the hitherto rather sedate concept of *veduta* (view) painting into a lively mode of expression that found great favor among his patrons, particularly the numerous English tourists who commissioned Canaletto to create pictorial souvenirs of their visits to Venice. However, Canaletto's *vedute* are more than literal renderings of scenes; he enhanced his observations by selecting the most agreeable aspects of Venetian life–colorfully dressed figures, sparkling water and pristine architecture–and excluding the unattractive street urchins, debris, aged people and weather-worn buildings. Then by slight changes in proportions of buildings, by careful arrangement of light and shade, and by calculated disposition of boats, market stalls and figures, he transformed these scenes into harmonious designs of a sybaritic Venice bathed in the bright sunlight of summer.[1]

This painting of about 1735[2] exemplifies Canaletto's mastery of this mode of expression. The varied Venetian architecture is given mass and substance by a skillfully organized pattern of strong sunlight and cool grey shadows and by the clear perspectival rendering which draws the eye down the long quay, through the clustered groups of people. Their brightly colored clothes–the scarlet hats, blue capes and white shirts–and the pristine white canvas of the stalls are contrasted with the dark gondolas and the shaded windows and arches of the sunlit buildings. The scene is enlivened by a variety of figures: boatmen poling their gondolas, gesturing vendors tempting potential buyers, and burdened tradesmen walking across the quay.

Canaletto primed this canvas with a ground of pale Venetian red, imbuing the thinly painted blue sky and white clouds with warmth and a distinct sense of the moist Venetian atmosphere. This hazy atmospheric quality and the calculated synthesis of motifs was employed by Canaletto as a stimulus of sensory recollection, to intensify and enhance his patrons' memories of Venice.

Since this scene is of one of the most important public areas of Venice, it is not surprising that Canaletto painted this view frequently. Two smaller versions, of the 1720s, from a lower viewpoint that includes the Doge's Palace at the right, are distinguished by isolated figures and a rather expansive treatment of the plaza.[3] A view of 1730 is taken from a point on the Bacino de San Marco, to the left of the Kimbell painting.[4] A large version of the early 1730s, from nearly the same point as the Kimbell painting, includes more water at the left and more of the library at the right.[5] This large number of variants and their related replicas is evidence of Canaletto's considerable reputation not only during his lifetime, but during the nineteenth century.

Description: A view in Venice, looking west, down the Molo (quay or wharf). At the viewer's right is the Column of St. Theodore and beyond are the Library, the Zecca (mint), the Public Granaries and the Fonteghetto della Farina. On the quay are a group of temporary booth awnings and numerous groups of more than thirty figures. At the left are gondolas and small craft beyond which is the entrance to the Grand Canal and Santa Maria della Salute in the distance.

Condition: Excellent. There is scattered inpainting in the sky and along the edges; a small hole (1/2 in. diam.) in the right foreground has been repaired and inpainted. On a glue lining and butt-end stretcher.

Exhibitions: None known.

Collections: Earl of Rosebery, Mentmore, to 1955. Brian Jenks, Astbury Hall, Shropshire, to 1969.[6]
Foundation Acquisition, AP 69.22.

Notes:

1 See W. G. Constable, *Canaletto . . .*, Oxford, 1962, vol. I, p. 116.

2 Constable, vol. II, p. 223, cat. no. 96.

3 17 × 23 in., unlocated, Constable, cat. no. 89; and 18 1/8 × 24 3/4, private collection, Constable, cat. no. 91.

4 23 × 40 in., the late Lord Egerton of Tatton, Constable, cat. no. 97.

5 43 1/2 × 73 in., Albertini Collection, Rome, Constable, cat. no. 95.

6 Constable, vol. II, p. 223, cat. no. 96.

Francesco Guardi, 1712–1793
Venice Viewed from the Bacino
Painted about 1780

Oil on canvas, 24 7/8 × 37 3/8 in. (31 1/4 × 95 cm.)

Considering his fame and popularity at the present time, in addition to the existence of a very large body of work produced over a long lifetime, it is remarkable that there is such a strange lack of documentation about Francesco Guardi. There are practically no letters, contracts, witness accounts of events, or even hearsay anecdotes as there are for most famous artists from even earlier periods. Except for his recorded birth date, the first certain personal record is Francesco's own signature on two allegorical pictures in the Ringling Museum at Sarasota, Florida, upon which there is also the date 1747, when the painter was already 35 years old. He did not become a member of the Venetian Guild of Painters until 1761 when he was nearly 50, and he was not elected to the Venetian Academy before he was 72, only nine years prior to his death. All of this is the more remarkable when we remind ourselves that Francesco was a member of a large and important family of artists, in which he must have received a good early training, as well as a young start as a practitioner. His father was an artist, as were both his brothers, Giovanni Antonio (1699–1760) and Niccolò (1715–85). Francesco's son Giacomo (1764–1835) also became a painter, and his sister married the mighty Giovanni Battista Tiepolo.

Although certainly hard at work from his youth, Francesco was probably eclipsed by his elder brother in a typical family shop, or *bottega*, situation. There are records that refer to works by "the Guardi brothers," implying a completely collaborative kind of system,[1] and the identity of the separate hands down to Antonio's death in 1760 is still a subject of the most conjecturable and variable opinion.[2] The *bottega* had a businesslike arrangement in which many copies of earlier masters' work were done, and this attitude made it easy for Francesco to begin making paintings from the precise, perspectival drawing and print views of Venice that Canaletto had begun producing during the early 1720s.[3] However, the brothers' shop collectively, as well as Antonio and Francesco as individual artists, did produce many original allegories, religious altarpieces and mythological "history" pieces. During this period Francesco absorbed influences from Solimena, Tiepolo, Longhi and Sebastiano and Marco Ricci. Fundamental to his development was the influence of the fantastic and evocative Alessandro Magnasco (1667–1749), especially that master's expressionistic *brio* in manipulating rich paint, although precisely how he imbibed this influence would make a knotty little subject for a seminar.[4]

After Antonio died, Francesco increasingly concentrated on views *(vedute)* rather than figurative compositions, particularly subsequent to the demise of Canaletto in 1768 when Francesco moved in to supply the growing demand that the older artist had filled. In the eyes of his patrons and contemporaries he became a specialist for recording particular places and notable events, such as the state visit of Pope Pius VI in 1782, the burning of the San Marcuola quarter of the city in 1789, the inauguration of Teatro la Fenice in 1792, or the first balloon ascension in Venice, 1784. An attitude of constraint toward this functional genre is indicated by the contract between Guardi and Signor Pietro Edwards who commissioned the four scenes to commemorate the Pope's visit; the artist had the obligation of "... taking the views on the spot... subject to the directions of the said Sig. Edwards as regards to the disposition and placing of the figures..."[5] One other rare document, the private diary of Senator Pietro Gradenigo, in an entry dated April 25, 1764, reveals a mixture of moderate admiration and deprecative description of an artist already well over 50 years of age: "Francesco Guardi ... is a good pupil of the famous Canaletto, and has been very successful in painting, with the help of the optic camera, two big canvases ordered by an Englishman of the view of Piazza San Marco. These have been put on exhibition today on the walls of the Procuratie and aroused universal applause."[6]

In spite of the ever increasing demand for his *vedute*, Guardi was paid relatively little for them as compared to the painters of portraits, religious subjects, or "histories." The academic Renaissance idea of a hierarchy of importance according to a picture's subject matter was still prevalent, and "views" were far down the ladder. For example, none of the *Vedutisti*, not even the elder Canaletto, is included in Alessandro Longhi's compendium of Venetian artists published in 1762.[7] But it is of much greater import, on purely aesthetic grounds, that as Guardi reached his full maturity of style with his familiar views, his art became more purely personal, entirely disengaged from academic formulas and precise optical representation. His nervous, exquisite draftsmanship and inventive use of melting colors drew him farther and farther from the path blazed by Canaletto. He focused less and less upon topographical fact and, through elusive formal means derived from his own imagination, he strove for that lyricism of total effect *(magia di effeto)* that contributes so much more to the beauty of his

canvases than the individual component parts. With this approach he became the supreme interpreter of that unique, unreal city of air, light and water where the shifting, unstable and ephemeral aspects of nature must be transmuted to canvas to capture the true spirit. For this achievement he is, for us today, the most renowned of all the painters of *vedute*, but in accomplishing his personal artistic end he went beyond the limits of rococo taste and had to wait a century or so for full recognition of his real qualities.

Inscription: On upper left quadrant of the back of the picture, in ink: *Margaret Ingram* (daughter of John Ingram who commissioned the picture from Guardi).

Description: Under a restless, mist-laden sky that occupies the upper two-thirds of the picture's surface, the classic view of Venice is taken from the middle of the Bacino di San Marco, that broad basin of water that constitutes the "front door" to the city. The line of sight is perpendicular to the Molo, or landing quay, sometimes called the *imbarco*. The entire facade of the official and ceremonial heart of the city stretches in a horizontal line between the two edges of the picture. First seen at the left is the Zecca, or mint, then the south end of the library, behind which soars the thin bell tower. A full view into the Piazetta is afforded, including the two columns of St. Theodore and the Lion of St. Mark at the near end, and the clock tower and front of St. Mark's Cathedral at the far end. One dome of the Cathedral peeks around the northeast corner of the Ducal Palace that bulks large slightly to the left of the central axis of the picture. Tied up in front of the Palace is a huge ship of state (the Bucentaur?), and just east of it are three smaller vessels with sails fully unfurled, drying in the still, sunny atmosphere. The whitish stone prison is right of center, and stretching eastward from it are the motley buildings along the Riva degli Schiavone. A variety of small craft and gondolas nose into the Molo, and these, in addition to the quay itself, are filled with deftly and economically sketched figures of that bustling, active type called *macchiette*. Three gondolas ply the middle waters of the deep blue-green Bacino, while a freight boat heads west in the near distance, and another of the same type is moored in the lower right foreground.

Condition: Excellent. Very fine general age crackle pattern through to red ground. Abrasions and some old flaking at edges. Lined, with glue-sized linen, now brittle. Numerous minor areas of strengthening, filling and inpainting. Old, vertical tear 2 3/4 inches long, lower left.[8]

Exhibitions: Burlington Fine Arts Club, London, 1934–35, cat. no. 78. *An Exhibition of Venetian Painting*, Matthiesen Galleries, London, 1939, cat. no. 71.[9] *European Masters of the 18th Century*, Royal Academy of Art, London, 1954-55, cat. no. 83. *Art Treasures Centenary, European Old Masters*, City of Manchester, England, 1957, cat. no. 164. *La Mostra dei Guardi*, Palazzo Grassi, Venice, 1965, cat. no. 140, illus. p. 268.

Collections: John Ingram, the Englishman who commissioned the picture, who lived in the Palazzo Mignanelli, Rome, and also had a residence in Venice. (He was born at Stainworth Hall, Durham, in 1767, by 1819 had removed all of his Guardis from Venice to Rome; in 1831 he was resident in London, but he died in Rome Jan. 31, 1841.)[10] Margaret Ingram, daughter of John Ingram. A. H. Godfrey, husband of Augusta Isabella Ingram, daughter of John Ingram. Lilian Godfrey, daughter of A. H. Godfrey. [Leggatts], London, about 1929. Capt. H. E. Rimington-Wilson, Broomhead Hall, Bolsterstone, Sheffield, to 1957. [Arthur Tooth & Sons, Ltd.], London, to 1963. David Wolfson, London.
Foundation Acquisition, AP 70.19.

Notes:

[1] The will of Count Giovanni Benedetto Giovanelli, dated 1736, as quoted in Vittorio Moschini, *Guardi*, London, 1956, p. 7; also Pietro Zampetti, *A Dictionary of Venetian Painters*, Leigh-on-Sea, England, 1971, p. 53. The Kimbell picture is illustrated in Zampetti with an unnumbered plate which would correspond to p. 146.

[2] Comune di Venezia, *Problemi Guardeschi, atti del Convegno di studi promosso dalla mostra dei Guardi . . .*, (Venice, Sept. 13–14, 1965), Venice, 1967; p. 66 ff.; p. 156 ff.; p. 161 ff.; p. 213 ff.

[3] Heribert Hutter, *Francesco Guardi in der Gemälde-galerie . . . Wien*, Vienna, 1967, p. 11 ff.

[4] Moschini, pp. 10, 12, 22, 26.

[5] Quoted in Moschini, p. 52.

[6] For an excellent analysis of the possible interpretation of "pupil of Canaletto," "help of the optic camera," and the relatively low prices paid to Francesco, see: J. Byam Shaw, *The Drawings of Francesco Guardi*, London, 1949, p. 16 ff.

[7] Alessandro Longhi, *Compendio delle Vite de' pittori Veneziani*, Venice, 1762.

[8] Thorough technical examination does not bear out Professor Arslan's doubts about the condition of the picture affecting its aesthetic quality, stated by him in August, 1965. See Comune di Venezia, *Problemi Guardeschi*, p. 21, note 140.

Giovanni Domenico Tiepolo, 1727–1804
Christ at Gethsemane with Saints Peter, James and John
Probably drawn shortly after 1770

On paper, brush and bistre wash over pen and ink, traces of chalk, 18 3/4 × 14 1/8 in. (46.2 × 35.9 cm.)

Giovanni Domenico Tiepolo, often called Giandomenico, was the eldest surviving son of the great Venetian painter Giovanni Battista Tiepolo and Cecilia Guardi, whose brothers were the renowned artists Giovanni Antonio and Francesco Guardi. The youngest child in the Tiepolo family, Lorenzo Baldissera, Giandomenico's junior by nine years, also became an artist, as did their much younger cousin, Giacomo Guardi. It was a large family of artists in the honored Venetian tradition, and there has been no stylistic or documentary evidence to suggest that Giovanni Domenico ever had any other master than his father. Until his father's death, he remained his assistant and collaborator, often doing whole walls, ceilings or rooms on his own as part of large commissions for churches or villas in the Veneto, for the Russian court, for the Ducal Palace in Würzburg, Bavaria, or for the Royal Palace in Madrid. After father and son had been working together for eight years in Madrid, the elder Tiepolo died in 1770, leaving Domenico to return to Venice alone.

Because of this long and close association, the reputation of the son suffered for more than a hundred years, as all pictures or drawings thought not to be of the greatest caliber were indiscriminately attributed to him, whereas anything superb was automatically credited to the father. In fact, with recent increase in art-historical knowledge, we know that Domenico was considered a distinguished artist in his own right by his contemporaries before he was thirty; and although he was certainly the complete heir of his father's glorious art, he transfigured it for his own personal and highly individual ends. Especially after his return to Venice from Madrid, his strong proclivities for pictorial episode, for dramatic narration and intimate human expressions of intense feeling began to coalesce in a pungent realism that embodies the essence of his individual style.

All of these qualities are distilled in this representation of Christ descending from his lonely prayer on the Mount of Olives: "Oh, my Father, if it is possible, let this cup pass from me; nevertheless, not as I will, but as Thou wilt," He had asked his three disciples to "Watch with me," but found them all asleep. "What, could ye not watch with me one hour?" St. Peter, awakened by Christ's return, and with a gesture appealing for forgiveness, looks up in shame and awe at the ethereal figure floating above him. Still with only partial comprehension, St. Peter also looks into a face that profoundly expresses the bitter agony of this hour. With miraculously sensitive drawing in pen and brush, and with theatrical staging of the human figures, Domenico achieves the intimate nuances of the psychological drama. In addition, in the very broadly treated elements of the landscape setting, the towering Mount of Olives at left, the looming clouds, the spiky pine that metaphorically repeats the human gestures, and in the murky foreground shadows, Domenico uses an operatic mode of composition learned from his father to heighten the surging drama.

Thus, although technically a drawing, the picture achieves a monumentality and haunting power seldom matched by large-scale paintings. The drawing's large size, as well as its technique, provenance, and manner of treating the subject,

[9] A review of the Matthiesen Galleries' exhibition appeared in *Burlington Magazine*, vol. 74, April, 1939, pp. 192–94, with the Kimbell picture illustrated, pl. B (g.), p. 193. This review said of the Kimbell picture: "Francesco Guardi has seldom been seen equally well represented in a London exhibition; and surely he never did anything finer . . . than [this picture] . . . which has the additional interest of having been painted for an English connoisseur, settled in Italy at the time."

[10] Francis Haskell, "Francesco Guardi as Vedutista and Some of His Patrons," *Journal of the Warburg and Courtauld Institutes*, vol. XXIII, nos. 3–4, December, 1960, pp. 256–76, illus. This article states that the Kimbell picture was among a group of three Guardis sold at Christie's, London, by Ingram's descendants; other Guardis from this provenance were sold, but not the Kimbell canvas.

Additional References:

Antonio Morassi, "Fasti e nefasti del Settecento Veneziano," *Emporium*, January, 1956, p. 21.
The International Studio, vol. 98, March, 1931, illus. p. 32. Caption reads: "The Ducal Palace and Piazzetta from the Lagoon, companion to the above [Straus-Houston Museum painting], has never before been published; it originally hung in Ingram's Palazzo Mignanelli and remained until recently with his descendants."

makes it one of an extensive series that J. Byam Shaw calls the "Large Bible Series," done shortly after the return to Venice from Madrid.[1] All of this series of more than 250 works are large in scale and were evidently done, according to Shaw, as "album drawings" for the collector's portfolio; in other words, as works of art in their own right, not studies for paintings or etchings. All are finished to a drawn margin line and have a strong pictorial effect; only three are unfinished. All are drawn with pen, extensively washed with brown bistre and grey watercolor, with underlying preliminary forms sketched in black chalk. In the Kimbell drawing Domenico used a simple device to achieve the visionary, ethereal quality in the white-robed Christ figure; before any of the aforementioned lines or washes were drawn, a thin wash of neutral grey was applied over the whole sheet, except where the figure was to be placed. Christ, therefore, plus some smaller reflection areas on Peter's flesh, exists in a visual value register that is slightly higher than that established for the light level of the rest of the scene.

Within the "Large Bible Series" there were other groupings, one of which, according to Shaw, was "The Life of St. Peter," to which the Kimbell drawing probably belongs.[2] Twenty-nine of this series, including this picture, were formerly in the collection of the Duc de Trevise,[3] and before that they were in the famed Cormier collection at Tours.[4] The latter contained a total of eighty-two drawings from the "Large Bible Series" which are now widely dispersed. The largest single group of the "Large Bible Series" in one place is the big folio volume in the Louvre known as the Recueil Fayet. The contents of this "folio," consisting of 138 drawings, were acquired by M. Fayet in Venice in 1833 and bequeathed by him to the museum in 1889.

Inscription: Between the bistre margin line drawn by the artist and the top edge of the sheet, beginning about four inches from the upper right corner, in pencil: two letters "M.Y." (?); a space, then two other letters "N.V." (?); a space and two illegible letters or numbers; then a dash and "39" in what seems a nineteenth-century hand. Finally, near the corner, in a modern hand, "304."

Description: Christ, slightly left of center, in a white robe stands in a frontal position with arms spread wide. He looks down at the kneeling St. Peter who gazes up into Christ's face with arms outstretched, his hands agitated. The other two disciples, James and John (the separate identities indistinguishable) lie asleep on the ground; one diagonally across the lower left corner, one beyond and to the right of Peter. At the extreme left are three deciduous trees, truncated at their tops. At the extreme right is a broken plank fence and in the middle ground, right of center, a large alpine pine tree. The steep Mount of Olives slopes from the upper margin, two inches in from the upper left corner, down to behind the pine tree and meets the right margin below center. A large cumulous cloud fills the right center of the picture behind the pine; another stretches horizontally from the upper right corner, along the upper margin, to within three inches of the mountain.

Condition: Good. Numerous small areas of old foxing stains, spotted generally.

Exhibitions: Forty-five Great Master Drawings and Prints from the 15th to the 20th Centuries, William H. Schab Gallery, New York, 1971, cat. no. 165, p. 164, color illus., color detail on cover.

Collections: Cormier collection, Tours, to 1921. Duc de Trevise, Paris, to 1947. Unknown collector, London, to 1967. [Sotheby's], London, July 6, 1967. [William H. Schab Gallery, New York.]
Foundation Acquisition, AP 71.9.

Notes:

1 J. Byam Shaw, *The Drawings of Domenico Tiepolo,* Boston, 1962, p. 36 ff. and p. 61.

2 Sotheby's, sale catalogue, London, July 6, 1967, lot 40, illus.; ref. to Shaw in note.

3 Hotel Drouot, Duc de Trevise, sale catalogue, Paris, Dec. 8, 1947, lot 36.

4 Galerie Georges Petit, Cormier collection, sale catalogue, Paris, April 30, 1921, lot 40.

François Boucher, 1703–1770
Four Classical Myths on the Theme of Fire
Painted in 1769

Oil on canvas, dimensions (stretcher size) given under individual titles.

With the exception of a very few blessed giants such as Rubens or Raphael, it is difficult to find in the history of art a major painter who was as perfectly attuned to the spirit of his time as François Boucher. His career spanned those very years during which princely patronage of art reached a lavish climax beyond compare. He died just as the worldwide reaction against this prodigal luxuriousness brought on the social, political and economic revolutions that wiped out the *Ancien Régime* forever. As the brothers de Goncourt wrote a century ago, "Boucher was one of those men who indicate the taste of a century, express, personify, embody it. In him, French eighteenth century taste was manifest in all the peculiarity of its character. Boucher was not only its painter but its chief witness, its chief representative, its very type."[1]

He was born with a highly sensual nature, but he also developed a keenly alert, historically sophisticated and analytical intellect, thus embracing that paradoxical range of accomplishments that forces us to think of his age as the epitome of decadent voluptuousness while calling it the Enlightenment, or Age of Reason. The four Kimbell Myths are a perfect synthesis of the manifold elements implied by this paradox. The four separate subjects taken from Greek and Roman mythology seem, at first, to be a whimsical selection from the practically infinite number of possible stories, simply an excuse to exploit this panoply of divine bodies, landscapes and narrative elements in a frivolous, disconnected decorative set of four canvases. Frivolity is indeed the attitude, but only a beginning hint at why the ensemble achieves a supremely unified scheme of sumptuous adornment is reached with the realization that each separate myth depicts one of the sources of fire to mankind. The intricacies of narration and symbolism reveal a profoundly intimate knowledge of classical mythology, in spite of which the artist's exuberantly humorous freedom of interpretation borders upon the outrageous. He is having *fun* with these grandiose allegories that once had the testamentary seriousness of a religion, and the foibles of that religion's gods could still evince the salient characteristics of the age of Louis XV and his mistress Madame de Pompadour. Moreover, those ancient gods, fashioned with mankind's most persistent frailties, still can poke fun grandly at our sensually intoxicated modern age.

This boisterous riot of bodies, draperies, clouds, fire, smoke, foliage, water, and color is disposed in such a deliberately and rationally planned series of compositions that nothing is out of control aesthetically and the whole achieves an incredibly rich orchestral integrity. The metaphorical repetition of shapes, gestures and movements by forms that represent entirely different natural objects bespeaks a masterful command of abstract, expressive composition worthy of a Mozart. But the ability to carry this out required an ingredient beyond deep feeling and judicious rationality; Boucher's technical dexterity and wizardry at manipulating paint is brought to bear so that the smallest detail of physical performance contributes to the swirling, passionate vitality of the whole. The economy and facility of his flowing brush, the precision and spontaneity of his drawing, augment the total effect of exhilaration. And as the de Goncourts so aptly put it, "His forms were modelled by a caress,"[2] thus maintaining that sense of silken luxury and loveliness so dear to Rococo taste. Seldom has so much rich variety born of a fertile imagination been so well ordered and technically controlled to achieve such unity.

Although the individual subjects depicted in the four Kimbell canvases had been treated separately and in other combinations at various times throughout Boucher's earlier career, none of them was ever done in these compositional arrangements; and, in addition to stylistic changes because of evolution in the master's development, none was ever used to serve the common theme of fire. They were originally done as designs for the royal tapestry works of Gobelin where Boucher was in charge, but they were evidently never carried out in that medium, probably because of the death of the artist the year following completion of the paintings and because the chill winds of a new moralizing and classicizing taste had already begun to blow, leading to a slackening activity at the Gobelin, especially upon the death of Louis XV (1774), and its suppression under the beginning revolution. During the nineteenth century the paintings were the principal adornment of the Hôtel de Marcilly, the private residence of the Countess de Marcilly at 3 Rue de Béranger (formerly Rue de Vendôme) in the Marais quarter of Paris.[3]

Juno Inducing Aeolus to Loose the Storm on Aeneas
9 ft. 1 1/2 in. × 6 ft. 7 3/4 in. (228 × 201.5 cm.)

Signature: F. Boucher 1769, on rock, lower right.

This picture, in concert with the one next described, *Venus Securing Arms from Vulcan for Aeneas*, orchestrates a contrapuntal theme derived generally from ancient classical mythology, but more specifically from Virgil's *Aeneid*.[4]

Juno, wife of Jupiter and keeper of heavenly fire, is also the goddess of the hearth, chastity, matrons and marriage. Venus is the goddess of love in its less pure, or undomesticated aspects. The eternal struggle between these two opposing facets of human nature is symbolized in the constant conflict between Juno and Venus. Their rivalry and mutual vindictiveness started when Paris awarded the golden apple, ordained by Jupiter, to Venus, passing over Juno and Athene. It should also be borne in mind that Paris was a Trojan, son of Priam and Hecuba, and was destined to be the "firebrand" who started the Trojan War by stealing Helen. But the gods never battle directly between themselves. Their quint-essential natures are immutable and immortal, and so their stratagems and tactics must be realized on the human level. The mortal pawn in this case is Aeneas, the issue of an illicit love affair between Venus and Anchises of Troy. Aeneas, after fleeing his burning homeland, was destined by Venus to found a new and even greater Troy, Rome; and this is why *Venus Genetrix* was so venerated along the Tiber's banks.

Juno, principal goddess of Carthage, plotting to prevent her rival's son from achieving such grandeur, goes to Aeolus and gives him her most beautiful attendant nymph Deiopea, shown here seated just below Juno who brandishes the heavenly flame, sceptre of her power. In return, Aeolus unleashes all the demons of wind and storm who promptly smash Aeneas' fleet against the African coast where the Trojans' long series of misadventures with Dido begin.[5]

Venus Securing Arms from Vulcan for Aeneas
7 ft. 3 1/2 in. × 6 ft. 8 5/8 in. (222.5 × 205.5 cm.)

Signature: F. Boucher 1769, on heavy wooden rail, lower right.

"An island rises near the Sicanian coast and Lipare, Aeolian land, steep over smoking rocks. Below them roars a cavern, hollow vaults scooped out for forges, where the Cyclops pound on the resounding anvils . . . Here Vulcan dwells,"[6] husband of Venus. The goddess has come, along with three of her seductive attendants, four beguiling *amores* (or *cupidines*) and eight of her symbolic doves, to entreat the master of fire from the bowels of the earth to forge new weapons. Responding to her lovemaking, Vulcan produces such splendid arms that Aeneas wins the war against the Latins and founds Rome.

The Birth of Bacchus
7 ft. 3 1/2 in. × 6 ft. 7 3/8 in. (222.5 × 203 cm.)

Signature: F. Boucher 1769, on large stone below urn at left edge.

In this story taken directly from Ovid,[7] the infant Bacchus has just been delivered by Mercury, shown seated upper center, to Ino and her company of nymphs, with orders from Jupiter to raise him safely in secrecy so that he will come to no harm because of the wrath of Jupiter's wife, Juno. The latter is angry because Bacchus was conceived as the result of Jupiter's illicit seduction of the beautiful nymph Semele, who was also Ino's mother. Semele no longer exists because, when Juno learned that Semele was six months pregnant by Jupiter, Juno tricked the nymph into an irreversible wish for Jupiter's appearance before her once more on earth. Jupiter appeared instantly in the form of a lightning bolt that consumed the mortal nymph who disappeared with the cloud generated by this stroke of celestial fire. Bacchus, however, being divinely sired, was untouched, and so Jupiter plucked him from the cloud and sewed him up in his own body for three more months until he was ripe for delivery. In this rendering of the myth, Jupiter is only symbolized by the large eagle who nestles the fire of lightning beneath himself in the smoke and clouds generated by this awesome power. A cherubic little figure symbolizing love, an *amore* or *cupidine*, flies down above Bacchus as though to crown him with a heavy bunch of ripe grapes. Two other *amores* frolic in the sky above Jupiter's eagle, struggling with a staff tipped with a pine cone and garlanded with grapevine. When Bacchus matured, this staff *(thyrsus)*, plus a crown of vines, became his symbols as the god of wine.

Zephyrus Transporting Psyche
7 ft. 3 in. × 6 ft. 8 $^{5}/_{8}$ in. (221 × 206 cm.)

Signature: F. Boucher 1769, on large rock, lower center.

106 Psyche, the soul, symbolizing the essential animating spirit in all living things as distinct from gross material existence, was so ineffably beautiful that she innocently provoked the jealousy of Venus. The goddess of love therefore dispatched her son Cupid to destroy or disfigure the young princess. Instead, Cupid fell in love with her and arranged to keep her in a secret palace where he visited her only at dark of night, keeping the palace absolutely black so that even his mistress could not know who her lover was. Thus Venus would never discover her son's disobedience. But, with the help of her sisters Psyche procured a lamp, and while Cupid slept she finally saw that her lover was the god of love himself. Cupid vanished, but fell ill because of a drop of oil from the lamp, and his mother discovered his affair. For years the watchful vengeance of the goddess of love forced poor Psyche to live in despondency, performing menial tasks wherever she went, always searching for her lost love. Eventually, distraught to the point of unseeing delirium, she threw herself from a high cliff and plunged into the unknown. But in mid-fall she was gathered up by Zephyrus, the west wind who brings fertile spring, and carried off to be nursed back to health by the nymphs who attend spring's flowers. By now, Jupiter had become aware of Psyche's tribulations. He made her immortal and helped arrange for her union forever in the palace of love with Cupid.[8]

The whole story is an allegory of the progress of the soul guided by love. Boucher has chosen to represent the moment when Zephyrus, accompanied by six jubilant *cupidines,* bears Psyche down onto a flower-strewn meadow where three nymphs are ready to attend her. One exultant *cupidine*

brandishes two torches aflame with the most subtle fire of all, while the palace in the background has already begun to smolder in anticipation.[9] The fusion of the soul with love is the reconciliation of all those paradoxical forces that create conflict.

Condition: Excellent. When the set of pictures was installed in the Hôtel de Marcilly, all four had a curved section of canvas at the center top, plus a small one at center bottom, to make the paintings and their enframements conform to the curvilinear boiserie, or woodwork, of the salon's walls. These curved sections have been lost during reinstallation in different locations in modern times. All canvases have been lined.

Juno and Aeolus has a horizontal join in the canvas, 49 inches from the bottom, a second horizontal join in canvas, 13 inches from the top. An exaggerated crack between butting members of the latter has been filled and inpainted. A horizontal piece, averaging 5 inches in width, at the very bottom, is a modern replacement.

Venus and Vulcan has a vertical join in the canvas, 33 inches from the right edge; old flaking along edges of the join has been filled and inpainted and is slightly discolored. Some old flaking at upper left corner has been inpainted, and there are pressure marks through to the surface from an old toggle, upper third of the picture.

Birth of Bacchus has a vertical join in the canvas, 30 inches from the left edge. An old tear, two inches diagonal, in the sky just above Mercury's left hand, has been repaired and inpainted. There is an approximately one-inch diameter hole and discolored inpaint in Nymph Ino's upper arm and drapery. Exaggerated crackle, once in a state of cleavage, has been put down, around the brass pitcher, lower left center. Pressure marks, irregularly through to the surface, resulted from an old bottom stretcher and upper toggle. The right hand of the forward nymph in the group at right, and the partially seen rear figure, are the only places where an assistant's hand is detectable.

Zephyrus and Psyche has a vertical join in the canvas, 35 inches in from left edge. There are two lap lines caused by uneven application of facing during a lining process, early in the 20th century; one at center, running vertically; a second, horizontal, 35 inches up from bottom edge; this being the only canvas of the four on which this condition exists. Four old diagonal tears, three to five inches long, have been repaired and inpainted along the extreme right edge. There are intermittent pressure marks through to the surface, from an old stretcher, plus two toggles.

Exhibitions: None known.

Collections: Countess de Marcilly, Paris, to before 1891. A Mr. Johnson, specific identity as yet not ascertained, to before 1907. Baron Edmond James Rothschild, Paris, by 1907. Maurice Charles Rothschild, Geneva. Baron Edmond A. M. J. J. de Rothschild, Paris.
Foundation Acquisition, AP 72.7, AP 72.8, AP 72.9, AP 72.10.

Notes:

1 Edmond de Goncourt and Jules de Goncourt, *French 18th Century Painters*, (written between 1856 and 1872), New York, 1948, p. 55.

2 de Goncourt and de Goncourt, p. 65.

3 A. de Champeau, "L'art décoratif dans le vièux Paris, le Marais," *Gazette des Beaux-Arts*, November, 1891, p. 412. See also: Pierre de Nolhac, *Boucher, Premier Peintre du Roi*, Paris, 1907, vol. I, *Zephyrus and Psyche* (as *Boreas and Orithyia*), illus. between pp. 90–91; *Birth of Bacchus*, illus. between pp. 96–97; in 1925 ed., cf. p. 189, illus. facing p. 184.

4 For the Juno and Aeolus story see Virgil, *Aeneid*, "The Landing Near Carthage," book I.

5 There is a beautiful drawing study by Boucher in the Louvre (R. F. 3879) for the sea nymph *(Nereid)*, reclining with her back to the viewer at the bottom of this picture. It is done in pencil and pastel, and was engraved by Jules de Goncourt when it was in the brothers' collection. Later, Edmond de Goncourt published it: *Gazette des Beaux-Arts*, 1896, p. 111. See, P. de Lavallée, *Musée du Louvre, collection de dessins*, vol. XIII, "François Boucher," n. d., no. 4.

6 Virgil, Aeneid, "Aeneus at the Site of Rome," book VIII.

7 Ovid, *The Metamorphoses*, 1st century B.C., book III, "Juno's Rage Against Semele." The de Goncourt brothers took delight in pointing out the "resemblance between these two painters of decadence, between these two masters of sensuality, Ovid and Boucher;" de Goncourt, p. 64.

8 Lucius Apuleius, *Metamorphoses*, or *The Golden Ass*, 2nd century A.D., books IV–VI.

9 An important lifelong influence upon Boucher's interpretation of mythology was also the writings of Jean de La Fontaine (1621–95), author of the world-famous *Fables*. Of especial pertinence to this *Psyche* canvas is: J. de La Fontaine, *Les Amours de Psyche*, Paris, 1669, from which Boucher took much of his feeling of subtle feminine sentiment and sly wit. Also see, Maurice Block, *François Boucher and the Beauvais Tapestries*, New York, 1933, pl. 13.

Jean-Baptiste Greuze, 1725–1805
Prince Sebastian Lubomirski, as a boy
Painted in the 1780s

Oil on panel, 15¾ × 12⅜ in. (40 × 31.4 cm.)

The soft sensuality of this painting is typical of Jean-Baptiste Greuze's portraits of the latter part of his life. It is thought to date from the 1780s,[1] a period when his previously substantial reputation was at a low ebb. His moralistic, rather melodramatic genre paintings, which had been highly extolled by Diderot, were losing vogue with the French public; he had disassociated himself from the Salon exhibitions where Neoclassic themes and modes of expression were growing in favor. Nonetheless, at this time he continued to be favored with small-scale portrait commissions. His long-standing acquaintance with some of the noble families of Imperial Russia then living in Paris was the basis of some of these commissions,[2] including this portrait of *Prince Sebastian Lubomirski* which was ordered by the sitter's father as a present for his wife.[3]

Greuze has presented this young boy with an air of knowing, but not quite sentimental, innocence. The fine, long hair and freely painted ruffles frame his partially shadowed face, concentrating attention on his rosy lips and large dark eyes. The variety of brushstrokes—delicate in the hair, vigorous in the fabric, and nearly smooth in the flesh—provides a lively contrast that is fresh and spontaneous.

Description: Bust-length portrait of a young boy. Seated in a three-quarter pose before a dark brown background with medium grey tones, he leans against a white pillow with a blue and rose print. His rosy-cheeked face is turned towards the viewer and his dark brown eyes confront the viewer directly beneath a mop of soft, light brown hair cut in a short bob. His long-sleeved, white silk shirt with a ruffle at the neckline has light grey shadows; a dark grey sash is around his waist.

Condition: Good. Oil paint is applied with moderate impasto. There is scattered overpaint throughout the hair, garment, chin line and over the ear and the varnish has yellowed and darkened.

Exhibitions: Behold the Child: An Exhibition of Portraits of Children throughout the Centuries, Baltimore Museum of Art, Nov. 7–Dec. 3, 1950, p. 8. *Twenty-One Paintings from the Kimbell Art Foundation*, Fort Worth Art Association, March 3–26, 1953, cat. no. 7, illus.

Collections: Prince Stanislaw Lubomirski, Warsaw; descended to Prince Sebastian Lubomirski (the sitter), Warsaw and Paris; descended to Prince Joseph Lubomirski, France. [Newhouse Galleries, Inc., New York.] Kimbell Bequest, ACK 50.2.

Notes:

1 This date was suggested by Edgar Munhall, Curator, The Frick Collection, New York, who is including this work in his catalogue raisonné of Greuze's paintings, now in preparation.

2 Anita Brookner, "Jean-Baptiste Greuze," *Burlington Magazine*, vol. 98, May–June, 1956, p. 196.

3 Another version on canvas (45 × 40 cm.), perhaps for another member of the family, was formerly in the Ernst Steiner Collection in 1948 and was sold at the Dorotheum, Vienna, Dec. 3–5, 1957, and illus. in *Weltkunst*, Nov. 15, 1957. This information was kindly provided by Mr. Munhall.

Jean-Honoré Fragonard, 1732–1806
The Pond
Painted about 1761–65

Oil on canvas, $25\,{}^{11}/_{16} \times 28\,{}^{3}/_{4}$ in. (65.2 × 73.1 cm.)

The scene depicted in this painting of a pond and sandy path in a wooded meadow with sweeping clouds above is painted in the manner of the seventeenth-century Dutch master Salomon van Ruysdael, but it is distinguished by a lyric grace and sparkle that reveal the facile hand of Jean-Honoré Fragonard. His characteristically light and lively touch is apparent in the fluidly painted women and animals and in the foliage and grasses as well. Although the vegetation is painted with the somber palette of Ruysdael, the beautiful blue of the sky is reminiscent of Fragonard's gardens burdened with roses and filled with lovers playing games. Something of his felicitous sensuality is evident here in the bushy vegetation on the low-lying hillock, lit by dappled sunshine, and the long grasses beneath the dark trees which shimmer in the moist light of summer. A branch projects from the tree at left, flinging its vigorously painted leaves to the sky. The harmony of the figures within this naturalistic setting sustains its mood of rustic tranquillity.

Famous as the painter of love, Fragonard is too often overlooked as one of the great French landscape painters. This neglect is perhaps partly due to the eminent de Goncourt brothers; their favorable evaluation of his work did not include a sympathetic treatment of the realistic landscapes, which they considered mere pastiches.[1] In Fragonard's lifetime, however, these landscapes were greatly admired, sold well, and were often copied and imitated. Their beauty and importance were recognized in 1880 by Fragonard's biographer Baron Portalis when he saw a large number assembled in the Walferdin collection which included the Kimbell painting. It was in that collection, he said, that Fragonard revealed himself as a great landscapist.[2] Today Fragonard is recognized as a precursor of Corot and the Barbizon painters of the nineteenth century in his instinctive appreciation of the poetry of nature and its expression in paintings of harmonious charm.

His first acquaintance with landscape painting doubtless came from his teacher Boucher, who himself copied the rustic scenes of Lowlands painters such as Teniers and Van Ostade, but Fragonard's direct experience of nature came during his years in Italy, from 1756 to 1761. As a student at the French Academy in Rome he was so overwhelmed by the great number of masterpieces to be seen there he lost faith in his own abilities and almost ceased to paint. With the encouragement of the Abbé de Saint-Non, and in the company of Hubert Robert, he began sketching landscapes in and around Rome, an exercise that wakened in him a profound love of nature while it helped restore his equilibrium as a painter. Back in Paris he turned to painting landscapes in the Dutch manner then fashionable, studying among others Hobbema, Wynants and Berghem, as well as Ruysdael. A possible trip to Holland has been conjectured, but seems unlikely. Sufficient numbers of Dutch landscapes were available for him to have studied in Paris, where their intimate views were preferred to the formal constructions of Italian landscape painting.

Fragonard's debt to Ruysdael in the Kimbell painting has been acknowledged since its first sale in 1780; then titled *Landscape Dotted with Trees*, its similarity to a Ruysdael in the collection of a M. Lempereur was remarked upon.[3] In the Walferdin collection, where it was titled *The Pond*,[4] the noted critic William Bürger [E. J. T. Thoré] pointed out its closeness to the manner of Ruysdael and dubbed it *Fishing for Crayfish*.[5] Although it may have figured in the Febvre sale under yet another title, *Pool in a Wood*,[6] Bürger's appellation has been the one most often used by scholars,[7] despite the fact the occupation of the two women is not clear. They may, as has been suggested,[8] simply be doing their laundry. Despite the confusion of titles, it can be said the Kimbell painting has consistently been acknowledged as a distinguished example of Fragonard's realistic landscapes.

Description: Scene of an open wooded field with two women wading in a pond in the foreground and to their right a dog barking at ducks. The woman on the left holds a basket and points across the pond while the woman on the right plunges both arms in the water. On the left of the painting two large trees stand by the pond and on the right a path curves up an embankment. At the far end of the path appear the head and shoulders of a man dressed in a straw hat and blue smock who is disappearing from view. A scattered mass of clouds, grey and white, leads down from the upper right, and dappled light plays over the water and field. Long spiky grasses under the dark umber trees at left are yellow-green and blue-green. The green woodland in the distance encloses the yellow-green meadow. Accents of red and blue appear in the dresses of the women.

Condition: Very good. Minor filling, inpainting and strengthening scattered throughout the painting; possible repair of a crescent-shaped tear in the lower right corner.

Exhibitions: None known.

Collections: Leroy de Senneville, Paris (sale of April 5, 1780, lot 49, not sold) to sale, April 26, 1784, lot 28, sold to M. Quenet, Paris. Anonymous sale, May 2, 1870, lot 13. Anonymous sale, April 27, 1872, lot 6. M. Walferdin, Paris, to sale April 3, 1880, lot 15, sold to [Brame]. A. Febvre, Paris, to sale April 17–20, 1882, lot 109. M. Courtin, Paris. A private American collection by 1925. [Newhouse Galleries, Inc., New York.]
Foundation Acquisition, AP 68.3.

Notes:

1 Jules de Goncourt and Edmond de Goncourt, *L'Art du dix-huitième siècle*, Paris, 1882, vol. II, p. 337: "... ses paysages froids, septentrionaux, ou il n'est qu'un pasticheur adroit, épris d'Hobbema et de Ruysdäel ..." The Kimbell painting is catalogued in vol. III, p. 334.

2 Baron Roger Portalis, "La Collection Walferdin et ses Fragonard," *Gazette des Beaux-Arts*, vol. XXI, 1880, p. 305. Georges Wildenstein, *The Paintings of Fragonard*, trans. by C. W. Chilton and Mrs. A. L. Kitson, Garden City and New York, 1960, p. 41, note 4, points out that it was the Walferdin collection which inspired Portalis to embark on his research on Fragonard.

3 Catalogue of the Leroy de Senneville sale, April 5, 1780, lot 49 *(Paysage touffu d'Arbres)*.

4 M. Walferdin sale, Paris, April 3, 1880, lot 15 *(La Mare)*.

5 See Portalis, *Honoré Fragonard: sa vie et son œuvre*, Paris, 1889, p. 127. Bürger is misquoted by Jacques Wilhelm in "Fragonard as a Painter of Realistic Landscapes," *Art Quarterly*, vol. XI, no. 4, autumn, 1948, p. 303, to the effect that Bürger thought of Wynants rather than Ruysdael.

6 *Étang dans un Bois.*

7 For example, Michel Florisoone, *Le dix-huitième siècle*, Paris, 1948, p. 104. Wilhelm calls it *Crabfishing*, p. 303.

8 Leroy de Senneville sale catalogues, 1780 and 1784, reflected in Wildenstein's preferred title, *The Two Washerwomen*, p. 241, cat. no. 185.

Additional References:

Baron Roger Portalis in ... *Fragonard* ... lists *Étang dans un Bois*, p. 276, *La Mare* and *Paysage touffu d'Arbres*, p. 282, as if they were separate works.
Pierre de Nolhac, *J. H. Fragonard, 1732–1808*, Paris, 1906, p. 138.
Louis Réau, *Fragonard: sa vie et son œuvre*, Brussels, 1956, p. 184.

Hubert Robert, 1733–1808
The Fountain
Painted about 1760–65

Oil on canvas, $44\,{}^{1}/_{2} \times 35\,{}^{1}/_{2}$ in. (113×90.2 cm.)

Although the scene in this painting depicts no actual site, it is quite obviously based on the architecture and setting of villas around Rome that Robert visited on sketching trips in the late 1750s and early 1760s. He had come to Rome in 1754 under the patronage of the Marquis de Marigny and the future Duc de Choiseul and became loosely associated with the French Academy there. Robert and Fragonard, who came to Rome in 1756, seem to have been influential in encouraging their fellow artists to leave their copying of the old masters and go outside to paint the marvels of the Italian countryside. In 1769 they were invited to spend the summer at the Villa d'Este in Tivoli by the art-loving Abbé de Saint-Non, with whom they also traveled the following year. These trips confirmed in Hubert Robert a love for the monumental Renaissance gardens of Italy which by the eighteenth century were frequently in a state of ruin. The appeal of these gardens has been eloquently described: "What increases the charm of the Roman gardens is that venerable impression of the hand of time. Created during the centuries of opulence, with a disposition according to the regular forms of art, the change of fortune and other natural causes have caused their upkeep to be neglected, and nature has in part resumed her rights. Her conquests over art and the intermingling of their efforts produce the most picturesque scenes. This negligence, this antiquity, and this impetuous vegetation compose the most wonderful pictures."[1] Robert seized on these remnants of past greatness with a passion that lasted his whole life; even after his return to France in 1765, one of his favorite painting subjects remained Italian landscapes. Ruins which provoked "ruminations upon irretrievable greatness" were a subject of inexhaustible interest in the eighteenth century. Their dramatic depiction became a new category in landscape painting in Italy, epitomized in the work of Robert's friend and teacher Giovanni Paolo Panini (1691–1765). Unlike those contemporary view painters who faithfully rendered specific locations, Panini often constructed landscapes combining fanciful ruins with actual sites, enlivened by human figures. Such caprices, as they were called, frequently conjured up in the viewers visions of the antique more compelling than those aroused by visits to actual sites.

Robert introduced this conception of landscape to France with imaginative paintings of ruins which owed a great deal to the dramatic talents of G. B. Piranesi, as well as to Panini. So popular did these paintings become, he was dubbed "*Robert des ruines*"; his friend, the artist Madame Vigée-Lebrun, observed, "It was fashionable and very magnificent. . . to have one's salon painted by Robert."[2] His amiable and decorative art, full of sentimentality and gentle fantasy, admirably suited the taste of his wealthy patrons.

In *The Fountain (Le jet d'eau)* the sense of neglect of the secluded terrace is conveyed by the overturned orange tub, the crumbling wall, the withered branch of the ancient tree and the overgrown arches in the background which lend an air of mossy decay. Contributing to the feeling of remoteness is the theatrical composition of the painting, with the villa and garden forming a hazy backdrop for the center stage action which takes place between the proscenium elements of the classical statue at left and the retaining wall at right. At the same time, the hazy atmosphere enveloping the villa and upper garden provides a quiet, melancholy and dreamlike mood. The papal tiara and keys on the wall at right suggest the former splendor of an estate which has now fallen into neglect and disrepair. Within this setting the figures play an important part in establishing the mood of the scene: no stalwart pope nor Renaissance prince is present now, only women and children passing the day. A sentimental note is interjected in the person of a man leaning on a cane who seems, like the garden, to have known better days. In the beautifully painted group of women by the fountain Robert reveals the talent for observation of detail which later made him a master in recording scenes of contemporary life in Paris. The light tonality of this painting is characteristic of Robert's early works and its compositional similarity to a painting dated 1760, *The Stair of the Park at Saint Cloud* in the Roxburghe collection,[3] suggests that *The Fountain* was painted before Robert left Rome in 1765.

Description: View of the sunken terrace of an Italian villa with figures, a large jet of water shooting upward at the left, and the facade of a Renaissance villa on the hill rising behind the terrace. A group of three women and a child standing beside the fountain are approached by a man extending his hat near the steps of the terrace. Behind him, in the immediate foreground, appear rubble, a ladder, and two tubs of orange trees, one overturned. Flanking the steps on the left is a balustrade surmounted at the turn by the statue of a woman and on the right a massive retaining wall with a dark doorway in its base and a gnarled overhanging tree. On the right, a woman and child disappear between two herms into a dark archway of the curved arcade enclosing the terrace. Trees in the garden above its wall closely surround the cream-colored villa in the background. The background, comprising the entire area behind the fountain, is distinguished by an overall blue-grey tonality, and the foreground by a greenish-ochre tonality. The man, leaning on a cane, wears a brown frock coat and the women are dressed in contemporary gowns of soft, dull, pastel colors.

Condition: Very good. There are abrasions along the lower edge and small scattered areas of filling and inpainting throughout. A large L-shaped tear in the center of the painting eight inches from the top has been repaired and inpainted.

Exhibitions: Three French Reigns (Louis XIV, XV, *and* XVI), 25 Park Lane [residence of Sir Philip Sassoon], London, 1933, cat. no. 33, illus. p. 48 *(Le jet d'eau).*

Collections: Duchess of Marlborough (née Consuelo Vanderbilt), later Madame Jacques Balsan, Paris, by 1928, through 1933. Marlborough Spencer Churchill family, to 1969. [Newhouse Galleries, Inc., New York.] Foundation Acquisition, AP 70.15.

Notes:

1 Quoted in Georgina Masson, *Italian Gardens*, London, 1966, p. 191.

2 Quoted in Louis Réau, *Histoire de la peinture française au* XVIIIe *siècle*, Paris and Brussels, 1926, vol. II, p. 49.

3 This painting, which also shows an Italianate wall at the right, water jet, steps with figures, arching tree and a classical statue, is illustrated in *France in the Eighteenth Century*, Royal Academy of Arts, London, winter exhibition, 1968, cat. no. 581, fig. 256.

Marie Louise Elizabeth Vigée-Lebrun, 1755–1842
Self-Portrait
Painted about 1776

Oil on canvas, $25\,^{3}/_{4} \times 22\,^{1}/_{4}$ in. (65.3×50.9 cm.)

Of the nearly twenty self-portraits executed by Marie Louise Elizabeth Vigée-Lebrun throughout her lifetime, this image is perhaps the most significant. The Kimbell portrait is the finest of several known surviving versions; none of the others presents such a deliciously fresh young face and none is done with such an assured yet spontaneous touch. Especially delightful is the artist's easy command of color composition within a palette as restricted in hue as that of Hals or Velasquez, yet possessing a pearly softening of color that is appropriate to the delicately feminine subject and the soft light fabrics. In addition, it is particularly expressive of the serene temper of the age of Louis XVI.

The face is framed within a nearly perfect oval of the dull black hat, so that it stands out, translucent and alive in its richly human complexity of coloring and contour and in its quietly animated expression. The half-parted lips and the candid encounter of the eyes convey a sense of the anticipatory promise of emerging adulthood, which is quixotically counterposed to the full maturity of the assured touch and the expert finish, representing an aesthetic coming-of-age for the young artist.

By the mid-1770s, when this painting must have been done,[1] the young artist, who was at most in her early twenties, was not limited to self-portraiture as a creative outlet or as a source of recognition and livelihood. By this time, she had given some posthumous portraits of French notables to the French Academy, and she had already begun that felicitous outpouring of handsome, sparkling likenesses[2] that capture the essence of aristocratic portraiture of the late eighteenth and early nineteenth centuries.

Inscription: Lower right: *L E Vigee*
Le Brun

Description: Life-size portrait of a girl, in half-length, facing the viewer, body turned three-quarters to her left. She has a pale, almost white complexion, with light pink cheeks and soft coral lips. Her eyes are a hazel green, a hue repeated in the background. Her hair is a dark ash brown, lightly powdered. She wears a dull black hat with a black feather and earrings of crystal (or pearls?) and gold. Her dress is made of a thin, soft white fabric with a bow and sash of soft coral, and a black shawl trimmed with two rows of fine black lace is placed around her arms.

Condition: Very good. The original canvas has been relined. The paint is applied with a low impasto and has developed a minor crackle system with some very slight cupping. The varnish is smooth and clear but rather heavy and has yellowed considerably.

Exhibitions: Twenty-One Paintings from the Kimbell Art Foundation, Fort Worth Art Association, March 3–26, 1953, cat. no. 21, illus. *France in the Eighteenth Century,* Royal Academy of Arts, London, Jan. 6–March 3, 1968, cat. no. 710, Academy of Arts, London, organized by Denys Sutton, Jan. 6–March 3, 1968, cat. no. 710, illus.

Collections: Gustave Muhlbacher, Paris, to sale, Paris, 1907, lot 57, illus. facing p. 44.[3] Baroness Springer-Rothschild, Vienna. Confiscated for the Kunsthistorisches Museum, Vienna, by 1940.[4] Returned to Baron and Baroness Springer-Rothschild, Paris. [Newhouse Galleries, Inc., New York.] Kimbell Bequest, ACK 49.2.

Related Versions: A number of other versions have been recorded, but their exact relation to this painting is not clear. They include a painting which Nolhac[5] identified as a copy of the Kimbell portrait; a painting belonging in 1919 to

L. Levy,[6] and a painting in an oval format belonging in 1940 to Mrs. William R. Timken of New York.[7]

Notes:

1 The only self-portrait definitely associated with this period is that mentioned by Mme. Vigée-Lebrun in her memoirs as having been executed in 1778; this painting, according to André Blum, *Madame Vigée-Lebrun, peintre des grandes dames du* XVIIIe *siécle*, Paris, 1919, p. 95, is associated by him with that belonging in 1909 to the Count of Greffulhe.

2 W. H. Helm, *Vigée-Lebrun: Her Life, Works and Friendships*, London, 1915, pp. 12–14. The Kimbell painting is recorded on p. 206.

3 Pierre de Nolhac, *Madame Vigée-Lebrun, peintre de la reine Marie-Antoinette, 1755–1842*, Paris, 1908, p. 135.

4 *Belvedere*, Jan. 13, 1938–43, vol. 13, p. 179, no. 164, illus.; *Kunsthistorisches Museum Gemäldegalerie Ausstellung der Neuerwerbungen 1940–41*, cat. no. 1988, pl. 13.

5 Nolhac, p. 135.

6 Blum, illus. facing p. 18.

7 Walter Pach, *Catalogue of European and American Paintings 1500–1900, (Masterpieces of Art*, New York World's Fair, May–October, 1940), New York, 1940, p. 154, illus. p. 152.

Marie Louise Elizabeth Vigée-Lebrun, 1755–1842
Comtesse Potocka
Painted in 1790–91

Oil on canvas, 56 × 49 3/4 in. (142.2 × 126.4 cm.)

An appealingly insouciant lady with handsome dark eyes and lips poised as if to smile is seated on a mossy ledge: behind her cascades of water spill down a rocky woodland hillside. The lady is a renowned Polish beauty, the setting is an evocation of the waterfalls at the Tivoli Gardens near Rome, and the artist is the talented, skillful Marie Louise Elizabeth Vigée-Lebrun.

Honored and admired in her native country, where she achieved a high reputation for her portraits of Queen Marie Antoinette and other highborn figures, Vigée-Lebrun left France at the outbreak of the French Revolution. For the next fifteen years she lived in gracious exile, painting the glittering international aristocracy of Europe in the major cities and fashionable spas of Italy, Austria, Germany and Russia. Rome was one of her first stops where she began painting this portrait shortly after her arrival in 1790, finishing it the following year. The sitter was born in 1754 as Anna, Comtesse Cetner, and this well-known portrait of her as Comtesse Potocka[1] was painted while she was visiting Italy just after her marriage to Kajetan, Comte Potocka.

This painting is, however, more than simply a portrait of a beautiful upper-class woman; it is a reassertion in the more favorable environment of Rome of just those qualities of aristocratic portraiture which had distinguished the artist's style in France. In the figure these include a pretty, sensitive face, a natural but well-bred elegance, and a sense of a sweet but lively intelligence. In the execution, there is a suave technique capable of modulation from meticulously precise figure to quickly brushed romantic landscape, assured draftsmanship, and the ability to render plastic form in light and shade and to establish complex rhythmic linear relationships of figures and background.

Repeating forms and contours of the poised woman and wild environment merge in a complex pictorial harmony that is one of Madame Vigée-Lebrun's major achievements as a painter. The right edge of the rocky ledge echoes the outline of the countess' left side and the two banks of hills at the right enlarge upon the forms of head and right arm; other repeating linear elements include the finger-like projections of the plant on the ledge and the pose of her right hand, the foliage to the right of the head and the curly coiffure.

No less notable are the varied textures achieved by subtle techniques. The satiny grey hue of the dress is warmed by the bronze ground showing through it; the skin, done in fine small blended strokes, has a translucent sheen; and the illusion of water running over a rocky course is established by transparent grey and white washes laid over a greenish-brown ground.

Inscription: Lower right: *L E Vigée Le Brun*
a Rome
1791

Description: Three-quarter-length view of a seated lady leaning against a mossy ledge before cascading waterfalls in a hilly, tree-filled landscape. She has blue eyes, pale lips and rosy cheeks; her golden brown hair is caught with a grey bow that matches her satin dress which has thin white ruffles at the sleeves and a gold sash. The dress reflects the vivid scarlet of her gold-trimmed shawl. A thin white scarf edged with gold is tucked into her bosom. The distant hills are painted in grey-green over a subdued sanguine underpaint, while the nearer hills are colored in green, cream, and a golden beige. The sky is the muted coral of early evening and reflects upon the distant reaches of water which is, overall, painted in white and grey over a greenish-brown. Also painted in warm brown and rich green is the rocky ledge on which the figure sits. A large green and brown tree is placed at the left of the figure and continues above her head.

Condition: Very good. The original canvas has been relined. The oil paint is applied with a low impasto and the varnish is very clear.

Exhibitions: Twenty-One Paintings from the Kimbell Art Foundation, Fort Worth Art Association, March 3–26, 1953, cat. no. 20, illus.

Collections: Count Charles Lanckoronski, Palais Lanckoronski, Vienna.[2] [Newhouse Galleries, Inc., New York.]
Kimbell Bequest, ACK 52.1.

Notes:

[1] Pierre de Nolhac, *Madame Vigée-LeBrun, peintre de la reine Marie-Antoinette*, 1755–1842, Paris, 1908, p. 94, illus. p. 91. Lionel Strachy, trans., *Memoirs of Madame Vigée Lebrun*, New York, 1903, pp. 57, 216.

[2] W. H. Helm, *Vigée-Lebrun: Her Life, Works and Friendships*, London, 1915, pp. 111, 216.

Additional References:

André Blum, *Madame Vigée Lebrun, peintre des grandes dames du* XVIIIe *siècle*, Paris, 1919, p. 103.
Louis Hautecœur, *Les Grandes Artistes–Mme. Vigée-Lebrun*, Paris, 1914, pp. 79–80.
Pierre de Nolhac, *Peintres français en Italie*, Paris, 1934, p. 128.

Marie Louise Elizabeth Vigée-Lebrun, 1755–1842
Angelica Catalani
Painted in 1806

Oil on canvas, 48 × 36 in. (122 × 91.4 cm.)

By 1805, Madame Marie Louise Elizabeth Vigée-Lebrun had returned to Paris from a long exile abroad. The mood of the French capital had changed to one of greater sobriety than that prevailing in the years before the French Revolution, when she had become renowned as official portraitist to Queen Marie Antoinette and painter of members of fashionable Parisian society as well as of foreign patrons of high rank. Nevertheless, Madame Lebrun, a gracious hostess and enthusiastic music-lover, resumed her evening *soirées* at which the principal singer was Angelica Catalani (1782–1849), whom she had met immediately upon her return to Paris.[1]

Perhaps inspired during one of these *soirées* by the young and beautiful singer's magnificent soprano voice and her dramatic presence, Madame Lebrun portrayed her friend singing the music from Rossini's opera *Semiramis*, while being accompanied on the piano. Conforming to the vogue for simplicity and severity in portraiture of the period, she placed her model before a modulated, dark background and spotlighted her face to emphasize her shy expression of hesitant anticipation. She sympathetically conveyed the mood of this vivacious and sensitive prima donna who was at the height of her career (having been acclaimed in Venice, London and Paris) when this portrait was painted in 1806 and had just married a dashing captain named Valabreque.[2]

Madame Lebrun regarded this portrait as one of her finest efforts and kept it in her home, hanging next to her portrait of another Italian singer, Madame Grassini, until her death in Paris in 1842.[3]

Inscription: Lower right, on piano:
L.E. Vigée Le Brun
a paris 1806
Lower right, on music book: *Opera Semiramis*

Description: Three-quarter-length portrait of a young woman singing. Standing before a darkly toned grey background, the singer is turned slightly toward her left, with her large, dark brown eyes looking upward. Over an opaque, white underdress, she wears a long, white, Empire-style dress of diaphanous fabric with a low neckline and long sleeves puffed at the shoulders; she wears a gold diadem with coral in her short, dark brown, curly hair. Standing behind a reddish-brown piano which stretches horizontally across the foreground, her right hand is extended in an expressive gesture over the piano. At the far left, some violets rest next to a red shawl embroidered in green which is draped over the edge of the piano. At the far right, a book bound in green leather and sheets of music rest on the piano stand.

Condition: Very good. This painting has been relined, cleaned and revarnished. The paint is applied with a low impasto and has developed a minor crackle system with some cupping. Minor losses, scattered throughout, have been filled and inpainted.

Exhibitions: None known.

Collections: In the artist's possession until her death in 1842. Prince de Talleyrand, Paris, to sale, Paris, 1847, lot 71. Gustave Muhlbacher, Paris, to sale, Paris, 1907, lot 58, illus. facing p. 46. [Julius Böhler], Munich, 1908. Le Comte de Normand, Paris.[4] [Newhouse Galleries, Inc., New York.] Kimbell Bequest, ACF 56.2.

Notes:

1 W. H. Helm, *Vigée-Lebrun: Her Life, Works and Friendships*, London, 1915, pp. 162–63.

2 Biographical information on Madame Catalani was supplied by the vendor.

3 Helm, p. 191.

4 Vendor information.

Additional References:

Souvenirs de Mme. Vigée Le Brun, Paris, n. d., vol. II, p. 374.
Lionel Strachey, trans., *Memoirs of Madame Vigée Lebrun*, New York, 1903, p. 226.
Pierre de Nolhac, *Madame Vigée-Lebrun, peintre de la reine Marie-Antoinette, 1755–1842*, Paris, 1908, p. 140.
André Blum, *Madame Vigée-Lebrun, peintre des grandes dames du XVIIIe siècle*, Paris, 1919, p. 103.

Peter Lely, 1618–1690, and assistants
Richard and Anne Gibson
Painted after 1640, probably about 1650–60

Oil on canvas, 65 1/6×48 1/6 in. (165.2×122.1 cm.)

Richard Gibson (1615–90)[1] is shown in this portrait with his wife, Anne Shepherd (1620–1709); both were dwarfs about 3 feet, 10 inches in height. From their marriage of about 1640 there were nine children, all of normal size, including several who became artists of minor recognition like their father.

Gibson had a varied and successful career as a painter of miniatures. After apparently receiving instruction from Frances Cleyn and Peter Lely he was employed at the court of Charles I (where his wife attended Queen Henrietta Maria), at Wilton House by Philip, fourth Earl of Pembroke, and possibly by Oliver Cromwell. He became drawing master to the daughters of James II and in 1677 accompanied one of them, Mary, to Holland where he lived off and on until 1688. About a dozen surviving works have been attributed to his hand, including a self-portrait related to the Kimbell portrait.

The origin of this painting probably derives from the close association between the Gibsons and the family of the Earl of Pembroke, who awarded an annuity to Richard Gibson that he was still receiving in 1677.[2] Anne Gibson also had close ties; she appears in a portrait of about 1637 with Mary Villiers, a daughter-in-law of the Earl of Pembroke.[3] Moreover, a portrait of the two dwarfs "hand in hand by Sir Peter Lely" was owned by the Earl of Pembroke until it was sold in 1712;[4] this painting has not been identified since then.[5]

Because the Kimbell work has traditionally been regarded as a seventeenth-century replica of the lost Lely painting[6] it is worth noting a possible explanation for the early existence of a replica. Sometime after 1663, Susan, daughter of the fifth Earl of Pembroke, married John, third Baron Poulett,[7] of Hinton St. George, the house from which the present painting is said to come. A replica made then might have had two possible dispositions. It could have been commissioned and sent to Hinton St. George as a sentimental remembrance of the bride's childhood home, or the original painting may have been sent there and a replica hung at Wilton House where it remained until sold in 1712. In any case, it is contended that the only painting known at the present time, the Kimbell work, is an original, albeit uneven, painting of the seventeenth century and not a copy.

The varying quality of different areas of this canvas provides good evidence that it is not merely a perfunctory replica. On the contrary, its marked unevenness suggests that it is a seventeenth-century shop production that reveals the hands of at least two artists. The inferior areas of painting are seen in the landscape setting and the figure of Anne Gibson. The former is not coherently composed and the body of the latter is somewhat flat and in a rather wooden pose. These subordinate areas of the painting are most likely the indifferent work of an uninspired assistant.

The figure of Gibson, however, is the work of a quite competent artist and is sufficiently accomplished to merit the attribution to Lely. Gibson's body is soundly posed and clearly presented through a well conceived and nicely painted system of highlights and shadows on the clothing. The direct gaze, firmly modeled chin and forthright pose

effectively communicate a distinctly proud, self-assured personality. The only discordant note is the rather amorphous, dark area of his neck. A possible explanation of this inconsistency may be found in a drawing, a self-portrait by Gibson that is in the British Museum.[8] Since it was first recorded in the late nineteenth century, this unsigned drawing has been regarded as an unquestioned work from Gibson's own hand. The drawing (of the head only) is of good quality and the view of the face corresponds exactly to that of this painting. The deft draftsmanship, the changed direction of the eyes and the variant hairstyle in the drawing precludes its being a mere copy of the painting. The correspondence of the profile outline, the facial features and, most importantly, the unmodeled shading under the chin strongly suggest that the drawing was the original basis for this portrait.[9]

This association of drawing and painting does not resolve, however, the questions of attribution or date of execution. Instead, it raises new questions: Should the drawing attribution be reconsidered; might it be by Lely? Did Gibson ever paint in oils, and could the work be a self-portrait? Pending further investigation, the proposed date of about 1650–60 is based on the apparent "middle age" of Anne Gibson.

Description: Two full-length figures of a man and a woman (both dwarfs) standing in front of a cliff that dominates a wooded landscape background. Both are turned to their right, with the man facing the viewer directly while the woman looks to her left. His left hand is placed squarely on his hip while his right hand gently grasps her left hand; she delicately holds a single white rose blossom in her right hand. (At the right of her little finger is a second white blossom whose stem is not visible and whose relative position in space is ambiguous.) His long dark hair is painted in tones of burnt umber and his eyes are grey. He wears a cape, painted in alizarin tones, over a red jacket that is secured by four buttons over a white shirt that shows at the neck and wrists. His boots are secured at the mid-calf by jeweled fasteners to red leggings. Her long, loosely curled hair is painted in tones of raw umber and her eyes are brown. She wears a long, loosely fitted gown of lustrous grey material, with a broad low neckline accented by a dark jeweled pin that secures a thin gauze scarf and a russet cloak over her left shoulder.

Condition: Fair. There is considerable inpainting, particularly in a vertical crack ten inches from the left edge, a second crack through the hand and left shoulder of the man, small areas of the faces and along the edges of the canvas. Since 1943 a jutting point on the cliff has been overpainted, increasing the amount of sky and giving the cliff a gentle curve. See: A. C. Cooper photograph of about 1943, negative no. 126756, Huntington Library archives.

Exhibitions: None known.

Collections: Eighth Earl of Pembroke (?). First Earl Poulett, Hinton St. George, Somersetshire.[10] Sir Berkeley Sheffield, Normanby Park, Scunthorpe, Lincolnshire, to sale: [Christie's], London, July 16, 1943, lot no. 76. [Newhouse Galleries, Inc., New York.]
Kimbell Bequest, ACF 44.1.

Notes:

1 See: Graham Reynolds, *English Portrait Miniatures*, London, 1952, pp. 76–82. David Piper, ... *Seventeenth-Century Portraits in the National Portrait Gallery ...* [London], Cambridge, 1963, p. 138. Edward Croft-Murray and Paul Hulton, *The British Museum: Catalogue of British Drawings*, XVI *and* XVII *Centuries*, London, 1960, p. 336–37.

2 Croft-Murray and Hulton, p. 337.

3 Mary Villiers (later Duchess of Richmond) married Charles Herbert (eldest son of the fourth earl) several months before his death in 1634–35. The double portrait,

GIBSON, RICHARD
Self-Portrait, pencil drawing, British Museum, London

attributed to Van Dyck, is known in two versions (at Wilton House and formerly at Newnham Paddox) and is recorded by: Sidney Herbert, Earl of Pembroke, *Catalogue of Paintings at Wilton House*, London, 1968, cat. no. 163, illus.; by Emil Schaeffer, *Van Dyck*, Stuttgart, 1909, pp. 364, 514, and Gustav Glück, *Van Dyck*, London, 1931, pp. 477, 573.

4 Horace Walpole, *Anecdotes of Painting in England*, 3rd ed., London, 1876, vol II, p. 150.

5 R. B. Beckett, *Lely*, London, 1951, p. 46, cat. no. 208.

6 Beckett, p. 46.

7 Peter Townend, ed., *Burke's . . . Peerage . . .*, 105th ed., London, 1970, pp. 2092, 2164.

8 8 7/8 × 7 in., no. 1881-6-11-157, Croft-Murray and Hulton, p. 337, pl. 139.

9 In the drawing, the shaded area not only suggests the neck but also encloses the bottom of the composition, a convention which appears to have been incorporated in the painting without the modification necessary to establish a positive connection between head and torso.

10 A painting of the two dwarfs in the possession of Lord Poulett in 1797 was attributed to Dobson (Musgrave Manuscripts, British Museum, Add. Ms. 6391, vol. 5, folios 175–176v.). Dallaway's notes to the 1826 edition of Walpole's *Anecdotes* refers to the painting at Hinton St. George and attributes it to Lely.

Additional References:

Oliver Millar has kindly shared his opinion that this painting is "an original Lely of the 1650s," letter to David Robb, Dec. 13, 1971.
J. J. Foster, *Samuel Cooper and the English Miniature Painters of the* XVII Century, 1914–16, p. 55.
B. Long, *British Miniaturists*, London, 1929, p. 171.
Robert R. Wark, *Early British Drawings in the Huntington Collection, 1600–1750*, San Marino, Calif., 1969, p. 57.

Attributed to George Beare, active 1744 to 1749
Mrs. Ann Burney (?)
Painted about 1740–50

Oil canvas, 30 × 25 in. (76.2 × 63.5 cm.)

This pleasant portrait of a comely young woman was painted in England at a time when there was a considerable increase in the number of practicing portrait painters. Knowledge of many of these artists is based on a few signed works and limited biographic data which are not always sufficient to establish clearly the evolution of a particular artist's style. Consequently, many competent portraits, including this example, have been misattributed to William Hogarth, the most accomplished English painter of the period. In this unpretentious portrait the forthright paint texture and the intricate arrangement of lace, bows and cuffs suggest that the artist, like Hogarth, favored the painterly tradition of contemporary French artists.

George Beare, a rather obscure artist in this tradition, is proposed as the most likely painter of this portrait. Unlike comparable contemporaries, such as George Knapton (1698–1778) or Joseph Highmore (1692–1780), there is no documentary evidence of Beare's life; his birth and death dates are unknown. The only record of his life is a group of about a dozen signed and dated portraits, dating from 1744 to 1749.[1] These share several characteristics—rather long noses and prominent chins, an emphasis on elaborate details of intensely colored clothing and sitters in erect poses—all evident in this portrait of Mrs. Burney. Her facial shadows are comparable to those of Beare's portrait of *Captain George Brydges Rodney*, dated 1744.[2] Beare's treatment of the fabrics of her dress and her squarely seated, proper posture is similar to that in his portrait of *Peg Woffington (?)*.[3]

The unconfirmed identification of the sitter as Mrs. Ann Burney (which has not been thoroughly investigated) provides no assistance in the attribution, although the style of her dress provides some corroborative evidence. The mode of full sleeves, with laces secured by large bows, is characteristic dress of the 1740s when Beare was active. Perhaps wider knowledge of the portrait through this publication will facilitate further investigation of Beare's work which shows, as Waterhouse remarked, a "friendly directness not unworthy of Hogarth."[4]

Description: Bust-length view in an oval format of a young woman, looking toward the viewer. She has a light complexion, dark blue eyes and rosy lips. Her brown hair is tied in back by a pale blue ribbon, and a white lace cap outlines her head. She wears earrings with three pearl drops and a double-strand choker of pearls. The loosely fitted sleeves of her light rose-colored dress are embellished at the elbows by large bows, from which two ruffles of white lace extend down each forearm. From her shoulders white lace drapes over the bodice to waist-length, secured at the low neckline by a pale blue bow. The background ranges from medium to darker brown at the perimeter.

Condition: Good. There is some inpainting about the edges.

Exhibitions: None known.

Collections: The Burney family, London (?). The Mountbatten collection, London (?). [Newhouse Galleries, Inc., New York.]
Kimbell Bequest, ACK 48.1.

Notes:

[1] Ellis Waterhouse, *Painting in Britain, 1530 to 1790*, 2nd ed., Baltimore and Harmondsworth, England, p. 128.

[2] 36 x 38 in., F. T. Sabin advertisement, *Apollo*, vol. XLV, January, 1969, p. XIV, illus.

[3] 30 x 25 in., undated, [Basil Taylor], *Painting in England, 1700–1850, from the Collection of Mr. and Mrs. Paul Mellon*, Royal Academy of Arts, London, 1964, cat. no. 218, illustration brochure, pl. 11.

[4] Waterhouse, p. 128.

Arthur Devis, 1711–1787
Edward Travers, Esq.
Probably painted in 1751

Oil on canvas, 29 7/8 × 24 7/8 in. (75.8 × 63.2 cm.)

The refreshing charm and graceful naiveté of a distinctive style mark the portraits of Arthur Devis, the most competent and successful of several minor masters of the small-scale, full-length portrait, a popular mode of the mid-eighteenth century. Born in Lancashire and possibly taught painting by Peter Tillemans (1684–1734), Devis enjoyed a considerable vogue from about 1742 to 1764. He specialized in portraits of middle-class owners of small country houses who found the diminutive full-length images appropriate for the moderate size of their rooms.

This painting of Mr. Travers, and its companion portrait of his wife, reveals many of the qualities which pleased Devis' patrons. Perhaps the most distinctive aspect of these portraits, and quite typical of the artist's style, is his fresh and quite personal use of color. The bright highlights and rich colors of the dress bring the figures forward from their paler-toned simple settings. Devis' considerable talent as a draftsman is revealed in the meticulously painted accessories of dress and details of setting. These precise details appealed no doubt to the proprietary interests of his sitters; now they are of great interest to social historians. The carefully tended and simply composed parkland settings, with their evocation of a serene and untrammeled atmosphere, are also characteristic of Devis' portraits. Individualization of character or personality was not one of Devis' major concerns. Instead, he emphasized the comfortable social situation of his sitters through detailed renderings of their correctly fashionable dress and their country estates.

Other than their names, the identity of this couple is not known. It might be presumed their home was near the coast, as a glimpse of the sea may be seen in the distant background of the portrait of Mr. Travers.

Inscription: Lower left: *Art. Devis fe./51*
The numerals are abraded and may originally have read: *1751* or *1761*.

Description: Full-length portrait of a man standing in a country landscape. He faces the viewer with his right leg crossed in front and his right arm resting on an aged tree stump. He holds a three-cornered hat at his hip in his left hand and a walking stick with the other. He wears dark blue breeches and coat, trimmed with gold; a long white satin waistcoat; black shoes with gold buckles, and white stockings. A tall tree behind the figure dominates the background; to the right is a distant view of two church towers and a small patch of ocean with one sail silhouetted on the far horizon. To the left are a winding river, trees and high hills.

Condition: Fair. There is extensive and skillful filling and inpainting of abrasions in the landscape, trees and clothing. A five-inch tear in the upper left corner has been filled and inpainted.

Exhibitions: None known.

Collections: [M. Knoedler & Co., Inc.] New York. Arthur Davis, New York, by 1932. [Newhouse Galleries, Inc., New York.]
Kimbell Bequest, ACF 64.4.

Reference:
Sidney H. Pavière, *The Devis Family of Painters*, Leigh-on-Sea, England, 1950, cat. no. 133, pl. 11.

Arthur Devis, 1711–1787
Mrs. Edward Travers
Painted about 1751

Oil on canvas, 29 3/4 × 24 3/4 in. (75.5 × 62.8 cm.)

This portrait of *Mrs. Edwards Travers* is reasonably presumed to have been painted by Arthur Devis as a contemporary pendant to the portrait of her husband in this collection, even though the present painting is unsigned. The two portraits share a common history and are painted in like styles except that the setting of this portrait of the wife is of somewhat darker tones.

Description: Full-length portrait of a woman standing in a country landscape. She faces the viewer with her left elbow resting on a weathered stone pedestal; her right hand raises the skirt of her lustrous pale blue dress to show the intricately worked edge of a blue petticoat. Sheer white ruffles extend from the elbow-length sleeves and edge the deep neckline which is accented by a blue ribbon bow. Her eyes are brown and a small cap frames her brown hair. In the left background is dark-toned foliage of trees and to the right a distant view of hills, trees, and a small classical building before a lake. The foreground is dominated by three different, meticulously painted, low plants.

Condition: Fair. There is extensive and skillful filling and inpainting of abrasions, particularly in the figure and the sky.

Exhibitions: None known.

Collections: [M. Knoedler & Co., Inc.] New York. Arthur Davis, New York, by 1932. [Newhouse Galleries, Inc., New York.]
Kimbell Bequest, ACF 64.5.

Reference:
Sidney H. Pavière, *The Devis Family of Painters*, Leigh-on-Sea, England, 1950, cat. no. 134, pl. 10.

Attributed to Tilly Kettle, 1735–1786
Mrs. Baldwin (?)
Painted in the late 1760s

Oil on canvas, 30 1/4 × 25 1/4 in. (76.8 × 64.1 cm.)

This attractive portrait of a lady is dated by the style of her dress to the 1760s. The attribution to Tilly Kettle[1] is provisional, however, as the early history of the painting is not clear and Kettle's paintings have not been studied in detail.[2]

Tilly Kettle, a little-known portraitist of the period, is a reasonable candidate as the artist of this painting because it has qualities consistent with his known works of the 1760s. Early in that decade his style derived mainly from the example of Joshua Reynolds, while later he was influenced by the style of Francis Cotes.[3] Not surprisingly, this painting has been attributed to both of these artists.[4] It can be excluded from their oeuvres, however, because of the combination of the relatively high intensity of the color scheme and the sitter's frontal position, looking directly at the viewer. More likely, it is the work of a younger artist searching for a distinctive style, and the oval-shaped head is a distinguishing characteristic of Kettle's portraits of this period.[5] The competent execution, in the fluent brushwork and the simple, triangular composition, suggests that this portrait would date from the late 1760s. At that time Kettle was in his early thirties and working in the Midlands and London, prior to his departure in 1769 for a successful six-year stay in India.

The traditional but unconfirmed, identity of the sitter derives from the portrait's presumed history in the collection of Lord Baldwin of Bewdley. Despite its meager history and uncertain attribution, the work remains a pleasant, unpretentious portrait in an interesting format.

Description: Half-length, frontal view of a seated lady, her arms folded across her waist. Looking directly at the viewer, she wears a loose-fitting cape of embroidered white silk or satin, edged in white lace, which reveals the center bodice of her bright blue dress with two large bows and white lace at the low neckline. Her accessories include a three-strand choker of pearls, matching earrings and an ornament of braided blue ribbon and white fabric which encircles the back of her head. She has alabaster skin, pink lips and her eyes and hair are dark brown. The background is very dark green.

Condition: Good. The canvas has been relined; there is minor strengthening in the face.

Exhibitions: None known.

Collections: Lord Baldwin of Bewdley.[6] Capt. R. O. R. Kenyon-Slaney, to [Sotheby's] sale,[7] London, Dec. 10, 1925, lot 119 (as by Francis Cotes), sold to Agnew. [Newhouse Galleries, Inc., New York.]
Kimbell Bequest, ACF 60.7.

Notes:

1 Suggested by Robert Wark, letter of Aug. 10, 1971.

2 The most recent investigation is J. D. Milner, "Tilly Kettle, 1735–1786," *Walpole Society*, vol. 15, Oxford, 1926–27, pp. 47–103, pl. 13–28.

3 Ellis Waterhouse, *Painting in Britain 1530–1790*, 2nd ed., Harmondsworth, England, and Baltimore, 1962, p. 186.

4 Cotes was shown as the artist when the painting was sold in 1925; it was attributed to Reynolds at the time of its acquisition.

5 Waterhouse, *Painting*, p. 186.

6 Vendor information.

7 Illustrated at time of sale, *Burlington Magazine*, December, 1925, p. 187.

Joshua Reynolds, 1723–1792
Miss Warren (?)
Painted in 1758–59

Oil on canvas, $93\,^{3}/_{4}\times 58\,^{1}/_{4}$ in. (238.1 × 147.8 cm.)

For more than thirty years after his return, in 1753, from his second trip to Italy, Joshua Reynolds was regarded as the most eminent painter in England. His paintings of these years and his *Discourses* (delivered as annual lectures at the Royal Academy) established him as "one of the most impressive minds and most formidable talents of the period."[1] Of the several modes of expression that Reynolds pursued during this period, his large-scale portraits, with their allusions to classical poses, dress and themes, were the most innovative. Their challenging intellectual content was intended by Reynolds "to raise the status of the portrait painter in Britain from that of a 'face painter' to that of a man of learning."[2] The development of this kind of portrait, heroic in concept and impressive in size, may have been stimulated by the inception of public exhibitions of paintings, an innovation which Reynolds encouraged and aided. These annual events provided English artists with their first institutional opportunities for exhibiting their paintings publicly. Reynolds saw them also as a means of public instruction in the fine arts and created the mode now referred to as the "grand manner style" to carry out his intent.

Painted six years after Reynolds' return from Italy,[3] this portrait is one of the earliest feminine full-length portraits in which most of the elements of the grand manner style can be seen. The languid pose echoes the "classic" forms of the Bolognese painters that Reynolds had admired. The long, loosely fitted gown alludes to a general concept of classical dress. The impassive facial expression of this statuesque woman imputes an atmosphere of dignified reserve. The cumulative effect is the public presentation of an idealistic, almost moralistic, point of view rather than an incisive characterization of a specific personality. Among the more than thirty full-length feminine portraits that Reynolds painted in this mode, only one other may predate the Kimbell work,[4] and another of quite similar composition was included in the first exhibition of the Society of Artists in 1760.[5] The restrained simplicity and absence of specific allusion in these portraits of the late 1750s contrast with the richness and complexity of his subsequent grand manner expressions, such as the painting in the 1765 Society of Artists exhibition, *Lady Bunbury Sacrificing to the Graces*,[6] which is replete with precise classical allusions and many levels of intellectual reference.[7]

The identity of the sitter and the history of the Kimbell portrait are not clear. The earliest published record of it, Frederick Bromely's mezzotint of the early 1860s, identifies the sitter as Lady Frances Warren and the owner of the painting as Sir Richard Bulkeley Williams-Bulkeley.[8] If correct, this painting represents Frances Bisshopp about four years before her marriage on February 4, 1764, as the second wife of Sir George Warren of Poynton, Cheshire.[9] On the other hand, the sitter has been variously identified as Viscountess of Bulkeley[10] and also as Miss Warren, sister of Sir George Warren.[11] Pending further investigation, the latter identity seems the most plausible and the least illogical.[12] Furthermore, it can be reasonably associated with sittings for a "Miss Warren" that Reynolds recorded in his sitter books in January, 1758, and May, 1759,[13] dates that correspond with the painting's inscribed date of 1759.

Inscription: On pedestal: *Reynolds pin/1759*

Description: Standing, full-length figure wearing a long blue gown with pink sash, white undersleeves and gold trimming at the deep neckline, on the sleeves and hemline. Her upswept hair is black and her slippers gold. Her right elbow rests on an ermine cape with rose-colored lining, draped on a pedestal which supports a large vase. The pastoral setting includes a large tree with foliage behind the pedestal on the left, a rolling lawn, trees and running brook in the lower right of the picture. The sky, ranging from white clouds at the horizon to deep blue above, is dominated by dark grey storm clouds.

Condition: Good. There is some overpaint in flesh tones of the head, bosom and her left arm and in dark areas on both sides of figure. A three-inch, C-shaped tear in the upper left quarter has been filled and inpainted.

Exhibitions: None known.

Collections: Sir George Warren, K. B., Poynton, Cheshire (?). Sir Richard Bulkeley Williams-Bulkeley, Beaumaris, Anglesey, by 1862, descended to Sir Richard Henry Williams-Bulkeley, until sale: [Christie's], London, April 28, 1922, lot 43, illus. William Randolph Hearst, New York, until sale: [Parke-Bernet], New York, Jan. 5–7, 1939. [Newhouse Galleries, Inc., New York.]
Kimbell Bequest, ACF 61.2.

Notes:

1 Frederick Cummings, *Romantic Art in Britain . . .*, Detroit Institute of Art and Philadelphia Museum of Art, 1968, p. 38.

2 Cummings, p. 40.

3 Ellis K. Waterhouse, *Reynolds*, London, 1941, p. 44, who dates the painting in 1758.

4 *Anne, Duchess of Grafton*, 236 × 146 cm., Duke of Grafton, Euston Hall; dated 1757–59 by Waterhouse, p. 43.

[5] *Elizabeth, Duchess of Hamilton*, 236 × 146 cm., Lady Lever Art Gallery, Port Sunlight, England; dated 1758–60 by Waterhouse, p. 45, pl. 67.

[6] 96 × 60 in., Art Institute of Chicago; Waterhouse, pl. 101.

[7] Cummings, p. 40.

[8] Freeman O'Donoghue, *Engraved British Portraits . . . in the British Museum*, London, 1914, vol. 4, p. 406, and published in the portfolio: R. E. Graves, *Engravings from the Works of Sir Joshua Reynolds, P. R. A.*, London, [1865].

[9] Algernon Graves and William Cronin, *A History of the Works of Sir Joshua Reynolds*, London, 1899–1901, vol. III, p. 1031. This source is not always reliable, however; this painting is associated by these authors with a June, 1757, sitter book listing for a Miss Bisshopp that is more logically related to another portrait, *Miss Catherine Bisshopp*. See: Graves and Cronin, vol. I, p. 48, and Waterhouse, p. 42.

[10] Walter Armstrong, *Sir Joshua Reynolds*, London, 1900, pp. 196, 235.

[11] Suggested by Algernon Graves; see: Armstrong, p. 235.

[12] In 1758 Reynolds did a full-length portrait of Sir George Warren's first wife, Lady Jane (Revell) Warren, who died in 1761. It seems possible that the identity of the sitter in this portrait may have become confused with that of the Kimbell painting, as both works share a common history from the early 1860s until sold at the Williams-Bulkeley sale April 28, 1922, lots 43 and 44. See: O'Donoghue, vol. 4, p. 406; Armstrong, pp. 196, 235, and Waterhouse, p. 44.

[13] C. R. Leslie and Tom Taylor, *Life and Times of Sir Joshua Reynolds*, London, 1865, vol. I, pp. 161, 177.

Joshua Reynolds, 1723–1792
Miss Charlotte Fish
Painted in 1761

Oil on canvas, 50×39 3/4 in. (127×101 cm.)

The commissioned portraits that Reynolds painted in his domestic mode contrast markedly to his heroic full-length portraits with their intellectual allusions and melodramatic poses. Characteristically smaller in size and informally posed, these private portraits are intimate in mood and dominated by distinct characterizations of the sitters.

Miss Charlotte Fish is typical of these portraits and clearly demonstrates Reynolds' advancement beyond the more sedate portraits of his teacher, Thomas Hudson, and his contemporaries such as Allen Ramsey. The strong presence of a definite personality is evoked by skillfully employed devices. The sitter's pose, almost but not quite demure, enlivens the portrait; she leans forward slightly with her arms in her lap in a relaxed attitude that naturally engages the viewer's attention. A charming look of amused inquiry is created by her direct glance and the hint of a smile. Her friendly attitude is emphasized by the varying pattern of casually arranged folds in the soft fabric of her dress. This intimate atmosphere is further enhanced by the warm colors of the creamy blue sky, the strawberry pink gown, and the pearly grey overskirt. Her enigmatic smile adds a piquant note to a mood of gracious informality.

The date of this portrait and the identity of Miss Fish can be positively confirmed, although there is little known of her life. It was painted in September, 1761, according to appointments recorded by Reynolds in his sitter book for a "Miss Charlotte Fish,"[1] and it dates from the early 1760s, one of the most prolific periods in Reynolds' career.[2] The sitter is explicitly identified by the inscription on a mezzotint made of the portrait in 1770 by James Watson.[3] This mezzotint also suggests that Reynolds considered the portrait one of his more successful efforts; such prints were usually commissioned by the artist to be made of his best paintings and then distributed through print-sellers as inexpensive advertisements.[4] The subsequent history of the painting provides further evidence of its quality: it was included in major Reynolds exhibitions of 1883 and 1937.

Description: Three-quarter-length view of a seated woman. She looks directly at the viewer and her arms are crossed in her lap. Her eyes are hazel and her hair is dark brown. A pearl choker encircles her neck, and she wears a black shawl over her shoulders. Her strawberry pink dress is embellished by elaborate lace cuffs and a white apron panel of tufted gauze fabric. A large tree at the right and a smaller one at the left, with foliage of warm browns and greens and scattered pink blossoms, frame a blue sky with puffy white clouds.

Condition: Good. Although areas of old, incompletely removed varnish have yellowed moderately and there is some inpainting of details in the face and hands, the painting is in sound condition for a Reynolds portrait of this period.

Exhibitions: Sir Joshua Reynolds, Grosvenor Galleries, London, 1883–84, cat. no. 49. Burlington Fine Arts Club, London, 1905, cat. no. 39. *Sir Joshua Reynolds*, 45 Park Lane, London, 1937, cat. no. 13, pl. 21. *Twenty-One Paintings from the Kimbell Art Foundation*, Fort Worth Art Association, March 3–26, 1953, cat. no. 16, illus.

Collections: Samuel Addington,[5] sold by 1883 to: Henry Louis Bischoffsheim, London, until [Christie's] sale, London, May 7, 1926, lot 81. Lady Fitzgerald (daughter of H. L. Bischoffsheim) by 1937, descended about 1947 to: Sir John Fitzgerald, until [Christie's] sale, June 23, 1950, lot 52. [Newhouse Galleries, Inc., New York.]
Kimbell Bequest, ACF 50.5.

Joshua Reynolds, 1723–1792
Miss Anna Ward with her Dog
Painted in 1787

Oil on canvas, 55 3/4 × 44 3/4 in. (141.6 × 113.7 cm.)

The increase in number of children's portraits is an intriguing and exceptional aspect of late eighteenth-century English painting. Reflecting changes in attitudes that are also evident in literary and social history,[1] these portraits are visual evidence of the evolving concept of childhood as a separate period in life, distinct from infancy and adulthood. A mode of expression in which the emphasis varies widely from beguiling innocence to trenchant self-awareness, children's portraits became an important category of painting for Joshua Reynolds; many of his most significant later works include children as a major motif.

Painted in March, 1787,[2] two years before Reynolds lost his sight, this portrait of Anna Ward was one of thirteen paintings that he exhibited in the Royal Academy exhibition of 1787.[3] It shows a young girl nestled on the ground in an unusual attitude between a rock and a tree, extending her left arm behind the head of a large dog while resting her right arm on the rock. The dog returns her affectionate gesture, with a friendly paw extended on her lap. Unlike more sentimental or ebullient expositions on the relation between a child and his pet, a pensive mood prevails. The child's serious expression and her direct look toward the dog contribute significantly to this restrained mood, a characteristic which this portrait shares with a number of other children's portraits that Reynolds painted in the 1780s.

The unusual status of the girl in this painting might have influenced Reynolds' restrained approach to this portrait. Anna Ward (1779 [?]–1837) was about eight years of age at the time it was

Notes:

1 C. R. Leslie and T. Taylor, *Life and Times of Sir Joshua Reynolds*, London, 1865, vol. I, p. 202, illus.

2 E. K. Waterhouse, *Reynolds*, London, 1941, pp. 11–12, 49.

3 Freeman O'Donoghue, ... *Engraved British Portraits* ... *in the British Museum*, London, 1910, vol. II, p. 213. Walter Armstrong, *Sir Joshua Reynolds*, London, 1900, p. 205.

4 Waterhouse, p. 10.

5 Algernon Graves and William V. Cronin, *A History of the Works of Sir Joshua Reynolds*, London, 1899, vol. I, p. 304, illus. These authors apparently confuse this portrait with one of *Miss Kitty Fisher* that Reynolds noted was to be sent to "the Secretary of the Dutch Embassy." See: Leslie and Taylor, vol. I, p. 202.

Additional Reference:

Walter Armstrong, *Sir Joshua Reynolds*, London, 1900, p. 205.

painted[4] and apparently the illegitimate daughter of John, second Viscount Dudley and Ward, and Mrs. Mary Baker, whom Lord Dudley married on July 15, 1788[5], more than a year after this portrait was painted. The commission of the portrait[6] and its subsequent public exhibition suggest that Lord Dudley had strong affection for his only child, and it was noted in 1790, two years after Lord Dudley's death, that the Viscountess Dudley "prevailed on herself to pay the residue of the price" for the painting.[7] Later, the painting was owned by the sitter and remained in her family until the death of her son at the end of the nineteenth century.

A distinctive feature of this portrait, the unusual pose of the sitter, may be an echo of Reynolds' interest in Italian painting. Although at first glance the young girl appears to lean back languidly against the tree, her body is not relaxed but twisted in a complex *contraposto*. Her legs are bent and curled beneath her skirt while her body twists to lean against the rock. Her right arm is shown in an awkward foreshortened attitude as it wraps about the rock, while the left arm extends to an abnormal length behind the head of the dog. This complex anatomical arrangement may constitute Reynolds' adaptation of the typically exaggerated gestures of seventeenth-century Mannerist painting. The absence of an identifiable prototype suggests that Reynolds may have evolved a unique attitude derived from a combination of antecedents.

Description: Full-length figure of a girl with long brown hair and dark eyes seated on the ground by a tree trunk. Her right forearm rests on a large grey rock; her left arm is extended behind the head of a brown-haired dog. She wears a pink dress with a white overskirt and a wide-brimmed white hat trimmed with white feathers. The foreground is freely painted in pale brown tones; the background is dominated by large white clouds in a dark blue sky.

Condition: Fair. Uneven drying rates of the different mediums used by Reynolds have caused considerable and widespread separations that have been filled and inpainted. Some overpaint is evident in the flesh tones.

Exhibitions: Royal Academy, London, 1787, cat. no. 33, *(Portrait of a Child with a Dog). Twenty-One Paintings from the Kimbell Art Foundation*, Fort Worth Art Association, March 3–26, 1953, cat. no. 15, illus.

Collections: Commissioned in 1787 by John, second Viscount Dudley and Ward and seventh Baron Ward. Partially paid for by Viscountess Dudley in 1790. With the sitter until her death in 1837, it passed to her husband, Horace David Cholwell St. Paul (1775–1840), and then to her son, Sir Horace St. Paul of Ewart Park, Northumberland, until 1891. T. H. Woods, London. Asher Wertheimer, London. Baron Nathaniel de Rothschild, by 1902.[8] [Newhouse Galleries, Inc., New York.]
Kimbell Bequest, ACF 48.3.

Notes:

1 William Blake's *Songs of Innocence* (1789) and William Wordsworth's *The Prelude* (1806) exemplify the literary parallels. The change in clothing worn by children is equally revealing: until about 1770 they are dressed as miniature adults; subsequently they wear distinctive attire different from that of infants and adults. See: Peter Quennell, "The Cult of Youth," *Romantic England, Writing and Painting*, 1717–1851, London, 1970, pp. 49–58.

2 In his sitter book for March, 1787, Reynolds made entries for "Miss Ward and her dog." See: C. R. Leslie and T. Taylor, ... *Sir Joshua Reynolds* ..., London, 1865, vol. II, p. 512.

3 Ellis Waterhouse, *Reynolds*, London, 1941, p. 78. Six of the thirteen paintings involved children. See: Waterhouse, pls. 272, 277, 284, 278, and 279.

4 Her birth date is not certain. She married Horace David Cholwell St. Paul in 1803 and died, at the age of 58, Jan. 26, 1837, leaving a son and five daughters.

5 Her father (born Feb. 22, 1724/25) was a member of Parliament from 1754 to 1774; he died on Oct. 10, 1788. His widow (and her presumed mother) married twice more before her death in 1810. See: Vicary Gibbs, ed., *The Complete Peerage*, 1916, vol. IV, p. 488.

6 Algernon Graves and William Cronin, ... *Sir Joshua Reynolds*, London, 1899–1901, vol. III, p. 1030, indicate that Lord Dudley paid £52 10s in February, 1787, for the portrait and that a final payment of £52 10s was made in April, 1790.

7 From "a newspaper, 1790," quoted by Graves and Cronin, p. 1030.

8 *The Connoisseur*, vol. II, January, 1902, pp. 39–40, illus.

Additional Reference:

Walter Armstrong, *Sir Joshua Reynolds*, 1900, p. 235.

Thomas Gainsborough, 1727–1788
Miss Lloyd (?)
Painted about 1750[1]

Oil on canvas, 27 3/8 × 20 7/8 in. (69.6 × 53 cm.)

During the ten years Thomas Gainsborough lived as a young man in Suffolk County, he frequently painted small, full-length portraits of figures in landscape settings. Although not as deftly composed as his later portraits of the gentry of Bath and London, these early works are distinguished by strong coloring and informally posed sitters which give them a freshness and charm that contrasts with the formal elegance of his later landscapes and portraits. These early portraits reveal Gainsborough's familiarity with seventeenth-century Dutch landscapes, French rococo design, and English "conversation pieces," particularly those of Francis Hayman. While the figures in these portraits, as Ellis Waterhouse notes, are occasionally somewhat gauche, his facile treatment of foliage and foreground details reveals his early predisposition for landscape, rather than portrait painting.

Although Gainsborough is thought to have made preparatory drawings for most of his portraits at this time in his career, relatively few are known to have survived. However, three preliminary drawings for the Kimbell portrait have been identified. These rapidly executed pencil sketches, now in the Morgan Library, clearly show the evolution of Gainsborough's ideas for the portrait from an initial summary outline of the figure with several lightly indicated trees,[2] through a second version with a varied disposition of the pedestal and tree trunks,[3] to the third version in which the background motifs are adjusted to positions similar to those in the painting.[4] Gainsborough's positive interest in establishing the appropriate landscape setting is evident in the varying disposition of

GAINSBOROUGH, THOMAS
Miss Lloyd (?), three pencil drawings for the Kimbell painting. The Pierpont Morgan Library, New York

foliage and architectural elements; in contrast, the summary outline of the figure is similar in all three drawings and the pannier at the right remains a slightly obtrusive compositional motif in the painting.

Precise dating of paintings and firm identification of sitters in Gainsborough's Suffolk period are often difficult. He dated very few of his paintings at this time and the identities of many of his sitters, including "Miss Lloyd," are obscure because they were rarely titled gentry whose lives are known through published documents. However, the distinctive stylistic qualities of *Miss Lloyd (?)* allow it to be reasonably associated with a group of Suffolk period portraits that date about 1750–55.

The Kimbell portrait is most closely related to Gainsborough's *Girl Seated with a Book in a Park*, which has been dated variously from 1750 to the mid-1750s.[5] The two paintings are almost the same size and format; brushstrokes and paint handling are quite similar, particularly in the foliage and foreground details. The architectural elements of classical urns, fountains, and statues in the backgrounds are treated in like styles. Moreover, the sitters' dispositions in woodland landscapes are nearly mirror images of each other.[6]

The earliest published record of the Kimbell painting identifies the sitter only as a "Miss Lloyd"[7] and suggests that it is a later portrait of the unidentified girl in Gainsborough's painting, *Heneage Lloyd and his Sister*, dated 1750–55, now in the Fitzwilliam Museum, Cambridge.[8] The girl appears to be about ten or eleven years of age in the Fitzwilliam painting, and the sitter in the Kimbell portrait appears to be at least seventeen. Since the styles of the two paintings are closer in date than the difference in ages would allow, the identity of the girl in the Kimbell painting is not certain.

Description: Full-length view of a young woman with brown hair, dark eyes, rosy cheeks and lips. Seated against a large tree in a wooded landscape, she faces the viewer with her body turned to her left. Her blue gown is accented by flowing white chemise sleeves and a loose white tucker on the bodice. The open-front skirt reveals a pink petticoat overlaid with transparent fabric. Her head is framed by a small white cap topped with a pink bow; a wide-brimmed hat of natural straw with pink tie ribbons lies in her lap. She wears white stockings and black, buckled slippers. Behind a detached blue pannier at her left is a paneled base supporting a large urn. Six trees with dense, olive green foliage (which almost obscures the urn) comprise the background.

Condition: Fair. It is thinly painted on an opaque light reddish-grey ground. Until cleaned in 1970 there was extensive overpaint in abraded areas, including the folds of the skirt and the trunk of the largest tree. The canvas is trimmed of the tacking edge and mounted on a relining. A small loss, 3 × 2 in., in the foliage between the left edge and the tree trunk, has been filled and inpainted. The face and upper torso bear minor inpainting. Two unusual meandering brushstrokes (most apparent on the urn) are worked in the ground; these may represent the artist's initial outlines of foliage.

Exhibitions: Paintings and Drawings by Thomas Gainsborough, Cincinnati Art Museum, May 1–31, 1931, cat. no. 34. *Selections from Fort Worth Collections*, Fort Worth Art Center, May, 1963.

Collections: Sir William Knighton (who died in 1837), Horndean, Hampshire.[9] W. M. de Zoate (Dezoete?), Layer Breton, Kelvedon, Essex.[10] [Scott and Fowles], New York, by 1931, to sale: [Parke-Bernet], March 28, 1946, lot 84. [Newhouse Galleries, Inc., New York.]
Kimbell Bequest, ACF 46.4.

Notes:

1 Suggested by Robert Wark, November, 1970, and by Ellis Waterhouse, *Gainsborough*, London, 1958, cat. no. 455. John Hayes, *The Drawings of Thomas Gainsborough*, London, 1970, p. 111, pl. 313, dates the painting in the "later 1740s."

2 18.7 × 14.9 cm., Pierpont Morgan Library, New York, no. III-46-c. Hayes, cat. no. 5, pl. 309.

3 18.7 × 14.9 cm., Pierpont Morgan Library no. III-46-a. Mary Woodall, *Gainsborough's Landscape Drawings*, London, 1939, cat. no. 463, pl. 25; Hayes, cat. no. 6, pl. 310.

4 18.7 × 14.3 cm., Pierpont Morgan Library no. III-46-b. Woodall, cat. no. 462, pl. 24; Hayes, cat. no. 7, pl. 311.

5 28 1/2 × 25 1/2 in., Paul Mellon, Upperville, Va. [Basil Taylor], *Painting in England, 1700–1850, from the Collection of Mr. and Mrs. Paul Mellon*, Royal Academy of Arts, London, 1964, cat. no. 226, dates the painting ca. 1750 (Illustration Souvenir, pl. 25). Waterhouse, cat. no. 754, dates the painting in the middle 1750s and regards it as the companion to Gainsborough's portrait of an unidentified man and wife, 29 1/4 × 25 1/4 in., at Dulwich College.

6 Because of this similarity, Woodall, pp. 31, 35 and pls. 22, 23, suggests that the same sitter appears in both paintings; a more reasonable explanation is that the paintings are merely compositional variants of about the same date.

7 Walter H. Siple, Preface, *Paintings and Drawings by Thomas Gainsborough*, Cincinnati Art Museum, May 1–31, 1931, p. 13 and cat. no. 34, pl. 3.

8 25 1/4 × 31 7/8 in., Carl Winter, *The Fitzwilliam Museum*, Cambridge, 1958, cat. no. 86, who notes that while the style is "nearer 1750," Heneage Lloyd was born 1743–44 and appears to be 11 or 12 years of age in the painting, making an approximate date of 1755 equally plausible. Woodall, p. 31, thinks the same sitter is in the Mellon, Fitzwilliam, and Kimbell paintings. Waterhouse, cat. no. 452, dates the painting about 1750.

9 Handwritten label on back of painting.

10 Cincinnati Art Museum, ... *Gainsborough*, 1931, cat. no. 34.

Thomas Gainsborough, 1727–1788
Suffolk Landscape
Painted in the mid-1750s

Oil on canvas, 24 1/4×29 in. (61.6×73.7 cm.)

As a young man, Thomas Gainsborough spent about ten years in Suffolk County before moving across England to Bath in 1759. In his landscapes of this period he explored themes and developed stylistic conventions that he was to use the rest of his life. A number of these paintings, and possibly *Suffolk Landscape*, were painted as chimney piece decorations for houses in Suffolk. Ellis Waterhouse describes these landscapes as "little anthologies of motives observed from life, put together in a landscape composed according to ornamental rules."[1]

This is certainly true of *Suffolk Landscape* with its sympathetically observed travelers set in a bucolic, but slightly artificial, landscape. The setting probably represents no specific place in Suffolk but is more likely derived from the general character of its well forested, rolling hills.

To this setting Gainsborough introduced an anecdotal motif, some travelers pausing on a country road. A tired mother nurses her child while her husband and their dog wait patiently at her side. Their fatigue is complemented by the somnolent donkeys and the aged trees. A deliberately structured composition accents these elements. One axis, formed by the pair of trees at left and the grove at the right, is crossed by a second diagonal axis that is defined by the travelers, the three donkeys, and the distant tower. In the generally even-toned setting, contrasting textures and patterns of lights and darks further emphasize the elements of these diagonals. The figures are set against a lightly colored area of the road, while the thinly-painted donkeys are nearly the same value as the bushes behind, and the tower is silhouetted against the sky. The dark, scudding clouds add a dramatic note to the bucolic mood.

As few of Gainsborough's paintings of this period are firmly dated, and only the recent history of this painting is known, stylistic comparisons are the major criteria for dating *Suffolk Landscape* about 1755.[2] Narrative treatment of small genre figures in a landscape of subdued tones is characteristic of Gainsborough's landscapes of the mid-1750s. The style of *Suffolk Landscape* is close to that of the pair of chimney pieces Gainsborough painted by May of 1755 for the Duke of Bedford[3] and the landscape in St. Louis, dated in the mid-1750s by Waterhouse.[4] It shares with these paintings, and a landscape in Montreal,[5] the motif of gnarled trees contrasted to trees with thick foliage. Gainsborough's earlier landscapes are distinguished by stronger color contrasts and more precise brushwork. By the late 1750s, contrasts of textures, motifs, and colors are less marked and variations in tone are smoother than in *Suffolk Landscape* and other paintings of the mid-1750s.

Inscription: Lower right, on end of log: TG

Description: Country landscape of brown and dark green tones. At the edge of a rutted dirt road, a woman rests, nursing her white-capped baby. Standing before them is a man lighting a clay pipe and carrying a knapsack over his shoulder. He wears a brown hat, jacket and leggings and a soiled red vest, and a small brown dog stands beside him. In the center of the painting are three donkeys on a small hill and two figures (barely visible), one walking down the road behind the hill and the other leaning on a wooden gate to the right. Dominating the left foreground are two gnarled tree trunks having branches with sparse leaves at the top. A distant tower punctuates the low horizon. To the right, a cottage roof is visible in the midst of a grove of trees. Dark clouds dominate the wide expanse of sky which is light blue at the right and creamy white above the horizon to the left.

Condition: Good. Two small tears, one in the upper right corner and the other above the gnarled trees, have been filled and inpainted. There are scattered fills and inpaint throughout the picture and some strengthening in the left foreground, on the dog and the roof of the cottage.

Exhibition: Wadsworth Atheneum, Hartford, Conn., (unconfirmed), after 1929.

Collections: F. E. Hills, Redleaf, to auction by Knight, Frank and Rutley, June 27, 1929, lot 23.[6] [Leggatt Brothers], London. [Scott and Fowles], New York. Private collection, eastern United States. [Newhouse Galleries, Inc., New York.]
Kimbell Bequest, ACF 42.2.

Notes:

1 Ellis Waterhouse, *Thomas Gainsborough*, London, 1958, p. 18.

2 Waterhouse, p. 109, lists the painting as cat. no. 848 *(Two Peasants with a Dog on a Sandy Road)* and dates it "probably 1750/55."

3 *Peasant with two Horses* ... and *Woodcutter Courting a Milkmaid*, Duke of Bedford, Woburn Abbey, Waterhouse, cat. nos. 833, 829, pls. 39, 41.

4 *River, with Horse Drinking, Lovers*, City Art Museum, St. Louis, 37 1/4 × 49 1/2 in., Waterhouse, cat. no. 834, pl. 47.

5 *Rustic Courtship (Milking Time)*, Museum of Fine Arts, Montreal, 29 × 47 1/2 in., Waterhouse, cat. no. 844, pl. 40.

6 Waterhouse, p. 109. Vendor information shows this owner as: "J. E. Hills, Readleave, Penshurst, Kent, England."

Additional Reference:

John Hayes, "Landscape with Woodcutter," article to be published by the Museum of Fine Arts, Houston, fig. 2.

Thomas Gainsborough, 1727–1788
Viscountess Harriet Tracy
Painted about 1760–65

Oil on canvas, 49 3/4 × 39 7/8 in. (126.3 × 100.7 cm.)

The portraits that Thomas Gainsborough painted while living in Bath from 1759 to 1774 show a marked change of style. Those of his early years in Bath, of which this portrait of Viscountess Tracy is a good example, are marked by a somber mood evoked by a combination of dark, muted backgrounds and deeply toned fabrics. In consequence, there is an emphasis on the figure which appears solid and thrust forward from the background.[1] It has been suggested that this change of style was Gainsborough's response to his greater familiarity with portraits by Van Dyck that he saw in the houses of his West Country patrons.[2] Striving for Van Dyck's elegance, Gainsborough adapted his own more informal style and evolved a portrait mode which depends on a carefully balanced narrow range of tones and a controlled rhythm of lines. Compared to the earlier, more brightly toned portraits of his Suffolk period and the more freely painted portraits after about 1765, these works are less beguiling. However, within these self-imposed limits Gainsborough mastered the technique of painting reflected highlights with a facility that is particularly evident in the rich pattern of blues and whites in the folds of Viscountess Tracy's dress. This solidly painted and carefully conceived area of glittering highlights and dark shadows appears to be good evidence that Gainsborough painted these areas himself.[3] Unlike many of his contemporaries, who employed industrious drapery painters to finish portraits in which only the face and hands had been worked up, Gainsborough preferred to paint these subordinate areas himself, a procedure that allowed him to control subtle nuances of mood and atmosphere.

Painted in the early 1760s[4] when Viscountess Tracy was apparently about fifty years old, this portrait was commissioned as a pendant to one of her husband,[5] Thomas Charles, sixth Baron and Viscount Tracy of Rathcoole (1719–92), whom she married on February 10, 1755.[6] Born as Harriet Bathurst, the daughter of Peter Bathurst of Clarendon Park, she married Viscount Tracy in her middle age, bore him no surviving children and after nearly forty years of marriage outlived him by three years before her burial on August 8, 1795.

Description: Three-quarter-length view of a woman of about 50 years of age. Turned to her left, she looks directly at the viewer, her right arm at her side and her left hand held in front at her waist. Her eyes are blue and her powdered hair is silver grey. She is dressed in a gown of a lustrous fabric of deep Prussian blue, trimmed with elaborate white laces on the elbow-length sleeves and at the square neckline. She wears an earring of white pearls and a wide black neck ribbon that is tied in a bow at the back (see *Condition*). The background is in dark umber tones with a freely painted deep red curtain at the left.

Condition: Good. Except for the face, where the eyebrows, eyes and mouth are rather abraded, the painting was found to be substantially intact when cleaned in 1971. At that time, cosmetic overpaint on the face (which reduced the apparent age of the sitter by about twenty years) was removed. A single strand of pearls, revealed by X-ray photography beneath the broad neckband, appears to have been painted over by the artist; the black paint of the neckband is clearly integrated with adjacent areas.

Exhibition: Paintings from the Kimbell Art Foundation of Fort Worth, Fort Worth Public Library, extended loan, 1960–66, cat. no. 7.

Collections: After the death of the sitter in 1795 the painting is presumed to have passed to the eighth Viscount Tracy (who died in 1797) and then to his daughter Henrietta who married in 1798 the first Baron Sudeley of Toddington Manor, Gloucester, in whose family it remained until sold in 1895 by the fourth Baron Sudeley.[7] With [S. T. Gooden]; sold to: E. M. Denny, until sale: [Christie's], London, March 31, 1906, lot 27, illus., bought by Vokins. Ernest James Wythes, Copped Hall, Epping, Essex, until sale: [Christie's], March 1, 1946, lot 3, bought by [Speelman]. [Newhouse Galleries, Inc., New York.]
Kimbell Bequest, ACF 49.2.

Notes:

1 Ellis Waterhouse, *Gainsborough*, 2nd ed., London, 1966, p. 20.

2 Waterhouse, p. 20.

3 Waterhouse, p. 22.

4 Waterhouse, p. 93, cat. no. 672.

5 49 × 39½ in., Dochfour, Baroness Burton, Waterhouse, cat. no. 671.

6 All biographical information is from *Burke's . . . Peerage* . . ., 105th ed., p. 2576.

7 Letter of Lord Sudeley, Aug. 17, 1967.

Additional References:

Walter Armstrong, *Gainsborough* . . ., London, 1898, p. 203.
Mortimer Menpes and James Greig, *Gainsborough*, London, 1909, p. 180.

Thomas Gainsborough, 1727–1788
Mrs. Alexander Champion
Painted in the mid-1770s

Oil on canvas, $29\,{}^1/_2 \times 24\,{}^3/_4$ in. (75×62.9 cm.)

For several years after he moved to London in 1774, Thomas Gainsborough apparently did not have a very large patronage. However, among the few portraits that can be dated with certainty to the years 1774–77, the artist's increasing concern for establishing poetic mood can be observed. *Mrs. Alexander Champion,* which is thought to date in the mid-1770s,[1] is characteristic of these works that Waterhouse describes as being painted with "remarkable formal elegance which almost overshadows the painter's concern for likeness."[2] Her erect pose, heavy-lidded eyes and impassive facial expression create a mien of imperious reserve. This lofty sensibility is brilliantly complemented by Gainsborough's extraordinarily facile command of painting techniques. The bravura of the quickly brushed, and completely convincing, golden fringe trimming the gown is deftly balanced by the controlled pattern in her hair of transparent greys, focusing attention on the intervening area of smoothly painted, unblemished flesh. In this painting Gainsborough is quite obviously in total command of the techniques that he used with such exceptional poetic effect in his ethereal landscapes of the 1780s.

This portrait of Mrs. Champion was probably painted shortly after 1776 when her husband, Col. Alexander Champion, resigned as commander-in-chief of the Bengal Army and returned to London. Born as Frances Hind, the daughter of William and Elizabeth Hind, she was married in 1758. After the death of her first husband at Bath in 1793, she married the Rev. Thomas Leman of Wenhaston House, Suffolk. When she died in January, 1818, the portrait passed to her adopted daughter, Frances Conway, the wife of Charles Cobbe of Dublin, in whose family it remained until 1913.[3]

Description: Bust-length portrait of a woman in a painted oval format. She faces the viewer directly and her torso is turned to her right. Her eyes are hazel and her upswept hair is light brown, with touches of grey at the hairline; the flesh tones are exceptionally pale. A golden fringe borders the edge of her transparent white gown beneath which are shades of pink; a single pendant pearl embellishes the edge of her right oversleeve. Warm brown and mahogany tones comprise the background and the painted oval outline.

Condition: Good. Aside from a small loss in the hair, now inpainted, some overpaint on her left cheek and stretcher marks about the edge, the painting is in reasonably sound condition.

Exhibitions: Dublin Exhibition Official Catalogue . . ., (inst. unk.), Dublin, 1872, p. 97, cat. no. 194. *English Paintings of the Late 18th and 19th Century,* California Palace of the Legion of Honor, San Francisco, 1933, cat. no. 9, illus. *Masterpieces of Art: European Paintings and Sculpture, 1300–1800,* New York World's Fair, May–October, 1939, cat. no. 135, ". . . Guide and Picture Book," pl. 112. *French and English Art Treasures of the* XVIII *Century,* loan exhibition, Parke-Bernet Galleries, New York, Dec. 20–30, 1942, cat. no. 382. *An English Exhibition to Honor Queen Elizabeth* II, Knoedler Galleries, New York, May 5–23, 1953, cat. no. 4, illus.

Collections: Mrs. Frances Conway Cobbe, Dublin; descended to: Charles Cobbe, Newbridge House, Dublin, by 1872, and to: Thomas Moberley Cobbe, Dublin, until 1913. Mrs. Daniel C. Jackling, San Francisco, by 1933. André de Coppet, New York, by 1939 until 1953. [Newhouse Galleries, Inc., New York.]
Kimbell Bequest, ACF 54.7.

Thomas Gainsborough, 1727–1788
Miss Sarah Buxton
Painted about 1776–77

Oil on canvas, 43 3/16 × 34 1/8 in. (109.7 × 86.7 cm.)

Late in his career Thomas Gainsborough began to develop means for making a portrait "an imaginative vehicle for conveying ideas very different from the mere establishment of a good likeness."[1] The beginnings of this evolution of his painting style can be seen in a number of portraits of the late 1770s including this portrait of Sarah Buxton which was painted about 1776–77.[2] By the early 1780s Gainsborough had successfully mastered this experimental mode in some full-length portraits that are among the most highly regarded efforts of his career.[3] Imbued with grandeur and poetic atmosphere, they are lyrical images of elegance rather than highly individualized likenesses. The active composition of the rich, vibrant settings not only complements the expression and pose of the figures but also, through a delicate balance in the intensity of colors and the pronounced rhythm of lines, plays an equal role in the design.

Miss Sarah Buxton can be regarded as an early investigation by Gainsborough of these expressive means. However, it is difficult to assess the overall effect of his intentions because the canvas has been reduced in size.[4] Originally a full-length composition in a more spacious setting, the painting is now dominated by the figure. Even so, the rich variety of textures and tones in the setting enhance the brilliantly rendered fabrics of the sitter's attire. The cool transparent blues and whites of her dress and sashes are painted in the same vigorous brushstrokes as the warm greens and browns of the leaves and trees. This gives an emphasis to the surface texture of the painting that is characteristic of Gainsborough's work of the 1770s as is the sitter's restrained, nearly erect pose. The mannered

Notes:

1 Ellis Waterhouse, *Gainsborough*, London, 1958, p. 59, cat. no. 129, dates it 1775–80.

2 Waterhouse, p. 26.

3 *An English Exhibition* ..., Knoedler Galleries, New York, 1953, cat. no. 4. John Francis Meehan, *Famous Houses of Bath and District*, Bath, 1901, p. 164.

Additional References:

Walter Armstrong, *Gainsborough* ..., London, 1898, p. 198: "Portrait of an unknown lady, coll. of Mrs. Cobbe ..."
Thomas Howe, "XVIII Century England in San Francisco," *The Fine Arts*, vol. XX, no. 3, July, 1933, p. 15, illus. p. 12.
E. K. Waterhouse, "... Portraits by Thomas Gainsborough," *Walpole Society*, vol. 33, Oxford, 1953, pp. 18–19.

gesture of her left arm, timorously raised to her breast, may be an instance in which Gainsborough tried to "elevate his portrait style by borrowing from the traditional European repertory of the history painter."[5] However, it should be noted that the relaxed position of her extended right arm is one that Gainsborough used again in the 1780s[6] when his sitters were posed in active, more natural poses.

Sarah Buxton (1757–83), was the daughter of Isaac and Sarah Buxton of Bellfield, Dorset. This portrait shows her at about the age of twenty just before her marriage in June, 1777, to Charles Dumbleton, of East Horsley near Epsom.[7] The mother of four children, she died in childbirth on December 5, 1783, about seven years after this portrait was painted. The painting remained in the family of her descendants until about 1917.

Inscription: Formerly on the back of the relining canvas that was replaced in 1971: "Sarah Buxton by Gainsborough. By the will of Ellen Dumbleton decd. Aug. 16, 1884, this picture with 3 others is left to her son Henry for his life, and from him in succession to her next surviving son to become the absolute property of the last holder."

Description: Figure of a woman, seated in a landscape, seen almost to the knees and turned one-quarter to her left while looking directly at the viewer. Her medium-brown hair (shaded grey at the hairline) is brushed high on her head and ornamented with jeweled pins; large curls drop to the sides of the neck. Her loosely fitted pale blue dress is cut low at the neck and fitted with long flowing sleeves. In her left hand, raised to her breast, and her right hand, extended in her lap, she holds the ends of a gold-fringed, transparent silk wrap that falls loosely off her shoulders and back. Around the waist is a loosely tied white sash, with long, freely hanging ends. The foliage background is in warm tones of green and brown except for a small area of creamy white sky at the left.

Condition: Good. Reduced in size (see note 3). When cleaned in 1971 the paint surface was found to be free of abrasions and relatively intact. There are several minor losses, now inpainted: a one-inch scratch on her right hand, a one-half-inch diameter loss on the bridge of her nose, a two-inch scratch in the upper left quarter and one-half-inch hole in the upper right quarter.

Exhibitions: None known.

Collections: Charles Dumbleton, Bath, Somerset; passed to Ellen Dumbleton by 1884, to Henry Dumbleton, Bronwylfa, Exmouth, Devonshire, by 1888, and then to: Col. Walter Dumbleton, Chichester, Sussex, until about 1917–18. Sold by [Duveen] to: Judge Elbert H. Gary, New York, until sale: American Art Association, New York, April 20, 1928, lot 34, sold to Edouard Jonas, Paris. Irving T. Bush, New York. [M. Knoedler & Co., Inc., New York.]
Kimbell Bequest, ACF 50.1.

Notes:

1 Ellis Waterhouse, *Gainsborough*, London, 1958, p. 27.

2 Waterhouse, p. 57, cat. no. 107.

3 For a discussion of these paintings, see Waterhouse, pp. 26–29.

4 Originally about 77 (or 67?) inches high, the painting was cut down in the mid-nineteenth century when a portion at the bottom was detached. In 1972 a fragment of the painting (showing a greyhound at the sitter's feet, 34 x 24 3/4 inches) was in the possession of the sitter's descendants, then living in South Africa. See: "On Works of Art in Devonshire," *Transactions of the Devonshire Association*, vol. XVIII, 1886, p. 121, and Waterhouse, pp. 57, 106. Correspondence with the sitter's descendants has also been informative.

5 Waterhouse, p. 28.

6 The placement of Sarah Buxton's right arm is quite similar to that in Gainsborough's portrait of *Mrs. "Perdita" Robinson* of 1781–82 (Wallace Collection, London), Waterhouse, cat. no. 579, pl. 238.

7 Peter Townend, ed., *Burke's . . . Peerage . . .*, 105th ed., 1970, p. 431, and ". . . Art in Devonshire," 1886, p. 121.

Additional Reference:

Ellis Waterhouse, ". . . Portraits by Thomas Gainsborough," *Walpole Society*, vol. 33, Oxford, 1953, p. 16.

Attributed to Thomas Gainsborough, 1727–1788
Louis-Edmond Quantin, Chevalier de Champcenetz(?)
Painted in the mid-1780s

Oil on canvas, 26 7/8 × 21 3/4 in. (68.3 × 55.2 cm.)

Among Thomas Gainsborough's portraits of the 1780s the most successful often involve sitters whose strong personalities stimulated Gainsborough to create incisive likenesses imbued with a positive atmosphere and presence. In this portrait it is this clearly evoked sense of a definite personality, proud and confident, that is the basis for its attribution to Gainsborough's hand, despite its puzzling omission from catalogues of his portraits.[1] The strongly modeled jaw, firmly set mouth, the clear and direct eyes are painted in layers of thin transparent glazes that are typical of Gainsborough's portraits of the middle 1780s.

Louis-Edmond Quantin de Richebourg, Chevalier de Champcenetz (1760–94), who is thought to be the sitter in this portrait, was a high-spirited French author and editor of political essays and books at the time of the French Revolution.[2] As a young man he was recognized as a duelist and a witty pamphleteer and is thought to have traveled to England in the 1780s.[3] As the result of an essay critical of the Prince d'Henin, he was confined from January, 1785, to October, 1786, in the chateau for French political prisoners at Ham, Picardy. After publishing *Petite traité de l'amour des femmes pour les sots* in 1788, he was the anonymous editor of several periodicals and wrote his best-known political essays including *Réponse aux lettres sur le caractère et les ouvrages de J. J. Rousseau* (against Mme. de Stael, 1789) and a *Petit dictionnaire des grands hommes de la Revolution* (1790). Arrested in June, 1793, he was released because of his early critical essays against the court. However, he was arrested again on March 19, 1794, and subsequently implicated in the Carmes prison conspiracy; his spirited remarks before he was beheaded on July 23, 1794, were particularly indicative of a proud and noble spirit.

The origin and early history of this painting is cloudy and does not assist in confirming the attribution to Gainsborough. Precisely when the Chevalier de Champcenetz visited England in the early 1780s has not been established. He is said to have known John Frederick Sackville (1745–99), third Duke of Dorset, and visited at Knole;[4] such an acquaintance may have dated from the duke's appointment as ambassador in Paris from 1783–89. Although the portrait was not among the six works that the duke purchased from Gainsborough in 1784,[5] it appears to have been added to the duke's collection at Knole by the early 1790s.[6] It is conceivable that when the duke learned of the death of his young friend, he recalled that Gainsborough had painted a portrait of him, went to Gainsborough's widow and purchased the portrait to hang at Knole where it remained until after the 1920s.[7]

Description: Bust-length oval portrait of a man 20 to 25 years of age. His eyes are hazel and his brown hair, which may be a wig, is lightly powdered. He wears a dark blue jacket with gold buttons that reveals a filled white jabot at the throat. The background is a vigorously brushed brown.

Condition: Good. Mounted on an oval stretcher. Discreet overpaint strengthens edges of the hair, face and clothing; there is considerable varnish on the background.

Exhibitions: None known.

Collections: John Frederick Sackville, third Duke of Dorset, Knole, by 1793 (?); descended in the Sackville family at Knole until after 1927. With Jacques Seligmann, London. Andre de Coppet, New York. [Newhouse Galleries, Inc., New York.]
Kimbell Bequest, ACF 54.8.

Johann Zoffany, 1734/35–1810
The Sayer Family
Painted about 1760–70

Oil on canvas, 40 1/16 × 50 3/16 in. (101.7 × 127.4 cm.)

The Sayer Family belongs to that class of paintings called conversation pieces,[1] which faithfully mirror the social history of England from the 1730s well into the nineteenth century. Unquestionably, the unrivaled master of this genre was Johann Zoffany, a German whose virtuosity lay in his complete and immediate assimilation of the English scene, his career dating from his arrival in London about 1760. The milieu which he recreated with such unerring exactitude was the elegant life of the times, often family groupings intimately portrayed among their prized possessions.

By 1765 Zoffany was already established as a painter of group portraits, known particulary for his theatrical scenes which record the celebrated actor David Garrick in his various roles. As a devotee of the theater, Zoffany created compositions which often resemble stage settings. Indeed, the Kimbell painting with its studied gestures[2] and backdrop-type scenery might almost be a scene from a play. Instead, we learn these are real people, the Sayer family being noted London print publishers, reputed to be close friends of the artist.[3]

The family is posed in the shallow foreground space which is clearly delineated by the leafy hedge to the left and rough stone wall to the right. Bright light shines through patches of blue sky illuminating an otherwise overcast day, creating alternating patterns of light and shade and focusing the viewer's attention on the domestic scene being enacted before him.

Mrs. Sayer is seated in the center of the family group, facing her son with her back to her husband. She is comfortably attired in country dress; her face, white apron and elaborately ruffled mobcap catch the sunlight. Her expression is intently serious as she addresses her son, her right arm raised toward him, book in hand. With this single admonishing gesture, the theme of the painting is set. Her son stands erect, slightly to the left of center, an elegantly attired young man, seemingly dressed for town. He faces his mother, but looks past her, bearing her lecture in stoic silence. Less reserved in his response is Mr. Sayer, whose flushed face, raised eyebrow and pursed mouth indicate his displeasure. Leaning toward his wife, he appears more the country squire than the London print publisher.

With Zoffany's skill as a landscapist, the conversation piece moved out-of-doors, and here we find the Sayer family posed against a view of their home near Richmond. In front of it stretches a smooth expanse of green lawn. In the valley to the left are trees, the dome of an arcadian gazebo,[4] and an arched bridge over the Thames, which winds peacefully into the distance. While all of this is flatly painted, the tree in the right foreground is dappled in a lively manner, this section of the composition reminiscent of *The Drummond Family*, dated about 1765–69.[5] Similarities of pose and accessories, in addition to the evidence of biographical material on Robert Sayer,[6] date the Kimbell painting contemporary with it.

Notes:

1 The portrait is mentioned but not catalogued by Ellis Waterhouse: "Preliminary Check List of Portraits by Thomas Gainsborough," *Walpole Society*, vol. 33, Oxford, 1953, p. 18. It is omitted in monographs on Gainsborough by George Fulcher (1856), Walter Armstrong (1898), and Waterhouse (1958).

2 Roman d'Amat, "Champcenetz," vol. 8 of *Dictionnaire de biographie française*, eds., M. Prevost and R. d'Amat, Paris, 1959, cols. 311–13, is the principal source of biographical information.

3 S. J. Mackie, *Knole House, its State Rooms, Pictures and Antiquities*, London, [1858], p. 88, cat. no. 209: "Mons. Champchinetz [*sic*]... frequently visited the Duke of Dorset at London and Knole." However, d'Amat, cols. 311–13, mentions no trips outside of France.

4 Mackie, p. 88, and Charles J. Phillips, *History of the Sackville Family... with a Description of Knole...*, London, [after 1927], vol. II, pp. 251, 436.

5 Phillips, p. 407.

6 Phillips, p. 191, notes that the Gainsborough portrait of the *Comte de Chamcenetz* [*sic*] was added to the Knole collection by the third Duke in "1793 (?)."

7 An alternate possibility is suggested by Waterhouse, "*Check List*," p. 18, who suggests that this portrait may be lot 2 of Mrs. Gainsborough's sale, May 10, 1797: "A portrait of the Marquis Champian, unfinished," bought by Walton.

Additional Reference:

George Scharf's "Trustees Sketch Book, VII," [1863], an unpublished notebook in the archives of the National Portrait Gallery, London, contains a sketch of this painting which he made at Knole. Mr. Robin Gibson kindly assisted in locating this reference.

Description: A family group of three figures posed against a landscape setting. The young man to the left wears a dark blue coat with brass buttons, a stock at his neck, a lapped pearl-grey waistcoat, buttoned buff knee breeches and white stockings. He is something of a dandy with his powdered hair and silver-buckled, pointed-toed black pumps. He holds a walking stick in his right hand, a black hat in his left. The seated figure in the center wears typical informal morning attire: mobcap and ochre gown trimmed with lace cuffs and covered by a white apron. Black wristlets complete her outfit. In her left arm she holds a black and brown spaniel, who looks directly at the viewer. The older man at the right is dressed in a rumpled dark green coat and waistcoat, with brass buttons, buckled black knee breeches, white stockings and stout silver-buckled shoes. His shirt is ruffled at the wrist and he holds a broad-brimmed black hat and walking stick in his left hand. In the verdant landscape behind can be seen a three-story residence, an arched bridge over a river and a small domed circular building.

Condition: Excellent. The paint layer has normal fine age craquelure.

Exhibitions: None known.

Collections: The Sayer family, Onslow Crescent, England. Lady Sayer, Onslow Crescent. A member of the Sayer family, London. [Newhouse Galleries, Inc., New York.] Foundation Acquisition, AP 69.21.

Notes:

1 Mario Praz, *Conversation Pieces: A Survey of the Informal Group Portrait in Europe and America*, London, 1971, p. 34.

2 While Zoffany was a master at capturing the significant gesture, he did not always achieve this at the first attempt. Some of the attitudes and positioning of figures in *The Sayer Family* were altered as the painting progressed, as evidenced by the *pentimenti* in the area of the son's right hand, the line of buttons on his coat, and the angle of the walking stick held by the father, which originally was a strong diagonal accent. Such changes in composition were characteristic of Zoffany.

3 Lady Victoria Manners, "John Zoffany, R. A.," *The Connoisseur*, vol. 48, June, 1917, p. 78.

4 This architectural motif, of which we see only the upper portion, was used in several of Zoffany's paintings and is thought to represent the temple on the banks of the Thames, near Hampton Court, which Garrick built to the memory of Shakespeare. See: Sacheverell Sitwell, *Conversation Pieces: A Study of English Domestic Portraits and their Painters*, London, 1969, illus. no. 39.

5 *Painting in England 1700–1850: Collection of Mr. and Mrs. Paul Mellon*, Virginia Museum of Fine Arts, Richmond, 1963, vol. I, p. 124; illus., vol. II, p. 229.

6 Robert Sayer is listed as an art dealer and probably also an engraver active in London about 1750–80; see: *Allgemeines Lexikon der bildenden Künstler*, eds., Thieme and Becker, Leipzig, vol. XXIX, p. 517.

Miss Susanna Randolph
Painted about 1771–79

Oil on canvas, 78×52 3/4 in. (198.2×134 cm.)

The concept of portraiture in this painting by an unidentified artist is an interpretation of the Grand Style that Joshua Reynolds articulated in his *Discourses* and demonstrated in his painting and which, by the 1770s, had become a convention in English portraits. Here the mode, which at times may evoke a contrived, rather artificial atmosphere, has been adapted in a rather forthright manner. The languid pose and detached mien of *Miss Susanna Randolph* derive from the Grand Style convention of posing English gentry in attitudes that allude to classical models; in this case, the "Venus Pudica" pose. In contrast, however, there is little of the theatrical atmosphere, created by unmotivated histrionic gestures, of many Grand Style portraits. For example, the arrangement of the sitter's hands is explicitly motivated: her right hand gently holds one end of the long, gauzy sash while her raised left hand lightly fingers it at her bosom. These straightforward details, her demure expression, and the rather somber tone of the background evoke in this portrait a tranquil, unpretentious atmosphere that distinguishes it from the more worldly mood of others painted in the grand classical manner.[1]

This portrait was probably painted in London between 1771 and 1779. Its style dates it later than about 1765 and before about 1785. The smaller time span is based on a presumed age of at least sixteen and a maximum of about twenty-two years for Susanna Randolph at the time this portrait was painted.[2] It might have been commissioned at the time of her twenty-first birthday when she received £1000 and the income of some Virginia property from her father's estate.[3] The explicit reference to "Chester, Virginia" in the inscription could argue

for a date before 1775 because specific mention of a colony might have been avoided after the Revolutionary War began. The painting certainly dates before 1783, when she was married; if later, her new surname surely would have been in the inscription. Other than the names of her five children little is known of the sitter's life.[4]

The painting's history is unknown before 1890 when it was exhibited at the Royal Academy and attributed to John Singleton Copley (1738–1815). In the next seventy years, during which the painting was sold three times and included in several books on Copley, this attribution was unchallenged until 1966 when Jules Prown omitted it from his comprehensive book on Copley.[5] Prown knows the painting but feels it to be "a good English portrait by someone other than Copley."[6] Even though a dating of the painting between 1771 and 1779 would allow Copley to have painted it soon after his arrival in England in 1774, the portrait has little in common with his early English paintings of comparable size.[7] However, research to date has not produced an artist who is more likely than any other to have done the portrait.

Inscription: Bottom center:
Susanna, the Daughter of the Ist Brett Randolph.
Born December 8th at Chester Virginia
(The year has been effaced.)

Description: Full-length figure looking to her right, standing before dark green foliage. Her left elbow rests beside a spray of jasmine on a stone parapet. She wears a gown of sky-blue silk with undersleeves of soft white fabric. A sheer white sash, striped with gold, is tied about her waist, extends over her right shoulder, passes through her left hand, and drapes loosely around her left side and in front to her right hand. A blue ribbon and a circlet of pearls are in her brown hair, which falls loosely across her left shoulder. At her right is a small area of blue sky with a creamy gold horizon.

Condition: Good. Small amount of filling and inpainting throughout background, particularly lower right and at the edges. Minor inpainting: cheeks, eyes and at edge of face, edges of the arms and in the parapet.

Exhibitions: ... *Works by Old Masters*, Royal Academy of Arts, London, 1890, cat. no. 57. Extended loan, Museum of Fine Arts, Boston, about 1910. *Twenty-one Paintings from the Kimbell Art Foundation*, Fort Worth Art Association, March 3–26, 1953, cat. no. 1, illus.

Collections: The Rev. William Cater Randolph, by 1890; by descent to: the Rev. Douglas C. Randolph, Gatehouse, Wickham Market, Suffolk, to sale: [Christie's], London, May 13, 1899, lot 49, sold to Wigzell.[8] T. J. Blakeslee, New York, to sale: [American Art Association], New York, March 9–10, 1900, lot 63,[9] sold to: Charles F. Sprague, Brookline, Mass., by descent to: Mrs. Charles. F. Sprague, Brookline, by 1904; by descent to: Mrs. Edward D. Brandagee (Mary Pratt Sprague), Boston, by 1910. [Newhouse Galleries, Inc., New York.]
Kimbell Bequest, ACF 48.1

Notes:

1 Compare to Joshua Reynolds' 1777 portrait, *Lady Bamfylde* (Tate Gallery, London).

2 Susanna Randolph was born on Dec. 9, 1755, 1756, or 1757 at "Chester," near Warwick, Chesterfield County, Va. Shortly thereafter she was taken to England, where she is said to have lived most of her early life. She was the only daughter of Brett Randolph (1732–59) and Mary Scott Randolph of Dursley, Gloucestershire, who were married in London on July 14, 1753, and had four children: Richard, born Aug. 17, 1754; Susanna; Henry, born Oct. 7, 1758, at Woodmancoate, Dursley, County Gloucester, England; Brett, 2nd, born in 1760. See: "Virginia Gleanings in England," *Virginia Magazine of History and Biography*, vol. 19, 1911, pp. 398–400.

3 She would have been 21 years old on Dec. 9, 1776, 1777, or 1778. Brett Randolph's will of Aug. 31, 1759, proved (in London?) Oct. 25, 1759, leaves: "To daughter Susannah [*sic*], my wife be not ensient at my decease, £2000 when 21; if my wife be ensient, the £2000 equally between the two children ..." Susanna Randolph would therefore have shared the legacy with Brett Randolph, 2nd. See "Virginia Gleanings ...," p. 398–99.

4 Susanna Randolph married Charles Douglas of Stansted, Mount Fitchet, Essex, on Aug. 23, 1783, at North Nibley, Gloucestershire, and had five children: Susan Mary Ann; Hearthy, born 1786; Charles Brett, born 1789; Albert Aberdeen, born 1789; and Eliza Randolph. See: Virginia Gleanings ...," p. 400, and Robert Isham Randolph, *The Randolphs of Virginia*, Chicago, 1930, entry nos. 52, 523, and 5231–35.

5 The painting is attributed to Copley in: *Masters in Art: Copley*, monograph no. 12, Bates and Guild, 1904, pp. 501–2, pl. VIII; Franck W. Bayley, *A Sketch of the Life and List of Some of the Works of John Singleton Copley*, Boston, 1910, p. 104; Bayley, *The Life and Works of John Singleton Copley* ..., Boston, 1915, p. 205.

6 Jules Prown, letter to Richard F. Brown, Sept. 16, 1968.

7 See Jules Prown, *John Singleton Copley* ..., Cambridge, 1966, vol. 2, pp. 245–310.

8 Algernon Graves, *Art Sales* ..., London, 1918, vol. 1, p. 149.

9 *American Art Annual*, 1900, p. 41 (63), illus. p. 40.

George Romney, 1734–1802
George B. Greaves, Esq.
Painted in 1786

Oil on canvas, 50 1/4 × 40 in. (121.7 × 101.6 cm.)

One of Romney's busiest and most productive years was 1786 when this portrait of George Greaves was painted. He was executing a vivacious image of a famous actress in one of her most popular roles, making studies of his favorite model as she enacted various moods and literary characters, and intensely involved in preliminaries for illustrating Shakespeare's plays, a project to which major English artists were asked to contribute.[1] In the midst of all this activity, commissioned portraits–his primary source of income and fame–continued unabated. His engagement book is crowded with appointments; his sitters included bishops, military men, lords and ladies, and large numbers of fashionable, though untitled, society.[2] George Bustard Greaves fits into this latter category.

Mr. Greaves was twenty-seven years old when he sat eight times to Romney for this portrait. These sittings were completed with unusual dispatch between June 1 and June 25, 1786.[3] Greaves' payment for the portrait (as well as for one painted of his wife at about the same time) was equally prompt; Romney records full payment two days before Greaves' last appointment with him.[4]

Greaves' portrait clearly demonstrates Romney's particular ability at painting commendably handsome masculine images. Greaves appears as an attractive man of moderate, not extreme, fashion, dignified yet youthful bearing, poised sobriety of countenance, and direct though unassertive gaze. The style is straightforward; uncomplicated outlines and simple smooth forms dominate the image with a lucid, almost blunt, effect. The flourish of decorative patterning often found in Romney's female portraits plays a far less prominent role in this painting, being confined to the enlivening curves of the left edge of his coat and the pleats and ruffles of stock and sleeves.

In most of Romney's portraits, as here, a reduction in the plasticity of arms and torso tends to emphasize the more fully modeled face and hands. Here, also, linear patterns produced by the spill of his stock, the wings of the vest, the line of the coat buttons, all direct attention to the face, as does the dark background. Yet other parts of the body, though less important, reinforce the masculine image, such as the sturdy muscular legs in their pale stockings and tightly fitted knee pants.

Romney frequently posed his sitter, as here, seated in an armchair, lit by a strong light from one side and viewed against a darkly cloudy sky. This convention enabled him to depict the sitter with plastic clarity, and gave him a background he could paint in swiftly after the figure was completed, harmonizing it in a lower key of the same hues, or, as in this portrait of Greaves, establishing a contrast of hue and value. The quick broad brushwork and blurred flat forms of this natural background are here a very effective foil to the sitter, who seems the more controlled, poised, and civilized by comparison. This is a purely painterly device, free of the intellectual artifice and cultural associations of the Grand Manner backgrounds consciously adopted by contemporaries like Reynolds; it does not result in revelation of the character of the sitter, but rather of superficial but widely admired features of upper-class social presence.

Description: A young man, shown in three-quarter view, is seated in an armchair. His head and body are turned to his left, his eyes facing the viewer. He sits erect, his forearms lightly poised on the chair arms, with his left arm almost fully extended, the hand hanging down loosely. His right arm is bent at the elbow and the right hand, holding white gloves, rests on his right knee. His legs are placed apart, visible to mid-calf. Greaves has powdered brown hair, dark brown eyes, and a fairly warm coloring of skin and lips. He wears a red coat with large, smooth gold buttons at the front and on the sleeves, a buff vest and knee pants fastened with gold, a pleated white cravat, white stockings, and white sleeve ruffles. The chair is covered in a yellow-green damask affixed with brass nails; it has scrolled arm ends of dark brown wood. Behind the figure is a turbulent sky in tones of black, red, blue, grey, white, rose and yellow; the horizon is streaked with pink, yellow, blue and brown. A faint indication of a dark brown vertical architectural element may be seen just to the left of the juncture of chair and shoulder.

Condition: Fair. The paint layer has extensive crawl throughout, and some areas of mechanical and age craquelure and traction cracks. There is no active cleavage. The somewhat unevenly cleaned surface has a fine craquelure and minor bloom. There is overpainting throughout the background and red jacket and extensively in the dexter arm. Small areas of inpainting may be seen in the dexter cheek, the forehead, and the vest, dexter ruffle, both hands and left thigh.

Exhibitions: None known.

Collections: The painting was commissioned by George B. Greaves, Esq., Page Hall, Sheffield, England; it later belonged to members of the Greaves family, his descendants, and still later was in the possession of Sir Austin E. Harris, London. [Newhouse Galleries, Inc., New York.] Kimbell Bequest, ACF 59.9.

Notes:

1 Arthur B. Chamberlain, *George Romney*, London, 1910, pp. 137–42.

2 Humphry Ward and W. Roberts, *Romney: A Biographical and Critical Essay with a Catalogue Raisonné of His Works*, London, 1904, vol. I, pp. 106–10.

3 Ward and Roberts, vol. I, p. 108.

4 The sum of £84 was paid for both portraits. Ward and Roberts, vol. II, p. 64.

George Romney, 1734–1802
A Lady Reading
Painted about 1777–80

Oil on canvas, 29 7/8 × 25 1/8 in. (75.8 × 63.8 cm.)

This portrait depicts an English gentlewoman who, eyes lowered, is totally absorbed in the open book on her lap. Her even-featured comeliness, elegant simplicity of dress and genteel deportment typify Romney's female images. What is more unusual is the lady's pose—her obliviousness to the viewer's presence—since an amiable sociability, if not a direct encounter with the viewer, is ordinarily suggested in the portraits of Romney's artistic maturity, from about 1775 to the late 1780s.

Romney is generally thought of as an earnest, single-minded craftsman with an acknowledged talent for rendering, within the prevailing polite convention, portraits characterized by straightforward likenesses, quick decisive brushwork, fresh color, simplicity and elegance of form, and careful pattern. These qualities are readily apparent in this portrait; the clear strong hues of the pink dress, the complexion and dark hair make the painting particularly memorable, as do the x-shaped linear patterns of book, arms and hands which boldly emphasize the activity of reading.

The sitter has been identified as Mrs. William Brown of Tallentyre Hall, Cumberland, England, and this name has been associated with a Mrs. Brown who sat four times to Romney in 1784, but there is no evidence to support this association.[1] On the contrary, the style of dress does not appear in Romney's portraits of the mid-1780s, although it is frequently encountered in those of the late 1770s.[2] Although the identity of the sitter is uncertain, the imagery of the painting is found in other near-contemporary paintings by the artist which depict women reading. In particular, Romney executed a number of paintings of Serena, the fictional heroine of an extremely popular poem, *The Triumph of Temper*, written in 1780 by Romney's intimate friend and eventual biographer, William Hayley.[3] Romney during the 1780s depicted Serena at least three times, dressed in nightgown and mobcap, engrossed in reading her book by the light of an almost guttered candle.[4] The Kimbell painting makes no allusion to the character of Serena or the circumstances of her activities (it may have been painted before the poem was written), but the Serena pictures contain similarities of pose: the bent head, the downward glance, the tranquil features and the air of total absorption; similar linear relationships focus attention on the book and link book and face in a tight compositional relationship. Hayley's poem puts a high value on the heroine's bookish pursuits as worthy of feminine emulation; in the Kimbell portrait, as in the Serena paintings, there is an equal stress on this absorbing and stylish pastime.

Description: A woman is shown seated against a background of trees, clouds and sky. A strong light falls upon her body from the upper right. She leans forward slightly, body turned slightly toward her right, her lowered head, which is seen in three-quarter view, turned more definitely toward her right. A dark red-brown book is open in the middle. It rests upon her right forearm and is supported in an open position by her right hand. Her left hand rests, relaxed, upon the right page as if to mark the limit of the passage which she is reading. Her right hand rests upon her knees which are placed close together on the center axis of her body. Her long, wavy dark brown tresses fall to the back of her head, with the front part lifted and drawn through a crescent-shaped pearl ornament. She also wears in her hair a narrow filmy white scarf striped in gold. Her skin is painted in clear fresh creams and pinks, lips in a muted tint of her bright coral-rose dress. The dress is full and loose in cut, except for the lower sleeves; it is wrapped in front to form a V-shaped bodice, secured at the shoulders with small clasps of blue sapphires, pearls and gold and at the waist by a gold-striped turquoise sash. A thin border of gold is visible at the edge of the bodice front; a filmy white undergarment may be seen at the neck and a narrow opaque white-banded ruffle edges her right sleeve.

The dark brown foliage behind her has touches of russet, gold and beige; the tree trunk at the right is a more intense dark brown with touches of vivid green and red. The distant trees in the lower left are painted in shades of green and gold with touches of turquoise. The sky and clouds above are broadly indicated in tones of beige, blue, pink, white and coral.

Condition: Good. An extensive age craquelure is visible, but there are no tears, cleavage, cupping, blisters or abrasions. Some minor filling and inpainting may be seen at the edges of the face. The dark areas have been incompletely cleaned.

Exhibitions: British Institution, 1866, no. 149 (as *A Lady Reading*).[5]

George Romney, 1734–1802
Lady Mary Sullivan
Painted in 1779 and 1784

Oil on canvas, 50 1/4 × 40 3/8 in. (127.6 × 102.6 cm.)

The serene comeliness of the image of Lady Mary Sullivan in this very fine and much-praised painting by George Romney is exemplary of the artist's portrait style.[1] Romney was a great admirer of womanly beauty; indeed, on a visit to Venice he once complained that he could not find enough of Titian's paintings of women to satisfy him.[2] It is not the robust and passionate sexuality of Titian's female images that appear in Romney's portraits of fashionable Englishwomen, however. Romney was attracted by the fresh strong color, the temperament-evoking gestures and the easy balance between painterly brushwork and linear pattern in Italian painting. All of these are strongly pictorial virtues, and in all of Romney's best portraits of women, as here, the establishment of pictorial beauty dominates, to the exclusion of drama, high seriousness or profound assessment of character.

Lady Mary, dressed in a modestly feminine costume of simple cut and delicate embellishment, displays the tranquil, yet natural elegance which was considered the ideal of aristocratic womanhood of Romney's day. The lovely face, the drapery, and landscape setting have been carefully defined and interrelated in a unified harmony manifest only in Romney's very best works. Large areas of strong color and fluid linear patterns serve to emphasize the sitter while relating her to the setting. The gently sensuous curves of head, torso, hips and knees are echoed more broadly in the large oval sweep of red drapery and pale skirt, and in the broad masses of tree and sky; the design is stabilized, however, by the strong vertical of the tree trunk at the left and the horizontals produced by the armrest, the clasped arms and the golden brown plain in the distance.

Collections: This appears to be *A Lady Reading*, which in 1866 belonged to John Bentley, Esq., Burch House, Lancashire, and Portland Place, London; Joseph Ruston, Monk's Manor, Lincoln, England, by 1913, when it was identified as Mrs. Brown (née Harris); [Arthur Tooth & Sons], London. [Newhouse Galleries, Inc., New York.] Kimbell Bequest, ACF 59.3.

Notes:

[1] The painting is said to be of a Mrs. Brown (née Harris) in a sale notice of the J. Ruston collection, July 4, 1913, where it appears as lot 123. This information is undoubtedly related to a handwritten paper label on the back of the Kimbell painting, which (although much obliterated), identifies the figures as "... /of Tallantyre Hall, Cumberland, / formerly Miss ... ris / incorrectly described in the catalogue as Mrs. Strangway." There is no evidence to associate this identification with the Mrs. Brown who sat for Romney in 1784 as recorded in Humphry Ward and W. Roberts, *Romney: A Biographical and Critical Essay with a Catalogue Raisonné of His Works*, London, 1904, vol. II, p. 19. A painting of *A Lady Reading* is recorded in a listing of "Anonymous Portraits," Ward and Roberts, vol. II, p. 190; it said to have been exhibited at the British Institution in 1866, as no. 149, lent by John Bentley, Esq.

[2] This costume is fairly common in Romney's paintings of 1776–79, for instance that of Caroline Gower, Countess of Carlisle (illus. in Ronald S. Gower, *George Romney*, London, 1904, facing p. 51) done in 1778–79 (Ward and Roberts, vol. II, p. 25); Lady Hanmer (illus. in Arthur B. Chamberlain, *George Romney*, London, 1910, fig. XXXI) done in 1777 (Ward and Roberts, vol. II, p. 88); and Elizabeth, Countess of Derby (illus. in Ward and Roberts, vol. I, p. 80), done in 1776–78 (Ward and Roberts, vol. II, p. 44).

[3] Chamberlain, pp. 99, 123, 129, 386–89.

[4] Ward and Roberts, vol. II, pp. 146–48.

[5] Algernon Graves, *A Century of Loan Exhibitions 1813–1912*, vol. III, pl. 1114; Ward and Roberts, vol. II, p. 190.

Nevertheless, the figure stands out from the setting through its higher value and its greater plasticity derived from the use of more carefully rendered outline and modeling.

The high quality of the painting may be in part explained by the rather large number of sittings—more than usual for Romney's female portraits of this size. The newlywed Lady Mary (at that time simply Mrs. Sullivan, for her husband had not yet received his baronetcy) sat for Romney nine times between March 20 and April 21, 1779, and again for seven times during April and May, 1784.[3] A companion portrait of her husband, Richard, was finished in eight sittings at about the same time; the same price, £37.16, was paid for each painting.[4]

Description: A three-quarter-length portrait of a lady posed against a landscape setting. She is seated frontally with her head turned to her left; her right arm is placed on a draped armrest while her left is bent at the elbow, the left hand resting lightly on her right wrist. Her costume is a creamy white long dress with a loosely fitting lapped bodice and full skirt. The bodice, worn over a filmy white under-garment, is adorned with a row of pearls; gold fillets catch the fullness of the upper sleeve; at the wrists is a thin blue ribbon centered between two rows of white ruching, the outermost one edged with pink. A rich bright blue sash, with touches of soft rose, is wrapped around the waist and falls to the left side of the skirt. She wears no jewelry and her auburn hair, powdered to a light brown, is dressed simply, with a narrow blue-and-white scarf woven through the crown and falling down the back. Her eyes are dark brown, her skin creamy fair, and her lips are colored a warm rose. Behind the figure is a drapery of a strong rose hue. At the left are two trees painted in hues of brown, dark brown, green, and gold, with dense foliage beyond and a blue sky above. To the sitter's right the landscape opens up onto a level plain, painted in fairly intense tones of brown, green, and gold; blue hills beyond merge into a cloudy sky painted in blue and rose.

Condition: Good. There is extensive craquelure in whites and flesh tones. Continuous cracks, two inches from the right edge, 1 3/4 inches from the lower edge and two inches from the left edge, have been partially filled and inpainted. There are minor retouches on the dress, and the shadow to the right of the chin has been reinforced.

Exhibitions: Old Masters Exhibition, Royal Academy of Arts, London, 1879, cat. no. 9. *Fair Women*, Grafton Gallery, London, 1894, cat. no. 100. *Twenty Masterpieces*, Agnew & Sons, London, 1895, cat. no. 16.

Collections: This portrait remained in family hands until at least 1894. By 1904 it was in the possession of James Ross of Montreal, Canada. On July 8, 1927, it was sold to [M. Knoedler & Co., Inc.], New York, and at some time later it belonged to Roy D. Chapin of Detroit, Mich., and a family named Hutton of New York. [Newhouse Galleries, Inc., New York.]
Kimbell Bequest, ACF 58.5.

Notes:

1 Arthur B. Chamberlain, *George Romney*, London, 1910, pp. 319–20; Humphry Ward and W. Roberts, *Romney, A Biographical and Critical Essay with a Catalogue Raisonné of His Works*, London, 1904, vol. I, pp. 88–89. It is observed that Ward and Roberts, vol. II, pp. 153–54, incorrectly describe Lady Mary as wearing a large hat; the description is otherwise accurate.

2 Chamberlain, p. 75.

3 Humphry and Ward, vol. II, pp. 153–54.

4 Humphry and Ward, vol. II, p. 153.

George Romney, 1734–1802
Miss Jemima Yorke
Painted in 1783–84

Oil on canvas, 30 × 25 in. (76.2 × 63.5 cm.)

This painting of Miss Jemima Yorke was commissioned by her father John Yorke, fourth son of the first Earl of Hardwicke.[1] She first sat for this portrait on May 28, 1783, shortly before her twentieth birthday.[2] After three more sittings the following week, work on the painting was interrupted until late October when five more sittings occurred. The painting was completed with a final sitting on June 7, 1784, not long before her marriage to Reginald Pole Carew who was, like his bride, a member of an aristocratic family.[3]

This portrait exemplifies a large proportion of Romney's portraits: images of lovely wellborn women, whose tranquil composure is well adapted to the modest format and deft but unassertive style. Here, Romney follows the time-hallowed convention of concentrating attention on the lovely face which is strongly modeled, its features incisively outlined and gently colored in pinks and creams. The clasped hands with their smoothly interwoven fingers typify Romney's tendency to reduce the less important elements of an image to a truly subordinate role. By reducing their formal plasticity and treating them as flat pattern, he creates a large oval curve which enframes head and torso without visually dominating them. Although the artist is not concerned here with communicating strong character or an inner psychological state, Miss Yorke's dignified and rather detached serenity is evoked by Romney's artifice, which is not simply confined to the pose. Easily noticed is the contribution to this establishment of polite temperament that is made by the color of the costume, which is cooler, on the whole, and less intense than that of the background, whose sharper

hue and value contrasts are compatible with the more angular abruptness of the rendering of cloud, sky and distant trees.

Description: Half-length portrait of a woman wearing a fitted white bodice, with long sleeves trimmed with narrow white lace ruffles and a vivid golden sash. Over the dress she wears a loose blue-grey robe, embroidered at the border with gold; its full short sleeves are gathered with pearl clasps. Her russet hair is slightly greyed, perhaps with powder, and a filmy blue-and-white scarf is pulled through her tresses; it is attached in front with a pearly ornament and hangs down her back. Her wavy hair is piled high on her head and falls at back and sides. Her eyes are dark brown, her lips and cheeks are tinted a delicate coral, her complexion is creamy white. In the background are a deep brown armrest, clouds of brown, coral and white, a sky of intense blue and trees of vivid-to-dark tones of gold, russet and brown. The figure is visible to just below the waist. Her torso is slightly inclined towards the supporting right arm, while her neck and head are turned to her left. Her right elbow and forearm are supported by an armrest at just above waist height. The left arm is bent at the elbow, forearm extended toward her right; the fingers of her hands are smoothly interwoven.

Condition: Good. The varnish is somewhat yellowed. A very fine craquelure is visible throughout much of the surface and traction cracking appears throughout the background and clothing. There is considerable filling and inpainting, especially at the left of the figure and throughout the clothing and hair; minor repairs are visible on chest, eyes and around the nose and mouth. Some strengthening has been added to the hair, left eyebrow and right eyelid.

Exhibitions: Old Masters Exhibition, Royal Academy of Arts, London, 1876, no. 46.[4]

Collections: Commissioned by the Hon. John Yorke, father of the sitter, in 1783, it remained in the family of Jemima Yorke and her husband, the Rt. Hon. Reginald Pole Carew, until at least 1876. It was subsequently in the possession of the Reid Topping family of New York. [Newhouse Galleries, Inc., New York.]
Kimbell Bequest, ACF 63.3.

Notes:

1 Humphry Ward and W. Roberts, *Romney: A Biographical and Critical Essay with a Catalogue Raisonné of His Works*, London, 1904, vol. II, p. 177. This may be the painting for which Romney, in December, 1785, "received of the Hon. Mr. Yorke for his daughter's portrait, 3-qrs., 10gs. and another 10gs., in all, 20gs.," according to Ward and Roberts, p. 176.

2 Ward and Roberts, vol. I, p. 102.

3 Ward and Roberts, vol. II, p. 177.

4 Algernon Graves, *A Century of Loan Exhibitions, 1813–1912*, vol. III, p. 1116.

Additional Reference:

The Connoisseur, April, 1963, vol. 152, no. 614, illus. p. LXXVIII, in color.

George Romney, 1734–1802
Edward and Randle Bootle
Painted in 1786

Oil on canvas, 86 7/8 × 60 1/8 in. (220.7 × 157.7 cm).

This double portrait of two adolescent boys, Edward and Randle Bootle, is one of a number of very fine paintings Romney executed of the Wilbraham Bootle family of Lancashire, England, between 1764 and 1793.[1] Romney was himself from Lancashire which may help to explain this early, and prolonged, patronage of the artist, which includes an early (1764) portrait of Mrs. Bootle, portraits of Mrs. Bootle and her husband done in 1780–81, this image of their sons, painted in 1786, and two half-length portraits of the elder son, Edward, in 1791 and 1793.

The fresh innocence and dignity of early adolescence are appealingly conveyed in both boys, Edward, who turned fifteen while the painting was in progress, and Randle, who became thirteen just after the sittings began.[2] Their gravely handsome faces, elegant and immaculate dress, self-assured yet natural poses, and their air of good breeding and good health are vivid indications of the ideals of the small and privileged society into which they were born. Edward, the elder son and heir, is given special prominence by his central position, his brilliant red coat (the uniform of his private school, Eton College), and the long line formed by his erect body; the pose of his slender figure, balancing the long gun against his hip, has a casual dignity befitting his approaching maturity. His face, however, surrounded by a tousled mane of hair, still has the rounded fullness of childhood, and he gazes with ingenuous charm at his brother. Young Randle is no less sympathetically rendered as he pensively muses, seated with legs spread casually apart on a rocky ledge; he appears less commanding, more casual and introspective than his brother.

The figures are posed in a rocky wooded landscape; at the right a waterfall plummets down a narrow course bordered by trees with autumnal foliage. In the distance, clouds veil a mountainous landscape. Although the figures are fully realized, the background, particularly the waterfall, may not be completely finished. Nevertheless, the softer outlines and blended tones of the setting provide a pleasant foil for the precise contours and strong clear colors of the figures.

Description: Two youths, posed full-length in a landscape. The younger boy sits on a high ledge at the left; he wears a black coat with smooth, round silver buttons, a white vest, cravat, and stockings, and black shoes with silver buckles. His long wavy hair is a bright chestnut brown. The older boy stands, his right elbow resting on the ledge and his left hand holding a long gun loosely against his hip. His wavy long hair is a brighter chestnut brown than his brother's, and his lips and cheeks are a vivid coral. He wears a long-tailed red coat with golden buttons, a white vest and cravat, fitted buff kneepants, brown and black boots. His long gun is brown with gleaming black fittings. Two black, broad-brimmed hats are piled on a rock at the lower right. The rocky ledge on which the boys are standing is painted in tones of brown, cream and green; a few green-leaved plants and a small brown bird appear in the center foreground. To the right, flowing between brown rocks and trees painted in browns, grey and green, is a steep, narrow waterfall indicated in white, brown and blue. Behind the boys may be seen distant blue hills, touched with brown, with bright russet foliage at their bases. The cloudy sky is composed of soft tones of white, pink, grey and brown.

Condition: Good. The paint and varnish have a consistent overall age craquelure; the surface is not completely clean in the darker areas. Numerous, minor repairs are scattered throughout the background and foreground and may be seen in the boys' hair and in the left eye of the standing figure.

Exhibitions: Eton Loan Exhibition, Eton College, Buckinghamshire, England, 1891, no. 52.

Collections: The painting was paid for by Mrs. Wilbraham Bootle in December, 1786. It remained in the possession of the Bootle family of Latham House, Lancashire, England (Mrs. Bootle's family home), until at least 1910, when it belonged to a direct descendant, the first Earl of Latham. Subsequently it was owned by an English private collector. [Newhouse Galleries, Inc., New York.]
Kimbell Bequest, ACF 61.1.

Notes:

1 Humphry Ward and W. Roberts, *Romney: A Biographical and Critical Essay with a Catalogue Raisonné of His Works*, London, 1904, vol. II, p. 15. Romney also painted in 1788 the Bootles' daughter Anne Dorothea, and her child, after her marriage to Richard Pepper Arden, afterwards Baron Alvanley, according to Ward and Roberts, vol. II, p. 5.

2 The sittings for the painting took place in 1786 on Jan. 4, 9, 12, 13, 24, 31, Feb. 11 and 18, March 4 and 11, April 13 and 20, June 5, 25, 27 and July 4. See Ward and Roberts, vol. I, p. 106–8. From the Ward and Roberts diary transcript, it appears that the boys posed separately for the double portrait. According to Ward and Roberts, vol. II, p. 15, Mr. and Mrs. Richard Wilbraham Bootle were first cousins, Mr. Bootle having assumed the additional surname of Bootle according to the will of his uncle, his wife's father, of whose estate, Latham House in Lancashire, they were co-heirs. Edward Wilbraham Bootle, their elder son, was born on March 7, 1771, and was later a member of Parliament from 1795 to 1828; on Jan. 30, 1828 he was created Baron Skelmersdale; he died on April 3, 1853. One of his descendants, Edward Bootle-Wilbraham, was created Earl of Latham in 1880. Randle Bootle, the younger son, was born on Jan. 10, 1773; he later became High Steward of Congleton; he died on Jan. 12, 1861.

Additional References:

Arthur B. Chamberlain, *George Romney*, London, 1910, pp. 135, 295–96.
Hilda Gamlin, *George Romney and His Art*, London, 1894, p. 186.
George Paxton, *George Romney*, London, 1903, p. 191.

Henry Raeburn, 1756–1823
Mrs. John Anderson of Inchyra
Painted in the late 1780s

Oil on canvas, 35 × 27 in. (88.9 × 68.7 cm.)

With an appraising gaze, Mrs. John Anderson looks out of the painting at the observer. Raeburn has achieved a striking documentary likeness, emphasizing her strong self-possession and her highly individualized features: a large straight nose, small thin mouth and steel grey eyes.

The artist posed the lady so that a strong cold light falls upon her face, bluntly revealing the somewhat shiny nose, the dispassionate eyes, the controlled sensuality of the mouth. This almost brutal candor is the strongest of Raeburn's gifts as an artist, but his portraits are further characterized by their somber colors and broad divisions of light and shade. The blunt strokes of paint, produced by a square-tipped brush, lie palpably separate and distinct upon the canvas. This technique is especially effective in the ruffle over her bosom which is so crisply starched it seems as forbidding as a crenellated fortification. Raeburn's straightforward method of painting is akin to that of Hals or Velasquez, to whom he was often compared, but is easily distinguished by its blunt descriptive directness.

Little is known of the sitter except for this memorable record of her appearance. The chronology of Raeburn's paintings is surprisingly obscure for an artist who is regarded as the first truly Scottish portrait painter of major stature, but Mrs. Anderson's costume is of a type which became fashionable during the late 1780s, suggesting a tentative dating for the portrait.

Henry Raeburn, 1756–1823
Mrs. John Parish
Painted in the 1780s

Oil on canvas, 50 1/8 × 40 1/8 in. (127.3 × 101.9 cm.)

Description: The painting shows a lady in three-quarter length, her arms clasped at the waist. She wears a white dress, gathered at the bust to a broad white ruffle into which a filmy white fichu is tucked; the long tight sleeves have narrower white ruffles at the wrists. A yellow sash is tied at the back. Her face is pale, her hair is powdered light brown and her eyes are grey. She is seated on a crimson chair, touched with splashes of white; the background is yellow, greenish-brown, and dark brown, relieved with touches of crimson.

Condition: Good. Some strengthening is visible in the face and hair, and small scattered areas of inpainting are found in the white dress and background. The varnish is somewhat yellowed.

Exhibitions: Raeburn Exhibition, Royal Academy, Edinburgh, Scotland, 1876, cat. no. 199. Royal Academy of Arts, London, 1907, cat. no. 130. French Gallery, London, 1910, cat. no. 15.[1]

Collections: John A. Wood, London. A. R. Wilson-Wood, London. Sir George Donaldson, London, by 1907. [Newhouse Galleries, Inc., New York.] Kimbell Bequest, ACF 54.6.

Note:

1 Algernon Graves, *A Century of Loan Exhibitions 1813–1912*, London, 1914, vol. III, pp. 972, 978, 989.

Additional References:

Walter Armstrong, *Sir Henry Raeburn*, London, 1901, p. 95.
James Grieg, *Sir Henry Raeburn, R. A., His Life and Works*, London, 1911, p. 37.
Edward Pinnington, *Sir Henry Raeburn, R. A.*, London, 1904, Appendix 1, page 218.

Raeburn's portrait of Mrs. John Parish is almost as interesting for its exciting and romantic history[1] as it is for the unassuming honesty of its representation of a pleasant Scots gentlewoman. The sitter is Henrietta Tod Parish, a member of an illustrious Edinburgh family who in 1773 married John Parish of another important Scottish family; they lived in Hamburg, Germany, where her husband was the head of a well-known and powerful banking house. Later their son took the painting with him to Czechoslovakia where it remained in the family home, Senftenberg Castle, until 1948, when the Parish family was forced to leave the country. The sitter's descendant, Baron Charles Parish, is said to have left on foot, his eldest son carrying the painting with him.

Because the painting was for such a long time in family hands in a distant part of Europe, it does not appear in the appreciative literature on Raeburn written at the beginning of the twentieth century. No complete modern catalogue of Raeburn's work exists, and few of his paintings may be firmly dated. From Mrs. Parish's costume, it appears likely that the portrait was executed during the 1780s. Despite the absence of scholarly attention, the painting is a characteristic example of Raeburn's style, and clearly indicates why the artist is so highly regarded and is admired as the chief figure of a native Scottish portraiture. Although the lady possesses the air of upper-class refinement typical of society portraits painted in Great Britain during the eighteenth century, Raeburn has depicted her with a blunt objectivity and sober, almost cautious, reserve, in a somber palette which seems to capture a distinctively Scottish temperament. The artist has not set out to

flatter his sitter, nor even to arrange her hands or her accessories in an elegant manner; he has simply recorded her image, with the candor of a camera lens, giving just those characteristic details of posture and gesture which reveal a sturdy unaffected character. Mrs. Parish's dark eyes are undoubtedly her best feature, enlivening an otherwise bland and unremarkable face with a direct, refreshingly human intelligence.

Description: A lady seated out-of-doors in three-quarter view with her body turned to the right and face turned toward the viewer. Her gloved left arm, holding a matching brown grey glove, rests in her lap; a long scarf, in olive green touched with russet and oxblood, enlivens a simple white dress trimmed with a black sash, a white bow, and softened at the neck with a filmy white fichu. The lady's complexion is fair, her mouth a very pale pink; her brown hair is lightly powdered. The rounded rock ledge on which her right arm rests is colored in browns and golds, with sparse green foliage at the base. Behind the figure are three leafy trees, painted in brown and green tones mixed with white where sunlight strikes the leftmost trunk. On the right, and beyond a dark green-brown strip of land, is golden parkland with a few brown trees. A distant green-brown field leads to two ranges of hills, the nearer indicated in blue, the farther in a greyed purple-pink. Brown-grey clouds may be seen above a bright blue strip of sky, below which are pink-brown clouds struck with white sunlight.

Condition: Good. General age craquelure and some mechanical cracks are visible in the paint layer; there is scattered strengthening and overpainting through much of the foliage and clothing, and on the forehead and cheeks. There is some abrasion of the paint surface, and three gouges have been repaired, one at the center of the upper edge and two along the lower edge.

Exhibitions: Twenty-One Paintings from the Kimbell Art Foundation, Fort Worth Art Association, March 3–26, 1953, cat. no. 13, illus.

Collections: John Parish, Esq., Hamburg, Germany; his son David Parish, Esq., Senftenberg Castle, Czechoslovakia; Parish family descendants; Baron Charles Parish, in 1948. [Newhouse Galleries, Inc., New York.]
Kimbell Bequest, ACK 51.2.

Note:

1 This history of the painting is based on information provided by the vendor.

John Hoppner, 1758–1810
Mrs. Sophia Fielding
Painted in 1787

Oil on canvas, 31 1/2 × 25 1/2 in. (80 × 64.8 cm.)

Mrs. Sophia Fielding, like John Hoppner himself, was closely associated with the royal court of King George III and his eldest son George Augustus Frederick, the Prince of Wales and later King George IV. She was governess to the children of King George III and woman of the bedchamber to his consort, Queen Charlotte.[1] Hoppner moved in the same lofty social circle: he was friendly throughout his life with the king's children and, not long after he painted this portrait, he was named Principal Painter in Ordinary to the King and Portrait Painter to the Prince of Wales.[2] It is said that it was through "the personal intervention of the King himself" that Hoppner was elected to associate (later full) membership in the Royal Academy.[3]

Mrs. Fielding, who was married in 1772 to Royal Navy Captain Charles Fielding, the grandson of the Fourth Earl of Denbigh, was a widow, probably in her mid-thirties, when this painting was done.[4] She is portrayed as a slender, even-featured lady with an almost girlish prettiness; indications of her maturity are confined to a slight fullness at the jawline. Her face, however, unlike those in portraits by Hoppner's contemporaries, Joshua Reynolds and George Romney, does not command the concentrated attention of the viewer; instead, her fashionable costume, extravagant hat and the distant parkland at the left are strongly emphasized. The latter, rendered in muted tones of brown, green and grey-blue and streaked with brilliant white and a vibrant red, reveals Hoppner's talent for romantic landscape painting.

Inscription: Lower left: *Mrs. Fielding/1787* (probably by another hand)

Description: Half-length view of a seated lady, who faces the viewer. She has blue-grey eyes and hair powdered to a light brown. Her satin dress is creamy white; over its wide collar is a pleated tippet of a thin white material. Her hat, secured under the chin with a black ribbon, is pale blue with a dark blue edge; it is lined with a white stripe-woven fabric which reflects tones of blue, pink and grey. The hat is ornamented with blue-and-white striped satin ribbon with two large white feathers atop the crown. The drapery above and to the right of the figure is a dark plum. To the left is a landscape view, topped by purple-grey clouds in a dark grey-blue sky; below is a lighter area of evening sky painted in blue, pink and cream. The distant parkland is painted in rich brown and green tones with bright streaks of red and white; at the edge of the park are grey-green trees and, beyond, a range of blue-grey hills.

Condition: Good. A characteristic age craquelure appears throughout the paint layer. There are numerous scattered areas of inpainting, and parts of the hat, dress and the pupils of both eyes have been strengthened. The varnish is heavy and yellowed, with considerable bloom.

Exhibitions: Twenty-One Paintings from the Kimbell Art Foundation, Fort Worth Art Association, March 3–26, 1953, cat. no. 10, illus.

Collections: Mrs. Sophia Fielding, until her death in 1815. W. Morley Pegge, by 1896. A private European collection. [Newhouse Galleries, Inc., New York.] Kimbell Bequest, ACF 52.1.

Notes:

1 William McKay and W. Roberts, *John Hoppner, R. A.*, London, 1914, p. 82.

2 McKay and Roberts, p. XIX.

3 McKay and Roberts, p. XIX.

4 Her husband died in 1783, six years before this portrait was done. See McKay and Roberts, p. 82.

Additional Reference:

H. P. K. Skipton, *John Hoppner*, London, 1905, p. 167.

John Hoppner, 1758–1810
Romantic Landscape
Painted about 1787

Oil on canvas 40 5/8 × 50 in. (103.2 × 127 cm.)

For John Hoppner, one of the most prolific of the major English portraitists, this painting is an unusual mode of expression. His landscapes were evidently few in number; no more than seven are recorded in the incomplete 1909 catalogue of Hoppner's works,[1] and they have not been the subject of major attention in critical literature. Nevertheless, "judging from some of the backgrounds of some of his portraits ... Hoppner, had circumstances permitted him to follow the bent of his genius, would have ranked as a landscape painter of high distinction."[2] The writer, William McKay, had not seen this landscape, but but many of his portraits, such as *Mrs. Sophia Fielding* in the Kimbell collection, possess a characteristically rich and vibrant landscape background.

Moreover, Hoppner's "love for country scenes amounted almost to a passion, and he was never happier than when making excursions into rural England, and drawing sketches of its scenery."[3] It was perhaps on one of these sketching tours, which extended from London to the north of England and to Wales in the west, that Hoppner observed, as later summer turned to autumn, a bucolic woodland scene which may have inspired this painting, executed in the studio at some later date. In this robustly colored, broadly painted, placid country scene, late afternoon sunlight streaks through a cloudy sky warmly illuminating an open woods whose trees display every stage of foliage turning to autumn colors.
The view, with its path, clear blue stream and low grassy knolls, is casual, as if spontaneously encountered from a bend in the path just at the point where the stream breaks the pattern of woodland to reveal open sky, a distant meadow and far-off hills.

The Kimbell painting is characteristic of Hoppner's recorded landscapes in its presentation of a natural environment that is touched by the presence of man; here the picturesque scene is inhabited by a pair of charming rustics: the man, stretched on the grass, is imploringly earnest; the woman, her full body turned towards him, turns her face poutingly away, a pose echoed in the somnolent dog at her feet.

Description: A shaded, dusky wooded landscape with a man, woman, and brown-and-white dog reclining beneath a tree at the right. The man wears a rose jacket, white shirt, tan pants with paler tan stockings, and brown shoes; he has coppery hair, a flushed complexion, and wears a dusty brown hat. The lady wears a grey skirt and bodice, trimmed with pink and purple-brown, with white sleeves and shawl. A straw hat with a blue ribbon tops her copper-brown curls. A stream, painted in blues, grey and cream, flows by on the left, between open woodlands. Both banks are a grassy green; the tree trunks and branches are mostly brown with predominantly green foliage accented with yellows, pale orange and bronze. In the distance is a glimpse of hilly meadow with trees at the crest in yellow, purple-grey and grey-green. The foliage of the large tree at the right which shelters the figures is more than half-turned to dark reds and oranges; the rough bark of its trunk is brown, grey and putty. The path at the lower right is painted in greys and brown. The sky is pale with purple-grey clouds and streaked with the very pale cream radiating rays of the setting sun.

Condition: Very good. The painting shows a characteristic age craquelure. Minor filling and inpainting may be seen throughout and there appears to be some strengthening in the sky and at the edges of the trees.

Exhibitions: None known.

Collections: Private collection, London. [Frost and Reed, Ltd.], London. [Newhouse Galleries, Inc., New York.] Kimbell Bequest, ACK 40.1.

Notes:

1 William McKay and W. Roberts, *John Hoppner, R. A.*, London, 1909, pp. 297–311. The date of about 1787 was suggested by Charles Holmes on an endorsed photograph, dated 1936, now in the archives of the Henry E. Huntington Library, San Marino, Calif.

2 McKay and Roberts, p. vii.

3 McKay and Roberts, p. vii.

James Ward, 1769–1859
Disobedience in Danger
Disobedience Detected
Painted in 1797

Oil on canvas, each 28 1/4 × 36 1/8 in. (71.8 × 91.7 cm.)

These colorful, anecdotal episodes were painted by James Ward early in his career when he was still under the influence of his brother-in-law George Morland, an accomplished genre painter who specialized in rustic scenes of a rather idyllic rural life. Already recognized as an outstanding mezzotint engraver before he turned to painting in the early 1790s, Ward achieved substantial success at the turn of the century as an *animalier*, painting impressively colored images of champion bulls, famous horses and other prized livestock in which he created considerable drama with contrasting colors and muscular draftsmanship. His incipient facility at handling contrasts of bright colors is evident in these two paintings which rely on this pictorial device for narrative emphasis.[1]

Probably based on an unidentified literary source, these paintings represent scenes of everyday domestic life in a realistic manner in which the figures are portrayed as types rather than as individuals. Concern for this kind of characterization is manifest in the concentration on emotional responses—the apprehensive glances of the children toward the bull in *Disobedience in Danger* and their remorseful expressions in *Disobedience Detected*—and the studied attitudes and gestures which heighten such domestic scenes into melodrama. Thus, Ward has created a mildly moralistic commentary on contemporary society. The suggestion of tension in *Disobedience in Danger* is augmented by Ward's inclusion of a gnarled oak tree, rocky terrain, the menacing bull at the right and the brooding masses of heavy storm clouds. By contrast, the play of light on the timorous figures in the pendant painting is a rather obvious symbolic device to suggest the

revelation of the children's misdeeds and the subsequent reprimanding. To be sure, there is a strong narrative quality which pervades these genre scenes, à la Hogarth, and corresponds closely to the mood of Morland's compositions, as well as his simple descriptive style.

Inscription: (Danger), lower right:
J. Ward
Pinx 1797
(Detected): none apparent.

Descriptions: Disobedience in Danger depicts four distressed children in a landscape with a bull and some cows. In the left foreground, three girls in long white dresses and a little boy in a red suit with white lace collar try to escape a menacing brown-and-white bull lurking behind a tan embankment and fence railing at the far right. Standing beneath a large oak tree, the eldest girl has a blue sash, brown gloves, red shoes and a yellow straw bonnet with blue ribbon trim. Resting at her feet is a nest with tiny birds. She holds a younger girl about the waist who is turned toward the brown wood fence behind the figures, her dark brown hair falling below her shoulders. To the far left next to a tall tree stump, the third girl, wearing a yellow sash, red shoes, and a white bonnet with a yellow tie, turns to mount the fence. She has one foot on the ground, her right foot on the bottom railing and both arms resting on the top railing. The little boy tries to scale the base of the old tree, holding a branch of it with his right hand and the skirt of the eldest girl with his left. The gnarled tree, with grey and tan bark and green and brown leaves, has been uprooted and leans against the fence, its heavy branches extending like tentacles. The menacing blue sky has medium grey clouds tinged in white. In the middle distance, six cows (two black, two brown and two white) graze peacefully in a green pasture to the right of center while green bushes form a foil behind the tree and the girls.

Disobedience Detected depicts an interior with six figures. The same four children appear, dressed as before, the boy holding a black hat filled with the bird's nest. In a room with green walls and off-white wainscoting and dado, they stand on a rug with a multicolored floral pattern before two women seated in chairs upholstered with green petit point at a brown wood table next to a large open window draped in red at the far right. On the far side of the table, a woman wearing a long white dress and white kerchief leans on the table with her arms folded. The other woman, who appears older, wears a black dress and black gloves, pale blue shawl and white ruffled bonnet with pale yellow bow. She faces the children, her feet resting on a petit point footstool, her left arm on the arm of the chair and her right arm on a large open book on the table. Visible through the window is a verdant landscape with a church tower at the low horizon under a blue sky with white, grey and rose clouds. At the far left, more landscape with green and ochre trees and a stormy sky can be seen through the doorway.

Condition: Both paintings are in good condition. The paint is applied with a low impasto. Minor losses throughout both paintings were filled and inpainted, probably when they were relined and cleaned. In *Disobedience in Danger*, a hole in the sky among the trees has been filled and inpainted. In *Disobedience Detected*, three tears (one between the seated women, another in the left seated woman, and another in the lower center) have been filled and inpainted.

Exhibitions: None known.

Collections: Private collection, United States. [Newhouse Galleries, Inc., New York.]
Kimbell Bequest, ACF 62.1 *(Danger)* and ACF 62.2 *(Detected)*.

Related Prints: Colored mezzotints were made of the paintings by W. Barnard about 1799.[2]

Notes:

1 Frederick Cummings, *Romantic Art in Britain, Paintings and Drawings, 1760–1860*, Detroit Institute of Arts, Jan. 9–Feb. 18, 1968, and Philadelphia Museum of Art, March 14–April 21, 1968, pp. 180–81.

2 C. Reginald Grundy, *James Ward, R. A., His Life and Works, with a Catalogue of His Engravings and Pictures*, London, 1909, p. 42, nos. 224, 224A; p. 70, nos. 31, 32; color illus., *Disobedience in Danger* mezzotint, facing p. lvi.

Francisco de Goya, 1746–1828
The Matador Pedro Romero
Painted about 1795–97

Oil on canvas, 33 1/8 × 25 9/16 in. (84.1 × 65 cm.)

For Francisco de Goya y Lucientes, the 1790s was a difficult and challenging period during which he created some of his most highly regarded paintings, including this portrait of his friend Pedro Romero, the famous matador. After a brilliant early career, capped by a coveted appointment as court painter to the royal Spanish family, Goya suffered a near-fatal illness in 1792 that left him completely deaf. His convalescence was a period of self-reflection that brought forth in him a heightened sensitivity that he strove to convey in his paintings when he resumed work in 1793. During the next six years he painted a prodigious number of works, many of which are distinguished by a straightforward, unaffected naturalism. Although he never flattered his sitters and was uncompromising in his standards, Goya revealed his concern for human qualities in sympathetic portraits of his friends, particularly those whose occupations, such as the stage and bullfighting, involved public exposition of drama and passion.

Goya's paintings of bullfight themes, his *Bulls of Bordeaux* lithographs and *Tauromaquia* etchings reveal exceptional knowledge of the sport that was founded not only on keen observation but also on Goya's first-hand experience as a bullfighter while a young man.[1]

Pedro Romero (1754–1839) is one of the most illustrious figures in the early history of Spanish bullfighting. Born at Tonda in Andalusia of a famous family of toreros, Romero fought in the bullring from 1771 until he retired in 1799, just after this portrait was painted. He was described by the poet Nicolás de Moratín as a brave young man, calm, self-controlled and very handsome.[2] One of Goya's etchings in the *Tauromaquia* series shows Romero killing a bull in the ring. In contrast to that objective view of a public performer, this portrait focuses upon the human qualities that de Moratín admired.

Goya's subtle rendering of Romero's distinctive character can be clearly perceived because the painting is in near-pristine condition. Romero's handsome appearance is revealed in the features of his cleanly modeled face, with its firm chin, high forehead and clear eyes. Immediacy and vitality are imparted by the slightly parted lips and by the close-up view of the figure (which fills the canvas to the sides) and most of all by the pose, which is unusual but convincingly natural. Romero leans forward both toward the viewer and to his right, thus connoting an erect carriage formed by taut, powerful muscles. His relaxed right arm, lightly supported by the draped table at his right, is brought forward in a remarkable foreshortening that ends in the superbly painted hand, which operates as an anchor for the complex composition of rich colors and varied patterns. Given mass by a deftly revealed glimpse of the thumb, this long-fingered hand has a prominence–unusual in Goya's portraits–that can be regarded as a means of indicating Romero's even temperament. That Romero's sword hand–which is said to have killed more than a thousand bulls–would be painted with such a smooth and a gentle modeling and in so relaxed an attitude is quite consistent with Goya's remarkable propensity for incisive visual irony.

Goya's balance of an exceptional combination of colors is equally beguiling. For example, the luminous greys and lustrous blacks of Romero's vest and jacket temper the brilliant crimson of the sash and jacket lining. The magenta-plum cape, revealed as a generalized area of dark tones beneath his right arm, extends behind Romero's back to envelop his left side in a triangular cascade of muted highlights and shadows. The psychological and compositional importance of this cape is emphasized by discoveries made in a recent laboratory examination of the painting which established that it is painted over portions of the jacket and sash that were originally more extensive. By enlarging the expanse of the cape and reducing the prominence of the more saturated colors, Goya judiciously balanced the composition. Hence, the evolutionary character of this design reveals Goya's conceptual process and indicates that the Kimbell painting was his initial portrait of Pedro Romero.

Published accounts of this painting's history present a complicated example of misidentification, misinterpretation, and outright confusion. Briefly, it has been mistaken for another Goya portrait; it has been published with incorrect dimensions, and it is alleged to have been in the possession of two collectors who never owned it. The existence of at least two other versions and the fact that two inches across the top of this canvas were once folded under explain much of the confusion. The following discussion is rather detailed because no fully accurate record of this painting's history has been published previously.

As with many of Goya's works, the nineteenth-century history of this painting is not entirely clear. It may be one of the paintings listed in the inventory made upon the death of Goya's wife in June, 1812, because their son, Xavier, was his mother's heir and entitled to half his parents' property.[3] In this inventory, painting number nineteen is a portrait of "Perico Romero" valued at 100 reales; this might refer to the Kimbell portrait, although the distinctive inscription found on other of Xavier's paintings is not on this canvas.[4]

In any case, by the middle of the nineteenth century the Kimbell painting was owned by Léon Lafitte in Madrid; this is clearly established by an inscription on the back of an old photograph of the painting that is now in the library of the Prado Museum.[5] Viuda de Vera of Seville[6] and Henri Rochefort of Paris,[7] have also been identified but not confirmed as nineteenth-century owners of this painting. Another alleged owner, Don Sebastián de Bourbon et Bragance, should be purged from the record because he never owned this painting or any version of it. Instead, he owned a Goya portrait of Romero's brother, who was also an illustrious bullfighter.[8] In an 1876 catalogue of his collection the portrait of José Romero is misidentified as being Pedro Romero,[9] a mistake that has been perpetuated in numerous studies of Goya's paintings. That Rodolphe Kann of Paris once owned the Kimbell portrait is well documented.[10] Apparently acquired after 1901,[11] it was included in the 1907 catalogue of Kann's distinguished collection.[12] Comparison of the painting with that catalogue's splendid photogravure plate (its earliest published illustration) reveals that a two-inch strip across the top of the canvas was turned over the edge of the stretcher, making its dimensions 31 × 25 1/4 in. (70 × 64 cm.) at that time.

Confusion abounds concerning the next owner of this painting. Despite a 1908 article asserting that the Goya portrait in the Kann Collection had been sold to Archer M. Huntington,[13] the noted New York collector of Spanish art, there is no corroborating evidence. Similarly, no Goya portrait of Pedro Romero has ever been owned by the Hispanic Society, New York, which was founded by Huntington.[14] Instead, it seems likely that Kann sold the portrait to Sir William Abdy of London, who died in August, 1910. While owned by Abdy, the canvas was relined and mounted on its present stretcher, which is confirmed by an inscription on the back of the top stretcher bar. When it was relined, the previously turned-under strip was laid flat, "enlarging" the painting to its present dimensions.

In the early 1920s the portrait entered the collection of its penultimate owner, Arthur Sachs, who was then living in New York.[15] This distinguished connoisseur loaned the painting to several important exhibitions in this country and, after moving to Paris, to the Louvre for the Goya exhibition of 1938.[16] Most recently, its inclusion in the major Goya exhibition of 1970 at the Mauritshuis and the Louvre is further testament to the painting's superior quality.[17]

Description: Half-length portrait of a mature man dressed as a matador. Seated and leaning forward slightly, he looks directly at the viewer with his dark brown eyes; his clean-shaven, olive-skinned face is in three-quarter, almost frontal view. His greying black hair is brushed back from his forehead; several locks curl in front of both ears. A black *coleta*, tied in a bow at the top, hangs down behind his head to just below his shoulders. On a surface draped in dark magenta fabric he lightly rests his right elbow and forearm with his relaxed hand hanging loosely over the edge; the tip of his thumb is just visible behind his forefinger. Over a brilliant white collar and frilled stock and a tightly fitted, shimmering pearl-grey vest he wears a blue-black jacket with a bright crimson lining revealed at the wrist and to the left of his waist. A similarly colored sash about his lower waist is partially covered by the light magenta cape that hangs loosely over his left shoulder. The warm blue-grey background is thinly painted over a ground of pale-red bole.

Condition: Excellent. The paint film of the figure is intact and unblemished. When a thin layer of discolored varnish was removed in 1970 the only losses observed were some minor surface abrasions about the edges and a small, one-inch diameter hole in the upper right corner that is now filled and inpainted. The most important revelation of the detailed examination made at this time was the discovery of two *pentimenti*, striking through from beneath the cape at the right: a downward extension of the black jacket and an extension to the right of the canvas of the red sash. This evidence certainly suggests that the Kimbell painting was Goya's initial portrait of Pedro Romero. A thin surface glaze now attenuates the transparency of the cape caused by time and preserves the integrity of Goya's final solution. The present relining canvas probably dates from about 1907–10 when a previously turned-under, two-inch band of canvas across the top of the painting was laid flat; a straight fracture in the paint film, parallel to the edge, indicates where it had been bent. No tacking edge remains.

Exhibitions: Opening Exhibition, Fogg Art Museum, Cambridge, Mass., June-November, 1927 (no catalogue published.) ... *Spanish Paintings from El Greco to Goya*, Metropolitan Museum of Art, New York, Feb. 17–April 1,

1928, cat. no. 23, illus. *Peintures de Goya des collections de France*, the Louvre: Musée de l'Orangerie, Paris, 1938, cat. no. 5, illus. *The Arthur Sachs Collection*, Santa Barbara Museum of Fine Arts and California Palace of the Legion of Honor, San Francisco, summer and fall, 1946 (no catalogue published). *Goya*, Mauritshuis, The Hague, and the Louvre: Orangerie des Tuileries, Paris, July – December, 1970, cat. no. 19, illus.

Collections: Possibly: Xavier Goya, Madrid, in 1812, Viuda de Vera, Seville, and Henri Rochefort, Paris. Léon Lafitte, Madrid. Rodolphe Kann, Paris, after 1901, by 1907. William Abdy, London, by 1910. [Wildenstein & Co.], New York, by 1920. Sold to Mr. and Mrs. Arthur Sachs, New York and subsequently Paris, by 1924, until 1966.
Foundation Acquisition, AP 66.12.

Related Versions: Goya made at least one replica of the Kimbell portrait of Pedro Romero: a second less-assured copy also exists. Since the late nineteenth century, the published records of these three paintings have been considerably confused, not only with each other but also with Goya's portrait of José Romero. Based largely on the extensive photographic archives of the Hispanic Society, New York, a clarifying summary of the recent histories of the two versions follows.

In 1900, Goya's replica was in the collection of the Duke of Veragua, Madrid, who loaned it to the Goya exhibition at the Prado that year.[18] After being exhibited again in 1908,[19] it entered the collection of Hermann Eissler of Vienna[20] and remained in his family until about 1960. Now in a Swiss collection,[21] it is a work of considerable quality which varies from the Kimbell portrait in some details. The two works can be distinguished by the omission of the thumb from Romero's right hand in the replica and by slight differences in the arrangement of hair about the ear and the outline of the jacket against the white stock. It has been suggested that the Kimbell portrait predates this version,[22] an observation that is confirmed by the *pentimenti* in the Kimbell painting.[23] The history and quality of the third painting are less easily established; its present location is unknown and it appears to have been illustrated only

once.[24] However, photographs of the painting suggest that it is a perfunctory copy; the modeling of the figure seems less substantial and its surface finish less appealing than either the Veragua/Eissler replica or the Kimbell portrait.

Notes:

1 Leandro de Moratín is the source for Goya's statement that he fought in the bullring. See the entry by Jeannine Baticle for this painting in the French edition of the catalogue for the exhibition, *Goya*, Orangerie des Tuileries, Paris, September–December, 1970, cat. no. 19.

2 See: Baticle, cat. no. 19.

3 Discussed in detail by F. J. Sánchez Cantón, "Cómo vivía Goya," *Archivo Español de Arte*, vol. XIX, 1946, pp. 73–109. See particularly pp. 85, 106.

4 Perico is the Spanish diminutive of Pedro. Sánchez Cantón identified a number of paintings in the inventory by associating them with an inscription in the lower left corner, consisting of an "X" followed by the inventory number.

5 Baticle, cat. no. 19.

6 Paul Lafond, *Goya*, Paris, [1902], p. 137, cat. no. 201.

7 Xavière Desparmet Fitz-Gerald, *L'Œuvre peint de Goya*, Paris, 1928–50, vol. II, cat. no. 427–1.

8 This confusion between the portrait of José Romero (which measures 36¼ x 29⅞ in., 92 x 76 cm., and is now in the Philadelphia Museum of Art) and that of Pedro Romero was initially clarified in the catalogue entry, no. 23, for *José Romero* in the 1928 *Goya* exhibition at the Prado Museum, Madrid. Also see: Baticle, cat. no. 19.

9 *Catalogue abregé des tableaux . . . appartenant aux héritiers de feu Mgr. l'Infant Don Sebastián de Bourbon et Bragance*, Pau, September, 1876, p. 71, cat. no. 633, "Portrait de Pedro Romero," 92 x 76 cm. Jeannine Baticle kindly provided this reference.

10 Valerian von Loga, *Francisco de Goya*, Berlin, 1903, p. 203, cat. no. 320; also, August Mayer, *Francisco de Goya*, London, 1924, cat. no. 404 (both of whom give incorrect dimensions of 92 x 76 cm.). Desparmet Fitz-Gerald, cat. no. 427–1. P. Gassier and J. Wilson, *Œuvre et vie de Francisco Goya*, Fribourg, 1970, cat. no. 671, illus. The immediate owner before Kann is not known; according to Desparmet Fitz-Gerald it was Henri Rochefort, while Mayer implies that it was the heirs of Léon Lafitte.

11 Emile Michel, "La Galerie de M. Rodolphe Kann," *Gazette des Beaux-Arts*, vol. XXV, June, 1901, p. 493, wrote: "L'école espagnole . . . est tout à fait absente de cette collection."

12 *Catalogue of the Rodolphe Kann Collection, Pictures*, Paris, 1907, vol. II, p. 49, pl. 142.

13 "Pictures Acquired by Mr. Archer M. Huntington," *Burlington Magazine*, vol. XIII, January, 1908, pp. 232–33, illus.

14 Priscilla Muller kindly verified that the records at the Hispanic Society contain no indication that Huntington or the Hispanic Society ever owned a Goya portrait of Pedro Romero, as asserted by Aureliano de Beruete y Moret, *Goya, pintor de retratos*, Madrid, 1915, vol. I, cat. no. 141, and subsequent editions, Madrid, 1917, cat. no. 149, and London, 1922, cat. no. 149.

15 Mayer, London, 1924 edition, cat. no. 404, shows Sachs as the owner, correcting his Munich, 1923 edition that shows the Hispanic Society as the owner.

16 Rather surprisingly, the catalogue of this exhibition shows incorrect dimensions of 92 x 72 cm.

17 Equally surprising is the omission of this painting from José Gudiol's *Catalogo analítico de las pinturas de Goya*, Barcelona, 1970; contrary to references in the 1970 Mauritshuis and Louvre exhibition catalogues, the Kimbell painting is *not* the work illustrated by Gudiol, cat. no. 405, fig. 616.

18 *Catalogo de las obras de Goya expuestatas en el Ministerio de Bellas Artes*, Madrid, May, 1900, cat. no. 68, 33½ x 25¼ in. (85 x 64 cm.).

19 Carl Moll, *Francisco José de Goya . . .*, Galerie Miethke, Vienna, March–April, 1908, cat. no. 3, 85 x 64 cm., "Früher Sammlung Duque de Veragua, Madrid," illus., p. 11.

20 Mayer, 1924 ed., cat. no. 405, pl. 95, with incorrect dimensions and an accurate record of its previous history and publications (erroneous in earlier editions). See also: Lafond, cat. no. 200; Von Loga, cat. no. 321; Beruete y Moret, cat. no. 139, pl. 16; Desparmet Fitz-Gerald, cat. no. 427.

21 Gudiol, cat. no. 404, figs. 614, 615.

22 Editor's note to article by H. W. Singer, "Pictures by Goya at the Galerie Miethke, Vienna," *Burlington Magazine*, vol. 13, [April], 1908, p. 99.

23 Mayer (1924), and Gassier-Wilson (1970), consider the Kimbell portrait to be Goya's initial painting and the Veragua/Eissler painting a replica. Lafond (1902), Desparmet Fitz-Gerald (1928–50) and, by implication, Gudiol (1970) give a contrary view. Von Loga (1903) and Beruete y Moret (1916) list both paintings without any designation of primacy.

24 Gudiol, cat. no. 405, fig. 616, with erroneous dimensions and history.

Francisco de Goya, 1746–1828
Rita Luna
Painted about 1814–15

Oil on canvas, 16 3/4 × 13 1/2 in. (42.5 × 34.2 cm.)

A highly regarded tragedienne, Rita Luna (Rita Vidal Alfonso Garcia, 1770–1832) achieved considerable success in the Spanish theatre, making her acting debut on the stage of her father's company in 1788. After playing leading roles for more than ten years she retired from the stage in 1804 to live a secluded life in El Pardo, a town about eight miles northwest of Madrid.[1]

Goya is thought to have painted this well-known portrait about 1814–15[2] when the sitter was about forty-four years old and living at El Pardo. Its small size, somber tonality, and the varying texture of the paint surface of the shadowed facial features are characteristic of several Goya portraits of 1808–20, the best known being his *Self-Portrait* of 1815 (Prado, Madrid). Portrayal of moments of intense emotion is a salient feature of Goya's late paintings. While the themes are often disturbing or violent—needless slaughter in *Third of May* of 1814 (Prado, Madrid), life-or-death combat in his bullfight prints of 1814–25, and cannibalism in *Saturn Devouring a Son* of 1819–23 (Prado, Madrid)—the expressively modeled, almost homely, face of Rita Luna demonstrates Goya's concurrent interest in more subjective themes. The deep introspection of the aging actress is charged with an intensity of feeling that verges on melancholia. This mood is evoked by her downcast glance and shadowed facial features. It is enhanced by the expressive qualities of Goya's varying technique. The flesh color of the face is applied with a loaded brush, leaving the black underdrawing visible in the eyebrows, corners of the eyes, the contour of the nose and at the left corner of the mouth. The dark, thinly painted hair and cloak contrast with the high impasto of the bright necklace and earrings.

Description: Bust-length portrait of a woman, frontal view, with head inclined slightly to her left, eyes looking downward. Her face is framed by curly brown hair and accented by her red lips, the gold necklace and earrings. The right side of her face is highlighted, and on the shadowed left side her cheek is light red. A black cloak over the shoulders covers her neck, except at the throat. At the left the background of olive green and brown tones is thinly painted, revealing the underlying reddish bole priming, while on the right it is more opaque.

Condition: Good. Small paint losses, now inpainted, are located in her left forehead and right shoulder. A larger area of repaint, probably covering an old tear, is in the upper left background and hair. The original canvas, which has been trimmed, is bounded on the right by a 5/8-inch-wide strip with a white ground rather than the original red.

Exhibitions: Exposición de Retratos de Goya, Museo del Prado, Madrid, 1902, cat. no. 989. *Exposición de Pinturas de Goya,* Museo del Prado, Madrid, April–May, 1928, cat. no. 83, pl. LXIII. *Goya,* Musée des Beaux-Arts, Bordeaux, May 16–June 30, 1951, cat. no. 41. *Exposición de Retratos de Goya,* Museo del Prado, Madrid, July, 1951, cat. no. 18.

Collections: Said to have been found in a closet of a country house in Eastern Spain by Goya's grandchild, Mariano Goya, about 1818.[3] Don Valentin de Carderera y Solano, Madrid, by 1877.[4] Duke of Béjar, Madrid; descended to his daughter, Dona Bernardina Roca de Togores y Tellez-Girón, XVI Condesa de Oliva; descended to Don Francisco Escrivá de Romaní y Roca de Togores, XVII Conde de Oliva, Madrid, by 1923; descended to Condes de Oliva, Madrid, by 1951. [Newhouse Galleries, Inc., New York.]
Kimbell Bequest, ACF 54.1.

Notes:

1 *Catálogo ilustrado de la Exposición de Pinturas de Goya*, Museo del Prado, Madrid, 1928, cat. no. 83. See also Véase Díaz de Escobar, *Rita Luna*, Málaga, 1900.

2 It is dated about 1814 by August L. Mayer, *Francisco de Goya*, Munich, 1923, p. 195, cat. no. 331, pl. 269. Xavière Desparmet Fitz-Gerald, *L'Œuvre peint de Goya*, Paris, 1928–50, vol. II, p. 174, cat. no. 401, dates the painting in 1808. José Gudiol, *Goya, 1746–1828...*, Barcelona, 1971, cat. no. 656, fig. 1065, dates it about 1815.

3 See: ... *Exposición de Pinturas de Goya.*

4 *Catálogo ... de retratos antiguos ... coleccionados por D. Valentín Cardedera y Solano*, Madrid, 1877, cat. no. 327.

Additional References:

Conde de la Viñaza, *Goya, su tiempo, su vida, sus obras*, Madrid, 1887, p. 239, cat. no. LXIX.
Paul Lafond, *Goya*, Paris, [1902], p. 132, cat. no. 154.
Valerian von Loga, *Francisco de Goya*, Berlin, 1903, pp. 88, 90, 199, cat. no. 268.
Albert F. Calvert, *Goya–An Account of His Life and Works*, London, 1908, p. 136, cat. no. 174.
Hugh Stokes, *Francisco de Goya*, London, 1914, p. 338, cat. no. 243.
Aureliano de Beruete y Moret, *Goya*, Madrid, 1915–19, vol. I, p. 176, cat. no. 162.
Leonardo Estarico, *Francisco de Goya, el hombre y el artista*, Buenos Aires, 1942, p. 269.
Connoisseur, vol. CXXXIV, no. 541, December, 1954, color illus. on cover and p. 169 (no text reference).
Pierre Gassier and Juliet Wilson, *The Life and Complete Work of Francisco de Goya*, New York, 1971, cat no. III, 1565, p. 377, illus. p. 298.

François-Henri Mulard, 1769–1850
Portrait of a Lady
Painted about 1810

Oil on canvas, 39 × 31 3/4 in. (99 × 80.7 cm.)

This portrait is a revealing example of the pervasive strength of Neoclassicism in French painting at the beginning of the nineteenth century. During the Napoleonic era in particular this viewpoint was dominated by an emphasis on history painting, especially with intellectual allusions to classical history. These narrative concerns stimulated the development of pictorial conventions suitable for dramatic emphasis that also dominated portraits of the period. Jacques-Louis David (1748–1825), the progenitor of this mode, was enormously influential during his long career and had many gifted and innovative followers (the most notable being J. A. D. Ingres), as well as numerous students. Many of the latter, such as François-Henri Mulard, are not well known.

By the time Mulard painted the Kimbell *Portrait of a Lady*, he was about forty years old and a mature artist. Having won the second annual Grand Prix de Rome in 1782, he also became recognized as a history painter for his works exhibited in the Paris Salons between 1808 and 1817. He appears to have been regarded as a competent follower of conventional standards, for he was appointed inspector of designs for the tapestries at the Gobelin Factory in Beauvais.[1]

His *Portrait of a Lady* is a general but slightly idealized treatment of a specific subject that conforms to the contemporary predilection for voluptuous, pampered femininity. Although the portrait lacks specific classical allusions, its style is fundamentally neoclassical in the use of strong local colors, precise draftsmanship, and attention to detail and pattern. Mulard strikes an equilibrium between simplicity and intricacy by isolating the figure against an austere, flat background that acts as a foil to the busy patterning of the sitter's costume and accessories and frames her face and the undulating outline of her silhouette. The upright pose of this young lady and the directness of her gaze may merely be Mulard's means of conveying the sitter's alert, individual temperament. An intriguing transformation of neoclassical conventions, this pose contrasts with the more relaxed attitudes of sitters in other portraits of the period. Many of these allude to specific classical antecedents, such as David's languidly posed portrait of *Madame de Verninac*, 1799, now in the Louvre, which is based on a Roman portrait of Agrippina.[2]

Another contrast can be observed in the rather active pattern of folds in the variously textured fabrics and the agitated distribution of evenly hued colors, accented by such details as the slightly eccentric arrangement of curls in her hair and of her sash and the skewed disposition of her red-beaded necklace. The effect is a subtle but distinct departure from the cool restraint that pervades more coherently arranged portraits by David and Ingres in which there is a more deliberate integration of pattern and color.

The sitter's identity is unknown but the fashionable nature of her high-waisted Empire dress and the plethora of colorful accessories suggest that she may be the wife or daughter of a successful Parisian bourgeois. The style of dress is also the basis for the estimated date of the painting.

Inscription: Lower left: *Mulard*

Description: Three-quarter-length view of a seated young woman silhouetted against a medium grey background. She is turned slightly to her right, her left arm resting on the back of a light brown wood chair. Her brown eyes are directed at the viewer and she has pale skin and rosy cheeks and lips. Her short, black, curly hair is parted in the center and she wears a gold tiara with red jewels. Her long, white dress is bound below the bustline in Empire style with a striped ribbon sash of light blue and cream which falls at her left side. Delicate white dotted lace is gathered in a ruffle at the neckline of the dress; there is a blue plaid scarf with kelly green stripes, violet shadows and multicolored fringe about her shoulders, knotted in front and tucked beneath the sash. The long sleeves of her dress are trimmed at the upper arm with eyelet lace, two rows of which also trim the wrists. A cream, fringed shawl with an embroidered or screen-printed floral pattern of red, green, blue and yellow is draped over her arms. Holding pale yellow gloves in her lap, she wears a red necklace with uniform beads and matching drop earrings.

Condition: Good. The paint is applied with low impasto which has been flattened slightly during a previous treatment, probably when the original canvas was relined. There is an old, large, L-shaped tear at the upper left which extends horizontally through her hair and the background and angles vertically down the canvas; this has been filled and inpainted. There is scattered inpainting in the background and the fabrics.

Exhibitions: None known.

Collections: Normand family, Paris.[3] [Newhouse Galleries, Inc., New York.]
Kimbell Bequest, ACF 58.6.

Notes:

1 E. Bénézit, *Dictionnaire critique et documentaire des peintres, sculpteurs, dessinateurs et graveurs*, Paris, 1966, vol. 6, p. 255.

2 Robert Rosenblum, *Jean-Auguste-Dominique Ingres*, New York, 1967, p. 122, illus.

3 Information supplied by vendor.

Thomas Lawrence, 1769–1830
Frederick H. Hemming
Painted about 1824–25

Oil on canvas, 30 × 25 3/8 in. (76.2 × 61.9 cm.)

This portrait of Frederick Herbert Hemming, and the companion portrait of his wife, date from late in Thomas Lawrence's career[1] when he was regarded as one of the outstanding portrait painters of his day. In England, where he was knighted in 1815, his distinguished reputation made him the almost unanimous choice as President of the Royal Academy in the 1820 election for the successor to Benjamin West. In continental Europe, after the exhibition of his impressive series of state portraits for the Waterloo Chamber of Windsor Castle, he was also widely acclaimed. Delacroix was impressed by his portrait of the Duc de Richelieu, and in Rome the fluid brushwork and rich color of his accomplished style were favorably compared to those of Titian.[2]

Lawrence earned this reputation with a prodigious talent and enormous skill. As a young painter he had quickly absorbed the calm classical conceptions of Joshua Reynolds and transformed them into vibrant and arresting images that depend for their effect not on intellectual allusion or balance of design, but on a dramatization of personality evoked by broad areas of dazzling color, strong tonal contrasts and long sweeping lines. Throughout his career, Lawrence's best portraits show that his "presentation of character is frequently highly individual and subtly attuned to the personality of the sitter."[3] Such distinctions of individual temperaments can be observed in this pair of portraits. The calculated reserve of Hemming's gaze, the vigorous modeling and long curving lines of his elegantly cut clothes and the strong contrasts of light and dark tones connote a self-assured, almost imperious temperament. In contrast, the young

woman faces the viewer with an innocent, rather dreamy directness and her portrait is dominated by warm flesh tones and gently rounded forms, all having a distinctly feminine (but very ladylike) sensuality that is enhanced by the delicate impasto of the fragile laces edging her dress.

The origin of these two paintings is informative;[4] it lies in Lawrence's passion for collecting old master drawings, which had resulted in a large and quite distinguished collection by the mid-1820s. Lawrence painted the portrait of Frederick Hemming in exchange for Giovanni Cipriani's original design for the diploma of the Royal Academy.[5] This drawing was owned by Richard Baker who, refusing Lawrence's attempt to purchase it, offered it to him as a gift. After Lawrence declined that gesture, they compromised on Lawrence's offer to paint a portrait and Baker nominated as the sitter his great-nephew, Frederick Hemming, who lived with him. Shortly thereafter Baker died, willing to Hemming his collection that included some drawings by Raphael. For these, Lawrence offered to paint a second portrait; Hemming agreed, proposing that Lawrence paint his fiancée, a Miss Bloxam, who was distantly related to Lawrence's brother-in-law. Subsequently, the acquaintance became a friendship and during the last years of his life Lawrence often passed the evening at the Hemmings' home on Sussex Place, Regent's Park, London. The commissioning of these two portraits at slightly different times accounts for their having been painted on different supports even though they appear as companions.

Description: Nearly half-length view of a clean-shaven young man, looking to his left. His eyes are brown and his curly hair is light brown. He wears a dark reddish-brown, double-breasted jacket with velvet lapels over a cream-colored waistcoat, a pale-blue undervest and a high white stock that is secured by a pale blue pearl stickpin. The loosely painted background is dark green except for a brown-toned area in the upper left corner, a yellowish-pink area at the lower left and a pale brown area at the lower right.

Condition: Very good. There is some superficial inpainting in the face and stock to attenuate the pattern of fine drying cracks.

Exhibitions: Institution for Promoting the Fine Arts, Birmingham, 1828.[6] *Old Masters Exhibition*, Royal Academy of Arts, London, 1873, cat. no. 9. *Exposition de Portraits Anciens et Modernes*, Galerie Charles Brunner, Paris, 1901, cat. no. 30. *Sir Thomas Lawrence as Painter and Collector*, Columbus Gallery of Fine Arts, 1955, cat. no. 17, illus.

Collections: Frederick H. Hemming, London, to sale: [Christie's], April 14, 1881, lot 245, sold to Notley. Possibly Adolph Hirsch, London, by 1913. [Henry Seligmann], New York, to sale: [Anderson Galleries], New York, March 29, 1934, lot 37, sold to: Mrs. C. F. Gould. [Duveen Gallery], New York, sold to: Thomas Manville, New York. Passed to Lorraine Manville (later Mrs. C. W. Dresselhuys), by 1954. [Newhouse Galleries, Inc., New York.]
Kimbell Bequest, ACF 63.1.

Notes:

1 Kenneth Garlick, "A Catalogue of the Paintings . . . by Sir Thomas Lawrence," *The Walpole Society*, vol. 39, 1964, pp. 104–5, and Garlick's earlier book, *Sir Thomas Lawrence*, London, 1954, p. 42.

2 Garlick, 1954, pp. 13–15.

3 Frederick Cummings, "Sir Thomas Lawrence," *Romantic Art in Britain . . . 1760–1860*, Detroit Institute of Arts and Philadelphia Museum of Art, January–April, 1968, p. 174.

[4] This narrative is based on that given by William T. Whitley, *Art in England, 1821–1837*, London, 1936, p. 200–201. Whitley's account is thought to be based on Hemming's own memoir, *The History of two portraits painted by Sir Thomas Lawrence with an episode in the life of that painter, by the original of one of the portraits*, London, 1872, 21 pages. Unfortunately, no copy of Hemming's pamphlet can be located.

[5] Cipriani's drawing had been given by his son to Lord Lansdowne with whom it remained until 1806 when it was acquired by George Baker, who died in 1811, leaving it to his brother, Richard Baker. After Lawrence's death it eventually entered the collection of the Royal Academy in 1847. See Whitley, p. 200.

[6] This portrait and its companion are said to have been loaned to this exhibition at Lawrence's request. See Walter Armstrong, *Lawrence*, London, 1913, p. 139.

Additional Reference:

Ronald S. Gower, *Sir Thomas Lawrence*, London and Paris, 1900, p. 136.

Thomas Lawrence, 1769–1830
Mrs. Frederick Hemming
Painted about 1824–25

Oil on panel, 30 × 24 1/2 in. (76.2 × 62.2 cm.)

The interesting origin of this pleasant portrait of Mrs. Hemming is detailed in the entry for the companion portrait of her husband. Although the sitter has been identified only as a Miss Bloxam, it is known that she was a distant cousin of Richard Bloxam,[1] the husband of Lawrence's older sister Anne. Even though commissioned while she was engaged, this portrait was apparently finished after her marriage because she wears a plain gold wedding band (behind a second ring with bluish stones) on the ring finger of her left hand. The slender brush she delicately holds in her right hand alludes to her abilities as "an accomplished painter on porcelain."[2]

Description: Half-length view of a seated young woman facing the viewer. She wears a white dress with a low-cut neckline and short sleeves, all trimmed with white lace. Her left arm rests on a low dark table at her side; her right hand, which also rests upon the table, holds a thin dark brush, poised as if about to paint the china dish on the table, beside which are a saucer and some brushes. Her eyes are dark hazel and her short brown hair is curled in ringlets. A strand of pearls, with a silver clasp, encircles her neck; a dark red pin is at her bosom and a pink sash about her waist. The background is a warm dark red curtain except for an opening beyond her right shoulder, which reveals a patch of blue sky and a barely indicated vase with flowers.

Condition: Very good. There is scattered inpainting of fine drying cracks in the flesh tones and in the background. It is mounted on a cradle.

Exhibitions: Institution for Promoting the Fine Arts, Birmingham, 1828, cat. no. 78. *Old Masters Exhibition*, Royal Academy of Arts, London, 1873, cat. no. 21. *Second National Loan Exhibition*, New Grosvenor Gallery, London, 1913, cat. no. 117, illus. p. 180. *Sir Thomas Lawrence as Painter and Collector*, Columbus Gallery of Fine Arts, 1955, cat. no. 18, illus.

Collections: Frederick H. Hemming, London, to sale: [Christie's], April 14, 1881, lot 246, sold to Notley. Adolph Hirsch, London, by 1913.[3] Possibly Mrs. C. F. Gould, about 1934. [Duveen Gallery], New York, sold to: Thomas Manville, New York. Passed to Lorraine Manville (later Mrs. C. W. Dresselhuys) by 1954. [Newhouse Galleries, Inc., New York.]
Kimbell Bequest, ACF 63.2.

Notes:

1 Walter Armstrong, *Lawrence*, London, 1913, p. 139, pl. XXII, facing p. 58. Kenneth Garlick, "A Catalogue of the Paintings . . . of Sir Thomas Lawrence," *The Walpole Society*, vol. 39, 1964, p. 105.

2 Armstrong, p. 139. This source also records an engraving of the portrait, by T. H. Greenhead, in 1893.

3 Armstrong, pl. XXII. Algernon Graves, *A Century of Loan Exhibitions*, London, 1913–15, p. 2020.

Additional Reference:

The Masterpieces of Lawrence, Gowan's Art Books, no. 52, London, 1913, illus. p. 42.
This portrait is also cited in most of the references given for Lawrence's portrait of Frederick Hemming.

J. M. W. Turner, 1775–1851
Glaucus and Scylla - Ovid's Metamorphoses
Painted in 1841

Oil on panel, 31 × 30 1/2 in. (79 × 77.5 cm.)

Joseph Mallord William Turner, the son of a London barber and wigmaker, received the most perfunctory elementary education while spending his boyhood doing sketches and watercolors to sell to his father's customers or brushing in the backgrounds of renderings produced in the architectural studios around Covent Garden. His natural aptitude for painting was so great that he had a watercolor accepted in the Royal Academy Exhibition when he was fifteen, and his father pronounced that he was to become a great artist. The prophecy came true, for Turner was a leading member of the Royal Academy himself when he was twenty-four. He more than compensated for his somewhat deprived upbringing and education by his native intelligence, boundless ambition, voracious curiosity, uncanny powers of observation and incredible energy. His entire career was an insatiable campaign to devour all that nature and the history of art had to teach and then outdo the old masters at the same tasks they had attempted. In the process, he progressed from one of the best meticulously representational painters in the English "topographical" school to an artist who, in his last decade, was reaching out into the borderland of abstract art one hundred years before its time.

Until the end of the 1830s Turner did not publicly exhibit his more experimental canvases in which expressive use of color was pushed to an extreme, even though his explorations in this direction affected such famous public pictures as *Ulysses Deriding Polyphemus* as early as the Academy show of 1829. Although he had already won a vast public, had achieved great official recognition, and had become rich thereby, contemporaneous opinion

of his more daring works was succinctly phrased by Hazlitt, the essayist: "They are pictures of nothing, and very like." In 1841 one of the pictures he chose for the Royal Academy Exhibition was *Glaucus and Scylla*;[1] about this time Punch Magazine said that his style, whatever he titled his painting, "is all the same; for it is quite as easy to fancy it one thing as another." The gap of incomprehension between avant-garde artist and newly democratized society, a phenomenon particularly endemic to the modern age, had already begun to widen. Although this attitude toward much of his later work caused Turner personal pain, it did not deter him from pushing steadfastly toward greater "abstraction." And he did have considerable support for this bent; the discerning collector B. G. Windus, a retired coachmaker, for example, bought *Glaucus and Scylla* out of the Academy show.[2]

What most of Turner's contemporaries could not see was the fact that his powerfully expressive use of color and light was not an arbitrarily or willfully imposed abstraction for formal reasons alone. What is represented in the picture always exactly obeys the conditions between nature and the human eye within the circumstances that the artist has chosen. In *Glaucus and Scylla* Turner chooses one of his favorite circumstances for good reason, that of looking directly into the setting sun, which blindingly reflects off the steaming sea and gossamer mists of a place steeped in myth, the Strait of Scylla and Charybdis at the lower tip of Italy. Dazzled and withheld by natural phenomena from too close scrutiny, we mortals witness the beautiful nymph's rejection of the water god, once a handsome fisherman, who became a frightening denizen of the sea because he loved it above all else, until he encountered Scylla. Water, air, land and light interpenetrate, as do history and legend, humanity and the gods, the natural and the supernatural. It is, indeed, a metamorphosis in the spirit of the ancient Ovid,[3] as well as a compendium of those elements Turner embraced in his ambitious career: grandiose landscapes with awesome natural effects, historical and mythological subject matter, scientifically analyzed perception, and classic two-dimensional and spatial composition in the spirit of Claude or Poussin.

Inscription: Written in the lower left corner, in Turner's hand, are partially legible lines which roughly parallel the horizontal edge of the picture, but the words are upside down as compared to the subject matter. Lying under the thin paint glazes, perhaps in soft pencil, Turner's partially legible words, which seem to be part of a reminder to himself, read: "... delay that then is a ... paint of the panel ... ground ... but the gesso for the ... but like I can get ... in the ...." Turner's technical methods were unorthodox, highly inventive, and sometimes bizarre. He disregarded conventions in such matters, so long as he could achieve his desired effect.

Description: The whole scene is dominated by a bright yellow-orange sun, setting on the horizon at left, its brilliant rays streaming forward toward the viewer and fanning out from left to right to set the dominant deep diagonals that control the composition and figural action. It was Circe, daughter of the sun, to whom Glaucus appealed when rejected by Scylla, and Circe transformed the beautiful nymph into the horrifying menace of the strait. Glaucus emerges from the sea in the near distance, left of center, and reaches out toward the naked Scylla who flees to lower right. Two little *amoretti*, airborne to her right, accentuate the fleeing action. A sheer cliff rises at the extreme left, at the bottom of which is a rocky beach strewn with varied, minute sea creatures uncovered by the tide. At the right rise two overhanging pinnacles (cf. Ovid), the tops crowned by fortresses, access to which is provided by a Roman-style bridge. In the far distance, just right of center, Mount Etna smokes unconcernedly, but its plume carefully participates in the fan-like compositional scheme dictated by the sun.

Condition: Excellent. Fine age crackle pattern reflecting wood structure of panel generally throughout paint structure. Double paint layer in upper corners, with original layer strengthened after abrasion caused by placement of picture in an arched frame at one point in recent history. Panel cradled at the back.

Exhibitions: Royal Academy of Art, London, 1841. *Bicentenary Exhibition*, Royal Academy, London, Dec. 10, 1968–March 2, 1969, cat. no. 166.

Collections: B. Godfrey Windus, London, who bought it from the Royal Academy Exhibition of 1841, until 1868. Louis Huth, London, 1872. [Arthur Tooth & Sons, Ltd.], London. José deMurietta, Marquis de Santurce, London, 1883. Sir Horatio Davies, Lord Mayor of London, 1901. Charles Sedelmeyer, Paris, 1902. A French collector until after 1950. Mrs. Chamberlin, United States, to 1966. Foundation Acquisition, AP 66.11.

Théodore Géricault, 1791–1824
Portrait Study of a Youth
Painted about 1818–20

Oil on canvas, 18 1/2×15 in. (47×38.1 cm.)

The remarkable psychological presence of the young man in this portrait is a salient characteristic of Théodore Géricault's paintings. A prolific painter, whose early death cut short an artistic career of less than fifteen years, Géricault infused his paintings with an intensity of emotion that is in marked contrast to the cool restraint of works by many of his academic contemporaries. In this painting, the long, glistening highlights in the hair, the deftly modeled planes of the face, and the vigorous brushstrokes of the collar communicate the intensity of the painter's rapid and assured technique.

Its unfinished condition is not surprising. Once Géricault had accomplished his basic objective, he felt no need to continue. Like many of his oil studies and sketches, this is a private investigation of a pictorial idea and not conceived as a vehicle for communicating the idea publicly. After finishing only the highlighted portion of the youth's head, Géricault had successfully suggested the ingenuous optimism of a youth just maturing into manhood; it was unnecessary for him to finish the summarily rendered undercolors of the shadowed side of the head. Thus, the painting is a revealing document of an aesthetic approach that is concerned primarily with definition of mood and feeling, rather than capturing a specific likeness.

Since the painting was intended as a study in psychology, the sitter's uncertain identity is not critical. The sitter may have been a son of Bro de Comères, Géricault's tenant and neighbor in Paris, or perhaps a member of the Dedreux-Dorcy family.[1] Whoever the sitter, Géricault's record of him is a masterful and incisive image of maturing youth.

Stylistically, this study dates after Géricault's most notable painting, *The Raft of the Medusa* of 1818–19, and was probably done in Paris before Géricault's sojourn in England in 1820–22.[2] Further investigation of the identity of the sitter may permit a firmer estimate of the painting's date.

Notes:

[1] Algernon Graves, *Royal Academy Exhibitions 1796–1904*, vol. VIII, London, 1906, p. 40, no. 542.

[2] Charles F. Bell, *A List of Works Contributed to Public Exhibitions by J. M. W. Turner, R. A.*, London, 1901, p. 143, no. 230.

[3] Ovid (43 B.C–A.D. 17), *Metamorphoses*, Book XIII, *Glaucus Becomes a Sea God.*

Additional References:

John Burnet, *Turner and His Works*, London, 1852, p. 119, no. 214.
W. Roberts, *Memorials of Christie's*, vol. II, London, 1897, p. 47.
Sir Walter Armstrong, *Turner*, London, 1902, pp. 147, 222.
Robert Chignell, *J. M. W. Turner*, Royal Academy, London, 1902, p. 200.
W. L. Wyllie, *J. M. W. Turner*, London, 1905, p. 174, no. 230.
Alex J. Finberg, *The Life of J. M. W. Turner, R. A.*, Oxford, 1939, p. 383, p. 506, no. 544.

Description: Frontal view of the head of a young man, age 13 to 18, with hazel eyes and long brown hair. The sitter looks slightly above and to the right of the viewer. His neck is framed by a broad, open-throat white collar, and he wears a green shirt. Only on the highlighted left side of the painting is the face completely finished; on the shadowed right side, hair details, facial modeling, and the collar are indicated in underpaint. The background is thinly painted in warm brown tones.

Condition: Very good. Several small flake losses, now inpainted, in scattered areas. Minor abrasion in the background. Cleaned and lined in 1969.

Exhibitions: Delacroix, ses maîtres, ses amis, ses élèves, Musée des Beaux-Arts, Bordeaux, 1963, cat. no. 286. *Géricault dans les collections privées françaises,* Galerie Claude Aubry, Paris, Nov. 6–Dec. 7, 1964, cat no. 28 *(Buste de jeune homme),* illus. *Géricault to Courbet ...*, Roland, Browse and Delbanco, London, May–June 1965, cat. no. 25 *(Portrait of a Young Man with Long Hair),* pl. VIII. *Géricault,* organized by Lorenz Eitner, Los Angeles County Museum of Art, Detroit Institute of Arts and Philadelphia Museum of Art, Oct. 12, 1971–May 14, 1972, cat. no. 55, illus. p. 95.

Collections: A. M. Leclerc, by 1879.[3] Pierre Dubaut, Paris, by 1963.[4] Private collection, Paris.
Foundation Acquisition, AP 69.7.

Notes:

[1] Lorenz Eitner, letter to Richard F. Brown, March 10, 1970.

[2] Eitner, *Géricault,* Los Angeles County Museum of Art, 1971, cat. no. 55.

[3] Charles Clément, *Géricault, étude biographique et critique ...*, Paris, 1879, cat. no. 129 *(Buste de jeune homme).*

[4] Red wax monogram *P D* on original stretcher.

Jean Baptiste Camille Corot, 1796–1875
View of the Ville-d'Avray
Painted about 1865–70

Oil on canvas, 22 3/4 × 38 1/2 in. (57.7 × 97.8 cm.)

By the 1860s, Jean Baptiste Camille Corot was recognized as one of the preeminent masters of French landscape painting. Like his predecessors Claude Lorrain and Nicolas Poussin, Corot journeyed to Italy early in his artistic career where he developed an extraordinarily facile style by making numerous studies of Rome and its environs. These are characterized by meticulously constructed compositions, precise drawing, carefully observed effects of light, and warm color tonalities. Toward the middle of his career, in the 1850s, however, his style changed. Soft, imaginary landscapes of lyrical themes gradually replaced his earlier, crisp paintings of specific places.[1]

View of the Ville-d'Avray is typical of many of Corot's paintings in the 1860s which evoke a mood of nostalgia. It depicts one of Corot's favorite scenes, the family property on the outskirts of Paris, but emphasis is placed on atmosphere and mood rather than on literal imagery. The figures in the scene, a child greeted by two women, a man poling his boat, and another woman carrying a bundle, impute the sense of a narrative event. The cool color harmonies complement the sense of calm on a late spring afternoon which is evoked by the long shadows cast by the figures, the stillness of the water reflecting the luminous sky, and the silvery light filtering through the feathery foliage of the young trees massed at the left. These elements, which are also seen in a smaller, later variation[2] of the Kimbell painting, appear repeatedly in the artist's landscapes of this period, although they are imaginatively varied.[3]

Inscription: Lower left: COROT

Description: Landscape with five figures. A man dressed in a beige shirt, brown pants, and red cap poles his wooden boat in a body of cream and grey water at the right side of the canvas. Near the center foreground on the light ochre and grey-green bank are two seated women dressed in blue-grey who greet a small child in a brown dress. A third woman dressed in brown, wearing a blue scarf over her head, walks toward the left side of the canvas carrying a beige bundle of wood. Behind her is a clump of trees with highlighted grey-green foliage. A screen of deep grey-green trees edges the pond in the middle ground, ending at the far right where cows graze in a green pasture. Behind them are beige farmhouses with reddish roofs before grey hills in the distance. The pale blue sky is veiled by creamy clouds.

Condition: Good. There is normal very fine age craquelure in the paint layer which is consistent with that in the varnish layer. Areas of minor overpaint are scattered throughout the canvas.

Exhibitions: Exposition Rétrospective de Tableaux et Dessins de Maîtres Modernes, Galerie Durand-Ruel, Paris, 1878, no. 64.[4]

Collections: Edwards Collection, Paris, to 1873. Bought by Henri Hecht, Paris, at sale May 10, 1876.[5] [Newhouse Galleries, Inc., New York.]
Kimbell Bequest, ACK 56.2.

Notes:

[1] Jean Leymarie, *Corot,* Geneva, 1966, pp. 79–83.

[2] Alfred Robaut, *L'Œuvre de Corot, catalogue raisonné et illustré,* Paris, 1905, vol. III, p. 352, cat. no. 2291 *(Ville-d'Avray, Le Bateau Quittant La Rive),* illus. p. 353. Robaut also notes that an etching reproducing this painting was made by Paul Emile Leterrier.

[3] James Merrill, "Notes on Corot," *Corot,* The Art Institute of Chicago, Oct. 6–Nov. 13, 1960, pp. 14–15.

[4] Robaut, p. 88, cat. no. 1503, illus. p. 89.

[5] Robaut, p. 88.

Jean Baptiste Camille Corot, 1796–1875
Orpheus Singing His Lament for Eurydice
Painted about 1865–70

Oil on canvas, 16 1/2 × 24 in. (41.9 × 61 cm.)

Of the three paintings by Jean Baptiste Camille Corot in this catalogue, *Orpheus Singing His Lament for Eurydice* best exemplifies the artist's idealized conception of landscape painting, coming closest to Claude Lorrain's style both in its mood of gentle reverie and its mythological subject. It is also perhaps the best example of the three of a "souvenir," or nostalgic distillation of arcadian landscapes Corot had painted earlier in his career.

Its theme was inspired by the famous opera, C. W. Gluck's "Orpheus and Eurydice." Originally produced in Vienna in 1762, it was first presented in Paris in 1774 at the Royal Academy. A new production at the Théâtre-Lyrique in Paris by Hector Berlioz in 1859[1] inspired Corot to paint several works on the Orpheus theme, the most important of which is his large *Orphée ramenant Eurydice*[2] which he exhibited in the Salon of 1861. The Kimbell painting depicts the beginning of the first act of this opera. In a grotto-like setting, Orpheus plays his lyre and sings with three friends who mourn the death of Orpheus' beautiful bride, Eurydice, who had succumbed to a serpent's bite.

The Kimbell painting can be regarded as a dual "souvenir," as it not only repeats this favorite theme but also a visual motif from a slightly earlier painting, *Souvenir of Italy, Castel Gandolfo,* 1865,[3] in which the same buildings on a hillside appear in the middle ground. Corot had actually painted studies from nature of the Castel Gandolfo on Lake Albano, Italy, in 1826–27[4] in which these geometric, architectural forms on a hill first appear. In the Kimbell work, they are employed to evoke the imaginary appearance of an idyllic setting.

Several elements in this painting had become standard by this point in Corot's career. The carefully constructed composition has a stage-like character, although Corot has eliminated the traditional proscenium of landscape painting and the figures are placed in the immediate foreground. The shadowed foreground is silhouetted against the sunlit lake and geometric forms of buildings in the middle ground. The background is comprised of a low horizon line and a light, atmospheric sky which occupies two-thirds of the composition. The mystical light filters through the loosely brushed, feathery trees in the foreground, rendering them almost transparent in the early spring light.[5]

Inscription: Lower left: COROT

Description: Landscape with four figures. Dressed in a pinkish-grey toga, the central figure with a lyre stands facing three young girls seated on green grass in the right foreground. At the right edge of the canvas is a tall tree. To the left of center is a mature tree with dark, grey-green foliage growing out of a rocky, brown cliff. Behind the figures in the middle ground is a light, blue-grey lake and blue buildings on an incline at the left. White clouds are suggested in the pale blue sky.

Condition: Very good. The paint layer has normal fine age craquelure and the varnish is slightly yellowed. Some small repairs and minor strengthening are evident in scattered areas of the canvas.

Exhibitions: Extended loan, Metropolitan Museum of Art, New York, 1886–1903; also, Jan. 31–May 6, 1941.[6] *The Serene World of Corot,* (Salvation Army War Fund), Wildenstein Gallery, New York, Nov. 11–Dec. 12, 1942, p. 41, no. 57, illus.

Collections: Alfred Sensier, Paris.[7] Brig. Gen. Cornelius Vanderbilt, New York; descended to Mrs. Cornelius Vanderbilt, New York, to 1945.[8] [Newhouse Galleries, Inc., New York.]
Kimbell Bequest, ACF 61.3.

Notes:

1 Gustave Kobbe, *Kobbe's Complete Opera Book*, New York, 1954, pp. 37–40. Hector Berlioz, *Gluck & His Operas*, London, n. d., pp. 1–3.

2 Alfred Robaut, *L'Œuvre de Corot, catalogue raisonné et illustré*, Paris, 1905, vol. III, cat. no. 1622 (Now in a private collection, Switzerland).

3 Robaut, cat. no. 1626.

4 Jean Leymarie, *Corot*, Geneva, 1966, p. 6.

5 S. Lane Faison, Jr., *Corot*, the Art Institute of Chicago, Oct. 6–Nov. 13, 1960, p. 6; also, James Merrill, "Notes on Corot," *Corot*, pp. 14–15.

6 The Kimbell painting was one of seven paintings loaned in 1941 by Col. and Mrs. Vanderbilt. *Bulletin of the Metropolitan Museum of Art*, New York, 1941, vol. 36, no. 4, p. 103.

7 Robaut, p. 174, cat. no. 1713 *(Orphée Charme les Humains)*, illus. p. 175; Robaut notes that this painting has been reproduced in an etching by Adolphe Lalauze and in a lithograph by Emile Vernier. Alfred Sensier was a friend of many of the French nineteenth-century landscape painters.

8 The preceding three collections were listed by the dealer at the date of purchase. Sold in Vanderbilt sale, April 18–19, 1945. See E. Bénézit, *Dictionnaire ... des peintres, sculpteurs, dessinateurs et graveurs*, [Paris], 1966, vol. II, p. 648.

Jean Baptiste Camille Corot, 1796–1875
Une Baie Napolitaine
Painted about 1872–73

Oil on canvas, 21 × 17¼ in. (53.3 × 43.8 cm.)

Painted very late in Corot's career, *Une Baie Napolitaine* is characteristic of the artist's landscapes at that time. The scene does not represent a specific place but is a "recollection" based on Corot's earlier visits to the rugged landscape around Naples. Corot had traveled extensively in Italy and made his third and last trip there in 1843,[1] about thirty years before he painted this landscape. It seems likely, therefore, that the artist intended this painting as an evocation from his memory of the lyrical mood of Italian scenery.

To create a tranquil mood of nostalgic melancholy, Corot employed several elements which recur throughout his late work. The buildings in the middle ground allude to ruins from antiquity. The large tree with vague, feathery foliage in the foreground dominates the composition, while the costume of the small figure at the base of the tree adds the singular warm note of color. The rocky cliff and expanse of blue sky with puffy white clouds complete the idyllic setting.

Corot's concern for natural appearances and the characteristically gentle touch and subdued colors of his late paintings are qualities that have consistently appealed to collectors since his lifetime.

Description: Landscape with one small figure dressed in brown pants, dark grey vest, and a red cap who stands at the base of a brown and green mature tree in the center of the painting. To the right is a brown and beige rocky precipice. In the middle ground at the left is a greyish building overlooking a white and grey-green body of water. The sky shades from medium blue at the top to pale blue at the horizon and has white clouds brushed in with a low impasto.

Condition: Fair. There is filling and inpainting in the center to repair a one-inch-square hole, as well as some minor strengthening in the foliage.

Exhibitions: None known.

Collections: Collection Verdier, Paris, June 1874.[2] Private collection, United States.[3] [Newhouse Galleries, Inc., New York.]
Kimbell Bequest, ACK 62.1.

Notes:

1 Jean Leymarie, *Corot*, Geneva, 1966, p. 7.

2 Alfred Robaut, *L'Œuvre de Corot, catalogue raisonné et illustré*, Paris, 1905, vol. III, p. 352, cat. no. 2295 bis, illus. p. 353.

3 This collection was listed by the dealer at the time of purchase.

Additional Reference:

The Connoisseur, vol. 149, March, 1962, color illus. on cover.

Richard Parkes Bonington, 1802–1828
Lake Como
Painted in 1826

Oil on panel, 7 1/4 × 6 3/4 in. (18.4 × 17.2 cm.)

This tiny painting was done by Richard Parkes Bonington while traveling in Italy during the spring of 1826. On his way back to Paris, he stopped in northern Lombardy at Lake Como, an idyllically lovely body of water which is surrounded by the Alps. Like many of his predecessors, Bonington continued the tradition of traveling to foreign lands to paint. During his stay in Italy he did some of his best works, and its short duration, from April 4 to June 20, marks the climax of his brief career. Unfortunately, he contracted tuberculosis on the trip and was subsequently able to work only sporadically until his death a month before his twenty-sixth birthday in Paris, 1828.[1]

Bonington made many pencil and watercolor sketches on his journey, as well as several oil sketches, which he developed further in his studio when he returned to Paris. Although he was born in England, he moved to Calais, France, as a youth and then to Paris where he came to know many of the young Romantic painters, especially Delacroix. They were very impressed with his almost exclusive use of watercolor, a medium which was relatively unknown in France but had a long tradition in Britain. His small works exhibited a spontaneous ease of handling which had great appeal on both sides of the Channel.[2]

Working in oil considerably less frequently, he used it much like watercolor, thinning the pigments down with oil to glazes with a transparent, wash-like consistency. The mountains, sky and the water in the Kimbell painting of *Lake Como* show how Bonington was able to render color and tonal nuances with great subtlety to capture transient

atmospheric qualities. By combining cool, delicate greys with warmer tones, he evoked the limpidity of the sky, the transparency of the shadows, and the fluidity of the water. He juxtaposed against these liquid glazes a minimum of minute details like the figures in the foreground which are rendered in brilliant opaque colors with crisp, flickering strokes. These small figures provide scale for the monumental mountains and lead the eye toward the curving diagonal entry into the deep picture space. His broad direct touch, deftly transferred from watercolor to oils, enabled him to make this sketch quickly, without hesitation, so that the painting possesses a memorably fresh effect and epitomizes the Romantic era's pictorial interpretation of nature.

Description: Mountainous landscape with a lake and two male figures. Before a large body of smooth grey water reflecting the white and pale grey clouds above, two travelers rest on a beige and light grey, rocky cliff in the lower right foreground. One man, wearing a blue-grey coat, sits facing the water on which a boat with a white sail floats in the distance; he appears to be sketching the scene. The other man, who wears a brown coat, beige slacks, and a grey cap, leans against the craggy cliff; a brown dog sits at his feet and behind him at the right are green and brown pine trees and tall, slender, brown and yellow deciduous trees. In the middle distance, the grey-toned mountains at each side rise majestically from the center, and beyond is a pale grey mountain, the pale yellow of the panel showing through.

Condition: Excellent. Oil paint is applied in low and moderate impasto and there is some very fine craquelure. The varnish is very fresh.

Exhibitions: None known.

Collections: Francis Neilson, New York; descended to Miss K. P. Evans, Locust Valley, N. Y.[3] [Newhouse Galleries, Inc., New York, by 1969.]
Foundation Acquisition, AP 70.20.

Notes:

1 Frederick Cummings and Allen Staley, *Romantic Art in Britain, Paintings and Drawings, 1760–1860*, The Detroit Institute of Arts, Jan. 9–Feb. 18, 1968, and the Philadelphia Museum of Art, March 4–April 21, 1968, p. 246.

2 Martin Hardie, *Water-colour Painting in Britain, vol. II: The Romantic Period*, London, 1967, pp. 173, 178.

3 Vendor information.

Théodore Rousseau, 1812–1867
Landscape in Normandy
Painted in 1832–33

Oil on canvas, 28 5/8 × 36 3/8 in. (72.7 × 92.3 cm.)

Pierre Etienne Théodore Rousseau was the guiding spirit of a loosely organized group of French landscape painters known as the Barbizon School, a name derived from the village at the edge of the forest of Fontainebleau not far from Paris. In this area, they made studies and drawings outdoors which were later completed in their studios. This practice, which was facilitated by the introduction of easily portable, lead paint tubes about 1840, later influenced the Impressionists. The Barbizon artists painted subjective landscapes that excluded concern for the social forces which were changing society's orientation from agrarian to urban. Although their work is noted for a great degree of naturalism, there is an underlying romanticism which embraces a "back-to-nature" attitude.[1]

Of all the Barbizon artists, Rousseau was the most controversial; the Salons would not accept his studies of wild nature, the critics gave him derisive reviews, and the public bought few of his paintings. This did not deter him from producing some of the most beautiful and personal work in the history of landscape painting.[2] Noted for its exactitude and realism, his work provided the transitional link between the classicists, Claude, Poussin and Corot, and the realists, Courbet and Manet.

Landscape in Normandy was painted early in Rousseau's career. After his first entry in the annual Paris Salon of 1831, he traveled through Brittany and Normandy in 1832.[3] The freshness of vision in the Kimbell painting is clearly represented by the way Rousseau captures the character of the marshy flat plains of rural Normandy, the forboding mood of the moisture-laden, stormy sky and the uneven

dispersal of light. Although the cows and people are painted with great plasticity, emphasis is placed on the elements of nature, reflecting Rousseau's overriding pantheistic philosophy.

Although he did not exhibit at the Salon between 1837 and 1847, he continued to be the most progressive influence as well as the focus for developments in French landscape painting.[4]

Inscription: Lower right: *Th. Rousseau*

Charles-François Daubigny, 1817–1878
French River Scene
Painted in 1871

Oil on panel, 15 1/4 × 26 3/4 in. (38.8 × 68 cm.)

Description: Landscape with cows and figures. At the lower edge of the canvas is brown underbrush; beyond this, in the left foreground is a russet and dark green incline which slopes down to an aqua pool where five cows are drinking. All highlighted with white, one cow is black, three are reddish-brown, and one is beige. At the right, a cowherd dressed in black stands watching the cows. In the center of the middle ground, a shepherd in a light blue-grey jacket stands watching his herd of beige and white sheep graze in a green pasture, as more sheep and cows graze at the right side of the canvas. Beyond is a clump of green and brown trees to the left of center and a screen of green poplar trees at the right. The land at the horizon shades to blue-grey below the cloudy, layered sky which occupies almost two-thirds of the composition. At the horizon, it is pearly grey; the layer above is medium grey intermixed with white clouds, while the stormy top layer is a much darker shade of grey.

Condition: Very good. The original canvas has been trimmed to the paint area and was relined in 1970. The impasto has been flattened slightly and there is normal old age craquelure. There is scattered minor filling and inpainting and one major tear in the upper right which has been repaired.

Exhibitions: None known.

Collections: Private collection, France.[5] [Pintura Establishment, Vaduz, Liechtenstein.]
Foundation Acquisition, AP 69.2.

Notes:

1 Robert L. Herbert, *Barbizon Revisited*, New York, 1962, pp. 15 ff.

2 Herbert, p. 174.

3 Herbert, p. 76.

4 Herbert, p. 174.

5 Information supplied at the time of purchase by the dealer who listed the title as *La Plaine en Normandie*.

By the 1850s Charles-François Daubigny had become one of the most original and strongest painters of the Barbizon School. Although he was only loosely associated with them (he never lived at Barbizon), he shared their great devotion to nature and was one of the few in the group who actually painted outdoors. In 1857 he set up a studio-boat, called "Le Botin," to drift down the Seine and Oise rivers and paint the transitory appearance of nature.[1] He thus initiated the so-called riverbank motif, which was to become immensely popular. Datable between 1859 and 1878, these poetic paintings of generally unidentifiable rural scenes show the artist's preoccupation with atmospheric effects and reflections of light on bodies of water.[2] Although the sketchy technique of these works disturbed the critics, the sober conventionality of Daubigny's compositions helped to get his work admitted to the Salon regularly.[3]

The Kimbell *French River Scene*, painted late in Daubigny's career, summarizes his impression of the verdant, bucolic countryside north of Paris. It exemplifies the originality of Daubigny's freshness of vision and technique and his quiet, lyrical romanticism, in contrast to the fervor and wildness of other Barbizon works. Dated 1871, this landscape was probably painted between May and September of that year. Having taken refuge in Holland and London during the Franco-Prussian war, he returned to his native town of Auvers in May; by September he was off again to Holland to seek more painting sites.[4] During his self-imposed exile, he saw landscapes of the English countryside by John Constable (1776–1837) and seascapes by his contemporary Eugène Boudin, and he painted landscapes alongside Claude Monet. Influenced by their concerns, his own work changed; his brushwork became looser and his palette lightened, qualities which became more marked in paintings during the last decade of his life.[5]

The luscious impastos in the sky of the Kimbell painting, as well as the bold brushstrokes in the foliage, the loaded color accents on the lilypads, and the abbreviated strokes used to suggest the form of the cows, reveal the effect of these artists' techniques on Daubigny's work. In addition, a serene mood is evoked by Daubigny's description of climatic conditions: the scene seems to be pervaded by the moist breeze of a late spring afternoon, and the clouds, which are reflected in the quiescent stream in the foreground, appear almost to be moving.

Daubigny combined his radical technique with a traditional approach to compositional structure in the riverbank motif which is naturally bilateral in its symmetry—a body of water with terrestrial borders on two sides. The composition is stabilized by Daubigny's prudent balance of the emphatic horizon with the vertical mass of dark trees in the middle distance that are silhouetted against the light sky. He used one compositional device in these later paintings, however, which is a departure from the conventions used in his earlier work. A more monumental focus for the panoramic view is created by pushing the foreground to the foremost plane, thus establishing an intimacy between the viewer and the painting. Even within its traditional format, the Kimbell painting has none of the historical or narrative connotations common to academic

landscapes that were being submitted to the Salon at that time. Daubigny's work, therefore, provides a strong link between the Barbizon tradition and the increasingly objective approach of the Impressionists, whose art he encouraged in the 1870s.

Inscription: Lower left: *Daubigny 1871*

Gustave Courbet, 1819–1877
Study for Man with a Pipe, Self-Portrait
Painted in 1845

Oil on canvas, 18 1/4 × 13 3/4 in. (46 × 35 cm.)

Description: River scene with a single figure and six cows. Beneath a light blue sky with grey and white clouds, a pale, blue-grey stream flows from the far left middle ground to the right foreground. Pale yellow lilypads float in the stream, which is bounded by verdant pastures. Left of center are two rows of tall trees with dense, dark olive foliage. At the left a woman in a black dress and white cap walks in the pasture. Three black cows rest in the center while one grey cow and two reddish-brown cows graze at the right. At the horizon, beyond a continuous line of dark green trees, is a yellow-green field with two dark grey windmills in the distance.

Condition: Excellent. There is scattered inpainting along the edges.

Exhibitions: None known.

Collections: Edith M. K. Wetmore, Newport, R. I., by about 1920 (?); descended to Maude A. K. Wetmore, Newport. [H. Terry-Engell Gallery, London.]
Foundation Acquisition, AP 69.20

Notes:

1 Robert L. Herbert, *Barbizon Revisited*, New York, 1962, p. 106.

2 Jerrold Lanes, "Daubigny Revisited," *Burlington Magazine*, vol. 106, October, 1964, p. 458.

3 Herbert, p. 106, and John Rewald, *The History of Impressionism*, rev. ed., New York, 1961, pp. 101–2.

4 Herbert, p. 82.

5 Charles Sterling and Margaretta M. Salinger, *French Paintings: A Catalogue of the Collection of the Metropolitan Museum of Art*, New York, 1966, vol. II, p. 95.

Gustave Courbet came to Paris from Ornans in 1840, a provincial youth who was in no way intimidated by the sophisticated world he encountered there. Confident in his own powers, he was sustained by the force of a driving ego and by a robust faith in his abilities as a painter. He painted an impressive number of self-portraits, undoubtedly prompted by a degree of narcissism, although "this propensity flowed from a more praiseworthy sentiment, that of research into his true personality rather than that of an egocentric cult. In this [respect] Courbet was indeed a Romantic."[1] Courbet's fascination with his own image, also evident from the numerous photographs made of him, continued throughout his life, but the stream of self-portraits tapered off as age coarsened his attractive features.[2]

This painting is a preliminary study for one of Courbet's best-known self-portraits, *Man with a Pipe*, of 1846, in the Montpellier Museum in France.[3] The study, like the finished work, has an immediate appeal based on the powerful, sensuous image it conveys. It presents a close-up view of the artist's strongly lighted face and shoulders which emerge dramatically from the shadows of the background. He appears in an attitude of bohemian nonchalance, with disheveled hair and half-closed eyes, his head inclined at an angle both languorous and watchful with a pipe held in the left corner of his mouth. The gaunt cheeks, slack corners of the mouth and sloping shoulders give the Kimbell portrait a rather dissolute air. It differs from the Montpellier painting in that the brushstrokes are looser, the eyes more shadowed and the cheeks more hollowed, giving a more agitated and intense effect. In the final work Courbet adjusted the angle of the right shoulder, straightened slightly the sloping ground line in the rear to differentiate it more clearly from the shoulder, imparted a slight smile to the lips and achieved a composition that is ultimately more harmonious than his initial study.[4] The romantic self-image underlying these works is equally apparent in another version, formerly in the Castagnary collection,[5] in which the eyes are somewhat less shadowed and the expression is disaffected and cynical.[6] Courbet himself viewed *Man with a Pipe* as "the portrait of a fanatic, an ascetic [or aesthete], a man without illusions concerning the nonsense that composed his education, one who is trying to establish himself in harmony with his principles."[7]

The concentrated form, generalized mood and psychological dimension of *Man with a Pipe* is unique among his early self-portraits. In it Courbet discarded the element of theatrical role-playing which led to the self-conscious conceptions and "obstructive arrangements" of other early self-portraits such as *The Guitar-Player*, *The Poet* and *Self-Portrait with the Black Dog*. Courbet considered *Man with a Pipe* a watershed in his œuvre. When it was rejected by the jury of the Salon of 1847 he wrote: "In former years, when my own style was less fully developed and I still painted a little like themselves, they accepted me; but now that I have become myself I must henceforth give up hope."[8] While there is not a little of Courbet's typical bombast in that remark, in 1854 he wrote Alfred Bruyas that *Man with a Pipe* was a "crucial element" in the "solution" of problems of realism.[9] Again we are reminded of the fact the Courbet's

"realism" is not solely to be found in his proletarian subject matter but in his sensuous approach to the physical world as well.

The Kimbell study remained with Courbet until his death when it passed to his sister Juliette; it is mentioned in contemporary inventories of the estate as "*portrait de l'auteur, inachevé*" ("self-portrait, unfinished").[10] Not long thereafter Juliette gave it in turn to Dr. Blondon, Courbet's lifelong friend and the executor of his estate.[11]

Inscription: In the upper left corner: *G.C.*

Description: Bust-length portrait of a bearded young man smoking a pipe. His right shoulder is turned back and his head inclined toward his left shoulder. His sensuous features, lighted on the forehead, nose and cheeks, are framed by a mane of dark brown hair and a short beard. Under half-closed lids his eyes are averted to his right. The ends of a delicate moustache curve around the corners of his mouth in which he holds a darkened clay pipe. He wears a blue jacket and white shirt; the brilliantly highlighted left tab of its collar interjects the single note of contrast in an overall scheme of muted blues and browns. The background consists of a dark brown vertical on the right of the painting and a deep blue-brown sky lightening to ochre above a dark blue horizon on the left.

Condition: Very good. Courbet's technique in this painting was not conducive to its sustained preservation: the priming was too thick for the supporting fabric, a gauze-like material with an open weave heavily sized with glue; and the stretcher, a strainer, allowed for no expansion, with consequent cupping, cracking and buckling of the paint surface.[12] In 1969, the painting was cleaned, areas of cleavage were laid down, and a lining applied with a wax-resin adhesive. At this time a circular loss at the upper left about four inches in diameter was inpainted as were small losses below the nose and in the beard.

Exhibitions: None known.

Collections: Juliette Courbet, La Tour-de-Peilz, Switzerland, 1878. Dr. Blondon, Besançon, France, before 1888. Charles Léger, Meudon, France. Family of Julien Degoumois, Grenoble, from about 1930.
Foundation Acquisition, AP 68.5.

Notes:

1 *Gustave Courbet*, Villa Medici, Rome, and Palazzo Reale, Milan, 1969–70, cat. no. 2, p. 4.

2 Rome–Milan exhibition, cat. no. 38, p. 86.

3 Dimensions of the Montpellier painting are 17 3/4 × 14 1/2 inches; it is illustrated in color in Robert Fernier, *Gustave Courbet*, London, 1969, pl. II, p. 21.

4 A discussion of early drawings for this portrait is presented by Linda Nochlin in "The Nature and Development of Realism in the Work of Gustave Courbet," unpublished dissertation for the Department of Fine Arts at New York University, October, 1963, pp. 47–48.

5 Gaston Delestre in a letter of July 31, 1968, notes that the self-portrait belonging to Antonin Proust exhibited at the *Exposition des œuvres de G. Courbet à l'École des Beaux-Arts*, Paris, May, 1882, cat. no. 37, was a profile view and not a version of *Man with a Pipe*, despite identical dimensions. A version signed in the lower left "G. Courbet," which belonged to Madame Castagnary, was exhibited at that time and reproduced in the photo album of the show but was not listed in the catalogue.

6 At least two other versions of *Man with a Pipe* are known, one in the Fogg Museum, Cambridge, Mass., and the other in a private collection in Paris, but their attribution to Courbet is doubtful at best. Illustrated in Charles Léger, *Courbet*, 2nd ed., Paris, 1929, p. 44, is a *Man with a Pipe* catalogued as a drawing which Léger in a letter to the Degoumois family asserts is in fact a painting, but he mistakenly identifies it with the work now in the Kimbell collection. The present location of that work is unknown.

7 Gerstle Mack, *Gustave Courbet*, New York, 1951, pp. 114–15. The bracketed translation was suggested by Mack.

8 Mack, p. 41.

9 Mack, p. 114.

10 No. 38 in an inventory of May 8, 1878, made at La Tour-de-Peilz by the notary Ansermet from a list prepared by Courbet shortly before his death; also: no. XII on the list prepared by Dr. Blondon of works not put up for sale in either of the auctions of Courbet's estate, Dec. 9, 1881, and June 28, 1882. See Léger, pp. 217–18.

11 In a letter to the critic Castagnary, who died in 1888, reference is made to a study for *Man with a Pipe* in the Montpellier Museum given by Juliette, Courbet's legatee, to Dr. Blondon, the executor of Courbet's estate. This study and the unfinished sketch mentioned in the inventories are doubtless one and the same painting. (Gaston Delestre in a letter of July 29, 1968, refers to Charles Léger's knowledge of the Castagnary letter.)

12 Jack Key Flanagan, conservator's report, September, 1969.

Gustave Courbet, 1819–1877

Roedeer at a Stream

Painted in 1868

Oil on canvas, 38 × 51 1/4 in. (96.5 × 130.2 cm.)

In 1868 when *Roedeer at a Stream (Chevreuils à la Rivière)* was painted, Courbet was at the height of his career. The violent attacks occasioned by the subjects of his earlier paintings had died down, for after the deaths of Ingres (1867) and Delacroix (1863), Courbet was undeniably the foremost painter of France. Today, looking at his pictures of peasants and deer and large-eyed, ample women it is hard to imagine the storm of protest his paintings provoked in the middle of the nineteenth century, but as one critic has summarized: "It was because they turned to a kind of subject which had not hitherto been considered acceptable and were painted as though these new subjects were just as important as any other—more so, perhaps. What was more, they seemed to be handled objectively in the sense that they were neither idealized nor emotionalized and it was obvious that the presence of beauty in the subject, or the painting of it, was of no consequence whatever to the artist."[1] By the 1860s the storm had abated, in part because Courbet had largely ceased to paint his most controversial subjects and in part because his genius as a painter could be appreciated in his relatively conservative manner of painting. As Gerstle Mack has pointed out, Courbet was never attacked with the relentless fury that marked critical assaults on the Impressionists whose manner of painting was like nothing ever seen before.[2]

Courbet was a great huntsman and painted deer and scenes of the hunt throughout his life, but the particular category of deer in covert seems to have originated[3] with a painting now in the Louvre, *Covert of the Roedeer at the Stream of Plaisir-Fontaine* which was exhibited at the Salon of 1866.[4] Its view of the secluded haunt of the deer was an immediate success: only a year later Castagnary reported that deer by Courbet were all the rage and that orders were pouring in. Courbet would paint the landscapes out-of-doors then finish them in his studio, adding the deer both from his own intimate knowledge of the animals and from sketches he made of stuffed deer he would rent to study at his leisure. There is a sufficient similarity in attitude between the deer with one hoof raised and head tossed up alertly in *Covert of the Roedeer*, in the Kimbell painting and in one entitled *Hunted Roebuck on the Alert, Spring*[5] to suggest a common model.

In *Roedeer at a Stream* three deer are seen in a valley identified as Bonnevaux, near Courbet's family home in Ornans.[6] The rich, dark and yet luminous colors are characteristic of Courbet's landscapes. He began with a dark brown ground plainly visible in the rocky bluff on the right; his reasons for this very traditional point of departure he once explained by saying, "Why are you surprised that my canvases are black? Matter without sunlight is black, and dark. I do what the light does. I bring out the salient points, and the picture is there."[7] To "do what the light does" within the limitations of pigment on canvas, he carefully ordered values in relation to one another to achieve an effect equivalent to that of light in nature. For Courbet landscape was "*une affaire des tons*" (a matter of tones) which in his masterful handling imparts an unprecedented density and solidity to the landscape and further defines the midday summery atmosphere of the green valley through the subtle and harmonious interplay of its various greens and browns. The figures of the deer, painted with beautiful feathery brushstrokes to suggest their soft fur, are the only elements in the painting that are modeled with the traditional technique of *chiaroscuro*. The boulder next to the roebuck in the foreground, for example, although equally solid in appearance, is executed by juxtaposing broad semi-tonal areas that rough out its shape. Courbet painted with his palette knife as no one had before; the freedom it allowed him can also be appreciated in the loose handling of the boulder and the bluff whose structure is suggested with Courbet's distinctive breadth of touch and evident love of his material.

Roedeer at a Stream differs from the Louvre's *Covert of the Roedeer*, done two years earlier, in the greater movement and openness of its composition. In the earlier work the leafy confines of the deer are still and somewhat airless, with movement confined to the play of dappled light and the arrested, impending motion of the deer. In the Kimbell painting structural elements which give a sense of depth and air are as important as the purely visual elements of tone and value: the bluff on the right, the boulder in the foreground and the stream at left are solid and assertive; the small patch of blue daringly brought down under the dark branch over the stream, the thrust into depth by the stream and the clearly expressed flow of its water all contribute to the dynamic vitality of the setting. Courbet himself considered *Roedeer at a Stream* one of his best works,[8] including it the same year it was painted among the eleven he sent to an exhibition of his work at Ghent, Belgium.

Inscription: Lower left: *G. Courbet, 68*

Description: Landscape of a shady dell with three roedeer at a broad stream. In the water a doe bends down to drink while a young buck looks to a larger one on the grassy bank at right, who raises his head alertly looking out at the viewer. Between them a large boulder rests at the edge of a small cascade in the stream. The background on the right is filled with a massive stone bluff, cleft in the middle by a jagged fissure and surrounded by trees, one of which angles over the stream. The wooded left bank opens into a wider valley which curves to the right behind the stream. The water is painted a grey-blue, the rocks in tones of ochre, and the grass and trees in a variety of somber greens; the deer are grey-brown.

Condition: Excellent. There is a small L-shaped tear in the center about eight inches from the top. Some minor scratches have been overpainted in small areas, with a few small strengthener retouches in spots where there is no damage. The surface varnish is lightly uneven and suffering from uneven bloom.

Exhibitions: Exposition Gustave Courbet, Ghent, Belgium, 1868. *Cinquante ans de peinture française*, Musée des arts décoratifs, Paris, 1925. There is also a label of the Moderne Galerie, Wertheim, on the back of the painting with the number 61 which would indicate it was exhibited at that gallery.

Collections: Vicomte de Curel, Paris,[9] to sale, [Galerie Georges Petit], Paris, May 3, 1919. Hans Duensing, Boisenburg; to his daughter, Alice von Guggenberger, Lugano.
Foundation Acquisition, AP 68.2.

Notes:

1 Joseph C. Sloane, *French Painting between the Past and the Present*, Princeton, 1951, p. 159.

2 Gerstle Mack, *Gustave Courbet*, New York, 1951, p. 95.

3 *Gustave Courbet*, Villa Medici, Rome, and Palazzo Reale, Milan, 1969–70, cat. no. 33, p. 76.

4 Charles Sterling and Hélène Adhémar, *Musée national du Louvre, Peintures de l'école française*, XIXe *siècle*, Paris, 1958, vol. I, cat. no. 479, pl. CXLVI.

5 Sterling and Adhémar, cat. no. 478, pl. CXLV.

6 Charles Léger in a letter to Hans Duensing dated Jan. 27, 1929.

7 Translated by Esther Rowland Clifford in *Gustave Courbet 1819–1877*, Philadelphia Museum of Art and Museum of Fine Arts, Boston, 1959–60, Boston, 1960, p. 24.

8 Charles Léger, *Courbet*, 2nd ed., Paris, 1929, p. 138. The Kimbell painting is illustrated, pl. 49.

9 The Vicomte de Curel, a noted dramatist, was like Courbet an avid huntsman.

Additional References:

George Riat, *Gustave Courbet*, Paris, 1906, p. 262.
Charles Léger, *Courbet*, Paris, 1925, p. 85.
Charles Léger, *Courbet et son temps*, Paris, 1948, p. 128.

Frederic Leighton, 1830–1896
Miss May Sartoris
Painted about 1860

Oil on canvas, 59 7/8 × 35 1/2 in. (152.1 × 90.2 cm.)

This portrait of a young sober-faced May Sartoris was painted by Frederic Leighton early in his career, just after he settled permanently in London in late 1859.[1] Having lived most of his prior life in the major cities of continental Europe, Leighton was well educated and fluent in several languages, thanks to his affluent parents. They encouraged his early interest in painting and he received thorough training from a number of competent teachers in France, Italy and Germany. Sociable and handsome, Leighton had a wide circle of acquaintances among academic artists including Ingres, Gerome and Bougereau, all of whom he met while living in Rome from 1853 until 1855. From this cosmopolitan background and with his superb draftsmanship, Leighton evolved a neoclassical mode of painting whose restrained drama, "coldly beautiful" elegance,[2] and serious-minded sentiment were later to bring him an enormous success that culminated with his election as President of the Royal Academy in 1878 and his elevation to the peerage (the only British painter so honored) just before his death.

Leighton's command of traditional academic techniques is clearly revealed in the skilled draftsmanship and sound anatomical rendering of this portrait. Figures were Leighton's major expressive means, and in this painting the carefully structured scheme of pose, colors, texture and scale is deliberately calculated to make the young girl dominate the setting. Generated by the frontal view of her face and the direct gaze of her dark eyes, the immediacy of this elegantly dressed girl is enhanced by compositional accents, such as the red scarf and the rising slope of the hill, which focus attention on the solemn expression of her face. The smoothly painted flesh and the meticulously rendered costume may reflect Leighton's familiarity with portraits by Ingres. Leighton, however, has placed this tightly painted figure of intense colors in a broadly painted, earthen-hued setting that is well within the painterly tradition of earlier English portraits. These contrasts of color and brushwork, and also the large size of the figure relative to the canvas, thrust the figure forward from the background details which operate primarily as figure-enhancing patterns and only secondarily to define ambient space. However, the details of the setting do firmly establish the figure in a specific and appropriate context, in this case the scenery of the sitter's home. Nevertheless, the uneven treatment of light, particularly the absence of a ground shadow as intense as the dramatic one across the brow, suggests that the background of this portrait was not painted out-of-doors but was done, like the figure, in his studio from sketches.

The uneven balance between figure and setting in this portrait might be explained by Leighton's intimate friendship with May Sartoris' parents, for whom he might have made an exceptional and atypical effort to particularize the setting of their Hampshire home.[3] Leighton had met Edward and Adelaide Sartoris in 1853 while living in Rome[4] and his subsequent letters of the 1850s mention frequent visits and dinners with them during their extended stays in Paris, Rome and London. He was particularly responsive to the artistic sensitivity of Adelaide Sartoris[5] who was the daughter of Charles Kemble, the actor, and the sister of Fanny Kemble, the writer. After marrying Edward Sartoris in 1843, she retired from a promising operatic career to live a cosmopolitan social life with numerous artistic, literary and theatrical acquaintances and, like her famous sister, to write several books. Their daughter Mary Theodosia, known as May, was born in 1845. In late 1859 the Sartorises had settled at Westbury House, near West Meon in Hampshire,[6] and this portrait of May Sartoris as a girl of about fifteen was probably painted there during the winter of 1859–60 when Leighton wrote that he spent "many a happy day there."[7] Leighton painted several other portraits of May Sartoris, including an unlocated study of her as a young girl[8] and another of her as a mature woman that was painted about 1875, after her marriage in 1871 to Henry E. Gordon.[9] Shortly thereafter she continued the Kemble artistic tradition by writing prefaces to revised editions of her mother's books. She died in 1925.[10]

Description: Full-length, frontal view of a young woman standing before an open landscape. This slight figure, who has dark eyes, a fair complexion and markedly red lips, is enveloped in the billowing loose folds of a long, dark blue riding habit, the front of which is gathered up to her waist by her right hand. The cuffs reveal the full white sleeves beneath, and she wears brown gloves. A brilliant red scarf is tied loosely about her neck and extends downward over her white lace collar to behind her left hand which holds a riding crop at her side. She wears a wide-brimmed dark blue hat with a large dark ostrich plume which curves down to her right shoulder. The folds of a matching head covering conceal her hair. At her left is the sawn face of a large tree trunk which recedes diagonally behind her, crossed by a limb with brown foliage at her right. Beyond, a rising dark green slope repeats the diagonal of the fallen tree and recedes to a distant slope with a field of haystacks and, at the right, to a wooded draw with a small cottage. In the upper left corner a windmill stands before the very high horizon and creamy blue sky beyond.

Condition: Very good. The painting was cleaned and lined in 1970. Isolated areas of very hard varnish and oil overpaint in the hat, skirt, and on the face were not removed. A few flake losses in the sky and two small places on the tree trunk were inpainted.

Exhibitions: Royal Academy, London, winter, 1897, cat. no. 43, *(Portrait of Miss May Sartoris [Mrs. H. E. Gordon] when a Child).*

Collections: The painting remained in the family of the sitter until about the early 1960s, descending to Mrs. M. Turner of London. [Newhouse Galleries, Inc., New York.] Kimbell Bequest, ACF 64.3.

Notes:

1 Mrs. Russell Barrington, *The Life, Letters and Works of Frederic Leighton*, London, 1906, vol. II, p. 49.

2 Initially applied by a reviewer to a painting that Leighton exhibited at the Royal Academy in 1859, the phrase "coldly beautiful" aptly describes the dispassionate and idealizing aesthetic infused by Leighton into English painting of the 1860s and 1870s. See: Allan Staley, "Frederic Leighton," *Romantic Art in Britain . . . 1760–1860*, Detroit Institute of Arts and Philadelphia Museum of Art, January–April, 1968, p. 325.

3 Comments about an unlocated Leighton painting of the Sartoris house may be indicative of his relative disinterest in landscape painting. Fanny Kemble, May Sartoris' aunt, wrote to Leighton, in a letter from Boston, dated March 15 [1861]: "... thank you a thousand times for the *portrait* of Westbury–it is exactly what I wished for–but, oh, why could there not be the lovely upland beyond, and the sheep slowly rolling up and down the slopes, and the tinkle of the bell, and you and she and they and all of us." See Barrington, vol. II, p. 74.

4 See Barrington, vol. I, pp. 27–28, 124.

5 Two drawings by Leighton of Mrs. Sartoris are illustrated by Barrington, vol. I, figs. 8, 51; see also, pp. 171–72, 184. See also: William Gaunt, *Victorian Olympus*, London, 1952, pp. 39–44.

6 Richard Ormond, letter to David Robb, Nov. 19, 1971.

7 Leighton letter to Robert Browning, Jan. 29, 1860; see Barrington, vol. II, pp. 51–52.

8 In a letter of 1855 Leighton mentions that he is painting a portrait of Mrs. Sartoris and another of "her little daughter May." See Barrington, vol. I, p. 184.

9 Now in the collection of Leighton House (no. 419), Royal Borough of Kensington and Chelsea, London, this portrait shows the sitter as a mature woman, seated in half-length view beside an attentive dog; it was exhibited at the Royal Academy in 1875, cat. no. 307. Information was kindly supplied by W. S. Hudson, letter to David Robb, Sept. 27, 1971. Another Leighton portrait of her, 20 x 16 1/2 in., was sold at Sotheby's, London, July 12, 1967, lot 110, and his portrait of her husband, 24 x 20 in., sold at Sotheby's, Jan. 7, 1970, lot 8.

10 Much of this biographic information was provided by Richard Ormond.

Camille Pissarro, 1830–1903

Near Sydenham Hill

Painted in 1871

Oil on canvas, 17 × 21 inches (43.5 × 53.5 cm.)

Jacob (Camille) Pissarro was the fourth and last son born into a family of Spanish-Jewish extraction which, after residing in France a number of generations, had emigrated to the Danish West Indies. As a boy he voluntarily adopted the singularly French name, Camille, a foreshadowing of the fact that, although he did not bother with the formalities of changing his Danish citizenship when he went to live in France, he became one of the most French of all artists. Degas, his friend and fellow artist, was French in his calculating intellect and acid wit. Renoir was French in his relish for everything sensuous, graceful and feminine. Pissarro, a man with immeasurable amplitude of heart and brain, was French in the manner of a great Gothic cathedral; an all-embracing rationality and generosity had a place to accommodate every sensitive nuance in the human spectrum.

The oldest of the many artists in the Impressionist group, with a large and patriarchal physical appearance, his temperament led the others naturally to think of him as Van Gogh defined him, "father to us all." Even though he was elder statesman, he was the first to see value in the experiments of the Neo-Impressionists, and he partook of those experiments. He remained young by being willing to learn from the young, just as he had learned earlier from the older Courbet and Corot. His transcendence of any kind of religious, racial or national chauvinism insulated him from the occasional prejudice he encountered, and he never showed any bitterness. Although he had to struggle against lack of recognition perhaps more than most of the other artists, and gained a modicum of financial success only when he was well over sixty, he never wavered

C. Pissarro

in his dedication to the misunderstood creativity of his art. He lived within the permissive society of the *fin de siècle*, but he always remained the devoted husband and father, even though married only after two children were born to the union. An intellectual and political liberal in a revolutionary age, his calm demeanor never left him, and he never had a fight with anyone.

In a truly profound sense, Pissarro was the child of that age which sought truth in the completely objective individual's sensual experience of the physical world, untrammeled by any kind of tradition, preconception, dogma, habit or convention. In the realm of art, Pissarro tried to achieve the same attitude that gave birth, during his own lifetime, to the age of modern science. Nature no longer was expected to fit a system; the system had to come from nature. The artist, therefore, had to go out and place his senses, as a passive and receptive medium, before nature. Thus, Pissarro became a major founder of open-air Impressionism.

The first fully mature fruits of this approach came with the pictures done just before and after 1870. In 1871 Monet and Pissarro were in England, fleeing from the Franco-Prussian War. While Pissarro was away, the German troops who occupied his house at Louveciennes destroyed nearly all his work from the first fifteen years of his career. Visiting English museums and galleries together, both Monet and Pissarro realized that their aesthetic direction was an extension of the contributions made by Constable and Turner, and a period of renewed conviction and intense activity followed. Painted while the grey mists of winter, 1871, still clung to the damp English countryside, *Near Sydenham Hill*, in its immediacy of visual sensation, is a culmination of the whole European Renaissance impulse toward realism. But, as the great critic Max J. Friedlander observed many years ago, the artist who can yield himself up to nature most completely is the one who reveals more of his own personal being; the pictures of the academicians were much more alike than those of the Impressionists. The French writer Emile Zola was one of the few who understood when he wrote about Pissarro and such then-novel pictures as *Near Sydenham Hill*: "The originality here is profoundly human. It is part of the very temperament of the painter. No pictures have ever appeared to me more of a masterful amplitude. One hears in them the deep voice of the soil, the powerful life of the trees. . . There is a man hidden here, a straight and vigorous personality, incapable of falsehood, making of art a pure and eternal truth."[1]

Inscription: Signed, lower left: *C. Pissarro*
On the back at the top of the stretcher are three lines in ink script of varying legibility:
Environs de Sydenham Hill pres Londres
vue du cimetiére de(?) Lower Norwood au Fond
1871 C Pissarro
At the side of the stretcher: *à ma femme . . .* (remainder illegible).

Description: The whole color harmony is controlled by a dank, silvery mist which permits only the cool greens and blues to emerge strongly. Spatially, the composition is organized by a series of parallel planes receding by subtly modulated tones into a far distance where the mist envelops everything. Forceful demarcation of the foreground plane is achieved by a dilapidated fence that stands on the far side of a drainage ditch, along which stand three large trees almost barren of leaves. The second plane is a broad green field, near the far edge of which, just left of center, stands a lone figure. This plane ends abruptly with the railroad cut for the suburban line to London. A white puff of steam from a passing engine rises from the cut, right of center. The town of Lower Norwood, where the relatives lived with whom Pissarro was staying, comprises the next plane. Finally, on a distant hill there is a cemetery and Gothic church tower.

Condition: Excellent.

Exhibitions: None known.

Collections: The picture was known by Pissarro's son, Ludovic Rodo, and a photograph of it was deposited at Bernheim-Jeune Gallery, Paris[2]; but early in the present century the painting disappeared. It was recently discovered in a South American private collection.
Foundation Acquisition, AP 71.21.

Notes:

1 Emile Zola, "Salon de 1868," in: *L'Evenement Illustré*; reprinted in F. W. J. Hemmings and R. J. Niess, *Emile Zola: Salons*, Paris and Geneva, 1959, p. 119.

2 Ludovic Rodo Pissarro and Lionello Venturi, *Camille Pissarro: son Art, son Œuvre*, Paris, 1939, vol. I, cat. no. 115, p. 95; vol. II, pl. 23, no. 115. See also: William Thornley, *Album of 25 Lithographs after the Works of C. Pissarro*, illus., n. d.

Camille Pissarro, 1830–1903
View Through the Trees: The Hermitage, Pontoise
Etched in 1879

Etching and aquatint on paper, fifth of five states, 8 5/8 × 10 8/16 in. (22 × 26.8 cm.)

View Through the Trees: The Hermitage, Pontoise is the print which Camille Pissarro contributed to *Le Jour et la Nuit*, a short-lived publication in the form of a print portfolio which was exhibited at the fifth Impressionist exhibition at Paris in April, 1880. The publication also contained works by Edgar Degas, who originated the idea, Félix Bracquemond, Mary Cassatt, J.-F. Raffaelli, and others. Proceeds from its sale were intended to help these struggling artists, but after this single exposure the project was abandoned because of indifferent public response. At this time, prints were primarily regarded as a medium to reproduce paintings and only a few other artists, such as Daumier and Manet, had begun to investigate the possibilities of expressing new visual concepts in graphic media.[1]

This print depicts a recurring theme in Pissarro's œuvre: a peasant standing before a row of trees which reveal a view of the houses in the Hermitage quarter of the rural town of Pontoise not far from Paris. Pissarro had settled there in 1866 and worked with his fellow artists in the hills surrounding the town, in the orchards, and along the Oise River.[2] The subject is typically Impressionist because it is directly inspired by Pissarro's response to nature without any anecdotal connotations, nor any pretext of political statement.

Considered one of Pissarro's finest graphic works,[3] this print is a superb example of technical mastery employed to achieve desired effects. To augment the fundamentally linear and spontaneous effects of etching, in contrast to the more rigid and disciplined engraving medium, Pissarro softened the image with an aquatint wash, in which the acid eats a fine grain into the copper plate. Soft, diffuse shading, varying from pale to dark tones, contrasts with the patches of light, creating the markedly atmospheric quality of the work. Thus, Pissarro transformed his painting style, which was concerned with contrasts of color and the momentary play of reflected light, into patterns of black and white.

From 1879 onwards, he used aquatint to heighten the tones in his work, vary his values, and obtain the same variety of greys from the copper plate that he achieved on his canvases.[4] Pissarro, like his friend Degas, was a prodigious printmaker who continually experimented with a variety of mediums, changing the impressions from state to state to enrich the original design until he had achieved the desired effect.[5] In the fifth and last state of this etching, of which the Kimbell print is an example, there is a different grain, created by the aquatint process, which gives form to the bushes in the foreground; the background is thinner and more harmonious than in the previous states; and the figure in the woods at the left, barely perceptible in the earlier states, is completely indicated.[6]

Inscription: Lower right, below plate, in pencil: *C. Pissarro.*

Description: Landscape with a single figure in a horizontal format. In the immediate foreground, a peasant, with his back to the viewer, stands in the brush beneath a grove of tall, slender trees with thin foliage. Beyond, in the middle ground, a pattern of flat and slanted planes is created by the houses and their roofs. The rather high horizon line in the background slopes in from the right and left sides toward the center of the composition; above, the sky is revealed through the scant foliage.

Condition: Excellent. There is evidence of bleaching of old foxing.

Exhibitions: None known.

Collections: Margo Pollins, New York, to 1969. Foundation Acquisition, AP 70.18.

Notes:

1 John Rewald, *The History of Impressionism*, rev. ed., New York, 1961, p. 439.

2 Rewald, p. 158.

3 Loys Delteil, *Pissarro, Sisley, Renoir*, vol. XVII of *Le Peintre-Graveur Illustré*, Paris, 1923, cat. no. 16 *[Paysage Sous Bois, à l'Hermitage (Pontoise)]*.

4 Claude Roger-Marx, *Graphic Art, the 19th Century*, New York, 1962, p. 165.

5 Rewald, *Camille Pissarro*, New York, 1963, p. 49.

6 Delteil, cat. no. 16, (fifth state).

Paul Camille Guigou, 1843–1871
Scene on the Durance River
Painted in 1866

Oil on canvas, 24 × 46 1/8 in. (66 × 116.8 cm.)

Paul Guigou, often overlooked or mentioned only briefly in appraisals of nineteenth-century painting, has only recently been recognized as a distinctive contributor to the rich and varied tradition of French landscape painting. His relative obscurity is partially explained by his short artistic career of about fifteen years, during which he received scant critical attention, and by his early death from lung congestion at the age of thirty-seven. He visited Paris and its environs from 1856 onward and entered the annual Salons between 1863 and 1870, but he spent most of his time in his native Provence, away from the mainstream of artistic developments in Paris.[1]

Guigou's formalistic concerns parallel those of other landscape painters of the 1860s whose new approaches constitute a departure from the tradition of idealized landscape painting. He shared the opinions of such painters as Renoir and Monet, with whom he became acquainted during lively discussions at the Café Guerbois in Paris, that pattern and shape were equal in importance to literal representation of a specific site. The influence of Gustave Courbet's realistic imagery is evident in Guigou's landscapes of southern France but the high values, intense light, and deliberate patterning to achieve an implied informality distinguish his work from Courbet's typically dark-hued, forest scenes. They more closely parallel works by another painter from southern France, Frédéric Bazille, who had been closely associated in his investigations with Monet and Renoir prior to the rise of Impressionism.

Guigou's straightforward objectivity of vision and sense for ordered grandeur are exemplified in *Scene*

on the Durance River. The character of the sun-drenched Provençal landscape is captured precisely by the taut compositional organization and the clear colors intensified by the luminous sunlight pervading the scene. The panoramic composition is traditionally conceived with emphatic horizontals, articulated by a systematic progression of alternately light and dark parallel bands and stabilized on the left side by massive cliffs and on the right side by low hills. This pattern is complemented by staggered vertical accents which create the perspective. Beginning with the focal point of the composition, two women and a mule, the line of vision recedes to two standing figures at the right, then to the left to three barely discernible figures in the distance, and finally to the pale buildings surmounting a cliff at the horizon.

The penetrating light imbues the scene with a sense of drama by imparting a crispness and clarity to the well-defined shapes. Using opaque primary colors for the figures, Guigou describes them with a broad technique of luscious impastos and dexterous brushwork. He contrasts these to the neutral tones of the rocks in the water and the craggy cliffs on the horizon at the left, while the trees in the distance are merely suggested with quick dabs of paint. In contrast to these opaque pigments, Guigou employed transparent, thinned-down tones for the sky and water. This combination of traditional composition, pellucid light, and pure hues is indicative of a dispassionate attitude toward nature, predominantly objective rather than philosophical, that reveals Guigou as an intriguing experimenter in the early development of this tradition.

Inscription: Lower right: *Paul Guigou. 66.*

Description: Landscape with mule and figures. Stretching across the immediate foreground, a light blue-grey, clear river scattered with beige and brown rocks flows before a rocky beige beach in the center of which stands a saddled greyish-brown mule facing to the left. Behind him are two women: one in a white blouse, blue skirt, and brown apron is standing; the other, wearing a red blouse, black vest and yellow-gold skirt, is leaning over to pick up a blue garment from a multicolored pile of clothing on the beach. In the middle ground, two figures at the right who are silhouetted against a light blue body of water, stroll along the sandy beach, while three men stand at the left in the far distance. At the horizon line to the left is a grey and tan, rocky cliff with green vegetation; in the center, the terrain stretches before pale green and tan slopes in the distance that are punctuated at various points by grey-green trees as they continue to the right. The pale blue sky, which occupies two-thirds of the composition, is accented with only a few horizontal, light rose and white clouds.

Condition: Excellent. This painting was relined and cleaned in 1968. Impasto is most noticeably evident in the mule, the central figures, and the rocks in the immediate center foreground, while the paint is so thin in the sky and water that the canvas is slightly apparent.

Exhibitions: Recent Acquisitions, Arthur Tooth & Sons, Ltd., London, November, 1968, cat. no. 3.

Collections: [Arthur Tooth & Sons, Ltd., London.] Foundation Acquisition, AP 69.4

Note:

1 For some recent discussions see: *Mon cher Guigou*, Galerie Daber, Paris, May 28–June 27, 1970; John Rewald, *The History of Impressionism*, rev. ed., New York, 1961, pp. 204–5; François Daulte, "Un Provençal pur, Paul Guigou," *Connaissance des Arts*, no. 98, April, 1960, pp. 70–77.

Edgar Degas, 1834–1917
Self-Portrait
Etched about 1857

Etching on paper, third of five states,
$9 \times 5^{5}/_{8}$ in. (22.9×14.4 cm.)

Hilaire-Germain-Edgar Degas was the eldest son of a wealthy Parisian banker who foresaw a law career for his son, but the young Degas, showing no aptitude for law or business, wanted to study art. He worked in the École des Beaux Arts and in the studio of Louis Lamothe (1822–1869), a former pupil of Jean-Auguste-Dominique Ingres, the leader of the Neoclassical movement whom Degas probably met around 1855. He also spent many hours in the Louvre studying and copying the works of such masters as Raphael, Mantegna, Dürer, and Rembrandt. More enthusiastic about Ingres' concept of art than his painting style, Degas was also drawn to the works of Delacroix, Rousseau, and probably Courbet.

Desiring to study more works by Italian masters, Degas left in 1856 for Italy where he is thought to have visited relatives in Naples a few years before. In Rome, he rendered several self-portraits, one as an etching and several in oil.[1] He had learned the technique of etching from a family friend, Prince Grégoire Soutzo, while still in Paris.[2] Although he had not yet developed full mastery of this graphic medium, he loved to experiment and modified his plate through many states, etching more lines, biting some areas with more acid, applying more ink or wiping some of the ink off until he got the desired effect.

The Kimbell *Self-Portrait* is a rare example of the third state in a total of five states of this etching.[3] It is closer to the impression in the Metropolitan Museum of Art, formerly in the H. O. Havemeyer collection, than any of the other impressions of the third state, although all differ in surface appearance and mood because of variations in inking and wiping.[4] The Kimbell impression demonstrates technical excellence in the way ink is wiped over the background to give a sense of space, as well as in the crosshatching, very dense in the jacket and hat but more open in the face and background, which yields rich contrasts between dark and light, intense blacks against the white of the paper. The facial features are modeled with a delicate combination of straight and curvilinear strokes. Revealing solid roots in the conventional artistic tradition of French nineteenth-century painting, and a particularly strong affinity with Ingres' conception of portraiture, Degas evokes a somber and very formal mood. The strict, simple placement of the figure against a blank background is also a device Rembrandt frequently used in etchings of himself. The intense expression gives us insight into Degas' character as a serious young man who is confident but sensitive and introspective.

Jean Sutherland Boggs, who has contributed valuable observations about Degas' portraiture, writes about this print: "His character had not been completely transformed from the Louvre portrait two years before, but his lower lip is somewhat withdrawn, he does wear his bulkier clothes more easily, and he stands with a greater independence as if ready, if not happy, to meet external challenges. In the play of light and shadow there is a suggestion of his increased response to the sensual side of his medium. . ."[5] The same qualities of his character are revealed in two related works in which the image is reversed, a drawing which was perhaps a preparatory study[6] and a self-portrait in oil,[7] both of which were done about the same time.

As one of the earliest of Degas' etchings, the Kimbell impression is distinguished by the dedicatory inscription to his intimate friend, the sculptor Paul Albert Bartholomé (1848–1928). There has been some question about the date of this etching and Degas' relative age. The traditional source, Delteil's catalogue of Degas' graphic works, dated it 1855, making Degas 21 years old. Jean Boggs redated it, stating that on November 8, 1857, Degas dated an impression now in the Bibliothèque Doucet, Paris, and she convincingly establishes that Degas went to Italy at the age of 22, subsequently executing the etching in Rome at 23.[8]

Inscription: Lower left, below plate, in pencil:

à Bartholomé
Degas

Description: Three-quarter-length self-portrait. Standing just to the right of center, he wears a dark jacket with a rolled collar and a dark hat with a flat crown and a broad, rolled brim which places his face partially in shadow. His dark, heavy-lidded eyes focus on the observer. His full lips are emphasized by a thin moustache; he has a thin, short beard and medium-length wispy hair. In the background, crosshatching is evident in the lower left portion. This area, as well as the far right edge and the center top of the print, show irregular traces of ink wiped on the plate.

Condition: Excellent.

Exhibitions: Alumni Treasures, Addison Gallery of American Art, Phillips Academy, Andover, Mass., May 19–June 18, 1967, cat. no. 206, illus.

Collections: Gift of the artist to Paul Albert Bartholomé, Paris. César M. de Hauke, Paris.[9] Robert M. Leylan, New York, to 1969.
Foundation Acquisition, AP 69.5.

Notes:

1 Paul-André Lemoisne, *Degas et son œuvre*, Paris, 1946, vol. II, cat. nos. 2–5, 11, 12, 37.

2 All biographical information is from John Rewald, *The History of Impressionism*, rev. ed., New York, 1961, pp. 11–27, and Jean Sutherland Boggs, *Portraits by Degas*, Berkeley and Los Angeles, 1962, pp. 5–11.

3 Loys Delteil, *Edgar Degas*, vol. IX of *Le Peintre-Graveur Illustré*, Paris, 1919, cat. no. 1, *(Edgar Degas, par lui-même)*.

4 Compare: *An Exhibition of the Works of Edgar Degas*, Sterling and Francine Clark Art Institute, Williamstown, Mass., Jan. 8–Feb. 22, 1970, cat. nos. 36–38, illus. p. 3.

5 Boggs, pp. 10–11.

6 *Self-Portrait*, 1857, black crayon heightened with white, 11 3/4 × 9 in., Walter C. Baker, New York. See: Rewald, illus. p. 27.

7 *Degas Wearing a Felt Hat, Self-Portrait*, about 1857, oil on paper mounted on canvas, 10 1/4 × 7 1/2 in. (260 × 190 cm.). See: Lemoisne, cat. no. 37, illus. p. 17.

8 Boggs, pp. 8–11 and p. 87, note 37.

9 De Hauke was the co-publisher, with Paul Brame, of Lemoisne's four-volume catalogue raisonné on this artist.

Edgar Degas, 1834–1917
Dancer with Upraised Arms
Drawn about 1887–90

Pastel on grey paper, 18 3/8 × 11 11/16 in.
(46.7 × 29.7 cm.)

By the mid-1880s, Edgar Degas had become almost a recluse. Plagued by impending blindness, he also became dependent on the sale of his work because his family's business, which had previously afforded him financial independence, was close to bankruptcy. Although he had never been particularly ingratiating or inclined to close personal relationships, he now completely disassociated himself from the Impressionist group with whom he had exhibited in the 1870s and early 1880s, an estrangement that allowed him to pursue new interests, unhampered by the sometimes conflicting opinions of his former friends. The emphasis of Degas' art was significantly transformed but his personal problems did not become primary concerns in his work.

He abandoned painting portraits and historical scenes to investigate new themes, including the ballet. In doing so, he set a precedent, for ballet was considered an unorthodox and unacademic subject for art. Degas' interest was motivated by a fascination with the complex movements of the dancers' bodies and their expressive gestures. Sketching quickly in pastel or charcoal, he captured their animated attitudes both at rehearsals and public performances. Although one senses Degas' empathy for the plight of the ballet dancers, or so-called "rats," who were often fatigued and depressed from long hours of strenuous practice, he never idealized them. He depicted them, with rare exceptions, as types rather than as individuals.[1]

The ungainly attitude of the Kimbell *Dancer with Upraised Arms*[2] heightens our perception of her anguish; one arm strains upward while the other is held to her forehead as if she is tired or in pain. The slightly oblique angle of vision placing the viewer just below the dancer, an unusual treatment of perspective adapted from Japanese print compositions, and her casual or off-guard attitude impute an informality to the composition. The spiraling, upward movement from her legs to her head culminates at her left arm which is thrust boldly off the paper, and the triangular shape of her skirt is echoed by the reversed triangle of her torso and arms.

Because of his deteriorating eyesight, Degas began to use pastels more than oils and abandoned the delicately precise, linear pencil technique of his early years. Pastels allowed him to capture the essence of a dancer's pose with an economy of means and to experiment with various additives such as water, turpentine, and gouache.[3] The spontaneity he strove for is evident in the Kimbell drawing, in which he first laid in the composition with brown pastel and then built up the forms with rhythmic strokes of dry but iridescent color. His adroit handling is manifest especially in the sculptural contours of the dancer's head and arms which are contrasted to the diaphanous net or gauze of her *tutu*.

The Kimbell image has been associated with the painting in the Metropolitan Museum of Art of *Dancers in the Rehearsal Room, with a Double Bass*[4] because it appears to be the antecedent for one of the dancers in the upper right corner of that painting. Since Degas inscribed dates on very few of his pastels and often reworked them at a later time, or did variants, it is difficult to establish a precise date for this pastel. Because the Kimbell pastel is quite

reasonably regarded as a study for the painting, however, it can be dated before 1891 when the painting was in the collection of Alexander Reid, a young dealer in Glasgow. Although Lillian Browse has suggested a date as early as 1880–83 for the painting,[5] Paul-André Lemoisne dated both the drawing and the painting 1887,[6] and Jean Sutherland Boggs dated the drawing about 1890.[7] The latter dates are stylistically reasonable both for the painting and the Kimbell pastel.

Inscription: Lower left, stamped in red: *Degas* (from 1918 Degas estate sale)

Description: Full-length view of a standing female dancer. Turned slightly to her right with her legs apart, she stretches her left arm upward and holds her right arm to her head which is elevated to the light. Her eyes are closed, her nostrils distended and her mouth open. Heavy, blonde bangs cover her forehead and her long hair flows down her back. She wears the traditional ballet costume that was worn for both rehearsals and performances; it has a generous, white gauze skirt with blue and violet shadows, a slightly decolleté white bodice, and a white sash tied at the waist. *Pentimenti* of blue bows are evident over her shoulders and the sketchy, blue and violet bow of her sash can be seen at the right side.

Condition: Excellent. Drawn on lightly textured, tinted paper that is laid down on rag board, mounted on a composition panel.

Exhibitions: Scènes et figures parisiennes, Galerie Charpentier, Paris, May–June, 1943, cat. no. 67, illus. *Degas: Paintings, Drawings, Prints, Sculpture,* Los Angeles County Museum, March, 1958, cat. no. 62. *Drawings by Degas,* City Art Museum of St. Louis, Philadelphia Museum of Art, and the Minneapolis Institute of Arts, January–June, 1967, cat. no. 130, illus. p. 197.

Collections: This work was sold in the second sale of Degas' estate, [Galerie Georges Petit], Paris, Dec. 11–13, 1918, lot 175, illus., and then was owned by René de Gas of Paris, the artist's younger brother, until his estate sale, Paris, Nov. 10, 1927.[8] It was in the collection of R. Nepveu de Gas by 1943[9] and passed to a private collection in England, where it remained until sold at [Sotheby's], London, Nov. 25, 1959, lot 54, illus., to [M. Knoedler & Co., Inc.], New York, who sold it to John D. Rockefeller, III, New York.[10] [Hirschl & Adler Galleries, Inc., New York.]
Foundation Acquisition, AP 68.4.

Notes:

1 John Rewald, *The History of Impressionism,* rev. ed., New York, 1961, pp. 273 ff., and Jean Sutherland Boggs, *Drawings by Degas,* City Art Museum of Saint Louis, 1966, pp. 17–18, 110, 122.

2 Paul-André Lemoisne, *Degas et son œuvre,* Paris, 1946, vol. III, cat. no. 910 *(Danseuse vue de face, le bras gauche levé),* illus. p. 531.

3 Pierre Cabanne, *Edgar Degas,* Paris, 1958, pp. 42–43.

4 Charles Sterling and Margaretta M. Salinger, *French Paintings: A Catalogue of the Collection of the Metropolitan Museum of Art,* New York, 1967, vol. III, pp. 84–85, illus. p. 85.

5 Lillian Browse, *Degas Dancers,* Boston, n.d., cat. no. 118, pl. 118.

6 Lemoisne, cat. no. 905 *(Danseuses au foyer, la contrebasse),* illus. p. 529.

7 Boggs, cat. no. 130, illus. p. 197.

8 Lemoisne, cat. no. 910.

9 Lender's name on the label for the 1943 exhibition in Paris.

10 Information supplied by the vendor.

Additional References:

Paul Lafond, *Degas,* Paris, 1919, vol. II, illus.
Denis Rouart, *Degas, à la récherche de sa technique,* Paris, 1945, illus. p. 75.

Claude Monet, 1840–1926
Pointe de la Hève, at Low Tide
Painted in 1864–65

Oil on canvas, 35 1/2 × 59 1/4 in. (90.2 × 150.5 cm.)

Pointe de la Hève is one of the two paintings that Claude Monet submitted for exhibition in the Paris Salon of 1865, the first Salon the unknown, twenty-four-year-old artist had entered.[1] Acceptance of these entries was important because the annual Salon was practically the only means for a young French artist of that time to establish his reputation.[2] Not only were both entries accepted, but several critics reviewed them favorably. Gonzague Privat wrote: "The two marines of M. Monet are unquestionably the best in the exhibition; the tone is frank, the breeze penetrates as on the open sea and the treatment is naive and young."[3] In the *Gazette des Beaux-Arts,* Paul Mantz wrote: "... the taste for harmonious colors in the play of analogous tones, the feeling for values, the striking view of the whole, a bold manner of seeing things and of catching the spectator's attention, these are qualities which M. Monet already possesses in high degree... We shall certainly be interested in following the future efforts of this sincere marine-painter."[4]

These critics do not comment on Monet's already distinctive and confident brushwork, one of the very aspects of these paintings on which current critical assessment focuses. Recently William Seitz has written: "Excepting the early sketches of Constable, and a few beach studies by Corot, the previous history of painting offers little precedent for such objective observation ... the skies are cloud-filled and the atmospheric tone ... is silvery. The hues are not brilliant but ... the [spontaneous] brushwork ... varies from one passage to another." He comments further on Monet's expressive brushstrokes that vary from the crisply-touched dabs of the beach stones to

the quivering strokes of the choppy water and the vigorously brushed clouds.[5] In his paintings of the later 1860s Monet was to use smaller brushstrokes and brighter colors.

The scene is the beach just west of his father's summer home at St. Adresse near Le Havre.[6] Monet probably began this canvas in the summer of 1864 and finished it that winter in Paris. It is apparently related to a small version of the same scene that bears an inscribed date of 1864.[7] After painting that version, Monet then decided to paint the scene as his Salon entry. He doubled the size of the canvas and then resolved some compositional problems by showing the scene at low, rather than high, tide; moving his viewpoint slightly; deleting a rowboat, and adding the horses and figures. The resulting composition is firmly organized and may reflect the artist's knowledge of marines by Johann Jongkind, whom Monet had met in the summer of 1862.[8]

The close relationship of these two paintings is not unusual in Monet's works of the 1860s. At least four other sets are known of related compositions in which figures have been added in the presumably later versions.[9] Although it is tempting to identify these as Monet's first series paintings, such as his later studies of haystacks, poplars, and Rouen Cathedral, their evolutionary character suggests that they were Monet's first known use of a procedure (different views of the same subject) that later evolved into a concept (the same subject in different conditions of light) which is fundamental to Impressionism. Later, Monet varied other aspects, such as format, size, and color value,[10] that he gradually evolved into the radical Impressionist paintings of the 1870s and 1880s.

Thus, *Pointe de la Hève* may be regarded as an exceptional "pre-impressionist" painting, whose expressive brushwork and deliberately resolved composition are indicative of Monet's later directions. Its well documented origin, its exhibition in the first Salon that Monet entered, and its relation to other paintings of the 1860s make it a key painting in Monet's oeuvre.[11]

Inscription: Lower right: *Claude Monet 1865*

Description: On a beach at low tide strewn with rounded stones of grey and ochre, a horsedrawn cart with a whip-cracking driver, a second team of horses with one rider, and a man wearing work clothes and a hat, all painted in greys and blacks, move away from the viewer through blue-grey rivulets of spent waves. At the left, white-capped, greenish water stretches to a low horizon, punctuated there by a boat with large black sails. To the right of the figures, the beach, divided by three breakwaters, rises toward a brown bluff topped by green vegetation which slopes downward to the horizon in the center of the painting. The blue sky is overcast with dark grey clouds except for a vigorously brushed opening of white in the center of the horizon.

Condition: Excellent. There are very minor abrasions at the edges and two small losses, now inpainted, in the lower left corner. The canvas was lined about 1950.

Exhibition: Le Salon de 1865, Palais de Champs Elysées, Paris, May–July, 1865, cat. no. 1525.

Collections: Leon Monet, Rouen, the artist's older brother. [Bernheim-Jeune, Paris.] Georges Bernheim, Paris. M. Y. de Saint-Albin, Paris. Remond Collection, Geneva. [Wildenstein & Co., Inc., New York.] Foundation Acquisition, AP 68.7.

Notes:

1 *Explication des ouvrages de peinture ... exposés au Palais de Champs Elysées. Le 1er Mai 1865, "Le Salon de 1865,"* p. 200, cat. no. 1525, (*La Pointe de la Hève à Marée Basse*). The other painting, cat. no. 1524, *Embouchure de la Seine à Honfleur*, is in private collection, Paris; see John Rewald, *The History of Impressionism*, New York, 1961 ed., illus., p. 122. The two paintings are the same size and bear identical inscriptions in the same location.

2 William C. Seitz, *Claude Monet*, New York, 1960, p. 16.

3 Gonzague Privat, *Place aux Jeanes, causeries critiques sur le Salon de 1865*, Paris, 1865, p. 190.

4 Paul Mantz, "Salon de 1865," *Gazette des Beaux-Arts*, vol. XIX, July, 1865, p. 26.

5 Seitz, *Monet*, p. 17.

6 A recent photograph of the scene is in Seitz, *Monet*, p. 15.

7 *Pointe de la Hève, Sainte Adresse*, 15 1/2 x 28 1/2 in. Illus.: Seitz, *Monet*, p. 15, and Phoebe Pool, *Impressionism*, 1967, fig. 46 (as *The Breakwater at Honfleur*). See: Lefevre Gallery, *Claude Monet, the Early Years*, London, 1969, cat. no. 2, for bibliography and history of the painting. A Christie's sale catalogue, June 19, 1964, lot 45, and Charles M. Mount, *Monet, A Biography*, 1966, p. 403, erroneously suggest that this painting was no. 1525 in the 1865 Salon.

8 Pool, p. 68, suggests that the small version was painted after a picture by Jongkind.

9 These sets include: two versions of *La Plage à St. Adresse*, ca. 1864, one, 22 7/16 x 31 7/8 in., Christie's sale, July 6, 1971, lot 8, and the second, 21 1/2 x 32 in., illustrated in *Monet and the Beginnings of Impressionism*, Currier Gallery of Art, Manchester, N. H., 1947, cat. no. 36; two versions of *Rue de la Bavolle, Honfleur*, ca. 1865, one in the Kunsthalle, Mannheim, Germany, and the other, 22 x 24 in., with figures, in the Museum of Fine Arts, Boston; two versions of the *Bas-Beau Road, Chailly* of 1865, one in the Louvre, 16 1/2 x 23 1/4 in., with no figures, a larger version, 38 5/8 x 50 3/8 in., with a lumber cart and figures, Frick Art Reference Library, photograph no. 517-3a; and a fourth set: *La Lieutenance de Honfleur* of about 1866, described by Joel

Isaacson, "Monet's Views of Paris," *Allen Memorial Art Museum Bulletin*, vol. XXIV, no. 1, Fall, 1966, p. 13, note 21.

10 Isaacson, p. 18, discusses this issue in detail.

11 Although its exhibition in 1865 is mentioned in numerous books and articles, the painting is not well known. It has not been exhibited publicly since 1865 and has been illustrated only once, by Arsene Alexandre in *Claude Monet*, Paris, 1921, facing p. 30. See also: D. Wildenstein, "Monet," in *Kindlers Malerei Lexikon*, Zurich, 1967, vol. IV, pp. 466, 470.

Additional References:

Theodore Duret, *Historie des peintres impressionistes*, Paris, 1906, p. 95.
Gustave Geffroy, *Claude Monet, sa vie, son temps, son œuvre*, Paris, 1924, vol. 1, pp. 36–37.
O. Reuterswärd, *Monet*, Stockholm, 1948, pp. 28, 30, 31.

Claude Monet, 1840–1926
Still Life with a Spanish Melon
Painted in 1880

Oil on canvas, 35 1/2 × 27 in. (90.2 × 68.6 cm.)

About 1878 Claude Monet resumed still life painting after an eight-year period in which he had painted landscapes almost exclusively, except for figure studies of friends and members of his family. These landscapes reveal an increasing emphasis on color harmonies and discrimination of textures. By the late 1870s, they had become less detailed, more varied in tone and mood, and increasingly concerned with the changing appearance of landscapes in fugitive conditions of sunlight. With this shift of aesthetic concerns, still life painting became a logical means of developing and refining his Impressionist ideas about color and composition.

Monet's return to still life painting coincided with his move in early 1878 to Vetheuil on the Seine where he lived four years during a most discouraging period in his life. Camille, his wife of thirteen years, died there in September, 1879, following an extended illness after the birth of their son, Michel. Grieving for his loss, burdened by medical bills, distracted by the care of his two young sons and receiving scant income from his paintings, Monet was forced to beg for loans from friends and former patrons. These unsettling conditions, however, may have contributed to his renewed interest in still life painting. Such painting would have been a logical activity during his wife's confinement when he had less opportunity to paint landscapes outdoors. Also, it may have been stimulated by public taste, since a still life was one of the few paintings that Monet sold in 1880.[1]

Still Life with a Spanish Melon is typical of the still lifes Monet painted at Vetheuil. It reflects his Impressionist theories and practices of the 1870s and his growing interest in color harmony. Unlike traditional, carefully balanced and deliberately arranged *trompe l'oeil* still lifes, it has an asymmetrical composition of casually arranged fruit dominated by diagonal axes formed by the edge of the cloth and the melon slice. In addition, the brushwork varies according to the nature of each object. Short, crisp touches of different colors and textures are deftly juxtaposed to describe the surfaces and to model the grapes and apples, the basket and the dappled cloth. This rich diversity of texture and color is set off by large areas of broadly painted color in the subdued background, the yellow melon slice and the reddish table edge. Monet skillfully integrated these qualities into the painting whose complexity results from his deliberate investigation of the relation between the inherent, tangible characteristics of objects and their representation in paint.

This play "between tactile and perceptual reality"[2] is particularly characteristic of a group of four related fruit still lifes, including the Kimbell work, that were painted in 1880, probably in late summer or early fall when all the fruits were in season. One of them, *Apples and Grapes* (Art Institute of Chicago), bearing Monet's inscribed date of 1880,[3] has a variety of textures and an asymmetrical composition comparable to the Kimbell painting. A second *Apples and Grapes* (Metropolitan Museum of Art, New York)[4] must have been painted from the same fruit arrangement as the Kimbell painting: the basket, fruit, cloth and table edge are nearly identical. However, the melon is absent and the viewpoint is at a slight angle to the table. The fourth still life (Kunsthalle, Hamburg), bearing Monet's

date of 1880,[5] shows less of the table than in the three other views. The vertical format of the Kimbell painting is distinctive; the other four versions are horizontal and of slightly smaller size.

This group of fruit still lifes provides a revealing document of a crucial phase of Monet's lifelong investigation of pictorial conventions. Soon after painting this group, Monet committed himself to a primary concern for harmony of colors. Subsequent still lifes of the 1880s, largely flower pieces, are less structured, more loosely painted and of stronger colors.[6] Fruit still lifes, with their challenging variety of textures, are conspicuously infrequent.[7]

Inscription: Lower right: *Claude Monet*

Description: View of a variety of fruits placed near the edge of a table almost covered by a white cloth. At the left, a woven reed basket is heaped with red and yellow-green apples and bunches of dark purple and pale, iridescent grapes; before it lie a large cluster of the pale grapes, a red apple and yellow-green apple. A Spanish melon at the far right, separated from the basket by two yellow-green apples, has a large slice cut from it which lies before it diagonally across the edge of the rumpled cloth. The dark surface of the table and its apron, edged with a bamboo design and brightened by strokes of burnt orange, are revealed at the right. The folded cloth hangs over the table edge, filling the lower left corner of the painting. The greenish-grey background ranges from a light, primed ground at the left to thickly painted dark tones at the right.

Condition: Excellent. The canvas has been relined: the prepared white ground is observable on the original tacking edge preserved about the perimeter. The surface has never been varnished.

Exhibitions: Monet, Pissarro, Sisley, Fogg Art Museum, Cambridge, Mass., 1931. Paul Rosenberg, New York, 1949, cat. no. 307. *Nineteenth Century French Paintings*, New York, 1954. *One Hundred Years of Impressionism: A Tribute to Durand-Ruel*, Wildenstein Gallery, New York, April 2–May 9, 1970, cat. no. 59, illus.

Collections: [Durand-Ruel], Paris. Private collection, Germany, about 1900. [Paul Rosenberg], Paris. Duncan Phillips, Washington, D. C., from 1926 to 1934. [Otto Wertheimer], Paris. Private collection, Switzerland, 1955–67. Foundation Acquisition, AP 67.5.

Notes:

1 The unidentified still life was sold to Georges Petit in January, 1880, for 500 francs. John Rewald, *The History of Impressionism*, New York, rev. ed., 1961, p. 434.

2 William C. Seitz, *Claude Monet*, New York, 1960, p. 114.

3 $25\frac{3}{4} \times 32\frac{1}{8}$ in., *Paintings in the Art Institute of Chicago*, Chicago, 1965, p. 319, and Seitz, 1960, fig. 34.

4 $26\frac{3}{8} \times 35\frac{1}{2}$ in., Charles Sterling and Margaretta M. Salinger, *French Paintings: A Catalogue of the Collection of the Metropolitan Museum of Art*, New York, 1967, vol. III, pp. 129–30, illus.

5 Alfred Hentzen, *Hamburger Kunsthalle, Official Guide*, Hamburg, 1967, pl. 56.

6 For example, *Sunflowers*, of 1881; Seitz, p. 114, illus.

7 The only known fruit still lifes are those that Monet painted in 1883–84 as part of the series of decorative panels for the apartment of Paul Durand-Ruel. See: *Claude Monet*, Durand-Ruel, Paris, Jan. 24–April 10, 1970, cat. nos. 33, 34, and *Claude Monet*, Arts Council of Great Britain, Tate Gallery, London, 1957, cat. no. 73.

Additional References:

Julius Meier-Graefe, *Entwicklungsgeschichte der modernen Kunst*, Stuttgart, 1904, vol. III, p. 99.
Meier-Graefe, *Modern Art*, London, 1908, vol. I, book III, illus. facing p. 304.
George Wildenstein, catalogue raisonné of Monet's paintings, in preparation.

Edouard Vuillard, 1868–1940

The Model in the Studio

Painted about 1905–6

Oil on board, mounted on cradled wood panel, 25×34 in. (61×86 cm.)

Edouard Vuillard and his close friend, Pierre Bonnard, are often referred to as Intimists because they painted genre and interior subjects observed at close range. *The Model in the Studio* epitomizes Vuillard's work as an Intimist. A master at capturing the informality and privacy of the petit-bourgeois interior at the turn of the century, Vuillard used the motif as a vehicle to articulate color and decorative pattern into a solid, architectonic composition. He created a tapestry-like effect by evenly deploying flat areas of subdued but rich colors, accented with black, over the surface and washing it with a diffused light. The flatness of the surface is emphasized in this work by the dull finish of the paint applied to absorbent pasteboard.

The Kimbell painting is characteristic of Vuillard's works of about the first decade of the twentieth century when the calculated tension of his earlier works began to ease and the mood of his pictures, as well as the structure, became more relaxed. The size of the panels and canvases increased, his brushwork loosened, his palette lightened, and color arrangements became more obvious, though no less delightful or exquisite. It is thought that these changes evolved because of his improved social and professional position; he was receiving commissions from wealthy clients for portraits.[1]

Vuillard compresses the picture space in *The Model in the Studio* by telescoping the perspective, flattening and tilting the planes into a taut spatial order of horizontals and verticals, and packing the composition with forms and shapes. This indicates the influence of Japanese prints, popular with late nineteenth-century artists. Vuillard favored using highly reflective surfaces as both decorative and space-expanding devices and simultaneously to establish and destroy order. The multitude of angled surfaces creates an intentionally ambiguous articulation of space. The figure, posed informally as if caught off guard, is placed in the center of the composition and is clearly defined as an entity. Vuillard's figures are usually shown marginally and, although engaged in routine duties, appear static and merge into the energetic surface pattern to create a unified design. This deviation from his more usual style reminds the viewer that, in all Vuillard's works, drama emanates from the power of the composition rather than from the actions of the figures. As Vuillard most often painted friends and relatives, the subject, because she is undressing, is probably a professional model.[2]

The setting of the painting helps to establish its date. The scene is the Parisian studio-apartment at 123 Rue de la Tour[3] where Vuillard lived between 1904 and 1907.[4] Stylistically, it seems reasonable to date the painting about 1905–6, the time during this period in which the artist most emphasized clarity of compositional structure and definition of shapes.

Inscription: Lower right: *E. Vuillard*

Description: A woman stands facing the corner of a room, hands to her back, untying the ribbons at the waist of her pinkish-white underclothing. A beige, pleated petticoat falls around her legs, the left leg extended beneath resting on a footstool. A bluish-black skirt lies over a wooden side chair at her left, and a matching printed blouse is draped over a moss-green armchair behind her. Pictures and aqua-colored portfolios are stacked against the wall, and printed fabric is draped over those near the corner. Above is a hanging shelf supporting more portfolios, with a narrow, horizontal tapestry attached beneath. On the wall to the left hangs a palette and, to the right, a pink and green tapestry. The left third of the painting is filled with a black fireplace with white inner facing and a large, gilt-framed mirror above. On the mantel are a blue jar, a white statuette (Aristide Maillol's *Leda*, 1900),[5] and a green vase filled with pink and green flowers, all reflected in the mirror and shiny mantel top. A black coal scuttle with scoop rests on the black and red hearth. The floor of light brown wood planks is covered by a brightly patterned rug in the lower right corner of the painting.

Condition: Very good. Minor abrasions in corners and scattered losses along the edges. Matte surface finish, with some adhering foreign matter. Unvarnished.

Exhibitions: Edouard Vuillard, œuvres récentes, Galerie Bernheim-Jeune, Paris, November, 1908, cat. no. 49. *Les Maîtres de l'Art Indépendant 1895–1937,* Petit Palais du Louvre, Paris, June-October, 1937, p. 58, cat. no. 2. *E. Vuillard,* the Louvre: Musée des Arts Décoratifs, Paris, May–July, 1938, cat. no. 58. *E. Vuillard,* Galerie Durand-Ruel, Paris, May 26–Sept. 29, 1961, cat. no. 45, illus. *Vuillard,* Kunstverein, Hamburg, 1964, cat. no. 52, color pl. 53; also shown at Kunstverein, Frankfurt, and Kunsthaus, Zurich, August–October, 1964. *Edouard Vuillard–K. X. Roussel,* Haus der Kunst, Munich, March 16–May 12, 1968, cat. no. 50, illus. p. 149; also shown at the Louvre: Orangerie des Tuileries, Paris, May 28–Sept. 12, 1968, cat. no. 116, illus. p. 217.

Collections: M. and Mme. Olivier Sainsère, Paris. Jacques Sainsère, Paris. Mme. Farjon, Paris. [M. Knoedler & Co., Inc., New York.]
Foundation Acquisition, AP 67.2.

Notes:

1 Andrew Carnduff Ritchie, *Edouard Vuillard,* New York, 1954, p. 24.

2 Jacques Salomon, *Vuillard, admiré,* Paris, 1961, p. 89, color illus. *(Le Modèle Se Déshabillant).*

3 Salomon, *Vuillard,* Paris, 1968, p. 206, color pl. 103, p. 103.

4 Haus der Kunst, *Edouard Vuillard-K. X. Roussel,* Munich, March 16–May 12, 1968, cat. no. 50, illus. p. 149; also shown at the Louvre: Orangerie des Tuileries, Paris, May 28–Sept. 12, 1968, cat. no. 116 *(Modèle Se Déshabillant dans l'Atelier. A Gauche, Une Cheminée Noire),* p. 33, illus. p. 217.

5 . . . *Vuillard* - . . . *Roussel,* p. 102.

Additional References:

Raymond Escholier, *La Peinture Française* XXe *Siècle,* Paris, 1937, illus. p. 20.
Claude Roger-Marx, *Vuillard et Son Temps,* Paris, 1945, p. 77.
André Chastel, *Edouard Vuillard 1868–1940,* Paris, 1946, illus. p. 59.
Curt Schweicher, *Edouard Vuillard,* Bern, 1955, pl. 19.
Jerome Mellquist, "The Badge of Identity," *Apollo,* vol. 75, July, 1961, pp. 16–19, illus. p. 16.
Jacques Salomon, "Edouard Vuillard als Chronist Seiner Epoche," *DU,* vol. 22, December, 1962, p. 37, color illus.
Stuart Preston, *Edouard Vuillard,* New York, 1971, pl. 48, p. 35.

André Derain, 1880–1954
The River Seine at Chatou
Painted in 1905

Oil on canvas, 27 7/8×43 5/8 in. (70.7×110.7 cm.)

The dramatic splash of seemingly irrational colors in *The River Seine at Chatou* represents a deliberate redefinition of the nature of painting, in subjective, emotional terms. By using color in a purely personal manner without regard for natural appearances, the artist created an almost abstract representation of his subject, divorcing it from the realism which had governed painting since the Renaissance.

André Derain achieves this effect in *The River Seine at Chatou* by a variety of means. He willingly distorts and simplifies his forms; he eliminates *chiaroscuro* and definition of space by geometric perspective; he gives the painting surface a variegated character by carefully disposing over it undulating lines of color, pure pigments directly from the tube, arbitrarily selected and spontaneously applied. The harmonies and dissonances of unmodulated color, while close in value, have a structural significance which builds the composition in terms of the surface rather than in depth.

Derain painted this landscape view of Chatou in 1905 while residing there. It exhibits his departure from a pointillist technique to a more liquid application of patches of color interwoven to form a cohesive composition. During his subsequent sojourn in London, the artist further pursued this method, producing watercolor-like effects.

These characteristics, radical for their time, typify the early paintings of Derain during his most interesting period, as well as early works of his Fauve colleagues, Maurice Vlaminck, with whom he shared a studio at Chatou, and Henri Matisse, who played a prominent, if not vital, part in furthering Fauvism. Derain's intellectual attitudes about painting were similar to those of Matisse, but his paintings most closely resemble those of Vlaminck; however, they are more graceful, polished, and pleasing to the eye, less harsh and violent, and never highly charged emotionally.

Fauvism, an outgrowth of the expressionistic tendencies of Vincent van Gogh and Paul Gauguin, was the first violent explosion of the twentieth century when artists were seeking reactive solutions to aesthetic problems. Begun in 1903, Fauvism made its public debut at the Autumn Salon of 1905 where the critic Louis Vauxcelles derisively referred to the small group of painters as "wild beasts" *(fauves)*. The loosely organized movement lasted only until about 1908 because it was primarily a decorative style without a cohesive system or formalized theory. It established a precedent for a series of artistic revolutions, however, and introduced a vital intuitive concept to art.

Inscription: Lower right: *A Derain*

Description: View of the town Chatou, a summer resort on the Seine River approximately eight miles northwest of Paris. The view is framed by a large, mature tree on the left and a smaller tree on the right, both predominantly green, highlighted with peach and silhouetted with strokes of blue. The trees provide a structural basis for leading the viewer's eye into the painting from a hill with heavy underbrush, perhaps flowers, divided in blocks of color and accented with color opposites, and saplings without foliage. These limbs and branches are drawn in warm tones, but farther down the hill, closer to the town, the trees have blue and green trunks with yellow-green and orange branches. A light yellow path in the lower right foreground descends to the bottom of the hill where a brick street is indicated with

short, broad strokes of blue, red and pink, with a yellow wall and green hedge beyond it. Medium blue underpainting shows through, outlining shapes throughout the composition. In the center of the painting, the roof and steeple of a church are revealed above the red roof of a blue-shadowed house. The church is flanked on the right by a row of three two-story houses with pink, green and purple pitched roofs and on the left by three other structures with deep red and purple roofs, partially obscured by the trees and branches in the foreground. The sides of the buildings facing the left are cream-colored, reflecting the light source from that direction, and the sides facing the viewer are shadowed in blue. In the background, a shimmering, pale green river bends around the opposite bank at the upper right, reflecting the overcast sky of light pink and blue and the red-orange trees on the river banks, whose reflections are chartreuse.

Condition: Very good. Minor buckling of the support in the upper right corner. Normal very fine age craquelure in isolated areas. Some inpainting in upper right corner and tree trunk on left.

Exhibitions: Recent Acquisitions XXI, Arthur Tooth & Sons, Ltd., London, Nov. 16–Dec. 3, 1966, cat. no. 3 *(La Seine à Chatou)*, color illus. on cover.

Collections: [Ambroise Vollard], Paris, by about 1905.[1]
Private collection, Switzerland. [Arthur Tooth & Sons, Ltd., London.]
Foundation Acquisition, AP 66.13.

Note:

1 This painting was either included in the contents of Derain's studio which Ambroise Vollard purchased in February, 1905, or painted while Derain was under contract to this important art dealer.

Edvard Munch, 1863–1944
Girls on a Bridge
Painted about 1904–7

Oil on canvas, 31 11/16 × 27 1/4 in. (78 × 69.3 cm.)

Girls on a Bridge was created by Edvard Munch as part of *The Frieze of Life*, his lifelong project. Begun in 1891, *The Frieze of Life* was conceived by Munch as a pessimistic panorama of the human condition in which he explored the fundamental theme of man's self-awareness in conflict with nature. Within this framework, he focused primarily on psychological relationships of individuals confronting love and death.[1] The imagery reveals Munch's preoccupation with such *fin de siècle* attitudes as personal isolation and introspection, despair, and sexual conflict–attitudes also reflected in the works of Munch's Nordic contemporaries, the playwrights Henrik Ibsen and August Strindberg. The paintings of this series share a common "form-language" of dynamic composition, expressionistic color and intensely subjective, often disturbing, imagery.[2]

The Frieze of Life is distinguished by recurring investigations of the same subjects because, when works sold, Munch painted subsequent versions to maintain a continuous record of his researches.[3] His innovative prints employ the same thematic motifs; while they generally postdate the oil versions, they are considered independent works, technically experimental in themselves.[4]

In the Kimbell painting, three girls contemplate the water on a quiet summer night, standing on a bridge at Aasgaardstrand, Norway, a village about forty miles south of Oslo.[5] Dominating the painting, the figures form a pivot on the bridge which thrusts diagonally through the composition, converging with the strong horizontal of the retaining wall and shoreline in the upper middle distance. This compositional and space-defining device, a strong diagonal combined with a vertical balance, was a radical one for the time. Borrowed from Henri de Toulouse-Lautrec, it had become a formula for Munch by 1906.[6] Foreground and background are related by the reflections in the water of the large trees, the shore, and the houses, which stand out sharply against the sky with its luminous midnight sun.[7]

The motif of figures isolated in a landscape is a consistent image in *The Frieze of Life*. In Munch's works of the 1890s these figures are often portrayed at moments of specific and intense emotion; anxiety, morbidity, and painful isolation are trenchantly analyzed and dramatically portrayed. By about 1900, the approximate date of Munch's first version of *Girls on a Bridge*, his statements on the human condition tend to be presented in images of less particularized situations, and a more tranquil mood emerges. The five successive versions[8] of *Girls on a Bridge* (based on a tentative chronology, as none of these paintings is firmly dated) reveal a progressive trend toward greater abstraction.

Stylistic considerations suggest that the Kimbell painting is the last of the five versions. The anonymous figures are clustered together without specific details of gesture or appearance. Some details are more subdued if not entirely omitted: the windows in the background are merely suggested with abbreviated strokes, and facial details are not delineated. The luminous quality of the paint and overall lighter tonality are characteristic of Munch's freer manner of painting around 1904, a departure from his earlier thinned-down, near-washes of somber colors.[9] The pigment is thickly applied in loose, almost separate strokes which leave the canvas visible in several places; the brushwork is quite aggressive, with a verve not seen in the related versions. Thus, the Kimbell painting is distinguished by a unique simplicity and directness.

Inscription: Lower right: *E. Munch*

Description: Landscape with three girls standing on a bridge. The focus of the composition is on the girls, who lean against the upper railing of the pink bridge which extends diagonally from the left foreground to converge with a road to the right in the middle distance. The full-length figure on the left faces the viewer, although facial details are not delineated; she wears a long-sleeved, light pink dress, has long, blonde hair, and rests her right elbow on the railing. Only the backs of her companions are revealed, the center figure in a bright red dress and yellow hat, the other wearing a light yellow dress with her long, reddish-blonde hair extending to waist level. Their heads, to the right center of the composition, are silhouetted against the pink, white and green shoreline and retaining wall beyond. The wall encloses almost the entire upper half of the painting which includes two light pink houses with blue pitched roofs, separated by a large clump of dark green trees, and other trees in the distance silhouetted against a light, blue-green sky. The light yellow midnight sun is above the house at the far left which is reflected, along with the dark green trees, in the blue water which occupies the lower left quarter of the painting.

Condition: Very good. Oil paint is applied with heavy impasto and is developing minor crackle system. The primed canvas was relined when the painting was cleaned in 1970.

Exhibitions: Edvard Munch, 1863–1944, Kunstmuseum, Bern, Oct. 7–Nov. 30, 1958, cat. no. 59. *Munch,* Kunstverein, Frankfurt am Main, Nov. 9, 1962–Jan. 6, 1963, cat. no. 21. *Munch,* Galerie Beyeler, Basel, September–December, 1965, cat. no. 31, color plate on front cover; the picture was used as the color poster for the exhibition.

Collections: Ake Bratt, Oslo. Hans Grether, Basel. Foundation Acquisition, AP 66.6.

Notes:

[1] Frederick B. Deknatel, *Edvard Munch,* New York, 1950, p. 26.

[2] Deknatel, p. 29.

[3] Deknatel, pp. 8, 28.

[4] Deknatel, p. 36.

[5] Deknatel, p. 39. Deknatel observes that the bridge is actually the pier to the dock.

[6] Gösta Svenæus, *Edvard Munch: Das Universum der Melancholie,* Lund, Sweden, 1968, pp. 36–38.

[7] Deknatel erroneously identifies the midnight sun as the moon, p. 39.

[8] Related versions: Kunsthalle, Hamburg, 1900, 13 3/8 × 11 3/8 in. (34 × 29 cm.); National Gallery, Oslo, 1899–1901, 53 1/2 × 49 1/2 in. (136 × 125.5 cm.); Norton Simon, Beverly Hills, 1902, 39 3/4 × 39 1/2 in. (100 × 101 cm.); Wallraf-Richartz Museum, Cologne, 1905, 49 5/8 × 49 5/8 in. (126 × 126 cm.).

[9] Deknatel, p. 42.

Emile Antoine Bourdelle, 1861–1929
Penelope
Dated 1909

Cast bronze, dark green patina, 47 1/8 × 17 × 14 3/4 in. (119.7 × 43.8 × 37.5 cm.)

Emile Antoine Bourdelle's sculpture of *Penelope* represents a character from the Greek literary classic, *The Odyssey*. Plagued by suitors while her husband Odysseus was away from Ithaca during the Trojan War, Penelope put them off by saying that she would choose between them when she had finished weaving a shroud for her father-in-law. However, she unraveled at night what she had woven by day. By the time the suitors discovered the ruse, Odysseus had returned to slay them and rescue Penelope from her dilemma. Bourdelle depicted her as a person of great strength of character and endowed her with a reflective expression. The remoteness of her expression allows for no sentimentality of feeling.

To attain this sense of detached objectivity for the piece, Bourdelle subordinated the symbolism of the theme in the interest of making a statement of universal form. While his preoccupation with mythological themes and his use of the human figure link him to the nineteenth century, he used these not as metaphors for the narration of an event but as points of departure to investigate the interaction between form and space. The figure, then, is used as a medium for the expression of proportion and is governed by a tendency for abstraction. In this way, Bourdelle attempted to reintroduce a sense of timeless monumentality to twentieth-century sculpture, in reaction against the stringent formulas of academic realism.

Although a close friend and one-time assistant of Auguste Rodin, whose aim was to capture spontaneity and movement, Bourdelle broke away from Rodin's influence. His predilection for clear structural formation and his interest in the tensions of strain and balance are evident in the way he composed *Penelope*. Reflecting his high regard for traditional sculptural concepts, especially those of Archaic Greek sculpture, Bourdelle treated the piece as a kind of monolith, or mass, to be activated and placed in a passive space. Compact forms are combined with rhythmic outlines and deeply modeled surfaces which define the concrete, self-contained shape of the sculpture. The mass and volume of the static figure interact with the implied movement of the gentle S-curve of the body which spirals upward from her heavy skirt to her head, focusing attention on her introspective expression. This emphasis on inner feeling, or psychological processes, anticipates one of the major concerns of twentieth-century art. However, the vitality of the surface and details of attire and physiognomy are subordinated to the unity of the whole. Thus, it is the exaggeration of the pose, the generalized modeling of forms, and the power of expression in the Kimbell *Penelope* which arrest one's attention.[1]

Dating from 1909, the Kimbell *Penelope* is one of four related versions of this theme which Bourdelle created between 1905 and 1912. Differing mainly in size, these versions are consistent in style and show a progressive refinement of an idea. Bourdelle's model for *Penelope* is thought to have been his first wife, Mrs. Van Parijs;[2] his 1906 drawing of her seated before a table shows an affinity in the gesture of the arms.[3]

The two earliest versions, seventeen and twenty-two inches high respectively, date from 1905 and show a pensive, heavy-hipped woman holding a spindle in

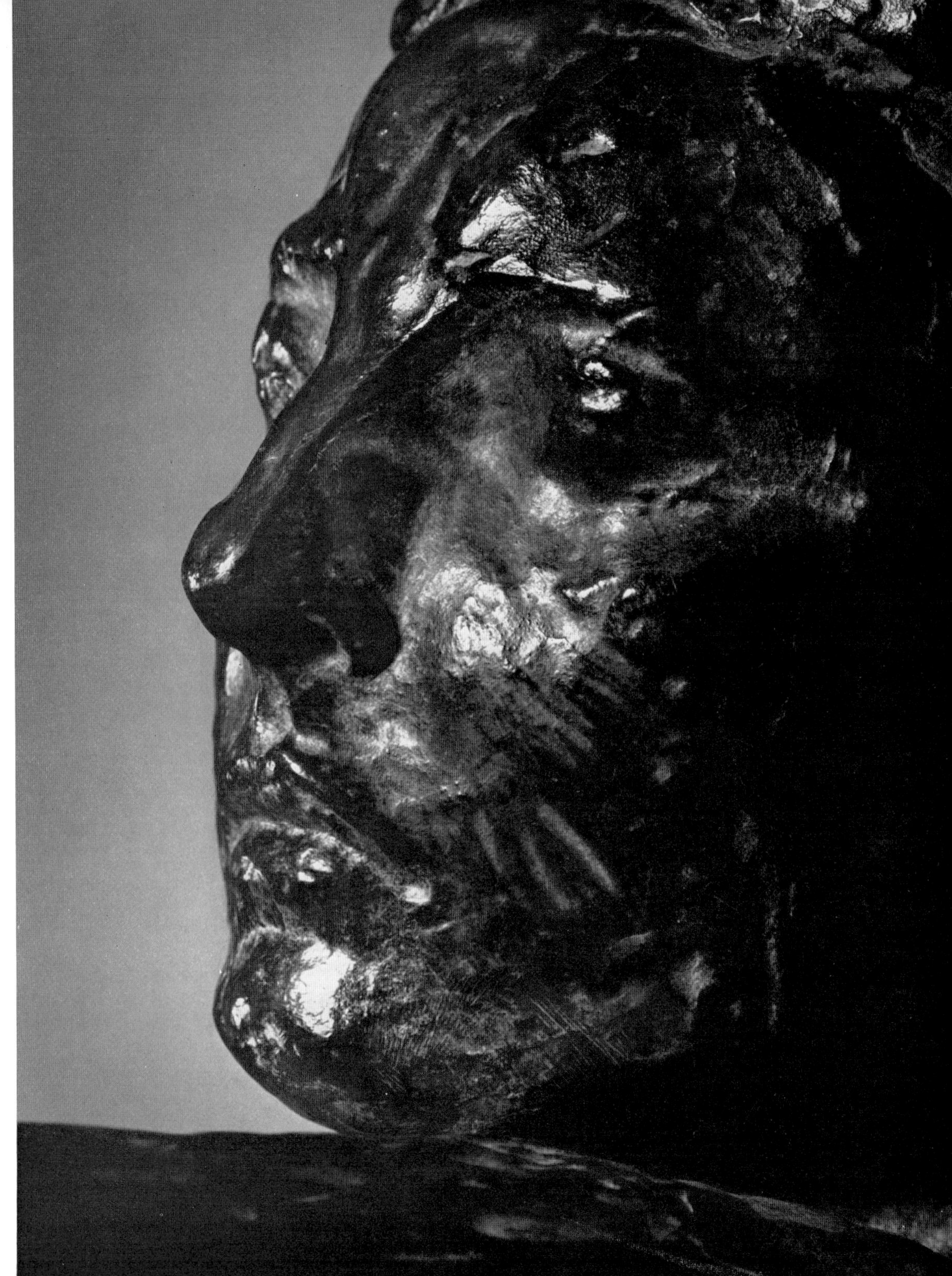

her right hand. Two years later, in a slightly larger version, the spindle is omitted as it is in all subsequent versions. In 1909 a version was modeled in which the size was doubled to forty-eight inches, giving the work a scale approaching the monumental solidity of its design. Apparently a further refinement of this version, the Kimbell *Penelope* includes for the first time a logical scale-defining detail near the base; the toes of her right foot now protrude from beneath the edge of her skirt. This detail plays a similarly important role in *La Grande Penelope*, the final version of 1912, which is 96 inches tall and more than double the size of the Kimbell work. Because of its similarity in all respects except size, the Kimbell *Penelope* may be considered the penultimate stage in the evolution of a sculptural idea realized in the heroic scale of *La Grande Penelope*.[4]

Inscriptions: Left side of base: Monogram 4
Lower left, back of base: *Susse Freres Fondeurs Paris*

Description: Cast bronze, full-length female figure. Free-standing on an integrated base, the figure is clothed in a long dress which falls to her feet in deep, fluted folds. The gathered ruffle at the neckline falls softly over her shoulders. Her weight rests on her left leg; the toes of her right foot protrude beneath her skirt. Her right arm, held close to her waist, supports her left arm and her left hand is held near her head, which is tilted slightly to her left and elevated to the light. Her hair is pulled back loosely over her head in a chignon.

Condition: Excellent. Dark green patina over entire sculpture. Bronze base is part of the whole.

Exhibitions: None known.

Collections: Private collection, Paris (obtained directly from the artist). [Pintura Establishment, Vaduz, Liechtenstein]. Foundation Acquisition, AP 69.3.

Notes:

1 Ionel Jianou and Michel Dufet, *Bourdelle*, Paris, 1965, pp. 27–29.

2 *Sculptures of the Rijksmuseum Kröller-Müller*, 2nd ed., Otterlo, The Netherlands, 1966, p. 46.

3 *Madame Bourdelle*, 1906, pen, ink and india wash, 14 1/8 x 8 in. See: *Antoine Bourdelle*, Charles E. Slatkin Galleries, New York, 1961, pl. 28.

4 For the various versions and their locations, see Jianou and Dufet, p. 85.

Pablo Picasso, born 1881
Man with a Pipe
Painted in 1911

Oil on canvas, 35 11/16 × 27 7/8 in. (90.7 × 71 cm.)

Cubism initiated one of the major aesthetic movements of the twentieth century by deliberately and systematically eliminating faithful rendering of the natural appearances of objects as a basic premise of art. Conceived by Pablo Picasso and Georges Braque as the logical development of Paul Cézanne's investigations of composition and form, the new convention established by this autonomous, internally consistent style has been a continuing influence on modern art.

After jointly exploring Cézanne's ideas for about four years, Picasso and Braque crystallized their own new style during a crucial period from the summer of 1910 to the winter of 1912, bringing Cubism to its purest expression and fullest maturity. *Man with a Pipe* is a salient example of this second stage of Cubism, the Analytical phase, when geometric fragmentation had become as much an artistic style as an innovative means of analysis. It is often difficult to distinguish Picasso's works of this period from those of Braque, since both artists espoused the primacy of the flat picture surface and abstract pattern over the identity of the subject matter. It has been pointed out, however, that Picasso's paintings generally tend to be more linear, angular, and immediate in their presentation, even sculptural in conception, while Braque's seem more painterly and cohesive.[1]

Man with a Pipe is one of the earliest[2] of about thirty-five oval pictures painted by Picasso mostly between 1911 and 1913.[3] It has been called "...a masterpiece, the classic in this series of works in which the crystalline structure of form achieves monumental clarity."[4] The oval format, an

unprecedented approach for that period, allowed Picasso to achieve a more solidly structured composition, focused in the center, with the surrounding space lighter both in tonality and weight.

The Kimbell painting's abstract quality derives from the fragmentation of forms into flat, monochromatic planes, as if observed from multiple viewpoints. Its complex design is organized within a linear grid near the surface of the painting. The man's presence is made evident by the concentration of geometric structure down the middle axis of the picture, with the composition less defined toward the edges, turning inward. The muted tones of the central mass are also present in the background, thus integrating it with the surrounding space. Spatial recession is minimized and no attempt is made to suggest texture. The brushstrokes, however, serve the important function of enriching the surface which is further unified by the elimination of a single light source.

Two elements in the painting disrupt the unity of the surface: the *trompe l'oeil* device and the typographical signs. The former is a pipe which appears to project from the canvas, thus disturbing the spatial continuity but providing clarity by implying a single point of view, in contradiction to the rest of the painting. The pipe also serves as a clue to the subject matter. The typographical signs–the letters *e s t* at the upper right and the block letters *H* and *L* below–contribute another level of reality, that of the third dimension. They prevent the surface from appearing absolutely flat and abstract by forcing the composition on which they are superimposed to be understood as a three-dimensional surface.

Inscription: Upper right: *Picasso*
Inscribed by Picasso in the 1950s at Mougins, France.

Description: Half-length figure of a mustachioed man seated frontally in a chair. Wearing a white collar and brown coat, he holds a pipe in his mouth and appears to hold a newspaper in his lap. Although the forms are fragmented, his nose and eye are slightly identifiable. Burnt and raw umbers with raw sienna predominate throughout, with the edges of planes delineated by black lines. Highlighting is defined by varying shades of ochres and greys and by white impasto on the pipe and the newspaper. In addition to typographical signs, geometric symbols in black outline are repeated throughout the work. The light ground on the canvas shows through only at the perimeter.

Condition: Excellent. The original canvas has been trimmed to the edge of the painting and mounted on a new support. There is a minor crackle system with minor cleavage at the lower left.

Exhibitions: Georges Braque, Wassily Kandinsky, Pablo Picasso, Kunsthaus, Zurich, Sept. 21–Oct. 20, 1946, cat. no. 136. *Pablo Picasso*, Palazzo Reale, Milan, Sept. 23–Dec. 31, 1953, cat. no. 21. *Picasso, 1900-Paris-1955*, Musée des Arts Décoratifs, Paris, June–October, 1955, cat. no. 25, illus. *Picasso*, Tate Gallery, London, July 6–Sept. 18, 1960, cat. no. 60, pl. 15a. *The Cubist Epoch*, Los Angeles County Museum of Art, Dec. 15, 1970–Feb. 21, 1971, cat. no. 237, color pl. 44; also shown at the Metropolitan Museum of Art, New York, April 7–June 7, 1971.

Collections: Private collection, Paris. [M. Knoedler & Co., Inc., New York.]
Foundation Acquisition, AP 66.8.

Notes:

1 Douglas Cooper, *The Cubist Epoch*, London, 1971, p. 44.

2 Picasso painted the picture while vacationing with Georges Braque at Céret in the French Pyrenees.

3 Antonina Vallentin, *Picasso*, New York, 1963, p. 118.

4 Hans Jaffé, *Pablo Picasso*, New York, 1964, p. 90, color illus., p. 91.

Additional References:

John Golding, *Cubism: A History and an Analysis, 1907–1914*, London, 1958, pl. 11; 2nd ed., Glasgow, 1968, p. 91, pl. 12.
Christian Zervos, *Pablo Picasso: Œuvres de 1912 à 1917*, Paris, 1942, vol. 2, part 2, pl. 323, no. 738 *(Homme à La Pipe)*.
Christian Zervos, "Portraits inédits de Picasso," *Cahiers d'Art*, vol. 29, 1954, pp. 209–20, color illus., p. 219.
Roland Penrose, *Picasso*, New York, 1971, color pl. 21.

Odilon Redon, 1840–1916
The Birth of Venus
Painted in 1912

Oil on canvas, 56 1/2 × 24 1/2 in. (143.4 × 62.6 cm.)

The Birth of Venus is a poetic example of Odilon Redon's mature work which retains the visionary character of his earlier somber prints of esoteric, nightmarish visions. It is typical of Redon's late works in its large size, narrow format, and vaguely suggested theme. This ethereal nude in the guise of a mythological heroine is an idealized and rather reserved figure. Her head is in profile and details of her face and hands are partially obscured, focusing attention on her well proportioned, youthful body. The familiar theme of Venus, the Roman goddess of love and beauty who arose on a shell from the sea, is evoked by the large shell that surrounds her like a mandorla and the smaller shells below. Unlike Redon's earlier, more decorative works painted about 1890–1910, the figure of Venus dominates the painting and less emphasis is given to small details.

This three-dimensional ensemble of figure and shell is vertically placed in the center of the composition, appears to rise in an indeterminate space of diaphanous clouds and sky, and is stabilized by the brightly colored shells below. The figure and shells have faint linear outlines, but the edges are generally softened, as if veiled by the atmosphere. The painting's ethereal quality is reinforced by thinly painted passages contrasted with heavy applications of opaque, scrubbed-on paint and delicately radiant pastel tones of primary and secondary colors juxtaposed in moist, opalescent patches.

One of eight versions of this theme by Redon, the Kimbell painting is perhaps his last treatment of it.[1] After about 1912, the artist's interest in mythological subjects waned and he began to create mostly flower paintings and nature studies. Among the eight versions, there seems to be no closely integrated evolutionary sequence. The variety of compositions and formats suggest that Redon investigated different approaches to the subject but considered each rendition as an independent work. However, Redon often incorporated earlier drawing studies of single objects into his paintings.[2] For example, *The Shell,* a pastel of 1912,[3] may be regarded as a study for the same motif in the lower right foreground of the Kimbell work.

Inscription: Lower right: *Odilon Redon*

Description: A full-length, frontal view of a nude maiden standing within a large shell. The flesh-toned figure is outlined in red. She stands on her left leg with her right leg partially behind it. Her right arm encircles her head, which is in profile facing downward to her right. Her left arm is at her side, partially obscured by golden hair which falls to below her knees. The pearly iridescence of the large shell surrounding the figure is achieved by a pattern of radiating strokes of cream, yellow, light green, aqua, and mauve with white highlights. The shell's undulating outline is silhouetted against a soft background of rich blues and creamy whites. Across the lower foreground are many smaller shells, painted in browns, greens and magentas at the left, with a small pink-and-white shell and a larger, carefully drawn shell in white and mauve at the right.

Condition: The painting is in good condition but is developing a minor crackle system. There is slight cupping and possible cleavage in the lower right corner. The surface has never been varnished.

Exhibitions: Kunstmuseum, Winterthur, Switzerland, 1919, cat. no. 81. *Exposition Rétrospective: Odilon Redon,* Galerie Barbazanges, Paris, May 18–June 15, 1920, cat. no. 2. *Odilon Redon,* Galerie Druet, Paris, 1923, cat. no. 54. *Odilon Redon,* the Louvre: Musée des Arts Décoratifs, Paris, 1926, cat.

no. 90. *Odilon Redon*, the Louvre: Musée du Petit Palais, Paris, 1934, cat. no. 53. Wildenstein Galleries, London, 1938, cat. no. 30. *Exposición de Pintura Francesca*, Montevideo, Uruguay, April–May, 1940, cat. no. 20. *The Painting of France since the French Revolution*, M. H. deYoung Museum, San Francisco, December, 1940–January, 1941, cat. no. 86. *French Paintings from David to Toulouse-Lautrec . . .*, Metropolitan Museum of Art, New York, Feb. 6–March 26, 1941, cat. no. 86. *Eugène Carrière et le Symbolisme*, the Louvre: Musée de l'Orangerie, Paris, December, 1949–January, 1950, cat. no. 142, illus. *Figures Nues de l'Ecole Française*, Galerie Charpentier, Paris, 1953. *Le Nu à Travers les Ages*, Galerie Bernheim-Jeune, Paris, May–June, 1954. *Odilon Redon*, the Louvre: Musée de l'Orangerie, Paris, October, 1956–January, 1957, cat. no. 190, pl. LI. *Odilon Redon*, Kunsthalle, Bern, August–October, 1958, cat. no. 199, illus. *Sources du XXe Siècle*, Musée d'Art Moderne, Paris, Nov. 9, 1960–Jan. 23, 1961, cat. no. 581. *Odilon Redon, Gustave Moreau, Rodolphe Bresdin*, Museum of Modern Art, New York, Dec. 4–Feb. 4, 1962, cat. no. 55, illus. p. 88; also shown at the Art Institute of Chicago, March 2–April 15, 1962. *Exposition Odilon Redon*, Galerie Bernheim-Jeune, Paris, May–July 1963, cat. no. 11. *Odilon Redon: For the Benefit of the Lenox Hill Hospital*, Acquavella Galleries, New York, Oct. 22–Nov. 21, 1970, cat. no. 47, illus.

Collections: Dr. and Emile Sabouraud, Paris, by 1920 to about 1940.[4] Roger Hauert, Paris, by 1949. Stephen Higgons, Paris, by 1961.
Foundation Acquisition, AP 66.14.

Notes:

[1] The Kimbell painting is dated 1912 by Klaus Berger, *Odilon Redon: Fantasy and Colour*, New York, 1965, p. 194, cat. no. 179, color illus. p. 105. He also lists, pp. 194, 210, five other versions: *The Birth of Venus*, 1908, oil, Galerie Druet, Paris; *The Birth of Venus*, 1912, oil, Bourgeat collection, Paris; *The Birth of Venus*, 1912, oil, J. B. van Gelder; *The Birth of Venus*, n. d., oil, $8^5/_8 \times 5^7/_8$ in., Dr. Saklatwalla, Crafton, Pa.; *The Birth of Venus*, 1912, pastel, $32^5/_8 \times 25^1/_4$ in., Musée du Petit Palais, by 1916. Two other versions should also be noted: *The Birth of Venus*, about 1890, oil, $21^3/_8 \times 28^5/_8$ in., Mr. and Mrs. Herman E. Cooper, New York; *The Birth of Venus, Venus with Shell* or *Eve* (?), about 1905, oil, 18 × 15 in., private collection, Paris.

[2] Translated quote from Redon's *Journal 1867–1915*, Berger, p. 113.

[3] Collection of Ari Redon, Paris, the artist's son.

[4] Acquired from the artist's studio in 1920 by the Galerie Barbazanges, Paris, and subsequently bought by Dr. Sabouraud. In 1908, Redon executed a portrait drawing in red chalk of his friend, Dr. Sabouraud; the preceding year, he did a pastel portrait of Madame Sabouraud. See: Berger, cat. nos. 771s, 401.

Additional References:

Odilon Redon, *A soi-même*, Paris, 1922.
Claude Roger-Marx, *Odilon Redon*, Paris, 1925.
Clarence Joseph Buillet, *The Significant Moderns and Their Pictures*, New York, 1936, pl. 125.
Charles Chassé, *Le Mouvement Symboliste dans l'Art du XIXe Siècle*, Paris, 1947, illus. p. 48.
S. Sandstrøm, *Le Monde imaginaire d'Odilon Redon*, Lund, Sweden, 1955.
Roseline Bacou, *Odilon Redon*, Geneva, 1956, pl. 106.
Werner Hofmann, *Art in the Nineteenth Century*, London, 1960, pl. 113.
René Huyghe, *L'art et l'homme*, Paris, 1961, vol. III, illus. p. 348.
H. H. Arnason, *History of Modern Art: Painting, Sculpture, Architecture*, New York, 1968, p. 71, color pl. 18, p. 85.
"René Huyghe renforce ses idées sur l'art," *Connaissance des Arts*, vol. 229, March, 1971, color illus. p. 93.

Henri Matisse, 1869–1954
Odalisque with Green Shawl
Painted about 1921–22

Oil on canvas, $34^7/_8 \times 45^3/_4$ in. (88.6 × 116.3 cm.)

Just before settling permanently in Nice in the south of France in 1921, Henri Matisse began to paint versions of a theme that he continued to explore for the remainder of his life. Typical of the period which lasted until about 1930, *Odalisque with Green Shawl*[1] is modest in size, pleasant in subject matter, and possesses a decorative charm; also, it is more conventionally realistic than any work he had produced since 1904.[2] The most pleasing pictures of this period are those of decorative interiors, frequently enhanced by the sophisticated elegance of odalisque figures. A delicate balance between the brilliance of light outside and the filtered light within pervades these pictures; this light, while not directional, helps build form and confirm mood.

During his Nice period, Matisse maintained restraint and simplicity by compressing space into flatter planes and filling the entire surface of the canvas with a unified decorative pattern. Although the provocative interactions of dissonant colors remain, a quieter and more simplified design replaces the sharp angles and vehement curves of earlier works. Details are delineated more emphatically than in any other period, but there is little differentiation of texture or sharpness of contour;[3] the paint is lush throughout, and the parts relate equally to the whole. However, the subdued decorative background of the Kimbell painting is atypical of works of this period, and the figure occupies more space proportionally than is usual. Although the model's identity is anonymous this unidealized odalisque belongs to the 1920s, as indicated by her hairstyle and the shape of her

H. Matisse

Matisse painting the Kimbell picture in his studio in Nice, 1921–22.

eyebrows; this was new for Matisse whose nudes generally have a timeless quality.

Matisse allowed life to dictate to art when painting these languorous harem women in bright costumes. He wrote: "My models are the principal theme in my work. I depend entirely on my model whom I observe at liberty, and then I decide on the pose that best suits her nature."[4] The images, which might otherwise be explicitly erotic, seem diffused into a luxurious, generalized sensuality. Suggestive of pleasure and the exotic Moroccan culture that Matisse loved, the odalisques evoke a nineteenth-century hedonistic culture. They are studies of pleasure and beauty in contrast to the bitter, psychological studies done concurrently by the German painters in the war-torn Europe of the 1920s.

Following the Nice period, Matisse returned to the flatter and more abstract presentation of the figure within an environment which he had often explored, always with a new and vital approach to the subject.

Inscription: Lower left: *H Matisse*

Description: Interior view with nude woman, reclining on a chaise draped with a vermilion cloth. Covered with a flowing, light green shawl, she rests on pillows covered with fabric of medium and light blue with a red diamond pattern. Her right elbow rests on a dark brown cloth, her hand bent at an angle almost parallel with her upper torso; her left arm rests on the pillow above her head. Her creamy-peach flesh is modeled with deeper shades of the same color; she has chestnut-brown, close-cropped hair; her eyes and mouth are closed. A red cloth with a peach-and-gold floral motif hangs in the background behind the chaise.

Condition: Excellent. Uneven coat of varnish, clear and clean. Large patterned age cracking in heavier areas of paint, especially on her body. Very small horizontal repair near left elbow (perhaps from original stretcher).

Exhibitions: XVI a *Esposizione Internationale d'Arte della Citta di Venezia*, Venice, April 15–Oct. 31, 1928, cat. no. 49 (as *Odalisca su fondo rosso*). XXVII *Esposizione Internationale d'Arte di Venezia*, Venice, June 19–Oct. 17, 1954, cat. no. 9, p. 253. *Exposition Rétrospective d'Œuvres de Henri Matisse*, Salon d'Automne, Paris, 1955, cat. no. 18. *Matisse*, Pavillon de Vendôme, Aix-en-Provence, July 9–Aug. 31, 1960, cat. no. 18, illus. *Dix Ans de la Biennale de Menton, les grands prix*, Musée Galliera, Paris, Nov. 4–20, 1960, cat. no. 4, illus. *Henri Matisse*, UCLA Art Galleries, Los Angeles, the Art Institute of Chicago, and the Museum of Fine Arts, Boston, January–June, 1966, cat. no. 57, color illus. p. 89.

Collections: Henri Matisse. Marguerite Matisse Duthuit, daughter of the artist. [M. Knoedler & Co., Inc., New York, by about 1966.][5]
Foundation Acquisition, AP 68.6.

Notes:

1 According to family records and photographs of Matisse painting this picture, it was executed in Nice during 1921–22.

2 Alfred H. Barr, *Matisse: His Art and His Public*, New York, 1966, p. 208.

3 Barr, pp. 209–10.

4 Lawrence Gowing, introd., *Matisse Retrospective*, Hayward Gallery, London, 1968, pp. 36–37.

5 The French title, *Nu au châle verte*, was supplied by the dealer.

Additional Reference:

Adolphe Basler, "Völkerbund der Malerei," *Kunst und Kuenstler*, vol. 27, no. 4, January, 1929, p. 151 (*Ruhende Frau*).

Aristide Maillol, 1861–1944
L'Air
1938

Bronze, blue-green patina, 60 1/2 × 94 × 38 in., including plinth (153.6 × 239.9 × 96.5 cm.)

Aristide Maillol's works exemplify one of the major directions of early twentieth-century sculpture, that of a kind of modern classicism, which recalls the serenity, balance and stability of ancient classical art. Although Maillol was an accomplished tapestry designer and book illustrator, he gained his greatest recognition as a sculptor, a discipline which he did not begin until the age of forty. The elegantly simplified forms of the female figures which preoccupied him are in contrast to the irregular surfaces and expressionistic forms of his older contemporary, Auguste Rodin, who openly praised Maillol's work.

The successful idealization of a graceful feminine figure and the airy, floating quality achieved on an heroic scale make *L'Air* one of the major works of Maillol's late career.[1] The nude figure reclines with her legs suspended in space and her left arm in the commanding gesture of pushing the clouds away. The face and figure are generalized, the surface texture is smooth and firm, and details are subordinated to the overall harmony of the finished work. This work was cast from the plaster model for one of the few monuments in Maillol's oeuvre, his memorial to French airmen who died in World War I.[2] It was commissioned by the city of Toulouse, in southern France, where many pilots had been trained.

Maillol developed the design for *L'Air* through an evolutionary process. He was first inspired by a small plaster study he had done in 1900 of a nude reclining on a billowing mass of clouds.[3] Like most of his works, it possessed a monumental character independent of its size and was easily translatable to a work of massive scale. To achieve the design for *L'Air*, Maillol had a large cast of his 1912–25 monument to Paul Cézanne[4] dismembered in order to rearrange the pieces. He changed the attitude of this nude, reclining on drapery and holding a laurel branch, by placing the new figure of *L'Air* on her side instead of her back and tilting her head, torso, and limbs forward. The swirling drapery beneath the plaster figure was retained in the final stone version chiseled by Maillol's assistant, Jean van Dongen,[5] which is installed in the Royal Garden at Toulouse.[6]

It was Maillol's intention to have sculpture cast from the plaster model. Although this was not done during his lifetime, the artist's will gave his executors permission to have Georges Rudier[7] make an edition of six casts. Maillol's lifelong principle was that a plaster model could not withstand more than six castings without losing some of the outline's purity and firmness.[8] In 1962 the edition was cast at the request of the Kröller-Müller Foundation in Otterlo, The Netherlands.[9] The stronger cast metal versions no longer required the supporting drapery of the plaster and stone versions; thus, it was omitted. This emphasized the floating attitude of the figure and revealed greater clarity of structure to achieve a more forceful visual statement.

Inscriptions: Plinth, front side: upper right, *A. Maillol;* lower right, *5/6*[10]; lower left, *Georges Rudier, Fondeur, Paris*

Plaster model for *L'Air*, 1938, in the artist's garden at Marly.

Description: Free-standing, bronze sculpture of nude female figure. The reclining figure is unsupported except at the right hip which rests on a rectangular plinth. Her head is tilted slightly downward and her hair is arranged in a chignon with loose curls falling about her finely chiseled, classic-featured face. Her right arm, bent at the elbow, would support the weight of her upper torso were she leaning on it. Her left arm is fully extended horizontally above her body with the hand gracefully cocked at the wrist. Her legs, separated and slightly bent at the knees, extend full-length.

Condition: Excellent.

Exhibitions: Extended loan to Cleveland Museum of Art, August, 1967–March, 1972.

Collections: [Marlborough-Gerson Gallery, New York.] Foundation Acquisition, AP 67.6.

Notes:

1 Waldemar-George, *Maillol*, Greenwich, Conn., 1965, p. 55.

2 John Rewald, *Maillol*, London, 1939, pp. 24–25, illus. pp. 86–87.

3 Rewald, illus. p. 86.

4 Rewald, illus. p. 85.

5 Brother of the painter Kees van Dongen.

6 *Sculptures of the Rijksmuseum Kröller-Müller*, 2nd English ed., Otterlo, The Netherlands, 1966, p. 80; also, Rewald, p. 87.

7 Georges Rudier is the son of Alexis Rudier, a favored foundryman of Maillol and Rodin until Alexis' death in 1917. However, the foundry continued to use Alexis' mark until the mid-1950s. Posthumous casts of both Rodin and Maillol works made after about 1952 usually bear the foundry mark of Georges Rudier. See Athena Tacha Spear, introd., *Rodin Sculpture in the Cleveland Museum of Art*, Cleveland, 1967, pp. 87–88.

8 Dina Vierny, "Notes on the Casting of Maillol's Work," *An Exhibition of Original Pieces of Sculpture by Aristide Maillol*, Paul Rosenberg and Co., New York, 1958–60.

9 *Sculptures . . . Kröller-Müller*, p. 80.

10 Number 5 of an edition of six, cast in 1962 by Georges Rudier, Paris, from the 1938 plaster model. Other casts of *L'Air* are located at: the Louvre: Les Jardins du Carroussel, Paris; Yale University Art Gallery, New Haven, Conn.; City of Hanover, Germany; Kröller-Müller Museum, Otterlo, The Netherlands; Norton Simon, Inc., Museum of Art, Los Angeles.

Additional References:

John Rewald, "Aristide Maillol achève . . . un monument aux aviateurs . . .," *Le Journal des Beaux Arts*, Feb. 3, 1939, p. 1 ff.
Andrew Carnduff Ritchie, *Aristide Maillol*, Buffalo, 1945, p. 117.
Henri Frère, *Conversations de Maillol*, Geneva, 1956, pp. 72, 81.
Rolf Linnenkamp, *Aristide Maillol*, Munich, 1960, illus. nos. 120, 133.

ASIA

Plate with King Peroz Hunting Boars
From Iran
About Seventh Century

Silver, partially gilt, 1 3/8×8 7/8 (diam.) in.
(3.5×22.6 cm.)

Ancient poets sang in praise of wine and beauty; of fine silver wares; of the conflict, man against beast, of a mounted king–Peroz, Kavad, Chosroes–charging in the hunt.

Let us pass round the golden cup
Persia has decked with divers images:
Chosroes in the midst and, on the sides,
antelopes pursued by raiders armed with bowes.[1]

Abu Nuwas, A.D. 762–815

The Sasanian drinking bowl or plate reflected the elegant, luxury-loving court life of a sophisticated nobility and conveyed a specific story to glorify the reigning monarch. While the great rock bas-relief sculptures at Taq-i-Bustan, on the old Silk Route, were an official representation of the monarch enthroned, the silver vessels, plates, bowls, ewers–only a hundred or so are known to have survived[2]–served a very private purpose, to be used on festive occasions of relaxation and entertainment to recall and toast the royal hunt.

A Sasanian king hunting wild boars appears on this magnificent silver plate. The main source and substance of power of the royal house came from astral affiliations. The Sasanian king displayed on his crown ancient astral motifs of sky, sun and moon.[3] Each monarch made his own selection of the emblems which constituted the principal ornament for his crown and the individual arrangement of the units which served to identify him[4] wherever his portrait appeared–on coins,[5] great rock sculpture[6] and on vessels such as the Kimbell silver plate.

The distinctive headgear worn by this king is a crenellated crown, symbolic of his sovereignty. The globe rests upon a crescent, beneath which are two eagle sky wings, emblems of royalty which reflect divine association.[7] The diadem, with flaring merlons and a moon symbol in the front, is a double-row band, punched to represent jewels. The elements and emblems on this crown distinctly identify this king as Peroz, who reigned A.D. 457/9–484.[8]

Peroz is represented in this seventh-century work[9] as a monarch with strong features, high cheekbones, moustache and a curled beard which is neatly tooled with a circle punch. Shown in profile, he has a prominent nose, with dilated nostril, and his wide-open eye is keen with the furor of the hunt. His arched eyebrow reflects this excitement. Over his head a light silk gauze is tightly drawn. From under the crown his long curly hair forms a mass in the nape of his neck over which flutters the royal Sasanian scarf which is attached to the investiture ring. His loosely fitting cloak of colorful supple silk, falling in multiple folds, is set off by his jeweled belt and scabbard. The apezat or braces which cross his chest are held together with a large jeweled medallion, all attributes of princely rank and royalty.[10]

In the ferocity of the royal hunt the king is shown here charging on his horse through a pack of wild hogs who scatter for their very lives. Peroz, seated high on his mount, swings around to launch a Parthian shot with his tautly held Sasanian bow, fully drawn. The bowstring is held by an unseen special archer's ring which fits over the thumb and is held steady by the two middle fingers, until released.[11] These bows were harder to manipulate than the more flexible type but they gave greater power and driving force to the arrow. They were used by the famous Iranian bowmen of the royal armies. Here it is used by Peroz to glorify his virtue and strength as a hunter.

The royal hunt was not a minor occasion or a day spent in the field. It was virtually a state ceremony with thousands of horsemen, nobles and their servants, prepared to spend a month upon the chase. Camels and elephants carried the king's pavilion and bore the turquoise throne, all bedecked in brocades of great color and beauty.[12]

The artist skillfully places the figure of Peroz on an imaginary vertical axis, while positioning the horse to carry the forward thrust of the horizontal. The circle of the plate dictates the placement of the fluttering scarf, the horse's front legs, the little pool with its fish, and the bodies of the wild boars. The instant depicted is one of wild fury; the design is one of all-encompassing circular motion. But for all the racing of the wild boars and the charging horse, the action is stopped like a single frame from a movie film. The artist has chosen this very instant to depict just a fragmentary glimpse of what a royal hunt was all about.[13]

Peroz was a monarch known for his deep religious feelings and famed for his efforts to overcome a famine which lasted for many years. In this silver plate the Sasanian artist, whose traditions looked back through many centuries, might have been drawing upon ancient astral symbols and cosmological meanings in showing Peroz hunting the wild boar, which is related to the moon and winter.

Perhaps the artist here depicts Peroz, concerned with the coming season to grow crops for his people and grain to feed his army, symbolically killing winter in this wild boar hunt.

Description: Silver plate, partially gilded, set on a ring foot, 3 5/16 in. diam. and 3/8 in. high, depicting a scene from a royal hunt. The outside of the plate is plain and there are no inscriptions. This refined representation of the king is executed in craftsmanship of highest quality, combining a variety of techniques of casting, repoussé and chasing. The plate is formed from two sheets of silver, one of which is worked from the back to develop the design; the other, when shaped and attached to the back, conceals the embossed area while giving strength to the whole plate.[14] The parts of decoration in highest relief were cut out, shaped, attached to the background by soldering and then tooled with various instruments to enrich the surface.[15] The plate, representing the king on horseback in full splendor, according to tradition, combines the solemn dignity of the monarch amid the liveliness of motion. The staid, sharply turned head of the king, set against the royal scarf which flutters back of his richly covered right arm; his flowing cloak, and the loose trousers, held at the instep and ankle by a jeweled clasp, are all carefully traced and modeled. The splendor of the harness of the royal mount is depicted with great care, adding to the surface brilliance and luster of the plate. The groups of animals and the individually placed bodies of three boars, partly modeled in relief, are against a gilded background. The plate is finished by a rolled rim which adds rigidity and strength. Combining all of these elements and techniques, the Kimbell plate reflects the quality of craftsmanship in Sasanian art at a moment of its highest attainment.

Condition: Excellent. There are no losses or damage and the evidence of surface wear is minimal.

Exhibitions: Treasures of Persian Art, J. B. Speed Art Museum, Louisville, Ky., March 1–April 3, 1966, no. 221, color illus. on cover. *Sasanian Silver, Late Antique and Early Medieval Arts of Luxury from Iran*, Oleg Grabar, The University of Michigan Museum of Art, Ann Arbor, August–September 17, 1967, cat. no. 5, illus. p. 95. *Masterpieces of Asian Art in American Collections* II, Asia House Gallery, New York, 1970, cat. no. 3, pp. 26–27, color illus. p. 25.

Collections: [Mehdi Mahboubian, New York.] Foundation Acquisition, AP 67.3.

Notes:

1 Roman Ghirshman, *Persian Art: The Parthian and Sassanian Dynasties, 249 B.C–A.D. 651*, New York, 1962, p. 209.

2 While the national economy of Iran was agricultural, the court and aristocracy supported a thriving commerce in luxury items. Silver ore was plentiful and silversmithing had been practiced from ancient times. Silver vessels were offered in trade for jewels and furs, which were in demand. Many of these vessels have been recovered in eastern Russia and are now in the Hermitage Museum, or have found their way into other collections. The Sasanians also traded with China. Successive reigning monarchs sent valued silver, such as the Kimbell plate, to foreign princes as gestures of good will. See Ghirshman, p. 203.

3 Phyllis Ackerman, "Some Problems of Early Iconography," *A Survey of Persian Art*, ed. by A. Upham Pope, New York, 1964–65, p. 879.

4 Edith Poroda, *The Art of Ancient Iran*, New York, 1965, p. 201.

5 Of the many fine Sasanian coins in the Cabinet des Médailles, Bibliothèque Nationale, Paris, the fifth-century silver coin shows Peroz facing right, his crenellated crown adorned in front with the crescent surmounted by another crescent containing the Korymous, paralleling the arrangement of the headdress on the Kimbell plate. Ghirshman, p. 250, fig. 318. See also: G. G. Belloni and L. F. Dall'Asèn, *Iranian Art*, London, 1969, pls. 62–69.

6 Ghirshman, p. 192, fig. 235.

7 Ackerman, "Standards, Banners and Badges," *A Survey of Persian Art*, ed. by A. Upham Pope, New York, 1964–65, p. 2771.

8 Kurt Erdmann, "Die Entwicklung der Sāsānidischen Krone," *Ars Islamica*, vols. XV–XVI, 1951, pp. 87–123, fig. 18.

9 The apparent discrepancy between the dates of Peroz' reign, A.D. 457/9–484, and the dating of this plate may be attributed to the fact that princely themes, especially the act of hunting, continue to be repeated and copied well into later periods. O. Grabar, "An Introduction to the Art of Sasanian Silver," *Sasanian Silver, Late Antique and Early Medieval Arts of Luxury from Iran*, Ann Arbor, Mich., 1967, pp. 33, 50, 60.

10 Hermann Goetz, "The History of Persian Costume," *A Survey of Persian Art*, ed. by A. Upham Pope, New York, 1964–65, p. 2227.

11 Ghirshman, *The Art of Ancient Iran: From its Origins to the Time of Alexander the Great*, New York, 1964, pp. 318–19, figs. 389–90.

12 Josef Orbeli, "Sasanian and Early Islamic Metal Work," *A Survey of Persian Art*, ed. by A. Upham Pope, New York, 1964–65, p. 723. This description of a royal hunt is given by the Director of the Hermitage Museum within a longer treatise on metalworking techniques.

13 Quite a different hunting scene with King Peroz, taken from Chahar Taxkhan, near Tehran, is to be found in a fifth-century composition of stucco plaques in the Philadelphia Museum of Art. Ghirshman, *Persian Art*, p. 187, fig. 229.

14 This highly developed technique of gold and silver-smithing was a contribution of Persia during the Parthian and Sasanian periods and has interesting parallels in Chinese metalwork. Bo Gyllensvärd, "T'ang Gold and Silver," *The Museum of Far Eastern Antiquities Bulletin No. 29*, Stockholm, 1957, pp. 30–31.

15 Grabar, p. 40.

Standing Buddha
From Gandhāra
Second Century

Grey schist limestone, figure:
48 1/8 × 20 3/4 × 8 1/2 in. (122.2 × 52.7 × 21.6 cm.);
including base: 51 1/2 in. (130.1 cm.) high

This early figure represents the Buddha as a monk. Half-closed eyes evoke his inward state of meditation while his tender, gentle nature is conveyed by the almost feminine softness of rounded cheeks and sensuous mouth. His cranial protuberance or *uṣṇīṣa* indicates the added wisdom of Enlightenment, and his earlobes remain elongated from the heavy ornaments worn in his royal youth and later abandoned for the simple robe of a monk. The halo, here only a fragment, originates in the tradition of Iranian solar deities rather than in Buddhist scripture.[1] The iconography is Indian in origin and was fully evolved prior to the first century when the first anthropomorphic Buddha images were made. A growing devotional cult occasioned these images, carved in high relief and destined for niches in Buddhist temples.[2]

The sculptural form of this Gandhāran Buddha image, as opposed to its iconography, seems more Mediterranean than Indian, a result in part of the geographic location of Gandhāra on the northwest frontier of India (now West Pakistan). The Kushans, rulers of Gandhāra, were a Central Asian tribe of a syncretic culture who maintained numerous contacts with the Roman world, especially during the first and second centuries when "the school reached its highest point of production and aesthetic effective-ness."[3] Graeco-Roman sculptors may have been at work in Gandhāra while Gandhāran sculptors may also have trained in Roman imperial studios.[4] Western stylistic traditions reveal themselves in the voluminous robe, draped like a Graeco-Roman toga; in the sensuous beauty of the face, reminiscent of Hellenistic images of Apollo, and in the Praxitelean *déhanchement* of the body (with the left knee visible

where it presses against the garment). Even the *uṣṇīṣa* itself, covered with soft, wavy hair, seems disguised as a Greek topknot.[5] The slight corpulence of the figure reflects Indian artistic tradition, but without the sensuality of the Indian tradition.

Dating sculptures of this school on stylistic grounds presents certain difficulties, as there was a great deal of repetition within the school as a whole. A date of the second century is based on the closeness of the features to Apollonian prototypes, a quality characteristic of second-century pieces, and the deeply carved, voluminous drapery, which in succeeding centuries loses weight and substance. The quiet, reflective expression becomes cold and mask-like in the third and fourth centuries. The robe's pattern of parallel, string-like folds, alternately deep and shallow, later becomes even more schematic, concealing rather than revealing the body which, in turn, becomes stiff and hieratic.

Similarities of the Kimbell Buddha to another in Berlin from Takht-i-Bāhī—in the handling of the drapery, in the forked folds by the left elbow, and in the soft, full face—point in all probability to the same site of origin.[6] A date of the second century places this figure in the high period of Gandhāran art.

Description: Full-length, fully draped figure of a Buddha in dark grey limestone. The wavy hair is drawn into a wide, full *uṣṇīṣa;* the round ūrṇā is placed low on the forehead and the earlobes are typically elongated and pierced. Draped over both shoulders and arms is the ankle-length monastic robe, a *saṃghāṭī*, with two undergarments, the *dhoṭī* and the *ūttarāsaṇga*, visible beneath it on the figure's right side. Through the clinging drapery the contours of the Buddha's chest, abdomen and left knee are revealed. Originally the right hand was raised in *abhaya mudrā*, the gesture of reassurance. The back of the sculpture is flat and unfinished. The figure stands, feet apart, on a square pedestal; the space between the legs has not been cut away.

Condition: Very good. The figure is well preserved, including the facial features and the full length of the body. Only a fragment of the halo remains and both arms are missing at the elbow. Some minor losses are evident on the right earlobe, on the folds in the drapery, and on the toes.

Exhibitions: None known.

Collections: [Nasli Heeramaneck, New York.] Foundation Acquisition, AP 67.1.

Notes:

1 Benjamin Rowland, Jr., introd., *The Evolution of the Buddha Image*, Asia House Gallery, New York, 1963, p. 9.

2 Rowland, *The Art and Architecture of India*, Baltimore, 1967, p. 79.

3 Rowland, *Art and Architecture*, p. 83.

4 Rowland, *Ancient Art from Afghanistan: Treasures of the Kabul Museum*, Asia House Gallery, New York, 1966, p. 74. Numerous Roman finds in Gandhāra have led to the proper identification of the Western influence at work in Gandhāran sculpture as Roman rather than Greek.

5 Rowland, *Art and Architecture*, p. 78.

6 Islay Lyons and Harald Ingholt, *Gandhāran Art in Pakistan*, New York, 1957, p. 113, cat. no. 222.

Standing Female Deity
From Rājasthān
Tenth or Eleventh Century

Pinkish tan sandstone, 56 3/4 × 22 1/4 × 11 1/4 in.
(143.8 × 56.5 × 28.6 cm.)

This delicately carved figure of a voluptuous goddess is an excellent example of the masterful stone sculpture produced in North India during the medieval period. Its large scale suggests it once formed part of the decoration of one of the many temples, Hindu and Jain, which were built in Rājasthān during this period. Although its identity and place of origin have not been clearly established, the stylistic characteristics are typical of the Rājasthān area; affinities with sculptures from Deogarh[1] and from Jodhpur[2] have been noted. The restraint, balance and symmetry of the figure recall the classical forms of the Gupta period (early fourth to late sixth century) while the dry and somewhat brittle handling is typically medieval. Identification of the goddess is hampered by the missing arms, originally four in number, which once held attributes that would have helped to place her. The partial remains of a sword provide the basis for further iconographic research.

The sculpture displays some passages which are finely observed and beautifully rendered and others which seem conventional and uninspired. The apparent inconsistency is accounted for by various factors. On the one hand, the technical virtuosity of North Indian art at its apogee is evidenced in the delicate precision of carving, interesting textural contrasts, and subtle relationships of form and ornament. The goddess' metallic armbands contrast with her rounded arms and the smooth pearls of the necklace complement the soft flesh of her breasts. Her pliant girdle conveys an appropriately drooping, sensuous heaviness; its lowermost swags confine the gentle sway of long tassels. The supple contours of the goddess are enhanced by the lively *channavīra*

tassel extending below the waist, which counters the opposing sway of her hips. These refinements of modeling account in part for the marvelous "living" quality of the sculpture. On the other hand, the tubular legs, devoid of muscle or bone, and the exaggerated round shoulders and breasts exhibit little anatomical accuracy. "The paradox has at least two explanations, one . . . [being] the particular importance of clay modelling as a foundation or memory image for the sculptor. The other rationalization is based in the Indian delight in metaphor, poetic and visual. We are familiar with it in Western literature, but the Indian sculptor applies it thoroughly and continuously to his figural imagery."[3] An eyebrow is conceived as "arched like a bent bow," breasts become "golden urns," an arm hangs down "like the trunk of an elephant." During the medieval period increased reliance on these stereotyped conventions led to more formalized renditions of the human body.

Description: Pinkish tan sandstone sculpture of a large female figure carved almost in the round with the back left rough. The goddess stands before a slab with rectangular opening at shoulder height: the slab is pierced around the head, forming a halo with a shallow relief border. At top left and right sits a cross-legged attendant wearing a *dhoṭī* and pearl *channavīra* and holding a disk, water jug, and fly whisk. Relaxed in the *tribhaṅga* attitude, the goddess wears a diaphanous sari and elaborate ornamentation. Her hair is coiled high in a jewel-wound, *mukuṭa*-like headdress with a pomegranate in the center and a delicate diadem of pearl strands suspended below; fat lovelocks cluster at the temples. Behind the head projects a sword blade in relief. Broad cheeks, a small chin, full lips, long nose, elliptical eyes with folds of the lids indicated, long, curving brows and a *tilaka* on the forehead constitute typically medieval facial features. The goddess wears large pointed armbands, a collar-like necklace of lotiform buds, a long pearl necklace of five strands, and a *channavīra*, rigid between the breasts, whose tassel curves over the pearl necklace. Her girdle, an *urū jālaka* consisting of three horizontal, looped chains of lotiform buds crisscrossing three long vertical tassels, rests low on the hips. One anklet remains; across the top of the lower ankle and over the crook of the elbows appear remnants of a jeweled garland.

Condition: Good. Surface and prime features are well preserved, with losses occurring mainly on the periphery. The stele is broken off on the figure's right side below the shoulder, and on the left at hip level. The arms are missing at the elbows and the feet from above the fragment of a garland, left, and below the ankle bracelet, right. The nose is damaged and abrasions are evident on the surface of the face and breasts. Minor losses occur in the earrings, headdress and halo. Both attendant figures are partially broken away, as is the sword.

Exhibitions: None known.

Collections: [Peter Marks, New York.] Foundation Acquisition, AP 68.1.

Notes:

1 Martin Lerner, letter to Peter Marks, May 20, 1970. Mr. Lerner refers to the goddesses of Temple 19, illustrated in Klaus Bruhn, *The Jina-Images of Deogarh*, 1969, figs. 244, 248. In comparison with these the Kimbell figure seems more softly modeled and differs in the anatomy of the torso.

2 Pramod Chandra, conversation with Nell Johnson, November, 1971. Reference was made to no particular site. As relatively little has been published on sites in Rājasthān it is not possible at this juncture to establish the goddess' place of origin.

3 Sherman E. Lee, introd., *Ancient Sculpture from India*, the Cleveland Museum of Art, 1964, p. 22.

Head of a Jina
From Rājasthān or Madhya Pradesh
Eleventh Century

Grey-pink sandstone, 30 3/8 × 26 1/4 × 21 in. (77.1 × 66.7 × 53.3 cm.)

This large head, originally part of a colossal sculpture, was made for members of the Jain religion, founded in the sixth century B.C. by Mahāvīra, a contemporary of the Buddha. During the medieval period Jain adherents had grown into a large and flourishing community, especially in Rājasthān and Gujarāt. There they built, high on mountaintops, numerous shrines and temples of which the most famous is Mount Abu, known for its intricate marble carvings. It was a period of great building activity for both Hindu and Jain in the face of the invading Muslim iconoclasts.

Most images in Jaina art are of Mahāvīra and his mythological predecessors who together constitute the twenty-four saviors of the Jain religion. "These saviors, the so-called 'Victors' *(jinas)* or 'Makers of the River Crossing' *(tīrthaṅkaras)*, lead the way across the whirling life-torrent of the unending cycle of rebirths,"[1] This head portrays one of these Jinas, although because of its fragmentary state it is not possible to distinguish which among the Jinas is represented. Both Jaina and Buddhist sculpture followed the general Indian tradition of identifying its saints or divinities by symbols; here the halo is the same symbol of divinity found throughout the world.[2] Buddhist iconographic elements are recognizable in this head in its snail-shell curls and elongated, pierced earlobes. It lacks the cranial protuberance *(uṣṇīṣa)* and dot between the brows *(ūrṇā)* which are attributes of the Buddha. The absence of earrings or turban indicates the Jina, like the Buddha, is an ascetic who has renounced material goods.

Through breadth and generalization of form, evident in the curves and countercurves of hairline, brows and eyelids, an impression is given "of the spiritual tranquillity and modest self-assurance of one who, having found the Truth, looks into the future with confidence, knowing the purpose of life."[3] The manner in which the eyes are carved to remain in shadow, creating an effect of inward meditation, is also characteristic of the subtle play of light and dark used effectively in Indian sculpture throughout the centuries. The long eyes, curving brows and full lips of the Jina are typical of North Indian medieval tradition. At the same time the additive handling of the features as discrete elements and the massive scale of the head reflect the coldness and ponderous rigidity of much Jain and Hindu sculpture of the period.

Description: Massive fragmentary head of a Jina in arcosic (?) sandstone. Facial features include thin, curving brows, arched like a bow; deep, broad eyelids, and eyes which are narrow slits, carved to remain in shadow. The nose is short, the lips full and pronounced, and the cheeks more round than broad. The elongated, pierced ears are thick and doughy. A cap of tight, bead-like curls in horizontal rows comes down low on the forehead; behind it the fragment of a lotus-petal halo is visible on his right.

Condition: Good. The head itself remains essentially intact, with minor damage to the curls, forehead and lips. The nose is broken. Peripheral losses occur in the area of the chin and ears, and most severely in the halo, which is almost entirely missing.

Exhibitions: None known.

Collections: Ben Heller, New York.
Gift of Ben Heller, AG 68.1.

Notes:

1 Heinrich Zimmer, *The Art of Indian Asia*, ed. by Joseph Campbell, New York, 1960, vol. I, p. 15. The terms *jina* and *tīrthaṅkara* are synonymous.

2 The fragmentary halo is obscured in the photograph.

3 J. E. van Lohuizen-de Leeuw, *Indian Sculptures in the von der Heydt Collection*, Museum Rietberg, Zurich, 1964, p. 24.

Khasarpaṇa Lokeśvara
From Bengal
Twelfth Century

Dark grey limestone, chlorite or dolomite,
49 3/16 × 31 5/8 × 14 1/8 in. (124.9 × 80.3 × 35.9 cm.)

The Pāla school of Bengal maintained the sculptural tradition of the Gupta period with increased elaboration and stylization. This image of a Khasarpaṇa Lokeśvara manifests the "comparative finesse and serenity" and "the fluent, rounded modelling characteristic of most Pāla work"[1] in its expression of tenderness and in the soft flesh of the torso. Late tendencies within the Pāla tradition toward the ornamental and decorative are evident in the complex profusion of detail. Such elaboration and intricacy in Pāla sculpture correspond iconographically to the proliferation of the Buddhist pantheon as it began to absorb elements of Hinduism. The worship of Khasarpaṇa Lokeśvara, a popular deity, began with the rise of Tantric Buddhism.[2]

Khasarpaṇa's posture of "royal ease" on the double lotus throne, which indicates the divine nature of its occupant, is the attitude of a prince. His right hand, with the small wheel symbolizing Buddhism in the palm, is extended in the gesture of boon-conferring. Streams of nectar pour forth from this gesture, and the needle-nosed demon Sūcīmukha, crouched below on the sculpture's left edge, raises his snout to receive a drop.[3] Khasarpaṇa holds in his left hand the long stem of a lotus flower, which in Buddhist art stands for spiritual birth or enlightenment. It is a salient attribute of Avalokiteśvara, the Bodhisattva of mercy, of whom Khasarpaṇa Lokeśvara is an esoteric Tantric form. "Avalokiteśvara is 'the being who is capable *(iśvara)* of enlightening insight *(avalokita)*,' but who, out of infinite mercy, postponed his own attainment of nirvāna."[4] He combines the virtues of the sexes, and in the soft contours of Khasarpaṇa's body we see the fusion of youthful male form and feminine grace.

Clad as a prince, befitting his Bodhisattva position in the Buddhist hierarchy, he nevertheless wears the ascetic's crown of matted curls.

In Buddhist art, each divinity was provided with specific symbols and placed precisely in relation to various spiritual planes. Thus, we find clustered around the figure of Khasarpaṇa the four deities commonly associated with him, their small scale indicative of their lesser importance.[5] By his right knee stands the goddess Tārā with her right hand raised in an expository gesture indicating a lotus bud. On the opposite side Bhṛkuṭī raises one hand in adoration while holding a staff and water vessel.[6] Below the lotus throne, Sudhanakumāra sits beneath the boon-giving hand with a tablet under his arm, his hands folded in worship. The squat demon Hayagrīva, one of the Defenders of Buddhism, sits opposite. His expression is fierce in contrast to the other deities, and his hand is held in an attitude expressing energy and activity.[7] Between Hayagrīva and the stalk of the lotus throne appears a large seed or bud with flame-like edges which seems to be the "light-giving, wish-granting" Jewel of Buddhism often associated with Khasarpaṇa.[8]

The small Dhyāni Buddha on the upper left of the sculpture was originally one of five. We can also conclude that the two small kneeling figures on the lower right corner of the Kimbell Khasarpaṇa represent the donor and his wife, for a different, single figure appears on a comparable relief in the John D. Rockefeller, III, collection.[9] Such donor figures are common in medieval Indian art.

Inscription: On the back, the name: *Janathika.*

Description: The Bodhisattva, Khasarpaṇa Lokeśvara, seated in *lalitāsana* and surrounded by eight small figures. The image is carved of warm grey stone, sandy in the crevices, with traces of red paint. The slab, pierced around the torso, is carved like a throne; a lotus rises on the left in front of a crossbar which has lotus scrolls and part of a flaming halo above it, with a Dhyani Buddha in the upper left corner. Khasarpaṇa sits on a pearl-bordered double lotus throne with his right hand in *varada mudrā* and his left holding a lotus. He wears a dhoṭī, whose pleated ends fall over the end of the throne, and an ornate jeweled girdle edged with bells. Details of the girdle and flattened contours of the torso are cursorily indicated on the back side of the relief. A scarf crosses the figure's chest and curls under the arm, its ends fanning out by the left elbow. Ornamentation includes three strands of pearls with a jeweled clasp, forming the sacred thread; an elaborate necklace and armbands; arm and foot bracelets, and a diadem. The hair is arranged in *jaṭāmukuṭa*, with lotiform knobs over the ears and on the earlobes and one tassel preserved on the right side. Marks of divinity include an elongated *ūrṇā*, signs in the palms, and webbed fingers. Female deities, Tārā and Bhṛkuṭī, stand by either knee, and the male deities, Sudhanakumāra and Hayagrīva, sit in *sukhāsana* below the lotus throne. On the outer edges, Sūcīmukha kneels at the left and a bearded donor holds a rosary with his wife behind him on the right. A flame-like bud juts out beside the stalk of the lotus throne.

Condition: Very good. The back slab is broken from just above the Buddha on the upper left to below the shoulder of the main figure on the right. Minor losses occur in the face, hands and headdress of Khasarpaṇa and the torso of Bhṛkuṭī.

Exhibitions: None known.

Collections: [Ben Heller, Inc., New York.]
Foundation Acquisition, AP 70.13.

Notes:

1 Pramod Chandra, introd., *Indian Sculpture from the Collection of Mr. and Mrs. Earl Morse*, Fogg Art Museum, Cambridge, Mass., 1963, pp. 8, 15.

[2] Benoytosh Bhattacharyya, *The Indian Buddhist Iconography*, Calcutta, 1968, p. 128.

[3] Stella Kramrisch, *Indian Sculpture in the Philadelphia Museum of Art*, Philadelphia, 1960, p. 81, cat. no. 33.

[4] Heinrich Zimmer, *The Art of Indian Asia*, New York, 1960, vol. I, p. 182.

[5] Bhattacharyya, pp. 128–30.

[6] The hand usually holding a rosary is missing.

[7] J. E. van Lohuizen-de Leeuw, *Indian Sculptures in the von der Heydt Collection*, Museum Rietberg, Zurich, 1964, p. 58, cat. no. 11, notes: "This mudrā, prescribed by some of the iconographical texts, is not often found in Indian images of Hayagrīva; it occurs more regularly in Tibet."

[8] Kramrisch, p. 81. The deep relief of this bud and certain other features, such as the difference in the size of the hands, indicate this relief was originally placed high above the viewer.

[9] Sherman E. Lee, *Asian Art: Selections from the Collection of Mr. and Mrs. John D. Rockefeller, 3rd*, Asia House Gallery, New York, 1970, p. 16, cat. no. 5.

Vishṇu
From South India
Thirteenth Century

Bronze, 33 3/4×13 3/8×12 7/8 in.
(85.7×34×32.7 cm.)

Vishṇu, Shiva and Brahma together constitute the Brahmanical (Hindu) Triad, with Vishṇu representing the Preserver, the mediator between those opposing forces whose energies are constantly active in the universe. Images of Vishṇu may take the shape of his avatars, like the boar or lion, depict one of his twenty-four emanations, or present him in his highest aspect *(Para)* as "the supreme cause and the final resting place of everything."[1] The Kimbell sculpture represents the last aspect, in which Vishṇu is shown in the straight, frontal, symmetrical posture called *samapādasthānakamūrti*. Immovable, he stands "At the still point of the turning world. Neither flesh nor fleshless;/Neither from nor towards; at the still point.../Where past and future are gathered."[2]

Visual images of Vishṇu were particularly important in the Vaishṇava cult which decreed that none of its followers "should stay for a single day or take food or drink in a house or village where there are no images of Viṣṇu."[3] Its members prayed to Vishṇu to gain specific ends, and Vishṇu images can be classified according to the results expected.[4] *Yoga* images, for example, were prayed to by those seeking spiritual self-realization; inauspicious *abhicārika* images by those who wished to inflict death on their enemies; and *bhoga* images, of which the Kimbell sculpture is an example, by those who sought prosperity and happiness. Needless to say, *bhoga* images are by far the most numerous.[5]

Recognition of the various types of Vishṇu images is dependent upon the disposition of the hands and the objects held; as with all the Hindu gods, Vishṇu's manifold powers and activities are symbolized by his many arms, their gestures and emblems.[6] Here his lower right hand expresses the gesture of reassurance *(abhaya mudrā)* while his lower left hand is held down beside his hip in an attitude *(kaṭyavalambita)* prescribed by the texts which dictated the iconography of religious sculptures.[7] Vishṇu holds two of his four attributes, the conch *(śaṅkha)* and the wheel *(chakra)*. These emblems, peculiar to Vishṇu, admit a variety of interpretations. The conch is an implement of war, blown to strike terror in the heart of the enemy;[8] it is also considered "the destroyer of ignorance"[9] and is furthermore thought to represent the sky—"probably the quality of primordial sound that pervades the sky."[10] The wheel recalls Vishṇu's Vedic origins as a solar deity, being "the sun in the shape of a wheel"; it is also a weapon of war, thrown to cut down the enemy, symbolizing Vishṇu's role as "chastizer of the wicked."[11] In a more general sense it is the wheel of life, the wheel of time, the wheel of the law.[12]

In this sculpture Vishṇu is magnificently attired, wearing a regal *kirītamukuṭa* crown and a richly draped and elaborately fastened *dhoṭī*. Visible in his palms are auspicious lines and on his chest a triangular *śrīvatsa*, the mark of beauty and fortune. His chest is raised with the breath of life which was thought to infuse each image as it became, by consecration, the god himself.[13] Falling over his chest is a sacred thread, a ubiquitous Brahmanical feature which symbolizes the Thread-spirit "on which all the individual existences in the universe are strung like gems, and by which all are inseparably linked to their source."[14] Thus attired, Vishṇu stands in hieratic splendor on the lotus pedestal of divinity connoting spiritual awakening. Lugs on the side of the base were used for the insertion of poles to support the image when carried in ritual processions.

Stylistic details of the ornamentation assist in determining the date of the sculpture. Features of Chola period bronzes include: the clasp of conjointed rings on the wavy, tripartite sacred thread; the shoulder tassels *(skandamālā)*, one a curl of hair, the other ending in a pipal leaf; the angle of the wheel; the division of the side sashes of the *dhoṭī* into two folds, and the mango motif discernible in the central *kaṇṭhī*-type necklace.[15] The Kimbell sculpture is similar in conception to twelfth-century Vishṇu images in the Tanjore Art Gallery and in the National Museum of India at New Delhi.[16] There is a sharpness to the facial features indicative of developments in the subsequent Vijayanagar period; however, there is a sense of liveliness in the figure as a whole, a subtlety of modeling, noticeable especially in the flesh of the torso, and an overall technical excellence which preclude its being dated later than the thirteenth century.

Description: A standing, four-armed image of Vishṇu on a low base, in bronze with a green patina. The god stands in *samabhaṅga*. His upper arms are raised in *kartarīmukha hasta*, holding flame-tipped disk and conch: the lower right hand expresses *abhaya mudrā;* the lower left is held in *kaṭyavalambita*. *Makara* (acquatic monster) forms are evident in the earrings and in the ornamentation of the armbands and the *kirīṭamukuṭa* headdress. Geometric patterns are incised into the headdress and the girdle, loops, and double side sashes of the lower garment *(antarīya)*. Tasseled ribbons extending from the mouth of the horned lion head on the clasp enclose a deep, squared-off median loop in the lowermost band of the girdle. Ridges set between parallel grooves constitute the schematic folds of the *antarīya*. The sacred thread, waving over the chest in three strands, runs the length of the body and loops up below the *antarīya* on the right ankle. Bracelets and other ornaments repeat a thick, triple-band motif. The stomach band is molded with an irregular, raised jewel motif. The base of the sculpture, comprised of a double lotus pedestal *(padmāsana)* and plinth *(bhadrāsana)*, is heavy, broad and low, with kidney-shaped lotus leaves incised above the curled edge of the *padmāsana*. A vertical tenon and two lugs appear on either side of the *bhadrāsana*.

Condition: Excellent. The *śiraśchakra* (lotus appendage) is missing at the back of the head, and the raised fingers of the god's upper right hand have been broken off and restored.

Exhibitions: None known.

Collections: Ben Heller, New York.
Gift of Ben Heller, AG 70.1.

Notes:

1 Jitendra Nath Banerjea, *The Development of Hindu Iconography*, Calcutta, 1956, p. 387. This complicated subject is dealt with at length in Banerjea and in Rao (see note four below).

2 T. S. Eliot, "Four Quartets: 'Burnt Norton-II' " in *Collected Poems 1909–1962*, New York, 1963, p. 177.

3 Banerjea, p. 395.

4 T. A. Gopinatha Rao, *Elements of Hindu Iconography*, 2nd ed., New York, 1968, vol. I, part 1, pp. 79–85 (unaltered reprint of the Madras, 1914 edition). As Banerjea notes, p. 398, these classifications were not always strictly followed.

5 Banerjea, p. 399.

6 Banerjea, pp. 81–82.

7 Some confusion exists concerning this gesture. There is no reason to assume that Vishṇu's attribute of a mace is missing from his lower left hand. See: Pratapaditya Pal, "South Indian Sculptures: A Reappraisal," *Boston Museum Bulletin*, vol. LXVII, no. 350, 1969, p. 156. P. R. Srinivasan in *Bronzes of South India*, Madras, 1963, identifies it throughout as *kaṭyavalambita*. J. E. van Lohuizen-de Leeuw in *Indian Sculptures in the von der Heydt Collection*, Museum Reitberg, Zurich, 1964, p. 202, identifies it as *āhūyavaramudrā*, the gesture which beckons "the devotee to come near and receive a boon," a gesture which would be especially appropriate to *bhoga* images of Vishṇu.

8 Banerjea, p. 300.

9 Rao, p. 295.

10 Pal, p. 156, based on the *Viṣṇudharmottarapurāṇa*.

11 Banerjea, p. 305.

12 Pal, p. 155.

13 Stella Kramrisch, *Indian Sculpture in the Philadelphia Museum of Art*, Philadelphia, 1960, pp. 24–25.

14 A. K. Coomaraswamy, note in Heinrich Zimmer, *Myths and Symbols in Indian Art and Civilization*, ed. by Joseph Campbell, New York, 1946, p. 185.

15 C. Sivirammamurti, *South Indian Bronzes*, New Delhi, 1963, pp. 24–43.

16 Siviramamurti, figs. 71a, 71b.

Additional References:

T. N. Srinivasan, *A Handbook of South Indian Images*, Tirupati, 1954, p. 43, fig. 21, captioned "Vishṇu as sthanaka murti-Sundaraperumal koil."
Sotheby's, sale catalogue, *Primitive Art and Indian Sculpture*, London, July 14, 1970, lot 25, illus.

Pārvatī
From South India
Fifteenth Century

Bronze, 35 3/4 × 11 × 9 5/8 in.
(90.7 × 27.8 × 24.5 cm.)

The Vijayanagar period (1336–1565) saw the last florescence of the great South Indian schools of Hindu metal sculpture just before a decline of the art set in because of increasing political instability.[1] The images produced, almost without exception, were "religious in purpose . . . designed to remind worshippers of the Divine, conceived by Hindu philosophy as the Impersonal Absolute and by Hindu Bhakti (devotion) as the Lord and Divine Lover of believers."[2] This figure represents the goddess Pārvatī, "the archetypal mother goddess, fertile, benevolent and gracious."[3] Her beauty reflects her position as the bride of Shiva and mediatress between the worshipper and the Divine.

Her shapely form corresponds to the Indian ideal of feminine beauty: heavy breasts, narrow waist and rounded hips, as determined by the *tālamānas* or systems of proportion. Every image conformed to traditional patterns known to the craftsman through the *silpa-śastras*, artistic-theological manuals. These guided the sculptor in creating an icon which, when consecrated and worshipped, became both symbol and actuality of the deity through a fusion of material form with the spiritual and cosmic world.

Within the highly traditional forms of Hindu religious sculpture, minor changes in ornamental motif became significant factors in determining the date of an object.[4] The high *keśamukuṭa* headdress with a lotus appendage, the waistband composed of several strips with a *makara* (aquatic monster) clasp, and the manner of draping the sari with its free end trailing along one leg are elements common in much earlier sculpture. Typical Vijayanagar characteristics are the thin wiriness of the few ornaments, the addorsed position of the *makaras* on the clasp, and Pārvatī's elongated eyes and sharply prominent nose. The stylization of the hem of her garment into flanges at hip and ankle and of the flesh of her torso into linear folds illustrate the increased formalism which distinguishes Vijayanagar sculpture from that of the preceding Choḷa Dynasty. Although Pārvatī's attitude and gestures are conventional, the dignity and vitality of her pose is enhanced by smooth modeling and long, flowing lines. She stands on a double lotus pedestal symbolizing her divinity. The image was originally placed in a temple among many such sculptures; its small scale enabled worshippers to carry it in religious processions.

Description: A standing figure of the goddess Pārvatī in the gently swayed *tribhaṅga* attitude, on a tall square base. The well-cast bronze has a warm, golden-brown patina. Pārvatī's right hand is raised in *kaṭakāmukha hasta;* her left hangs in the graceful *lola* position. The *keśamukuṭa* headdress, fringed with flat curls around the face and below the bulbous cushion at the top, is ornamented with a jewel-like motif at four points. The hair in back forms the same flat curls below a protruding *śiraśchakra* composed of sixteen ribbed, blade-like points around a series of rings from which a tassel falls. Necklaces, arm and leg ornaments are simple and wire-like, save for pendulous ear ornaments of an indistinct organic shape. The goddess wears a sari whose folds are delicately incised on the legs, the hem ends fanning out at hip, ankle and various points on the girdle. The girdle, with three decorative beaded bands in front and four in back, includes a small frontal panel of beaded folds. From the girdle's clasp of addorsed *makaras* issue ribbons which encircle this panel and the swag of the lowermost band. The base incorporates a round double lotus pedestal with incised leaves set on a square plinth consisting of two registers separated by double moldings, with panels of an incised crosshatch pattern above and lotus petals below.

Standing Maitreya Buddha
From Pra Kon Chai
Probably Eighth or Ninth Century

Bronze, 48 1/4 × 20 × 12 1/2 in.
(122 1/2 × 51 × 31 1/2 cm.)

Condition: Excellent. *The śiraśchakra,* broken off and restored, has a different, rather greenish patina.

Exhibitions: None known.

Collections: [N.V. Hammer, Inc., New York.] Foundation Acquisition, AP 69.13.

After a particularly heavy rainfall during the monsoon of 1964, one of the most startling artistic discoveries in recent years was made accidentally by local residents near Pra Kon Chai, a small village in Thailand, about 150 miles northeast of Bangkok, near the northern border of present-day Cambodia. Adjacent to an abandoned and derelict small temple datable to the seventh century,[1] a burial chamber was revealed, inside which was a hoard of bronze figures wrapped in heavy cloth. There were ten large figures, ranging from about three feet in height to slightly over four feet, and about two dozen smaller pieces variously measuring from three to eighteen inches.[2]

All the figures are Buddhist in subject and are of a pre-Angkor type hitherto unknown. Accordingly, extended study of this important group will alter and enlarge considerably our interpretation and understanding of the art of this entire period and region. A number of factors, however, make it still premature to arrive at precise conclusions concerning dating, place of production, and even iconography. In contrast to our relatively extensive knowledge of chronological events during the Angkor period (802–1431), derived mostly from carved inscriptions upon known temples, there is very little ascertainable historical fact from pre-Angkor times. Almost everything we know about the Funan period (first century to A.D. 550), most of which is legend, derives from references in reports of Chinese envoys and travelers; the very name we apply to the country at that period, Funan, is a Chinese transcription of a native name now unknown to us.[3] That it was undoubtedly the earliest of the Indianized states of Southeast Asia becomes apparent, however, as we move into the Chenla Period (A.D. 550–802) and find large numbers of Hindu and Buddhist buildings and sculpture with strong Pallava Indian antecedents. Inscriptions, also in the Pallava tradition, begin to proliferate, and although they identify individual rulers, dates and names of cities, it is often impossible to reconcile dates with personages, or to locate capital cities geographically.[4]

Drawing upon a vast intimacy of knowledge and feeling for the art of Cambodia, Jean Boisselier has theorized that the type of Buddhist bronzes from Pra Kon Chai may represent the religious art of the Canāśa Kingdom (ca. seventh to tenth centuries).[5] A key object in this suggestion is the large bronze *Bodhisattva* in the Pra Kon Chai style recently found at Ban Tahnot on the Korat Plateau, which was where the Canāśa Kingdom was located. Emma C. Bunker has tentatively summarized this possibility: "The stylistic development of the Pra Kon Chai bronzes does not fit into the mainstream of pre-Angkor art from Cambodia, which was primarily Brahmanic, nor does it belong to the formative period of Thailand, which is basically Hinayana (Buddhist), although it borrows from both areas. Instead, the style . . . would seem to bear out Boisselier's theory, representing an extremely homogenous, local artistic phenomenon: the development of the religious art of the little known Kingdom of Canāśa, which must have played a very important role in the spread of Mahayana Buddhism in Southeast Asia."[6] As pointed out by Mrs. Bunker, "The religion (of Canāśa) was originally Buddhist, but became Sivaite early in the tenth century, a radical change of faith which could account for the cache at Pra Kon Chai." The paucity

Notes:

1 Although such metal sculptures are commonly referred to as bronzes, they are, strictly speaking, an amalgam of copper, silver, gold, brass and white lead.

2 F. H. Gravely and T. N. Ramachandran, *Catalogue of Hindu Metal Images in the Madras Government Museum,* Madras, 1932, vol. I, part 2, p. 1, quoted by P. R. Srinivasan, *Bronzes of South India,* Bulletin of the Madras Government Museum, new series, vol. VIII, 1963, pp. 2–3.

3 Pramod Chandra, introd., *Master Bronzes of India,* the Art Institute of Chicago, 1965, unpaginated.

4 To a certain extent, variations were inevitable as the lost-wax method of casting ensured the uniqueness of every piece. An excellent discussion of motifs is presented in G. Siviramamurti, *South Indian Bronzes,* New Delhi, 1963.

of information about the Canāśa Kingdom, however, makes it necessary to emphasize the hypothetical nature of these suggestions.

Whatever the origins of this extraordinary sculptural art, as Sherman Lee has so well written, "We must imagine an emerging aristocracy of wealth and power, fervent in their preoccupation with the new-found Buddhist and Hindu faiths and their material embodiment in images—objects of worship—rather than in large temples or other tokens of luxury and display, and deluged with imported concrete manifestations of their newly embraced faiths and culture. These things came from India, largely by sea, and were probably small, portable images, usually of metal, from various centers of the faiths in all parts of India. The resulting, almost chaotic, possibilities were refined and solidified by ruling groups, with inexorable will and purpose. The results are their aesthetic justification."[7]

A large proportion of pre-Angkor bronzes represents either Avalokiteśvara or Maitreya, the two principal members of Buddha's celestial congregation, who were vouchsafed a vision of the "Body of Bliss" *(Sambhogakaya)*. There are innumerable representations of the Buddha in which the presence of an architectural relic mound (stupa) is known to symbolize his final attainment of bliss (nirvana), and such a stupa is represented on the Kimbell figure just above the forehead, at the front of the tall chignon *(jaṭāmukuṭa)*. Thus, the figure undoubtedly represents Maitreya, or the "Buddha of the future." The positions of the four arms and the precise articulation of the hands and fingers cannot be related to a definite pose *(mudrā)* with Buddhist iconography. Since some of the Pra Kon Chai figures, as well as those from other areas, still carry such attributes as the pilgrim's bottle and the lotus bud, it is possible that the Kimbell figure also once did. The heavily pierced, pendulous earlobes also suggest other movable attributes such as earrings, now lost. But a more basic religious symbolism in the exact positions of arms and hand gestures is suggested by the constancy with which most of these Maitreya and Avalokiteśvara figures hold the right forward arm slightly back and higher than the left forward arm which extends outward and down, whereas the two rear arms are crooked upward to exactly the same level at the hands.[8]

Although Maitreya was practically never represented in stone, which was the predominant medium at this period, there are certain aspects of the bronze Kimbell Maitreya that recall the early Cambodian's innate feeling for the more obdurate, unmalleable material. A monolithic solidity and robustness is maintained in spite of the tensile strength of bronze, which makes the extension of four arms possible. No detail is permitted to disrupt the taut surface contexture of the rich, smooth bronze (an alloy with copper, silver and gold, known to the Cambodians as *samrit*). Thus, the single garmet *(sampot)* is very nearly only "inscribed" onto the figure in a manner to reveal most solidly and subtly the anatomy of the lower torso, while the pectoral cleft and other details of the upper torso are so understated as to become subsumed in a body bursting with energy. The hair, stupa and chignon, forming an appropriate "crown" because of their relatively greater complexity, still subserve this generalized figure of supernatural vigor by being deliberately geometrized. Moreover, the sense of free-standing stability and *poise* in this bronze figure is an expression seldom matched in stone because of the early sculptors' inability to achieve such a pose in the less tensile medium without recourse to secondary supporting elements such as niches, mandorlas or attachment to flat backgrounds. In sum, the Kimbell Maitreya, in which the facial expression performs an essential consonant part, exalts an archaic intensity of strength along with an expectant jubilation that expresses both the early time of its making and its subject, the Buddha of the future.

Description: A youthful male figure standing formally erect in what seems a strongly frontal pose, but subtleties of modeling, anatomy and surface qualities invite viewing in the round. The figure is almost entirely nude but for a very short lower garment that resembles the *sampot*, except the cloth is not drawn back between the legs. There are four arms, the hands of which are held in a pose which is similar to, but not, the *vitarka mudrā;* they may once have held attributes of Maitreya, as the pierced ears may have supported earrings. A restrained, archaic smile is on the lips, not the broader smile of later Cambodian Buddhas that usually appears with partially closed eyes; here the eyes are alert and wide open. A very thin curving moustache is on the upper lip. The hair is pulled up severely in parallel furrows from brow, temples and the back of the head and is gathered in a high, cylindrical chignon *(jaṭāmukuṭa)* that is made up of six horizontal rows of curls running all around the whole shape. At the front center of this chignon is a small stupa, which gives the iconographic identity of the figure as Maitreya.

Condition: Excellent. Cast in an accomplished and subtle lost wax process, nearly solid, but probably with a heavy clay core, the surface in many areas still retains a soft, silvery sheen resulting from the bronze alloy with copper, silver, and perhaps other precious metals *(samrit)*. When found, both double arms were broken off, and these in turn were broken variously at a number of places; they have been repinned during restoration. Both legs, just below the knee, were cracked through, and the extremity of the right heel had been lost. The silver inlay on the right-hand side of the left eye is missing.

Exhibitions: None known.

Collections: (Ellsworth & Goldie, Ltd., New York.) Foundation Acquisition, AP 65.1.

Notes:

1 The brick construction method, with shallow engaged pilasters, projecting main piers, and corbelled entablature is comparable to many small temples around Sambor Prei Kuk and Phnom Bayang.

2 The tallest of the group, an Avalokiteśvara, now in the Metropolitan Museum of Art, New York, is about 1/2 inch larger than the Kimbell piece; one of the smaller figures of the group of 10 big ones, with superbly sensitive casting, is now in the John D. Rockefeller, III, Collection, New York, and measures 38 3/8 inches.

3 Lawrence Palmer Briggs, *The Ancient Khmer Empire*, American Philosophical Society, Philadelphia, 1951, p. 12 ff.

4 Briggs, p. 52.

5 Jean Boisselier, "Notes sur l'art du bronze dans l'ancien Cambodge," in *Artibus Asiae*, Ascona, Switzerland, vol. XXIX, 4, 1967, p. 275.

6 Emma C. Bunker, *Pre-Angkor Bronzes from Pra Kon Chai*, Colorado College and Denver Art Museum. We are deeply grateful to Mrs. Bunker for sharing the results of her research and all her photographic material prior to publication of her article.

7 Sherman E. Lee, *Ancient Cambodian Sculpture*, The Asia Society, New York, 1969, p. 16.

8 Pierre Dupont, *La statuaire prèangkorienne*, Ascona, Switzerland, 1955, p. 202, Also see: Madeleine Giteau, *Khmer Sculpture and the Angkor Civilization*, New York, 1965, p. 129.

Buddha Enthroned
Tenth or Eleventh Century

Bronze, 68 1/8 × 27 1/4 × 16 5/8 in.
(173 × 69.5 × 42.5 cm.)

The origins of the Khmers are lost in legends of a mythical progenitor named King Kambu, founder of the race of Kambuja, who named their country Kambujadesa (Cambodia), "land of the descendants of Kambu." It is impossible to say now whether this primal myth of royalty helped shape Khmer character to an extent that it had a bearing upon religion and society during the period of ascendancy of the Khmer Empire (802–1431). But at the very heart of the entire culture generated by that empire was the old Indian concept of a world ruler as the God King (Chakravartin), which in Cambodia became the Devarāja. The king was divine, and upon his death he became one with a major deity, usually Shiva or Vishṇu, since the dominant religion was Hindu. Upon rare occasions the Devarāja was a Buddhist of the Mahayana ("Great Vehicle") faith that emphasized the formally theistic worship of the god, as opposed to Hinayana ("Small Vehicle") Buddhism that stressed more of the compassionately humanistic doctrine he propounded.

Khmer art, as well as religion, was largely taken from India, but it was not a provincial offshoot. It was truly indigenous in conception, style, technique, and ceremonial function, and its overriding function was to effect the identity of the king with his deity. Consequently, upon the accession of each king, all of society was organized and pressed into service to build temples and temple complexes to glorify and deify the monarch, his family, and even his ancestors. Each succeeding royal line, of which there were many because of incessant civil and external wars, aspired to surpass what had been built, carved and decorated before. Teeming masses of the populace at the peasant and slave level were bound by their state religion into these vast symbolic and artistic efforts. Although myriad temples were modest, or even small, and the larger complexes were functionally related to the basic rice-growing economy, these successive efforts became more and more of a strain. Nevertheless, for more than 400 years (ninth through early thirteenth centuries) the system produced a prodigious recurrent vitality that filled the domain with cities, artificial lakes, canals, palaces and temple complexes laden with religious sculpture.

When Angkor Wāt, the largest single religious edifice in the world, was rising under the reign of the follower of Vishṇu, Sūryavarman II (1113–50), the capital city of Angkor was one of the most populous in the world. However, by the time Jayavarwan VII (1181–1215) was unsuccessfully trying to complete the Bayon, on which are gigantic heads of the Bodhisattva Lokeśvara in the king's own image, the nation was exhausted. An iconoclastic revolution ensued, during which Mahayana Buddhism was suppressed. By the end of the thirteenth century a "fifth column" with simpler, humbler and more democratic principles had firmly penetrated the land of the Devarājas in the form of Hinayana Buddhism, and a little later Theravada Buddhism. Comparatively, these created a religion for the masses which had little use for huge symbolic monuments. They were faiths of compassion, submission and renunciation.

The rising kingdom of the Thais (Siam), as well as other neighbors, militarily ransacked Cambodia a number of times during the fourteenth century, and when the last Khmer administrators had to move out of Angkor in 1432 the empire was finished. Nearly 500 years later, during the latter half of the nineteenth century, the world was amazed at the discoveries of French archaeologists as they started tearing away the smothering jungle that had conquered all.

Discovery still goes on, and the Kimbell *Buddha Enthroned* is one of the more recent pieces to emerge. Unless a sculpture is still on a known and identified building, precise location of provenance is hardly ever possible; there is argument even about many of the famous individual pieces in the museums of Cambodia or Thailand. When it comes to dating a particular work, one is on somewhat firmer ground because of the magnificent and prolonged scholarly contributions made by the French during the last century, mainly by that intrepid confraternity of l'École Française d'Extrême Orient founded in 1898. (Cambodia had become a French Protectorate in 1864.) This vast tapestry of fact, theory and comparative stylistic analysis, although inevitably the foundation upon which all present and future studies must rest, is bewildering and sometimes confounding. For the general reader it may be interesting to point out that most of the dating in the bibliography down through 1927, and especially in relation to Angkor's two most famous monuments, Angkor Wāt and the Bayon, have been completely reversed by periods ranging from 100 to 400 years![1] Such a monumental reminder of fallibility must be borne in mind when any assertions of date based upon stylistic analysis are made, although the most rigorous and honest attempts must continue, of course.

Because of its pertinence in dating the Kimbell Buddha, based upon: (1) affinities in general conception and iconography of the subject, (2) parallels in formal style, (3) precise similarities of decorative details, and (4) known historical circumstances that logically relate to all the foregoing, the dating of one of Cambodia's most beautiful temple complexes, Banteay Srei, needs to be discussed as briefly as possible here.

As the result of generally correct facts and a chronology derived from carved inscriptions, it was long accepted that Banteay Srei was built under the reign of Rajendravarman II (944–68) and his son Jayavarman V (968–1001). In 1926 Louis Finot reread the inscriptions and concluded that this monument was not completed until the first years of the fourteenth century,[2] although, in the same year, Victor Goloubew's stylistic analysis maintained the old dating.[3] In 1928, Georges Coedès reconsidered the inscriptions (which are in both Sanskrit and Khmer, and often damaged or fragmentary) and maintained the late tenth-century dating.[4] During the early 1930s Guilberte Coral-Rémusat turned her attention to reconciling styles with inscriptions[5] and her excellent book, which appeared in 1940, claimed that only the foundations of Banteay Srei date from the tenth century, whereas the rest was done under King Indravarman III (1296–1308) in 1304.[6] The second edition of her book, however, which appeared in 1951, consistently and firmly reestablished the earlier date.[7] Also published in 1951 was Laurence Palmer Briggs' exhaustive study that approached the subject from a purely historical and epigraphical point of view; and he inflexibly affirms the earlier dating of Banteay Srei, including quotations from inscriptions that state the temple was not only founded but dedicated at the earlier period (A.D. 967).[8]

Because many elements of the Banteay Srei style are floridly "baroque" there was a natural proclivity on the part of Western scholars to see it as a late evolution of what, in Europe, would have been an historical progression from archaic to classic to baroque to rococo; and Madame Coral-Rémusat's initial hypothesis of a later dating seemed to make eminent sense. Benjamin Rowland, for example, whose fine survey was at the press for its first edition as Rémusat's second edition began to appear, built a plausible aesthetic for a "... final rococo phase of Khmer art" at Banteay Srei.[9] Heinrich Zimmer taught this same hypothesis at Columbia University from 1941 until his death in 1943, and the two posthumous editions (1955, 1960) of his large interpretive study, based upon his Columbia lectures, still lend credence to the later dating.[10] Even though most other students of the subject insist upon the tenth-century placement in time,[11] enough confusion was inserted in an already complex question to encourage generalized conclusions of late dating for Cambodian objects containing stylistic affinities with Banteay Srei's luxuriance. The temple's dedication date (967) should be taken as a closer approximation for dating the Kimbell *Buddha Enthroned*.

But why this attention to an edifice that was dedicated, in any case, to Vishṇu? Because, not only did the unprecedented and astonishing richness of its style give a universally accepted name to a whole novel stylistic development, but, whenever Banteay

Srei was done, the Kimbell *Buddha Enthroned* was done also.

The image is eminently Mahayana, aloof, monumental, powerful, hieratic, bejeweled and richly adorned, although the body itself is generalized and simplified to enhance its regal strength. Not only is such a conception unlikely at the later date, none in fact, has been discovered. As Jean Boisselier recently wrote, "... today we do not possess a single large-scale Khmer bronze later than the Bayon style (1181–ca. 1200) ... and there is little chance of discovering one someday because of known events in Cambodia since well before the end of the thirteenth century and, above all, from the beginning of the fourteenth century."[12] Nevertheless, Sherman Lee may be right in asserting that the Kimbell Buddha is the "isolated and remarkable" example.[13] By following George Groslier's exhaustive stylistic analysis, however, and by comparison with certain pieces known to have been found at Banteay Srei, the Kimbell piece closely relates to a group from this site, as discussed by Groslier.[14] Although nearly all of this group represent Hindu figures, they share an important general stylistic element with the Kimbell Buddha; the body is almost archaic in its sturdy, robust simplicity, whereas the accoutrements of dress and surrounding adornment are elaborated beyond anything seen down to this time. This duality is not only to be found in the single figures; it is a salient feature of the temple itself. Massive, simplified figures and whole scenes are shown in a bulky, smooth symmetry, whereas they are surrounded with architectural decoration of an almost overwhelming, jungle-like luxuriance. The constant tension between these divergent elements is one of the means, in the case of the imperturbable Kimbell Buddha, to express the eternal conflict between spirituality and sensuality that is at the heart of the religious message.

There are innumerable precise motifs at Banteay Srei that compare in detail to those on the *Buddha Enthroned*. The sinuous, polylobed arch of the embrasure (*toraṇa*) in which the Buddha sits exactly matches the arches that embrace the many tympana on the temple. These snake-like (*nāga*) arches terminate at their lower ends in fantastically stylized crocodile heads (*makaras*) in the manner of Banteay Srei's florid elaboration. The continuously repeating lozenge motif, with the rosette in the center of these horizontal diamond shapes, which appears on the two flat surfaces at the base of the Buddha's throne, is a major motif used on the stylobate of the temple. The colonnettes that support the *torana*, with shallow geometrically treated capitals, seem to be truncated, or sliced flat, at their inner edges; and this too is done on the temple.

Although there are other parallels of an architectural nature, brief mention should be made of the diadem and conical headpiece (*mukuṭa*) that the Buddha wears, as well as the necklace. According to the exhaustive analysis made by Boisselier, the forms of these adornments began before the period of the Banteay Srei style and continued, in variations, down to the Bayon and beyond; but the preponderance of their application in these specific types and shapes appears most frequently in the late tenth and eleventh centuries.[15] After the thirteenth century the treatment of a Buddha head tends in two directions: (1) the coiffure is a tight, cap-like arrangement of the hair in the so-called "snail curl" style, with no diadem or *mukuṭa*, and a more traditional *uṣṇīṣa*, or (2) the *mukuṭa* becomes higher, thinner and more elaborate.

Without implying that a direct connection has been established between a known historical person and the Kimbell Buddha, but simply to help vivify this period in Khmer history, it is perhaps valid to introduce Kavindrarimathana, who was King Rajendravarman's Minister of Public Works (944–68) and most probably in charge of building Banteay Srei. He was one of the most influential ministers in Khmer history, and, although the King was a Vishnaite, the minister was a great Buddhist leader. Under him the first large Buddhist temple complex was constructed at Phimai. He also built, as patron and donor, a charming Buddhist temple at Bat Chum. According to an inscription datable in 960, found at Bat Chum and translated by Coedès, "He restored the holy city ... and rendered it charming ... with shining gold, palaces glittering with precious stones ... This minister, dear to the gods, who knew the arts like Visvaharman (god of architects), was charged by this king to make ... a charming palace."[16] This inscription dedicates the sanctuary to the Buddha and Bodhisattvas, and it contains a long list of the minister's donations of images, mostly of Mahayana Buddhas, to temples in many widely scattered parts of the realm.[17]

Description: The Buddha, with interlocked legs, and naked to the waist, but adorned with armlets, a large flat necklace, a diadem and conical headpiece *(mukuṭa)*, sits in the "earth-touching" pose *(bhūmisparśa mudrā)*, in which the right hand reaches down for contact with the whole earth for strength. His left hand, holding a stylized lotus bud *(padma)* symbolizing all that is pure in the universe, is in the pose of inward contemplation *(dhyāna mudrā)*. This combination of *mudrās* may signify that the Buddha is at that point of meditation when the evil god Mara sent his host of demons to prevent the Enlightenment. The agitating figures on the altar base may be the demons. The entablature containing these little figures is embraced at the top by a flat architrave, at the bottom by a flat plinth, each faced with a lozenge pattern and bordered on its inner side with a repeating foliate motif. The two colonnettes that support the embrasure *(toraṇa)* are also faced with a floral pattern. The dragon, or crocodile, heads *(makaras)* at the top of each column are conceived as guardians, and their scaly tails become the polylobed arch which forms a kind of holy nimbus *(probhāvali)* around the Buddha figure. These tails relate to the traditional snake gods of Cambodia *(nāgas)*, who were also guardians, and they recall the legend according to which King Kambu became progenitor of the Khmer race through union with a snake goddess *(nagini)*.

Around the outer edges of the pillars and the arch are depicted twenty-four mortal Buddhas, with a slightly larger twenty-fifth one above the summit of the arch. The luxuriously stylized foliate motif above the arch is the Bodhi tree, under which Enlightenment was achieved. At its summit is a trident *(triśūla)*, also a main attribute of Shiva, symbolizing indestructible power.

Condition: Good. The whole was originally encrusted with jewels, now missing. It was cast in eighteen pieces, five of which comprise the central figure. The base is in three separate horizontal sections. All of these and the remaining pieces are now attached to a modern iron armature. A large jagged loss is right of center on the plinth of the base. Over all is a patina of ashen green corrosion, with earth accretions in many scattered spots. Evidence of bronze disease (now arrested?) can be found in numerous places.

Exhibitions: Ancient Cambodian Sculpture, Asia House Gallery, organized by Sherman E. Lee, New York, Oct. 9–Dec. 7, 1969, cat. no. 61, p. 114; also pp. 30, 33, color pl. 61.

Collections: [Ellsworth & Goldie, Ltd., New York.] Foundation Acquisition, AP 66.9.

Notes:

1 Based upon a rigorous system of stylistic analysis, especially of sculptural decoration, the establishment of a whole new chronology was started by: Philippe Stern, *Le Bayon et l'évolution de l'art khmer*, Paris, 1927. These conclusions were then correlated with the then-known and translated inscriptions, further establishing the validity of the new dating, by Georges Coedès in *Bulletin de l'École Française d'Extrême Orient*, Hanoi. Between 1911–1940 this scholar published translations of inscriptions and their significance for dating and understanding style 294 times. Stern's brilliant pupil synthesized these approaches during the 1930s and published her admirable summation: Guilberte de Coral-Rémusat, *L'Art khmer; Les grandes étapes de son évolution*, 1st ed., Paris, 1940.

2 Louis Finot, "Le Temple d'Icvarapura," *Mémoires Archéologiques*, Paris, 1926, pp. 69–133.

3 Victor Goloubew, "Le Temple d'Icvarapura," *Mémoires Archéologiques*, 1926, pp. 51–67.

4 Coedès, "La date du temple de Bantay Srei," pp. 289–96, and "Quatre nouvelles inscriptions de Bantay Srei," pp. 143–57, both in *Bulletin de l'École Française d'Extrême Orient*, 1928.

5 Coral-Rémusat, "Le problème de la chronologie," *Bulletin de la Commission Archéologique Indochinoise*, Paris, 1934, pp. 35–44.

6 Coral-Rémusat, *L'Art khmer*, pp. 112–13.

7 Paul Pelliot, "Memoires sur les coutumes de Cambodge par Tcheou Ta-Kouan," *Bulletin de l'École Française d'Extrême Orient*, 1902, pp. 123–77.

8 L. P. Briggs, *The Ancient Khmer Empire*, Philadelphia, 1951, pp. 135, 141, 243, 251–52.

9 Benjamin Rowland, *The Art and Architecture of India*, 3rd ed., Baltimore, 1967, p. 240.

10 Heinrich Zimmer, *The Art of Indian Asia*, New York, vol. I, p. 423.

11 Louis Frédéric, *The Art of Southeast Asia*, English ed., New York, 1965, pp. 276, 286. Madeleine Giteau, *Khmer Sculpture*, New York, 1965, p. 78. B. F. Groslier, *The Art of Indochina*, New York, 1962, p. 113 ff.

12 Jean Boisselier, "Notes sur l'art du bronze dans l'ancien Cambodge," *Artibus Asiae*, vol. XXIX, tome 4, 1967, p. 282.

13 Sherman E. Lee, *Ancient Cambodian Sculpture*, Asia House Gallery, New York, 1969, p. 33.

14 George Groslier, "Les Collections khmères du Musée Albert Sarraut à Phnom-Penh," *Ars Asiatica*, vol. XVI, Paris, 1931, p. 82 ff.

15 Boisselier, *La statuaire khmère et son évolution*, Saigon, 1955, pp. 112, 137, 159.

16 Coedès, *Études cambodgiennes*, 1908, pp. 203–54.

17 Briggs, p. 131.

Amphora-shaped Vase
Seventh or Eighth Century

Stoneware, with transparent glaze,
$14^{7/8} \times 7^{5/8}$ (diam.) in. (37.8×19.4 cm.)

A typical shape of the T'ang period, the amphora appears to be based on Hellenistic prototypes, which became known in China via trading routes through the Near East. However, the Chinese transformations of this Western form give a distinctly different character to the Mediterranean vase type.[1] The body is generally fatter and the handles evolve into elaborately constructed lip-biting phoenixes or dragons. The handles may be heavy single pieces of clay or, as in this vase, double-stranded loops embellished with nodules and a delicately modeled crest.

This simple, gracefully proportioned vase is quite restrained when compared to more elaborately decorated T'ang amphorae. The neck is plain, without rings or grooves and the shoulders are unadorned, without applied medallions or scrolls. The barely tinted glaze is swagged over only the upper body and allows the turning pattern in the dense, hard clay to complement the chastely shaped neck and body. In other examples, bright three-color glazes may be splashed in colorful random patterns that obscure the turning pattern while descending nearly to the foot. This austerity of design in the Kimbell vase allows the possibility of an early seventh-century date as exemplified by a similarly unpretentious vase at Yale University that is dated in the Sui Dynasty.[2]

Description: High-fired, greyish-white stoneware amphora, with transparent glaze. Two double-stranded, dragon-headed handles "bite" the sides of the wide mouth which rises from a plain neck with incurving sides. The slightly flared base melds smoothly into a plain ovoid body. The finely crackled neutral glaze is swagged over the upper body, tinting it to a straw color where thin and a slightly greenish color where thick. The lower third of the body and the flat base are unglazed.

Condition: Very good. Except for small losses in the "crests" of the dragon heads and a small chip in the glaze on the lip, the vase is unblemished.

Exhibitions: None known.

Collections: [N. V. Hammer, Inc., New York.] Foundation Acquisition, AP 69.16.

Notes:

1 Celia Carrington Riely, *Chinese Art from the Cloud Wampler and other Collections in the Everson Museum*, Syracuse, 1968, cat. no. 23.

2 George J. Lee, *Selected Far Eastern Art in the Yale University Art Gallery*, New Haven, 1970, p. 19, cat. no. 25.

Jar with Cover
About Ninth Century

Earthenware with white and blue glazes,
8 7/8 × 8 7/8 (diam.) in. (22.5 × 22.5 cm.)

If nobility is a quality that can be imparted to a conventional ceramic form, this covered vessel is eminently qualified for consideration as a "noble jar." Its straightforward shape is handsome and gracefully proportioned; its colorful glazing is masterfully applied and its condition exceptional. Jars of this shape, known as *wan-nien-hu* (meaning, very roughly, a 10,000-year wine vessel,) are not uncommon; containing grain, they were placed as mortuary gifts in T'ang tombs. Comparable examples covered with a rich amber or deep blue glaze are well known, but only a few have been recorded that still retain their original covers and bear glaze patterns that complement the shape so positively as the one embellishing this jar.[1]

Above the slightly flared foot, the body of fine white clay swells out rapidly, as if expanding against the skin of the glaze, before receding sharply above the rounded shoulder to meet the neck. The flare of the body's flattened lip matches the flange of the cover whose profile rises in a gentle flat curve that repeats the swelling outline of the body's upper shoulder.

The cobalt-blue glaze pattern varies considerably. About the mouth are nine deliberately spaced touches that descend partway down the inner neck and trail over the outer lip. Only smallish spots and spatters decorate the cover, while on the body larger splashes mottle into blurred streaks where the glaze ran more freely down the incurve of the sides. These shapes appear to be climbing up the ample curve of the shoulder toward the mouth, thus enhancing the jar's assertive shape.

This exceptionally attractive glazing was obtained by a complex process. Initially, the cover and the upper body were covered with white slip. Next, deliberate touches of the blue glaze were laid about the rim of the mouth and perhaps also at random points on the shoulder. Finally, spatters from a brush were flicked upon the surface with an intuitive spacing that comes only with the assurance of long experience. The spontaneity implicit in this predominantly random pattern is very appealing to the modern taste for chance effects. The artist's use of this very personal technique on this jar and other freely glazed T'ang vases can be regarded as a relatively early example of deliberate pursuit of the accidental quality of natural effects. The varying visibility of the crazing pattern, which resulted from exposure to different aging agents while interred in the ground, provides a complementary texture that enhances the naturalness of the glaze pattern.

Description: Globular jar with high flat shoulders, short neck and everted mouth rim. The matching low cover has a central knob and a flat flange. Except for the lower third, the low-fired, white body is covered with a creamy-white glaze slip. The shoulders and the cover are dappled and streaked with numerous spots and splashes of cobalt blue glaze except for two anomalies: one deliberate streak of green and a greenish-yellow spot. The partially glazed interior is creamy-white; the inner neck is glazed and deliberately spotted, while the underside of the cover is unglazed. The body flares slightly at the crisply cut foot, and the unglazed base forms a broad ring about a shallow flat depression.

Condition: Very good. It is unblemished except for some scattered dull crazing in the glaze and two very small repaired chips in the edge of the foot.

Exhibitions: None known.

Collections: [N. V. Hammer, Inc., New York.] Foundation Acquisition, AP 71.18a, b.

Note:

1 A similarly shaped vase (20.2 x 20.8 cm.) bearing a more open, less assertive pattern of blue glaze splashes is illustrated by Hsien-ch'i Tseng and Robert Paul Dart, *The Charles B. Hoyt Collection in the Museum of Fine Arts...*, Boston, 1964, cat. no. 102.

Wine Jar with Cover, Chekiang ware
Eleventh or Twelfth Century

Stoneware, olive-green glaze,
12 1/2 × 5 5/8 (diam.) in. (31.7 × 14.3 cm.)

This gracefully proportioned jar, with the beguiling little dog surmounting its cover, probably contained a funerary offering, most likely wine (because of the allusion in its unusual inscription). A comparable inscription on a jar of plainer shape not only refers to wine but also bears an inscribed date equivalent to A.D. 1080.[1] However, the purpose of the five upright tubes on the shoulder is obscure. In similar vases, the tubes may be solid or terminate in animal heads; so a suggested initial use of the tubes as flower-holders is not likely.[2]

Chekiang province, located on the east coast of China north of Taiwan, was noted for its potteries early in the Sung Dynasty.[3] Recently this jar has been convincingly associated with a group of ceramics from the Li-shui region in the center of the province.[4] The Lung-ch'üan area, about fifty miles southwest of Li-shui, has also been suggested as this jar's place of origin.[5] However, it has a combination of features characteristic of ceramics that are thought to have been made near Li-shui: thick walls, a rather broad shape, pale olive-green glaze, an unglazed base, and incised designs with an abundance of combed detail.

Inscription: Around the tubular neck of the cover, under the glaze, are indented characters that translate as: "Ch'ih Shih-pa-lang's Thousand Year Wine Shop."[6]

Description: Covered wine jar of greyish-red, porcelaneous stoneware with tall, ovoid body and short, straight neck. It is covered with a crackled, transparent, olive-green glaze. On the body five vertical tubes surmount the shoulder, four diagonally scored rolls embrace the middle, and carved overlapping petals encircle the lower portion. A small reclining dog surmounts the floral-shaped cover which has a five-foil, spreading rim. The glazed foot ring surrounds a shallow depression to which rough unglazed clay adheres.

Condition: Excellent.

Exhibitions: Chinese Ceramics, Los Angeles County Museum, 1952, cat. no. 154. *Selections of Chinese Art from Private Collections…,* China Institute in America, New York, Nov. 15, 1966–Feb. 15, 1967, cat. no. 44.

Collections: Warren E. Cox, by 1944. Dr. and Mrs. Robert Dickes, by 1966. [N.V. Hammer, Inc., New York.] Foundation Acquisition, AP 70.8 a, b.

Notes:

1 R. L. Hobson, *Catalogue of Chinese Pottery and Porcelain in the Collection of Sir Percival David…,* London, 1934, pl. CLXXIX (from Ayers) and Warren E. Cox, *The Book of Pottery and Porcelain,* New York, 1944, pl. 41a.

2 John Ayers, *The Seligman Collection …,* London, 1964, vol. 2, p. 80, illustrates two jars, nos. D155 and D156, and discusses others in the British Museum, the Honolulu Academy of Fine Arts, the Percival David Foundation, London, the Yamato Bunka-Kan, Osaka. The flower-holding theory is advanced by Cox, pl. 41b.

3 Hobson, *Chinese Pottery and Porcelain,* London, 1915, vol. 1, p. 76.

4 Ayers, pp. 16, 80. See also: Herbert Ingram, "Form, an Early Factor in the Dating of Early Chinese Ceramics," *Ethnos,* no. 4, 1946, p. 162 ff., and G. St. G. M. Gompertz, *Chinese Celadon Wares,* London, 1958, pp. 23–24.

5 Cox, pl. 41b. Henry Trubner, *Chinese Ceramics,* Los Angeles County Museum, 1952, cat no. 154. Mrs. Gilbert Katz, *Selections of Chinese Art,* China Institute in America, New York, 1966, cat. no. 44.

6 Trubner, *Chinese Ceramics,* cat. no. 154. The characters have also been read as *chu shih pa lang ch'en nien chiu ku tzu,* or "Chu the 18th thousand-year-wine store made" by Cox, pl. 41b, who also shows a view of the characters on the neck of the cover.

Bowl with wave design, northern celadon ware
Twelfth or Thirteenth Century

Stoneware, olive-green glaze,
2 1/2×6 1/4 (diam.) in. (6.4×15.9 cm.)

Elegant graceful shapes, rich greenish glazes and distinctly carved designs are salient features of the restrained jade-like ware known as "northern celadon."[1] The somewhat ambiguous name alludes to its development in the northern provinces of Shensi and Honan during the Northern Sung period (960–1127). Celadon is a European term originally designating a color; it derives from the distinctively colored grey-green robe of a French theatrical figure of the seventeenth century.[2] Since then the term has enlarged in meaning to describe a distinctive variety of ceramic types of which this bowl is but one example.

The pleasingly crisp profile of this bowl more than mitigates a small blemish in its glaze. Both the foot and the thin flared lip are clearly cut in sharp outlines. These features are balanced by the bowl's relatively thin walls and emphasized by the carved surface decoration. The allover pattern of deftly carved waves in the interior of this bowl is clearly revealed by the dark tint of the thicker glaze that fills the deep cuts of the design. Also long random fractures in the glaze, appearing as a filigree of pale brown lines, further enhance the gentle curve of the sides. They occur mostly where the thicker glaze overlies the carved area and disappear where the glaze is thinner over the plain band just below the lip. On the exterior the irregularly spaced parallel grooves are neatly stopped just below the flaring rim.

Close inspection of the very thin surface glaze on parts of the foot rim and the pronounced craquelure of glaze over carved areas suggests that two layers of glaze may have been applied: an initial surface film over the bowl, including the foot, and a second glaze overlying only the carved areas, giving it a smooth finish.

Description: Shallow bowl of grey stoneware with extensive carved designs, a slightly flared lip, and pale celadon glaze. The interior design is an intricate "comb" pattern of interlocking wave crests with a radiating petal pattern at the bottom. The exterior bears a pattern of irregular vertical grooves. The smoothly finished shallow recess of the foot (1 7/8 in. diam.) is unglazed and bears a faint center indentation (7/8 in. diam.); the bottom rim is very thinly glazed. The glaze has a pronounced craquelure pattern and varies from pale to dark olive-green (in the carved areas).

Condition: Good. In addition to normal hairline scratches, there is an old, skillfully filled, loss of glaze, 1 1/2×3/4 in., at the bottom of the interior.

Exhibitions: Selections of Chinese Art from Private Collections..., China Institute in America, New York, November, 1966–February, 1967, p. 31, cat. no. 45, illus.

Collections: Dr. and Mrs. Robert Dickes, New York, by 1966. [N. V. Hammer, Inc., New York.]
Foundation Acquisition, AP 70.9.

Notes:

1 G. St. G. M. Gompertz, *Chinese Celadon Wares*, London, 1958, p. 35.

2 R. L. Hobson, *Chinese Pottery and Porcelain*, London, 1915, vol. I, pp. 77–78.

Bowl with lotus design, northern celadon ware
Twelfth or Thirteenth Century

Stoneware, olive-green glaze,
2 3/4 × 7 1/4 (diam.) in. (7.1 × 18.4 cm.)

This particular type of northern celadon bowl, which appears to have been a rather popular Sung form, reveals a consummate mastery of ceramic techniques. Although the substantial hard-fired body, with its thick rounded lip and summarily formed foot, has a solid unpretentious shape, the ornately carved lotus design and subtly enhancing glaze combine to produce a vigorous effect of considerable elegance.

The long curving incisions that form the carved design were cut into the damp clay at an angle. Consequently, one side of a cut slopes gradually down from the surface while the other side is bounded by a slight ridge of clay that was pushed aside during the cutting. This varying relief of the carved area has a marked effect on the thin glaze. Its surface undulates and its intensity of color varies according to the underlying carving, thus reinforcing the boldly cut pattern. Of medium intensity in uncarved areas, the glaze appears darker where it collected in the furrowed lines. It is thinner over the adjacent ridges, forming pale upraised lines that are further enhanced by the varying reflections from the undulating surface.

The large number of bowls and shallow dishes with the design motif of this bowl suggests that a particular meaning associated with the design may have prompted the production of these containers for ceremonial usage.[1] An atypical feature of the Kimbell bowl is the counterclockwise orientation of the fan-shaped leaf which is the opposite of most bowls, such as the one that is said to have originated from Tung chou in Honan province.[2] However, one bowl with a design similar to that of the Kimbell bowl has also been recorded.[3] A further variation of the motif may be found in a more naturalistic and slightly later Tz'u-chou ware bowl. In it, the blossom and leaf design, in overglaze enamel, expands to fill the entire circular design, and the ornate foliage is eliminated.[4]

Description: Shallow conical bowl of grey porcelaneous stoneware with a deeply carved lotus design and a darkish yellow-green celadon glaze. In the interior medallion an open bloom and a naturalistic leaf dominate the surrounding scrolls of ornate foliage. The exterior is plain except for a prominent bead paralleling the rounded rim. The thick foot ring, whose bottom is beveled slightly, surrounds a shallow glazed recess. The thin layer of glaze has only minute crazing; its color is consistent except for three small brown spots in the interior and similar coloring about the foot.

Condition: Very good. It is unblemished except for scattered areas of very slight surface clouding in the otherwise lustrous glaze and one narrow quarter-inch lacuna on the exterior.

Exhibitions: None known.

Collections: [N. V. Hammer, Inc., New York.]
Foundation Acquisition, AP 71.16.

Notes:

1 For other examples, see: *Illustrated Catalogues of the Tokyo National Museum: Chinese Ceramics*, Tokyo, 1965, cat. nos. 205, 206, illus.; also Sotheby's sale catalogues: June 2, 1970, lot 50, illus.; Dec. 14, 1971, lot 220, illus.; and March 14, 1972, lot 111. A bowl in the Ashmolean Museum, Oxford, is illustrated by Peter Swann, *Art of China, Korea and Japan*, New York, 1963, p. 138.

2 François Fourcade, *Art Treasures of the Peking Museum*, trans. by Norbert Guterman, New York, 1965, p. 143, illus.

3 *Old Chinese Ceramics from the Robert Hilton Simmon Collection*, Pasadena Art Institute, 1953, cat. no. 24, illus.

4 Henry Trubner, *Royal Ontario Museum: The Far Eastern Collection*, [Toronto], 1968, p. 23, cat. no. 13.

Attributed to Hsia Kuei, about 1180–1230
Mountain Landscape by Moonlight
Painted about 1200–1225

Hanging scroll, ink on silk, 20 7/8 × 14 in.
(53 × 35.6 cm.)

Southern Sung landscape painting is a form of poetry, concerned less with outward appearance than with expressive qualities such as mood and feeling. In this hanging scroll, the elements of nature have been distilled to their very essence, their presence not described, merely suggested. The mountain has been simplified, reduced, concentrated into a steeply falling, expressively jagged edge, whose silhouette is intensified by the darker ink tones and angular strokes of the trees and foliage. This strong diagonal dramatically divides the composition, separating the material world from infinite space, confining the principal detail of the landscape to the lower third of the painting.

What is left, however, is not emptiness or a meaningless void.[1] Instead, the delicately graded washes of the background create an atmosphere of mist which permeates the painting, obscuring detail, enveloping individual elements and merging them into the whole. This all-pervading space has a spiritual quality, evoking a mood of stillness and silence, in which the fragmentary and unstated become powerfully suggestive elements. What is omitted becomes as important as what is included; it remains for the viewer to fill in the missing detail.

Plainly, the dominant theme of this painting is the vastness and harmony of nature. The time is nightfall; the mood is one of serenity as the moon shines through the haze illuminating a promontory in the middle distance. Silhouetted against this patch of moonlight are two small figures, a man on a donkey and his servant, following on foot. These human figures are inconspicuous, dwarfed by nature and absorbed into it, just as are the moon, mountains and trees. Man is not in conflict with nature; he neither dominates nor is dominated by it.[2] Instead, he is part of the unity of the universe. In *The Mustard Seed Garden Manual of Painting*, the artist is instructed that in addition to scenery, landscape painting should include figures *(jên)* and other living things *(wu)*, which should all bear a relationship to each other: "A figure should seem to be contemplating the mountain; the mountain, in turn, should seem to be bending over watching the figure. ... Figures should, in fact, be depicted in such a way that people looking at a painting wish they could change places with them."[3]

In China, painting and writing are related arts, sharing the same technique, using the same equipment—brush and ink. The basis of judging both painting and calligraphy has always been the quality of the brushwork. *The Manual of Painting* states that "each brushstroke should be a living idea *(shêng i)*,"[4] purposeful, expressive and related to the whole. By the very nature of the materials, there can be no corrections or second thoughts; the moment the brush touches the silk (or paper), the artist is committed. He must, therefore, have a clearly formed mental image in addition to a spontaneous, unfaltering technique. Consistent with this economy of means is the use of monochrome ink which is capable of an incredibly wide range of subtle tones. Hence, the familiar Chinese expression, "If you have ink, you have the Five Colors."[5]

Mountain Landscape by Moonlight reflects the style of the Ma-Hsai school,[6] named after its founders Ma Yüan and Hsai Kuei, who dominated the Southern Sung Academy at Hang-Chou during the first quarter of the thirteenth century. Its tranquil, introspective mood is perhaps symptomatic of the times, for this was a period when China, surrounded by hostile neighbors, looked inward upon herself. In terms of monumental landscape painting, this was a moment which "may well have marked the apogee of Sung art; no other painting style combines, as does theirs [Ma Yüan and Hsai Kuei], the ultimate of formal elegance with metaphysical depth."[7]

Inscription: The eulogy *(tsan)* translates as follows: *Who is mounted on Tu's mule?/ Through the universe his name resounds!/ With (wind-) blown steps he rides the donkey away/ Cheerfully, intoxicated with heaven and earth!/*
This poem refers to Tu Fu (712–770). Its author signs with his *hao*, Yün-feng (san-jen); his secular name was Hsia Yüan-ting. He was from Yung-chia (Chekiang) and lived in the late Sung period.[8]

Seals: There are two. The vase-shaped seal may be that of the painter. It possibly reads *An-chai;* not identified thus far.

Description: Hanging scroll of silk, painted in monochrome ink. The pinnacle of the mountain, which represents its furthest distance, is marked by pine trees. The face of the mountain plummets sharply, its silhouette marked by the edge of the wash, accented by foliage. In the middle distance is a flat promontory which extends outward in two points. This space opens up as the moon illuminates a pathway on which travels a man on a donkey followed by a hunched-over figure, bearing a bundle. The foreground is close to the picture plane, its line delineated by the edge of the wash, further defined by bushes and ground cover. A branch of pine reaches downward from the lower left margin of the painting, in contraposition to the main downward diagonal thrust of the composition. Far below, an expanse of land marked by a pathway is suggested in the distance. At the top, the inscription extends to the left in five columns, the end of which is marked by a seal. Just below the right center margin is another seal.

Condition: Fair. There are numerous cracks and small losses, most of which appear to be quite ancient and have been filled. This painting is thought to have been remounted in Japan during the Muromachi Period (1392–1573). A vellum-like material has been attached to its back to provide support; narrow strips of paper have been set horizontally and vertically as reinforcements between the mounting and the silk. In spite of this, continuous horizontal striations have been brought about by handling and rolling. The stresses which have caused this horizontal dishing originate from within the supporting structures.

Exhibitions: None known.

Collections: This painting is thought to have been in a Japanese collection by the Muromachi Period. [N. V. Hammer, Inc., New York.]
Foundation Acquisition, AP 71.17.

Notes:

[1] Space is filled with the *Ch'i,* the Spirit or Vital Force. See: Mai-Mai Sze, *The Tao of Painting: A Study of the Ritual Disposition of Chinese Painting, with a translation of the Chieh Tzu Yüan Hua Chuan or Mustard Seed Garden Manual of Painting 1679–1701,* Bollingen Series XLIX, New York, 1963, vol. I, p. 95; vol. II, p. 630.

[2] George Rowley, *Principles of Chinese Painting,* 3rd ed., Princeton, 1970, p. 20.

[3] Mai-Mai Sze, vol. II, p. 220.

[4] Mai-Mai Sze, vol. II, p. 364.

[5] Mai-Mai Sze, vol. I, p. 66.

[6] For a discussion of the Ma-Hsia School, see: James Cahill, *Treasures of Asia: Chinese Painting,* Cleveland, 1960, pp. 80–84, and Laurence Sickman and Alexander Soper, *The Art and Architecture of China,* 3rd ed., Baltimore, 1968, pp. 134–35.

[7] Max Loehr, "Chinese Painting," *Chinese Calligraphy and Painting in the Collection of John M. Crawford, Jr.,* New York, 1962, p. 35.

[8] Translated in a letter from Max Loehr to Ruth S. Wilkins, April 18, 1972. Our appreciation also extends to Mrs. Fumiko Cranston and Harvey Molé, Cambridge, Mass., who aided in deciphering the inscription and identifying its writer.

CHINESE, SUNG DYNASTY, 960–1279, OR YÜAN DYNASTY, 1280–1368

Vase, Tz'u-chou ware

Thirteenth or Fourteenth Century

Stoneware, greenish-brown glaze,
15 1/2 × 11 5/8 (diam.) in. (39.4 × 29.6 cm.)

Tz'u-chou ware constitutes a large ceramic category within which there is a considerable variety of slips, glazes and shapes. They all share, however, a distinctive decoration in which large-scale motifs are incised or painted in bold slip patterns of strongly contrasting colors. Developed during the Sung Dynasty, this ware is named for a kiln at Tz'u-chou (meaning "Porcelain Prefecture") in Hopei Province with which it was initially associated by historians. Tz'u-chou wares like this vase, bearing a dark slip carved to reveal the color of the body, are thought now to date from the Yüan Dynasty although they have frequently been dated to the earlier Sung period.[1] This gaily decorated dark-on-light ware, of which numerous examples are known, appears to have been a predominantly middle-class and utilitarian ceramic style that flourished independently from the more delicate and refined stonewares and porcelains made for upper-class and imperial usage.[2]

On this jar the striking boldness of the simple design was obtained by a straightforward technique. Initially, the dark slip covered the body; then it was cut away from the lower third of the jar, and deeply incised outlines of the floral design and some details (most notably the eyes and scale pattern of the fish) were cut through the slip. Finally, the background of the floral design was removed from within the areas bounded by the still discernible incisions, thus revealing the underlying cream color of the stoneware body. The resulting dark-light contrasts are balanced in a pleasing manner and enhanced by the differing textures presented by the sheen of the smooth slip and the rough matte dryness of the hard-fired body.

In comparison with similarly decorated Tz'u-chou vases several atypical aspects of this vase may be noted. The fish motif is uncommon although not unique.[3] The difference between the base and shoulder diameters of this jar is relatively small, giving it a robust quality in comparison to the more typical squat, almost spherical form. Moreover, its sturdy appearance is enhanced by its height which is several inches greater than most Tz'u-chou vases with dark-light designs.

Description: Baluster-shaped jar, with sloping shoulders, two small loop handles and a short, straight-necked mouth. The upper body is covered in a chocolate brown slip that has an olive tint in the area below the neck. On the lower shoulder and side a stylized foliage design containing the outline of a fish is carved through the glaze revealing the cream body as the background. Several spatters of dark glaze can be seen in the lower third of the body. The interior is glazed and the cleanly cut foot encompasses a flat, shallow and unglazed recess.

Condition: Excellent. It is unblemished except for superficial surface scratches and a few minute chips at the edge of the foot.

Exhibitions: None known.

Collections: [N. V. Hammer, Inc., New York.] Foundation Acquisition, AP 70.6.

Notes:

1 Sherman E. Lee, "The Art of the Yüan Dynasty" in *Chinese Art Under the Mongols: The Yüan Dynasty 1279–1368*, by Lee and Wai-kam Ho, Cleveland Museum of Art, 1968, p. 13.

2 Lee, p. 11.

3 A similarly colored Tz'u-chou vase with a two-fish design is in the Victoria and Albert Museum, London, no. C. 209–1916.

CHINESE, YÜAN DYNASTY, 1280–1368

Mei-p'ing Vase, Ch'ing-pai ware

First half, Fourteenth Century

Porcelain, pale greenish-blue glaze,
12 1/2 × 7 1/8 (diam.) in. (31.8 × 18.1 cm.)

Called a *mei-p'ing* vase because its shape resembles that of an inverted pear *(mei-p'ing)*, the swelling, almost bloated profile of this jar dominates its typical slight asymmetry and imbalance. The wall is relatively thick compared to earlier, more fragile Sung Dynasty wares. This heavy, massive body is complemented by bold, vigorously carved decoration.[1] A variety of carving techniques are employed in the definition of the dragon-dominated design. Broad, deep cuts, tinted dark by the greater amount of glaze, outline the major elements, such as the floral scrolls on the shoulder, the lotus petals at the foot and, in the major panel, the head, claws and expanded chest of the dragon. In contrast, thin parallel cuts define and texture the light puffy clouds and the borders. Once identified as *ying-ch'ing* ware, meaning "shadowy-blue," this type of ceramic ware is now called *ch'ing-pai* (blue-white) ware as it is thought to be of the type described by that name in Chinese ceramic literature as early as the fourteenth century.[2]

Although earlier *ch'ing-pai* ware of the Sung Dynasty is more common,[3] the shape and decoration of this jar is more typical of Yüan Dynasty ceramics of the fourteenth century.[4] It is recorded that *ch'ing-pai* ware was then being produced near the northern Kiangsi Province town of Ch'ing-tê-chên, which was subsequently the location of an important imperial kiln in the Ming Dynasty. Thus, it is not surprising that the monumental shape of Yüan Dynasty wares of this type appear to be antecedents to more delicate Ming ceramics.

Description: Inverted pear-shaped vase with carved designs under a thin transparent glaze, tinted greenish-blue. Below the short contracted neck with a flared lip, the high broad shoulder bears a band of carved floral scrolls. A carved design of a dragon, twisting through stylized clouds, encircles the middle above a band of false gadroons around the lower third. Within the scraped, unglazed foot rim, the 3/8 in.-deep recess is glazed.

Condition: Excellent. "Pinhole" voids are scattered throughout the glaze.

Exhibitions: None known.

Collections: [N. V. Hammer, Inc., New York.] Foundation Acquisition, AP 68.8.

Notes:

1 Sherman E. Lee, "The Art of the Yüan Dynasty" in *Chinese Art Under the Mongols: The Yüan Dynasty 1279–1368*, by Lee and Wai-kam Ho, Cleveland Museum of Art, 1968, p. 17.

2 Celia Carrington Riely, *Chinese Art from the Cloud Wampler and other Collections in the Everson Museum*, Syracuse, 1968, p. 92.

3 Riely, p. 93.

4 Vases with similar dragon embellishments are recorded by: Lee and Ho, cat. no. 99 (10 1/2 in. high) and by Henry Trubner, *Chinese Ceramics*, Los Angeles County Museum, 1952, cat. no. 187 (11 in. high).

Chu Te-jun, 1294–1365
Returning from a Visit
About mid-Fourteenth Century

Handscroll, ink on paper, 11 1/4 × 47 in.
(28.2 × 119.3 cm.)

The Kimbell handscroll, with its sweeping view of mountains and winding waters, is an extraordinarily well documented work formerly in the Manchu Household Collection, bearing an inscription and seals of Emperor Ch'ien-lung and an earlier poem by Tu Mu. Dating from the Yüan Dynasty, it is by the artist Chu Te-jun, a man known for his exceptional refinement who was highly trained as a literary writer and poet.

It is generally accepted that the Yüan Dynasty marks a break in the continuity of Chinese painting,[1] which parallels and inevitably reflects the political situation of the day, namely that of China under the Mongol conquerors. Faced with this barbaric presence, the cultivated Yüan painters withdrew unto themselves, turning nostalgically to the art of the distant past, seeking the strength of the Northern Sung masters while renouncing the ideals of Southern Sung.

Chu Te-jun, like other Yüan artists, worked in an archaic style, landscapes such as this scroll clearly deriving from the Li Ch'eng-Kuo Hsi tradition. While individual forms are almost identical to earlier models, the overall mood has been reinterpreted. The clumps of bare cedar trees might have been taken directly from Li Ch'eng, but in their transposition they have lost the tortuous, writhing quality which marked their earlier existence.[2] Similarly, the boulders and mountain formations, which in Kuo Hsi were expressions of power and twisting movement,[3] have assumed the soft billowing quality of inflated clouds. In short, despite the use of specific formal elements from an earlier epoch, the total effect has been softened and subdued. The austerity and grandeur of Kuo Hsi gives way to a more personal, human expression.

The Kimbell scroll has an intimate, inviting quality which would have been unacceptable to the Northern Sung masters. This is achieved partly by the scale of the scroll, the manner in which the viewer is led into the composition, and the introduction of human figures.

The viewer enters the landscape through the right foreground which is closest to the picture plane. Twin cedars stand silhouetted against a distant mountain, their gnarled roots reaching into the sparsely vegetated boulders from which they spring. Between the billowing rock form to the right and the spit of land to the left, a pavilion with thatched roof rises out of the shallow waters. A frontal view through the window reveals a scholar at his books; almost incidentally, the head of a woman is visible through a right side window. Beyond, in the distant hills, a pagoda is lightly indicated among the blurred forms of faraway pines.

The scroll recedes in space from right to left, the middle ground marked by an island, which subtly repeats the forms of the foreground: disproportionately huge boulders, covered by scrub and jaggedly outlined cedars, almost conceal hastily sketched cottages. Looming monumentally in the background is a tall rounded mountain, in an almost cloudlike formation, spotted with dots of vegetation.

The last third of the scroll has become progressively atmospheric. The still waters of the bay ripple lightly in the foreground, two fishing boats barely visible offshore. The horizon line is lost in hazy mists from which emerge suggestions of trees and pagodas, the distant mountains expressed in more naturalistic forms.

The principal drama of the scroll is enacted almost inconspicuously on the footbridge, spanning island and foreground. The inscription tells us that a man, returning from a visit with a friend, finds it past sunset as he makes his way homeward. He is accompanied by a servant because the bridge is slippery and he may need help. The mood is one of cordial sociability, perhaps reflecting the quiet life of the sage-scholar who has withdrawn from the world of affairs to the untouched countryside, a theme ever popular in Chinese art.

Inscriptions and Seals: The eulogy (*tsan*) of Emperor Ch'ien-lung (1711–99) is dated midsummer of 1781 and is followed by two seals: Ku-hsi T'ien-tzu and Yu-jih Tzu-tzu. *Peaks are piled up, a stream encircles the place. / The superior man chooses his dwelling by the oracle. / There are times when he visits cloud and water. / At leisure, he cares for insects and fish. / Crossing the log-bridge, he walks [very] carefully. / In his study, a friend is waiting anxiously. / Meeting each other, the two talk about farming fields. / They are not drawing up ten-thousand-word memorials./*[4]

The second eulogy is that of the noted scholar and art historian Tu Mu (about 1459–1525), and is followed by a seal: Huang-t'ao Chieh-mu. *On my return from visiting an old friend, it is already twilight. / Passing the slippery bridge, I lean on my young servant. / At home there is only the children's*

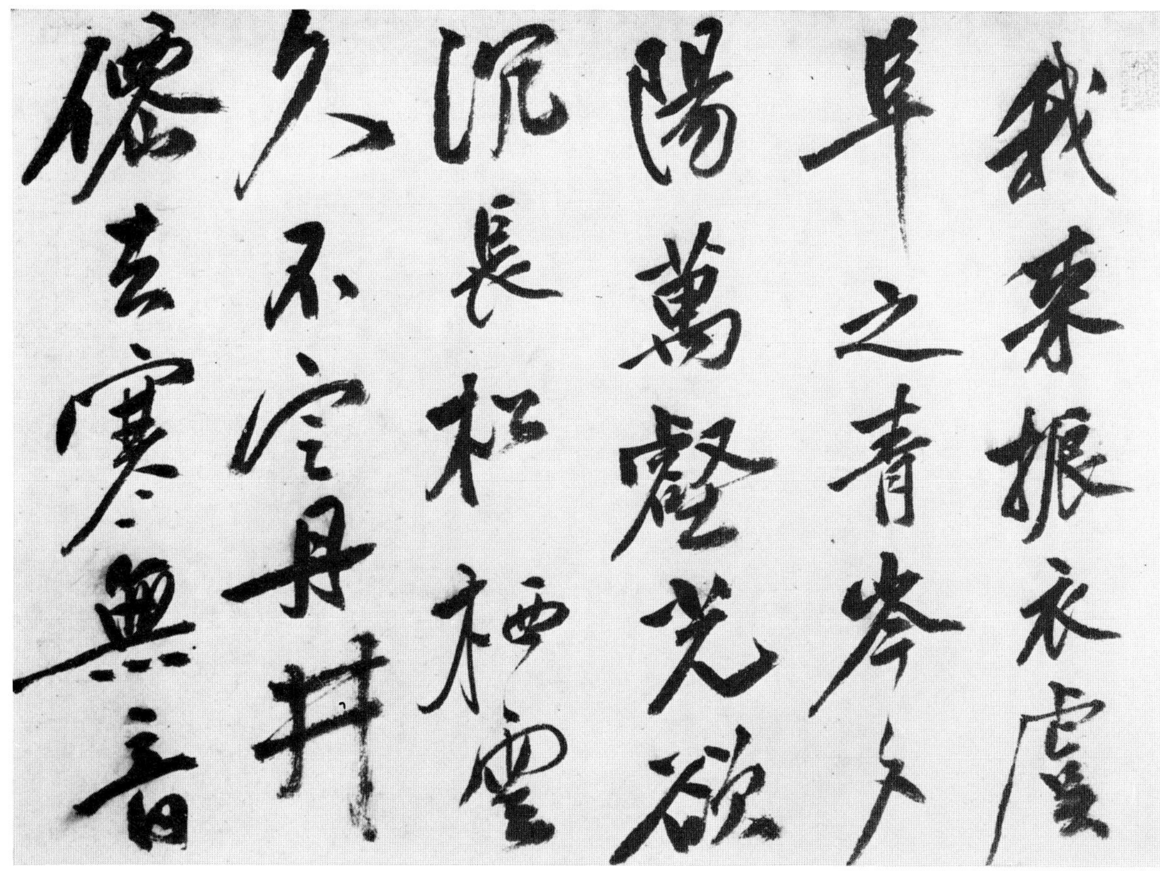

noise and laughter, / And the clothes they wear are badly soiled. /

Artist's seal in lower right corner: Chu-shih Tse-min; colophon and 3 seals of Wang Feng-nien (active about second half of sixteenth century); colophon dated 1696 and 3 seals of Cha Shih-piao (1615–about 1698); 12 additional seals of Chien-lung; 2 seals of Chia-ch'ing (1736–95); 6 seals of Po Ch'eng-liang (before 1793); 2 seals of Hsuan-t'ung (1906–67).

Description: Handscroll, monochrome ink on paper. High mountains form the background against which is set a view of a wide bay. Boulders and hills in the right foreground are covered with trees and scrub, an island occupies the middle ground, and in the far distance the winding waters and mist-covered mountains are enveloped into the atmosphere. Two men set forth across a bridge, their destination presumably the pavilion in the foreground. The scroll is abundantly marked with collectors' seals which cover both right and left edges and are spaced intermittently across the top and down the center. To the upper right of center is the eulogy of Ch'ien-lung and on the upper left margin, the eulogy of Tu Mu. The painting is followed by two colophons.

Condition: Very good. There appear to be minor ancient mends which occur in unimportant areas of the scroll.

Exhibitions: Chinese Art Under the Mongols: The Yüan Dynasty (1279–1368), The Cleveland Museum of Art, Oct. 2–Nov. 24, 1968, cat. no. 217, illus.

Collections: Manchu Household Collection, Zen-ichior Takeuchi, Tokyo.
Foundation Acquisition, AP 72.6.

Bowl with secret decoration, white ware
Early Fifteenth Century, possibly Yung-Lo period, 1403–24

Porcelain, transparent glaze tinting to pale blue, 4×8 1/4 (diam.) in. (10.1×21 cm.)

Purity of form and restrained decoration are the distinguishing characteristics of an elegant class of white porcelains that is thought to have originated during the early fifteenth century. Such qualities are quite appropriate for ceramics of this period; it was at this time that the early Ming emperors consolidated their rule and established the unquestioned primacy of the Imperial Court. Moreover, their patronage and high standards of excellence had made the porcelain kilns in the Ch'ing-tê-chên area of Kiangsi Province the most important ceramic center of China by the middle of the century. The hard, dense body of these Ming wares and the clear, nearly colorless glaze that is positively fused with the body can be attributed to the better control of higher firing temperature that could be obtained by this time.

This handsome bowl's nearly hemispheric profile, which resembles the seed pod of a lotus flower *(lien-tzu)*, is a shape that dates from the early fifteenth century. Its deep sides, plain rim and small foot distinguish it from shallower, more substantial shapes of its fourteenth century antecedents.[1] The remarkably thin walls rise from the foot with a grace and fragility that clearly reveal an extraordinarily facile technique. Equally impressive is the barely discernible decorative pattern on the bowl, known as *an-hua* or "secret decoration," that is lightly incised and deftly molded into the fine-grained body and made perceptible by the greater amount of slightly tinted glaze which fills the recesses. Appearing as lacy bluish-white filigree floating in the whiteness of the body, this subtle embellishment of the simple shape is enriched by the lustrous sheen of the hard glaze.

Notes:

1 Max Loehr, *Chinese Painting After Sung*, Yale Art Gallery, Ryerson Lecture, March 2, 1967.

2 Osvald Sirén, *Chinese Painting: Leading Masters and Principles*, London, 1956, vol. I, p. 199.

3 Sirén, p. 218.

4 Eulogies translated in a letter to Ruth S. Wilkins from Mrs. Fumiko Cranston, Cambridge, Mass., June 8, 1972.

Additional References:

Ch'en Jen-t'ao, *Ku-kung i-i shu hua-mu chiao-chu (An Annotated List of the Lost Calligraphies and Paintings from the [Ch'ing] Palace Collection)*, Hong Kong, 1956, p. 13 B.
Harada Kinjiro, *Shina meiga hokan (Pageant of Chinese Painting)*, Tokyo, 1936, pl. 300.
Shih-ch'ü pao-chi, (Catalogue of Calligraphies and Paintings of the Imperial Collection), part II, 1793, reprinted Shanghai, 1948, p. 241 a–b.
So-Gen-Min-Shin meiga taikan, (Painting Masterpieces of the Sung, Yüan, Ming, and Ch'ing Dynasties), Tokyo, 1931, pl. 37.

Tentatively dated in the Yung-Lo period, this bowl might date from the mid-fifteenth century. Definition of Yung-Lo style is difficult because only a very few pieces bearing this reign mark are known, in contrast to the more frequently marked wares of the Hsüan-tê and later periods. The clean shape, dimensions and foot of this bowl are similar to several bowls that have been dated to the early fifteenth century.[2] On the other hand, its shape, decoration and dimensions are close to two slightly later bowls from Ch'ing-tê-chên now in the Kempe collection.[3]

Description: Nearly hemispherical bowl with *an-hua* designs and a very thin body, the upper part of which is translucent. In the interior there is a barely discernible pattern, molded in relief, of radiating petals and a cresting wave border. The incised design on the exterior is a scrolling vine with six open blossoms and abundant foliage below a geometric border. The transparent glaze, tinting to an icy pale greyish-blue in the recesses, is very smooth and highly reflective. The plain deep foot ring (7.5 cm. diam.) is straight-sided and encloses a glazed recess showing the convex curve of the bowl. The unglazed rim is cut flat, revealing the very fine grain of the white paste.

Condition: Excellent. There are some superficial surface scratches and several black specks of impurities in the glaze.

Exhibitions: None known.

Collections: [N. V. Hammer, Inc., New York.]
Foundation Acquisition, APX 71.20.

Notes:

1 John A. Pope, *Chinese Porcelains from the Ardebil Shrine*, Washington, D.C., 1956, p. 86.

2 See Suzanne G. Valenstein, introd., *Ming Porcelains: A Retrospective*, China House Gallery, New York, October, 1970–January, 1971, p. 12, and cat. no. 5, illus. (blue-and-white bowl, 8 1/4 in. diam., Indianapolis Museum of Art) and cat. no. 8, illus. (*lien-tzu* bowl with floral patterns in *an-hua*, 8 1/4 in. diam., Falk collection).

3 See Bo Gyllensvärd, *Chinese Ceramics in the Carl Kempe Collection*, Stockholm, 1964, p. 201, cat. no. 676, illus. ("Hsüan-tê mark," 10.2 x 21.2 cm.) and cat. no. 686, illus., ("fifteenth century," 10.4 x 20.7 cm.).

Dish with melon design, blue-and-white ware
Early Fifteenth Century

Porcelain, blue underglaze decoration,
3 × 17 1/16 (diam.) in. (7.7 × 43.4 cm.)

The uniform quality of this large dish is characteristic of the distinguished Ming Dynasty porcelains of the early fifteenth century. Its considerable size and near-perfect shape demonstrate the mastery of ceramic skill that had been achieved by that time. The decorative scheme is orderly and spacious, in contrast to more crowded designs of fourteenth-century ware. The underglaze decoration of intense blue, rendered in cobalt that was imported to China from Persia at that time, is expertly applied and evenly toned. Proficiency of technique is particularly evident in the modeling of the fruit and leaves in which unpainted areas of white are skillfully transformed into highlights and interior outlines.

An enriching variety of three different patterns decorates the upper surfaces of this dish. The flat outer rim is embellished by a dense stylized band of rolling waves alternating with evenly distributed cresting waves. A spacious pattern of blossoms on a scrolling vine is similarly distributed about the cavetto wall. The rhythmical patterns of these two areas surround the center medallion containing an exuberant arrangement of twisting tendrils, large fruit, and ragged leaves. The melon motif and asymmetry of this center design are unusual; axial or symmetrical arrangements of grapes, peony, and lotus blossoms are found more frequently on dishes of this type.[1] Equally distinctive is the subtlety of details (such as the wash modeling of the fruit and the leaves overlapping the fruit to give the design dimension and value). The exceptional spaciousness of the design becomes apparent when it is compared to similar melon designs on two contemporary but smaller dishes (both 14 1/2 in. diam.) in the British Museum[2] and the Ardebil Shrine collection, Tehran.[3]

Lotus Bowl, blue-and-white ware
Hsüan-tê period, 1426–35

Porcelain, blue underglaze decoration,
4 3/16 × 8 3/16 (diam.) in. (10.6 × 20.8 cm.)

"Hsüan-tê blue and white porcelains are elegant, they are charming, they are beautiful–they are among the great joys of Chinese ceramics."[1] This highly regarded ceramic style is well represented by this hemispheric bowl. Its body clay is dense, pure and fine-grained; its balanced shape is rationally proportioned (the diameter is twice the height) and fits the hands comfortably. The cobalt-blue underglaze is strong and brilliant; the glaze is even and clear. Finally, its orderly, spacious decoration complements the shape and is applied in assured, graceful strokes.

The shape of this bowl is the source of its name: it resembles the seed pod of the lotus flower *(lien-tzu)*. Surrounding the bowl's exterior are stylized petals that rise from the base and embrace the shape of the bowl like fingers of a hand. Association of this pattern with this shape of bowl is unusual and "seems to have been limited to the early part of the [fifteenth] century."[2] The strong effect of this vigorous design is apparent when it is compared to the very subtle decoration of similarly shaped bowls with lightly incised *(an-hua)* designs.

The six-character Hsüan-tê reign mark on this bowl is a distinctive feature; such reign marks are uncommon before this period. Although they are also found on later replicas of highly regarded Hsüan-tê wares, the calligraphy of this bowl's inscription is consistent with that of pieces of the Hsüan-tê period.[3] Among nine similar bowls that have been published and dated to the early fifteenth century, only one other bowl is reported to bear a Hsüan-tê mark.[4]

Inscription: On bottom, in blue underglaze, within a double ring are six characters: *Ta-Ming Hsüan-tê nien chih*, that translate as "Made in the period of the Hsüan-tê reign of the Ming Dynasty."

Description: A large, deep dish with everted, flat rim and designs in underglaze blue enamel. In the center, a sprawling vine with tendrils, leaves and three melons–two large ones and a small one–rises from a thin line of earth. It is surrounded on the well by a band of seven blossoms on a scrolling vine, separated from the center by a double-line border. An allover pattern of breaking waves covers the rim and six sprays of fruits and flowers are evenly distributed about the exterior. The unmarked base and the shallow, wedge-shaped rim of the foot are unglazed.

Condition: Excellent. Except for a very small imperfection in the white background, at the edge of the fruit, and hairline scratches on the glaze, this dish is in pristine condition.

Exhibitions: None known.

Collections: [Spink & Son, Ltd., London.]
Foundation Acquisition, AP 70.3.

Notes:

1 John A. Pope, *Chinese Porcelains from the Ardebil Shrine*, Washington, D.C., 1956, p. 94.

2 Harry Garner, *Oriental Blue and White*, London, 3rd ed., 1970, pl. 15.

3 Pope, cat. no. 29.61, pl. 40.

Description: Deep bowl with curving sides and cobalt-blue underglaze decoration. The exterior design consists of 32 plain, dark blue petals radiating up from the foot toward a thunder pattern border on the lip. In the interior, a center design of leaves and nine small berries is surrounded by a floral scroll of leaves, buds and six blossoms (three large chrysanthemums (?) and three small peonies (?) and edged by a lip border of loosely painted breaking waves. The sections are separated by double-line borders. The 3 in. (7.6 cm.) diameter foot is decorated with a double ring around the exterior and has traces of red on the unglazed rim; the interior recess is glazed and there are no spur marks.

Condition: Excellent. In the glaze of the interior, besides normal hairline scratches, there is one "pinhole" void.

Exhibitions: None known.

Collections: [J. Pierre Dubosc, Paris.]
Foundation Acquisition, AP 70.14.

Notes:

1 Suzanne G. Valenstein, introd., *Ming Porcelains*, China House Gallery, New York, 1970, p. 13.

2 John A. Pope, *Chinese Porcelains from the Ardebil Shrine*, Washington, D. C., 1956, p. 97.

3 Compare the inscription to those illustrated by Harry Garner, *Oriental Blue and White*, London, 3rd ed., 1970, pl. 97a, b and c.

4 The similar bowl with a Hsüan-tê mark is published in an advertisement: *Oriental Art*, n. s., vol. XVI, no. 1, spring, 1970, p. 25. Other bowls, without Hsüan-tê marks, are in Tehran (Pope, cat. nos. 29.324, 29.325, 29.326, pp. 50, 86, 97 and pl. 47); the Indianapolis Museum of Art (Valenstein, *Ming Porcelains*, cat. no. 5, illus.); the Freer Gallery, Washington, D. C. (Pope, *Ming Porcelains in the Freer Gallery of Art*, Washington, D. C., 1953, cat. no. 51.14, pl. 3, p. 13); the David Foundation, London (Margaret Medley, *Porcelains Decorated in Underglaze Blue*, London, 1963, cat. no. B-637) and the Los Angeles County Museum of Art (see its *Quarterly*, vol. 11, no. 2, summer, 1954, pls. 24, 25).

Flask, blue-and-white ware
Late Fifteenth Century

Porcelain, blue underglaze decoration,
13 1/8 × 7 11/16 × 5 1/4 in. (33.3 × 19.5 × 13.3 cm.)

The dense, almost crowded, decoration of this flask is characteristic of late fifteenth-century blue-and-white ware.[1] The blue underglaze dominates the color of the body, appearing almost as a blue appliqué on the white surface. The smooth, glossy glaze creates sparkling highlights that are sharper and more brilliant than those of the dappled, "orange skin" surface of earlier glazes. Equally characteristic of late fifteenth-century flasks of this type is the sharp crisp profile, particularly of the neck. Like that of a flask in the Ardebil Shrine collection,[2] the neck rises as a tube, straight from the body, flares out above the loop handles and then constricts to its initial diameter just below a swollen lip.

Initially deriving from an Islamic metal form,[3] earlier flasks resemble a double gourd design, having a smooth, flowing outline and a bulbous upper swelling instead of the sharp angles in the neck of this flask. Also their white backgrounds tend to be more expansive than in later works.[4] Thus, the shape of this flask constitutes an instructive example of the transformation of an originally metallic shape into a distinctive ceramic form.

The complex shape of this piece required that the body be formed in pieces and then carefully joined together. Visual inspection suggests that the bottom was formed in two parts and joined vertically with the neck on top. The solid, flat base appears to be an integral part of the bottom gourd.

Description: Flask *(pien hu)* with small mouth, two loop handles, a flat foot and cobalt-blue underglaze designs. On the neck is a scroll pattern, a row of five stylized lotus-petal panels and, between the handles at the narrowing, a row of six stylized pointed leaves. On each side, circular bands of scrolling vines with blossoms (separated by a single band of stylized petals) frame identical, large circular designs. In these circular designs the overlapping shell motifs in the center depressions are encompassed by a narrow scrolling band and a large pattern of six radiating crosshatched panels. The effervescent glaze gives a slight tint of pale blue to the milk-white body. The broad foot is flat, unglazed and bears no spur marks.

Condition: Excellent. There are four scattered "pinhole" voids and a narrow, 1/8 in.-long fissure in the glaze; a small piece of excess clay adheres to the lip.

Exhibitions: Exhibition of Chinese Art, Palazzo Ducale, Venice, 1954, cat. no. 644, illus.

Collections: The von Pflugk family, Castle of Strehla, near Dresden, Germany, from about 1683 to after 1938.[5] Percival David collection, London. [N. V. Hammer, Inc., New York.] Foundation Acquisition, AP 68.11.

Notes:

1 John A. Pope, *Chinese Porcelains from the Ardebil Shrine*, Washington, D. C., 1956, p. 115.

2 Pope, p. 116, pl. 69, cat. no. 29.459, 13 3/8 in. high, "late fifteenth century." He also illustrates, pl. 136 D, another late fifteenth-century flask, broken at the neck, in the Victoria and Albert Museum, London, cat. no. 1335–1876.

3 See Basil Gray, "The Influence of Near Eastern Metalwork on Chinese Ceramics," *Transactions of the Oriental Ceramic Society*, vol. 18, 1940–41, pp. 47–60.

4 See Pope, pl. 55, cat. no. 29.458; Margaret Medley, *Porcelains Decorated in Underglaze Blue . . . in the Percival David Foundation*, London, 1963, cat. nos. 600–674, illus.; and Harry Garner, *Oriental Blue and White*, London, 3rd ed., 1970, pl. 31 A; and *Blue-and-White Ware of the Ming Dynasty*, Book II, part 1, National Palace Museum, Taichung, Taiwan, pub. Hong Kong, 1963, Hsüan-tê Period: pls. 9, 10.

5 W. W. Winkworth, "A Fifteenth Century Blue and White Vase from Saxony," included as a note to the article by Gray, on pp. 59–60.

Lan Ying, 1585–about 1664
Steep Peaks and Tall Pines of Mt. T'ien-t'ai
Painted about 1635–40

Hanging scroll, ink and light color on silk, 71 3/4 × 22 1/2 in. (182.3 × 57 cm.)

The tradition of monumental landscape painting represented by this scroll was one established very early in Chinese art. The subject of mountain and water, of man and nature, a theme of inexhaustible complexity treated with the simple means of ink and brush, has been a continuing interest of the Chinese artist. Kuo Hsi, a Sung master whose treatise on painting is one of the most important documents of Chinese art theory, "maintained that the value of landscape painting lay in its capacity to make the viewer feel as if he were really in the place depicted. A genuine lover of the wilderness . . . may be prevented by circumstances from carrying out his dreamed-of wanderings among mountains and streams; but he can experience imaginary journeys by gazing at paintings."[1]

To be "really in the place depicted" is often more a state of mind than an actual locale; Lan Ying's subject is the famous Buddhist mountain T'ien-t'ai, whose name in this instance serves as an evocative focus for the quiet pleasures of scholarly pursuits. The Chinese painting is not organized according to the Western system of linear perspective but by areas, each of which is seen frontally, without foreshortening. Like the traveler in the scroll, we move through the composition from one area to another, sequentially, in contemplative participation in nature and the work of art.

Lan Ying is classed with the Chê school of late Ming professional painters, although he frequently followed the example of the Wu school *literati* in copying the monumental landscapes of the Southern school painters. This scroll was inspired by the work of Wang Mêng, who was active in the fourteenth

century. He is one of the Four Great Yüan Masters, all of whom exerted tremendous influence on subsequent developments in Chinese painting, especially in the seventeenth century about the time of Lan Ying. The Kimbell scroll is not a literal copy of any painting, but belongs to an important category of Chinese paintings which comprises "signed works of well-known painters of different periods that are deliberately couched in the distinct manners of some earlier masters."[2] Thus, it is especially interesting for what it reveals of the formal and stylistic concerns of the different periods involved.

The tall, narrow format of Lan Ying's scroll, containing a high mountain peak brought close to the picture surface and extending downward to trees clumped by the edge of a stream, is a pictorial formula derived from Wang Mêng. Picture surfaces of the earlier master are almost entirely filled with the density of innumerable dots and wrinkles and surging masses that contribute to an unprecedented sense of structural solidity and dynamic vitality.[3] In his paintings the mountain becomes a living entity of incredible complexity, with ravines that trap mists, boulders that thrust through the heavy weight of streams, and trees that jut over bluffs above deep gorges.

In *Steep Peaks and Tall Pines* there is movement, texture, complexity, a wide range of tonal variations, and a variety of formal elements and brush idioms found in the work of Wang Mêng, but the force with which we are drawn into an experience of the mountain has yielded to the more decorative and calligraphic surface concerns of the Ming period and of the Chê school in particular. There is a greater emphasis on individual areas as the focus shifts from the structural logic of forms to the decorative possibilities of ink and brush: interesting contrasts of texture and tonality in the foliage justify the arbitrarily large scale of the trees in the foreground. Graceful curves of bending grasses offer fascinating calligraphic possibilities, but there is little differentiation in brushstrokes between the water flowing over rocks in the stream and the claw-like roots of trees. These differences in the work of Lan Ying and Wang Mêng reflect changes in outlook which in the Ming-Ch'ing phase "meant a greater concern, not with the embodiment of ideas in essential forms, but rather with the sensuous qualities belonging to those forms."[4]

Nevertheless, Lan Ying was exceptionally conscientious in his efforts to grasp the forms and spirit of the earlier master. In this respect, as well as in his choice of subject, Lan Ying reveals his concern with the ideals of the nonprofessional Wu school *literati*. The Chinese consider him the last of the Chê school painters whose academic, decorative manner is ultimately derived from such prototypes as Ma Yüan and Hsia Kuei. Lan Ying himself, however, followed *literati* ideals to the extent that he wrote poetry, belonged to literary groups and, together with a painter friend, re-edited the *Tu Hui Pao-Chien*, introducing in this thirteenth-century compilation of artists changes which reflected contemporary preferences. Despite these activities he remained a professional painter and must have had an important atelier for, beginning with his son and grandsons, there are many painters associated with him as followers.[5]

Inscription: The poem, in four lines of seven characters, may be paraphrased thus:
Steep peaks reach so far into the heavens that the clouds cannot pass.
Mount T'ien-t'ai is easy to see as one nears Dragon-pool falls;
The tall pines enhance the green of the cold stream.
Pure conversation and yellowed volumes provide pleasures beyond those of this world.
The accompanying text reads: "(Painted) in the manner of Wang Mêng (Wang Shu-ming) and inscribed in the Z-i Shan-t'ang by Hsi-ch'i by Lan Ying for Mr. . . .'s delectation."[6]

Seals: Two, the artist's own, in red: *Lan Ying chih yin* and *T'ien shu.*

Description: Hanging scroll of silk mounted on paper with gold brocade borders. A single mountain massif, its base hidden in mists, towers above groves of trees that rise from the shrub-clad rocky shores of streams below. The complex composition, filling almost the entire picture surface, is contained by spaces of water, mists and sky. Our eyes enter the composition by the stubby tree in the lower left corner and move back and up through myriad strokes and dots of accent and texture, following a sinuous line which leads up the tall pine and ridge above it to the boulder-strewn top of the mountain. Hemp-fiber *ts'un*, bent in a manner characteristic of Lan Ying, structure the surface of the rocks. Halfway up the mountainside an isolated building nestles near the source of the waterfall. Misty peaks of distant mountains rise to the left of the massif, beyond two rocky ledges that angle down to the gorge of the falls hidden behind a boulder rimmed with trees. Below, wrapped round by mists, a grove of trees with delicately contrasting foliage stands on the left bank of the stream. A traveler on a narrow bridge approaches the exaggeratedly tall clump of trees that dominate the foreground. Beyond, the thatched buildings of a mountain retreat cluster in woods set just below a rocky outcrop of the mountain. Within the buildings two scholars indulge in the "pure conversation and yellowed volumes" mentioned in the inscription. Executed on now-yellowed silk in ink and blue-green and russet washes of varying tonalities, the painting has a subdued and pleasant warmth. Inscription and seals appear in the upper right.

Condition: Very good. Several small, scattered losses have been filled and inpainted; minor scratches and abrasions appear throughout. There is apparently some strengthening in the washes of the large pine, the tree immediately below it to the left, the little tree in the lower left corner and the broad-leafed tree to the right of the scholars' pavilion. A 5/8-inch strip has been added across the top.

Exhibitions: None known.

Collections: The fact that there are no collectors' seals on the painting indicates that it was most likely preserved for a considerable length of time in Japan, where collectors' seals were seldom used. Hiraki collection, [N. V. Hammer, Inc., New York.]
Foundation Acquisition, AP 69.17.

Notes:

1 James Cahill, *Chinese Painting*, Cleveland, 1960, p. 35.

2 Wen C. Fong, "Towards a Structural Analysis of Chinese Landscape Paintings," *Symposium in Honor of Dr. Chiang Fu-Tsung on his Seventieth Birthday*, reprint, n. d., p. 8.

3 For an example of his work, see: Laurence Sickman and Alexander Soper, *The Art and Architecture of China*, Baltimore, 1968, pl. 116.

4 George Rowley, *Principles of Chinese Painting*, Princeton, 1959, p. 25.

5 Hugh Wass of Mills College, Oakland, Calif., in a letter to Nell Johnson, April 14, 1972, kindly dated this painting and supplied biographical material on Lan Ying.

6 Translated from the Chinese by David Roy (University of Chicago, 1971), who adds "Hsi-ch'i is the name of a famous stream near Hangchow in Chekiang province. It winds for eighteen *li* through scenic mountains and is famous for its groves of plum trees."

Female Figurine

Latest Jōmon Period, about 1000–200 B.C.

Low-fired clay, 7 7/8 × 5 1/8 × 2 3/8 in.
(20.1 × 13 × 6 cm.)

Among the oldest artistic legacies of Japan are the small clay figurines or *dogu* whose assertive presence and aura of magic potency belie their relatively small scale. They have in common with early pottery vessels a type of cord-marked decoration whose name, *jōmon*, is used to designate the neolithic period as a whole. About a thousand of these *dogu*, representing both human and animal forms, have survived; the majority are human in form and date from the latter part of the neolithic period, from about 2000 B.C. to 200 B.C. They were made in Honshū, Kyūshū, and Hokkaidō, but primarily in the populous areas of central and northeast Honshū, until fundamental cultural changes at the end of the neolithic era brought an end to this art form.

Most often the figurines were found singly or in small groups deposited in the pit dwellings of the neolithic Japanese, less frequently in shell mound burial sites or ritual shrines. Although apparently domestic in nature, their use and symbolism is still unclear. The frequently bizarre interpretation of physical form in these figurines seems to result from the artists' consideration of form and decoration as of equal value, rather than from dictates of a symbolic or ritualistic nature.[1] The smaller figurines were carried as talismen, to judge from worn and rubbed examples, while the larger ones perhaps served as household gods.[2] They may have been charms for warding off or healing disease, or for protecting women during childbirth.[3] Female figures, often depicted as pregnant, apparently were symbols of the Mother Goddess, intended to foster the fertility of man and nature.

In the latest Jōmon period, when this figurine was produced, technical improvements were introduced and decoration was more consistently applied, with figures conforming more strongly to uniform stylistic conventions.

This example, from Yamagata Prefecture in the Tōhoku region,[4] is typical of a large category of figurines which is distinguished by the hollow technique, square shoulders and large, undifferentiated, straddled legs with large pad-like feet that solidly support the figurine.[5] A similar figurine in the Tokyo National Museum also has spirals on the knees, a triangle or "plunging neckline" on the chest, hatched ridges marking eyes and mouth, and large areas of polished, undecorated surface.[6] The chins and noses of these figurines are tilted upward, an attitude which J. E. Kidder suggests may have resulted from their usual position near the floor—if true, a very early and sophisticated accommodation of perspective![7] There is in this figure a harmonious balance between the decoration, confined to zones, and the polished surfaces; between the columnar verticals of trunk and legs and the repeated horizontal markings around the face, across the shoulders and in the hip zone. The spiral grooves and cord impressions of the hip zone are continued on the back of the figure, as are the flat grooves on the shoulders, indicating that the artist had begun to conceive of the figure in the round, abondoning the earlier treatment of front and back as totally unrelated areas.

Description: Hollow clay figurine of a standing female decorated with incised designs. The body has wide, square shoulders, small overhanging breasts and very short, attenuated arms. Below the trunk of the body, hips and thighs are fused into disproportionately thick, stubby legs. The feet are round, flat pads with grooves, perhaps indicating toes, on the right foot. The head is squat in proportion with a raised chin, prominent upturned nose and a headdress of piled-up swirls with a crescent at the back. The eyes, mouth and wide contour of the face are outlined with grooves and hatched ridges. Decoration includes a deep inverted triangle with hatched ridges on the chest, cord impressions and spiral grooves in the central zone of the hips. The rest of the body is smoothly polished, with scattered traces of red ochre paint. The back is decorated with long grooves across the shoulders and back of the head and spirals and cord impressions in the hip zone. The buff color of the clay is slightly darker in the left leg, which may indicate it was found some distance from the body.

Condition: Good. The left leg has been broken off and rejoined. Areas of restoration include the left shoulder and arm, the tip of the right arm and right breast and the outside, flat portion of the right foot. The entire headpiece, save for the crescent at back, is a reconstruction.

Exhibitions: Masterpieces of Japanese Art, Dallas Museum of Fine Arts, Dallas, 1969, cat. no. 3.

Collections: Okura collection, Tokyo. [Kochukyo Co., Ltd.], Tokyo. [N.V. Hammer, Inc., New York.]
Foundation Acquisition, AP 71.15.

Notes:

1 J. Edward Kidder, Jr., *The Birth of Japanese Art*, London, 1965, p. 11.

2 Kidder, *Japan Before Buddhism*, New York and Washington, D.C., 1966, p. 71.

3 Kidder, *Birth*, p. 66.

4 Professor Matsubara, in information supplied the vendor.

5 Kidder, *Birth*, p. 46.

6 Kidder, *Birth*, illus. p. 65, pl. VI.

7 Kidder, *Birth*, p. 46.

Haniwa Figure: Seated Man
Fifth Century

Reddish-tan terra cotta, 29 3/4 × 10 3/4 × 10 3/4 (76.2 × 27.3 × 27.3 cm.)

Distinguished by a lively expressiveness and simplified forms, *haniwa* (meaning "circle of clay") figures served as tomb ornaments for about two centuries during the mound-building culture of protohistoric Japan. These hollow cylindrical forms were placed upright in the ground, sometimes in rows several deep, on and around the burial tumuli of high-ranking personages both to inhibit erosion of the sloping sides of the tombs and also to form a symbolic barrier around the precincts of the dead.[1] Of the numerous surviving *haniwa*, relatively few are surmounted by sculptures, unadorned examples being far more common. Legions of priests, warriors, shamans, dancers, and peasants were created, as well as houses, animals and objects of everyday use. Seen across the moats which surrounded the tombs, they must have presented an extraordinary sight indeed.

The origin of these figures is obscure, and numerous theories have been put forward to explain them. Early stories suggest they ware created as substitutes for human sacrifice, but there is some doubt this custom ever existed in Japan. A more recent theory proposes that they served as "permanent memorials of the important persons . . . who took part in the funeral observances."[2] It is also thought that they may reflect influence from China where figurines played a large part in the funerary cult, although the *haniwa*, unlike Chinese burial sculptures, were placed on the outside of the tomb and endowed with a very different communicative power and psychic presence. "The probability was that clay workers, while making cylinders for the prevention of soil-erosion, were inspired by Chinese mortuary customs to produce sculptural pieces."[3]

Haniwa figures exhibit a freedom and vitality that is captured in a form "simplified to the point of being a mere outline,"[4] partly because of the large numbers which were made. The gigantic tumulus of the Emperor Nintoku reputedly was adorned with some 20,000 *haniwa* cylinders alone.[5] The outdoor setting, at a considerable remove from the spectator, must also have contributed to the simplification of form, for there was little need to go into much detail. The crude techniques and materials used, however, were the most salient factor in determining the cubistic form of *haniwa* figures. In this type of sculpture there is no carving and little modeling; the flat and round elements suggest the clay medium with a minimum of transformation and the figures are accordingly solid and rigid. The Kimbell *Seated Man* is built up of coils of clay smoothed flat and tempered with grit, giving an interesting texture to the surface. Decoration, which is common on such figures, most frequently consists of rolled strips of clay such as the ties on his boots, patterns incised and combed in the clay and a red pigment, hermatite or cinnabar, which is here painted on the clothing and the face. Eyes and mouth, made merely by punching holes through to the hollow core, are crudely rendered but convey an expression that is hauntingly alive.

Like the majority of sculpted *haniwa*, this figure comes from Ibaragi Prefecture in the Kantō region northeast of Tokyo[6] where society had flourished since the neolithic period. His elevated, seated posture, sword and long garment suggest that he represents a person of high standing, although differences among social classes were never very marked. The distortion of his dwarf-like legs, typical of those few *haniwa* on which legs were attempted, is characteristic of the fundamental abstraction of these pieces. His braids are also a typical male headdress, but his conical hat is an unusual feature, as is the extreme sparseness of ornamentation, indicated only by red paint. The significance of facial painting which appears on many *haniwa* is not clearly understood; it is variously considered an indication of status, a protective disguise for the spirit world[7] or perhaps tattooing. Stylistically, this figure is closest to another seated male figure with a conical hat and triangular facial painting in the Tokyo National Museum.[8] These two figures are further alike in their distinctive air of "austerity and sadness"[9] which makes them to the modern eye all the more powerfully expressive as funerary figures from the remote past.

Description: Low-fired clay figure of a seated man. He sits on a cushion atop a large cylinder which has a comb-textured surface and a raised rim near its top with holes at either side. The walls of the hollow sculpture are almost half an inch thick. The head is proportionately large, the arched arms short, and the dangling legs shorter still; the doll-like feet barely reach a supporting platform. The figure's right hand is affixed to his waist and the left is about to clasp the short sword at his side. He wears a conical hat with a slightly flared peak, a long garment and boots with ties at the outside. Thick round braids extend to his shoulders. He has a long flat chin, small hooked nose and slots of approximately the same size for eyes and mouth. Traces of red pigment are found in radial stripes on the hat, triangles on the cheeks, chin and nose, and bands at the neck and waist of his garment. The back, both in the hair and garment, has a lightly combed texture.

Condition: Good. As in most *haniwa* the soft clay has broken in several places, but the major segments are intact. Repaired breaks occur in the neck just above the collarbone, in both arms near the shoulder and in the torso at the level of the waist. The fingers, areas of the lap and the left rear of the hat are restorations. The cylindrical base is a patchwork of breaks and repairs.

Exhibitions: None known.

Collections: Hisashi Okura, Tokyo, before 1958. [Mayuyama and Co., Ltd.], Tokyo. Jean Daridan, Paris, before 1966. [N.V. Hammer, Inc., New York.]
Foundation Acquisition, AP 72.2.

Notes:

1 S. Goto, *Study of the Ancient Japanese Culture*, pp. 90–91, mentioned in J. Edward Kidder, Jr., *Japan Before Buddhism*, New York, 1959, p. 196.

2 Fumio Miki, *Haniwa: The Clay Sculpture of Protohistoric Japan*, trans. by Roy Andrew Miller, Rutland, Vt., and Tokyo, 1960, p. 43.

3 Seiroku Noma, "Haniwa: Protohistoric Sculpture of Japan," *Oriental Art*, new series I, Spring, 1955, p. 5.

4 Noma, introd., *Haniwa*, Asia House Gallery, New York, 1960, unpaginated.

5 Miki, p. 149, pl. C.

6 Miki, cat. no. 10, p. 152.

7 Kidder, *The Birth of Japanese Art*, London, 1965, p. 156.

8 Miki, cat. no. 41, p. 156.

9 Miki, cat. no. 10, p. 152.

Additional References:

Yukio Kobayashi, *Haniwa*, vol. I of *Toki Zenshu* ("Ceramic Series: Collective Catalogue of Pottery and Porcelain of Different Periods in Japan, China, and Korea"), ed. by Fujio Koyama, Tokyo, 1960, color pl. II and fig. 11.
Nihon genshi bijutsu ("Primitive Art of Japan"), Tokyo, 1964, vol. VI, pl. 105.
Junkichi Mayuyama, ed., *Japanese Art in the West*, Tokyo, 1966, p. 363; p. 332, fig. 424.

Tsuina Mask
About Thirteenth Century

Lacquered and polychromed wood,
$10\,^3/_8 \times 8\,^1/_2 \times 5\,^7/_8$ in. (26.3 × 21.7 × 14.9 cm.)

This extraordinary mask was created for the annual Tsuina (goblin-expelling) ceremony on the evening of the "border of the seasons" (*setsubun*) between winter and spring.[1] This ritual ceremony culminates three days of religious services (*Shuni-e*) that begin the first week of February. In the Tsuina rite the simulated punishment and expulsion of a man wearing a goblin mask takes place, a custom that still survives in parts of Japan. Because of their rough usage in the violent movements of the wearers, few Tsuina masks of the Kamakura period have survived. Like comparable Bugaku and Gyōdō masks, they were discarded when they became dilapidated in the course of repeated use.

The Kimbell mask came originally from the famous temple complex of Hōryū-ji, located near Nara; it was probably removed during the Buddhist persecutions of the Meiji period. Later preserved in the eminent Hara collection, it remained unrecorded until its recent discovery by Shōichi Uehara, who considers it "probably the oldest example of a Tsuina mask in existence."

Other Kamakura period Tsuina masks from the Hōryū-ji provide us with a totally different type of goblin image.[2] They represent horned monsters, marvelous in their grotesque abstraction and far closer to those in contemporary picture scrolls, such as the Haseo Sōshi (a story about the courtier Haseo and a goblin) and the Jigoku Sōshi (illustrations of the Buddhist hells). In sharp contrast to imaginary spirits, the Kimbell mask presents "a strikingly realistic portrayal of a wrathful face." The realism of its expression of violent fury is conveyed by brows brought sharply down over bulging eyes, lips drawn back to expose pointed fangs, cheeks tightened into ridges and angular jaw thrust forward. In this vigorous expression it also "differs from the Batō and Sanju masks used in the Bugaku dance, or from the Hachibu-shū (the eight supernatural guardians of the Buddha) and other guardian demigods in the Gyōdō ceremony."

Realism in Kamakura sculpture, as Langdon Warner observed, was in part the contribution of Zen Buddhism with its emphasis on individual character and in part a consequence of technical innovations of Unkei (about 1175–1218), who introduced a new sculptural style at the beginning of the Kamakura period.[3] Unkei innovations included whittling the mask down to a thin shell which enabled the sculptor to proceed with greater finesse than if he were working with a heavy block. Hence, this thinly carved mask can be attributed to an unidentified sculptor of the Unkei school.

The Kimbell Tsuina mask is, as Mr. Uehara notes, "a precious piece of Japanese sculpture. . . . It may not be exaggerating to say that its superb chisel work can vie with that of the Gigaku masks from the prime of the Tempyō period" (729–48). Its taut, vigorous carving and precise modeling define an unforgettable image of fury.

Description: Face mask of a goblin expressing rage. The mask is carved in wood, lacquered black and subsequently coated with a priming of white clay, over which the entire surface is painted in verdigris. The eyes, the zigzagged teeth and the protruding fangs are covered with gold leaf. The gums and the linings of the eyes are shaded a realistic pink. Originally the mask had an extensive moustache and beard. It is very thin-walled and the back is smoothly finished.

Condition: Very good, although fragile. The wood base is exposed where the coloring has come off at abraded spots on the eyebrows and the tip of the nose. The planted hairs for the moustache and beard have been cut at their roots. The lacquered paint layer is brittle and there are extensive flake losses.

Exhibitions: None known.

Collections: Hara collection, Yokohama. [Mayuyama & Co., Ltd., Tokyo.]
Foundation Acquisition, AP 71.13.

Notes:

[1] The text of this entry is based on an unpublished English translation of the article on this mask by Shōichi Uehara of the Nara National Museum, *Kobijutsu*, no. 30, June, 1970. All quotes, unless otherwise indicated, are from this source.

[2] The abstract type of Kamakura horned goblin mask is illustrated in *Treasures Originally from the Hōryū-ji*, Tokyo National Museum, 1959, p. 97, cat. no. 186. A more realistic Tsuina mask, closer to the present example and also from the Hōryū-ji, appears in Seiroku Noma, *Nihon ko-gaku-men* ("Old Japanese Masks"), the Imperial Household Museum of Tokyo, 1935, pl. 117.

[3] Langdon Warner, *The Craft of the Japanese Sculptor*, New York, 1936, p. 34.

Attributed to Soga Dasoku, active about 1452–1483
Calligraphy attributed to Ikkyū Sōjun, 1394–1481
Portrait of Daruma
Painted about 1452–81; calligraphy, 1473–81

Hanging scroll, ink on paper, 36 1/2×13 1/2 in. (92.8×34.5 cm.)

Ikkyū Sōjun, the famous Zen Buddhist monk and calligrapher, was closely associated with Soga Dasoku; his calligraphy appears on four of Dasoku's paintings.[1] Dasoku seems to have had connections with the Daitokuji temple to which Ikkyū came as abbot in 1473, but their association goes back considerably further: the first extant painting by Dasoku, done in 1452, was a portrait of Ikkyū. An eccentric and influential Zen master, Ikkyū's "great strength of character and sense of conviction stand out in his calligraphy, which is renowned for its uniqueness and vitality."[2] Much less is known about Dasoku, who was nevertheless an influential painter; the Soga school in Kyoto continued his powerful linear style throughout the sixteenth and seventeenth centuries.

Zen Buddhist religious images were often deliberately unorthodox, as in this portrait of Daruma (Bodhidharma), the Indian patriarch honored as having introduced Ch'an (Zen) Buddhism to China. Seen in an unusual profile view, the bearded monk is hunched under his robe with only his face visible. His eyes are half-closed in meditation, but otherwise a long-standing convention of depicting Daruma with beard, downturned mouth and large nose has been observed; the image lacks the usual glowering expression and bulging eyes. The figure is outlined with a broad, wet brush in a few sharp strokes so quick and dynamic they seem almost to disrupt the stillness of the monk. The power of the brushstroke becomes the concentrated means by which the physical immobility and spiritual vitality of meditation is suggested. Washes of grey ink, darkening as they surround the figure, further emphasize the isolation of the patriarch. These contradictions of immediacy and remoteness, energy and stillness, visually express the paradoxical concept in the fourth line of the accompanying poem: "The half portrait shows his wholeness."

A specific episode in Daruma's apocryphal life, a meeting with the Emperor Wu of Liang, is referred to in the first two lines of Ikkyū's poem on this scroll: "Why does he exert his spirit at Shao-lin?" and "There is beauty at the court of the Emperor Liang." According to an account of the incident in *The Record of the Transmission of the Lamp*, vol. III, "... the Emperor ... first questioned Bodhidharma about how much Buddhist merit would accrue to him for his having erected temples, having sutras copied and supporting monks. Bodhidharma replied curtly, 'none at all'. ... Bodhidharma soon departed from the Liang Kindom and went north to the state of Wei, where he spent nine years in 'wall contemplation' at the Shao-lin temple."[3]

The word "beauty" in the poem signifies the Emperor Wu's active patronage of Buddhism, while "Shao-lin" in the first line obviously refers to the location of the Nine-Year Wall-Gazing. Ikkyū was well known for his criticism of the Zen sect of his time; the spiritual message of his poem may well reflect his censure of the worldly preoccupations of the official Zen church. The poem and painting together point out that Enlightenment comes not as the result of good works but from unyielding devotion to a difficult and paradoxical way of life.

The practice of Zen Buddhism involved long years of hardship and rigorous training as a disciple before its mind-boggling contradictions yielded to the

sudden insight of Enlightenment. Paintings of the Buddha, patriarchs and others undergoing these hardships form an important category of Zen subjects. Just when the first representations of the Nine-Year Wall-Gazing appeared is not known. The earliest Japanese example shows Daruma facing foward in a vine-hung cave; other versions show him turned toward a wall.[4] In the Kimbell's more austere conception Daruma's isolation, heightened through the profile view, is complete. One episode during the Nine-Year Wall-Gazing takes place in dead of winter; thus, the single detail of the monk's robe closely enveloping his body suggests this period of meditation. Restraint of rendering and limitation of color to black ink tones are especially suited to the Zen attempt to clear the way for direct perception of the truth. In this type of painting (*suiboku-ga*) the swift, incisive manner of using the brush becomes a statement of the purity of Enlightenment.

Inscription: Colophon: "This colophon is humbly presented by the venerable Jun Ikkyū, former bishop of the Daitokuji Zen temple in Murasaki-no [a section of Kyoto]."

Poem: *Why does he exert his spirit at Shao-lin?*
There is beauty at the court of the Emperor Liang.
[undeciphered]
The half portrait shows his wholeness.[5]

Description: Ink monochrome painting *(suiboku-ga)* on paper with a bearded old man, wrapped in a long robe, seated in profile to his right. In the upper part of the scroll appears a colophon with the calligrapher's seal on the right and a four-line poem to the left.

Condition: Good. Age cracks throughout the painting have been inpainted, and there are minor tears and abrasions which have been repaired.

Exhibitions: None known.

Collections: Viscount Matsudaira. Baron Kuki. Mrs. Kinta Muto Hyogo. [N. V. Hammer, Inc., New York.] Foundation Acquisition, AP 70.7.

Notes:

1 Background information is taken from Jan Fontein and Money L. Hickman, *Zen Painting and Calligraphy*, Museum of Fine Arts, Boston, 1971. The alternate spelling of Dasoku is Jasoku.

2 Fontein and Hickman, introd., pp. XLIV–XLV.

3 Fontein and Hickman, cat. no. 7, pp. 21–22.

4 Fontein and Hickman, cat. no. 55, p. 135.

5 Translated by Molly Garrett Bang with the assistance of staff at the Freer Gallery of Art, Washington, D. C., and the Museum of Fine Arts, Boston.

JAPANESE, MUROMACHI PERIOD, 1392–1573

Attributed to Tosa Mitsushige, active mid-sixteenth century
An Exiled Emperor on Okinoshima Island
Painted about 1550

Six-fold screen, ink, gold and color on paper, 58 1/4 × 137 in. (148 × 348 cm.)

The narrative focus and delicate rendering of the panoramic scene on this screen are characteristic of paintings of the Tosa school. Named for Tosa Yukihiro in the early fifteenth century, it became the official studio of the imperial court, reviving the native Japanese *(Yamato-e)* tradition of narrative handscrolls and reinterpreting it in a refined classical manner. In the sixteenth and seventeenth centuries members of this school, including Tosa Mitsushige, a descendant of Tosa Mitsunobu (died 1522), enlarged the intimate views of handscrolls to a monumental scale on folding screens. In this screen the literary theme of *Yamato-e* tradition is retained, as is a typical richness of descriptive detail, evident in the gate and boats. *Yamato-e* techniques such as the bird's-eye perspective of the cottage are also employed, but the vivid color and dramatic liveliness of *Yamato-e* are sacrificed to a more restrained manner. Color is limited to an almost monochromatic scheme which reflects the influence of the Chinese renaissance in Ashikaga Japan, as does the calligraphic draftsmanship of the waves. The screen is typically Tosa in the spotting of light and dark, the vividly detailed drawing, and the poetic, evocative atmosphere.

The isolated subject is thought to represent one of two emperors who were exiled to the desolate island of Okinoshima off Kochi Prefecture, Shikoku, as recorded in two accounts in the literary classic *Masukagama*.[1] The later exile, that of the Emperor Go-Daigo, is perhaps the more likely. He is known to have been sent to Okinoshima in the earliest years of the Nambokuchō Schism, about 1337, and to have escaped a year later in a fishing boat brought by his

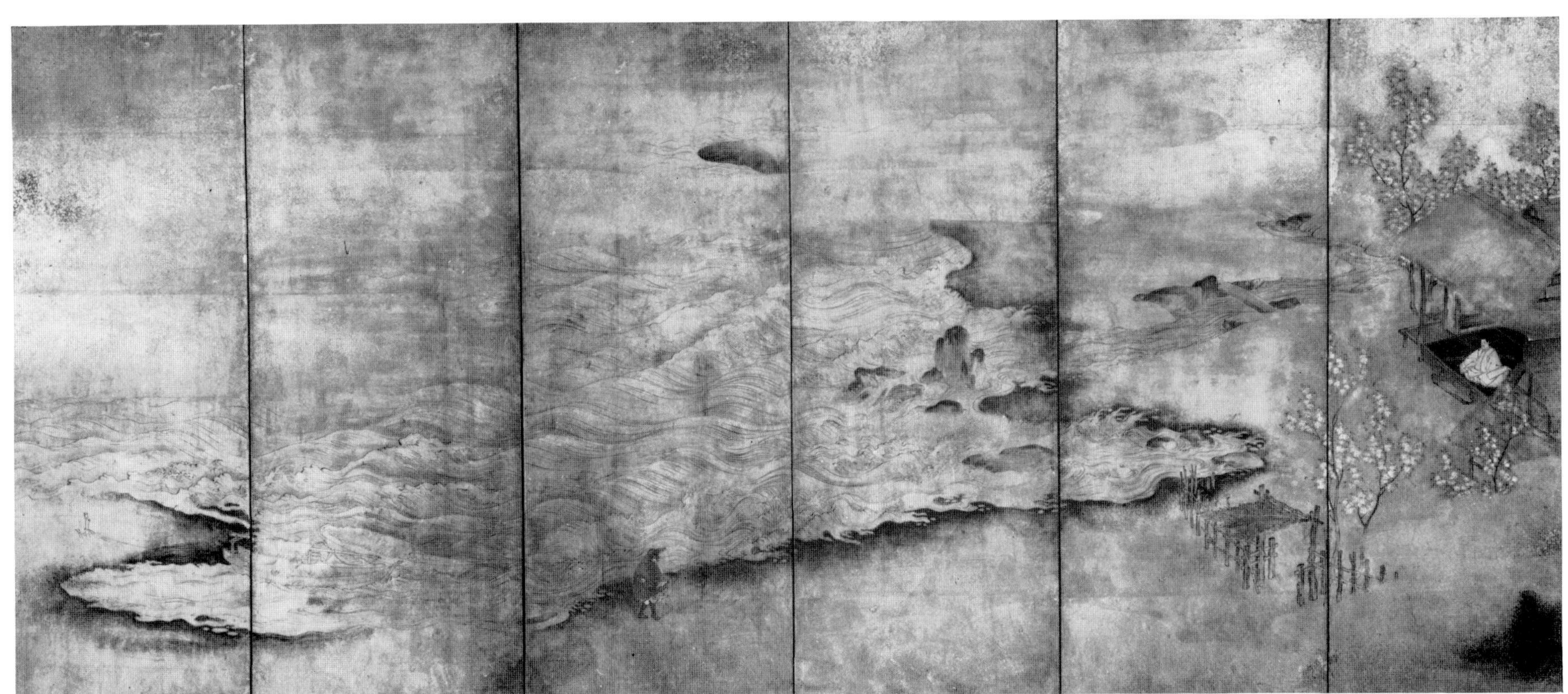

loyal follower, Takaoki Chidane. A passage in *Masukagama* describing springtime during his exile is admirably suited to the scenery of this screen: "Even after spring has come to the island, the breeze from the sea is cold, the waves are rough, and the ice on the shore has hardly melted." This description, plus details of the man in a fisherman's straw raincoat and the two boats, would seem to indicate that this screen represents the impending escape of the Emperor Go-Daigo.

On the other hand, accounts of the Emperor Go-Toba are sufficiently similar to make it possible that the screen depicts his exile in 1145. The emperor laments: "I left the city where the flowers were blooming and I came to this desolate, remote country. Searching for some sign of my past home, I see only fishermen in fishing boats through the misty, smoky air. On the edge of the shore within the shadow of the mountains, I live in a temporary abode with poles of pine. Year after year looking at the hazy sky I can't keep the tears from coming. My home is a sad memory in this desolate, lonely land." The poignant contrast between the delicate cherry blossoms and rough sea would seem to convey visually the emperor's distress at the contrast between his remembered home and his present surroundings.

The sense of isolation in both passages is eloquently captured in this screen by extremes of scale and marked contrasts between intimate details and the broad expanse of the sea. The main figure, the single strong color accent of the floor, and the majority of detail are confined to a single panel at the extreme right, and the rest of the screen is filled with the boundless stretches of a wild and turbulent sea. Its vast scale is emphasized by the solitary windswept figure of a fisherman in the foreground; the two boats behind him are barely visible against the waves. Although this figure and the boats are not small, they appear tiny beside the foaming ocean, so well has the artist captured the effect of its limitless, mist-shrouded reaches. The lonely figure of the emperor in his open house, the trees near him, and the gate are sharply and solidly drawn–stable elements in a fluid world. The narrative subject of the screen is thus carried to an epic scale by these contrasts and by the monumental sweep of its composition. At the same time the unobtrusive, restrained coloration and the poetic rendering are sustained and made viable on the large screen through the sympathetic participation demanded of the viewer by its sentimental theme.

Description: In the extreme right panel a nobleman sits in a thatched cottage with a musical instrument *(koto)* at his side surveying the world of mists and waves stretching before him. Blossoming cherry trees surround the cottage and a swift stream runs behind it to the sea. A fisherman in a straw raincoat walks along the shore in the foreground toward the rude gate of the nobleman's cottage. Two small open boats behind him are staked to the shore at left. High in the center panels a distant shore and rooftops are barely visible through the mists. The panels are painted in ink and gold, with white in the trees and *Yamato-e* green in the floor of the cottage.

Condition: Fair. The screen is somewhat stained and abraded, with several scattered losses. Touches of white in the far left panel indicate the waves were once highlighted by white.

Exhibitions: None known.

Collections: Kawakatwu collection, Yokohama. [J. Pierre Dubosc, Paris.]
Foundation Acquisition, AP 71.11.

Note:

1 Ichimatwu Tanaka, "On a Folding Screen Picture of an Exile on Okinoshima Island," *Kokka*, no. 824, November, 1960, describes this screen at length, providing the basis for discussion of the exiles.

Attributed to Sesson Shūkei, about 1504–1589
Evening Landscape
Painted in the Sixteenth Century

Hanging scroll, ink and light color on paper, $11\,^{7}/_{16} \times 18\,^{3}/_{16}$ in. (29×46.2 cm.)

This painting, like most landscape paintings of the Muromachi period, reflects the strong Chinese influence then prevailing in Japan. Zen Buddhism was the dominant cultural force, and its values of reticence and simplicity found expression in the tea ceremony and in the understatement of ink monochrome painting. The misty, poetic landscapes of the Southern Sung school of Ma Yüan and Hsia Kuei "became the standards for Japanese taste," for in this style "little was explicitly shown; suggestion was everything. The spectator furnished more than his usual share and this was ideal for either discussion after tea or for the insertion of a new and Japanese viewpoint into the silken voids."[1] In Sesson's painting, elements of the Ma-Hsia tradition are evident in the forms dissolving into mist, the mountains silhouetted in the distance, and the numerous needle peaks, as well as in motifs such as the man on a donkey and the angular ledge in one corner of the foreground.[2] These elements are subordinated, however, to pictorial concerns that are peculiarly Japanese.

Like other painters inspired by the Southern Sung tradition, Sesson "thinks in terms of large units of design, which he disposes for effect or formal considerations; he is less concerned with mist or haze, or generally, illusionistic rendition, than with brushwork, the relative weight of a line, and the relationships of his form elements."[3] The formalized shapes and abstract design of the whole are especially effective in conveying specific emotional content: the bulk of the mountain looming up from the distant valleys takes on the compelling mystery of a vision, enhanced by the misty evening stillness; the response it demands is spelled out in the figure of the

bearded man in the foreground who stands before it bent over in an attitude of incredulous awe. Similarly intense expressive feeling is imputed to the entire image by the markedly contrasting values, linear emphasis and exaggerated space, whose bold drama is distinctly Japanese as compared to its more softly suggestive Chinese antecedents.

Sesson was a very prolific monk-painter who worked in the north, apart from main centers of Japanese art in the sixteenth century such as Kyoto. He continued the linear *kanga* (Chinese painting) style of Sesshū (1420–1506) in a poetic and eccentric manner uniquely his own. Influences of Sesshū and of Mu Ch'i (mid-thirteenth century) can be seen here in the use of the *haboku* or "splash ink" technique to suggest birds flapping about in water in the middle distance and in the addition of Sesshū color accents to what was previously an exclusively monochromatic scheme. In the foreground the little figures drawn with light touches of the brush are very characteristic of Sesson, whose "figure drawing especially seems weird at times, but . . . reveals a very powerful imagination."[4] His work was greatly prized in the eighteenth century; no less a person than Ogata Kōrin found in the decorative emphasis and expressive exaggerations of Sesson's style the first distinctive Japanese aesthetic.

Description: A misty open landscape panorama dominated by vertical mountain peaks rising abruptly through the vapors just beyond two ledges in the foreground. The major cluster of mountains, asymmetrically placed, has large, geometric boulders of a bulging type in the foreground, modeled with strong *chiaroscuro*, with summary structural definition provided by a few "ax-stroke" *ts'un* at the top. Scattered accents of dark "lichen-dot" *ts'un* are concentrated about the edges of the shapes. On the right a large waterfall curves out in a frozen arc between the boulders. Behind them tall needle peaks contain the rooftops of buildings among their misty crevices; the moon appears at the center left margin beside an isolated needle peak. On the right, hazy mountains in the distance rim a valley above which some birds are flying and others, executed in the *haboku* technique, are splashing in the waters of the lake below. The foreground consists of two angular planes with contours executed in rich ink tones; crisp, black leaves of sparse bamboo punctuate the edges. Two men stand on the nearer ledge at right with a boy behind them; on the left a man on a donkey with his servant trotting behind heads toward a rough bridge at right. The painting is executed on paper in sharply contrasting tones of black ink with touches of pale reddish-brown in the bearded man, rooftops and bridge.

Condition: Fair. There is a quadrifoil-shaped paper loss about two inches wide in the lower left. Numerous flake losses throughout the painting have been inpainted; one small untouched loss near the lower center is located one inch from the bottom. Colors are quite faded.

Exhibitions: None known.

Collections: Baron Koyata Iwasaki, Tokyo. S. Kumita, Tokyo. Baron Fukuoka Kotei. [N. V. Hammer, Inc., New York.]
Foundation Acquisition, AP 69.15.

Notes:

1 Sherman E. Lee, *Tea Taste in Japanese Art*, New York, Asia House Gallery, 1963, p. 26.

2 Laurence Sickman in *Chinese Calligraphy and Painting in the Collection of John M. Crawford, Jr.*, New York, 1962, cat. no. 55, p. 123.

3 Max Loehr in . . . *Collection of John M. Crawford, Jr.*, cat. no. 34, p. 89.

4 Robert Treat Paine and Alexander Soper, *The Art and Architecture of Japan*, Baltimore, 1960, p. 85.

Attributed to Kanō Dōmi, active prior to 1603
Europeans Arriving in Japan (Namban Byōbu)
Painted in 1592–1602

Pair of six-fold screens, ink, gold and color on paper, each 41 3/8 × 102 5/8 in. (105 × 260.6 cm.)

The shock of encounter between two highly developed civilizations such as Japan and Western Europe in the sixteenth century is hard to imagine today. The Japanese preserved their impressions of the marvelous ships and strange appearances of the Portuguese, who were the first to discover Japan, on the six-fold paired screens (*byōbu*) which were the glory of the Momoyama period. They called the Europeans "Southern Barbarians" (*namban*) because they came up to Japan from the south, landing at the port of Nagasaki on Kyūshū. Contacts between the Japanese and their "discoverers" revolved around trade and missionary activities, but in 1614 an edict was published prohibiting Christianity, and about 1636 Japan again closed her doors to the outside world. In the fierce persecutions of Christians which followed, European religious influence was eradicated. (The size of these screens, about 50 cm. shorter than usual, suggests they were cut down, probably when the retable was effaced, to remove the cross atop the church and avoid any association with Christianity.) No profound confluence of civilizations took place during the hundred years Japan was open to the West, although the introduction of firearms radically altered Japanese society. Nevertheless, this early exposure to European culture was not forgotten; in the later seventeenth and eighteenth centuries, it greatly influenced Japanese art, literature, medicine and other disciplines.

The Kimbell screens depict on the left the ship's arrival and unloading and on the right the Portuguese procession through town to a church. This composition is typical of the majority of *namban* screens, including the earliest ones. The screen of the arrival is dominated by the ship of the

Portuguese, whose East India carracks were the largest in the world and a source of wonder to the Japanese.[1] Its open deck affords a clear view of the barbarians at ease; Moors seem to have been especially interesting and appear frequently on both screens. The air of calm about the landing is dispelled in the right screen where the Europeans are surrounded by numerous curious onlookers. An English captain, John Saris, writing in 1613 of the reception his party received in Japan, reported that both children and adults surrounded them, jumping about, turning somersaults, poking at them, and finally ending up by throwing rocks at them.[2] Such exaggerated reactions to the strange appearances of the foreigners can be seen here in the group of six men in a house who make a great commotion over the procession. The Japanese, although traditionally quite polite, were amused and amazed by their exotic visitors, and *namban byōbu* became very popular; some fifty examples have come down to us from the short period, the 1590s through the 1630s, during which they were made. Westerners, for their part, were not untouched by Japanese customs; in the background of the right screen we find European priests playing the oriental game of Gō together.

Most early screens were the work of Kanō school painters, and in a recent study on *namban byōbu* Tadao Takamizawa suggests that the Kimbell screens are the work of Kanō Dōmi.[3] In composition and details, such as the Chinese courtesans in the procession, they are most similar to a pair in the Freer Gallery of Art, Washington, D.C., which Takamizawa also attributes to Dōmi. The Freer screens, however, are usually considered to be by one of the so-called town painters, or *machi-eshi*, whose untrained and spontaneous renderings of urban genre scenes preceded the development of the *ukiyo-e* school.[4] Mr. Takamizawa's argument rests on stylistic similarities to Dōmi's work which include the long bodies with thick bull necks, the heads thrust forward, and the glaring eyes. Kanō Dōmi, a Christian convert, is known to have visited Kyūshū, and probably Nagasaki, in 1592, where he may well have seen the arrival of a Portuguese ship. He was at work in Kyoto in 1602 and left Japan the next year for Christian headquarters at Manila. He was associated with the Franciscan friars, who appear on the Kimbell screens. A story which demonstrates the close relations between Kanō painters and Christian missionaries relates that Dōmi signed a letter at the instigation of the Franciscans, vilifying the Jesuits, which he later had to retract under oath.[5]

Regardless of whether the Kimbell screens are by Kanō Dōmi or by a *machi-eshi* painter, they are a splendid example of Momoyama screen art. Screens were painted with mineral pigments using lapis lazuli and malachite among other substances; the brown incursions tinged with green in the cloud areas may be a kind of silver, now darkened.[6] Executed in softly gleaming gold leaf, the clouds act as unifying elements and compositional foils to set off the ship and procession. Although *namban* screens form a link to Christian art, they reflect little of the Western-style art being taught in the seminaries; *namban* screens, except for very small areas of shading, are painted exactly like genre paintings (*fuzokuga*) of that time. These early screens often showed the foreigners with grotesque features and long noses.[7]

Description: In both screens the colors are predominantly subdued, warm shades of brown, dull green and pale orange-red, with the water a dark greenish-black.

On the left screen a three-masted brown carrack stands in water just off a tree-shaded shore at the right, with a tender at the stern. Three boatmen unload another tender at the shore where two priests and attendants wait among boxes and jars. Aboard ship the captain's party sits around a tea table in the center while sailors lounge on the fore and aft decks. The figures are clad in full pantaloons with some wearing tall, broad-brimmed hats.

On the right screen the *namban* cortege, which includes three Chinese courtesans, is preceded by some goats; it moves along the wharf toward a church complex surrounded by a moat on the right. Attendants bring up two horses in the rear. Small crowds of Japanese are fascinated by the travelers, chasing after the group, peering out of houses, and gaping along the path. Domestic and business activities are shown in the interiors of houses: traders and a distracted scale-tender in shops along the wharf, a woman spinning silk, Japanese and European priests playing a game. In the church Franciscan and Dominican priests pray before an altar whose retable is now effaced.

Condition: Very good. Both screens have been recently renovated. Wear marks, some losses and restorations are evident along all the fold seams. Some abrasions, losses, and stains are scattered throughout both screens. They have been cut down from their original size. The present greenish-black of the water and the dark green foliage may have darkened from originally lighter values.

Exhibitions: None known.

Collections: Tachibana family collection, Fukui, Japan.
[Mayuyama & Co., Ltd., Tokyo.]
Foundation Acquisition, AP 71.14 a, b.

Notes:

1 C. R. Boxer, *The Christian Century in Japan, 1549–1650*, Berkeley and Los Angeles, 1967, p. 122.

2 Nobuo Tsuji, "Namban Byōbu," *Kobijutsu*, no. 21, March, 1968, pp. 103–5. Translation was kindly provided by Molly Garrett Bang.

3 Tadao Takamizawa, *Nanban Byobu* [*sic*], Tokyo, 1970, vol. I, cat. no. 5, pp. 126–28; vol. II, pp. 29–33.

4 *The Freer Gallery of Art*, part II (Japan), Tokyo, 1971, cat. no. 31–32, illus. p. 162.

5 Boxer, p. 202.

6 Suggested by Nobuo Tsuji.

7 *The Freer Gallery of Art*, p. 161.

Additional Reference:

Invitation to Art in Japan, Tokyo, 1968, Mayuyama & Co. advertisement on inside back cover, color illus.

Tea Bowl, Karatsu ware
Late Sixteenth or early Seventeenth Century

Stoneware, grey and brown glazes,
$3\,^1/_2 \times 4$ (diam.) in. (8.9×10.3 cm.)

The discreet modulation of plain shapes and simple decoration is the salient quality of the quite varied and numerous type of Japanese ceramics known as Karatsu ware. Named for a port town on the west coast of Kyushu Island, Karatsu ware quite understandably reflects earlier Korean designs because many potteries in that area were established by Korean emigrants who crossed the Tsushima Straits and settled there in the sixteenth and early seventeenth centuries. A great number of kilns flourished in this area until the mid-seventeenth century when the increasing development of porcelain techniques supplanted its production.[1] "There is nothing lofty or noble" about Karatsu ware; it was initially made for daily use "by common people."[2] Later, its characteristic simplicity and sobriety of color appealed enormously to practitioners of the tea ceremony whose avid patronage inspired the evolution of a large number of distinct types of decoration.

Among the different categories of Karatsu wares, *E-Karatsu* (painted Karatsu) ware, of which this bowl is a splendid example, is one of the most important and most numerous types.[3] Painted in the dark brown colors of iron oxide glazes, its designs retain the characteristic restraint of Korean ware of the early Yi Dynasty (1392–1910), but the more earthy colors of the Japanese ware are combined in rather muted contrasts as compared to the brighter color contrasts on the Korean ware. This evolution of design may have been induced by the temperate taste of the tea masters or it may simply reflect the availability of different natural glazes in Japan.

Elaborate classifications of Karatsu ware according to kilns have been recently proposed.[4] Preliminary investigation suggests that this bowl may be tentatively associated with the outstanding painted ware designated as Kishidake style which was developed by artisans who moved from a kiln of that name near Karatsu in the latter part of the sixteenth century.[5]

Description: Straight-sided cup with low foot and glazed designs. The cylindrical shape is articulated into three lobes by vertical indentions that are pronounced at the lip and diminish down the sides to meet a horizontal indention around the bottom. Below the slightly flared bottom edge of the sides, the nearly horizontal bottom recedes sharply toward the crisply cut foot ring (2 1/8 in. diam.). A thin pearly-grey glaze covers the interior (except for one "skip") and forms the background of the exterior designs in a dark ferrous brown glaze. An open spray of lightly leafed foliage decorates two lobes, and on the third lobe three gently curved branches with sparse round buds (?) descend from the thin, brown-edged rim. Except for the unglazed foot, which reveals the dark brown body, the surface is covered by a transparent overglaze with fine crackle.

Condition: Excellent. There are two superficial chips from the glaze on the bottom rim of the side. On the exterior just below the rim, the crackle pattern is accentuated by very faint staining.

Exhibitions: None known.

Collections: [J. Pierre Dubosc, Paris.]
Foundation Acquisition, AP 71.12.

Notes:

1 Soame Jenyns, *Japanese Pottery*, London, 1971, p. 166.

2 Shinzo Sato, in *Tosetsu*, no. 61, and *Toki Zenshu*, no. 3, as quoted by Jenyns, pp. 164–65.

3 Jenyns, p. 170. An alternate spelling of *E-Karatsu* is *egaratsu*.

4 Jenyns, p. 170–77, provides a bibliography and summaries of the classifications advanced by Shinzo Sato, Kyoichi Kimbara and Wasaburo Mitzumachi.

5 Jenyns, p. 172, pl. 73 A. See also Fujio Koyama and John Figgess, *Two Thousand Years of Oriental Ceramics*, New York, 1961, pl. 111, who illustrate fragments from kilns in the Kishidake area.

JAPANESE, MOMOYAMA PERIOD, 1573–1615, OR EDO PERIOD, 1615–1868

Jar, Shigaraki ware
Late Sixteenth or early Seventeenth Century

Earthenware, orange and green glazes,
14×11 5/8 (diam.) in. (35.6×29.5 cm.)

Shigaraki ware takes its name from a small town at the southern end of Shiga Prefecture in the central part of Honshu Island, where it was initially produced as a functional ware to store seeds and tea. This region is rich in clay deposits and Shigaraki is regarded as one of the six "ancient kilns" of Japan, ceramic production having begun there perhaps as early as the thirteenth century.[1] However, by the sixteenth century the unassuming naturalness of the robust shapes, dark colors, and rustic decoration of this folk ware had come to be highly regarded by the masters of the tea ceremony. They delighted in the "sense of materiality" of its surface and the opportunity for a "fortunate accident" in its patterns,[2] and patronized the Shigaraki kilns with enthusiasm. Used as flower-holders during the tea ceremony,[3] Shigaraki vases were felt to be rich in *shibui* (a sense of unaffected astringency or sobriety) that was a highly regarded ideal of the tea masters.[4]

This sturdy jar is thought to have been made in the Shigaraki area about the end of the sixteenth century when there was a great increase in pottery production throughout Japan. The sense of natural ruggedness and freedom found in much of this rustic ware is evident in the slightly asymmetrical shape of this jar's body, its coarse surface texture and the random pattern of the green glaze. The unpretentious appearance of the rough, earth-colored body of Shigaraki ware is accented by the characteristic abundance of white nodules of partially fired stone particles that are distributed throughout the clay. The green splash of wood-ash glaze is equally typical of Shigaraki ware, but it is also found on contemporary Tamba and Iga wares from other folk kilns of central Honshu.

Description: High-shouldered jar with a short neck and wide mouth. The granular surface of the coarse greyish-white body is smoothly finished except for turning marks on the lower third; numerous white silicon speckles project through the opaque orange glaze of varying intensity which covers most of the body and the interior neck. One side is covered by a pale, finely crackled, mint-green "throw" of wood-ash glaze, having several thick rivulets of darker green, one of which runs to the bottom. The interior is roughly turned and unglazed. The flat foot (5 3/4 in. diam.) shows two support marks and several unfused quartz-like granules embedded in the clay.

Condition: Good. Three are three small chip losses on the lip and the shoulder and two vertical hairline cracks in the neck.

Exhibitions: None known.

Collections: [J. Pierre Dubosc, Paris.]
Foundation Acquisition, AP 69.8.

Notes:

1 See Soame Jenyns, *Japanese Pottery*, London, 1971, pp. 114–17 for an informative summary.

2 Sherman E. Lee, introd., *Tea Taste in Japanese Art*, Asia House Gallery, New York, 1963, pp. 30, 35.

3 Jenyns, p. 130.

4 Lee, p. 10, and Jenyns, p. 18.

Kanō Shigenobu, active about 1635
Wheat, Poppies and Bamboo
Painted in the early Seventeenth Century

Six-fold screen, ink, colors and *gofun* on gold leaf paper, 61×140 in. (152.5×355.8 cm.)

Large-scale paintings using rich colors on a gold background were a development of the Momoyama period. As screens (*byōbu*) and sliding wall panels (*fusuma*) they were designed to be splendid embellishments for the vast, dim interiors of the fortified palaces then being built. This highly decorative style of painting was initiated by members of the Kanō family whose consistent style influenced several generations of painters. Originally conceived on an overwhelmingly grand and impressive scale, this type of screen painting by the beginning of the seventeenth century had softened to a more elegant and refined expression epitomized in the work of Kanō Sanraku. The Kimbell screen was painted in this later idiom by Kanō Shigenobu. Little is known about him other than that he had connections with Kanō Sanraku (died 1635) and Lord Mitsuhiro Karasumara (died 1635) and is thus believed to have been active in the early part of the century.[1]

The brilliance of Kanō painting, beyond its grandeur of scale and flaunting color, derives from the contrast between vibrant gold-foil backgrounds and the heavy, flat tempera in which color was applied, as well as the use of ink lines to sharpen contours and heighten details.[2] In the Kimbell screen this precisely applied line renders veins in the spathes of the bamboo and defines the contours of the poppy blooms. Further definition is given to the poppies and to the wheat by the use of *moriage*, a technique by which details are modeled in raised areas of gesso. Clarity of execution allows especially effective plays of rhythm as seen in the crisscrossing, smoothly bending wheat leaves and jagged poppy leaves which contrast with their fragile stems.

Natural forms in Kanō painting become stylized components in a complex, carefully arranged decorative design. Unfortunately, we are unable to appreciate the entire sweep of Kanō Shigenobu's original design as this screen is but one of an original pair. An intact pair of Shigenobu screens in the Seattle Museum depicting poppies and bamboo furnishes an example of a continuous composition.[3] Through comparison of the screens, it is evident that the Kimbell screen once stood on the right, as borne out by the jar-shaped Kanō seal by its right edge. The screens are similar in conception and execution, but the Kimbell screen employs a more rigid composition. Poppies, bamboo and wheat are disposed in separate clumps within a framework established by the vertical grid of the screen's folds. In this compartmentalized composition, dominated by the central mass of poppies, the different elements are unified by the repeating verticals of their slender stems. Only in the second panel from the right do different forms appear in the same panel; a small pair of poppies and a pair of bamboo sprouts crossed by a curving frond act as grace notes in the composition–studied, precious and elegant.

Seals: Two in the lower right: a jar-shaped Kanō seal and an incomplete Shigenobu seal.

Description: Gold-leafed, six-fold screen with wheat left, poppies center, and bamboo right. The wheat, in varying stages of ripeness, stands in two clumps on a low ground in the leftmost panel. Poppies, with blooms of gold, white, red and various pinks, occupy the next three panels. Their leaves are painted in varying shades of green with veins picked out in gold, and the occasional pods are a pale grey-green. On the right, dark green bamboo extends the full height of the screen.

Condition: Good. The outer panels are relatively unblemished while the two central panels have darkened considerably and been abraded. Losses are not filled but have been inpainted. None of the color variations in the poppies of the central panels remain; blooms are a greyish white and leaves a uniform dark green.

Exhibitions: None known.

Collections: [Mayuyama & Co., Ltd., Tokyo.] Foundation Acquisition, AP 69.10.

Notes:

1 *Kokka*, vol. 50, no. 601, December, 1940. This information was kindly supplied by Catherine Kaputa of the Seattle Art Museum.

2 *Gofun*, the material used for white, was composed of ground oyster shells.

3 Junkichi Mayuyama, ed., *Japanese Art in the West*, Tokyo, 1966, pp. 182–83, illus., no. 220.

Jar, Arita ware, Kakiemon enamels

Shoo or Kambun period, 1652–72

Porcelain, blue underglaze, colored enamels, 19 1/4 × 13 7/8 (diam.) in. (48.9 × 35.3 cm.)

This magnificent jar is one of a small group of Kakiemon vases whose ovoid shape, bold decoration and exceptionally large size constitute an impressive demonstration of ceramic artistry. On these jars the brightly colored enameled decoration is formed in dense patterns of ornamental designs that accentuate three large panels on the sides containing more open designs of naturalistic motifs. The panels on jars of this type often contain blossoming plants, such as the blue flower on the Kimbell jar, the red and yellow flowers of a jar in the Freer Gallery[1] or a bird and flower design on the jar in the British Museum.[2] Other jars of this size bear panels depicting several standing figures in a naturalistic setting; some of these were designed for export to Europe.[3] The design of these large jars contrasts with that of another, more numerous, group of generally smaller Kakiemon vases that are distinguished by more open, circumferential designs with extensive areas of white and by broad diameters nearly equal to their height.[4]

In the jars of the Kimbell class the elaborate decoration is subtly arranged to complement its simple vertical shape. For example, the varying width of a panel, narrow at the bottom and broad at the top, is deliberately correlated to the changing diameter of the jar; a center view of one panel shows only that panel and none of the others. These three designs are integral parts of an overall scheme that includes the floral interstices between the panels and, above, a system of decorative bands whose varying widths and colors enhance the incoming curve of the shoulder.

Since the chronological development of early Japanese porcelain is not definitely established, dates

assigned to pieces are tentative. The suggested date of 1652–72 for this jar is based on the one proposed by Soame Jenyns for the repaired "magnificent wreck" of the British Museum jar. Like this jar and the Freer jar, the Kimbell jar is a technical *tour de force* which has considerable presence and dignity.

Inscription: Beneath the glaze of the recess is a deliberate mark in a pale brown color, 1 3/8 in. long, which might have been intended as an identifying character.

Description: Tall jar of dense fine clay with high curved shoulder, short straight-sided neck and wide mouth. It is decorated in light and dark blue underglazes and red-orange, pale blue-green and yellow enamels. On the sides are three panels with different combinations of butterfly, peony, chrysanthemum, and bamboo motifs, separated by nearly identical interstices of symmetrical leaf and blossom designs. The background is white except for a blue-green overglaze in the upper part of the interstices. On the shoulder are bands of floral and geometric designs, three in blue underglaze and two of colored enamels. Around the neck is a false gadroon design in blue underglaze. White glaze covers the interior surface except the lip and part of the neck which may have been intended to receive a fitted cover, now missing.[5] The slightly slanted foot (7 1/8 in. diam.) encloses a shallow glazed recess bearing several faint spur marks; the rim is unglazed.

Condition: Excellent. The surface is impeccably preserved except for several faint hairline scratches and some stain in the crackle of glaze on the lower part of one side. In one interstice, a small area of green overglaze is slightly discolored from uneven firing.

Exhibitions: None known.

Collections: [N. V. Hammer, Inc., New York.] Foundation Acquisition, AP 68.10.

Notes:

1 A fine color illustration of this jar, which is almost 16 in. high, is in *The Freer Gallery of Art*, Washington, D. C., [1970], vol. II (Japan), pl. 105.

2 20.2 in. high; see: Soame Jenyns, *Japanese Porcelain*, New York, 1965, pl. 50 A and B.

3 A vase of this type is represented in a painted ceiling of about 1695 in the Oranienburg Palace near Berlin. The vase that probably served as the model for this image is now in the Charlottenburg Palace, Berlin. See: Jenyns, p. 129, who refers to illustrations of the vase and ceiling in an article by L. Reidemeister, "Die Porzellan Kabinette der Brandenburgisch-Preussischen Schlösser," *Jahrbuch der Preussischen Kunstsammlungen*, 1934, p. 272, pls. 7, 8. Two other vases with similar scenes have also been recorded, one in the Victoria and Albert Museum, London (no. 1736–76, 50.1 x 34.3 cm.); see: J. Mayuyama, *Japanese Art in the West*, Tokyo, 1966, fig. 380, and one that was formerly in the collection of Richard de la Mare (61.5 cm. high, with cover); see: Jenyns, pl. 57B, and Sotheby's auction catalogue, London, May 19, 1971, lot 66.

4 See: Jenyns, pls. 31A, 49B, 49C, 51A, 54A, 54B, and 84A.

5 This cover may have been enameled and dome-shaped like the one on the vase that was formerly in the de la Mare collection; see note 3.

Octagonal Bowl, Arita ware, Kakiemon enamels
Late Seventeenth Century

Porcelain, colored enamels,
4 1/8 × 8 1/4 (diam.) in. (10.4 × 21 cm.)

Arita ware is named for the town in Hizen Province on Kyushu (the southernmost major island of Japan) near where the first porcelain was made in Japan in the early seventeenth century. The kaolin found in this area is easily worked and, when fired, fuses into a warm milk-white porcelain. By the mid-seventeenth century this porcelain was being decorated with colored enamels applied on the surface of transparent glazes. The overglaze decoration on this bowl is called "Kakiemon style" after Sakaido Kakiemon, traditionally regarded as the originator of this technique and the founder of an illustrious family of potters; his name derives from the persimmon (*kaki*) color of a red enamel that he developed.[1] Kakiemon style is, however, more than just an overglaze enamel technique; it is a style of enamel decoration that is generally feminine, lyrical and elegant. Its popularity in Europe influenced designs of Meissen and other wares.[2]

In this bowl, this distinctive mode is exemplified in the restrained and delicate enamel designs that enhance the warm white of the porcelain and emphasize the simplicity of the bowl's octagonal shape. Its shape and size are typical; similar bowls of contemporary date are well known.[3] However, each has a distinctive design scheme, possibly the result of different enamel painters decorating bowls from the same kiln.

Description: Octagonal bowl with flared lip. On the exterior: a branch with blossoms, in yellow and orange-red enamels, and leaves, in blue, yellow and green enamels, extends around five panels; on the three remaining sides are two small bird-like designs and a long-tailed *hoho* bird in blue, green, yellow and red enamels. On the interior are scattered five small designs of leaves and buds enameled in the same colors. The designs were originally outlined and the leaves veined with black enamel lines. The lip is edged in brown, and the round foot rim (10 cm. diam.) encloses a shallow glazed recess that bears one small spur mark in the center.

Condition: Very good. In the interior there are some superficial hairline scratches. The black enamel outlines and leaf veins are partially abraded.

Exhibitions: None known.

Collections: [N. V. Hammer, Inc., New York.] Foundation Acquisition, AP 68.9.

Notes:

1 Several versions of this legendary explanation are known; see: *Art Treasures From Japan*, Los Angeles County Museum of Art, 1965, p. 165, and Richard S. Cleveland, introd., *200 Years of Japanese Porcelain*, City Art Museum of St. Louis, 1970, p. 12.

2 Sherman E. Lee, *A History of Far Eastern Art*, New York, 1964, p. 497.

3 There are similar bowls in: the Victoria and Albert Museum, London (7 7/8 in. diam., illus. by W. B. Honey, *The Ceramic Art of China and Other Countries . . .*, London, 1945, pl. 182 a); the Museum of Fine Arts, Boston (no. 50.1551, 10.1 x 19.9 cm., illus. in *The Charles B. Hoyt Collection*, Boston, 1952, cat. no. 715); the Seattle Art Museum (3 7/8 x 7 5/8 in., illus. by S. E. Lee, *Japanese Decorative Style*, Cleveland Museum of Art, 1961, cat. no. 144); the City Art Museum of St. Louis (11.2 x 25.5 cm., illus. by R. S. Cleveland, cat. no. 90). Several later bowls of the same form are also illustrated by R. S. Cleveland, cat. nos. 93, 95.

Ogata Kōrin, 1658–1716

Seiōbo

Painted about 1705

Hanging scroll, ink and color on silk over paper, 37 1/2 × 14 5/8 in. (95.2 × 37.1 cm.)

Renowned for his colorful and sumptuous style of painting, Ogata Kōrin is a major figure in the history of Japanese art and the foremost decorative painter of the early Edo period. Born to a Kyoto family with strong artistic traditions, both Kōrin and his brother Ogata Kenzan (1663–1743) were trained in the arts at an early age. They inherited a fine sensibility for draftsmanship and design from their father who was an accomplished calligrapher as well as a wealthy cloth merchant who dealt with the latest fashions in decorative design. Kōrin's familiarity with these textile designs may have influenced the development of his remarkable talent for pattern and composition, color and texture. Other artistic influences on Kōrin were the screen painter and ceramicist Kōetsu (1558–1637) and, more significantly, the artisan-painter Sōtatsu (first half of the seventeenth century), whose vigorous brushwork and beautiful colors were absorbed into Kōrin's more graceful style.

Kōrin in his younger years indulged a taste for aesthetic pleasures and sumptuous, elegant living until financial circumstances forced him to make a living at his art.[1] He produced exquisite lacquers, collaborated with Kenzan in ceramic design, and continued to paint; in 1701 he was awarded the honorific title Hōkkyō in recognition of his artistry. Shortly thereafter he went or was exiled to Edo (Tokyo) where he remained until 1711; this painting of the legendary Seiōbo, like most of his major works, dates from his Edo sojourn.[2]

Less forceful and abstract than his larger works, the Kimbell painting is quiet and lyrical; the influence of Sōtatsu is felt in the harmonious colors, the beautiful brushwork of the ample robes and trailing scarves, and the soft, fumbling contours of the chair. An appreciation for the beauty of naiveté and clumsiness that characterizes the Rimpa (Sōtatsu-Kōrin) aesthetic is apparent. Kōrin's interest in calligraphic line and pattern is most evident in the flowing contours of the sleeves, executed in the double-line technique, and in the complicated contrasts of shapes in the lower right.

Seiōbo, or Hsi Wang Mu, was the Chinese queen of the fairies, or more properly the Western Royal Mother, the female principle *(yin)* of life.[3] According to legend she lived high in the mountains in a jade palace surrounded by golden walls on the edge of a jasper lake, and in her garden grew the peaches of immortality. These peaches ripened only once every 3,000 years, on her birthday, the occasion of a marvelous feast. She was depicted, as here, in Chinese dress, sometimes as a beautiful princess, other times as a noble matron. E. T. C. Werner notes a custom of presenting to women fifty years old, presumably on their birthdays, an image of Seiōbo to which they prayed for long life and happiness.[4] This scroll may have been such a birthday gift. Its composition, with the figure seated in a chair and holding a flower, is found in other paintings of the *ukiyo-e* school which depict beautiful women of the period.

Inscription: Hōkkyō Kōrin

Seal: Dōshū

Description: Seiōbo, a woman in Chinese dress, is seated on a chair. She wears a flowing white garment, open at the neck, beneath a full-sleeved dull green coat with an embroidered grey-green border which envelops her left hand. A blue shawl covers her shoulders with long streamers falling on the ground. A broad red apron is adorned with a two-fold panel hanging down the center. Bright blue bows ornament her sandals. She wears a headdress of pale blue and gold and her hair is tied back with a red ribbon. She holds to her chest a peach (?) blossom in her right hand. The curving grey chair is upholstered with a panel of pink peonies and grey-green leaves.

Condition: Excellent. There are some small stains scattered in the figure and the background.

Exhibitions: None known.

Collections: Hosomi Collection, Japan. [Ellsworth & Goldie, Ltd., New York.]
Foundation Acquisition, AP 67.8.

Notes:

1 Historians often detail occasions of Kōrin's extravagance; Langdon Warner includes many of the stories in *The Enduring Art of Japan*, Cambridge, Mass., 1965, pp. 71–72.

2 The date of about 1705 was assigned to the scroll when it was published in *Kokka*, no. 842, May, 1962; illus. pl. 1, and in color on the frontispiece.

3 Information about Seiōbo is taken from E.T.C. Werner, *Dictionary of Chinese Mythology*, New York, 1961, pp. 163–64, and V.F. Weber, *Ko-Ji Hô-Ten*, Paris, 1923, vol. II, pp. 264–65.

4 Werner, p. 64.

Kaigetsudō Ando, active early eighteenth century; traditional dates 1671–1743
Standing Beauty
Painted before 1714

Hanging scroll, ink, color and *gofun* on paper, 39 7/8 × 18 3/8 in. (101.3 × 46.7 cm.)

Ukiyo-e or "pictures of the floating world" are familiar in the West through the Japanese print, but the term itself is applicable to a larger cultural phenomenon embracing all the arts and reflecting new social developments in Japan. Courtesans such as the one depicted in this scroll represented but one aspect of the pleasure-seeking culture of Edo (Tokyo), the new capital of the Tokugawa shoguns. The growth of industry and commerce had brought prosperity to an emergent middle class, but rigid social restrictions "left the townsmen little choice but to spend their new wealth on themselves and a variety of social activities."[1] In the entertainment quarters of the city where the courtesans were to be found, teahouses sprang up in abundance, Kabuki theater was born, and all the arts of a popular nature took on new dimensions. *Ukiyo-e* painting of various types portraying everyday pursuits served as the basis for the woodblock print which came into its own at this time. One of these classic types as it appears in this *kakemono* was the single standing courtesan, majestic and self-contained, isolated against a plain background, the innovation of Kaigetsudō Ando. Ando's style with its heavy contour lines and masses of color was admirably suited to the woodblock technique and the prints of his pupils and followers are among the most sought after, although he himself did none.

In this scroll the attitude of the courtesan as she stops to look back was one frequently employed in *ukiyo-e* to allow the most advantageous display of the beautiful kimono. Most often the empty sleeve is left dangling, as in the Kimbell painting by Eishun, a follower of the Kaigetsudō. Here the courtesan sweeps up her full sleeve ahead of her, creating a dynamic counterthrust to the inclination of her head and her other backswept sleeve. The grace and broad, sensuous curves of this attitude are matched by the boldly painted decoration of her kimono. This elegant effect is tempered by the monumental stillness of the image as a whole which derives from the flat pattern imposed by the black outlines and from the courtesan's air of detachment. Dominating her elaborate robes, she conveys the extraordinary aloofness which makes the pensive courtesans of Kaigetsudō Ando timeless symbols of the floating world.

Inscription: Nihon giga Kaigetsudō kore wo zu su ("Kaigetsudō drew this picture for fun in the Japanese style.")

Seals: Two in lower right: *Kandoshi* and *Ando Giboku.*

Description: Against a tan background a standing woman turned to her left, her body arched, her face looking down to her right. She holds her long kimono gathered up in front and sweeps its left sleeve forward over her arm. Her blue kimono is lined in gold and painted with gold sails and green reeds behind ambiguous but effective white and black leaves and tendrils. Its obi is brown striped, tied in front. The underkimono is red with broad five-petaled flowers of white and gold and a tiny hatched pattern of tie-dye; below, half of her small bare foot protrudes. Her flowing hair is tied with a red ribbon.

Condition: Excellent.

Exhibition: Images du temps qui passe, Musée des arts décoratifs, Paris, 1966, cat. no. 32.

Collections: Saga collection. [N. V. Hammer, Inc., New York.]
Foundation Acquisition, AP 71.19.

Note:

1 Muneshige Narazaki, *Masterworks of Ukiyo-e: Early Paintings,* Tokyo and Palo Alto, Calif., 1968, p. 16.

Additional Reference:

Nihonga Taisei, *(Great Collection of Japanese Paintings),* Tokyo, 1931–34, vol. 41, pl. 2.

Ogata Kenzan, 1663–1743
Tea Bowl with bamboo leaf design
Late Seventeenth or early Eighteenth Century

Stoneware, glazes and colored enamels,
2 3/8 × 4 3/4 (diam.) in. (6.2 × 12 cm.)

Among the three great masters of painted ceramics of the Edo period, Ogata Kenzan "did the most to elevate the craft to the rank of a recognized art."[1] He developed an imaginative ceramic style whose salient characteristic is a consistent harmony between the suave dignity of his painted designs and the sober precision of his ceramic forms. Distinguished by masterly brushwork and solid forthright shapes, Kenzan's ceramic idiom initiated a tradition that has been enormously influential on generations of ceramicists, even to the present day.

Having turned as a young man to Zen meditation as a basis for his aesthetic ideas, Kenzan's style developed a restrained assurance that contrasts with the more exuberant mode of his equally renowned older brother, the decorative painter Ogata Korin, 1658–1716. Reared in a family with strong artistic interests, the brothers were well acquainted with the many writers and artists of the Kyoto area. Kenzan may have known and was certainly influenced by the first of the three great ceramicists of the Edo period, Ninsei, who is regarded as the major innovator of enamel decoration on stoneware.[2] Kenzan became the inheritor of Ninsei's tradition during the period from about 1689 to about 1712, when he lived at Omura and Narutaki. Even though he had moved to these rural retreats from the bustling life of nearby Kyoto, he maintained association with that vibrant center of artistic activity, particularly with his brother who painted designs on a number of Kenzan's ceramic pieces.

The refined simplicity of this bowl's austere shape and the emphatic colors of its bold design are typical of the ceramics that Kenzan is thought to have done at Narutaki. His early training as a painter is certainly evident in its powerful asymmetrical design and the superb brushwork whose thinness and variations in tone are evocative of ink painting. The sensitive disposition of the large leaves clearly reveals the simple and incisive qualities of Kenzan's style. Painted in a muted harmony of earthen pigments, these blades "grow up" quite naturally from the base in varying directions and aspects, overlapping each other and occasionally appearing to extend beyond the lip. Laid on a lustrous creamy ground, some of the grass blades are defined by richly textured single strokes of opaque matte brown while others reveal an underlying glaze of pale yellow-green beneath very spare dry strokes of a thin layer of brown.

Kenzan's thorough knowledge of the aesthetics of tea taste is quite evident in this bowl's painted design. The sharp-edged bamboo leaves, the contrasting colors and textures of the glazes, and the crisp silhouette of its shape are carefully balanced to produce a vessel that is designed to appeal to different senses during the extended ritual of serving, drinking and quiet conversation. The large scale of the leaf pattern has an intimacy of design that is only gradually perceived when it is realized that the same motif covers both interior and exterior surfaces. Furthermore, the ascetic effect of the lean dry strokes that define the brown blades of grass imbues this bowl with *shibui,* the austere quality that was so highly prized by the tea masters.

Inscription: Within the ring foot, two characters in brown paint form the signature of Kenzan.

Description: Straight-sided bowl, flaring slightly toward the top, with a low foot. On both interior and exterior the cream-colored ground is decorated with leaf designs in blackish-brown and a pale green, streaked with brown. A lustrous transparent glaze with a fine crackle pattern covers the background and the greenish leaves but not the brown leaves and brown rim which are substantially matte. The unglazed bevel and shallow recess of the crispy cut ring foot reveal the dense, hard body of fine greyish-white clay.

Condition: Excellent. The crackle pattern in the bottom of the interior is emphasized by faint staining.

Exhibitions: None known.

Collections: [J. Pierre Dubosc, Paris.]
Foundation Acquisition, AP 69.9.

Notes:

1 Peter Swann, *Art of China, Korea and Japan*, New York, 1963, p. 254.

2 The year of Ninsei's death is not clearly established. He may have died in the early 1660s, but Bernard Leach believes that he lived until 1699 and passed his private notebook on ceramic techniques directly to Kenzan. See Leach, *Kenzan and his Tradition*, New York, 1967, pp. 81–83, and Soame Jenyns, *Japanese Pottery*, London, 1971, pp. 219–20.

Ogata Kenzan, 1663–1743
Tea Bowl with reed design
Early Eighteenth Century

Stoneware, colored glazes and enamels,
$2\frac{3}{4} \times 5\frac{3}{4}$ (diam.) in. (6.9×13.1 cm.)

Within the wide scope of tea ceremony aesthetics, the sense of materiality is a fundamental concern that was consistently pursued in a variety of approaches. It ranged from delight in designs dominated by naturally occurring chance effects to those having an unassuming naturalness that was deliberately achieved through artful dexterity.

That Ogata Kenzan was an accomplished master of the "controlled accidents" of the latter approach is quite evident in the expressive combination of motifs in the design of this bowl. The apparently fortuitous irregularity of the bottom edge of the dark green ground that drapes down from the rim was, in fact, established before its application. Its undulating outline was deliberately defined by the absence of the white ground that was initially applied elsewhere. The seemingly natural disposition of the bent shapes of the long grey and black reeds is equally purposeful. Their graceful outlines are intentionally calculated to form countercurves that complement and echo the round shape of the bowl. Moreover, they are carefully and evenly distributed over the surface, intersecting and overlapping to form a sinuous open pattern that integrates the green areas into the overall design.

The artful informality of these deliberately controlled motifs is emphasized by their contrast with other effects which are inherent in the material or the technique. The tremulous edges of the reeds reveal the slight waver of the hand in a long extended brushstroke, at the same time evoking the natural distortions of windblown, water-soaked reeds. In the white ground, the pebbly texture and numerous random black specks are intrinsic qualities of the enamel that were deliberately preserved, just as the small rough contractions in the thick green glaze at the bottom of the interior are serendipitous contrasts to its otherwise rich luster.

The reed motif on this bowl has been called a *Musashino* design, referring to the name of a large marshy area with high grasses on the outskirts of Edo (Tokyo). Its appearance here might indicate that Kenzan made this bowl between about 1712 and 1731 when he is thought to have lived near Edo.[1]

Inscription: Within the ring foot, characters in brown paint form the signature of Kenzan.

Description: Curving-sided bowl on a high foot. Decorated with long intersecting strokes of thin grey and black paint, a pebbly surfaced, creamy white ground covers approximately half the interior and exterior. On the remainder, a brilliant mint-green ground covers the bottom of the interior, most of the areas adjacent to the rim and an irregular shape encompassing the foot. The unglazed recess and ring foot ($\frac{7}{16} \times 2\frac{1}{16}$ in.) reveal a hard body of slightly granular cream clay.

Condition: Excellent. The crackle pattern of the interior is articulated by faint staining.

Exhibitions: None known.

Collections: [J. Pierre Dubosc, Paris.]
Foundation Acquisition, AP 71.10.

Note:

1 Soame Jenyns, *Japanese Pottery*, London, 1971, pp. 221, 223, who notes that according to some writers Kenzan may have moved to the Edo area as late as 1731.

Baiōken Eishun, active about 1720–1750
Courtesan in a Procession
Painted about 1720–30

Ink, color and *gofun* on paper, 35 7/16 × 17 5/16 in. (90 × 44 cm.)

Little is known about Eishun other than that he was a follower of the Kaigetsudō (see Kaigetsudō Ando, *Standing Beauty*) and like them painted pictures of the courtesans who lived in the Yoshiwara, entertainment quarter of Edo (Tokyo). Depictions of the courtesan's procession, showing a stately courtesan of the *tayû* rank followed by one or more female attendants and a male retainer holding an umbrella over the *tayû* as an emblem of her status, were apparently quite popular during the 1720s and early 1730s when the Kimbell version was painted. It is hard to say when the subject originated; a version in the Gale Collection is dated by Jack Hillier to the final decade of the seventeenth century.[1] The *Nishikawa Fude no Yama* of about 1720 opens with a double-page illustration of this subject.[2] It appears twice in Sukenobu's *Ehon Tokiwagusa* of 1730 where it is used to introduce the sections dealing with the pleasure quarters of Kyoto and Osaka respectively. A similar procession, with an older woman rather than a male retainer holding the umbrella, appears at the beginning of the second volume of Sukenobu's *Hyakunin Jorô Shina-sadame* of 1723. Such processions were a daily occurrence in the Yoshiwara as we learn from Seikaku, a chronicler of the period, who chided those who followed the fashions set by the courtesans: "A courtesan's daily parade of splendour is made in the cause of earning a living. Amateur beauties ... can manage well enough without dressing in layers of conspicuous silks."[3]

In this painting the *tayû* turns to look at her young attendant who pads along happily wearing the long-sleeved *furisode* reserved for unmarried girls. The courtesan's pose as she turns to look back, her

full left sleeve hanging empty at her side, was given its classic formulation by the Kaigetsudō artists and appears again and again in their work and that of their followers. The same basic pose also appears in the so-called "Beauties of the Three Capitals" prints which became fashionable in the late 1720s.

Another Eishun painting is in many respects very close to this one.[4] It shows a courtesan in an almost identical pose turning to look at a girl attendant, whose pose is also very close to that of the girl in this picture. The two figures stand further apart, however, and there are other adjustments in their relationship to one another; but the biggest difference is in the absence of the male servant. In the Kimbell work the retainer and his umbrella form an interesting addition to the composition; he is carefully distinguished as separate and subordinate by his clothes and position, as well as by his disinterested air.

Inscription: Signed at the lower left: *Baiōken.*

Description: Three figures walking left, a woman, young girl and man holding an umbrella. The man, dressed in pale brown (considered the sign of prosperous times)[5] and wearing pale blue *tabi* socks, carries a tan umbrella with a broad, dull blue border. The courtesan turns back to her left, holding up her kimono in her right hand with her left hand drawn up inside the kimono. It is of a fashionable pale blue, lined in the red which symbolized happiness and good fortune.[6] The kimono darkens to a deep blue sprigged with flowers on the skirt and has a single white circle on the sleeve. Her underkimono is light orange and the obi, front-tied, is dark green with a black geometric stamp. The courtesan's hair is smoothly knotted and stuck with a single comb. The girl, barefoot like the *tayû,* wears a red-lined *furisode* tied with trailing green ribbons at the sleeves. The *furisode* is red with large, five-petaled white flowers at the top fading to a solid pale blue at the bottom. Broad stripes of brown and white appear on the full part of the sleeves, and her obi, tied in back, is dark blue with scrolled flowers. Her hair is tied up with a white ribbon. All are set against a plain tan background.

Condition: Good. Small losses have been filled and inpainted.

Exhibitions: None known.

Collections: Baron Seikai Kuki. Ryuichi Kuki by 1932. [N.V. Hammer, Inc., New York.] Foundation Acquisition, AP 70.10.

Notes:

1 Jack Hillier, *Japanese Paintings and Prints in the Collection of Mr. and Mrs. Richard P. Gale,* Minneapolis, 1970, vol. I, no. 18.

2 Donald Jenkins, *Ukiyo-e Prints and Paintings: The Primitive Period,* Art Institute of Chicago, 1971, cat. no. 172.

3 Sherman E. Lee, *Japanese Decorative Style,* Cleveland Museum of Art, 1961, p. 95.

4 *Ukiyo-e Taika Shûsei,* Tokyo, 1931–32, vol. 3, pl. 44.

5 Helen Benton Minnich, *Japanese Costume,* Rutland, Vt., and Tokyo, 1963, p. 343.

6 Minnich, p. 342.

Footed Dish, Nabeshima ware
Early Eighteenth Century

Porcelain, blue underglaze and colored enamels, 2 1/4×8 5/8 (diam.) in. (5.8×22.1 cm.)

Of all the Arita wares from Kyushu Island in Southern Japan, the finest in quality is Nabeshima ware, named for a local noble family for whose exclusive use it was made.[1] Since only perfectly conceived and executed pieces were accepted, the quality of the porcelain, design, and enameling technique in Nabeshima ware is consistently superior. Generally, its carefully calculated designs dominate the surface with a characteristically cool and deliberate feeling.

The shape of this piece, a shallow bowl on a ring foot, is typical of Nabeshima ware, as are the blue comb-tooth pattern on the foot and the blue floral designs on the underside of the bowl. The work's restrained character derives from its subtle design and intricate enameling technique, evident in the discretely rendered leaf veins of blue underglaze that show through the overlying transparent glaze and in the modulated distribution of the red-orange cherry blossoms. A very subtle device is employed in the enameling of the leaves: if a leaf surface is yellow enamel, the tip is green enamel, and if the surface is green, the tip is yellow.

The circular *mon* motif of three dark blue "commas" is the heraldic design of a Japanese noble family that was used somewhat as a coat of arms was used in Medieval Europe. Its presence suggests that this plate may have been part of a service decorated for a particular family which, however, cannot be identified because this *mon* motif was used by at least ten families.[2]

Description: Shallow bowl on a raised foot (3/4 × 4 5/8 in.). On the exterior, in blue underglaze, there are four floral motifs on the underside and a comb-tooth pattern around the foot. The interior has a horizontal design, with a pale grey "cloud" above and three parallel stripes, in blue underglaze, below. Across the middle is a design of three blue *mon* motifs, in a field of five-petaled cherry blossoms and foliage in blue underglaze and red-orange and yellow enamels.

Condition: Very good. Light hairline scratches. Partial loss of enamel in two yellow leaves; crazing and cleavage in several other yellow leaves.

Exhibitions: None known.

Collections: [N. V. Hammer, Inc., New York.] Foundation Acquisition, AP 68.12.

Notes:

[1] Richard S. Cleveland, introd., *200 Years of Japanese Porcelain*, City Art Museum of St. Louis, 1970, p. 15, and Peter Swann, *The Art of China, Korea and Japan*, New York, 1963, p. 252.

[2] V. F. Weber, *Ko-ji-Hô-ten*, Paris, 1923, vol. I, pp. 33–34; vol. II, appendix IX, p. 78, pl. 27, no. 353.

Maruyama Ōkyo, 1733–1795
Crows
Painted in 1766

Pair of six-fold screens, ink and gold on paper, each 60 1/2 × 141 5/8 in. (153.5 × 359.6 cm.)

The eighteenth century in Japan saw a new influx of realism in painting best exemplified in the innovative work of Maruyama Ōkyo. A major factor in the development of his style was his direct and intensive study of nature. In the Kimbell screens every attitude of the crows as they dart up, swoop down and rest on the ground reveals the most patient and detailed observation of actual birds. The malevolent, scraggly look of crows is wonderfully captured. The lifelike stance of the two crows under bamboo on the right screen is particularly convincing; one can almost hear their raucous cries. Ōkyo was obviously delighted with the challenge of conveying the rapacious nature of these birds and their varying attitudes. His interest in natural forms led to his being "strongly criticized by the existing painting schools for being too concerned with physical appearances . . . no more than a slave to subject matter . . . entirely lacking in dignity. . . ."[1] Nevertheless, his work enjoyed wide popular appeal.

The Kimbell screens are bold and striking in effect, retaining the monumental sweep of earlier screen painting while employing different technical means. Ōkyo's birds "are not generalized blots like the flying birds of Kano, nor are they all line like the careful birds of Sesshu."[2] The backbone of his style is in his technique of laying down the ink with the side of the brush rather than drawing with its tip in the more conventional calligraphic fashion.[3] A fused brushstroke is thus achieved; among its mixed ink tones strong lights and darks predominate. Through this technique Ōkyo rendered details such as the knobby claws and tufts over the beaks of the crows and contrasted the long wing feathers and downy chest feathers without his image becoming finicky and overworked. The immediacy of the brushwork is enhanced by the artist's practice of isolating a single motif against the sketchiest background. The complex silhouettes of the different configurations of crows stand out compellingly against the pale gold washes of the background which suggest vast airy spaces.

Influences from Chinese and Western realism were additional factors in the development of Ōkyo's naturalism. The somewhat awkward attitude of the ascending bird high on the right screen might be the ambiguous result of a misunderstood application of the principles of foreshortening. Whatever his experiments, Ōkyo had developed his own style fairly early as is evident from the 1766 date of the Kimbell screens.[4] His satisfaction with more successful representations is reflected in his repetition of several motifs in later works: the pair of flying birds on the left screen appears in approximately the same configuration on screens of geese in the Enmanin temple, Kyoto, and the clump of bamboo on the right is similar to one in *Bamboo in Wind and Rain*, now in the Enkōji temple.[5]

Inscription: In the lower left of left-hand screen: *Hei-ju Chū-tō Heian Ōkyo* ["Winter of 1766, Heian Ōkyo"].

Seals: Two, in the lower left of left-hand screen: *Ōkyo no In* and *Chū-sen*.

Description: Pair of six-fold screens painted in *suiboku* (black ink) technique with four crows and bamboo to the right, five crows and plum branches at the left. Misty, evocative space is suggested by a background of gold washes. The crows are carefully disposed, from right to left, in rhythms of 2-1-1 on the right and 1-2-2 on the left.

On the right screen two crows under bamboo caw at a third who flies toward them; a fourth darts up to the left. On the left screen a crow coming in over a softly suggested stream brings his wings forward in a landing attitude. Two crows perch in plum branches, one looking down and one up at two crows winging by overhead. The general composition is spare, the contrast between near and far, light and dark, exaggerated.

Condition: Excellent.

Exhibitions: None known.

Collections: Bunzo Nakanishi collection, Kyoto.
[Mayuyama & Co., Ltd., Tokyo.]
Foundation Acquisition, AP 69.11 a, b.

Notes:

1 Noma Seiroku, *The Arts of Japan: Late Medieval to Modern*, trans. by Glenn T. Webb, Tokyo and Palo Alto, Calif., 1967, vol. II, p. 116.

2 Ernest F. Fenollosa, *Epochs of Chinese and Japanese Art*, New York, 1963, (reprint of 1913 ed.), vol. II, p. 170.

3 Robert Treat Paine and Alexander Soper, *The Art and Architecture of Japan*, Baltimore, 1960, p. 89.

4 Tanio Nakamura of the Tokyo National Museum notes in private correspondence: "It is important that the seal of Ōkyo saying 'Ōkyo no In' was used by him for the first time since from the third year of Meiwa."

5 Nakamura correspondence. The screens, *Flying Geese*, were also done by Ōkyo during the Meiwa era (1764–71).

Wine Cup and Stand, celadon ware

Twelfth Century

Stoneware, celadon glaze, overall height, 3 7/8 in. (10 cm); stand, 5 3/4 (diam.) in. (14.5 cm.)

Celadon glazed wares of the Koryo period are distinguished by muted colors, gently rounded naturalistic forms and restrained decoration. Developed during the first two centuries of the Koryo Dynasty, they initially reflected the forms and designs of Chinese celadon wares of the Sung Dynasty. By the twelfth century, however, a distinctive reticence of ceramic expression had become a salient feature of these Korean wares, which are thought to have been made not for daily use, but to contain burial offerings.

The graceful, restrained decoration and simple form of this cup-and-stand set suggest that it may be a relatively early example of mature Koryo celadon and date from about the mid-twelfth century. Laid on a pinkish-grey body, the bluish-green color of the glaze is typical of Korean celadon glazes which are consistently modulated within a fairly predictable range that is rarely very bright or pale. Sets with shapes similar to this one are rather common. It has an unpretentious intimacy of design that is typically Korean, evident in the light indentations and gently curved outlines. This simplicity and the small amount of decorative embellishment suggest that this set is a relatively early example in a stylistic development that led to more ornate designs. The plain surface is articulated only by the engraved lobes on the cup's exterior; three small fish are lightly incised about the bottom of the cup's interior and there are three small floral motifs on the flange. Cup-and-stand sets of probably later date often bear markedly incised (or molded) lotus-leaf patterns around the curving shoulder of the platform[1] or more extensive incised or inlay patterns on the exterior of the cup[2] and on the flange of the stand.[3]

Description: Six-lobed cup and stand of celadon glazed stoneware. The cup, 2 3/8 × 3 1/4 (diam.) in. (6 × 8.2 cm.), has straight sides and a scalloped edge defining engraved lobes that descend into a short splayed foot. Three circling fish are incised on the bottom of the interior. The 3/8 in.-deep recess of the foot is glazed; four spur marks on the rim have been ground smooth. The stand has a raised central platform bordered by a bead rim with a faintly incised circular design of thirteen swirling petals in the center. The raised flange, with six light indentions about the edge, bears faintly incised floral motifs in three lobes. The 1 1/4 in.-deep recess of the base is glazed; its circular foot ring bears the remains of five or six spur marks that have been ground smooth. The light-grey porcelaneous body is covered with a thin blue-green celadon glaze with no crackle.

Condition: Excellent. Only several typical scattered glaze imperfections affect the appearance of this otherwise pristine piece.

Exhibitions: None known.

Collections: [N.V. Hammer, Inc., New York.] Foundation Acquisition, AP 70.12 a, b.

Notes:

1 Two such pieces in the National Museum of Korea were published by R.T. Paine and H. P. Stern, *Masterpieces of Korean Art*, National Gallery of Art, Washington, D.C., 1957, cat. nos. 82, 83, illus. See also: Robert P. Griffing, *The Art of the Korean Potter*, Asia House Gallery, New York, 1968, cat. no. 42, illus. p. 80.

2 A cup with extensive exterior incising is illustrated by G. St. G. M. Gompertz, *Korean Celadon . . .*, London, 1963, pl. 12 A. Another with inlay pattern is illustrated by Michael Sullivan, *Chinese Ceramics . . . in the Collection of Sir Alan and Lady Barlow*, London, 1963, cat. no. C. 299, pl. 139 a.

3 Other elaborately decorated examples with floral inlay on both the cup's exterior and the stand's wide rim are in the Hakone Art Museum, Japan, (see Gompertz, pl. 53 A) and the Daksoo Palace Museum of Fine Arts (see Paine and Stern, cat. no. 113, illus.).

Bowl, inlaid celadon ware
Twelfth or Thirteenth Century

Stoneware, dark green and white inlay, celadon glaze, 2 1/4 × 7 1/4 (diam.) in. (5.8 × 18.4 cm.)

The distinctive inlaid decoration known as *zōgan* is the major ceramic achievement of the Koryo Dynasty potters.[1] Its technique is a logical step beyond the earlier practice of cutting linear designs into soft clay. In *zōgan* ware, the valleys of the incised or stamped design were filled with white or black paste after which any excess slip was carefully scraped away before application of the overlying glaze.

This shallow bowl, from which wine or water may have been sipped, demonstrates the variety of decorative effects obtainable with this technique. The blossoms about the exterior and in the center of the interior medallions were stamped and then filled with white slip. Their nearly perfect circular outlines and slight imbalance of pattern reveal the imprint of a carefully carved relief mold that was gently pressed into the clay at a slight angle. The greenish black leaves and surrounding arabesque design of curling leaves are equally revealing of the deft freehand excavations of a v-shaped knife. However, the background of this curling foliage, rather than the leaves themselves, was cut and filled with white inlay. In this technique, known as "reverse inlay," the inlay thus outlines the foliage which has the grey-green color of the celadon glaze. Finally, the random crackle pattern of the glaze, which can only be influenced but not controlled by the potter, also contributes to the unassuming naturalness of this bowl's discreet decoration.

The combination of the deliberate and accidental variations inherent in these differing techniques imparts a gentle natural grace to the unpretentious decoration of this bowl. The occasional gaps or "skips" in the incised patterns and in the reverse inlay outlines complement the uneven impressions of the stamped designs and enliven the overall effect just as the typical sparing use of dark elements judiciously accents the predominantly white design.

Bowls of this shape and size are common, but they bear a considerable variety of decorative patterns.[2] One such bowl in the National Museum of Korea, bearing chrysanthemum head designs and elaborate reverse inlay in white similar to that of this bowl, is the earliest dated piece of inlaid celadon ware, having been found in a tomb dated to 1159. The assurance of its technique and design suggests, however, that the inlay technique had been fully mastered much earlier in the twelfth century.[3]

Description: Low, shallow bowl with curving sides, inlaid designs and greyish-green celadon glaze. About the side of the interior, edged by a scrolling white band below the lip, there is a band in reverse inlay of celadon-colored leaf scrolls with a white background containing four evenly spaced roundels. Each of these roundels, edged in dark-green, and another in the bottom, contains a circular design of a white chrysanthemum blossom and dark-green leaves. Four similar blossom and leaf designs are evenly spaced about the exterior between two bands of parallel lines. Within the shallow glazed recess of the low glazed foot ring are three sandy spur marks.

Condition: Very good. There are scattered imperfections in the glaze.

Exhibitions: None known.

Collections: [N. V. Hammer, Inc., New York.] Foundation Acquisition, AP 70.11.

Notes:

1 *Zōgan* means "inlay" in Japanese and corresponds to the less frequently used Korean *sanggam*. See G. St. G. M. Gompertz, *Korean Celadon . . .*, London, 1963, p. 62, note 1.

2 See R. T. Paine and H. P. Stern, *Masterpieces of Korean Art*, National Gallery of Art, Washington, D. C., 1957, cat. nos. 106–9, all illus.; also Robert P. Griffing, *The Art of the Korean Potter*, Asia House Gallery, New York, 1968, p. 39, cat. nos. 61, 62, both illus.

3 Chewon Kim and Gompertz, *The Ceramic Art of Korea*, London, 1961, p. 84, pl. 32.

Bottle, inlaid celadon ware

Late Twelfth or early Thirteenth Century

Stoneware, black and white inlay, celadon glaze, $12\,^3/_{16} \times 6\,^7/_8$ (diam.) in. (31×17.5 cm.)

The harmonious balance between natural forms and regular patterns found in the shape and decoration of this svelte vase endows it with the quiescent strength of a sturdy tree. Emphasis on the details and character of natural forms, as manifest in the gourd-like ribs and the twisting vine, is characteristic of twelfth-century Koryo celadon ware. Similarly shaped bottles of that period with lightly incised articulation of numerous convex ribs and no inlaid design appear to be the stylistic antecedents of this vase.[1] In the later thirteenth century the alternating disposition of ribs and inlaid vertical patterns on this and similar bottles[2] was apparently superseded by designs without ribbing and with more extensive inlay patterns.[3]

In this bottle an inlaid vertical design of incised black vines and leaves and stamped white blossoms is isolated in the center of each of the six panels. The sinuous vines ascend the sides, each supporting a staggered chain of blossoms until it approaches the constriction of the neck. There the pattern changes: the black vine disappears and is replaced by a row of three white blossoms and sets of black leaves, whose regular arrangement relates it rather emphatically to the corresponding rows of the adjacent panels. This discreet transformation of the same motif from a staggered pattern into a regular one subtly integrates its design with the shape of the bottle and is clear evidence of the potter's respect for the complementary character of decorative pattern and ceramic form.

Description: Teardrop-shaped bottle, with grey body, flared mouth and inlay designs. Indented lines, from the base to the constriction of the neck, define six panels with similar *mishima* designs of stamped chrysanthemum blossoms in white inlay and vines and leaves in black inlay. The crackled glaze varies from a cool green-grey on the bulge of the body to a warmer grey-tinted olive green on the neck and mouth. The mouth is glazed down to the constriction of the neck; the interior is unglazed. The low foot rim is unglazed and encloses a shallow, partially glazed recess to which considerable sand still adheres.

Condition: Good. There are some scattered "pinhole" voids in the glaze; on the flare of the mouth, most of the glaze has been skillfully resurfaced.

Exhibitions: None known.

Collections: [N.V. Hammer, Inc., New York.] Foundation Acquisition, AP 69.12.

Notes:

1 G. St. G. M. Gompertz, *Korean Celadon . . .*, London, 1963, illustrates, pl. 15, an early twelfth-century bottle (11.5 in. high) with no inlay or ribbing. Ribbed bottles without inlay are illustrated by Lorraine d'O. Warner, "Kōrai Celadon in America," *Eastern Art*, vol. 2, 1930, fig. 10 (40 cm. high), and by Robert P. Griffing, *The Art of the Korean Potter, Asia House Gallery*, New York, 1968, cat. no. 43, illus., twelfth century (13 5/8 in. high), Museum of Fine Arts, Boston, no. 11.1819.

2 Bottles comparable to this one, with alternating ribs and vertical inlay patterns, are in the Metropolitan Museum of Art, New York (see Warner, fig. 70, 34.9 cm. high), and the Museum of Fine Arts, Boston, no. 11.1816 (see Griffing, cat. no. 67, illus., thirteenth century, 15 5/8 in. high). Another bottle with a vertical inlay pattern of pairs of ascending floral vines and no indented ribs is in the collection of Jae Hung Yu (see *Korean Ceramics*, Museum of Far Eastern Antiquities, Stockholm, February–April, 1966, cat. no. 51, 31.5 cm. high).

3 Two thirteenth-century bottles with extensive horizontally disposed inlay designs are in the Freer Gallery of Art, Washington, D. C. (14 in. high), and a Japanese collection (13 in, high); see Gompertz, pls. 71, 76A, thirteenth century.

AFRICA

BINI TRIBE, THIRTEENTH OR FOURTEENTH (?) TO NINETEENTH CENTURY

Standing Oba
From Benin City
Late Eighteenth to Nineteenth Century

Bronze, 22 5/8 × 7 1/8 × 7 3/4 in. (57.4 × 18.1 × 19.7 cm.)

Silent and darkly enigmatic, *Standing Oba* is a representation of a Benin king, divine ruler of the Bini tribe. It is not intended as a portrait of a particular Oba, but rather as a generalized representation of the office. Cast in solid bronze, it is a weighty figure, surmounted by a twisted loop handle. Together with bronze memorial heads of past Obas, it would have adorned one of the royal ancestor altars, *aru-erha*, at which the elaborate state rituals were performed. It, therefore, reflects the highly formalized court art of the Oba's palace rather than the freer, more imaginative Bini tribal style.

The Kimbell *Standing Oba* displays what William Fagg refers to as typically African proportions,[1] its head forming more than one quarter of its full height. This disproportionate emphasis given to certain parts of the body, notably the head and hands, is undoubtedly associated with their importance as cult objects—the head signifying "the seat of judgment,"[2] the hand, man's power to accomplish things. In the case of the Oba, the cults of his head and hand had an even wider significance, involving the achievements and well-being of the entire kingdom.[3]

The annual sacrifices to the king's own head and to the heads of past Obas can be regarded as the central rite of the royal ancestor cult, and Benin art has survived today principally in the form of these bronze memorial heads. Full-length figures, such as the Kimbell *Standing Oba*, are exceedingly rare by comparison. For this reason most studies of Benin iconography have centered almost exclusively on the bronze heads.

According to legend, the technique of bronze casting was introduced into Benin about 1400 by a master craftsman, Iguegha, who was sent from the sacred city of Ife, in central Yorubaland, to instruct Bini craftsmen in the making of these memorial heads.[4] The earliest Benin bronzes were thin, fragile castings expressing a sensitive naturalism which derived from the classical style of Ife. However, by the mid-sixteenth century, with the arrival of copious supplies of Portuguese bronze,[5] these heads increased in size and weight, their emphasis gradually shifting from human qualities to an overelaboration of sumptuous detail, the coral bead ornamentation of collar and headdress eventually encasing and dominating the face.

While the basic iconography of the bronze memorial heads remained essentially unchanged over the centuries, tradition has long held that in the reign of Oba Osemwede (1816–48) elaborate wing pieces were added to the crown, together with appendages representing carnelian beads wired to protrude on either side of the face. It now appears likely that these features originated as early as the late eighteenth century.[6] This is particularly pertinent in determining the date of the Kimbell *Standing Oba*, whose headdress bears these embellishments. It should be noted, however, that in comparison to later examples, the wings on the Kimbell piece are relatively stubby, not yet extended nor exaggerated. The carnelian bead appendage is equally unobtrusive, falling in a graceful curve from the edge of the cap to the line of the collar. Indeed, it would appear that the Kimbell figure may be a transitional piece, dating from the very beginning of the "wing" tradition, because it carries over a curious element from an earlier period. Underneath the wing to the viewer's right, and rising visibly above it, is a feather of the type which might have adorned the cap of a warrior in one of the bronze plaques of the middle period (about 1550–1650).

While the combined use of wing and feather does not seem to have appeared on the bronze memorial heads, it does occur on other full-length standing figures which bear comparison to the Kimbell example. *Figure of Oba*, in the British Museum,[7] is more naturalistically conceived than the Kimbell Oba, thereby suggesting an earlier date. The headdress of the British figure is distinctive because its wings curve forward horizontally rather than vertically, clinging to the cap with a feather rising jauntily from the right side. In its pose, facial expression, overall proportions, and in such details as the delineation of the eyes, tribal marks and body scarification, it is reminiscent of works of the middle period.

Figure of a King, in the Chicago Natural History Museum,[8] appears to be more nearly contemporary to the Kimbell Oba, sharing similar iconographic details. Like the Kimbell figure, he stands rigidly posed, grasping in his right hand the leaf-shaped ceremonial sword, *eben*, in his left, a gong. Both are lavishly attired in beaded collar, netted shirt and winged headdress with feather, but the Kimbell Oba has a greater assurance, a more majestic presence.

It is perhaps inevitable that Benin art which served an intricately ritualistic religion should itself eventually become schematized, reduced to a

formula, as found in the elaborate stylization of its later works. In the Kimbell piece, however, this stylization has not yet completely extinguished the human qualities of the subject. Although he is almost completely covered by his ornate coral-beaded regalia, he is not overpowered by it. Indeed, his personality dominates, expressing his absolute mastery and control. His eyes, widely spaced, are watchful and all-seeing; his nose and mouth are firmly structured, adding to his positive presence. If he is flamboyant, it is with a complete self-awareness of his religious and political role as a symbol of divine kingship.

Description: About one-third life-size figure of an Oba in bronze, surmounted by a twisted loop. He has strongly Negroid features. His eyes are outlined with deeply incised eyelashes and the pupils protrude prominently, giving him a bright-eyed look. His eyes are further emphasized by radiating lines above and circular punch marks forming a triangular pattern below. Evenly spaced above the eyes are three tribal marks, traditional scarification of the Bini. The Oba is richly attired in ceremonial garb including the winged headdress, which terminates in a cylindrical pike; coral-beaded collar with biblike extensions front and back, and kilt ornamented with two rows of guilloche pattern alternating with two rows of mixed *eben* and conventionalized head motifs. His kilt is bound up in a band behind his left shoulder. He is further adorned with wristlets and anklets, bands of beads across his chest and back and a band of bells around his hips. In his powerful hands he holds attributes of his office, which are attached to his shoulders with supports which would have acted as gates during the bronze casting process.

Condition: Very good. There is a slight loss to the rim of the wing piece to the viewer's left.

Exhibitions: None known.

Collections: Pitt Rivers Museum, Farnham, Dorset.[9] [Ben Heller, Inc., New York.]
Foundation Acquisition, AP 70.4.

Notes:

[1] William Fagg, *Tribes and Forms in African Art*, New York, 1965, p. 32. Benin bronzes were so technically advanced that when they first appeared in London after the capture of Benin City by the British in 1897, their origins were sought in a non-African tradition.

[2] W. Forman, B. Forman and Philip Dark, *Benin Art*, London, 1960, p. 15.

[3] Fagg, *Divine Kingship in Africa*, London, 1970, p. 20.

[4] See Forman, Forman and Dark, p. 26, for a complete description of the *cire-perdue*, or lost-wax technique of casting.

[5] From this period, the weight of the memorial heads quadrupled. See: William Fagg and Herbert List, *Nigerian Images: The Splendor of African Sculpture*, New York, 1963, p. 35.

[6] Fagg and List, *Nigerian Images*, p. 37.

[7] Forman, Forman and Dark, cat. nos. 60–62, illus.

[8] Dark, *The Art of Benin: A Catalogue of an Exhibition of the A. W. F. Fuller and Chicago Natural History Museum*, Chicago, 1962, cat. no. 103, illus. pl. XXIV.

[9] Lt. Gen. Pitt Rivers, *Antique Works of Art from Benin*, London, 1900, reprinted New York, 1968, p. 62, lists the Kimbell Oba as having been obtained from the Liverpool Museum.

Additional Reference:

Felix von Luschan, *Die Altertümer von Benin*, Berlin, 1919, reprinted New York, 1968, pp. 294–96, presents a different interpretation of the Standing Oba as the Sword-King, *Ebere-König*, personifying the ceremonial sword, *eben*.

PRE-COLUMBIAN AMERICA

Seated Figure
From Veracruz, Mexico
Middle Pre-Classic Period, about 800–300 B.C.

Whiteware, 10 7/8 × 9 1/8 × 6 1/8 in.
(27.7 × 23.2 × 15.6 cm.)

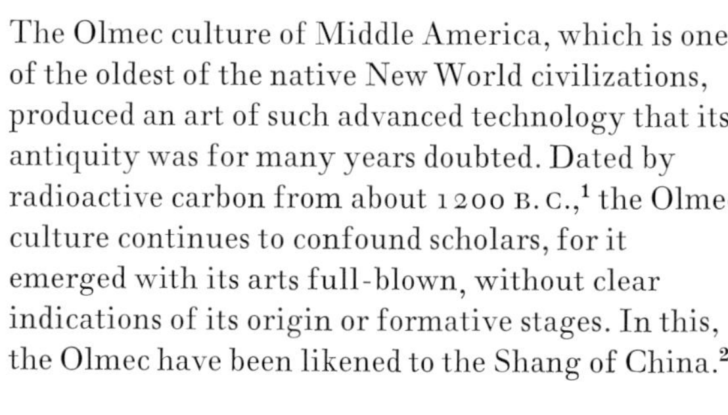

The Olmec culture of Middle America, which is one of the oldest of the native New World civilizations, produced an art of such advanced technology that its antiquity was for many years doubted. Dated by radioactive carbon from about 1200 B.C.,[1] the Olmec culture continues to confound scholars, for it emerged with its arts full-blown, without clear indications of its origin or formative stages. In this, the Olmec have been likened to the Shang of China.[2]

The Kimbell *Seated Figure* embodies the enigmatic quality which permeates Olmec art, at once attracting and mystifying the viewer. His snarling face dominates his stunted trunk. Though small in stature, he is a forceful figure of enormous vitality. Seated upright, with a hands-on-hips gesture, he appears at once impudent and challenging. His elongated, deformed head rests on a thick-set neck, joining a powerful squat body. Initially the proportions of the figure suggest its resemblance to a human baby. However, the short arms and legs reflect strength and physical stamina rather than childlike chubbiness. No attempt has been made at naturalism. Two small breasts are indicated in a tentative way, but they bear no relationship to actual anatomy. Though nude, the figure remains of indeterminate sex.

While he is conceived in human forms and might even be characterized as Mongoloid in appearance, this *Seated Figure* has an indefinable quality which might best be described in terms of a snarling animal. The large voracious mouth, trapezoidal in shape, has been likened to that of a jaguar, the dreaded animal which roamed the ancient jungles and was worshipped as a deity by the Olmec. This man-jaguar concept permeates Olmec art, where the combination of jaguar and human features occurs in varying degrees, from the jaguar in slightly humanized form to the human with only superficial jaguar traits. The Kimbell figure falls into this second category and is thought to be a representation of the powerful Olmec rain god.[3]

The hollow clay construction of the Kimbell *Seated Figure* incorporates a technique which made possible the execution of large-scale ceramic figures and permitted the Olmec artist to model in the rounded, simplified forms which apparently satisfied his aesthetic ideal. While the Olmec were primarily stonecarvers known for their lapidary skills, their competence carried over into their modeling of clay. An examination of the Kimbell figure reveals that they were able to impart to clay surfaces a smooth, burnished finish which has the quality of highly polished stone.

In pose, the Kimbell *Seated Figure* can be compared to the seated child in the collection of Dr. and Mrs. Josué Sáenz, Mexico City,[4] which has an animation and childlike vitality. Both share the device of the hands resting on the legs which, in the case of the Kimbell figure, become inseparably joined. A similar pose is repeated in the sitting male figure in the collection of F. Feuchtwanger, Mexico,[5] which is engagingly alert and has more infantile features than either of the former examples. A more naturalistic portrayal of the Olmec seated figure as a baby can be found in the hollow figurine from Las Bocas, now in the Museum of Primitive Art, New York,[6] whose plump body is truly infant-like, as he sits with head thrust back, passively sucking his finger.

The Kimbell *Seated Figure* might bear superficial resemblances to such benign and childlike images, but one has only to recall his savage mouth with sharply filed teeth to be reminded of his essential animal ferocity. He may, indeed, be identified as one of the "Jaguar's Children."[7]

Description: Seated baby-like figure, in clay. He sits upright, with broad shoulders and muscular arms, his short legs pointed outward. The sculpture is hollow, with firing vents provided at the top back of the head, on the bottom of the figure, underneath the arms and through the open mouth. The head is elongated and flattened, curving gently backward. The hair, painted black with an incised design, has the appearance of a helmet, with straps hanging down on either side of the face. Traces of black paint mark the upper ears and soles of the feet. The white, burnished surface of the face and upper torso is interrupted in the area beneath the navel and reappears on the legs below the knees. Vestiges of pale orange accent the lips and lower ears. The eyes are elongated, diagonal slits, with deeply drilled pupils. The nose is small, placed high in the face. The mouth is the most prominent feature, the widely flaring top lip curving upward almost to the nose and the lower lip protruding conspicuously. The ears are notably elongated and stylized, with large, pierced lobes.

Condition: Fair. The head, once broken from the body, has been reattached with no apparent loss. This is an ancient break, repaired in Pre-Columbian times with a tar-like material. His right foot is missing below the instep, his left foot damaged in the area of his upper foot and toes. A number of fractures in the body of the figure have been repaired and filled.

Exhibitions: None known.

Collections: Foundation Acquisition, AP 71.2.

Seated Woman
From Guerrero, Mexico
Middle Pre-Classic Period, about 800–300 B.C.

Clay, 4 3/8 × 3 1/8 × 2 7/8 in. (11.1 × 8 × 7.3 cm.)

Notes:

[1] Michael D. Coe, "San Lorenzo and the Olmec Civilization" in *Dumbarton Oaks Conference on the Olmec* (Oct. 28–29, 1967), ed. by Elizabeth P. Benson, Washington, D. C., 1968, pp. 60–61.

[2] Coe, p. 64.

[3] Coe, *The Jaguar's Children: Pre-Classic Central Mexico*, the Museum of Primitive Art, New York, pub. Greenwich, Conn., 1965, pp. 14, 105.

[4] Elizabeth Kennedy Easby and John F. Scott, *Before Cortés: Sculpture of Middle America*, Metropolitan Museum of Art, New York, 1970, cat. no. 19, illus.

[5] *Master Works of Mexican Art: From Pre-Columbian Times to the Present*, Los Angeles County Museum of Art, 1964, p. 10, cat. no. 145, illus. p. 13.

[6] Coe, *Jaguar's Children*, illus. pp. 104, 106, 107.

[7] Coe, *Jaguar's Children*, p. 105.

Modeled in clay with a deliberate economy of means, the Kimbell *Seated Woman* has a lively presence which belies her small size. She is obviously one of the people of the village, a simple woman with a broad peasant face. She sits erect with arched back, her head leaning forward, tilted as if in conversation with a companion. She is a person completely at home in her environment, self-assured, with a benevolent interest in all that is happening around her. Only slightly more than four inches tall, she was conceived as a tomb figurine to be buried with the dead as a companion in the future life. Such figures were not thought to have served any religious function. They exist today as a prime source of information on ancient life, mirroring the customs, hairstyles and dress of the times.

The Kimbell figure was excavated near Xochipala, a remote village in the state of Guerrero. While this region is geographically part of Western Mexico, its art is related to the great Olmec civilization, which so vastly influenced the various other cultures of Middle America. Guerrero is rich in archaeological sites, but there has been little scientific investigation of this area and it remains the least known of Mexico's regions.

The features of the Kimbell *Seated Woman* are typically Olmec, but they are portrayed naturalistically, unlike the highly stylized representations of the colossal heads from La Venta and San Lorenzo. Her head is flattened and elongated, reflecting the cranial deformation of the skull which was practiced by the Olmec.[1] Her features are indicated with quick, deft strokes. The eyes are small, slightly slanted, with the pupils clearly defined by a round hole, giving her an alert look. The nose and mouth are proportionately larger and coarser, which becomes particularly apparent when viewed in profile. The nose is broad at the base, with nostrils prominently indicated. The mouth with its flaring lips recalls the ancient man-jaguar theme, but here there is no indication of ferocity. On the contrary, hers is an amiable, highly sociable expression.

In contrast to the impressionistic modeling of her features, the hair is painstakingly delineated by parallel incised lines, which seemingly correspond strand for strand. It is parted in the middle and falls into a stylized arrangement, spilling down her back in a long flat panel.[2] This same fineness of detail and careful attention to decorative pattern can also be found in the border motif of the shawl and the definition of the toes.

The artist was a highly skilled technician with a complete mastery of his material. No part of the figure is overworked; the whole has an immediacy and sureness of execution. The body, wrapped in a shawl, is treated as a simplified, monumental mass. When viewed frontally, the figure seems perfectly straightforward; when viewed from the side, the artistry of the piece reveals itself—the thrust of the shoulders, the gracefully arched back, the curve of the arm beneath the shawl.

318 *Description:* Small seated figurine of a woman, in solid clay. Her body is flattened and broadened, her left shoulder slightly higher than the right. She is cloaked in a simple shawl which wraps around her body from right to left, covering her crossed arms and extending past her knees. Her legs are crossed right over left; her right foot is gracefully arched. She has highly individualized features; her face is framed by a carefully arranged hairdo, and she wears earrings. In profile, she has a strong chin, thick lips, and her teeth protrude. There are faint traces of red paint in the incised lines of her hair in back and slight overall indications of original white pigment.

Condition: Good. The head has been broken off and reattached to the torso. There are minor losses in the area where the shawl overlaps.

Exhibitions: None known.

Collections: Foundation Acquisition, AP 71.4.

Notes:

[1] Michael D. Coe, *The Jaguar's Children: Pre-Classic Central Mexico*, the Museum of Primitive Art, New York, pub. Greenwich, Conn., 1965, p. 26.

[2] This same convention appears centuries later in the large, hollow Chinesco figures of Nyarit, Western Mexico, where the delineation of the hair becomes the most striking feature, falling in long, straight, finely incised strands. See: Gordon F. Ekholm, introd., *Ancient Mexico and Central America*, the American Museum of Natural History, New York, 1970, illus. p. 18.

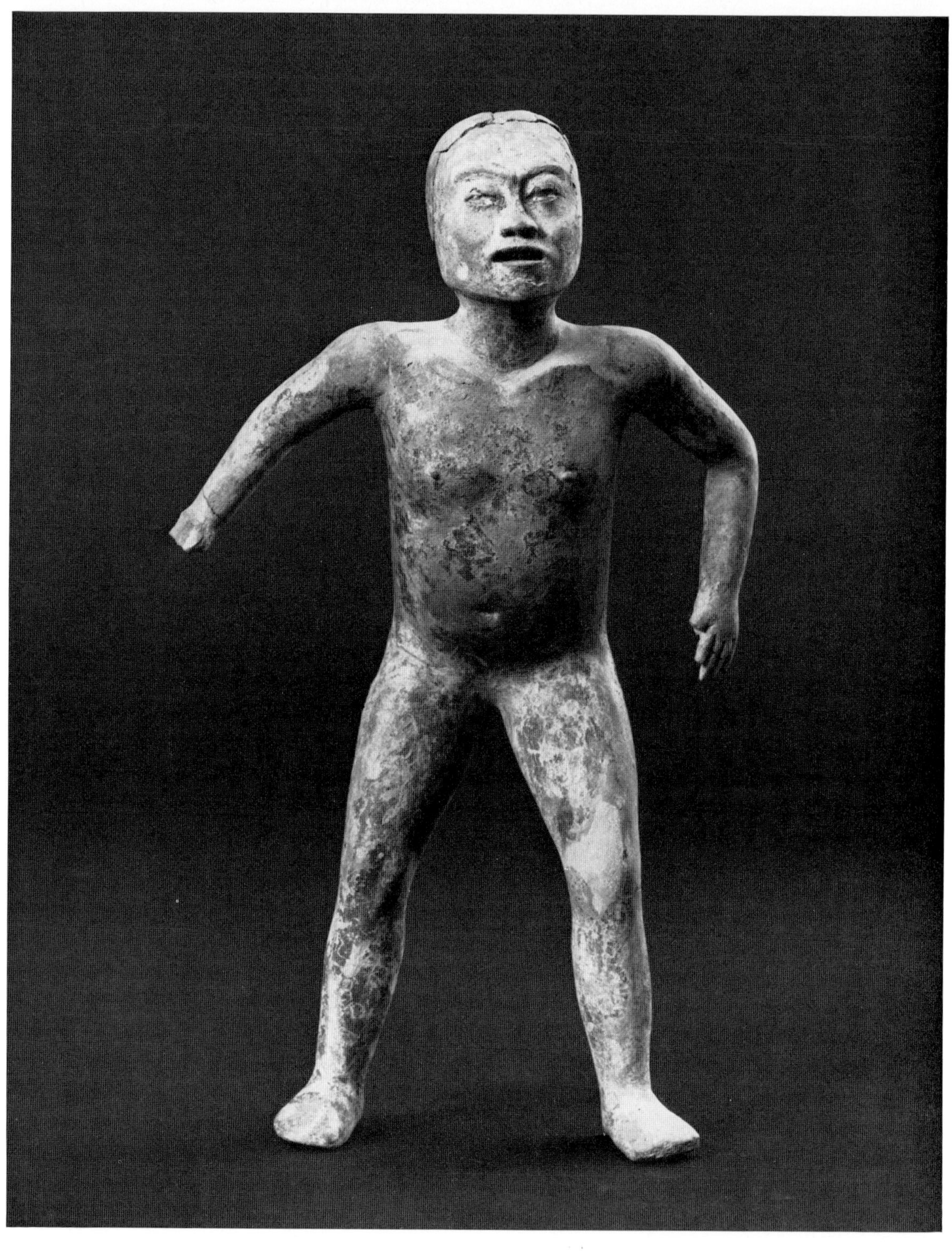

Standing Man
Middle Pre-Classic Period, about 800–300 B.C.

Clay, 8 1/2 × 5 1/16 × 2 7/8 in. (21.6 × 12.9 × 7.3 cm.)

The Kimbell *Standing Man* is a purposeful figure, his entire body alive with anticipated excitement. He displays the tense posture of an athlete—challenging, poised to meet an opponent. This attitude is enhanced by his open mouth, deep-set eyes and dilated nostrils. His feet are planted wide apart, his knees slightly bent, and his body is thrust forward. He seems ready to spring into action, his outstretched arms giving him balance and stability. This same stance can be seen today in a ball player or wrestler.

This *Standing Man* comes from near Xochipala, state of Guerrero, Mexico, and was probably conceived as a tomb figure—one of the multitude of clay figurines which has been preserved through burial and excavated from the graves of ancient Middle American villages. As a group, they represent a wide variety of subjects including dancers, musicians, ritual performers, acrobats, ball players, warriors, hunchbacks and women taking care of babies.[1]

The Kimbell figure is naturalistically proportioned and well coordinated. His features are highly individualized and might even be considered to approach portraiture. His is not a stereotyped jaguar face: his mouth is wide and horizontal; his lips thin, not flaring, and his eyes are neither slanted nor Mongoloid. Yet, this figure remains indefinably Olmec in feeling.

The *Standing Man* is a highly evolved figure, conceived in three dimensions, as compared to the flat, symmetrical, solid clay "gingerbread" type of western Mexico.[2] While the artist clearly understood human anatomy and was even able to impart a sense of energy to his figure, he appears to have been pushing his clay medium to its furthest limit. The Kimbell man closely approaches the maximum size at which a solid clay figure can be made without risking firing cracks caused by the uneven shrinkage of the clay body during production.[3] It is for this reason that larger figures required hollow clay construction.

Description: Figurine of nude standing man, in clay. He supports himself in an upright position, his entire body tensed for action. He is broad through the shoulders and chest. His navel, breast and collarbone are prominently marked, but his genitalia are not indicated. His face is strongly structured and, while his eyes are not clearly delineated, his glance is direct and penetrating. There are indications of a layer of pigment which has darkened.

Condition: Fair. The top and back of the reassembled head have suffered some losses. A horizontal crack seemingly corresponds to the hairline, while a deep vertical fissure, probably a firing crack, bisects the back of the head. Various related cracks are apparent, and fracturing has occurred in layers. Four fingers of his left hand have been broken off; three have been repaired, but the thumb and top of the index finger remain missing. His right arm has suffered a break above the wrist and the loss of the entire hand. His right leg has been reattached at the hip; his left leg, broken off below the knee, has also been rejoined. His head and both arms were also at one time severed. Losses to the back shoulder, right knee and neck above the collarbone have been filled.

Exhibitions: None known.

Collection: Foundation Acquisition, AP 71.3.

Notes:

1 For an interesting variety of figurine types, see: Michael Kan, Clement Meighan and H. B. Nicholson, *Sculpture of Ancient West Mexico: Nayarit, Jalisco, Colima, the Proctor Stafford Collection*, Los Angeles County Museum of Art, 1970, pp. 42–49, illus. 20–38.

2 John L. Alsberg and Rodolfo Petschek, *The Evolution of Artistic Form: Ancient Sculpture from Western Mexico*, Berkeley, 1968, p. 21, fig. 7.

3 Elizabeth Kennedy Easby and John F. Scott, *Before Cortés: Sculpture of Middle America*, Metropolitan Museum of Art, New York, 1970, p. 49.

Presentation of Captives to a Maya Ruler
About A.D. 750

Limestone and water-based paint, 45 3/8 × 35 in. (115.3 × 88.9 cm.)

This wall panel, carved in low relief and painted in once-vivid hues of black, blue and red-orange, was made for a major room of a Maya palace, a large masonry building used for special rites and ceremonies. Its rectangular shape suggests that it was a lintel, placed on the inner side of a doorway which opened directly onto the exterior.[1] The interior in which this lintel was placed, to judge from that in a surviving palace at Piedras Negras, must have looked very much like that seen in the wall panel itself: a small shallow floor area and a step leading up to a platform on which was placed, opposite the doorway, the ruler's stone seat; civic events like the one shown here would thus have been visible to spectators in the courtyard below.[2]

Three rope-bound captives at the lower left are being presented to a Maya leader, probably the regional ruler or *halach uinic*, by a subordinate, probably a *batab* who served as military and administrative governer of a single small city or ceremonial center.[3] The unusual prominence given this subordinate may be more fully explained by the hieroglyph inscription, which has not yet been deciphered; the identifying glyph is unlike any that is known to be associated with a major ceremonial center.[4] It is possible that the lintel may have been made for a small city; this hypothesis would explain the emphasis given to its immediate governor, rather than the regional ruler.

The captives possibly were taken in raids on a neighboring city-state to assure a supply of slaves[5] or sacrificial victims required by the Maya religion.[6] These prisoners are obviously of Maya stock, for each has the characteristic almond-shaped eyes, high cheekbones, fleshy aquiline nose, large lower lip, and slightly receding chin, as well as the artificially deformed head with sloping forehead.[7] However, their headdresses are of different styles and their features are coarser than those of their conquerors. Also, the ruler and his subordinate are more elegantly dressed, with earrings, necklaces and other jewelry and quetzal-feathered headdresses trimmed with disks or plaques.

The colors used in the wall panel are, considering the artist's limited palette, naturalistic and consistent with its narrative content. Color is also used, as far as can be congruent with this naturalistic aim, to distinguish forms from setting (i. e., jewelry against skin, skin against wall) and to clarify the hierarchic structure. For instance, the higher status of the main ruler is emphasized by the more varied polychrome of his dress (the only one that includes solid black) as compared to the nearly mono-chromatic rendering of the captives.

Wall panels like this one are the narrative complements to the monumental ruler images on Classical Maya stelae like that in the Kimbell collection *(Stela with a Ruler-Priest)*. Both types of images, which are characteristic of the art of the lowland Maya,[8] undoubtedly represent individual rulers at precise moments in their reigns; the hieroglyphs on the wall panel may eventually identify the ruler and his dates, the specific event depicted and even the names of his prisoners. The style of both Maya sculptures in the Kimbell collection is fundamentally the same, involving low relief carving in a limited number of planes, a hieratic buildup of forms to emphasize the ruler, an even and harmonious disposition of figurative and glyphic elements over the surface of the panel, and a precisely detailed rendering of the figures, their features, costumes and gestures.

Although the style of the wall panel is no less disciplined and technically adept than that of the Kimbell stela, the narrative and secular content of the panel determines a livelier and more dynamic image. The specific historical episode is conveyed by vivid, convincing gestures and poses: the ruler leans forward as if listening attentively; the subordinate's intermediary character is defined by his half-kneeling, half-standing pose on the steps; the captives' attitudes are highly individualized, but for the moment they are ignored by their captors. The figures, though related through fluid linear patterns produced by gesture and costume, remain distinct units because of their hieratic placement and the intervening hieroglyphs. This type of aesthetic order is fundamentally akin to the hierarchical order of Maya society.

Inscription: The four sets of glyphs on this panel had not been transcribed at the time this catalogue was written.

Description: A low-relief panel of limestone which depicts three prisoners presented to a ruler by a subordinate; there are also four panels of hieroglyph inscriptions, and further hieroglyphs adorn the ruler's dais. The setting is an interior hung with shallow drapery swags; a high step leads up to a platform with the glyph-ornamented dais supported by two wedge-shaped legs (the right-hand edges of which are visible between the glyph panel and the heads of the first and third captives).

The ruler *(halach uinic)* is seated on his dais; he wears sandals, a loincloth, a tassel and quetzal-feathered headdress; also earrings, necklace, pectoral and bracelets all made of disks and plaques. He is seated crosslegged, his torso inclined toward his subordinate, his right hand clasping his right knee; his left hand is poised across his chest, with his left elbow resting on his left knee. His subordinate *(batab)* wears a knotted loincloth, the ends of which hang in front and back; tasseled sandals; a shoulder cape; a pendant necklace bearing the image of a jaguar-head (the Maya jaguar god of war), and a disk and quetzal-feathered headdress. He carries a war club in his left hand and gestures toward the ruler with his right, which holds a tassel-ornamented attribute (a sling?). His right knee rests on the platform; his left foot is poised, balancing his weight, on the step.

Below the dais, at the ground level, are three figures, one seated and two kneeling, the left one only partly visible. Ropes are clearly visible about the upper arms and backs of the first two figures and may be indicated below the right hand of the prisoner at the left. All wear loincloths, elaborate earrings and turban-like knotted headdresses. The right-hand figure is seated with crossed legs; his left hand is presented palm upwards while his right rests on his thigh and holds a striated rectangular object. His head and body are seen in vertical profile, and his headdress is more carefully articulated than that of the other captives. They both kneel while raising their left hands to head level; their headdresses and earrings are ornamented with a zigzag motif. The center captive, whose hair hangs down in three long strands, bows his head; a drapery hangs over his right forearm. The third captive's body is seen in frontal view, his upturned head clearly revealing an elaborate necklace; his lips are slightly parted.

Considerable color from a water-based paint survives on the panel; red-orange and a typical Maya blue are the most common hues, and black is used occasionally. (It is most visible on the ruler's loincloth and the hair of the foremost captive.) The surviving pigment suggests that the panel was once completely covered with paint. The red-orange hue is found on all the hieroglyph groups, on the curtain and platform, in the skin coloring for all the figures (in some areas apparently mixed with black) and also on the headdresses and sandals of ruler and subordinate, as well as on the latter's cape fringe and war club. Traces of the red-orange pigment show on the loincloths, headdresses and necklaces of the captives, and also on their ropes. The blue-green hue is used for the wall, dais and step of the throneroom and on the quetzal-feathers and jewelry worn by the ruler and the subordinate, the center strap of the ruler's sandal, the subordinate's cape, loincloth and attribute.

Condition: Very good. An extensive amount remains of the water-soluble pigments that originally covered much of the surface; some of it is covered by white crystalline deposits of unknown character. Most of the facial features and accessories are intact except the profile of the ruler whose nose has suffered several chip losses. When the panel was acquired it had been cut into four sections; these have been backed with a honeycomb phenolic core and laminated to aluminum plates for reassembly and mounting.

Exhibitions: None known.

Collections: [New York art market, by March 1970.] Foundation Acquisition, AP 71.7.

Notes:

1 In size and proportion, the Kimbell wall panel is very similar to Lintels 15, 16, 17 and 25 from Building F, Yaxchilán, Chiapas, Mexico, now in the British Museum, illustrated in Jacques Soustelle, *Arts of Ancient Mexico*, London, 1967, pls. 110, 111, 113, 114.

2 Sylvanus G. Morley, *The Ancient Maya*, Palo Alto, Calif., 1946, pl. 70a, fig. 39.

3 J. Eric S. Thompson, *The Rise and Fall of Maya Civilization*, Norman, Okla., 1966, p. 91.

4 Michael D. Coe, *The Maya*, New York, 1966, fig. 49; Thompson, p. 97.

5 Thompson, p. 93.

6 Thompson, p. 98.

7 Thompson, p. 61.

8 The lowland Maya region centers around the valley of the Usumacinta River, which today forms part of the border between Mexico and Guatemala.

Stela with a Ruler-Priest

From the Usumacinta River Valley
About A.D. 700–750

Limestone, 107 3/8 × 68 3/8 in. (172.7 × 73.7 cm.)

This imposing portrait of a ruler, stolid and impassive beneath his elaborate costume, is one of the finest surviving artifacts from the vanished cities of the Classical, or florescent, period of Maya culture. Such a stone monument, or stela, would probably have been set up in a great ceremonial courtyard before the approach to an imposing pyramid temple and usually next to a simple stone altar, where it seems to have served the double purpose of supplicating the gods and glorifying the ruler of the community.[1] The male figures depicted on Maya stelae are now thought to represent specific individuals who held the title of *halach uinic*, and who possessed both civil and priestly authority.[2] The temporal power and high status of this stalwart figure is indicated by his sturdy body, his scepter and tasseled shield, as well as by his lavishly ornamented loincloth, breastplate, sandals, quetzal-feathered headdress and jewelry.

Many Maya portrait stelae are apparently also costumed as impersonations of some major deity. The deity here represented is without question Itzam Na, the omnipresent and omnipotent iguana god, "the creator to whom all men owed their very existence ... [for they] depended upon his caprice as giver of the two essential requisites of life: rains at the right time and fertile soils."[3] Artistic representations of the god emphasize, as here, the "large square eye with rounded corners (a Maya convention for deities of animal origin)," reptile jaws and protruding tongue, vegetation sprouting from the head, and particularly the motif of a fish nibbling at a water-lily blossom.[4] In the Kimbell image, these attributes are concentrated in the large mask-headdress worn by the figure, but the fish-nibbling-blossom motif also occurs at either side of the loincloth hem. "Maya art of the Classical period," according to Eric Thompson, "... is seldom free of representations of Itzam Na ... [not only] a reflection of the overwhelming importance of this god, but [also] ... the outcome of efforts of members of the ruling class to identify themselves with this supreme power."[5] The accompanying hieroglyphic texts, in the Kimbell example as yet undeciphered, may record dynastic data or reflect the fundamental Maya preoccupation with "the mystery of time and its influences on every side of life."[6]

The royal figure on the Kimbell stela is a remarkable embodiment of the calm and dignified self-assurance which characterizes the best of these Maya monuments. A near stasis—although a subtle and extremely varied one—is achieved by the balanced disposition of the dominant horizontal and vertical elements, by the careful arrangement of figure, costume and hieroglyphs to fill the available surface completely, and by the use of bold diagonals in the arms and in the headdress to enframe the profile head. The immobility of the powerful figure is further assured by the masterful technique of carving, which here defines only a few artificially flattened shallow planes of space.

Although the study of Maya figure style is both complex and difficult, the difference is readily apparent between the static monumentality achieved in this stela and the fluid dynamic narrative of the Kimbell wall panel, *Presentation of Captives to a Maya Ruler;* such comparison provides clear evidence of the tremendous range and versatility of Maya sculpture during the Classical period. Maya

stelae have been found frequently in the lowland regions adjoining the Usumacinta River, which today forms the boundary between Mexico and Guatemala. The Kimbell stela, on the basis of its general style, may without hesitation be assigned to this area, although its original specific location is unknown and it is not possible to link it to any known site.

A figure in a similar costume and headdress is represented on Stela 3 from Machaquilá, Petén, Guatemala, and the fish-nibbling-blossom motifs are encountered more than once at this site.[7] An elaborate, multimasked breastplate, disked bracelets and tall sandal ornaments may be found on a ruler portrayed on Lintel 53 from Yaxchilàn, Chiapas, Mexico,[8] as well as on Stela 16 at Tikal, Guatemala.[9] The latter figure demonstrates a similar delineation of the quetzal feathers of the headdress and a somewhat similar (and equally unusual) depiction of the hand holding the shield. Another figure, on Stela 1, Bonampak, Chiapas, Mexico, clutches a tall staff in an almost identical manner.[10]

Inscription: There are two sets of glyphs to the right of the figure that had not been completely transcribed at the time this catalogue was written.

Description: Stone sculpture bearing the image, in low relief, of a male figure and two panels of hieroglyphs. The figure stands in a frontal position, toes turned outward, with the head turned to his left. His left arm is bent at the elbow with forearm raised; the left wrist and hand, palm outward, support a small double-strapped shield adorned with tassels. The right arm, bent slightly at the elbow, holds a scepter, head downwards, formed by a stylized serpent and a blossom. Parts of the figure's body are clearly visible: his right eye, lower nose, mouth and chin, long straight hair clasped at the neck, parts of the shoulders, arms and hands, the outer edges of the thighs, the upper half of the lower leg. He wears a large three-part headpiece consisting of: (1) a multi-feathered headdress, with mask face, trimmed with large tassels, round disks and a fish nibbling a blossom, (2) an ornate nosepiece trimmed with disks and extending out from the face, and (3) a tasseled chinpiece. His costume also includes a collar of plaques and disks; a large breastpiece formed of mask heads, disks and tassels; two wide wristlets and two single-strand armlets; a short patterned loincloth with a central pendant ornament and fish-nibbling-blossom motifs at each edge of the hem, and sandals trimmed with feathers, disks and tassels.

Condition: Good. Although the stela has some losses about the edges, the figure is intact except for the upper portion of the headpiece and some chip losses on the jaws. Some surface details are somewhat eroded from prolonged contact with moist ground. At the time of acquisition, the work had been broken and cut into separate pieces; these were backed with a honeycomb phenolic core and laminated to aluminum plates for reassembly and mounting.

Exhibitions: None known.

Collections: [New York art market, by 1969.] Foundation Acquisition, AP 70.2.

Notes:

1 Eric H. Thompson, *The Rise and Fall of Maya Civilization*, Norman, Okla., 1966, p. 63.

2 Thompson, *Rise and Fall*, p. 97.

3 Thompson, *Maya History and Religion*, Norman, Okla., 1970, p. 232.

4 Thompson, *Maya History*, pp. 203, 212, 218, 221, 222, and figs. 1, 4g, 5b.

5 Thompson, *Maya History*, p. 232.

6 Thompson, *Rise and Fall*, p. 9.

7 Elizabeth K. Easby and John F. Scott, *Before Cortés*, Metropolitan Museum of Art, New York, January–June, 1970, fig. 171. See also: Thompson, *Maya History*, fig. 8.

8 Easby and Scott, fig. 173.

9 Gilbert Médioni, *Art Maya de Mexique et du Guatémala*, Paris, 1950, fig. 20. This stela bears a date corresponding to Dec. 5, A.D. 711.

10 Manuel A. Bravo and others, eds., *Flor y Canto del Arte Prehispánico de México*, Mexico City, 1964, fig. 280.

Maya, *Stela with a Ruler-Priest*, AP 70.2.

Additional Reference:

R. D. Buck and R. Merrill, "Honeycomb Core Construction for Supporting Panels," *Bulletin of the American Group – The International Institute for Conservation of Historic and Artistic Works*, vol. 12, no. 2, 1972, pp. 62–67.

Male Face
From Chiapas, Mexico
About 700–900

Stucco, 10 1/4×8 7/8×6 1/2 in. (26×22.7×16.5 cm.)

The Kimbell *Male Face* is dominated by a powerful, high-bridged nose which appears to extend well into the forehead, thereby achieving the ideal Maya profile. Originally conceived as an architectural decoration, this face is sculpted in high relief, meant to be seen from below. While its eyes are treated in a conventionalized manner, its nose and mouth are highly naturalistic, obviously modeled after an actual person. Indeed, with its strongly structured nose and lips, almond-shaped eyes and narrow forehead, this face relates stylistically to the numerous representations of Maya rulers vividly depicted in profile in the low relief stelae which are among the masterworks of the Late Classic period.

The Kimbell *Male Face* can be compared to other architectural fragments of the Late Classic, which range from decorative representations to actual portraiture. The *Profile Fragment* from Campeche, now in the Dayton Art Institute, displays features similar to the Kimbell face—a slanted, crescent-shaped eye, beak nose and sensual mouth—but these become exaggerated patterns, assuming a grotesque, menacing quality.[1] In contrast, *Head of a Prince* from Comalcalco (Museo Nacional de Antropología, Mexico),[2] is conceived frontally, an imposing bearded image with strongly naturalistic features. Like the Kimbell example, this is a secular representation, presumably a portrait of a high-ranking Maya. Even more strikingly realistic, however, is the *Modeled Face* from Palenque (Museo Nacional de Antropología),[3] which is sometimes referred to as the "Juárez Sculpture," because of its strong resemblance to the nineteenth-century Mexican president, Benito Juárez. This worn, aged face goes beyond mere physical appearance to become a penetrating character study. The Kimbell *Male Face*, on the other hand, describes but does not attempt to interpret.

Description: Larger-than-life male face, in white stucco with traces of red and brown pigment. This is a massive face, broad through the cheeks and jaw, with bold, asymmetrical features. The prominent nose is high-bridged, curving to the viewer's left, the right nostril flaring upward. The eyes are conventionalized and set at an angle, the left higher than the right. The lips are slightly parted, sagging downward to the right. The forehead is low and narrow; the edge of a headdress is suggested by a protruding ridge on the right side.

Condition: Good. The face is intact with losses occurring on the upper sides and above the forehead. There are traces of the original finishing layer of stucco, but most of the surface is coarse, deeply pitted and embedded with dirt and foreign matter. No repairs or restorations have been made.

Exhibitions: None known.

Collections: Foundation Acquisition, AP 71.5.

Notes:

1 Hasso von Winning, *Pre-Columbian Art of Mexico and Central America*, London, 1969, p. 293, pl. 474.

2 Ferdinand Anton, *Art of the Maya*, trans. by Mary Whittall, London, 1970, p. 318, pl. 147.

3 Elizabeth Kennedy Easby and John F. Scott, *Before Cortés: Sculpture of Middle America*, Metropolitan Museum of Art, New York, 1970, cat. no. 203, illus.

Additional Reference:

Michael D. Coe, *The Maya*, vol. 52 of *Ancient Peoples and Places*, ed. by Glyn Daniel, New York, 1966.

Seated Man, possibly Huehueteotl

About 1500

Basalt, 25 1/4 × 15 1/4 × 12 1/8 in.
(64.1 × 38.7 × 30.8 cm.)

The Kimbell *Seated Man* has been identified as the "Old God," Huehueteotl, Aztec patron of fire.[1] Indeed, his desiccated face, with its taut modeling, is the personification of old age. His skin appears to stretch to cover the high cheekbones which, in turn, accentuate the deeply sunken eyes and hollow cheeks. His hair fits closely like a cap; his forehead is low, with prominent brows. His lower lip and jaw jut forward strongly.

The powerful simplicity of the Kimbell sculpture reflects the fierce vitality of the Aztec conquerors who assimilated the cultures and deities of the older, more highly refined civilizations which they vanquished. Earlier peoples had represented the fire god Huehueteotl stooped over with age, bearing a huge brazier on his head or back, which was thought to hold the sacred fire from which all life emanated.[2] The Aztecs were sun-worshippers, and at the end of every fifty-two-year cycle, the sacred fire had to be kindled anew to assure that the sun continue burning. Often the attributes of Huehueteotl included blinders for his eyes.[3]

In the Kimbell version, however, the old man's eyes are unprotected and he appears to squint up into the light with a painful grimace. The lines of scarification intensify this expression, particularly around the eyes, and delineate the tightened muscles of the cheeks and the upper lip which is stretched and flattened. Seated with crossed legs, his rigidly frontal pose suggests that he may originally have served as a guardian figure for ceremonial purposes and, in this, he might be compared to the *Seated Standard-bearer*, Metropolitan Museum of Art.[4] In any event, his coarse features suggest that he was modeled after a *macéhual*, a simple man of the village.

Aztec art reflects a highly formalized and ritualistic society; it is in no way unsophisticated. In the Kimbell sculpture, body contours are skillfully transposed into rhythmical decorative patterns—the collarbone becoming a design element; the knees marked by barely visible chevrons, the toes flattened and repeated uniformly for purposes of composition. The loincloth *(maxtlatl)*, knotted decoratively in low relief at the navel, reappears in the back supported by a waistband. Above it, the vertebrae are stylized into a vertical pattern of three circles, and the shoulder blades are indicated by a very subtle curve.

The Kimbell *Seated Man* relates to several representations of aged, seated figures, which seem to have been a frequent theme of Aztec art. It bears certain stylistic resemblances to the seated man in the Museo Nacional de Antropología, Mexico City,[5] which presents a starkly emaciated body but has certain similarities in anatomical detail. Perhaps a more valid comparison can be made with the *Kneeling Old Woman* in the collection of Pierre Langlois, Paris,[6] who shares with the Kimbell figure the same squat proportions, the stylized scarification of the face, and the quality of venerable old age. She is no deity, however. Her broad features, pursed mouth, and hanging bosoms are notably naturalistic, not godlike in any conceivable way.

What, then, makes the Kimbell figure a deity? Is he indeed the fire god Huehueteotl? Or is he just an aged man staring into the blinding Aztec sun, seeking divine revelation, perhaps in quest of his own death and deification?

Description: Seated figure of an old man, carved in basalt. He sits erect on a small platform, his legs crossed, right in front of left. His wrists rest on his raised knees; his wrist bones are particularly prominent. The position of his right hand indicates he might at one time have held a staff. His head rests on a short, powerful neck. His shoulders are broad, his chest narrow. His forehead, cheeks and upper lips are incised in parallel lines. His ears are highly stylized with pierced lobes. He is clad in a loincloth, knotted in front.

Condition: Good. Part of the nose is missing below the bridge. Both ears have suffered losses, the right more so than the left. The fingers and thumb of the right hand are missing, while the entire left hand below the wrist is lost. The large toe of the right foot is noticeably chipped.

Exhibitions: None known.

Collections: Jacques Ullmann, Paris. [Judith Small Galleries, New York.]
Foundation Acquisition: AP 69.19.

Notes:

1 When in the collection of Jacques Ullmann, Paris, the Kimbell *Seated Man* was catalogued as the "Old God," *Huehueteotl.*

2 Pedro Ramirez Vazquez, *The National Museum of Anthropology, Mexico,* New York, 1968, pp. 64, 136.

3 Carlo Ludovico Ragghianti and Licia Ragghianti Collobi, *National Museum of Anthropology, Mexico City,* New York, 1970, p. 81.

4 Elizabeth Kennedy Easby and John F. Scott, *Before Cortés: Sculpture of Middle America,* Metropolitan Museum of Art, New York, 1970, cat. no. 275, illus.

[5] Ignacio Bernal, *Museo Nacional de Antropología de México: Arqueología*, [Mexico City], 1967, p. 200, illus. 137.

[6] Hasso von Winning, *Pre-Columbian Art of Mexico and Central America*, London, 1969, p. 270, pl. 385; see also p. 271, pl. 388.

Additional Reference:

George C. Vaillant, *Aztecs of Mexico: Origin, Rise and Fall of the Aztec Nation*, rev. by Suzannah B. Vaillant, Garden City, N. Y., 1962.

Index

Artists' names are CAPITALIZED; titles are *italicized*. All objects are illustrated.

Illustrations of Works in Other Collections